THOMAS GRENNES
North Carolina State University

INTERNATIONAL ECONOMICS

PRENTICE-HALL, INC., Englewood Cliffs, New Jersey 07632

Library of Congress Cataloging in Publication Data

GRENNES, THOMAS (DATE)
   International economics.

   Includes bibliographies and index.
   1. International economic relations.   I. Title.
HF1411.G713 1984   337   83-27064
ISBN 0-13-472713-4

To *Janet* and *Daniel*

Editorial/production supervision and interior design: **Joan Foley**
Cover design: **Debra Watson**
Cover caricatures (Adam Smith, David Hume, David Ricardo, John Stuart Mill):
Frances M. Kasturas
Manufacturing buyer: **Ed O'Dougherty**

Printed in the United States of America

10 9 8 7 6 5 4 3 2 1

ISBN 0-13-472713-4

Prentice-Hall International, Inc., *London*
Prentice-Hall of Australia Pty. Limited, *Sydney*
Editora Prentice-Hall do Brasil, Ltda., *Rio de Janeiro*
Prentice-Hall Canada Inc., *Toronto*
Prentice-Hall of India Private Limited, *New Delhi*
Prentice-Hall of Japan, Inc., *Tokyo*
Prentice-Hall of Southeast Asia Pte. Ltd., *Singapore*
Whitehall Books Limited, *Wellington, New Zealand*

CONTENTS

PART II INTERNATIONAL MONETARY ECONOMICS

PREFACE

This book is an introduction to the subject of international economics. The reader is assumed to have had a course in the principles of economics. All the major topics in international trade and international finance are discussed. This text would be an appropriate textbook in a one-semester college course. It could also be combined with supplementary readings in a two-semester course. The purpose of *International Economics* is to help the student to understand events in the international economy. Principles intended to be a guide to the real world are followed by frequent examples. Extensive economic data are presented, and current and historical international institutions are described.

A fundamental premise of this text is that theory and facts are inseparable. Facts do not interpret themselves, and the validity of theories cannot be determined without consulting facts. Each chapter presents theoretical material and attempts to apply the principles to economic problems. *Part I* consists of the first 13 chapters, which deal with international trade. They treat the traditional pure or barter theory that largely abstracts from the use of money in exchange. *Part II*, which consists of Chapters 14 through 22, emphasizes international monetary economics.

There is an inevitable lag between developments in the literature in professional journals and changes in textbook discussions of comparable topics. Because of developments in recent research, the gap between textbooks and journals has greatly widened in the subject of international finance. A major goal of Part II is to narrow this gap. This text employs both partial and general equilibrium analysis. However, the applied nature of the book has led to a more extensive and consistent use of supply and demand diagrams than is the case in some other books. Readers interested in more advanced or more detailed literature may consult the general references following Chapter 1 or specific references following the appropriate chapter. Major sources of international economic data are listed at the end of Chapter 1.

Many useful comments were made by my colleagues at North Carolina State University, by Donald McCrickard, and by anonymous reviewers. The manuscript was ably typed by Robin Kueffer and Kay Jones.

CHAPTER ONE
INTRODUCTION

1.1 THE SUBJECT
OF INTERNATIONAL
ECONOMICS

International economics is the study of trade among nations. It includes the exchange of goods and services and the international movement of factors of production. Trade is closely related to the concept of specialization. A country is self-sufficient if its residents produce exactly the same goods that they consume. The condition of self-sufficiency logically precludes trade with the rest of the world. Specialization is the opposite of self-sufficiency. It means that residents restrict production to certain goods, while relying on foreigners to supply them with other goods. International trade consists of each country's exchanging part of its specialized production for the specialties of its trading partners. Trade can be thought of as indirect production. For example, an additional unit of coffee can be produced directly by moving factors of production from growing corn to growing coffee. The opportunity to trade also permits indirect production whereby coffee can be obtained by producing additional corn and exchanging it for coffee. The choice between direct and indirect production can be made on the basis of relative cost. Trade and specialization, also called division of labor, are inextricably linked. The same forces that determine the pattern of trade simultaneously determine the international pattern of production, employment, and consumption. Trade is a mechanism that increases the interdependence of world economies. Interdependence increases world income, but it also makes producers and consumers vulnerable to a disruption of the normal pattern of trade.

The profitability of trade is based on the existence of differences between trading partners. The principles of international trade also apply to trade between regions of a country, trade between households and firms, and even trade within households. In traditional households, husbands specialized in employment outside the home, while wives specialized in managing the home and caring for children. In recent years, this pattern of household specialization has changed. Women's participation in the labor force has increased sharply, women have entered traditionally male occupations, and the birth rate has declined. Differences between the economic behavior of men and women have declined, and specialization within the household has changed. There are many interesting aspects of the economics of the family, some of which can be analyzed in terms of the same principles that are applicable to international trade.

Some relevant issues are (1) Should each family member perform the same economic tasks or should they specialize? (2) If specialization is chosen, how should tasks be assigned to different members? (3) How is family specialization affected by the prospect of family dissolution due to death or divorce? Some closely analogous issues will be considered in analyzing trade among nations. International economics is merely an application of the general principles of economics to the world trade situation.

International trade is a substitute for international migration and international investment. Labor and capital are employed in production, and products can be thought of as embodying the services of factors of production. Importing labor-intensive goods is an indirect way to import the services of labor. Exporting capital-intensive goods is an indirect way to export the services of capital. For example, wages are lower in Mexico than in the United States. Exports of labor-intensive products from Mexico are a substitute for emigration of workers from Mexico to the United States. The erection of trade barriers by the United States increases the incentive for Mexican workers to emigrate. Similarly, U.S. machinery exports to Mexico are a substitute for direct investment in Mexico by U.S. firms. Protectionist trade policies by Mexico increase the profitability of foreign investment in that country. Thus, trade policies between countries are inseparable from migration and international investment policies. Substitution between mobility of goods and mobility of factors of production illustrates the important interdependence between product and factor markets in the world economy.

All trade is based on differences in cost or demand between trading partners. In this respect, international trade is not fundamentally different from interregional trade. The traditional reasons for treating international economics as a separate subject from interregional trade are the following:

1. Factors of production are more mobile within a country than between countries.
2. Knowledge of technology is more uniform within a country than between countries.
3. Governments tend to impose greater trade barriers between countries than between regions.

4. Laws, regulations, and taxes affecting production and consumption are more uniform within countries than between countries.
5. Interregional trade nearly always involves a single currency, but international trade usually involves two or more different currencies.
6. Language and culture are more uniform within countries than between countries.

Thus, trade between New York and California is similar in some ways to trade between New York and Mexico, but in other respects it is quite different. Tariffs, capital controls, immigration barriers, tax differences, language, foreign exchange risk, and technological differences are all factors that make trade between countries different from trade between regions.

Whether a given transaction is classified as international trade or domestic trade depends on the location of national borders. New countries are formed as regions separate from larger units. Old countries lose their separate identity as a result of political union. National borders also change as a result of war or purchase of territory. The original 13 United States have grown to 50 states, which include some territory that previously belonged to England, France, Spain, Mexico, and Russia. Puerto Rico and the U.S. Virgin Islands have territorial status, but Commerce Department officials have vacillated about whether oil brought in from the Virgin Islands is imported or domestic. The United Kingdom of England, Scotland, Wales, and Northern Ireland was not always united, and separatist movements threaten the current union. Many modern nation states did not become unified until the nineteenth century. Unification transformed some international trade into interregional trade. For example, trade between Prussia and Bavaria was once international trade, but the unification of Germany transformed it into internal trade. Dividing the country into West and East Germany following World War II again made commerce between Prussia and Bavaria part of international trade.

The European Economic Community is an ambitious attempt to convert 10 independent nations into a single economic unit. The Community has already abolished nearly all of the barriers to trade and factor mobility among member states, and a program to adopt a single currency is underway. If full economic union is achieved, a large volume of international trade will become interregional trade. The unification movement reduced the number of autonomous political units in the world, but the demise of colonialism since World War II has increased the number of separate countries.

Although some governments continue to restrict domestic trade, internal trade is generally freer than international trade. Since the rise of the modern nation state has resulted in the elimination of many trade barriers between smaller political units, there is some concern that the recent proliferation of small countries may increase the number of barriers to world trade. The decline of colonialism has increased the number of independent nation states from 70 at the close of World War II to more than 140 at the beginning of 1981. The precise number of countries depends on the authority being consulted, but the U.S. State Department acknowledged in 1981 the existence of 165 independent countries, and the U.S. government maintained diplomatic relations with 148 of them. An example of a dispute that affects the numbers is the annexation of Lithuania, Latvia, and Estonia by the USSR, which is not recognized by the United States. The International Monetary Fund had 143 members at the end of 1981, and the United Nations had 154 members.

The size of countries, measured by population or area, varies greatly. Countries range in population from the People's Republic of China, with approximately 1 billion people (nearly 25 percent of the world's population), to Tuvalu, an island in the south Pacific Ocean with a population of 6,000 people. The country of Monaco has a smaller area than Tuvalu, but it has 26,000 people. The area for selected countries is shown in Table 1-1. Among the smaller countries are Luxembourg, Hong Kong, and the United Arab Emirates with less than 1,000 square miles each. The USSR is by far the largest country (8,650 million square miles). Other countries with more than 3 million square miles are Canada, China, the United States, and Brazil. In these large countries, trade among regions with diverse climate and terrain may substitute for international trade. Similarly, countries with large populations and incomes can obtain the economies of large-scale production in the domestic market that smaller economies can obtain only through international trade. Thus, international trade may be less important for large countries than for small countries.

The determination of national borders is only one way in which governments affect international trade. Government policies with respect to tariffs, foreign exchange rates, taxation, spending, money, and regulation can all influence trade in important ways. National governments are also a major source of statistics related to international trade. Although international agencies publish trade data, virtually all the information is obtained from national government sources.

1.2 BASIC FEATURES OF INTERNATIONAL TRADE

The importance of international trade varies substantially among countries. A closed economy is one that does not trade. A conventional measure of openness is the ratio of exports of goods and services to gross domestic product.[1] This index of openness is shown for selected countries in Table 1-1. It varies from more than 80 percent for Luxembourg to less than 1 percent for the USSR and China. Differences in the relative importance of trade are partly explained by each country's size. As previously mentioned, countries with large area may

---

[1] In most cases the ratio of imports to gross national product (GNP) gives approximately the same results. If there is a large difference between a country's imports and exports, the average of the two may be a more appropriate measure. Gross domestic product (GDP) is equal to gross national product minus net factor payments from abroad. GDP is used because of its greater availability.

TABLE 1-1 Exports, Gross Domestic Product, and Area of Selected Countries, 1980

COUNTRY	EXPORTS DIVIDED BY GROSS DOMESTIC PRODUCT	AREA (THOUSANDS OF SQUARE MILES)
Luxembourg	85%	1
Kuwait	84	8
Hong Kong	74	1*
United Arab Emirates	72	1*
Saudi Arabia	68	850
Taiwan	58	14
Iraq	58	116
Libya	57	680
Ireland	55	27
The Netherlands	55	13
Belgium	55	12
Israel	49	8
Norway	48	125
Panama	40	29
Austria	39	32
Korea	36	36
Ivory Coast	37	183
South Africa	36	473
Switzerland	35	16
Nigeria	26	356
Iran	31	628
Indonesia	33	735
Sweden	31	173
Denmark	23	17
West Germany	29	96
Canada	29	3,852
Kenya	26	220
Egypt	26	386
New Zealand	29	104
United Kingdom	28	94
Italy	23	116
Chile	23	286
France	21	213
Philippines	20	116
Greece	19	51
Australia	18	2,974
Spain	15	195
Japan	13	143
Mexico	12	760
Pakistan	13	364
Argentina	12	1,078
Brazil	7	3,286

TABLE 1-1   **Exports, Gross Domestic Product, and Area of Selected Countries, 1980** *(Continued)*

COUNTRY	EXPORTS DIVIDED BY GROSS DOMESTIC PRODUCT	AREA (THOUSANDS OF SQUARE MILES)
India	7	1,197
Turkey	7	301
United States	10	3,615
USSR	1 †	8,650
China	1 †	3,705

*Less than 1,000 square miles.
†Less than 1%.

Source: International Monetary Fund, *International Financial Statistics Yearbook, 1981,* published by IMF, Washington, D.C., and *Statistical Abstract of the United States,* published by the U.S. Government Printing Office, Washington, D.C.

substitute domestic trade between diverse regions for international trade. Most of the countries for which exports are less than 10 percent of gross domestic product (GDP) have more than 1 million square miles. This group includes the United States, Brazil, India, and Argentina. Conversely, most of the extremely open economies are small countries. All the countries for which exports are more than 50 percent of GDP are extremely small, except for the specialized oil exporters, namely, Saudi Arabia, Libya, and Iraq.

With the exception of oil exporting countries (e.g., Norway, Nigeria, and Iran), Table 1-1 shows that the openness of a country is inversely related to its size. In the exceptional cases, petroleum production is a large fraction of GDP, and since most of it is exported, the country is more open. The significance of oil has increased dramatically since the sharp price increases of 1974 and 1980. These events increased both the real income and the openness of the oil exporting countries.

Although the ratio of exports to GDP is a convenient measure of openness, it understates the importance of trade to a country. International conditions affect the prices of domestic substitutes for imports and exports as well as the traded goods themselves. If foreign conditions lower the prices of imported oil, steel, and automobiles, then the prices of substitute goods produced in the United States will also decline. Even if the import share in these markets is only 25 percent, 100 percent of the prices will be affected by international trade.

The concept of an importable is an attempt to represent the pervasive effect of imports. Importables are the sum of imports and domestic substitutes for imports. Thus, 100 percent of automobiles are importables even if only 25 percent are imports. Employees and owners of General Motors, Ford Motor

Company, and Chrysler Corporation are painfully aware of the pervasive influence of auto imports.

A similar relationship holds for the export sector. Even if only 50 percent of the U.S. grain crop is exported, 100 percent of the grain prices are affected by foreign economic conditions. Exportables are defined as the sum of exports and export substitutes. The ratio of exportables to GDP would be a better measure of the importance of trade than exports. A practical reason for not using exportables is that some products are imperfect substitutes for exports, and it is difficult to know where the list should stop. Wheat that remains at home is a perfect substitute for exported wheat. Barley and oats are imperfect substitutes for wheat. But what about grass that is used for grazing? If the foreign wheat crop is small, the price of exported and domestically consumed wheat will increase. As the demand for wheat substitutes increases, eventually the price of grazing land will be bid up. If the concepts of exportable and importable are defined broadly to include weak substitutes, nearly all products are affected by international trade.

Importables and exportables taken collectively are called tradable goods. Even some products that are not tradable goods are influenced by foreign trade through the markets for factors of production. The services of taxicabs have no close substitutes that are exported or imported. However, taxicabs use inputs that are importable (e.g., automobiles and gasoline), and the wages of drivers are influenced by wages in the tradable goods sector. Thus the ratio of exports to GDP can be interpreted as a minimum or lower-bound estimate of the effect of trade on the domestic economy.

Table 1-1 shows the importance of trade for various countries in 1980. Has trade become more or less important to the world economy over time? Table 1-2 shows the growth of world trade and world commodity output from 1963 through 1979. The figures appear in an annual publication of the General Agreement on Tariffs and Trade (GATT) in Geneva, Switzerland. The volume of world exports and world commodity output are measured by index numbers with 1963 as the base year, or 1963 = 100. By 1979 exports had increased to 300, whereas commodity output increased to 223. Thus, international trade has become more important in recent years. The increase in the relative importance of trade during this 17-year period is a result of many economic forces such as consumer preferences, supplies of factors of production, technology, transport costs, and trade barriers. When total exports are divided into commodity groups, it can be seen that exports grew more rapidly than did output for manufactures and agricultural products, but not for minerals. Manufactured exports grew to 381 in 1979, whereas manufactured output grew to 249. Agricultural exports increased to 194 in 1979, whereas agricultural output grew to only 145. In the case of minerals, exports and output (mining is approximately the same category) grew at the same rate to 199. Petroleum is the most important mineral, and the slow growth of real export volume and production were partly responsible for the sharp price increase for minerals.

TABLE 1-2   World Trade and World Production, 1963 and 1973–1979

	1963	1973	1974	1975	1976	1977	1978	1979
World export volume (1963 = 100)								
Total	100	231	239	232	258	269	284	300
Agricultural products	100	147	142	149	163	166	182	194
Minerals*	100	195	190	176	184	188	191	199
Manufactures	100	280	304	290	328	344	361	381
World export prices Unit value (1963 = 100)								
Total	100	161	227	244	249	271	297	351
Agricultural products	100	185	235	225	230	255	262	302
Minerals*	100	192	445	460	510	550	563	780
Manufactures	100	152	185	212	212	232	266	303
World commodity output Volume (1963 = 100)								
All commodities	100	180	185	183	196	205	214	223
Agricultural products	100	128	130	134	137	139	145	145
Minerals*	100	171	174	171	181	191	189	199
Manufactures	100	197	203	200	216	227	237	249

*Including fuels and nonferrous metals.

Source: General Agreement on Tariffs and Trade, *International Trade 1978/79* (Geneva: GATT, 1979).

The behavior of prices is shown in the row for export unit values, which represent a kind of average export price obtained by dividing the total value of exports by the real export volume. When all exports are considered, prices rose from 100 in 1963 to 351 in 1979. When the three export categories are considered separately, agricultural prices rose to 302, manufactured prices rose to 303, and minerals prices increased to 780. The sharp increase in the relative price of minerals, particularly petroleum, represented a major structural change in the world economy during this period. Thus, the period from 1963 to 1979 was characterized by (1) an increase in the relative importance of world trade and (2) a major change in relative product prices.

Just as world trade has grown more rapidly than has world production in recent years, the commodity composition of trade has also changed. Table 1-3 shows trade for various commodity groups expressed as a percentage of total world trade. Fuels are shown as a separate category to emphasize the important change they have undergone. The first point to notice is the decline in the relative importance of agricultural trade. From 1960 to 1979, the share of agricultural products in total world trade declined from 32 percent to 16 percent. This experience is a continuation of a decline that has been occurring throughout this century. This trend is partly attributable to a low response of the demand for agricultural products to income growth.

TABLE 1-3 Distribution of World Trade by Commodity Groups, Selected Years 1960–1979 (in percent)

	1960	1970	1973	1974	1979
Agricultural products	32%	21%	19%	18%	16%
Ores, minerals, and nonferrous metals	7	7	6	6	4
Fuels	10	9	12	20	20
Manufactures	51	62	64	56	60

Source: General Agreement on Tariffs and Trade, International Trade, 1979/80 (Geneva: GATT, 1980).

Engel's law is the widely observed empirical proposition that the demand for food grows less rapidly than income. Food constitutes a large fraction of agricultural output. Growth in demand for the remaining agricultural output has been retarded by the development of synthetic materials. Although the relative importance of agricultural trade has declined for the world as a whole, it has not declined for the United States. Agricultural exports have remained approximately 20 percent of U.S. exports for many years. There is evidence that the U.S. comparative advantage in agricultural production has increased in recent years.

As the share of world agricultural trade has declined, the share of trade in manufactured goods has increased. The share of manufactures in world trade increased from 51 percent in 1960 to 62 percent in 1970 and remained at 60 percent in 1979. The relatively rapid growth of manufactures traded in the last 20 years is also a continuation of a longer trend in world economic development.

The third category, ores, minerals, and nonferrous metals, experienced a decline from 7 percent in 1960 to 4 percent in 1979. This experience contrasted sharply to the increased importance of fuels, whose share increased from 10 percent of world commerce to 20 percent during the same period. As shown, the growth in the value of fuels traded was associated with a large price increase and slow growth in trade volume. This development is conventionally explained by the monopolization of the world petroleum market by the Organization of Petroleum Exporting Countries (OPEC).[2] Petroleum has a pervasive economic effect because it is an input in the production of many other products. Thus, some major changes have occurred in the entire pattern of world trade in the last two decades. The increased share of manufactured goods and the decreased share of agricultural goods are a continuation of a longer-term trend. However, the doubling of the share of fuels trade was an entirely new development. These product categories are extremely broad aggregates that

[2]The original members of OPEC, formed in 1960, were Iran, Iraq, Kuwait, Saudi Arabia, and Venezuela. Other members are Qatar, Indonesia, Libya, Abu Dhabi, Algeria, Nigeria, Ecuador, and Gabon.

provide some general information about the pattern of world trade. Data on more specific products will be considered in some detail in later chapters.

Another aspect of trade is the relative importance of individual countries and groups of countries. The export shares of individual countries are more closely related to economic variables such as national income than to size variables such as population and area. A set of high-income countries that contains a minority of the world's population carries out most of the world's international trade.

Table 1-4 shows the dollar value of world exports and the share of world exports for various groups of countries for the years 1970 and 1980. The countries are grouped according to the standard categories used by international agencies such as the United Nations, the International Monetary Fund, and the World Bank. Developed countries are the high-income countries of North America, Western Europe, Japan, and Oceania. Communist countries include the USSR, the People's Republic of China, and nations in Eastern Europe. Developing countries are all the remaining low-income countries, divided into members of the Organization of Petroleum Exporting Countries and others. One of the main features of Table 1-4 is the concentration of exports among the developed countries.

In 1970 the developed countries accounted for 72 percent of world commerce. This share declined to 63 percent in 1980, largely because of the increased importance of OPEC trade. The share of developing countries in world exports increased from 17 percent in 1970 to 27 percent in 1980, but nearly all the increase was attributable to OPEC. The contribution of Communist countries to world trade has been small and stable. Their export share was 11 percent in 1970 and 10 percent in 1980. Thus, the major change in relative export shares was a switch from developed countries to OPEC countries.

All the largest individual exporters were developed countries. The largest exporter in 1980 was the United States, with 11 percent of world exports, followed by West Germany (10 percent), Japan (6 percent), the United Kingdom (6 percent), and France (6 percent). Several members of the 10-country European Community (EC)[3] are prominent exporters, which illustrates the sensitivity of international trade statistics to the location of national boundaries.

Although the 10 members remain separate countries, they have eliminated nearly all tariffs and import quotas among members. They have achieved free mobility of factors of production among members, and they have made some other progress toward complete economic union. When current trade among EC members is treated as international trade, aggregate exports of the EC comprise 34 percent of world trade. If trade among members were treated as domestic trade, as, for example, in the case of trade between California and New York, the EC would appear to be a much less important trading unit.

---

[3]The original six members of the EC, founded in 1957, were West Germany, France, Italy, Belgium, The Netherlands, and Luxembourg. In 1973 the United Kingdom, Denmark, and Ireland joined. Greece became a member in 1981.

TABLE 1-4 World Trade by Country Groups, 1970 and 1980

COUNTRY AND GROUP	VALUE OF EXPORTS IN 1970 (BILLIONS OF DOLLARS)	SHARE OF WORLD EXPORTS IN 1970	VALUE OF EXPORTS IN 1980 (BILLIONS OF DOLLARS)	SHARE OF WORLD EXPORTS IN 1980
Developed countries	$226.0	72%	$1,281.1	63%
United States	43.2	14	222.4	11
Canada	16.7	5	65.9	3
Japan	19.3	6	128.7	6
European Economic Community	113.0	36	677.9	34
France	18.1	6	115.0	9
West Germany	34.2	11	196.6	10
Italy	13.2	4	81.6	4
United Kingdom	19.6	6	117.4	6
Other developed countries	33.7	11	186.2	9
Developing countries	53.8	17	535.1	27
OPEC	17.6	6	292.6	14
Other	36.2	12	242.5	12
Communist countries	34.7	11	202.1	10
USSR	12.8	4	76.0	4
Eastern Europe	18.2	6	87.4	4
China	2.1	1	18.5	1
Total	$314.5	100%	$2,018.3	100%

Source: Council of Economic Advisers, *Economic Report of the President, 1981* (Washington: U.S. Government Printing Office).

The importance of the developed countries in world trade is noted here, and it will be referred to again when theories of international trade are discussed.

1.3 TRADE AS A SOURCE OF INFORMATION

International trade is an important source of new information. Trade makes familiar products available at a lower cost than would otherwise prevail and also provides information about new products and new technology. Some cultures have gone through permanent changes as a consequence of trade, particularly in the area of food importation. Many foods and beverages now closely identified with particular countries, such as coffee, were not known in those countries until they were introduced through international trade. Coffee is native to Arabia and East Africa, but it had a profound effect on European consumption after it was introduced there in the seventeenth century via trade with Constantinople. Europeans introduced coffee growing to Java in 1690 and later to Brazil in 1722, resulting in coffee's becoming the major Brazilian export for many years since. Another example is tea. It is now the national drink of the United Kingdom, but was not known in that country until 1664. It was brought to continental Europe from China in 1610 by the Dutch. Today, India is the world's leading exporter of tea, but tea was not grown there until 1870.

A third example is chocolate. Chocolate was not known in Europe until the seventeenth century, when it was brought from Mexico. Tomatoes and pimientos are further examples of products that came to Europe from Mexico. The potato, which is an important item in the diets of Northern Europeans, was not introduced to Europe from its native Peru until the eighteenth century. Pasta is an essential Italian dish, but noodles were brought to Italy from China by Marco Polo in the thirteenth century. Red peppers, an essential ingredient of curry, were brought to India from America by the Portuguese. Ice cream and sherbet came to Paris in the seventeenth century via Italy, Arabia, and China. Beef is an important part of American diets, but cattle were introduced to America from Europe, as were the horses used in cattle production. Food is only one of the many ways in which trade transmits information between countries.

Technological information is embodied in commodity exports and international investment. High-technology exports are important for the United States, and much foreign direct investment by American-based, multinational corporations is attributable to technological superiority. American net service exports are large ($41 billion in 1981), and much of that revenue can be considered payment for information.

In addition to technology transfer, language and culture are transmitted through trade. For better or for worse, American culture is being exported in the form of rock music, blue jeans, television programs, and movies. The importance of the United States and the United Kingdom in world trade has promoted the use of English as the de facto world commercial language. The development of Swahili in East Africa is an earlier example of the interaction of commerce and language. In absence of a common language, East African traders found it expedient to develop a hybrid language to promote commerce. Many cities began as trading posts, where merchants exchanged information as well as products. Most of the great cities of the world continue to be centers of commerce. Trade and specialization imply that producers of goods are different from the people who consume them. Thus, successful trade must include a thorough exchange of information.

1.4 THEORY
AND EVIDENCE

To help the reader understand events and institutions in the world economy, some pertinent facts about trade and finance will be presented, and important international institutions will be discussed. However, facts do not interpret themselves. A theory of international trade and finance is indispensable in interpreting data. In some cases, theories provide hypotheses that can be tested by comparing the implications with empirical data. For example, the factor endowments theory implies that U.S. imports should be more labor-intensive than U.S. exports. The hypothesis has considerable intuitive appeal to many observers, but a series of empirical studies has found little support for it in its simple form.

In other cases, theory provides guidance in organizing data. Without the guidance of economic theory, it would not be possible to know which facts are relevant to a given problem. For example, if one were interested in explaining the appreciation of the U.S. dollar relative to the pound sterling, which of the infinite number of facts should one consult? Only with the guidance of a theory can one choose among average rainfall, soccer scores, inflation rates, monetary policy, and other potential explanations. Certain practical people deny that they employ theories in interpreting economic behavior, but their giving more weight to certain facts over others indicates the use of an implicit theory. Much time and confusion will be saved if theories are made explicit. Thus, this book will emphasize the essential interdependence between theory and evidence.

Some sources of international economic data are listed at the end of this chapter. The list is intended to assist readers interested in pursuing research in international economics. Sources of general data are also listed at the end of this chapter. Sources of specialized data (e.g., the largest multinational corporations) are listed at the end of the appropriate chapter. All national governments publish economic data, but it is not always comparable. An advantage of using data published by international organizations is that the institutions attempt to present data that is consistent. The United Nations is a basic source of trade data for its members. The International Monetary Fund (IMF) is a basic source of international financial data. At the beginning of 1982, the IMF published internationally comparable data for 128 countries in its monthly *International Financial Statistics*. A thorough understanding of international economics requires some knowledge of institutions such as the IMF, the General Agreement on Tariffs and Trade (GATT) and the International Trade Commission (ITC).

However, economic institutions and business practices change more rapidly than does economic theory. The amount of detailed institutional information that is worth acquiring depends on how rapidly it is expected to become obsolete. The IMF, the GATT, and the ITC were all created since World War II, and they have all undergone major changes since. For example, the original IMF charter prohibited floating exchange rates by member countries. In 1974 most members adopted floating rates in spite of the charter. Later the charter was amended to legitimize the nearly universal practice. Conversely, the principles of comparative advantage and purchasing power parity are already much older, and they are likely to be much more durable. Thus, international economic institutions will not be ignored, but basic economic principles will be emphasized.

1.5 THE PLAN OF THE BOOK

This book is divided into two parts. Part I (Chapters 2 through 13) discusses the real or barter theory of trade, which largely abstracts from the use of money in exchange. Barter is the exchange of some goods for other goods (rather than for money), and barter theory emphasizes that ultimately the residents of a country must pay for imports of goods and services with exports of goods and services. In fact, nearly all international trade involves the use of money. However, in the long run, money payments may conceal the more fundamental determinants of trade. Money has been described as a "veil" that obscures important economic relationships. A theory of trade that abstracts from the use of money may be a useful simplification.

Part II (Chapters 14 through 22) deals with international monetary economics, sometimes called international finance. Money may be unimportant for certain purposes, such as explaining the long-run determinants of the commodity composition of a nation's trade. At the same time it may be extremely important for financial issues, such as the determinants of inflation, currency exchange rates, and nominal interest rates. In Part I, Chapters 2 through 5 introduce the basic principles of international trade. Chapter 2 introduces the concepts of absolute and comparative advantage and considers the case of trade under constant cost. Chapter 3 considers the role of relative factor supplies under conditions of increasing cost. Chapter 4 considers the effect of trade on factor prices and the distribution of income. Chapter 5 presents alternative theories used to explain the pattern of trade. Chapters 6 through 8 discuss the economic effects of barriers to trade. Transport costs, a natural barrier to trade, are reviewed in Chapter 6. Chapter 7 considers the economic effects of tariffs. Quotas and other nontariff barriers are analyzed in Chapter 8. Chapter 9 is about industrial policy, which is the set of domestic economic policies that influence trade indirectly. Chapter 10 considers the effect of monopoly power on both import and export markets. International migration of labor is the subject of Chapter 11, and international investment is the subject of Chapter 12. Chapter 13, the conclusion of Part I, considers the relationship between economic growth and international trade.

International monetary economics is the subject of Part II. The existence of many currencies is a distinguishing feature of an open economy. Foreign exchange is simply foreign money, and each foreign currency will have an exchange rate in terms of domestic money. Chapter 14 introduces some financial institutions that participate in the foreign exchange market, and Chapter 15 provides an economic analysis of the market. Balance-of-payments accounts, which record the international transactions of a nation, are the subject of Chapter 16. A major change in the world economy occurred in 1974, when most governments adopted some form of floating exchange rates. Floating replaced the adjustable peg system, which had been in effect since 1946. Chapters 17 and 18 analyze various aspects of floating exchange rates. Chapter 19 considers some of the determinants of exchange rates, including inflation, monetary and fiscal policy, and the current account balance. A permanently fixed exchange rate system is the polar opposite of a floating system. The gold standard, the most important historical example of a fixed rate system, is the main topic of Chapter 20. The adjustable peg system, which is a compromise between permanently fixed rates and freely floating rates, is analyzed in Chapter 21. Chapter 22 concludes with a discussion of worldwide inflation and the mechanism by which it is transmitted among countries. Suggested references and sources of data appear at the end of each chapter.

REFERENCES

General Works on International Economics

Collected Readings

ADAMS, JOHN. *The Contemporary International Economy: A Reader*. New York: St. Martins, 1979.
BALASSA, BELA, ed. *Changing Patterns in Foreign Trade and Payments*, 3rd ed. New York: W. W. Norton, 1978.

BALDWIN, ROBERT E., and J. DAVID RICHARDSON, eds. *International Trade and Finance: Readings*, 2nd ed. Boston: Little, Brown, 1981.
BHAGWATI, JAGDISH, ed. *International Trade: Selected Readings*. Hammondsworth, England: Penguin, 1969.
————, ed. *International Trade: Selected Readings*. Cambridge, Mass.: M.I.T. Press, 1981.
CAVES, RICHARD E., and HARRY G. JOHNSON, eds. *Readings in International Economics*. Homewood, Ill.: Richard D. Irwin, 1968.
COOPER, RICHARD, ed. *International Finance: Selected Readings*. Baltimore: Penguin, 1969.
DORNBUSCH, RUDIGER, and JACOB FRENKEL, eds. *International Economic Policy: Theory and Evidence*. Baltimore: Johns Hopkins University Press, 1979.
ELLIS, HOWARD S., and LLOYD A. METZLER, eds. *Readings in the Theory of International Trade*. Homewood, Ill.: Richard D. Irwin, 1949.
FRENKEL, JACOB A., and HARRY G. JOHNSON, eds. *The Economics of Exchange Rates*. Reading, Mass.: Addison-Wesley, 1978.
KINDELBERGER, CHARLES P. *International Money: A Collection of Essays*. London: George Allen and Unwin, 1981.
LESSARD, DONALD, ed. *International Financial Management: Theory and Application*. Boston: Warren, Gorham, and Lamont, 1979.
SARNAT, MARSHALL, and GIORGIO SZEGO, eds. *International Finance and Trade*, 2 vols. Cambridge, Mass.: Ballinger, 1980.
TAUSSIG, FRANK W., ed. *Selected Readings in International Trade and Tariff Problems*. Lexington, Mass.: Ginn, 1921.

Historical Interest

ALLEN, WILLIAM R. *International Trade Theory: Hume to Ohlin*. New York : Random House, 1965.
BASTIAT, FREDERIC. *Economic Sophisms*. New York: D. Van Nostrand, 1964.
CAVES, RICHARD E. *Trade and Economic Structure: Models and Methods*. Cambridge, Mass.: Harvard University Press, 1960.
HABERLER, GOTTFRIED. *The Theory of International Trade with Its Applications to Commercial Policy* (1936). New York: Macmillan, 1937.
MARSHALL, ALFRED. *Money, Credit, and Commerce*. London: Macmillan, 1923.
OHLIN, BERTIL. *Interregional and International Trade*. Cambridge, Mass.: Harvard University Press, 1933.
RICARDO, DAVID. *On the Principles of Political Economy and Taxation*. In Ricardo, *Works and Correspondences*, Piero Sraffa, ed. Cambridge: Cambridge University Press, 1951.
ROTWEIN, EUGENE, ed. *David Hume: Writings on Economics*. Madison: University of Wisconsin Press, 1970.
SMITH, ADAM. *An Inquiry into the Nature and Causes of the Wealth of Nations* (1776). New York: Random House/Modern Library Edition, 1936.
TAUSSIG, FRANK W. *International Trade*. New York: Macmillan, 1927.
VINER, JACOB. *Studies in the Theory of International Trade*. London: George Allen and Unwin, 1937.

Advanced Material

BHAGWATI, JAGDISH. "The Pure Theory of International Trade: A Survey." *Economic Journal*, March 1964.
CHACHOLIADES, MILTIADES. *International Trade Theory and Policy*. New York: McGraw-Hill, 1978.

CHIPMAN, JOHN S. "A Survey of the Theory of International Trade." *Econometrica*, 1965.

CORDEN, W. M. *Inflation, Exchange Rates, and the World Economy*. Chicago: University of Chicago Press, 1977.

DIXIT, A. K., and V. NORMAN. *Theory of International Trade*. London: Cambridge University Press, 1980.

DORNBUSCH, RUDIGER. *Open Economy Macroeconomics*. New York: Basic Books, 1980.

HELPMAN, ELHANAN, and ASSAF RAZIN. *A Theory of International Trade Under Uncertainty*. New York: Academic Press, 1978.

JOHNSON, HARRY G. *International Trade and Economic Growth*. Cambridge, Mass.: Harvard University Press, 1961.

JONES, RONALD W. *International Trade: Essays in Theory*. Amsterdam: North-Holland, 1979.

KEMP, MURRAY. *The Pure Theory of International Trade and Investment*. Englewood Cliffs, N.J.: Prentice-Hall, 1969.

KRAUSS, MELVYN B. *A Geometric Approach to International Trade*. New York: John Wiley, 1978.

LEAMER, EDWARD E., and ROBERT STERN. *Quantitative International Economics*. Boston: Allyn and Bacon, 1970.

MEADE, JAMES E. *The Balance of Payments*. London: Oxford University Press, 1951.

———. *A Geometry of International Trade*. London: George Allen and Uwin, 1952.

———. *Trade and Welfare*. London: Oxford University Press, 1955.

MUNDELL, ROBERT A. *International Economics*. New York: Macmillan, 1968.

STERN, ROBERT. *The Balance of Payments: Theory and Economic Policy*. Chicago: Aldine, 1973.

TAKAYAMA, AKIRA. *International Trade: An Approach to the Theory*. New York: Holt, Rinehart and Winston, 1972.

YEAGER, LELAND. *International Monetary Relations*, 2nd ed. New York: Harper & Row, 1976.

Sources of Data
on International Trade
and Finance

U.S. Government

Council of Economic Advisers. *Economic Report of the President*, Washington, D.C.: U.S. Government Printing Office, annually.

Federal Reserve Board of Governors. *Federal Reserve Bulletin*, Washington, D.C., monthly.

Federal Reserve Board of Chicago. *International Letter*, biweekly.

Federal Reserve Bank of St. Louis. *International Economic Conditions*, quarterly.

U.S. Department of Agriculture. *U.S. Foreign Agricultural Trade Statistical Report*, Washington, D.C., annually.

U.S. Department of Commerce. *Historical Statistics of the United States*. Washington, D.C.: U.S. Government Printing Office, 1975.

———. *Statistical Abstract of the United States*. Washington, D.C.: U.S. Government Printing Office, annually.

United Nations

United Nations. *Commodity Trade Statistics*, New York, quarterly and annually.
―――. Food and Agriculture Organization. *Trade Yearbook*, New York, annually.
―――. *Monthly Bulletin of Statistics*, New York, monthly.
―――. *Statistical Yearbook*, New York, annually.
―――. *Yearbook of International Trade Statistics*, New York, annually.

International Monetary Fund

IMF. *Annual Report*, Washington, D.C., annually.
―――. *Balance of Payments Yearbook*, Washington, D.C., annually.
―――. *Direction of Trade Yearbook*, Washington, D.C., annually.
―――. *International Financial Statistics*, Washington, D.C., monthly.
―――. *International Financial Statistics Yearbook*, Washington, D.C., annually.
―――. *Survey*, Washington, D.C., weekly.

World Bank

World Bank. *Atlas*, Washington, D.C., annually.
―――. *Finance and Development*, Washington, D.C., monthly.
―――. *World Bank Tables*, Washington, D.C.
―――. *World Development Report*, Washington, D.C., annually.

Organization for Economic Cooperation and Development

OECD. *Financial Statistics*, Paris, monthly.
―――. *Main Economic Indicators*, Paris, monthly.
―――. *Quarterly Oil Statistics*, Paris, quarterly.
―――. *Statistics of Foreign Trade. Series A: Monthly Bulletin*, Paris, monthly.
―――. *Statistics of Foreign Trade. Series B: Annual Tables by Reporting Country*, Paris, annually, discontinued 1982.
―――. *Statistics of Foreign Trade. Series C: Annual Tables by Commodity*, Paris, annually.

Other Sources

Capital International Perspective. Geneva: Capital International, S.A. Provides international stock market data.
Euromoney Publications Limited. *Euromoney*, London, monthly.
Fortune. New York: Time-Life, biweekly. Provides annual data on performance of largest domestic and foreign corporations.
General Agreement on Tariffs and Trade. *International Trade*, Geneva, annually.
Harris Bank. *Harris Bank Newsletter*. Chicago, monthly.
International Wheat Council. *World Wheat Statistics*. London, annually.
Morgan Guaranty Trust Company. *World Financial Markets*, New York, monthly.
Oil and Gas Journal. Tulsa: PennWell Publishing Company, weekly. December 1982 issue gives world oil production by country.
Pick, Franz. *Currency Yearbook*. New York, annually.
The Wall Street Journal. Chicopee Falls, Mass.: Dow Jones, Monday–Friday.

CHAPTER TWO
COMPARATIVE
ADVANTAGE
WITH CONSTANT COST

2.1 ABSOLUTE
ADVANTAGE

The purpose of this chapter is to introduce the fundamental determinants of international trade. Both supply and demand factors influence trade. This chapter considers the simple case of supply when the marginal cost of production is constant. Constant cost means that an additional unit of a product can always be produced at the same additional cost as the previous unit. Economies characterized by constant cost are sometimes called Ricardian economies, because David Ricardo (1772–1823), the British classical economist, made extensive use of the constant cost concept. Supply under conditions of increasing cost will be analyzed in Chapter 3.

The fundamental concepts of absolute and comparative advantage are introduced in the discussion of comparative costs. Comparative advantage is a determinant of the pattern of a country's trade and specialization. Specifically, comparative advantage determines the commodity composition of trade, which is the list of products that a country exports and imports. Under conditions of constant cost, trade is likely to result in completely specialized production in both countries. The nature of the gains to both trading partners will be demonstrated. Exchange tends to equalize prices between countries. The level at which prices are equalized depends partly on demand and partly on cost, which is a component of supply. However, a range of permissible prices is determined solely by relative cost of production. Relative costs also determine a range for relative wages and for exchange rates between national currencies.

Alfred Marshall (1842–1924), the British economist, emphasized that product prices and quantities bought and sold are determined by both supply and demand forces. In his famous "scissors" analogy, he pointed out that it is fruitless to argue that paper is cut either by the upper blade or the lower blade of a pair of scissors. Just as the blades of scissors interact to cut paper, the forces of demand and supply interact to determine prices and quantities. In the special case of constant cost for a closed economy, it will be shown that price is determined by cost and that quantity is determined by demand. However, the introduction of trade to an economy characterized by constant cost permits both demand and supply to influence price.

An aspect of demand considered in this chapter is the demand for differentiated products. Much of international trade consists of intraindustry trade, which involves countries exporting and importing goods simultaneously in the same product category. For example, the United States is both an exporter and importer of machinery, and Germany exports and imports automobiles. A partial explanation for this phenomenon is that consumers demand specific product characteristics. Since the object of theory is to explain facts, the chapter closes by presenting some trade data for the United States. The observed pattern of exports and imports is the result of the interaction among comparative costs, demand, and barriers to trade.

A discussion of absolute and comparative advantage requires at least two products and two countries. The basic principles apply to the general case of many trading countries and many products, but the simple case must be considered first. Let the two products be cloth (to be designated X_C) and food (to be designated X_F). Let the two countries be the home country and the rest of the world (designated ROW). ROW is a single aggregate representing all the other countries in the world. It will be convenient to designate foreign variables by an asterisk ($\star$), so if X_F is the quantity of food produced in the home country, then $X_F^{\star}$ will indicate the quantity of food produced in ROW. What is foreign to one country is domestic to the other country, and the product that is imported into one country is necessarily exported from the other country. With only two countries in the world, any food exports from the home country (E_F) must equal the food imports ($I_F^{\star}$) by the rest of the world. There is nowhere else for the food to go. By the same logic, any imports of cloth into the home country (I_C) must equal the exports of cloth by ROW ($E_C^{\star}$). It is the only place from which the cloth can come. Thus, a curve showing the supply of imported cloth into the home country (I_C^s) can also be interpreted as the supply of cloth exports ($E_C^{\star s}$) from the perspective of the rest of the world. The point is simply that petroleum shipped from Ras Tanura to New York is part of the import supply of the United States and the export supply of Saudi Arabia.

A country's national income is limited by its supply of factors of production (also called resources or inputs) and technology. One way to employ the scarce factors is to produce all the goods that are consumed in the country.

This is the case of economic self-sufficiency or autarky discussed in Chapter 1. An alternative allocation of scare domestic resources is to produce only a few goods at home and acquire the remaining goods through trade. If the costs of production differ between countries, it is not difficult to see why two countries would benefit from specialized production and trade. Each country could produce the good for which its costs were lower, and this specialization would allow more of both goods to be produced for a given amount of labor effort.

Of course, not all specialization is productive. If the United States specialized in producing coffee and Brazil specialized in producing computers, U.S.-Brazilian trade would lower the incomes of both countries. For trade to be beneficial, the pattern of specialization must be based on costs of production. A classic statement of the advantages of specialization was made by Adam Smith (1723–1790) in his 1776 classic, the *Wealth of Nations:*

> It is the maxim of every prudent master of a family never to attempt to make at home what it will cost him more to make than to buy. The tailor does not attempt to make his own shoes, but buys them of the shoemaker. The shoemaker does not attempt to make his own clothes, but employs a tailor. The farmer attempts to make neither one nor the other, but employs those different artificers. All of them find it for their interest to employ their whole industry in a way in which they have some advantage over neighbors, and to purchase with a part of its produce, or what is the same thing, with the price of a part of it whatever else they have occasion for.
>
> What is prudence in the conduct of every private family can scarce be folly in that of a great kingdom. If a foreign country can supply us with a commodity cheaper than we ourselves can make it, better buy it of them with some part of our own industry, employed in a way in which we have some advantage.[1]

This cost advantage that Smith referred to is called absolute advantage. It explains why profitable trade might occur when one country has a cost advantage in the production of *some* products, but not *all* products. Brazilians are better at growing coffee than are residents of the United States, but Americans are better at producing some other products (e.g., computers and airplanes) than Brazilians are. First, consider the gains from specialization and trade when each country has a cost advantage in the production of one good. This case is Adam Smith's example of absolute advantage. We will then consider the more complicated case where one country has a cost advantage in all products, which requires a distinction between absolute advantage and comparative advantage. In terms of the U.S.-Brazil example, would there be any gains from trade if Brazilians were better at producing *all* products than were U.S. residents?

First, consider the case of absolute advantage, where each country has lower costs for one product. To simplify the discussion in this chapter, let labor (designated L and measured in man-hours) be the only variable factor of

---

[1] Adam Smith, *An Inquiry into the Nature and Causes of the Wealth of Nations* (1776) (New York: Random House/Modern Library Edition, 1936), p. 424.

production in both countries. Other factors of production may exist but their quantities are fixed, and firms can alter their output of the products, cloth and food, only by varying the amount of labor employed. However, the existence of different quantities of these cooperating factors (e.g., climate, technology, soil fertility) may explain why labor is more productive in one country than in another. Labor productivity is measured by output per unit of labor. Labor cost is the inverse of labor productivity (i.e., labor per unit of output). Labor cost will be represented by labor coefficients a_{LC} and a_{LF}. The coefficient a_{LC} represents the amount of labor necessary to produce 1 unit of cloth in the home country, while a_{LF} represents the amount of labor required to produce 1 unit of food at home. The coefficients measure the labor cost of each product. Since labor cost per unit is assumed to be the same at all levels of output, the coefficients measure both average and marginal labor cost. Labor cost will be different in the rest of the world, and ROW labor coefficients are represented by $a_{LC}^\star$ and $a_{LF}^\star$. Labor cost per unit of output at home and abroad in the cloth and food industries can be summarized as follows:

	Home	ROW
Cloth (X_C)	a_{LC}	$a_{LC}^\star$
Food (X_F)	a_{LF}	$a_{LF}^\star$

Suppose that in the home country 1 unit of cloth costs 8 man-hours to produce and a unit of food requires 1 man-hour. The unit labor costs are assumed to be constant no matter how much food or cloth is produced. The corresponding figures for cloth and food in ROW are 4 man-hours and 3 man-hours. The labor costs can be summarized as follows:

	Home	ROW
X_C	$a_{LC}=8$	$a_{LC}^\star=4$
X_F	$a_{LF}=1$	$a_{LF}^\star=3$

A country is said to have an absolute advantage in the production of a product if its labor costs are lower for that product. In this example, ROW has an absolute advantage in the production of cloth, whereas the home country has an absolute advantage in food production:

$$a_{LC}=8>a_{LC}^\star=4$$
$$a_{LF}=1<a_{LF}^\star=3$$

Thus, absolute advantage depends solely on home and ROW labor costs for the same product. In this example, each country has an absolute advantage in one product and an absolute disadvantage in the remaining product. Since absolute advantage depends solely on labor costs, it is logically possible for one country to have an absolute advantage in both products.

An alternative to labor cost is the concept of forgone opportunity cost. Labor can be employed to produce either cloth or food, and the opportunity cost of employing labor in cloth production is the forgone output of food. In the example, 8 man-hours can be employed to produce either 1 unit of cloth or 8 units of food. Thus, the opportunity cost of producing 1 unit of cloth at home is 8 units of food forgone. The opportunity cost or marginal cost of a unit of cloth (MC_C) is equal to the ratio of the home labor coefficients for cloth and food:

$$MC_C = \frac{a_{LC}}{a_{LF}} = \frac{8}{1}$$

Similarly, the opportunity cost of a unit of cloth in ROW is $1\frac{1}{3}$ units of food forgone:

$$MC_C^\star = \frac{a_{LC}^\star}{a_{LF}^\star} = \frac{4}{3}$$

In this example, cloth is cheaper to produce in ROW and food is cheaper at home[2] regardless of whether cost is measured by labor cost or forgone opportunity cost. However, these two cost measures do not generally produce the same results. Following Adam Smith's maxim that a prudent country should not produce at home those products that can be produced more cheaply abroad, the home country would benefit from importing cloth from ROW. Cloth production is cheaper abroad in terms of labor costs or forgone output of wheat:

$$a_{LC} = 8 > a_{LC}^\star = 4$$
$$MC_C = 8 > MC_C^\star = 1\frac{1}{3}$$

Because of international cost differences, trade is profitable. Arbitragers have an incentive to buy cloth in ROW and sell it in the home country. Arbitrage is the simultaneous purchase of a product at a low price and sale of the same product at a higher price. Cloth imports of the home country would be paid for with food exports, which would require a reallocation of labor from the cloth industry to the food industry. The home country benefits from food specialization, because unit labor costs are lower in the expanding food industry than in the contracting cloth industry. For example, 8 man-hours can be used in the home country to produce either 1 unit of cloth or 8 units of food. The withdrawal of 8 man-hours from cloth production would reduce cloth output by 1 unit and increase food production by 8 units. The additional home food production could be transformed into cloth by trading with the rest of the world. In absence of trade, the cost of cloth in ROW was $1\frac{1}{3}$ units of food. If ROW residents are willing to trade at that price (4 units of food for 3 units

[2] Notice that the opportunity cost of a unit of food is the inverse of the cost of cloth.

of cloth), the home country's additional 8 units of food can be exchanged for 6 units of ROW cloth. Thus, the 8 man-hours that could have produced 1 unit of cloth directly at home can produce 6 units of cloth indirectly by producing food at home and exchanging it for cloth. The net gain is 5 units of cloth for each 8 man-hours reallocated to more productive food employment. Thus, trade can be considered a form of indirect production. Because of trading opportunities, individuals and entire societies can be well dressed without producing any clothes. Similarly, the people can be well fed without growing their own food, provided that they produce something else of value.

It has been shown that the home country can benefit from exchanging some food for cloth, but the magnitude of the gain depends on the volume of trade and the prices of food and cloth. The information presented so far pertains to cost, which is a component of supply, but nothing has been said about the demand for food and cloth in the two countries. Without information about how much food and cloth people demand at various prices, the exact volume of trade and equilibrium prices cannot be determined. Cost differences lead arbitragers to buy cloth in ROW and sell it in the home country. The result is an excess demand for cloth in ROW and an excess supply of cloth in the home country. The cloth price will rise in ROW and fall in the home country until trade has equalized prices in the two countries. As long as prices differ between countries, arbitragers have an opportunity to earn a riskless profit.

The observation that riskless profit opportunities do not persist in the real world suggests that arbitrage occurs quickly. If 1 ounce of gold sells for $500 in New York on a given day, the gold price in London will be very close to $500. If it were not, a fortune could be made by arbitrage. Thus, trade will equalize prices between the home country and ROW. Without information about demand, the equilibrium level of prices cannot be determined. As importers of cloth and exporters of food, home country residents would benefit from a low cloth price and a high food price. ROW residents have exactly opposite interests.

The pattern of international specialization is determined by cost of production. In this case cloth is cheaper to produce in ROW and food is cheaper in the home country. ROW will export cloth, while the home country will export food. In this example cloth is cheaper in ROW in terms of both labor costs and forgone opportunity cost. Absolute advantage depends on home and ROW labor costs for the same product. Since $a_{LC}^{\star} = 4 < a_{LC} = 8$, ROW has an absolute advantage in cloth production. Since $a_{LF} = 1 < a_{LF}^{\star} = 3$, the home country has an absolute advantage in food production. Here each country has an absolute advantage in one product, but there is nothing inherent in the concept that prevents one country from having an absolute advantage in both goods. One country could have lower labor costs for both goods. Since labor productivity is the inverse of labor cost, an equivalent statement is that productivity could be higher in one country for both goods. In that situation, a mutually profitable pattern of trade could not be established without further information about the two economies. In terms of Adam Smith's example, what would the tailor do if he were not only better at making clothes than the shoemaker but also better at making shoes? The concept of comparative advantage provides that information.

2.2 COMPARATIVE ADVANTAGE

Suppose that the one country is better at producing all goods than the rest of the world. Does it follow that the two countries cannot benefit from trade? This question was posed by David Ricardo, and its applicability transcends international trade. Suppose that some plot of land is better suited to produce potatoes than is any other plot in the world. Does this information by itself imply that the land should be devoted to potato production? Alternatively, if a musician is the best violinist in the orchestra, does this imply that playing the violin is his best position in the orchestra? In both cases the answer is uncertain because more information is needed about the superiority of the resources.

The economic cost of employing a resource in a given activity is its alternative opportunity cost, which is the output lost by not employing the resource in the best alternative use. The economic cost of employing land in potato production or of a musician's playing the violin is the forgone output from the best alternative employment. Information is needed about the productivity of the land and the musician in alternative uses. The location of the productive potato land may also make it the best seaport in the world. Manhattan Island was once productive farmland. Thus, the land may be superior to other plots (i.e., it may have an absolute advantage) for both potato production and shipping. The relative superiority (comparative advantage) of the land over other plots should determine its optimum economic use. Similarly, the violinist may also be the best conductor, and if his conducting superiority is greater than his superiority over other violinists, the best use of the musician would be as a conductor.

In these examples resources have an absolute advantage in some activity, but it is necessary to know whether they also have a comparative advantage in that same activity. It follows that a country may have an absolute advantage in all goods, in the sense of lower labor costs, but it cannot have a relative or comparative advantage in all goods.

David Ricardo made the first formal statement of the principle of comparative advantage in discussing trade between England and Portugal. He stated that labor costs were higher in England for both cloth and wine but that costs were relatively higher for wine. Thus, both countries would benefit from trade if England specialized in cloth and Portugal specialized in wine.

The principle of comparative advantage can be precisely stated in terms of the four coefficients for cloth and food for the home country and ROW. In contrast to the first example, let the home country have an absolute advantage in both goods. Change the value of one coefficient so that the home country has lower labor costs for both goods. Let the ROW coefficients and the home food coefficient remain the same, but change the home cloth coefficient from $a_{LC} = 8$ to $a_{LC} = 2$. The situation in the two countries before trade will be the following:

	Home	ROW
Cloth	$a_{LC} = 2$	$a_{LC}^{\star} = 4$
Food	$a_{LF} = 1$	$a_{LF}^{\star} = 3$
MC_C	$\dfrac{a_{LC}}{a_{LF}} = 2$	$\dfrac{a_{LC}^{\star}}{a_{LF}^{\star}} = 1\tfrac{1}{3}$

In this example the home country has an absolute advantage in both goods, because labor costs are lower for both cloth and food:

Cloth	$a_{LC} = 2 < a_{LC}^{\star} = 4$
Food	$a_{LF} = 1 < a_{LF}^{\star} = 3$

However, the economic cost of a unit of cloth is the forgone opportunity cost. Specifically, the opportunity cost of an additional unit of cloth in the home country is the amount of food that could have been produced with the labor necessary to produce cloth. The appropriate measure of opportunity cost is marginal cost, which is the change in total cost associated with a 1-unit change in output. Since a unit of cloth requires twice as much labor as 1 unit of food, the marginal cost (MC_C) of cloth is 2 units of food:

$$MC_C = \frac{a_{LC}}{a_{LF}} = \frac{2}{1}$$

Because the labor coefficients are assumed to be constant at all levels of cloth and food output, the marginal cost of cloth is also constant at all levels of output. In the rest of the world the labor cost of cloth is $1\tfrac{1}{3}$ times the labor cost of food. It follows that the opportunity cost of cloth in ROW is $1\tfrac{1}{3}$ units of food forgone:

$$MC_C^{\star} = \frac{a_{LC}^{\star}}{a_{LF}^{\star}} = \frac{4}{3}$$

The comparative cost of a product is the home cost relative to the foreign cost, when both costs are expressed in terms of forgone output of the remaining product. Thus, the comparative cost of cloth is

$$MC_C = 2 > MC_C^\star = 1\tfrac{1}{3}$$

The country with the higher comparative cost has a comparative disadvantage in that product. In this case the rest of the world has a comparative advantage in cloth, leaving the home country with a comparative disadvantage in cloth. The home country necessarily has a comparative advantage in food.

The paradox in this example is that, in one sense, both products are cheaper to produce in the home country, but in another sense, cloth is more expensive to produce at home. The paradox is resolved when it is recognized that two different cost concepts are involved. Labor costs, which determine absolute advantage, are lower at home for both goods. However, the forgone opportunity cost of cloth, which determines comparative advantage, is higher in the home country. In what sense is it cheaper to produce an additional unit of cloth in ROW at a labor cost of 4 man-hours when the same cloth could be produced at home for only 2 hours of labor? The cost of employing 4 man-hours to produce a unit of cloth in ROW is $1\tfrac{1}{3}$ units of food forgone. However, the cost of employing enough additional labor (2 man-hours) to produce another unit of cloth at home is 2 units of food. Thus, cloth is more costly at home in terms of forgone food production, even though labor costs are lower at home. A simple comparison of labor costs for the same product gives a misleading impression of the true economic costs in the two economies. The relevant economic cost is opportunity cost, which depends on the relative cost of cloth and food in the two countries. The comparative cost relationship stated earlier in terms of marginal cost can be restated equivalently in terms of relative labor costs:

$$\frac{a_{LF}}{a_{LF}^\star} = \frac{1}{3} = 33\% < \frac{a_{LC}}{a_{LC}^\star} = \frac{2}{4} = 50\%$$

Home country labor costs are 33 percent of ROW labor costs in the food industry, but they are 50 percent of ROW labor costs in cloth. Even though home labor costs are lower in both industries, they are relatively lower in food production. Recall that labor productivity is the inverse of labor cost. It follows that home labor productivity is three times ROW productivity in food, but it is only twice as great in cloth.

With respect to the earlier question of how to allocate musicians within an orchestra, it is not sufficient to know one's skill at the violin; it is also necessary to know one's productivity in other activities. If the musician is 120 percent as good as the next best violinist and 150 percent as good as the next best conductor, he has an absolute advantage in both activities and a comparative advantage in conducting. Adam Smith's tailor may be superior to the shoemaker in making both clothes and shoes. Whether it is prudent for him to trade with the shoemaker depends on the tailor's relative productivity in clothes and shoes compared with that of the shoemaker.

The cost of cloth (MC_C) has been stated in terms of forgone food production. Alternatively, the cost of food (MC_F) can be expressed as forgone cloth output. It is important to recognize that these expressions are not independent, since the second is merely the reciprocal of the first:

$$MC_F = \frac{1}{MC_C} = \frac{a_{LF}}{a_{LC}} = \frac{1}{2}$$

The cost of producing an additional unit of food at home is $\frac{1}{2}$ unit of cloth forgone. Because of the reciprocal relationship, knowledge that the comparative cost of cloth is greater at home necessarily implies that the comparative cost of food is lower in the home country. The relationship can be formally stated as follows:

If

$$MC_C = 2 > MC_C^\star = 1\frac{1}{3}$$

then

$$MC_F = \frac{1}{2} < MC_F^\star = \frac{3}{4}$$

The home country's comparative disadvantage in cloth implies a comparative advantage in food. The important general implication is that a country cannot have a comparative advantage (or disadvantage) in all goods. In this example, the home country has an absolute advantage in both goods and a comparative advantage in food.

Another relationship relevant to comparative advantage is the one between labor cost and labor productivity. The labor coefficients measure unit labor costs:

$$a_{LC} = \frac{L_C}{X_C} \qquad a_{LF} = \frac{L_F}{X_F}$$

where L_C and L_F are the quantities of labor employed in cloth and food, respectively, and X_C and X_F are the quantities of cloth and food produced. A conventional measure of labor productivity is output per man-hour or average product of labor (λ):

$$\lambda_C = \frac{X_C}{L_C} = \frac{1}{a_{LC}} \qquad \lambda_F = \frac{X_F}{L_F} = \frac{1}{a_{LF}}$$

Labor productivity is the inverse of labor cost. Thus, MC_C can be interpreted either as the relative cost of cloth or as the productivity of labor in food relative to cloth:

$$MC_C = \frac{a_{LC}}{a_{LF}} = \frac{\lambda_F}{\lambda_C}$$

If the relative labor cost of cloth is greater in the home country, the productivity of labor in food relative to cloth must be greater in the home country. The formal relationship is the following:

If

$$\frac{a_{LC}}{a_{LF}} > \frac{a^{\star}_{LC}}{a^{\star}_{LF}}$$

then

$$\frac{\lambda_F}{\lambda_C} > \frac{\lambda^{\star}_F}{\lambda^{\star}_C}$$

In the example, cloth costs twice as much as food at home and $1\frac{1}{3}$ times as much in ROW. At the same time labor productivity in food is twice the productivity in cloth at home, whereas ROW productivity is $1\frac{1}{3}$ times as great in food as in cloth. Comparative advantage can be expressed either in terms of comparative labor cost or relative labor productivity. Absolute labor productivity can be greater in one country for both goods, as in the current example. However, relative labor productivity cannot be greater in one country for both goods. It follows that one country cannot have a comparative advantage in all goods.

The fact that home and ROW marginal costs are different in the absence of trade indicates that there are potential gains from international specialization. World income will rise if production is transferred from the high-cost to the low-cost country. Since the cost of cloth is lower in ROW, there would be a net benefit if 1 unit of cloth production were transferred from the home country to ROW. Total cost of cloth would rise by $1\frac{1}{3}$ units of food in ROW ($= MC^{\star}_C$), whereas the total cost of cloth would fall by 2 units of food in the home country. The net effect would be an increase in world food production of $\frac{2}{3}$ units with no change in cloth production. A further reallocation of world cloth production in ROW would lead to greater gains, but the total gain depends on the equilibrium prices of cloth and food. Prices depend on demand as well as cost. The comparative cost information is sufficient to demonstrate that greater specialization could lead to greater food production for a given level of cloth output. Alternatively, one can use the expressions for the marginal cost of food (MC_F, $MC^{\star}_F$) to show that specialization would lead to greater production of cloth for a given level of food output. In general, it would be possible to have more of both goods through specialization and trade. The pattern of comparative advantage and the potential gains from trade can be seen more clearly with the use of the production possibilities curves of the two countries.

2.3 COMPARATIVE
ADVANTAGE
AND PRODUCTION
POSSIBILITIES

A production possibilities curve represents a country's productive capacity. All countries have a limited productive capacity, and a production possibilities curve (also called production frontier) is a kind of boundary between those combinations of goods that are attainable and those that are not. A nation's production possibilities are determined by the existing technology and the total supply of factors of production. The market in which factor services are traded is called the factor market, which is to be distinguished from the product market where goods or products are traded.

Figure 2-1 shows the production possibilities curve (R_1R_2) for the home country under conditions of constant marginal cost. The geometrical interpretation is that for any given amount of one product, the curve shows the maximum amount of the other product that can be produced by the home economy. For example, if OG units of cloth are chosen, the maximum amount of food that could be produced is OE units. If all resources are employed in cloth production, output will be 50 units. If all resources are employed in food, 100 units will be produced. The equation of the production possibilities curve can be derived from the labor coefficients and information about the total supply of labor in the economy. A simple production process is assumed in which fixed quantities of labor are required to produce a unit of cloth or food. The labor coefficients in the home country can be expressed as

$$a_{LC} = \frac{L_C}{X_C} \qquad a_{LF} = \frac{L_F}{X_F}$$

L_C and L_F are the quantities of labor employed in the cloth and food industries, respectively, and X_C and X_F are the quantities of cloth and food produced. Thus, the labor coefficients are a measure of labor requirements per unit of output. A production function is a relationship between the quantity of a product (output produced) and the minimum quantity of factors of production necessary to produce the product. It is a summary of the best technology available.

These expressions can be written as production functions for cloth and food:

$$X_C = \frac{1}{a_{LC}} L_C \qquad X_F = \frac{1}{a_{LF}} L_F$$

The reciprocals of the labor coefficients ($1/a_{LC}$ and $1/a_{LF}$) can be interpreted as average labor productivity, which is sometimes expressed as output

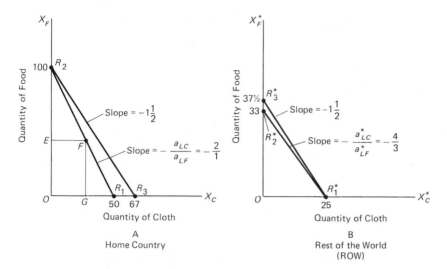

FIGURE 2-1   Production Possibilities

per hour of labor. These production functions simply say that the amount produced in each industry depends on both employment in that industry (L_C, L_F) and output per hour (a_{LC}, a_{LC}) in the industry. This information completely summarizes the technology, and with information about the total labor supply, the production possibilities curve can be derived.

Assume that the total labor supply is fixed at 100 man-hours. If full employment of labor prevails, everyone will be employed either in the cloth industry or in the food industry:

$$L = L_C + L_F = a_{LC}X_C + a_{LF}X_F$$

The interpretation of the right-hand side of the equation is that employment in each industry depends on the labor coefficients and the amount produced in each industry (X_C, X_F). This equation defines the home production possibilities curve, and it can be written as the equation of a line with the quantity of cloth on the horizontal axis and the quantity of food on the vertical axis (see R_1R_2 in Figure 2-1):

$$X_F = \frac{L}{a_{LF}} - \frac{a_{LC}}{a_{LF}} X_C$$

According to this production possibilities curve, the amount of food that can be produced depends on three variables: the total labor supply in the home economy (L), the labor coefficients (a_{LF}, a_{LC}), and the amount of cloth produced (X_C). The intercept on the horizontal axis is L/a_{LF}, and the slope of the curve is $-a_{LC}/a_{LF}$, indicating that the more cloth is produced, the less wheat can be produced. Since the total labor supply is $L = 100$ and the home labor coefficients are $a_{LC} = 2$ and $a_{LF} = 1$, the specific functional form of the production possibilities curve is

$$X_F = \frac{100}{1} - \frac{2}{1} X_C = 100 - 2 X_C$$

The production possibilities curve for ROW can be derived similarly by assuming a total labor supply of $L^\star = 100$ and labor coefficients $a_{LC}^\star = 4$ and $a_{LF}^\star = 3$:

$$X_F^\star = \frac{L^\star}{a_{LF}^\star} - \frac{a_{LC}^\star}{a_{LF}^\star} X_C^\star = \frac{100}{3} - \frac{4}{3} X_C$$

The graph of the ROW production possibilities curve is shown in panel B of Figure 2-1. The slope of the curve is $-\frac{4}{3}$, the coefficient of $X_C^\star$ in the equation. Since the slope of the home production possibilities curve is $-\frac{2}{1}$, the home curve is steeper or more vertical. This relationship is important because these slopes reflect the marginal cost of cloth in each country. It was shown that marginal costs determine the comparative advantage of each country. The comparative cost of cloth is the marginal cost at home relative to the marginal cost in ROW:

$$MC = \frac{a_{LC}}{a_{LF}} = \frac{2}{1} > MC_C^\star = \frac{a_{LC}^\star}{a_{LF}^\star} = \frac{4}{3}$$

Cloth is more costly to produce at home than abroad, and this fact can be seen by inspecting the two production possibilities curves. The left-hand side of the inequality is the slope of the home production possibilities curve, and the right-hand side is the slope of the ROW production possibilities curve. The flatter slope of the ROW curve indicates a comparative advantage in cloth. Thus, a country's comparative advantage can be determined without explicit knowledge of the home and ROW labor coefficients. The fact that marginal costs differ indicates that the total cost of producing a given amount of cloth can be reduced by shifting some production to ROW.

2.4 RANGE OF EQUILIBRIUM PRICES

Arbitrage will equalize product prices in the two countries. The permissible range of prices is determined by marginal costs, which are reflected in the slopes of the production possibilities curves. The price lines $P_C^\star$ and P_C in Figure 2-

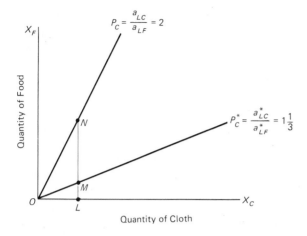

FIGURE 2-2   Range of Equilibrium Prices

2 show the possible range of equilibrium prices. The slopes represent marginal costs at home and abroad. The minimum price that ROW exporters will accept for cloth is $1\frac{1}{3}$ units of food, the ROW production cost. The maximum price that home importers will pay for cloth is 2 units of food, the home production cost. The area between the curves P_C and P_C^* represents possible equilibrium prices at which both countries gain from trade. For example, ROW exporters would offer OL units of cloth for at least ML units of food. Home importers would be willing to pay as much as NL units of food for OL of cloth. If any quantity of food within that range were traded for OL of cloth, both countries would benefit. Thus, the equilibrium price (P_C^0) must fall within the range established by marginal costs:

$$MC_C^* < P_C^0 < MC_C$$

The home country will benefit more the closer the equilibrium price is to ROW's cost of production. The equilibrium price with trade can be represented by lines R_2R_3 and $R_2^*R_3^*$ in Figure 2-1. The lines can be interpreted as consumption possibilities curves for the two countries. Because trade equalizes prices, the slopes of R_2R_3 and $R_2^*R_3^*$ must be equal. To lie within the permissible range, the slopes must be steeper than R_1R_2 and flatter than $R_1^*R_2^*$. Trade is potentially beneficial because it permits residents of both countries to consume beyond their production possibilities. Combinations of cloth and food lying on R_2R_3 and $R_2^*R_3^*$ are now attainable, whereas only points on R_1R_2 and $R_1^*R_2^*$ were attainable without trade.

Once the equilibrium price is established, the potential gains from trade may be measured. Suppose that the equilibrium price of cloth is $1\frac{1}{2}$ units of food. This price lies within the permissible range, and it is represented in Figure 2-1 by the slopes of lines R_2R_3 and $R_2^\star R_3^\star$. The home country will completely specialize in cloth production at point R_2, and ROW will completely specialize in food at $R_1^\star$.[3] The home country will produce 100 units of food, which can be exported for 67 units of cloth.

In the absence of trade, the maximum amount of cloth the home country could produce is 50 units. Thus, the home country's potential gain from trade is 17 units of cloth. The actual gain depends on the equilibrium price and the actual trade volume. Similarly, the ROW gains can be expressed in terms of food. At $R_1^\star$ ROW will produce 25 units of cloth, which can be exchanged for $37\frac{1}{2}$ units of food at the equilibrium price. In absence of trade, ROW could produce only 33 units of food. Thus, the potential gain is $4\frac{1}{2}$ units of food. It can be seen that trade provides consumption opportunities for both countries that would not be available under economic autonomy, or autarky.

Trade will bring about specialization in both countries. As long as the equilibrium price lies between $1\frac{1}{3}$ and 2, both countries will completely specialize in the production of one good. ROW will produce all the cloth for both countries, and the home country will produce all of the food. However, if the equilibrium price is at one of the extremes ($1\frac{1}{3}$ or 2), one country will produce both goods.

The relationship between prices and specialization is shown in Figure 2-3. The curve P_1DF is the supply curve of cloth for the rest of the world, the low-cost producer. It is horizontal at the price of $1\frac{1}{3}$ until the entire labor force produces cloth at point D. The ROW supply curve becomes vertical (DF) once capacity is reached. Because costs are higher, no cloth will be produced in the home country unless world demand exceeds the capacity of ROW. If world demand is so great that the price rises to 2, cloth production will begin in the home country. The contribution of the high-cost production at home adds the horizontal segment FG to the world supply curve of cloth. The assumption of constant costs that are different in the two countries implies that the world supply curve of cloth is a step function, P_1DFG.

If demand intersects the supply curve between points F and D, the equilibrium price will lie between $1\frac{1}{3}$ and 2. ROW will specialize completely in cloth, and the home country will specialize completely in food. Demand curve X_1^d with equilibrium at point E is an example of complete specialization in both countries.

If world demand for cloth is higher than ROW's productive capacity, both countries will produce cloth. Demand curve X_2^d with equilibrium at point H is an example of this case. At the equilibrium price of 2, ROW produces P_2F units of cloth, while the home country produces FH units. Thus, ROW is completely specialized, but the home country produces both goods. A final possibility is that world cloth demand is small relative to ROW capacity. ROW will produce both goods, while the home country completely specializes in food.

---

[3] Complete specialization will occur if each country's productive capacity is large enough to satisfy both domestic demand and foreign demand.

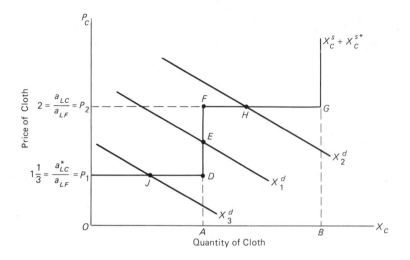

FIGURE 2-3   Prices and Specialization

Demand curve X_3^d with equilibrium at point $\mathcal{J}$ is an example of this case. At the price of $1\frac{1}{3}$, ROW produces $P_1\mathcal{J}$ units of cloth. The remaining labor that could have produced $\mathcal{J}D$ units of cloth will be employed in food production. Thus, if the equilibrium price lies within the range determined by comparative costs, both countries will be completely specialized. If the equilibrium price lies at one of the extremes, one country will produce both goods.

Relative costs also determine a range for relative wages at home and abroad. Since labor is the only variable factor of production, labor cost is the only relevant cost. Home country productivity is greater for both goods. In equilibrium, home country wages must be high enough to make each country competitive in one product. Higher wages in the home country will make ROW competitive in spite of lower productivity. Higher wages also serve the function of rewarding home country workers for higher productivity. Equilibrium-relative wages $(W/W^\star)$ must lie within the range determined by relative productivity in the two industries, which is the inverse of relative labor costs:

$$\frac{a_{LC}^\star}{a_{LC}} = 2 < \frac{W}{W^\star} < \frac{a_{LF}^\star}{a_{LF}} = 3$$

In equilibrium, home country wages must be between two and three times the wages in ROW. If home wages are more than three times ROW wages, home country costs will be higher for both products. For example, if home country wages are four times ROW wages, home country costs will be twice as high in cloth and $1\frac{1}{3}$ times as high in food. (See Table 2-1.) At the opposite extreme, if home wages are less than twice ROW wages, home costs will be lower for both goods. For example, if home wages are only 1.5 times ROW

TABLE 2-1   Relative Wages and Costs

RELATIVE WAGE	HOME RELATIVE COST OF CLOTH	HOME RELATIVE COST OF FOOD
$\dfrac{W}{W^\star}$	$\left(\dfrac{W}{W^\star}\right)\left(\dfrac{a_{LC}}{a_{LC}^\star}\right)$	$\left(\dfrac{W}{W^\star}\right)\left(\dfrac{a_{LF}}{a_{LF}^\star}\right)$
4.00	2.00	1.33
1.50	0.75	0.50
2.50	1.25	0.83

wages, the home cost of cloth will be 0.75 times ROW cost, and the home cost of food will be 0.50 times the foreign cost. At these wages ROW producers will not be competitive in either product. Within the permissible range, one country will be competitive in each product. For example, if relative wages are 2.5, home costs are 1.25 times ROW costs for cloth and 0.83 times ROW costs for food. Thus, relative labor productivity establishes a range for relative wages.

Once money costs are determined in each country, the equilibrium exchange rate (π) between the two national currencies is determined by relative labor productivity. Let money costs be given by the following table:

TABLE 2-2   Relative Money Costs

PRODUCT	HOME MONEY COST	ROW MONEY COST FOREIGN CURRENCY COST	$\Pi = \$0.60$	$\Pi = \$0.30$	$\Pi = \$0.40$
Cloth	$2	F4	$2.40	$1.20	$1.60
Food	1	F3	1.80	.90	1.20

When the dollar is taken as the home currency, home costs are $2.00 per unit of cloth and $1.00 per unit of food. ROW costs are 4 units of foreign exchange per unit of cloth and 3 units of foreign exchange per unit of food. Since home and ROW costs are expressed in different currencies, an exchange rate must be used to compare them. The range of permissible exchange rates is determined by relative labor productivity. If the foreign currency is too expensive, ROW will not be competitive in either product. For example, if the exchange rate is $0.60 per unit of foreign currency ($\pi = \$0.60$), cloth will cost $2.40 in ROW and $2.00 at home, whereas food will cost $1.80 abroad and $1.00 at home. Conversely, if the foreign currency is too cheap, the home country will be unable to compete in either product. For example, at an exchange rate of $0.30 per unit of foreign exchange, cloth will cost $2.00 at home and $1.20 in ROW, while food will cost $1.00 at home and $0.90 in ROW. Equilibrium requires that each country be competitive in one product, which will occur when the exchange rate lies between $0.33 and $0.50. In general, the range of possible exchange rates depends on relative labor productivity:

$$\$0.33 = \frac{a_{LF}}{a_{LF}^{\star}} < \pi < \frac{a_{LC}}{a_{LC}^{\star}} = \$0.50$$

2.5 DEMAND AND TRADE

It has been shown that both countries can benefit from some trade. The actual volume of trade and prices depend on demand conditions as well as cost. Demand conditions for a closed economy are shown in Figure 2-4. Consumer preferences can be represented by an indifference map, which consists of a set of indifference curves between cloth and food. Indifference curves represent the preferences of consumers; that is, curves farther from the origin are preferred to those nearer the origin. Thus, curve U_3 is preferred to U_2 and U_2 is preferred to U_1. The general properties of indifference curves are (1) negative slope, (2) convex to the origin, (3) nonintersecting.[4] Since these curves repre-

FIGURE 2-4   Demand in a Closed Economy

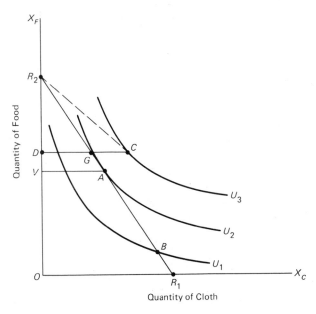

[4]For a comprehensive treatment of household indifference curves, see an intermediate textbook such as Edwin Mansfield, *Microeconomics: Theory and Applications*, 4th ed. (New York: W. W. Norton, 1982). For a discussion of community indifference curves, see Melvyn B. Krauss and Harry G. Johnson, *General Equilibrium Analysis: A Microeconomic Text* (Chicago: Aldine, 1974), Chap. 1; or Wassily W. Leontief, "The Use of Indifference Curves in the Analysis of Foreign Trade," in Howard S. Ellis and Lloyd A. Metzler, eds., *Readings in the Theory of International Trade* (Homewood, Ill.: Richard D. Irwin, 1950).

sent all the consumers in the economy, they are more complex than those for individuals.

The aggregate curves are called community indifference curves. They can be thought of as portraying a representative consumer or an average of all consumers. In Figure 2-4, U_3 is the preferred indifference curve, but no point on U_3 is attainable when the home country is a closed economy. The production possibilities curve is simultaneously a consumption possibilities curve in the absence of trade. Point A on U_2 is the highest attainable combination of cloth and food without trade. The employment of enough factors to produce VA units of cloth requires that home consumers forgo R_2V units of food. With trade, the home country will be able to obtain more cloth for the same food cost. Point B on U_1 is attainable by the home economy, but consumers consider that bundle of goods to be inferior to the bundle at point A.

Since ROW has a comparative advantage in cloth, trade will lower the price of cloth faced by home country consumers. The new price will lie between $1\frac{1}{3}$ and 2. In Figure 2-5 the new price line R_2R_3 must be flatter than line R_1R_2. In equilibrium with trade, production will be at R_2 and consumption will be at C. At R_2 the home country will specialize completely in cloth, which can now be sold at a more favorable price. In a closed economy DG units of cloth could be produced at a cost of R_2D units of food. With trade, DC units of cloth can be obtained for the same cost in terms of cloth. Thus, the gain from trade is GC units of cloth. The equilibrium consumption bundle at point C was not attainable under autarky. The fact that point C on U_4 is on a higher indifference curve than point A is on U_3 indicates that the home country has gained from trade. The total gain is a combination of a consumption gain and a production gain. The consumption gain comes from the opportunity to choose

FIGURE 2-5   Demand in an Open Economy

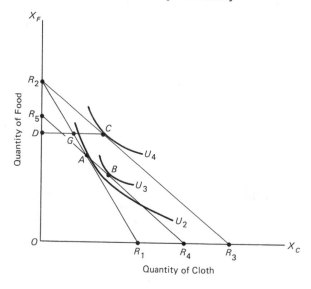

Quantity of Cloth

a combination of cloth and food that was not available under autarky. The production gain comes from the opportunity to specialize in producing the product (food) whose cost is lower at home.

The separate consumption and production gains can be shown by letting consumption respond to world prices while requiring that production be the same as under autarky. That situation is represented by curve R_4R_5, which passed through point A and is parallel to curve R_2R_3. Point B on indifference curve U_3 is the preferred point on consumption possibilities curve R_4R_5. Since U_3 is a higher curve than U_2, there are consumption gains even when production is constant. When production is also permitted to respond to world prices, the relevant consumption possibilities curve becomes R_2R_3. Since U_4 is above U_3, there are additional gains from specialization in production.

A trade triangle can be formed by connecting the production point R_2, the consumption point C, and point D. Exports are R_2D units of food, the difference between production and domestic consumption. Imports are DC units of cloth, the difference between consumption and domestic production. The slope of the hypotenuse (RC) represents the price of cloth in terms of food. If domestic residents had different preferences, such as a stronger preference for cloth, the equilibrium would be altered. If preferences for cloth were stronger, the equilibrium would be southeast of A along curve R_2R_1 without trade and southeast of C along curve R_2R_3 with trade. The diagram shows only the gains to the home country. A separate diagram is necessary to show the situation in ROW, and readers are encouraged to test their understanding by constructing it themselves.

The previous section has shown the gains from trade when the equilibrium price has been determined. The effect of demand on the equilibrium price can be shown using an offer curve or reciprocal demand curve.[5] Let the home country demand for cloth be shown by the demand curve in panel A of Figure 2-6. The curve shows the quantity of cloth demanded at each price in terms of food. Four points on the demand curve are given by the following data:

P_C	X_C	$P_CX_C=X_F$
40	20	800
30	40	1,200
25	50	1,250
10	80	800

At the price of 40 units of food, 20 units of cloth are demanded. Since the price is 40 units of food per unit of cloth, the total amount of food offered for 20 units of cloth is

$$X_F = P_CX_C = (20)(40) = 800$$

---

[5] A simplified derivation of the offer curve is presented here. For a more detailed treatment, see James E. Meade, *A Geometry of International Trade* (London: George Allen and Unwin, 1952), Chaps. 2–3; or Krauss and Johnson, *General Equilibrium Analysis: A Microeconomic Text*, Chap. 6.

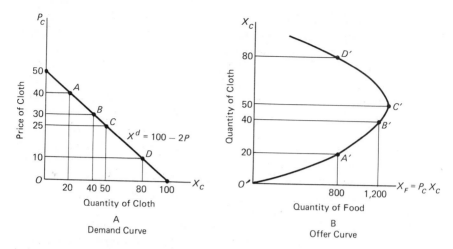

FIGURE 2-6   Demand Curve and Offer Curve

Panel A shows quantity of cloth demanded as a function of price. Panel B shows the home country's offer curve with quantities of cloth and food on the two axes. Point A' on the offer curve corresponds to point A on the demand curve. For 20 units of cloth, residents of A will pay 40 units of food per unit of cloth or a total offer of 800 units of food. For 40 units of cloth, home residents will pay 30 units each or a total offer of 1,200 units of food. For 50 units of cloth the price is 25 and the total offer is 1,250. As long as demand is elastic, a larger quantity of cloth will bring about a larger offer of food.

The demand curve is elastic to the northwest of point C and inelastic to the southeast of point C. When demand is elastic, the offer curve has a positive slope (from O' to C') and when demand is inelastic, the offer curve has a negative slope (C' to D'). For example, for the quantity of 80, the price paid is 10 units of food, and the offer is 800 units of food. Each point on the upper curve shows the quantity of food exports offered by home residents for each quantity of cloth imports. The offer curve represents demand conditions in the home country. An offer curve for ROW can be derived analogously. World equilibrium occurs when the home country's offer of food for cloth intersects ROW's offer of cloth for food.

Equilibrium is shown in Figure 2-7 at point A. The home country will export OD units of food for DA units of cloth. Since an offer curve shows the quantity of one product offered for a given quantity of the other product, the price cannot be read directly from the curve. However, the price is given by the slope of a ray (straight line) from the origin to the curve. At point B, the price is given by the slope of the line OB. At that price the home country will accept BC units of cloth for OC of food, but ROW will offer GC of cloth for OC of food. There is an excess supply of cloth and an excess demand for food. At the equilibrium point A the price is given by the slope of OA. In this ex-

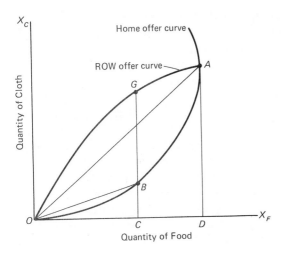

FIGURE 2-7   Equilibrium Price with Free Trade

ample, cost conditions determine that the equilibrium price must lie between $1\frac{1}{3}$ and 2, and demand conditions determine the exact price.

2.6 DEMAND AND DIFFERENTIATED PRODUCTS

The discussion of comparative cost implies that countries will export products in which they have a comparative advantage and import products in which they have a comparative disadvantage. An apparent implication is that the goods exported by a country will be different from the goods imported by the same country. However, much of the observed world trade consists of countries simultaneously exporting and importing the same category of products. For example, the United States is both a large exporter and importer of automobiles. Germany is a significant exporter and importer of wine. This pattern of trade is called cross-hauling or intraindustry trade, and it appears to involve some unnecessary transport costs. If American auto importers and exporters could get together, perhaps they could avoid some international transport costs by trading with each other. However, the fact that intraindustry trade in automobiles is so widespread and has persisted for years suggests that there may be good reasons for it to occur. The first reason is that most consumers are not interested in merely automobiles or wine but, rather, in specific product characteristics. Products contain different combinations of specific characteristics. Passenger space, reliability, gasoline mileage, and durability are important to auto buyers, and these features may vary substantially from one car to another.

An important task of each auto company is to incorporate in its product a set of characteristics that consumers view as superior to those of its rivals. This practice is called product differentiation, and it is an important way in which firms compete with each other on a nonprice basis. If some countries specialize in X-type autos and other countries specialize in Y-type autos, one would expect both countries to simultaneously export and import cars. In the case of the United States, imported cars have been smaller, with better gasoline mileage, than exported cars. Product differentiation appears to be a fact of life, but what remains unexplained is why countries specialize in certain product characteristics. In the case of autos, the price of gasoline is probably an important factor. Gasoline has been cheaper in the United States for many years, and this has encouraged the use of larger cars. If firms develop their products primarily with domestic sales in mind, this would explain the emphasis on large cars by U.S. companies. Apparently, American firms have been slow to respond to the higher price of gasoline, and profits have been low because of it.

The wine situation is similar. Consumers may choose from a bewilderingly large number of kinds of wine. They may be categorized in many ways including country of origin, specific district within a country, grape variety, vintage, and color of wine. Consumers do not consider a bottle of French wine from Chateau Margaux to be a perfect substitute for a bottle of Rhine wine from Germany. Because of product differentiation, France and Germany engage in intraindustry trade in wine and other products. In the case of wine, the product characteristics in which countries specialize seem to be partly based on national differences in soil and climate. David Ricardo regarded these features as the basis of comparative advantage. The interaction between comparative advantage and consumer demand for differentiated products helps to explain intraindustry trade.

An examination of trade statistics indicates that the amount of intraindustry trade depends on the level of aggregation of the data. For example, are the product categories broad, such as agricultural products and minerals, or are they narrow, such as durum wheat and copper? If the categories are broad, a country such as the United States that imports coffee and exports wheat would appear to be both an exporter and an importer of agricultural products. However, this high level of aggregation would conceal the fact that the agricultural products exported are quite different from those imported. If the narrower categories are chosen, the United States would be shown to be only an exporter of durum wheat and only an importer of copper. Therefore, trade data organized according to lower levels of product aggregation will show less intraindustry trade.

The standard format for presenting trade data is the United Nations' Standard International Trade Classification (SITC) system. The highest level of product aggregation (broadest categories) consists of ten single-digit categories that are shown in Table 2-3. The categories include food and live ani-

TABLE 2-3   Standard International Trade
Classification

0	Food and live animals
01	Meat and preparations
011	Meat, fresh, chilled, frozen
0111	Bovine meat, fresh and frozen
1	Beverages and tobacco
2	Crude materials, excluding fuels
3	Minerals and fuels
4	Animal, vegetable oil, fat
5	Chemicals
6	Basic manufactures
7	Machines and transport equipment
8	Miscellaneous manufactured goods
9	Other

Source: United Nations, *Yearbook of International Trade
Statistics* (New York: United Nations, 1978).

mals (0), beverages and tobacco (1), crude materials, excluding fuels (2), and minerals and fuels (3). At this single-digit level of aggregation, there is a large volume of intraindustry trade. The United States is a large exporter and importer of food and live animals, machines and transport equipment, and chemicals.

The two-digit level defines products more narrowly and includes categories such as meat and preparations (01), which are components of food and live animals. The United States exports wheat and imports meat. These products are in the same category at the single-digit level (food and live animals), but they are different categories at the two-digit level. At the single-digit level, products would appear to be part of intraindustry trade; at the two-digit level they would not.

The three-digit level of aggregation has narrower categories, including meat: fresh, chilled, and frozen (011). The four-digit level is the lowest level of aggregation that is readily available, and it consists of 625 categories, including bovine meat, fresh and frozen (0111). The volume of intraindustry trade declines at lower levels of product aggregation, but it is still significant at the four-digit level. Thus, the phenomenon of intraindustry trade is partly attributable to the manner in which trade statistics are presented.

There are also other reasons to expect intraindustry trade. The first reason is border trade attributable to transport costs. The United States, Canada, and Mexico are all large countries in terms of area. This means that people near the border may find it cheaper to trade with foreign neighbors than to trade with fellow citizens in distant regions. The same product may be simultaneously exported from Washington state to British Columbia and imported from Nova Scotia to Maine because international transport costs are lower than domestic transport costs.

A second reason is seasonal trade and time aggregation. Because the growing seasons in the Northern and Southern Hemispheres do not coincide, countries in the North may export agricultural products during the northern growing season and import the same products during the southern growing season. The choice of a year as the proper time period (aggregate) conceals the fact that during each particular growing season, each country is solely an exporter or an importer. This information would be preserved and intraindustry trade would diminish if trade were reported on a monthly or a quarterly basis.

A final reason for intraindustry trade is that some countries have a comparative advantage in providing marketing or middlemen's services. Such middlemen (also called *entrepôts*) import certain products and re-export the same products. Their function may be based on location or the provision of specialized banking or transport services. Singapore, Hong Kong, and The Netherlands are examples of such countries. Intraindustry trade is an important fact in the real world, and there is an apparent conflict between such trade and the concept of comparative advantage. If a country has a comparative advantage in X, it should not be expected to both export and also import X. However, the theory can be reconciled with the facts by considering product differentiation, the services of middlemen, and some peculiarities in the presentation of trade data.

2.7 U.S. TRADE EXPERIENCE

This chapter has discussed the basic principles of absolute and comparative advantage, which are the determinants of the supply of traded goods. It has also considered the general aspects of demand, including differentiated products. If these theoretical concepts have any validity, they must be consistent with the facts of the real world of commerce. This section presents some trade data for the United States that must be explained by international trade theories. A common measure of a country's reliance on international trade (openness) is the ratio of exports to gross national product (GNP). This ratio was presented for a number of countries in Table 1-1, and a time series for the U.S. ratio is shown in Table 2-4. The main point of this table is that the U.S. economy has not been very open, since exports have rarely been as large as 10 percent of the GNP. The only exceptions are the period before 1800 and the period since 1974. In the pre-1800 period most of the population lived near the Atlantic Ocean, where cheap transport was readily available and inland transportation was primitive. Since 1974, the U.S. economy has been more open to international trade than in any period in nearly two centuries. Between these two extreme periods the ratio of exports to GNP has been low and remarkably stable.

From 1834 to 1899, the ratio was always between 5 and 7 percent. From 1900 to 1968, the range was nearly the same (4 to 8 percent) with two minor

TABLE 2-4   U.S. Exports as a Percentage of
GNP, 1710–1980

PERIOD	PERCENTAGE OF GNP
1710–1720	20–30%
1790–1800	10–15
1834–1899	5–7
1900–1968	4–8
1969–1973	8
1974–1978	10
1979–1982	8

Source: Lance Davis et al., *American Economic Growth:* An Economic History of the United States (New York: Harper & Row, 1972), p. 554; and Council of Economic Advisers, *Economic Report of the President,* 1981 (Washington, D.C.: U.S. Government Printing Office, 1981), p. 344.

exceptions. During the decade that includes World War I (1909 to 1918), the ratio rose to 8.1 percent. For much of the War period the United States was the major supplier of the combatants whose economies were seriously disrupted. The second exception was the period that includes the Great Depression, when exports fell to 3.8 percent of the GNP. The United States imposed the restrictive Smoot-Hawley tariff (see Chapter 7) in 1930, and most trading partners retaliated with their own trade barriers.

The major explanation for the relative historical unimportance of trade is that the United States is a large economy in which interregional trade substitutes for international trade. However, in one important sense, the ratio of exports to GNP understates the importance of trade to the economy. Many products are directly affected by trade even if they are not imported or exported. Domestic products that compete with imports have competitive prices. Competition from imports has forced U.S. producers of textiles, shoes, steel, and autos to keep their prices lower than they otherwise would have been. Domestically produced products that are consumed at home but are good substitutes for exports must also sell for competitive prices. In recent years half the U.S. grain crop has been exported, but the half that remained at home sold for a higher price than it otherwise would have because the export alternative was available. The term "importable" refers to both imports and also their domestic substitutes. The term "exportable" includes both exports and also substitutes that remain at home. Thus, all U.S. wheat is exportable, even if only half the crop is exported. International trade has a direct effect on the prices of all importables and exportables, not just imports and exports. Therefore, the influence of trade is greater than that indicated by the ratio of exports to the GNP.

In the absence of trade barriers, the United States should export products in which it has a comparative advantage and import those goods in which it has a comparative disadvantage. The commodity composition of trade for the United States for 1982 is shown in Table 2-5. It should provide some information about the comparative advantage of the United States.

On the import side petroleum was most important at $61.2 billion or 25 percent of total imports. Other important imports were consumer goods at $39.7 billion (16 percent of imports), capital goods at $35.5 billion (14%), and automotive vehicles at $33.3 billion (13 percent). Exports should reflect comparative advantage, and the largest exports were machinery at $62.0 billion (29 percent of total exports) and agricultural products at $37.4 billion (18 percent). Other export categories are: automotive vehicles (8 percent), and consumer goods (7 percent). Notice that these product categories are fairly broad, and at this level of aggregation, there is considerable intraindustry trade. The United States was a large exporter and importer of agricultural products, industrial supplies and materials, automotive vehicles, and consumer goods.

Measured by the value of imports, the major comparative disadvantage for the United States is in petroleum. This was not always true, and the large

TABLE 2-5   Commodity Composition of U.S. Trade, 1982

	1982 VALUE (IN BILLIONS OF DOLLARS)	PERCENTAGE OF TOTAL
Exports		
Agricultural products	$ 37.4	18%
Industrial supplies and materials	63.6	30
Machinery	62.0	29
Civilian aircraft	10.0	5
Automotive vehicles	16.7	8
Consumer goods, excluding food, and autos	14.7	7
Other	7.0	3
Total exports	$211.4	
Imports		
Foods, feeds, beverages	$ 17.1	7%
Industrial supplies and materials	114.8	46
Petroleum and products	61.2	25
Capital goods except autos	35.5	14
Automotive vehicles	33.3	13
Consumer goods	39.7	16
Other	7.3	3
Total imports	$308.9	

Source: U.S. Department of Commerce, *Survey of Current Business* (Washington, D.C.: U.S. Government Printing Office, March 1983), pp. 53–54.

TABLE 2-6   U.S. Petroleum Imports, 1970–1982

YEAR	PRICE (CURRENT DOLLARS)	PRICE (CONSTANT 1967 DOLLARS)	IMPORT VOLUME (MILLIONS OF BARRELS PER DAY)	VALUE OF IMPORTS (BILLIONS OF DOLLARS PER YEAR)	OIL IMPORTS (AS A PERCENTAGE OF TOTAL IMPORTS)
1970	$ 2.16	$ 1.86	3.75 bbl	$ 2.9	7%
1971	2.43	2.00	4.14	3.6	8
1972	2.57	2.05	5.00	4.6	8
1973	3.33	2.50	6.83	8.4	12
1974	10.98	7.43	6.61	26.6	26
1975	11.45	7.10	6.50	27.0	28
1976	12.14	7.12	7.81	34.6	28
1977	13.29	7.23	9.30	45.0	30
1978	13.28	6.80	8.74	42.3	24
1979	18.67	8.59	8.81	60.0	28
1980	30.46	12.35	7.09	78.9	32
1981	34.02	12.49	6.25	77.6	29
1982	31.26	10.81	5.36	61.2	25

Source: Board of Governors of the Federal Reserve System, *Federal Reserve Bulletin,* April 1981, p. 271, and U.S. Department of Commerce, *Survey of Current Business* (Washington, D.C.: U.S. Government Printing Office, March 1983).

value of recent petroleum imports was partly due to the change in the structure of the petroleum market that occurred in 1974 and partly due to U.S. oil price policy.

Table 2-6 shows a time series of U.S. oil import data for the period from 1970 to 1982. It includes prices paid for imported oil in current and constant 1967 dollars, the volume of imported oil in millions of barrels per day, the value of imports in dollars per year, and petroleum imports as a percentage of total imports. The column showing prices in current dollars shows the first significant price increase in 1973 from $2.57 per barrel to $3.33. In 1974 the price more than tripled from $3.33 to $10.98. From 1974 through 1978 oil prices rose more slowly than inflation, but in 1979 there was sharp increase to $18.67 and larger increase to $30.46 in 1980. The money price declined to $31.26 in 1982.

The inflation factor is removed in the column showing oil prices in constant 1967 dollars. That column shows a $0.45 increase in 1973 and a nearly $5.00-per-barrel increase in 1974. Real prices fell in 1975 and remained below the 1974 level until the $1.79-per-barrel increase in 1979 and the $3.76-per-barrel increase in 1980. The real price fell to $10.81 in 1982. These are the average prices paid by Americans for imported oil.

Prices received by domestic producers were held below this level by regulation. The volume of oil imports fell slightly after the price increase of 1974 (from 6.83 million barrels per day in 1973 to 6.61 million barrels per day in 1974), but imports increased in 1976 and reached their peak in 1977 at 9.30 million barrels per day. Import volume decreased after 1977; in 1978 and 1979, and in 1981 oil imports were below the 1973 level. Until 1982 prices increased much more than quantity of imports decreased. Consequently the dollar value of oil imports increased. The largest increases in value were in 1974 (from $8.4 billion to $26.6 billion), in 1979 (from $43.3 billion to $60.0 billion), and in 1980 (from $60.0 billion to $78.9 billion). Petroleum was not a particularly important import category before 1973, with a steady share of 7 to 8 percent. The share jumped to 26 percent in 1974 and to 32 percent in 1980. The oil share declined to 25 percent in 1982. Thus, the overwhelming importance of oil imports is a rather recent phenomenon. It remains to be seen whether the dominance of oil imports constitutes a permanent change in comparative advantage or a transitory change in the structure of the world oil market.

Export figures shown in Table 2-7 indicate a large and growing comparative advantage for the United States in agricultural products. For the world as a whole, the agricultural share of total trade has been declining for many years. For the United States, the agricultural share of total exports has remained near 20 percent since 1965. The United States did not become a consistent net exporter of agricultural products until 1960, but agricultural surpluses have occurred every year since then. The surpluses before 1973 overstate the U.S. agricultural comparative advantage because the government pursued an active export subsidy program associated with foreign aid.

During the period from 1955 to 1980 the average fraction of U.S. agricultural exports that was subsidized was 11 percent. The peak of the subsidy share was 41 percent in 1957, and the minimum was 4 percent in 1980. The

TABLE 2-7   U.S. Agricultural Exports, 1935–1980

PERIOD	NET AGRICULTURAL EXPORTS (IN BILLIONS OF DOLLARS PER YEAR)	AGRICULTURAL EXPORTS (AS A PERCENTAGE OF TOTAL EXPORTS)
1935–39	$ −0.4	27%
1940–44	−0.2	14
1945–49	+0.7	29
1950–54	−1.1	23
1955–59	0.0	22
1960–64	+1.5	24
1965–69	+1.8	20
1970–74	+5.5	20
1975–79	+13.5	20
1980	+24.0	20

Source: U.S. Department of Agriculture, U.S. Foreign Agricultural Trade Statistical Report, 1979 (Washington, D.C.: USDA, October, 1980).

TABLE 2-8   U.S. Service Transactions, 1970 and 1980 (in billions of dollars)

	1970			1980		
	EXPORTS	IMPORTS	NET	EXPORTS	IMPORTS	NET
U.S. government Transactions	$ 1.8	$ 5.6	$−3.8	$ 8.6	$12.5	$−3.9
Travel	2.3	4.0	−1.7	10.1	10.4	−0.3
Passenger fares	0.5	1.2	−0.7	2.6	3.6	−1.0
Transportation	3.1	2.8	0.3	11.4	10.9	0.5
Royalties and fees	2.3	0.2	2.2	6.9	0.8	6.1
Miscellaneous	1.3	0.8	0.5	5.2	3.2	2.0
Investment income	11.7	5.5	6.2	75.9	43.2	32.7
Total	$23.0	$20.1	$ 3.0	$120.7	$84.6	$ 36.1

Source: U.S. Department of Commerce, *Survey of Current Business* (Washington, D.C.: U.S. Government Printing Office, November 1981), pp. 30–31.

magnitude of net agricultural exports increased sharply from $3 billion to $9 billion in 1973. There is some evidence that the dollar devaluations of 1971 and 1973, which made U.S. exports cheaper to foreigners, stimulated agricultural exports. Net agricultural exports continued to increase, and by 1980 they were $24 billion. The composition of agricultural exports has changed over time, as grain and soybeans have displaced the traditional exports of cotton and tobacco. In 1980 exports were as follows: feed grain (mainly corn), $10 billion; wheat, $7 billion; soybeans, $6 billion; and cotton, $3 billion. Feed grain and soybeans are usually fed to animals and then are consumed indirectly by humans as meat.

The major U.S. agricultural imports in 1980 were coffee ($4 billion), meat ($2 billion), and sugar ($2 billion). Because imports of meat, sugar, and dairy products were restrained by import quotas, the United States probably had a greater comparative disadvantage in these products than the observed volume of imports would indicate. Traditional agricultural trade has been heavily influenced by climate and soil. Modern agriculture has been altered by the application of new technology, machinery, and human capital. Capital is relatively abundant in the United States, and agriculture is one of the most capital-intensive industries in the country.

International trade in services has become quite important for the United States. Merchandise trade is trade in tangible products such as automobiles, grain, and machinery. Merchandise includes the set of goods that passes through customs and is subject to tariffs. Service trade, on the other hand, is trade in intangibles, such as shipping services, research and development, and the return on capital invested abroad. The distinction between goods (merchandise) and services made in the trade accounts is the same as the one made in the GNP accounts. Table 2-8 shows U.S. service trade in 1970 and 1980. Net service exports were $3.0 billion in 1970 and $36.1 billion in 1980, indicating a large and growing comparative advantage in services. Since the service surplus was $25.4 in 1978 and $34.8 in 1979, the comparative advantage does not appear to be transitory.

Services are growing relative to the major merchandise categories. U.S. service exports in 1980 of $120.7 billion were 54 percent of total merchandise exports. Direct investment income, or the annual repatriated income from American-owned businesses abroad, has been the dominant service export, at $75.9 billion in 1980. Exports of the services of capital substitute for capital-intensive merchandise exports. Investment income was much larger than any single merchandise export category, including machinery and agricultural products. Other service exports were transportation ($11.4 billion), travel ($10.1 billion), and fees and royalties ($6.9 billion). Transportation includes the foreign income earned by U.S. airlines and ships. Travel consists of expenditures made by foreign tourists in the United States. Fees and royalties are payments made by firms abroad (including foreign branches of American-owned companies) for the use of technology developed in the United States. After subtracting service imports of $84.6 billion, net exports were $36.1 billion.

Investment income, the repatriated income of foreign firms from their American operations, was also the largest service import. The importance of U.S. service trade can be seen by considering balance-of-payments figures for 1980 and 1981. When only merchandise trade is considered (balance of trade), there were deficits of $25.3 billion in 1980 and $27.8 billion in 1981. When both merchandise and service trade are included, there were surpluses of $3.7 billion in 1980 and $6.6 billion in 1981. Obviously, service trade made an important contribution to these surpluses, but service trade and merchandise trade are interdependent. Reducing the service surplus by only one dollar would not necessarily reduce the total surplus by only one dollar, but by more. Some of the service exports substituted for capital-intensive merchandise exports. A satisfactory theory of trade must explain trade in both goods and services.

SUMMARY

This chapter introduced the concepts of absolute and comparative advantage. In conjunction with demand, they form the basis of international exchange. Because absolute advantage is defined in terms of labor costs or labor productivity, it is possible for one country to have an absolute advantage in all products. Since comparative advantage is defined in terms of forgone opportunity cost or relative labor productivity, each country must have a comparative advantage in some product. Comparative advantage may be determined geometrically by comparing the slopes of home with ROW production possibilities curves. In the simple case of one variable factor of production, the production possibilities curve is a straight line, indicating constant marginal cost. International trade permits residents of a country to choose points on a consumption possibilities curve that lie beyond the production possibilities curve. The total national gains from trade depend on the equilibrium level of prices. A permissible range of prices is determined by costs in the trading countries. Demand conditions interact with costs to determine equilibrium prices within the range. The same relative costs also determine a range for wages and exchange rates between national currencies. Comparative advantage implies specializing in a limited number of products. However, the specialties may be narrowly differentiated products rather than broad product categories. Thus, the large volume of intraindustry trade observed in the real world does not necessarily conflict with the notion of comparative advantage. Since the usefulness of a theory depends on its ability to explain facts, this chapter's final section presented summary data on U.S. trade in goods and services.

The present chapter has attempted to explain trade patterns in terms of comparative costs, without attempting to explain the sources of comparative cost differences. Chapter 3 will offer an explanation of differences in relative factor supplies between countries.

REFERENCES

ALLEN, WILLIAM, ed. *International Trade Theory: Hume to Ohlin.* New York: Random House, 1965. Contains classic works by Smith, Ricardo, and Hume.

BALASSA, BELA. "An Empirical Demonstration of Classical Comparative Cost Theory." *Review of Economics and Statistics*, August 1963.

GRUBEL, HERBERT, and P. J. LLOYD. *Intraindustry Trade: The Theory and Measurement of International Trade in Differentiated Products.* London: Macmillan, 1975.

HABERLER, GOTTFRIED. *The Theory of International Trade.* London: Hodge, 1936.

KRAUSS, MELVYN B., and HARRY G. JOHNSON. *General Equilibrium Analysis: A Microeconomic Text.* Chicago: Aldine, 1974.

LEONTIEF, WASSILY W. "The Use of Indifference Curves in the Analysis of Foreign Trade." In *Readings in the Theory of International Trade*, Howard S. Ellis and Lloyd A. Metzler, eds. Homewood, Ill.: Richard D. Irwin, 1950.

MACDOUGALL, G. D. A. "British and American Exports: A Study Suggested by the Theory of Comparative Costs." *Economic Journal*, December 1951, pp. 697–724. Reprinted in *Readings in International Economics*. Richard E. Caves and Harry G. Johnson, eds. Homewood, Ill.: Richard D. Irwin, 1968. Contains an early empirical study of comparative costs.

MARSHALL, ALFRED. *Money, Credit, and Commerce.* London: Macmillan, 1923. Appendix J, which was written earlier (1869–1873), contains an influential geometrical treatment of trade relationships.

MEADE, JAMES E. *A Geometry of International Trade.* London: George Allen and Unwin, 1952.

RICARDO, DAVID. *Principles of Political Economy and Taxation* (1817), Vol. I of Piero Sraffa, ed., *The Works and Correspondence of David Ricardo.* Cambridge: Cambridge University Press, 1953. The first formal statement of comparative advantage.

SMITH, ADAM. *An Inquiry into the Nature and Causes of the Wealth of Nations* (1776). New York: Random House Modern Library Edition, 1937. A paperback reprint was published in 1976 by the University of Chicago Press.

STERN, ROBERT. "British and American Productivity and Comparative Costs in International Trade." *Oxford Economic Papers*, October 1962.
UNITED NATIONS. *Yearbook of International Trade Statistics*, New York, annually. Presents trade data using SITC categories.
U.S. DEPARTMENT OF COMMERCE. *Survey of Current Business*, monthly. Presents detailed data on U.S. trade.
VINER, JACOB. *Studies in the Theory of International Trade.* London: George Allen and Unwin, 1937. Thoroughly documented history of economic thought on trade.

CHAPTER THREE
TRADE WITH INCREASING MARGINAL COST

3.1 INTRODUCTION

Trade conditions for a simple economy were discussed in Chapter 2. It was shown that an economy employing one variable factor of production has a straight-line production possibilities curve. Since the slope of a production possibilities curve represents marginal cost, such an economy is characterized by constant cost of production. The cost of an additional unit of a product, X, is always the same, no matter what volume of X is being produced. In the example of Chapter 2, the marginal cost of cloth was 2 units of food for any level of cloth output. Complete specialization is an implication of constant costs.

The present chapter analyzes economies characterized by increasing marginal cost of production. Increasing costs occur because of the existence of two distinct factors of production used in different proportions in the production of different goods. In contrast to the case of constant cost, increasing cost tends to bring about incomplete specialization between countries. The division of factors of production into two or more groups makes it possible to discuss relative supplies of factors of production in different countries. One explanation of comparative cost differences is that relative factor supplies differ between countries. This chapter will show that a country's production possibilities curve may be derived from information about technology and relative supplies of factors of production. If demand conditions are similar at home and abroad, the pattern of a country's trade will be determined by relative factor supplies. An important empirical implication of this factor proportions theory is that countries will export products that use large quantities of their relatively abundant factor of production and import products that use large amounts of their relatively scarce factor. A second implication is that trade will increase the price of the abundant factor of production and decrease the price of the scarce factor.

Supply and demand curves for importables and exportables can be derived from the nation's production possibilities curve and the community indifference map. The home country's import demand and export supply curves can be derived from the conditions in the importable and exportable markets. With the use of these analytical devices, one can distinguish between the economic effects of a domestic sales tax and the effect of a tariff. It will be shown that the effects differ because the elasticities of demand and supply for imports and exports are greater than the corresponding domestic elasticities. The significance of trade elasticities will be illustrated by considering the U.S. energy policy.

3.2 PRODUCTION POSSIBILITIES, TECHNOLOGY, AND FACTOR SUPPLIES

Relative slopes of home and foreign production possibilities curves reflect comparative costs. Classical writers such as David Ricardo did not offer a detailed explanation of why costs might differ between countries. They made vague references to differences in climate, soil, and culture that would generate differences in national productivity. Explaining international trade by comparing differences in national productivity has the virtue of being a simple theory with modest data requirements for testing.[1] A shortcoming of such a simple theory is that it fails to distinguish between alternative sources of productivity differences. One possibility is that productivity differences are fully explained by national differences in technology.

An alternative explanation of comparative cost is that technology is identical in all countries, but relative factor supplies and factor prices differ among countries. The latter explanation is called the factor supply or factor endowments theory of trade. It is also called the Heckscher-Ohlin theory after the Swedish economists, Eli Heckscher (1879–1952) and Bertil Ohlin (1899–1979).[2] Of course, technological differences do not preclude factor supply differences. Thus, the Ricardian theory does not necessarily conflict with the Heckscher-Ohlin theory. However, the Heckscher-Ohlin theory is more ambitious in that it attempts to explain both the pattern of each country's trade and also the

---

[1] See Chapter 5 for a discussion of empirical studies by G. D. A. MacDougall and others.

[2] See Eli Heckscher, "The Effect of Foreign Trade on the Distribution of Income," *Economisk Tidskrift*, 1919, reprinted in Howard S. Ellis and Lloyd A. Metzler, eds., *Readings in the Theory of International Trade* (Homewood, Ill.: Richard D. Irwin, 1950); and Bertil Ohlin, *Interregional and International Trade* (Cambridge, Mass.: Harvard University Press, 1933).

source of comparative cost differences between countries. The relationship between factor supplies and comparative cost can be shown by deriving the production possibilities curve from information about technology and national factor endowments.

Let all factors of production be divided into two categories: capital and labor. To justify this grouping, one must assume that the components of each category are relatively homogeneous. This assumption abstracts from differences between skilled and unskilled labor and differences between natural resources and produced capital. The consequences of treating diverse factors of production as homogeneous units will be discussed in Chapter 5.

Let each country be endowed with fixed quantities of capital and labor. Capital and labor move freely between industries to maintain full employment, but they are not mobile between countries. Assume that technology, as represented by the production functions for cloth and food, is identical in both countries. Capital and labor can be continuously substituted for each other in both cloth and food production. The substitutability between labor and capital is given by the slopes of the unit isoquants $X_C = 1$ and $X_F = 1$ in Figure 3-1. A unit isoquant shows all the technically efficient combinations of capital and labor that are capable of producing one unit of output.

If the prices of capital and labor are given by the slope of C_1C_2, points A and B are the least cost combinations of capital and labor for producing 1 unit of food and cloth, respectively. The proportions in which capital and labor are employed in the two industries are given by the slopes of the lines $OAGX_F$ and $OBHX_C$. Thus, food production is more capital intensive than is

FIGURE 3-1 Technology, Factor Prices, and Factor Intensity

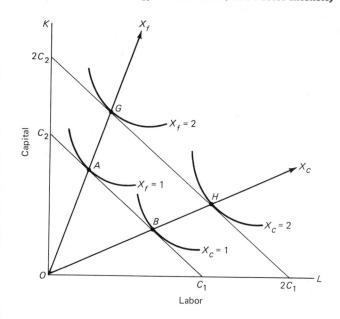

cloth production at the initial factor prices. Factor proportions will vary with factor prices, but it may be assumed that food production is more capital intensive than is cloth at all possible factor prices.[3] Assume that production is subject to constant returns to scale, which means that a doubling of all inputs will also double output. Since factor prices are given, costs will also double. The equilibrium points G and H represent twice as much output as points A and B and twice the quantities of inputs. Under these assumptions, technology determines which product will be more capital intensive. Relative factor supplies determine factor prices and comparative cost between the home country and ROW. For example, if technology determines that food is more capital intensive than is cloth production, the cost of food should be lower in the capital-abundant country.

Information about factor supplies and technology determines the shape of a nation's production possibilities curve. The relationship can be shown with the assistance of an Edgeworth box. The box diagram, named after the British economist Francis Y. Edgeworth (1845–1926), is shown in Figure 3-2, panel

FIGURE 3-2   Factor Supplies Technology and Production Possibilities

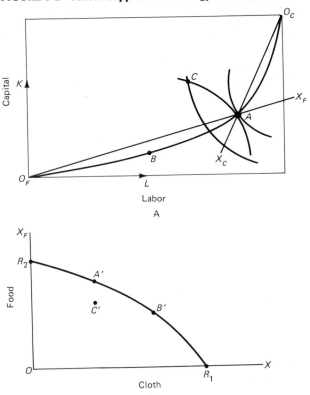

[3] A violation of this assumption is called a factor intensity reversal, which will be considered in Chapter 5.

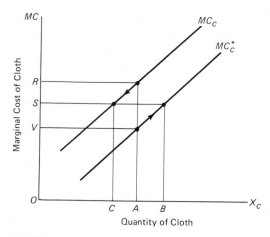

FIGURE 3-3 **Increasing Marginal Cost and Specialization**

A. The dimensions of the box represent the total endowment of labor and capital in the economy. Output of food is measured along isoquants originating at O_F, and output of cloth is measured from O_C. The contract curve $O_F BAO_C$ shows the maximum amount of one product that can be produced for a given amount of the other product. From any point along the contract curve, an increase in output of one product requires a decrease in output of the remaining product. For example, a movement along the contract curve from A to B represents an increase in output of cloth and a decrease in production of food. At point A, the relative slopes of $O_F X_F$ and $O_C X_C$ indicate that cloth production is more capital intensive than is food production. The amount of cloth given up to increase food output can be determined from knowledge of the isoquants. The shape of the production possibilities curve $R_1 R_2$ in panel B is determined by the shape of the contract curve in panel A, and both are determined by the interaction of factor supplies and technology. Points A' and B' on the production possibilities curve are comparable to points A and B on the contract curve. Points off the contract curve, such as C, represent technically inefficient combinations of capital and labor. Point C is inefficient because a movement from C to A results in an increase in food output with no decrease in cloth output. Point C' inside the production possibilities curve is comparable to point C. A change in factor supplies will alter the dimensions of the Edgeworth box and the shape of the production possibilities curve. Since the slope of the production possibilities curve measures the marginal cost of cloth, a change in relative factor supplies will alter comparative cost.

The concave (to the origin) production possibilities curve $R_1 R_2$ implies increasing marginal cost. Specifically, the cost of producing an additional unit of cloth is greater at B' than at A'. Increasing cost tends to bring about incomplete specialization, because marginal cost increases as output expands in the low-cost country, whereas marginal cost decreases as output contracts in the high-cost country. Figure 3-3 shows the case of increasing cost for both the home country and also ROW. At the output level OA, the marginal cost of cloth is greater in the home country (OR) than it is abroad (OV). Expansion of cloth output in ROW will increase cost along the $MC^\star$ curve and contraction at home will decrease cost along the MC curve. Trade will equalize marginal cost in both countries at the level OS, with the home country producing OC units of cloth and ROW producing OB units. Variability of marginal cost in both countries retards specialization. Notice in Figure 3-3 that if specialization went farther, ROW would produce more cloth than OB and the home country would produce less cloth than OC. Specialization would be excessive, since marginal cost would be greater in ROW $(MC^\star)$ than in the home country (MC).

3.3 CLOSED AND OPEN ECONOMY EQUILIBRIUM WITH INCREASING COST

The effects of increasing cost on home country equilibrium is shown in Figure 3-4. The shape of the production possibilities curve R_1R_2 depends on technology and relative factor supplies. Demand conditions are represented by the indifference curves U_1, U_2, and U_3. In the absence of trade, the equilibrium is at point A on curve U_1. Point A represents both production and consumption, and R_1R_2 represents both production possibilities and consumption possibilities. Since the home country has a comparative disadvantage in cloth, international trade will reduce the relative price of cloth. Point B is the equilibrium production point, and point C is the equilibrium consumption point on the free trade price line BC.

Trade causes domestic food production to increase, but the home country does not completely specialize in food. Production of food is restrained before complete specialization occurs. Each additional unit of exportable food can be produced only at a higher cost than the previous unit. The trade triangle BEC shows that BE units of food are exported in exchange for EC units of imported cloth. Since point C is on a higher indifference curve (U_3) than is point A (U_1), the home country benefits from trade. There would be consumption gains for residents even if production did not respond to world prices. The line AD indicates that there are consumption gains from trade. Curve AD passes through the initial production point A and is parallel to BC. If AD were the consumption possibilities curve, point D on U_2 would be the consumption point. Trade would permit home residents to move to a higher indifference curve (U_2) without altering production. When production is permitted to respond to prices, production moves to point B and consumption moves to point C on curve U_3. The movement from U_2 to U_3 indicates production gains from trade. Under conditions of increasing cost, specialization tends to be incomplete. However, an exception occurs when one country is much larger than the

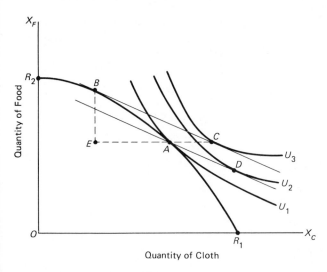

FIGURE 3-4   Home Country Equilibrium with Increasing Marginal Cost

other. An example would be a small exporter of food, such as Argentina, trading with a large importer of food, such as the USSR. If Argentina specialized only in food production and the USSR produced both food and other products, Argentina might be unable to satisfy both domestic food demand and USSR demand for food. Although complete specialization based on size differences is a logical possibility, it is not frequently observed in the real world.

It has been shown that the pattern of international trade depends on both demand and supply considerations. Specifically, trade depends on consumer preferences, real income,[4] technology, and relative factor supplies. Of all these explanatory variables, Heckscher and Ohlin emphasized factor supplies. To derive clear theoretical implications, one must assume that factor supplies dominate international differences in demand and technology. If preferences, income,[5] and technology are identical in all countries, the pattern of trade is solely determined by relative factor supplies. Labor-abundant countries should export labor-intensive goods; capital-abundant countries should export capital-intensive goods. The case in which preferences, income, and technology are identical in both countries is shown in Figure 3-5. The home country's production possibilities curve R_1R_2 is steeper than ROW's production possibilities curve at a given level of cloth output. Technology is assumed to be the same in both countries. The shapes of the curves reflect greater labor abundance in ROW, which indicates a lower marginal cost of cloth in ROW. Because of identical preferences, a single indifference map is used for both countries. Both

---

[4] Real income is the purchasing power of a given money income over goods and services. It is commonly measured by money income divided by a price index.

[5] It would be sufficient to assume that consumers' budget shares are the same at all income levels. This requirement is met when preferences are homothetic, which implies that all income elasticities equal 1.

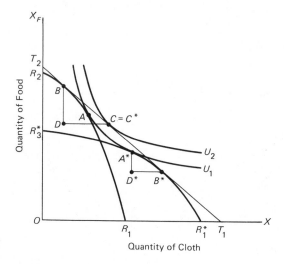

FIGURE 3-5   Trade Equilibrium with Identical Demand in Both Countries

countries start on the same indifference curve U_1 because they have equal real-incomes. In the absence of trade, the home country will produce and consume at point A, and ROW will produce and consume at point A^*. Cloth will be more expensive in the home country, and food will be more expensive in ROW. Trade will equalize prices at a level shown by the slope of $T_1 T_2$. Because preferences and income are identical, both countries will consume at point $C = C^*$ on curve U_2. The home country will specialize in the production of food at point B, and ROW will specialize in cloth at point B^*. The home country will export BD units of food in exchange for DC units of cloth. ROW will export D^*B^* of cloth and import A^*D^* of food. To clear the world markets for food and cloth, home exports of food must equal ROW imports of food, and home cloth imports must equal ROW cloth exports. In this case the pattern of specialization is completely determined by relative factor supplies. The proposition that the pattern of trade depends on relative factor supplies is called the Heckscher-Ohlin theory.

However, if technology and demand are not identical in all countries, it is possible for these variables to overwhelm factor supplies as determinants of trade. The case in which demand differences dominate cost differences is called a demand reversal. For example, let the home country's demand be strongly biased toward food, the labor-intensive good. If the demand bias is strong enough, the autarky price of food will be higher in the home country in spite of the labor abundance at home. The autarky equilibrium will be located northwest of Point A along curve R_1R_2. When trade is introduced, the home country will become an importer of food. The reader is invited to demonstrate this possibility geometrically.

Another possibility is that technological differences between countries dominate factor supplies. For example, a country possessing a superior technology for a labor-intensive good might export that good even if the country were capital abundant. The employment of less labor per unit of food could result in lower cost, in spite of higher wages. This case will be discussed in Chapter 5 under the subject of trade based on a technological gap and the product cycle. Thus, the importance of factor supplies as a determinant of trade depends on the similarity of demand and technology between trading countries.

By altering relative product prices, international trade changes the pattern of world production. Food production expands at home and cloth production expands abroad. Trade also alters the distribution of income within each country. As food production expands in the home country, the demand for capital and labor increases. As cloth production contracts at home, the demand for labor and capital declines. Since food production is more capital intensive than is cloth production, there is a net increase in the demand for capital and a net decrease in the demand for labor. The effects of trade on factor prices is an increase in the rental on capital goods and a decrease in wages in the home country. Trade will redistribute national income in favor of owners of capital and against labor.

The opposite effect will occur in ROW. Expansion of labor-intensive cloth production and contraction of capital-intensive food production tends to raise wages and lower the rental on capital in ROW. In general, trade increases the price of a country's abundant factor and decreases the price of the scarce factor. Trade tends to equalize both product prices and factor prices between countries. Although there are net gains from trade for each country, some individuals in each country lose from trade. Specifically, workers in the home country are harmed by lower wages that are attributable to trade. Trade relationships have been expressed in terms of production possibilities curves and community indifference curves. The relationship of trade to supply and demand curves for importables and exportables will be discussed in the next section.

3.4 IMPORTABLE DEMAND, IMPORTABLE SUPPLY, AND THE DEMAND FOR IMPORTS

The production possibilities curve shows that the amount of a good that can be produced in a country depends on the amount of the other good produced in the same country. An indifference curve shows that the amount of one good desired by consumers depends on the amount of the other good chosen by consumers. These analytical techniques stress the interdependence between consumption and production of various goods. The set of tools that analyze market interdependency is called general equilibrium analysis. The previous analysis stressed the interdependence between the markets for importable cloth and exportable food and between labor and capital.

A simpler analytical technique is partial equilibrium analysis, commonly called supply and demand. Partial equilibrium focuses on a single market, holding conditions in related market constant. For example, a demand curve expresses quantity demanded as a function of the product's own price, while holding constant related prices, real income, and consumer preferences. Partial equilibrium analysis permits the study of a particular market in more detail than with general equilibrium analysis. However, the analyst may overlook important market interdependency with this method. A more practical advantage to partial equilibrium analysis is that students are more familiar with supply and demand. In the following section the market for the home country's importable product, cloth, will be analyzed in detail. This same product is an exportable from the perspective of the rest of the world (ROW) ($I^s = E^{s\star}$). The same partial equilibrium analysis is applicable to the home country's exportable market, food, which is simultaneously an importable for ROW ($E^d = I^{d\star}$).

The home country's supply and demand curves for importable cloth are derived from the underlying production possibilities curve and indifference map in Figure 3-6. The supply curve of cloth, which shows quantity supplied as a function of the price of cloth, is the marginal cost curve for cloth. The supply curve or marginal cost curve for cloth in panel B is derived from the production possibilities curve in panel A. Specifically, the vertical distance $A'X_O$ in panel B is equal to the slope of the production possibilities curve at point A in panel A. Other points on the supply curve X_C^s are obtained in a similar fashion. Since the maximum amount of cloth is OR_1 in panel A, the supply curve in panel B must become vertical at that quantity. The positive slope of the supply curve indicates increasing marginal cost. The vertical distance up to the supply curve for any quantity is the supply price, the minimum price that sellers will accept for supplying that amount.

The home country's demand curve for importable cloth can be derived from the indifference map. The slope of indifference curve U_0 indicates the amount of food that consumers are willing to give up to acquire one more unit of cloth. This amount is plotted in panel B as the demand price. Thus, the slope of U_0 at point A in panel A is plotted in panel B as the vertical distance X_0A'. Since the indifference curve is convex to the origin, the amount that consumers are willing to pay for additional units of cloth declines with the quantity of cloth. Hence, the demand curve for cloth has a negative slope. In the absence of trade, equilibrium occurs for the home economy at the intersection of the importable supply curve and the importable demand curve. At point A' the equilibrium price is O_2P_2 and the equilibrium quantity is O_2X_0. Of course, domestic production of cloth must equal domestic consumption of cloth. Thus, panel B of Figure 3-6 is a supply and demand representation of the closed economy equilibrium in panel A.

The effect of international trade on the home country is shown in panel

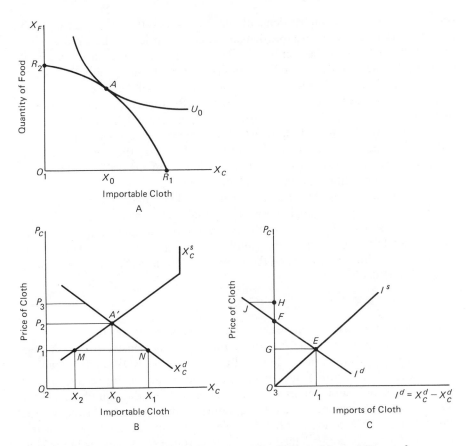

FIGURE 3-6 ·Supply and Demand for Importable Cloth and Import Demand

C of Figure 3-6. The import demand curve (I^d) is derived from the demand
and supply curves for importable cloth. Specifically, import demand is defined
as the difference between the demand for the importable and domestic supply
of the importable:

$$I^d = X_C^d - X_C^s$$

Geometrically, import demand in panel C is the horizontal distance between X_C^d and X_C^s in panel B. Import demand is a kind of excess demand curve.
For example, at price O_2P_1 the quantity demanded by domestic residents is
O_2X_1 and the quantity supplied by domestic firms is O_2X_2. At that price the
excess demand $(MN = X_2X_1)$ is plotted in panel C as GE, a point on the import demand curve. At the higher price P_2, the quantity demanded of the importable equals the quantity supplied, and the zero excess demand is plotted
as point F in panel C. The import demand curve is determined by connecting

points E and F. The import demand curve has a negative slope and is necessarily flatter than the importable demand curve.[6] A price increase reduces import demand through the combined effects of (1) a decrease in quantity demanded of the importable and (2) an increase in quantity supplied of the importable. At prices below O_3F, the home country will be a net importer of cloth. At the price O_3F, the home country is self-sufficient; at higher prices it will be a net exporter of cloth. For example, at the price O_3H, the home country will export HJ units of cloth, which are shown as negative imports. The import demand curve shows the quantity of cloth that the home country is willing to import at various prices. Information about import supply must be obtained from conditions in the rest of the world.

Import supply is shown as I^s in panel C. The import supply curve (I^s) can be derived from the supply curve of exportable cloth and the demand curve for cloth in ROW (not shown in the diagram). It is a kind of excess supply curve for ROW. Specifically, the supply of imported cloth facing the home country is the difference between the supply of cloth in ROW and the demand for cloth in ROW:

$$I_C^s = X_C^{s\star} - X_C^{d\star}$$

The I^s curve has a positive slope and is necessarily flatter than the supply curve of cloth in ROW. The I^s curve is more price responsive than is X_C^s because, at a higher price, more cloth will be produced in ROW and less will be consumed. World equilibrium under free trade occurs at the intersection of the import supply and import demand curves (E). At the equilibrium price $(O_2P_2 = O_3G)$, the quantity of cloth that home residents want to buy equals the amount that ROW residents offer for sale. The home demand for cloth imports (O_3I_1) equals home demand for the importable (P_1N) minus home supply of the importable (P_1M). Any price below O_3G would result in a world cloth shortage, and any higher price would generate a surplus. The result of trade is to make cloth cheaper in the home country and more expensive in ROW than it otherwise would have been. The price change induces an excess demand at home and an excess supply in ROW equal to the volume of world trade in cloth.

Home country residents must pay for cloth by exporting food. The home country's export supply of food and ROW's demand for exported food depend on conditions in the domestic food market in the two countries.

The derivation of export demand and supply is perfectly analogous to that of import demand and supply. The demand and supply curves for imports and

---

[6] The slope of import demand is

$$\frac{dI^d}{dP} = \frac{dX_C^d}{dP} - \frac{dX_C^s}{dP}$$

which is necessarily more negative than $\dfrac{dX_C^d}{dP}$

exports will be employed to analyze a wide variety of trade problems, such as the effect that tariffs, import quotas, and transport costs have on world trade. Before considering the economic effect of a tariff, it is instructive to acknowledge some issues associated with multilateral trade.

3.5 MULTIPLE TRADING PARTNERS AND THE DIRECTION OF TRADE

The analysis so far has considered only two trading partners, the home country and the rest of the world. This relationship, called bilateral trade, is simpler than that in a world of many trading countries. But when ROW is divided into its component parts, some multilateral trade problems emerge. For example, an importing country may impose different tariffs against a product, depending on the source of imports. Similarly, an exporting country may face different tariffs imposed against each of its exports in each destination.

For certain purposes it is convenient to treat ROW as a single economic unit. However, ROW is a diverse aggregate of more than 100 countries, and some information is lost by treating them as a single entity. In addition to concealing the diversity of trading partners, aggregating those countries into a single unit may give the misleading impression that the home country is as large as the rest of the world. In fact, most individual countries are so small that they are unable to affect the prices of goods that they trade.

When the individual countries comprising ROW are treated separately, one must consider the source of home country imports and the destination of home country exports. For example, one must explain the total volume of U.S. oil imports and the amount imported from Saudi Arabia, Mexico, Nigeria, and other sources. In the case of exports, one must explain total U.S. grain exports and the amount shipped to Japan, China, the USSR, and other destinations. Thus, there are two separate issues involving a country's trade pattern. The first issue, the commodity composition of trade, is the determination of which products a country will export and import. The second issue, the direction of trade, is the determination of the source of a country's imports and the destination of its exports. When the world is divided into only two trading partners, the trade direction problem does not arise. The direction of trade for a single country can be shown by listing the destination of its exports and the source of its imports. (These data are shown for the United States, with imports in Table 3-2 and exports in Table 3-3. The complete multilateral pattern of trade is described by a world trade matrix, which is shown for 1978 trade in Table 3-4.)

Table 3-1 shows the relative importance in world trade of various countries that comprise the rest of the world. It shows the value of exports in 1978 for major country groups and selected individual countries. If the United States is taken as the home country, the rest of the world was responsible for 86 per-

TABLE 3-1   World Trade by Country Groups, 1978
(in billions of dollars)

	VALUE OF EXPORTS	PERCENTAGE OF WORLD EXPORTS
World	$1,216.6	100%
Industrial countries	781.4	64
United States	167.0	14
West Germany	111.0	9
Japan	70.4	6
United Kingdom	69.0	6
The Netherlands	58.0	5
Italy	53.0	4
Belgium	49.0	4
Canada	40.8	3
Other European countries	69.5	6
Australia, New Zealand, South Africa	24.4	2
Oil exporting countries	93.5	8
Saudi Arabia	20.0	2
Other less-developed countries	197.6	16
USSR, China, Eastern Europe	48.7	4

Source: International Monetary Fund. Direction of Trade Yearbook, 1979 (Washington, D.C.).

cent of world exports in 1978. The group of industrial countries dominated world trade with 64 percent of total exports. Less developed countries are grouped according to whether they were oil exporters. Other less developed countries (without oil) were responsible for 16 percent of total exports. Oil exporting countries had 8 percent of exports. The centrally planned economies of the USSR, China, and Eastern Europe accounted for only 4 percent of world exports, although they had more than 30 percent of the world's population. Five factors explain their low share of exports: (1) low income, (2) substitution of interregional trade for international trade, (3) inconvertible currencies, (4) national security considerations, and (5) incompatibility of unrestricted trade and central planning.

Most trade is concentrated among a relatively small number of industrial countries. Among individual countries in 1978 the United States was largest exporter, with 14 percent of world exports. The next largest national exporters were all industrial countries: West Germany (9 percent), France (7 percent), United Kingdom (6 percent), Japan (6 percent), The Netherlands (5 percent), and Italy (4 percent). Within the group of less developed countries, the largest exporter was Saudi Arabia, with 2 percent of world exports. Petroleum accounted for nearly all of Saudi Arabia's export earnings, demonstrating a feature that less developed countries have in common: exports tend to be concentrated in a small number of products. Some potential problems associated with export concentration will be considered in Chapter 12.

The commodity composition of a country's exports depends on comparative cost. When there are many trading countries, the destination of one's exports depends on characteristics of export demanders in alternative destinations. The relevant characteristics include transportation costs, income, population, and barriers to trade. Thus, exports from the United States are more likely to be sent to countries characterized by (1) nearness to the United States, (2) high income, (3) large population, and (4) few barriers to U.S. products.

The direction of U.S. export trade for 1978 is shown in Table 3-2. Total exports were $144 billion, of which $76 billion (53 percent) was sent to industrial countries. Oil exporting countries received 11 percent of U.S. exports, while other less developed countries received 26 percent. The remaining 10 percent of exports was divided evenly among the remaining regions.

Among individual countries, the most important destination for U.S. exports was Canada, which received 20 percent of the total. The next four largest markets were Japan (9 percent), United Kingdom (5 percent), West Germany (5 percent), and Mexico (5 percent). The importance of Canada and Mexico for U.S. exports must be partly attributable to low transport costs. Although Canada's population (24 million) is much smaller than Mexico's (65 million), Canada is a larger market for U.S. products than is Mexico because of higher annual per capita income (Canada, $8,350; Mexico, $1,160). The importance of Western Europe and Japan as markets for U.S. products is attributable to high income and, to a lesser extent, low transport costs.

The sources of U.S. imports were very similar to the destinations of U.S.

TABLE 3-2   Direction of U.S. Trade: Exports, 1978
(in billions of dollars)

	VALUE OF EXPORTS	PERCENTAGE OF WORLD EXPORTS
Total U.S. exports	$143.7	100%
Industrial countries	76.4	53
Canada	28.4	20
Japan	12.9	9
United Kingdom	7.1	5
West Germany	7.0	5
The Netherlands	5.7	3
France	4.2	2
Other European countries	5.2	3
Australia, New Zealand, South Africa	4.4	3
Oil exporting countries	16.0	11
Saudi Arabia	4.4	3
Other less developed countries	37.4	26
Mexico	6.7	5
USSR, China, and Eastern Europe	4.2	3

Source: International Monetary Fund. *Direction of Trade Yearbook, 1979* (Washington, D.C.).

exports. Table 3-3 shows that U.S. imports were $183 billion in 1978, of which $97 billion or 53 percent came from industrial countries. Thus, the import share (53 percent) from industrial countries was exactly the same as their export share. Oil exporting countries were the source of 18 percent of U.S. imports, whereas they were the destination for only 11 percent of U.S. exports. Other less developed countries were the source of 24 percent of U.S. imports. Among individual countries, Canada was the largest source of U.S. imports with 19 percent. Thus, Canada was the most important trading partner for the United States in terms of both imports and exports. The next most important sources of imports were Japan (14 percent), Germany (6 percent), United Kingdom (4 percent), and Mexico (3 percent). The same five nations that appeared at the top of the U.S. export list were also at the top of the import list. Certain individual less developed countries have become important sources of U.S. imports. Brazil, Taiwan, Hong Kong, and Korea now rival Italy and France as import suppliers. Because of their economic success, these countries are sometimes treated as a separate group called newly industrializing countries.[7]

TABLE 3-3   Direction of U.S. Trade: Imports, 1978
(in billions of dollars)

	VALUE OF IMPORTS	PERCENTAGE OF WORLD IMPORTS
Total U.S. imports	$183.1	100%
Industrial countries	96.7	53
Canada	34.6	19
Japan	26.5	14
West Germany	10.6	6
United Kingdom	6.8	4
Italy	4.5	2
France	4.3	2
Other European countries	3.7	2
Australia, New Zealand, South Africa	4.8	3
Oil exporting countries	32.3	18
Saudi Arabia	5.8	3
Nigeria	5.0	3
Other less developed countries	44.0	24
Brazil	3.0	2
Mexico	6.2	3
Republic of China (Taiwan)	5.7	3
Hong Kong	3.8	2
Korea	4.1	2
USSR, China, and Eastern Europe	1.6	1

Source: International Monetary Fund. *Direction of Trade Yearbook, 1979* (Washington, D.C.).

[7] See Chapter 13 for a discussion of trade policies of newly industrializing countries (NICs). The category of NICs has been used by several international agencies, and it usually includes the following 8 countries: South Korea, Hong Kong, Taiwan, Singapore (the "Gang of Four"), Brazil, Mexico, Argentina, and India. When Colombia, Chile, Israel, and Yugoslavia are added, the re-

The pattern of trade of the United States has been shown by listing the destinations of U.S. exports and the sources of U.S. imports. This representation completely describes U.S. trade, but it omits all trade in which Americans are not directly involved. The most complete description of the direction of world trade is provided by a world trade matrix, which is a rectangular array of numbers, showing the value of each country's or region's exports to each of its trading partners. If the value of country 1's exports to country 2 is E_{12}, then the value of country 1's exports to country 3 would be E_{13}, and the value of country 1's exports to country n would be E_{1n}. The first row of the world trade matrix would be

$$E_{11} \ E_{12} \ E_{13} \cdots E_{1n}$$

The first entry (E_{11}) represents purely domestic trade, that is, country 1's exports to itself. Total exports (E_1) of country one are the sum of the entries in row 1, after domestic trade is deleted:

$$E_1 = \sum_{j \neq 1} E_{1j}$$

Similarly, row 2 shows exports of country 2 to its trading partners:

$$E_{21} \ E_{22} \ E_{23} \cdots E_{2n}$$

The sum of entries in row 2, after deleting domestic trade (E_{22}), represents total exports of country 2. If there are n countries, there will be n rows. A typical entry, E_{ij}, represents the exports of country i to country j. The complete world trade matrix is given by:

$$
\begin{array}{cccc|c}
E_{11} & E_{12} & \cdots & E_{1n} & E_1 \\
E_{21} & E_{22} & \cdots & E_{2n} & E_2 \\
\cdot & & & & \\
\cdot & & & & \\
\cdot & & & & \\
E_{n1} & E_{n2} & \cdots & E_{nn} & E_n \\
\hline
I_1 & I_2 & \cdots & I_n & I = E
\end{array}
$$

The elements on the diagonal, $E_{11}, E_{22}, \ldots , E_{nn}$, show purely domestic trade. The sum of entries in column 1 (after deleting E_{11}) shows total imports (I_1) of country 1. Adding the entries in column 1 will give total imports of country 1.

sulting 12 countries accounted for 83 percent of manufactured exports of developing countries in 1973. See Louis Turner and Neil McMullen, *The Newly Industrializing Countries: Trade and Adjustment* (London: George Allen and Unwin, 1982), Chap. 1.

(I). When trade is accurately and systematically measured, world exports (E) should equal world imports (I).

A trade matrix for 1981 that divides the world into five country groups is shown in Table 3-4. Since each group consists of several countries, the diagonal elements show international trade of that group with other members of the same group. It is apparent that domestic trade has already been eliminated from the diagonal elements.

It has already been shown that industrial countries are responsible for the majority of world trade, and Table 3-4 shows that most of their exports go to other industrial countries. In 1981 industrial countries' exports to other industrial countries reached $793 billion or 65 percent of their total exports. Industrial countries also sent $248 (20 percent) of exports to non-oil developing countries, $115 billion to oil exporters, and $35 billion to the USSR and Eastern Europe. Since the Heckscher-Ohlin theory explains trade by differences in factor proportions, the large volume of trade among industrial countries has been cited as evidence against the theory. Factor proportions appear to vary less among different industrial countries than between industrial countries and less developed countries.

Row 2 of Table 3-4 shows that oil exporting countries specialize in exports to industrial countries, $196 billion (72 percent) in 1981. Oil exporters sold very little to each other or to the USSR and Eastern Europe.

Row 3 shows that non-oil developing countries sent $182 billion of exports (56 percent) to industrial countries. Thus, industrial countries are a larger market for developing countries' exports (56 percent) than are developing countries as a market for industrial countries' exports (20 percent). Measurement errors and inconsistencies in national reporting practices prevent world exports (sum of last column entries) from equaling world imports (sum of last row entries).

3.6 TRADE EQUILIBRIUM, DOMESTIC TAXES, AND TARIFFS

This section will treat the rest of the world as a single trading unit. The supply and demand analysis of Section 3.4 can be employed to show the establishment of free trade equilibrium and to demonstrate the differential effects of domestic taxes and tariffs. First, consider the effect of a domestic sales tax in a closed economy. For example, let the demand for cloth by domestic consumers be represented by the following equation:

$$X^d = 60 - 2P^d$$

P^d is the demand price, the maximum price that consumers are willing to pay for each quantity of X rather than doing without it. It is a price that includes

TABLE 3-4 World Trade Matrix, 1981
(in billions of dollars)

EXPORTS TO → EXPORTS FROM ↓	INDUSTRIAL COUNTRIES	OIL EXPORTERS	NON-OIL, DEVELOPING	USSR, E. EUROPE	WORLD*
Industrial countries	$ 793	$115	$248	$35	$1,219
Oil exporting countries	196	4	63	1	270
Non-oil developing countries	182	23	77	21	322
USSR, Eastern Europe	31	3	17	—	51
World	$1,202	$145	$405	$57	$1,862

*Totals may not equal the sum of components because of omitted countries and measurement errors.

Source: International Monetary Fund. *Direction of Trade Statistics Yearbook, 1982* (Washington, D.C.).

any taxes that may be levied on the product. The equation indicates that if X were free $(P=0)$, consumers would demand 60 units, and for each one-dollar increase in the price, quantity demanded would fall by 2 units. The coefficient -2 on the price variable is the slope of the demand curve for X shown in Figure 3-7, and 60 is the intercept on the quantity axis. Let the supply of X by domestic business firms be represented by following the supply equation:

$$X^s = 2P^s$$

P^s is the supply price, which is the minimum price that firms will accept in order to supply a given amount of X. It is a net price that firms receive after paying any taxes that may be levied on X. The demand price (P^d) determines consumer demand, the supply price (P^s) determines producer supply, and the difference between them is equal to the sales tax per unit:

$$P^d - P^s = \tau$$

Consider first the case where there is no sales tax on X. Equilibrium occurs where the quantity that consumers demand is equal to the quantity that firms supply:

$$X^d = X^s$$
$$60 - 2P^d = 2P^s$$
$$P^d = \frac{60}{4} = \$15.00$$

The equilibrium, which is shown as point A in Figure 3-7, occurs at a price of $15. To find the equilibrium quantity, substitute $P^d = 15$ in either the demand or supply equation:

$$X^d = 60 - 2\,(15) = 30$$

In the absence of a tax, the equilibrium price of X will be $15, and the quantity produced and consumed will be 30 units.

Let this equilibrium be disturbed by a $1-per-unit sales tax on X. An example might be the state or federal tax on gasoline. What will be the effect of the sales tax on the price of X and the amount produced and consumed? In the presence of the tax, sellers must remit part of the price paid by consumers to the government, and the supply price will exceed the demand price by the amount of the tax:

$$P^s = P^d - \tau = P^d - 1$$

The firms' supply depends on the after-tax price $(P^d - \tau)$, and the new equilibrium can be found by substituting this expression for P^s in the supply equation:

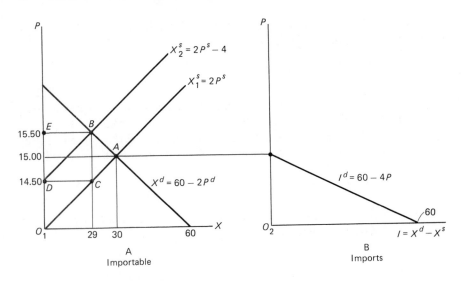

FIGURE 3-7 Domestic Sales Tax

$$X^s = 2P^s = 2\ (P^d - \tau) = 2\ (P^d - 1) = 2P^d - 2$$

Substitute this tax-inclusive supply equation for the earlier one, and find the new equilibrium where

$$X^s = X^d$$
$$2P^d - 2 = 60 - 2P^d$$
$$P^d = \$15.50$$

The \$1-per-unit sales tax raises the consumer price from \$15.00 to \$15.50, and the remainder of the sales tax is borne by producers:

$$P^s = P^d - 1 = \$15.50 - \$1.00 = \$14.50$$

Market conditions prevent sellers from shifting the entire \$1 tax onto consumers. Consequently, sellers are forced to accept a lower after-tax price of \$14.50. Equilibrium is at point B. The paradoxical effect of a sales tax is that it simultaneously raises and lowers prices. The resolution of the paradox is that with a sales tax there are two prices, $P^d \neq P^s$. The consumer price goes up, but the producer price goes down. Thus, a sales tax tends to discourage both domestic consumption and domestic production.

The effect of a sales tax on domestic production distinguishes it from a tariff, as will be shown in later equations. The effect of the tax on demand is found by substituting \$15.50 for the demand price in the demand equation:

$$X^d = 60 - 2P^d = 60 - 2(\$15.50) = 29$$

The effect on domestic production is obtained by substituting $14.50 for the supply price for in the supply equation:

$$X^s = 2P^s = 2(\$14.50) = 29$$

In the absence of trade, the quantity demanded must equal the quantity supplied by domestic firms. The tax reduces both quantities from 30 units to 29. The final effect of the sales tax is to raise revenue (T) for the government by an amount depending on the tax per unit (τ) and the number of units sold (X):

$$T = \tau X = 1(29) = \$29.00$$

The economic effects of a $1-per-unit sales tax on X in a closed economy can be summarized as follows:

	No Tax	Sales Tax ($\tau = \$1$)
Consumer price (P^d)	$15.00	$15.50
Producer price (P^s)	15.00	14.50
Consumption (X^d)	30.00	29.00
Production (X^s)	30.00	29.00
Tax revenue (T)	0.00	29.00

The tax revenue is represented in Figure 3-7 by the area of the rectangle $DEBC$.

To show the effect of a tariff, let the same economy engage in international trade, and let the sales tax on X be zero. The import demand for X depends on the difference between domestic demand and supply:

$$I^d = X^d - X^s$$
$$I^d = 60 - 2P^d - (2P^s) = 60 - 4P^d$$

$(P^d = P^s$ when $\tau = 0)$.

The import demand equation is shown in panel B of Figure 3-7. At a price of $15.00, no imports are demanded. For each $1.00 decrease in the price, the quantity demanded increases by 2 units, the quantity supplied by domestic firms decreases by 2 units, and the quantity of imports demanded increases by 4 units. If imports were given away $(P = 0)$, 60 units would be demanded.

The import demand equation summarizes the terms on which home country residents are willing to trade, but equilibrium cannot be established without information about the terms on which the ROW suppliers are willing to sell. The import supply (export supply from the perspective of ROW) is the difference between total supply in ROW $(X^\star_s)$ and domestic demand $(X^\star_d)$ in ROW. Suppose that import supply is given $\star$

$$I^s = X^\star_s - X^\star_d = 11P^\star$$

Import supply depends on the price prevailing in ROW ($P^\star$). This price will be different from the home country price, if the latter imposes a tariff:

$$P = P^\star + t$$

A tariff is a tax levied on imported X, but not on domestically produced X. A tariff can be thought of as a sales tax from which domestic production is exempt. The initial import supply curve is shown in Figure 3-8. The equilibrium with free trade ($P = P^\star$) occurs at point A, where the quantity of imports demanded equals the quantity of imports supplied:

$$I^d = I^s$$
$$60 - 4P = 11P^\star = 11P$$
$$P = \$4.00$$

The volume of imports is found by substituting this price into either the import supply or import demand equation:

$$I^d = 60 - 4(4) = 44$$

The equilibrium volume of imports must be 44 units, the difference between home country consumption and production. Consumption is obtained by substituting the equilibrium price of $4 for P in the domestic demand equation:

$$X^d = 60 - 2P = 60 - 2(4) = 52$$

Production is obtained from the domestic supply equation:

$$X^s = 2P = 2(4) = 8$$

FIGURE 3-8   Effects of a Tariff

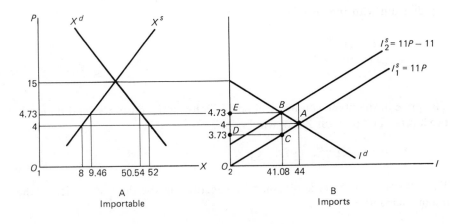

A
Importable

B
Imports

The results are consistent (see Figure 3-8), since imports equal the difference between domestic consumption and production:

$$I = X^d - X^s = 52 - 8 = 44$$

This example is applicable to any importable product, such as oil in the United States. In the absence of trade, there would be some price ($P = \$15.00$ in the example in Figure 3-3) high enough to equalize domestic demand and domestic supply ($X^d = X^s = 30$). The existence of cheaper imported oil would cause the price of domestic oil to fall (from $15.00 to $4.00). U.S. consumers would benefit from the lower price and increase their consumption (from 30 to 52). U.S. oil producers would be harmed by the lower price, and production would decline (from 30 to 8). Employment of capital and labor in the oil industry would also decline. For the 8 units of oil that are produced with free trade, domestic firms receive only $4.00 per unit instead of the previous $15.00. This $11.00 per unit is a pure transfer to U.S. consumers.

Starting from the free trade equilibrium at point A in Figure 3-8, consider the economic effects of a tariff of $1 per unit levied by the home country on imports of product X. A tariff is a discriminatory tax in the sense that it applies to imports but not to domestic production of the same product. In the posttariff equilibrium, the domestic price (P) must exceed the foreign price ($P^\star$) by the amount of the tariff:

$$P^\star = P - t = P - 1$$

To determine the tariff-inclusive import supply, substitute the tariff in the initial import supply equation:

$$I^s = 11P^\star$$
$$I = 11(P - t) = 11(P - 1) = 11P - 11$$

Equilibrium with the tariff occurs where

$$I^s = 11P^\star$$
$$11P - 11 = 60 - 4P$$
$$P = \$4.73$$

The price in the home country will be $4.73 for both consumers and domestic producers. The price in ROW will be lower:

$$P^\star = P - 1 = \$4.73 - \$1.00 = \$3.73$$

The volume of imports is obtained by substituting the domestic price in the import demand equation:

$$I^d = \$60.00 - 4(\$4.73) = \$41.08$$

The posttariff equilibrium is summarized in Figure 3-8. The tariff of \$1 causes the import supply curve to shift upward to $I_2^s = 11P - 11$. The new equilibrium at point B shows that the domestic price has risen from \$4.00 to \$4.73, while the quantity imported declined from 44 to 41.08. Since the domestic price rises by less than the amount of the tariff, the foreign price falls:

$$P^\star = P - t = \$4.73 - \$1.00 = \$3.73$$

Part of the tariff (\$1.00 - \$0.73 = \$.27) has been shifted to foreign suppliers in the form of a lower foreign price, but domestic consumers do not benefit directly from this lower price. The domestic treasury captures the difference between the lower foreign price and the higher domestic price. Total treasury revenue from the tariff is

$$T = tI = 1(\$41.08) = \$41.08$$

Tariff revenue is shown by the area of the rectangle $DEBC$. At the domestic price of \$4.73, consumption is

$$X^d = 60.00 - 2(4.73) = 60.00 - 9.46 = 50.54$$

Domestic production is

$$X^s = 2(4.73) = 9.46$$

Import demand is the difference between domestic consumption and production:

$$I^d = X^d - X^s = 50.54 - 9.46 = 41.08$$

Imports have declined (44.00 - 41.08 = 2.92) because of a decrease in domestic consumption (52.00 - 50.54 = 1.46) and an increase in domestic production (9.46 - 8.00 = 1.46). The consumption and production effects of the tariff occur because the domestic price rises for both consumers and producers.

The increase in both prices illustrates an important difference between a tariff and a sales tax. A sales tax raises the price to consumers, but it lowers the price to domestic producers. Consequently, both tariffs and sales taxes decrease consumption, but a tariff increases domestic production while a sales tax decreases it. The increase in domestic production caused by a tariff is called the protective effect of a tariff. It protects domestic producers from foreign competition, but it harms domestic consumers. The effects of the tariff can be summarized as follows:

	Free Trade	Tariff = $1.00
Domestic price	$ 4.00	$ 4.73
Foreign price	4.00	3.73
Consumption	52.00	50.54
Production	8.00	9.46
Imports	44.00	41.08
Tariff revenue	0.00	41.08

3.7 TRADE AND DIFFERENCES IN DEMAND AND SUPPLY

Potential trade between countries depends on the existence of international price differences in the absence of trade. The initial price differences may be attributable either to differences in supply or demand or both. It was shown in Figure 3-5 that supply differences determine the pattern of trade when demand conditions are identical. Supply differences were represented by production possibilities curves with different shapes.

The effect of demand differences and supply differences on trade can also be shown in terms of import supply and demand curves. Panel A of Figure 3-9 shows the case in which supply conditions differ between the home country and ROW but demand is identical. The demand curves X^d and X^{d*} are identical. The supply curves (X^s and X^{s*}) are drawn so that the home country's costs at each output level are higher than ROW's. It follows that the price of X will be higher in the home country (P_1) than in ROW (P_2) in the absence of trade. The home country's import demand curve (I^d) and ROW's import supply curve (I^s) are derived from the underlying domestic demand and supply curves in the two countries.

The free trade equilibrium is at point C, where the price is P_3 in both countries. Because of its comparative disadvantage in X, the home country is an importer of X. In this case home country imports of X are attributable to higher costs. The difference in cost may be due either to differences in relative factor supplies or to international differences in technology. Without additional information, one cannot discriminate between these alternative explanations of trade.

Alternatively, international trade may be attributable to differences in demand, when supply conditions are the same in both countries. Demand conditions may differ because of differences in preferences, which are influenced by culture, or because of differences in income. For example, Orthodox Moslems are prohibited from consuming alcoholic beverages. Consequently, Moslem North Africans might be expected to demand less wine than Frenchmen with the same income. France and Algeria have been major wine producers, but Algeria has traditionally shipped most of its wine to France. Preferences

FIGURE 3-9 Trade Based on Differences in Supply or Demand

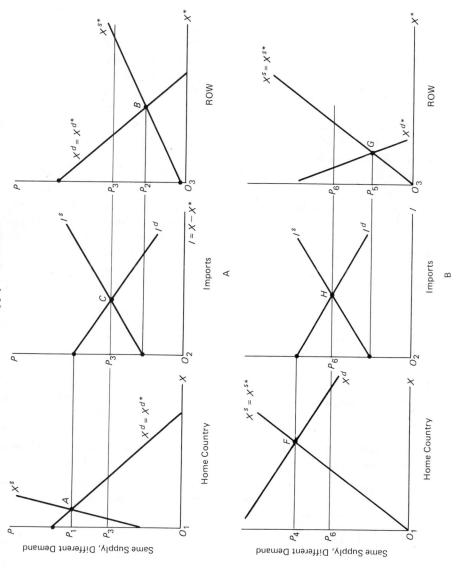

may be partly responsible for the French-Algerian wine trade. Demand may also differ between countries with identical preferences, because of differences in per capita income. As long as income elasticities of demand are different from unity, the proportions in which products are consumed will vary with income even when preferences are identical. In fact, income per capita varies substantially across countries. In 1978 income per capita for the world as a whole was $2110, but income ranged from $9660 per person in North America to $280 per person in Asia.[8] Engel's Law is a well-known empirical relationship, which states that the fraction of income spent on food is inversely related to income. Thus, the pattern of food demand would be quite different in North America and Asia even if preferences were the same on both continents.

The case in which international trade is based on demand differences is shown in Panel B of Figure 3–9. Supply curves for the home country (X^s) and ROW $(X^{s\star})$ are assumed to be identical, but the home country has a greater demand for X at each price. Consequently, the price of X would be greater in the home country (P_4) than in ROW (P_5) in absence of trade. Under free trade the home country would import X even though cost conditions were identical in both countries. The equilibrium price would be P_6 in both countries. The two extreme cases have been shown in which trade is solely attributable to either supply differences or demand differences. The Heckscher-Ohlin theory explains trade by supply differences attributable to variations in factor supplies among countries. More generally, trade may be based on international differences in both supply and demand.

3.8 ELASTICITY OF IMPORT DEMAND

It is often important to measure the sensitivity of trade to price changes. The elasticity of import demand (η_{IP}) measures the percentage change in the demand for imports with respect to a given percentage change in the price of imports. Since import demand is an excess demand, the elasticity of import demand may be expressed in terms of the underlying domestic elasticities of demand and supply:[9]

[8] Data on income per capita for all major countries appears in the annual *World Bank Atlas*.

[9] To find the effect of a price change on import demand, differentiate the expression for imports with respect to price:

$$\frac{dI}{dP} = \frac{dX^d}{dP} - \frac{dX^s}{dP}$$

To express the left-hand side of the equation as an elasticity, multiply both sides by P/I:

$$\frac{dI}{dP}\frac{P}{I} = \frac{dX^d}{dP}\frac{P}{I} - \frac{dX^s}{dP}\frac{P}{I}$$

Express the right-hand-side terms of the equation as elasticities by multiplying the first term by P/X^d and by its reciprocal, X^d/P, and the second term by P/X^s and by its reciprocal, X^s/P, to obtain

$$\eta_{IP} = \left(\frac{dX^d}{dP}\frac{P}{X^d}\right)\frac{X^d}{I} - \left(\frac{dX^s}{dP}\frac{P}{X^s}\right)\frac{X^s}{I}$$

$$\eta_{IP} = \eta_{XP} \frac{X^d}{I} - \epsilon_{XP} \frac{X^s}{I}$$

The domestic price elasticity of demand for X is represented by η_{XP}, which measures the percentage change in the demand for X associated with a given percentage change in the price of X. The price elasticity of the supply of X made available by domestic producers is represented by ϵ_{XP}, which measures the percentage change in domestic supply associated with a given percentage change in price. Because of the law of demand, η_{XP} has a negative sign. Because of the law of supply, ϵ_{XP} has a positive sign. Since the quantities X^d, X^s, and I must all be positive numbers and since ϵ_{XP} is multiplied by -1, both terms on the right-hand side of the equation must be negative. It follows that the elasticity of import demand must be more negative (larger in absolute value) than the elasticity of domestic demand. Therefore, import demand is more elastic than domestic demand. For example, the elasticity of demand for imported automobiles, steel, and petroleum is more elastic than the domestic demand for automobiles, steel, and petroleum.

A product with an inelastic demand ($|\eta_{IP}| < 1$) may have an elastic import demand ($|\eta_{IP}| > 1$). If import demand is elastic, a 10 percent price increase will reduce the volume of import demand by more than 10 percent, which will reduce the total value of imports.

In a country with an elastic import demand for oil, an increase in the price of imported oil would decrease the amount of money spent on imported oil. The economic explanation for this relationship is that a price change brings about a change in the imports partly through a change in domestic demand, but also through a change in domestic production. It is the induced change in domestic production that makes import demand more elastic than domestic demand. If a country were unable to produce a product ($X^s = \epsilon_{XP} = 0$), domestic demand would equal imports ($X^d = I$), and import demand elasticity would equal demand elasticity ($\eta_{IP} = \eta_{XP}$).

It is sometimes convenient to express the import demand elasticity in terms of the share of imports in total demand ($s = I/X^d$). An expression using the import share that is equivalent to the one just given is

$$\eta_{IP} = \frac{1}{s}\eta_{XP} - \left(\frac{1-s}{s}\right)\epsilon_{XP}$$

Since the import share (s) is necessarily a positive fraction, η_{IP} is more negative than is η_{XP}. In general, the magnitude of the import demand elasticity depends on

1. Domestic demand elasticity (η_{XP})
2. Domestic supply elasticity (ϵ_{XP})
3. Share of imports in total demand (s)

Specifically, import demand is more elastic (1) the more elastic domestic demand is, (2) the more elastic domestic supply is, and (3) the smaller the market share of imports is.

The concept of import demand elasticity can be illustrated by using some values that might represent conditions in the U.S. oil market. Let the initial domestic quantities demanded and supplied be

$X^d = 15$ million barrels per day (m.b.d.)
$X^s = 9$ m.b.d.

It follows that the initial volume of imports must be

$I = X^d - X^s = 6$ m.b.d.

Suppose that the domestic demand and supply elasticities are

$\eta_{XP} = -0.2$ and $\epsilon_{XP} = +0.6$

Substituting these values in the equation for the import elasticity yields

$$\eta_{IP}^{\star} = \frac{X^d}{I}\eta_{XP} - \frac{X^s}{I}\epsilon_{XP}$$

$$\eta_{IP} = \frac{15}{6}(-0.2) - \frac{9}{6}(+0.6) = -1.4$$

In this case a 10 percent increase in the price of the oil would induce a 14 percent decrease in the quantity of imported oil and a decrease in the amount of money spent on imported oil. This result illustrates that a product with a highly inelastic domestic demand (-0.2) can still have an elastic import demand. The same result can be shown in terms of the import share of the market, where s equals market share. In the example, imports are 40 percent $(s = 6/15)$ of domestic consumption, and

$$\eta_{IP} = \frac{1}{s}\eta_{XP} - \frac{1-s}{s}\epsilon_{XP} = (\frac{1}{0.4})(-0.2) - (\frac{1-0.4}{0.4})(+0.6) = -1.4$$

In this case import demand is elastic because the relatively unresponsive domestic demand is dominated by a more responsive domestic supply and a small import share.

As long as domestic prices respond to foreign prices, the expression for the import elasticity measures the response of imports to a foreign disturbance. For example, the formation of a cartel in the rest of the world would increase the foreign price of the imported good. Unrestricted arbitrage would transmit the price increase to the home country. However, if trade were restricted, by a quota, for example, the domestic price need not respond to the foreign price change. U.S. domestic prices were insulated from foreign prices from 1973 to 1981. Regulation held domestic prices below world prices, producing an incentive to buy oil in the United States and to sell it abroad. Exports were blocked by a quota. Since the demand for oil in the United States and the supply of oil by domestic producers depend on the domestic price, there was little incentive for consumers to conserve oil or for producers to expand output. The federal price control system prevented the foreign price increase from being transmitted to domestic prices.

The quantity of oil imports may be quite responsive to domestic prices, but unresponsive to foreign prices, if domestic prices are not permitted to respond to foreign prices. Partly because of the price insulation policy, the foreign oil price increases of 1974 and 1979 to 1980 resulted in large increases in the value of oil imported into the United States. The quantity of oil imported responded to the low domestic price rather than to the high foreign price. It is possible that the U.S. import elasticity is less than 1, because the true elasticities for η_{XP} and ϵ_{XP} are smaller than the values assumed. An alternative explanation is that η_{IP} is greater than 1, but imports were unresponsive to the foreign price increase, because price signals were not transmitted to domestic producers and consumers.

A government policy of insulating domestic prices from changes in foreign prices has a direct effect on the demand for imports. Since any elasticity is the percentage change in one variable in response to a given percentage change in another variable, the response of domestic prices to foreign prices can be expressed as an elasticity. The price transmission elasticity is defined as follows, when T equals price transmission:

$$T = \frac{dP}{dP^\star}\left(\frac{P^\star}{P}\right)$$

It is the percentage change in the domestic price associated with a given percentage change in the foreign price of the same product.

If foreign prices were always fully transmitted to the domestic economy, a 10 percent increase in foreign prices would induce a 10 percent increase in domestic prices, and T would equal 1. At the opposite extreme, if domestic prices never responded to foreign prices, T would equal zero. The latter case could be described as complete insulation of domestic prices. In intermediate cases, where domestic prices are partially responsive, T is between zero and 1.

The U.S. oil policy was complicated because domestic producers and consumers faced different prices. The domestic producer price was essentially fixed, but the consumer price was partly responsive to the world price. Consumers buying domestic oil paid a low price (subject to rationing), while consumers buying foreign oil paid the world price. This complication requires separate transmission for domestic demand (T^d) and domestic supply (T^s), and the magnitude of insulation can be measured by each transmission elasticity. The effect of insulation is to reduce the response of import demand to a foreign price change, as can be seen from the following expression:

$$\eta_{IP}{}^{\star} = T^d \frac{X^d}{I} \eta_{XP} - T^s \frac{X^s}{I} \epsilon_{XP}$$

If $\eta_{IP}{}^{\star}$ is the response of import demand to foreign prices, then T^d is the transmission elasticity for consumer prices, and T^s is the transmission elasticity for domestic producer prices. If $T^d = T^s = 1$, then the expression reduces to the simple equation

$$\eta_{IP}{}^{\star} = \frac{X^d}{I} \eta_{XP} - \frac{X^s}{I} \epsilon_{XP}$$

If $T^d = T^s = 0$, then $\eta_{IP}{}^{\star} = 0$, no matter how large η_{XP} and ϵ_{XP} are. Thus, $\eta_{IP}{}^{\star}$ can be zero, even when $\eta_{IP} = 1.4$. In general, a policy of insulation reduces the value of T, which reduces the response of imports to foreign prices.

In the case of U.S. oil policy, the price received by domestic producers was not permitted to rise when world prices rose, and therefore T_s was small or zero. The consumer price was more complicated because buyers had to pay the world price for imported oil. Otherwise foreign suppliers would turn to other national markets. However, the price paid for domestic oil was artificially low and the resulting shortage brought about a complicated rationing program. Thus, on the demand side, T_d was less than 1 but probably greater than the value of T_s. An extreme empirical example of insulating trade policy is the European Economic Community's variable grain levy, which essentially reduces the values of T_d, T_s, and $\eta_{IP}{}^{\star}$ to zero. Each \$1 decrease in the foreign price is completely offset by a \$1 increase in the EEC grain tariff. Another example of insulation is the English Corn Laws (1689–1846), which used a variable levy to reduce grain imports. The case of the variable levy will be considered in Chapter 7.

3.9 U.S. ENERGY PRICE POLICY AND IMPORT DEMAND

Since the demand for imports varies inversely with the domestic price, one can calculate the increase in imports brought about by a given price decrease. The U.S. energy price controls kept prices lower than they would have been from 1973 to 1981. A paper by Hall and Pindyck (1977)[10] attempted to estimate the magnitude of the increase in energy imports caused by this policy. They dealt with total energy units instead of just petroleum by converting other forms of energy into oil equivalents in terms of B.T.U.s. Natural gas was the next most important source of energy, and its price was also held far below the price abroad. For 1977, the observed levels of domestic demand, production, and imports were

[10] See Robert Hall and R. S. Pindyck. "The Conflicting Goals of National Energy Policy," *Public Interest*. Spring 1977.

$X^d = 38$ m.b.d.
$X^s = 31$ m.b.d.
$I = 38$ m.b.d. $- 31$ m.b.d. $= 7$ m.b.d.

They assumed that the demand and supply elasticities for energy were

$$\eta_{XP} = -0.25 \qquad \epsilon_{XP} = +0.20$$

As previously noted, these elasticities are applicable to all energy rather than just oil. The reader can show that these figures imply an import elasticity of demand for energy of -1.76. Domestic energy prices were assumed to be held 30 percent below the level of world prices, which is 30 percent lower than they would have been in the absence of controls:

$$\frac{dP}{P} = \frac{P - P^\star}{P} = -0.30$$

Price controls are shown as a decrease from P_1 to P_2 in Figure 3-10. Expressing the changes in domestic demand and supply as elasticities[11] yields the following expression for the change in imports:

$$dI = X^d \eta_{XP} \frac{dP}{P} - X^s \epsilon_{XP} \frac{dP}{P}$$

FIGURE 3-10   The Effect of Energy Price Controls in the U.S.

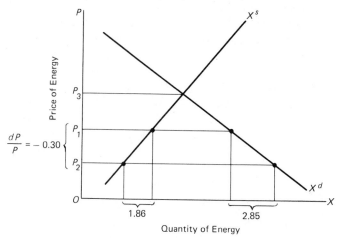

Quantity of Energy

[11] For discrete changes, the elasticity of demand may be written as
$$\eta_{XP} = \frac{dX^d/X^d}{dP/P} \quad \text{and} \quad dX^d = X^d \eta_{XP} \frac{dP}{P}$$
Similarly, the change in quantity supplied is $dX^s = X^s \epsilon_{XP} \frac{dP}{P}$.

The effect of price controls on imports can be expressed in terms of the domestic demand and supply components:

$$dI = dX^d - dX^s$$

The change in import demand depends on the initial level of demand, the domestic price elasticity of demand, and the percentage decrease in price. All of this information is available:

$$dX^d = (38)(-1.25)(-0.30) = +2.85 \text{ m.b.d.}$$

Price controls that held the domestic price 30 percent below the world price increased the U.S. demand for energy by 2.85 m.b.d. Similarly, the effect on the domestic supply of energy can be expressed as

$$dX^s = X^s \epsilon_{XP} \frac{dP}{P}$$
$$dX^s = 21(+0.20)(-0.30) = -1.86 \text{ m.b.d.}$$

Price controls curtailed domestic energy production by 1.86 m.b.d. The effect of the program on energy imports was the sum of these two components:

$$dI = dX^d - dX^s = +2.85 - (-1.86) = +4.71 \text{ m.b.d.}$$

Price controls increased energy imports by 4.71 m.b.d.

Despite frequent statements that official U.S. policy favored greater energy independence, the effect of the U.S. price policy was to promote greater dependence on energy imports. If complete energy independence were the national policy goal, it could have been achieved by setting a price high enough (P_3 in Figure 3-10) to make the nation self-sufficient in energy. If these elasticities are constant over the range of prices being considered, the price at which domestic demand equals domestic supply can be determined. What is needed is a price increase necessary to reduce the initial level of imports (7 m.b.d.) to zero.

$$dI^d = (X^d \eta_{XP} - X^s \epsilon_{XP})\frac{dP}{dP} = -7$$
$$-7 = [38(-0.25) - 31(0.20)]\frac{dP}{P}$$
$$\frac{dP}{P} = +44.6$$

Under the assumed conditions, a price increase of 44.6 percent would have brought about energy self-sufficiency in the United States. This energy price increase assumes that other prices are constant. Because of inflation in recent years, a larger price increase would have been necessary to accomplish the same relative price rise. It is ironic that during this period every president and every Congress espoused a goal of energy independence, but the actual price policies carried out led to greater dependence on energy imports. The policy of keeping domestic energy prices below foreign prices increased the demand for imported energy. The policy of insulating the domestic price from foreign price changes reduced the elasticity of demand for imported energy. Since the United States is the world's largest oil importer, these price policies put upward pressure on world energy prices. By distorting the pattern of U.S. imports, this policy made the American apparent comparative disadvantage in energy look larger than it actually was. Since energy imports are capital intensive, this policy made total imports more capital intensive than they otherwise would have been.

SUMMARY

This chapter has extended the discussion of comparative advantage to the case of increasing cost of production. By introducing two factors of production, it permits relative factor supplies to influence comparative cost. The general determinants of international trade are factor supplies and technology on the supply side and preferences and income on the demand side. Factor supplies and technology can be represented by an Edgeworth box, from which a production possibilities curve can be derived. Increasing cost will result in incomplete specialization unless the size of trading countries is vastly different.

The Heckscher-Ohlin theory explains trade by differences in relative factor supplies, assuming that demand and technology are similar between countries. Import demand can be derived from the underlying domestic demand and supply curves for importable goods. Because it is derived from both demand and supply, import demand is more price elastic than domestic demand. The relationship between these two demand curves can be used to show the contrasting economic effects of a domestic sales tax and a tariff. The elasticity of import demand measures the responsiveness of import demand to a price change.

Some governments have attempted to insulate their domestic economies from foreign disturbances by preventing domestic prices from following foreign prices. The amount of interference can be measured by the price transmission elasticity. The import elasticity concepts were employed to show the effect of U.S. energy price policies of the 1970s. This chapter has emphasized how trade affects product markets in both trading countries. In addition, trade alters both prices of factors of production and the distribution of income in each country. This topic will be the subject of Chapter 4.

REFERENCES

BALDWIN, ROBERT E., and J. DAVID RICHARDSON, eds. *International Trade and Finance: Readings*, 2nd. ed. Boston: Little, Brown, 1981.

BHAGWATI, JAGDISH. "The Pure Theory of International Trade: A Survey." *Economic Journal*, March 1964.

BRANSON, WILLIAM. "Trends in U.S. International Trade and Investment Since World War II." In *The American Economy in Transition*. Martin Feldstein, ed. Chicago: University of Chicago Press, 1980.

ELLIS, HOWARD, and LLOYD METZLER, eds. *Readings in the Theory of International Trade*. Homewood, Ill.: Richard D. Irwin, 1949. A collection of landmark papers on the development of trade theory.

General Agreement on Tariffs and Trade. *International Trade*, Geneva, annually. Contains data on the volume and value of trade for countries and country groups.

GRUBEL, HERBERT G. "The Theory of Intra-Industry Trade." In *International Trade and Finance: Readings*, Robert E. Baldwin and J. David Richardson, eds., 2nd ed. Boston: Little, Brown, 1931.

HALL, ROBERT, and R. S. PINDYCK. "The Conflicting Goals of National Energy Policy." *Public Interest*, Spring 1977. The source of the energy study cited in the text.

HECKSCHER, ELI. "The Effect of Foreign Trade on the Distribution of Income," *Economisk Tidskrift*, 1919. Reprinted in *Readings in the Theory of International Trade*, Howard S. Ellis and Lloyd A. Metzler, eds. Homewood, Ill.: Richard D. Irwin, 1950. An early statement of the factor proportions theory.

JOHNSON, HARRY G. "Factor Endowment, International Trade, and Factor Prices," *Manchester School of Economic and Social Studies*, September 1957. Reprinted in *Readings in International Economics*, Richard E. Caves and Harry G. Johnson, eds. Homewood, Ill.: Richard D. Irwin, 1968. A detailed treatment of the relationship between product markets and factor markets.

JONES, RONALD W. *International Trade: Essays in Theory*. Amsterdam: North-Holland, 1979. Contains advanced papers on the theory of trade.

INTERNATIONAL MONETARY FUND. *Direction of Trade Yearbook*, Washington, D.C., annually. Contains data on the source of imports and destination of exports by country and country groups.

KRAUSS, MELVYN B., and HARRY G. JOHNSON. *General Equilibrium Analysis: A Microeconomic Text*. Chicago: Aldine, 1974, Chap. 6, including Appendix A. Derives the import demand curve from the underlying production possibilities and indifference curves.

MACDOUGALL, G. D. A. "British and American Exports: A Study Suggested by the Theory of Comparative Costs." *Economic Journal*, December 1951 and September 1952. Reprinted in *Readings in International Economics*, Richard Caves and Harry G. Johnson, eds. Homewood, Ill.: Richard D. Irwin, 1968.

OHLIN, BERTIL. *Interregional and International Trade*. Cambridge, Mass.: Harvard University Press, 1933. An early formal statement of the factor proportions theory by a student of Heckscher.

TURNER, LOUIS, and NEIL MCMULLEN. *The Newly Industrializing Countries: Trade and Adjustment*. London: George Allen and Unwin, 1982. A collection of empirical studies on trade problems of Newly Industrializing Countries.

WORLD BANK. *World Bank Atlas*, Washington, D.C., annually. Contains data on income and population by country.

CHAPTER FOUR
GAINS FROM TRADE
AND THE DISTRIBUTION
OF INCOME

4.1 THE NATURE
OF THE GAINS
FROM TRADE

The conventional modern view of international trade is that voluntary exchange benefits both trading countries. Mutual benefits can be measured by
increases in the national incomes of both countries. The sources of additional
income are the additional consumption and production opportunities made
available to households and firms by trade. The proposition that both trading
partners gain from exchange does not imply that both countries benefit equally.
There are circumstances in which a single country may appropriate most of the
gains from trade. However, the case of unequal gains is logically distinct from
the stronger proposition that the welfare of one country declines as a result of
trade.

The exploitation of one trading country by another is a popular theme in
Marxist literature, and some classical Greek writers also denied that there are
mutual benefits from trade. Aristotle considered trade to be unproductive because the benefits received by one trader are offset by the losses of the trading
partners. Mercantilist writers,[1] who were criticized by Adam Smith (1723–1790)
and David Hume (1711–1776), also denied that international trade provides
benefits to both trading partners.

Mercantilists considered exports to be beneficial to a nation, though im-

---

[1] For a detailed discussion of mercantilist thought see Eli Heckscher, *Mercantilism*, 2nd ed.,
2 vols. (London: George Allen and Unwin, 1955); and Jacob Viner, *Studies in the Theory of International Trade* (London: George Allen and Unwin, 1937).

ports were considered harmful. Exports earned gold and created domestic jobs, but imports used gold and destroyed jobs at home. The main policy prescription of mercantilism was that countries should seek a balance of trade surplus, an excess of exports over imports. Modern economic thought is not sympathetic to most mercantilist ideas about trade, but modern political leaders continue to find the ideas appealing. Implicit in much of modern trade policy is the notion that exporting countries gain from trade, but importing countries lose. Commercial policies that protect domestic producers from cheap imports ignore the damage done to domestic consumers. Policies that subsidize exports to unfriendly nations are sometimes defended on the ground that all the benefits from trade accrue to the exporting country. Several presidents of the United States have sent subsidized grain to the USSR during periods of unfriendly relations.

Another example of trade policy that overlooks the mutual gains from trade is the strategy used at multilateral trade negotiations. The object of negotiations is to reduce trade barriers, but no country will reduce its tariff unless other countries will reciprocate. The implicit assumption of participants is that a unilateral tariff reduction would be harmful because it would increase imports relative to exports. These policies stress the benefits that accrue to exporting countries.

Conversely, a trade embargo is based on the assumption that importing countries receive most or all the benefits from trade. Presumably, the object of an embargo is to punish a trading partner by denying that country access to one's exports. However, proponents of an embargo must assume that restricting exports does little damage to the exporting country. Underlying all trade policy is a theory of the gains from trade. This chapter will analyze the gains from trade, including the total gains and the distribution of gains among countries and regions.

Although international trade provides net benefits for residents of a country, every individual does not gain. Indeed the incomes of some individual households will decline as a result of trade. This chapter will consider the effect of trade on the distribution of income within countries. Trade has different effects on producers and consumers. Consumers of importables benefit from trade, but domestic producers of importables are harmed. Producers of exportables benefit from trade, but consumers of exportables are adversely affected.

Trade also has different effects on different factors of production. If exports use large amounts of a nation's abundant factor, trade will increase the net demand for that factor and reduce the net demand for the scarce factor. Trade will be beneficial to owners of the abundant factor and harmful to owners of the scarce factor. Trade tends to equalize product prices between countries. By altering relative factor demands, trade also tends to equalize factor prices between countries. By equalizing international factor prices, trade functions as a substitute for international factor mobility.

Since some specific households and firms lose from trade, it might be in their interest to lobby against free trade. As long as there are net national gains from trade, the gainers can potentially compensate the losers. If an effective compensation mechanism could be designed, stronger political support for free trade would develop. The adverse effects of trade on certain industries, factors, and regions cannot be denied. However, all favorable economic innovations have adverse effects on someone and should not be discouraged for that reason only. The effects of trade on the distribution of income are comparable to the effects of economic growth from any source.

4.2 PRODUCTION AND CONSUMPTION GAINS

The benefits from trade may be measured in terms of additional income. The increase in national income brought about by trade may be broken down into separate consumption and production gains. Consumption gains result from the opportunity to trade with a country whose initial prices are different from those in the home country. By providing consumers with more options, trade permits consumers to obtain a preferred combination of goods. Trade permits consumers to buy existing products at lower prices, but it also offers them information about entirely new products. For example, Marco Polo's discovery of pasta in China had a significant and lasting effect on Italian cuisine. Today international trade is an important mechanism for introducing new technology to potential users. By offering cheaper imports, trade also reduces the prices of domestically produced importables. The additional competition from imports also discourages the development of domestic monopoly.

Production gains result from a more efficient employment of factors of production. If the productivity of factors of production is different between countries, production gains can be obtained by employing factors in these industries where they are more productive. The concept of comparative advantage implies that there are production gains even if the factors in one country are more productive in all industries. Comparative advantage is determined by relative productivity. Every country and every factor will have a relative advantage in something.

Production gains are brought about by moving factors from less productive to more productive employment. It is sometimes said that imports are harmful, because they destroy jobs in the import-competing sector. In one sense the statement is misleading because the total number of jobs is not fixed for a single firm, industry, or the entire economy. Employment depends on the prices of labor, capital, and technology as well as on the demand for the product produced by labor. If wages fall, firms have an incentive to increase employment. Also, jobs are not the only consideration. If they were, people would welcome such job-creating natural disasters as earthquakes and hurricanes.

Trade does destroy jobs in the import-competing sector, but it creates jobs in the export sector. If specialization follows comparative advantage, employment in the expanding export sector will be more productive than will employment in the contracting import-competing sector. The production gains from trade depend on labor and capital being mobile between industries. If imports simply reduced employment in the import-competing sector without stimulating output in more productive industries, there would be no production gains from trade. However, this cannot happen in the long run because a country cannot import goods without exporting something to pay for them. The export sector is necessarily the one in which domestic factors of production are relatively more productive. In the real world, factors of production do not change employment without cost, which may include transitional unemployment. However, in a dynamic economy, trade is only one of many reasons why factors must change employment.

The development of new products and the invention of new techniques for producing old products causes entire industries and professions to become obsolete. The reallocation of factors of production between industries in response to change is a necessary cost of economic growth and a necessary cost of trade. The tradititional theory of international trade assumes that factors of production are mobile between the industries of a country, but they do not move between countries. In this case, trade is a substitute for international factor mobility. For example, the importation of certain labor-intensive products from Mexico to the United States is a partial substitute for migration of Mexican workers to the United States.

Similarly, the exportation of capital-intensive products from the United States is a partial substitute for the investment of U.S. capital in Mexico. Just as part of the consumption gains come from discovering new products to consume, part of the production gains come from discovering new technology that is applicable to domestic production. The money value of the benefits from any given level of international trade is measurable. The same technique may be applied to measure the gains from increasing the trade volume (e.g., by lowering transport costs) or the costs of reducing trade (e.g., by imposing a tariff). Finally, the same principles are employed in measuring the gains from international trade as in assessing the gains from interregional trade or interpersonal trade among households.

The main advantage of international trade is that additional production and consumption opportunities result in higher income. However, there may be disadvantages as well. Adam Smith illustrated this point in his famous "pin factory" example in the *Wealth of Nations*. He argued that more pins could be produced in a day if each worker specialized in producing one part of a pin than if each worker produced an entire pin. All workers could specialize in the tasks they did best and improve their skill by repetition. However, there may be disadvantages to specialization. The most important potential disadvantage is that trade creates dependency. Consumers depend on factories to provide pins. Factories depend on access to pin markets, and pin workers depend on demand for their specialized skills.

A specialized nation becomes dependent on imports to supply certain products and on foreign markets to demand its own products. Dependency becomes a problem only if there is an unexpected interruption to the supply of imports or the sale of exports. Examples would be the oil embargo imposed by some Arab countries against the United States in 1973 and the grain embargo applied by the United States against the USSR in 1980. Since the oil embargo, there has been concern that the United States is too dependent on imported oil and other minerals.

Uncertainty about import supply may have become more important in recent years as governments have shown a greater willingness to apply economic sanctions as part of their foreign policy. After a series of embargoes, U.S. producers are now regarded as unreliable suppliers.[2] A traditional way to hedge against the possibility of a supply interruption is for the importing country to hold an inventory of the imported product in reserve. If imports are cut off, domestic demand may be satisfied by drawing down the inventory. Many countries have held strategic stockpiles of products deemed essential for national defense, and the United States is now accumulating a strategic oil stockpile. An unexpected supply interruption may cause temporary problems for an importing country, but a persistent interruption cannot impose greater costs on a country than if it had never imported that commodity. An effective 20-year embargo (probably not enforceable) against a country cannot be more damaging to that country than if it were always self-sufficient. The temporary problem caused by dependency is that domestic supply may be less elastic in the short run than it would have been without trade. Long-run domestic supply is not affected. Another common remedy for uncertain supply is a tariff, whose costs and benefits will be discussed in Chapter 7.

Two other criticisms of trade have little economic merit, but they are frequently heard in popular political discussions. The first criticism is that imports represent failure of the domestic economy. Large-scale food imports by China and the USSR have been interpreted as failures of those economies rather than prudent specialization. Similarly, auto and steel imports into the United States have been popularly interpreted as a failure of the U.S. economy rather than as a change in comparative advantage. According to this view, a successful economy should produce all its own goods, which is a denial of the gains from trade.

A related criticism of trade is based on a crude form of egalitarianism. An equitable international division of labor is said to be one for which each nation produces the same goods. According to this view, any form of interna-

---

[2] Following the U.S. soybean embargo of 1973, the Japanese diversified their sources of supply. Following several U.S. grain embargoes, the Soviet Union has reduced its reliance on imports from the U.S. See I. M. Destler, *Making Foreign Economic Policy* (Washington, D.C.: The Brookings Institution, 1980).

tional specialization confers inferiority on some nations. In particular, the production of primary products, such as minerals and agricultural goods, has been viewed as an inferior economic activity. Some proponents of this view see international trade as a means of reinforcing an inequitable division of labor among countries. However, the massive redistribution of world income toward oil producers that occurred between 1973 and 1974 and between 1979 and 1980 has changed the minds of some people who thought that primary production is necessarily unremunerative.

Another possible disadvantage of trade is that the information associated with new products is not always welcome to all residents. In particular, trade may undermine the traditional culture of a country. Certain Moslem leaders have complained that Western music and programs that follow imports of television sets and phonographs have undermined traditional morality. This trade disadvantage also influences the distribution of income.

Finally, trade may be a source of instability to the domestic economy, through dependency, on either the import or export side. However, trade may also stabilize the economy by offsetting domestic disturbances. For example, a country may offset bad weather and a small domestic crop by importing additional food from abroad. Trade may transmit foreign disturbances or offset domestic disturbances. Whether trade is a stabilizing or destabilizing influence is an empirical question involving the source, frequency, and magnitude of economic disturbances. This topic will be pursued in Chapter 13.

4.3 GAINS FROM TRADE
IN GENERAL EQUILIBRIUM

The most general representation of the national gains from trade employs the production possibilities curve and the indifference map. Figure 4-1 reproduces

FIGURE 4-1   Gains from Trade in General Equilibrium

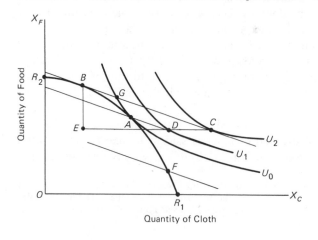

Quantity of Food

Quantity of Cloth

the essential features of Figure 3-4 in Chapter 3. The total gains are divided into production and consumption gains using a concave production possibilities curve. These gains were also previously shown in terms of linear production possibilities. (See Figure 2-2 in Chapter 2.) The main difference between these two representations is that constant cost tends to bring about complete specialization but that increasing cost results in incomplete specialization.

In the absence of trade, the nation's production possibilities curve (R_1R_2) would also define its consumption possibilities. The nation's residents must consume exactly those goods that they produce. Consequently they can choose only those points lying on curve R_1R_2. Point A is the preferred point because it lies on the highest indifference curve (U_0), touching R_1R_2. Pretrade domestic prices are represented by the slope of the production possibilities curve at point A. Notice that points B and F are both attainable production and consumption points, but they lie on lower indifference curves than U_0. When trade is introduced, residents can deal at world prices represented by the slope of the lines through points B, A, and F.

The new equilibrium may be determined in a two-stage process. First, find the production point that maximizes national income at world prices. Then choose a consumption point that maximizes national utility. The production point that maximizes the value of national output is point B, because it produces a budget line or consumption possibilities curve (BGC) that is farther from the origin than all other attainable curves. For example, the budget lines passing through points A and F, which represent the value of those outputs at world prices, lie entirely inside curve BGC. Once production has been set at point B, any point on BC is available for consumption, and the optimal point is C on indifference curve U_2.

Other points such as G are available to domestic consumers, but they all lie on indifference curves below U_2. The home country would import EC units of cloth and export BE units of food. Trade may be thought of as indirect production, because part of the cloth consumed in the home country is obtained by producing food and exchanging it for cloth. Thus, consumers may be well dressed without producing any cloth at all.

The total gains from trade may be seen from the fact that the nontrade indifference curve (U_0) is below the free trade indifference curve (U_2). The separate consumption and production gains can be found by introducing world prices and examining the situation when domestic production is constant at the no-trade level (point A). The resulting consumption possibilities are represented by line AD, for which the optimal consumption point is D on indifference curve U_1. Since U_1 is above U_0, there are consumption gains from trade, even if domestic production is constant. The movement from U_0 to U_1 represents the benefits to home consumers of substituting relatively cheaper cloth for more expensive food. Thus, trade would be beneficial even if domestic factors of production were completely immobile between the food and cloth industries.

To find the production gains, let domestic suppliers respond to the higher world price of food. They will bid capital and labor away from the cloth industry, causing production to move to point B, where the value of national output is maximum along BGC. The optimal consumption point is C on indifference curve U_2. Production gains are shown by the fact that U_2 lies above U_1. The movement from U_1 to U_2 represents the gains from specialized production according to comparative advantage. An analogous figure would show the gains to the rest of the world from specializing in the production of cloth and importing food.

4.4 GAINS IN TERMS OF SUPPLY AND DEMAND FOR IMPORTS

The previous representation stresses the interdependence between the consumption and production of food and cloth. The production possibilities curve shows that the amount of one good that can be produced depends directly on the quantity of the other good produced. Each indifference curve shows that the amount of one good consumed depends on the amount of the other good consumed. The information about the gains from trade may also be expressed in terms of the supply and demand for imports.

In Figure 4-2 the domestic supply and demand curves for importable cloth are derived from the underlying production possibilities curve and indifferences map in panel A. As shown in Chapter 3, the supply price of cloth is equal to the slope of R_1R_2, and the demand price for cloth is equal to the slope of the indifference curve U_0. Cloth is the importable good (both produced at home and imported), with production and consumption measured in panel B and the volume of imports measured in panel C. The import demand curve (I_1^d) in panel C is derived from the domestic demand and supply curves (X_C^d, X_C^s) as shown in Chapter 3.

The gains from trade may be measured in terms of consumer and producer surplus. In an organized competitive market, a single price prevails. All buyers and sellers deal at the same price, even though some consumers are willing to pay a higher price and some sellers are willing to accept a lower price. The difference between the maximum amount consumers are willing to pay and the actual amount paid is called consumer surplus. The difference between the actual amount received by sellers and the minimum amount they are willing to accept is called producer surplus (or rent). These two surplus measures appear on the graph in Figure 4-2 as the areas under supply and demand curves above the price.

In Figure 4-3, consumer surplus is the area of the triangle DBA, whereas producer surplus is the area of the triangle CDA. Each point on the demand curve (X^d) represents the demand price, the maximum amount consumers will

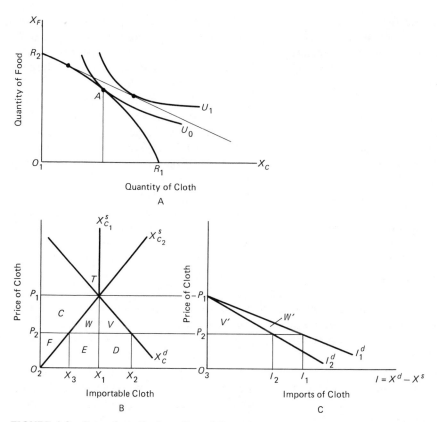

FIGURE 4-2   Gains from Trade in Partial Equilibrium

FIGURE 4-3   Consumer and Producer Surplus

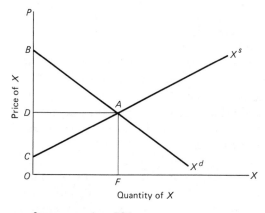

Consumer surplus = DBA
Producer surplus = CDA

pay for that quantity. Each point on the supply curve (X^s) represents the minimum price sellers will accept for that quantity. The equilibrium price is OD, and the equilibrium quantity is OF. For the quantity OF, consumers would be willing to pay, at most, price $OBAF$, but they actually pay price $ODAF$. The difference, DBA, is consumer surplus. For OF units, sellers would be willing to accept the amount $OCAF$, but they actually receive the amount $ODAF$. The difference, CDA, is producer surplus. These two surplus measures may be used to measure the gains from trade. Since the import demand curve (I^d) is derived from the domestic demand (X^d) and supply (X^s) curves, the same producer and consumer surplus can be measured either under the domestic curves or under the import demand curve.

Returning to Figure 4-2 the domestic supply and demand curves are X_C^s and X_C^d, and the pretrade equilibrium is at point T, where the price is P_1 and the quantity is X_1. With trade, the price of cloth falls to P_2, consumption increases to O_2X_2, production decreases to O_2X_3, and imports increase to $X_2X_3 = O_3I_1$ (in panel C). The total gains from trade are measured by the areas $W + V = W' + V'$ (in panel C), which are the increase in consumer and producer surplus attributable to trade.

The total gain may be divided into consumption and production gains by first assuming that domestic supply is constant at O_2X_1 along supply curve X_{C1}^s and later letting supply respond along curve X_{C2}^s. The perfectly inelastic supply curve (X_{C1}^s) implies that the import curve is I_2^d, which is steeper than I_1^d. As the price falls to P_2, consumption increases to X_2, production remains at X_1, and imports increase to I_2. The consumption gain equals the area under the domestic demand curve (V), which also equals the area under the import demand curve (V^1).

Recall that the vertical distance up to X_C^d and I^d indicates the maximum price that domestic consumers are willing to pay for various quantities of cloth, and areas V and V' measure the excess of what consumers are willing to pay for cloth over what they actually have to pay (P_2). The production gains are obtained by letting domestic firms respond to the lower prices of cloth by moving along curve X_{C2}^s. This domestic supply curve is associated with the more price-responsive import demand curve I_1^d. In this case, production falls to X_3, imports rise to I_1, and the production gains are measured by the area $W = W'$. The vertical distance up to the supply curve measures the marginal cost of cloth in terms of a predetermined quantity of food. Since P_2 measures the actual cost of importing cloth, the area $W = W'$ measures the resource saving from replacing high-cost domestic production with lower-cost imports. Flatter (more elastic) domestic demand and supply curves result in larger total gains from trade.

Since market supply and demand curves may be estimated from empirical data, the gains from trade are objectively measurable. Such empirical measures are commonly used to estimate the cost of reducing trade by imposing trade barriers. Figure 4-2 shows the gains from trade enjoyed by the home

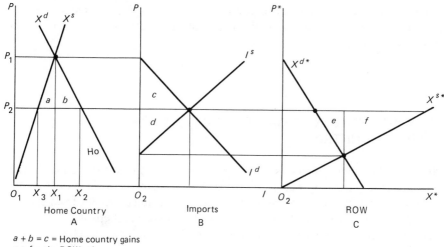

a + b = c = Home country gains
e + f = d = ROW gains
c + d = World gains

FIGURE 4-4   World Gains from Trade

country. There will also be benefits to the rest of the world, and the resulting sum of the home country's and ROW's gains measures the world gains from trade.

Figure 4-4 shows the world gains as area $c+d$, where c measures home country gains and d measures ROW gains. Each of these national gains may be divided into production and consumption gains:

$$c = a + b \qquad d = e + f$$

The total world gains depend on the elasticities of demand and supply. When trade is reduced (e.g., by higher transport costs), the total cost and the distribution of these costs between trading countries depends upon the elasticities of the import demand and supply curves. The graph shows that b is the area of a triangle whose base $(X_1 X_2)$ is the change in quantity demanded and whose height $(P_1 P_2)$ is the change in price. Thus it is

$$\text{area } b = \tfrac{1}{2} dX^d dP$$

Similarly, a is the area of a triangle whose base $(X_3 X_1)$ is the change in quantity supplied and whose height $(P_1 P_2)$ is the change in price:

$$\text{area } b = \tfrac{1}{2} dX^s dP$$
$$\text{area } c = \text{area } b + \text{area } a$$
$$= \tfrac{1}{2} dX^d dP + \tfrac{1}{2} dX^s dP$$
$$= \tfrac{1}{2}(dX^d - dX^s)dP$$
$$= \tfrac{1}{2} dI dP$$

Thus, home country gains depend on the elasticity of import demand, which is derived from the underlying elasticities of demand and supply for the importable. Similarly,

area $d = \frac{1}{2}dIdP^{\star}$

4.5 DISTRIBUTION OF GAINS
WITHIN COUNTRIES

International trade confers net gains on the world as a whole and on both trading countries separately, but it also redistributes income between various groups within these economies. In the home country, consumers benefit from cheaper cloth, but producers of cloth are harmed by imports. There is a transfer of income within the domestic economy from cloth producers to cloth consumers. The money value of this transfer is area C in Figure 4-2. This area represents the excess of the pretrade price of cloth over the domestic marginal cost of producing cloth, which is eliminated by trade. In the absence of trade, this area represents producer surplus, or rent to the owners of scarce factors employed in the cloth industry. Consequently, one would expect owners of such factors to oppose free trade.

An example of how trade redistributes income is the English Corn Laws, which existed for centuries until their repeal in 1845. They were a tariff on grain (called "corn" in England) whose effect was to increase the domestic price of grain and the rent on English land that produced grain. The laws benefited landowners, whose political power was enhanced by rules that restricted voting to property owners. Repeal of the Corn Laws brought about an income transfer such as area C in Figure 4-2 from landlords to consumers of grain. The Common Agricultural Policy of the European Economic Community has been described as a "modern Corn Law" because it redistributes a substantial amount of income from European consumers to landlords and producers.

Of course, imports must be paid for. Thus, in the absence of international borrowing (which will be considered in later chapters), the value of exports must equal the value of imports, represented by the area $E + D$ in Figure 4-2, and in this case, it must equal exports. Area D is the increase in the value of cloth consumption induced by the lower price, and area E is the decrease in the value of domestic cloth production. Thus, factors of production worth $D + E$ must be moved into food production to pay for cloth imports. Because of the concave production possibilities curve, cloth production does not cease, and the area F is the remaining producer surplus in the cloth industry.

Since the gross consumer gains in Figure 4-2 are $C + W + V$ and the loss to domestic producers is area C, the net gains to the home country are $W + V$. However, the consumers who benefit from trade may be different people from the producers who are harmed by trade. As a result, trade is likely to redistribute national income at the same time that it increases total income. This redistribution is a specific example of the general principle that all economic changes, no matter how beneficial, have adverse effects on someone.

The invention of a new product or a new technique that lowers the cost of an old product necessarily harms those with a vested interest in the old product or the old technique. In the words of the British economist Philip Wicksteed (1844–1927), "If the sanitary habits of the public suddenly improved, there would be a slump in the business of the undertaker, and if no one committed murder, the hangman would be out of a job."[3] Because imports cause the price of cloth to fall to P_2, domestic cloth production falls. Employment of all factors will decline in the cloth industry. The factor that is employed intensively in cloth production will suffer a greater decrease in the demand for its services. Competition from imports will reduce the price of that factor and its income.[4] Thus, international trade has a direct effect on product prices and an indirect effect on the prices and incomes of factors of production.

If labor is the factor employed intensively in the cloth industry in the home country, trade will lower the wage of labor as well as the price of cloth. In this case, imports of labor-intensive cloth have the same effect on domestic wages as immigration of labor. Even though trade confers net benefits on the nation as a whole, people are harmed insofar as they are wage earners. Of course, the same people must gain as consumers of cloth, and they will gain further if they are owners of capital. Conversely, the gainers from trade are the sellers of food and the owners of the factor (e.g., capital) used intensively in food production. These gains may be shown with the use of the home country's supply curve of exported food and ROW's demand for imported food. It is left to the reader to construct this food diagram, which is analogous to Figure 4-2 for cloth.

Although trade provides net benefits to residents of a country taken as a group, it has adverse effects on groups associated with the import-competing sector. Business firms producing a product that is a substitute for imports, factors of production employed in that sector, and regions of the country in which production of import-competing goods may be concentrated are all adversely affected by imports. The United States as a whole benefits from trade, but residents of Michigan are harmed by auto imports, Pennsylvanians are harmed by steel imports, and North Carolinians are adversely affected by textile imports. However, horse ranchers and blacksmiths were adversely affected by the invention of the automobile. The fact that trade or inventions are harmful to particular people or regions does not imply that they are harmful to society as a whole. Trade does redistribute income, and recognition of this fact helps to

---

[3] Philip Wicksteed, *The Common Political Economy* (London: Routledge, 1933).

[4] The income reduction is called the Stolper-Samuelson effect. For details, see the article by Wolfgang Stolper and Paul A. Samuelson, "Protecion and Real Wages," in *Readings in the Theory of International Trade*, Howard A. Ellis and Lloyd A. Metzler, eds. (Homewood, Ill.: Richard D. Irwin, 1949).

understand why particular groups have opposed trade for as long as trade has existed.

The French essayist Frederic Bastiat (1801–1850) was an ardent proponent of free trade who wrote a famous satirical essay in which the French candlemakers complained that they were harmed by imports:

> We are suffering from the ruinous competition of a foreign rival who apparently works under conditions so far superior to our own for the production of light that he is flooding the domestic market with it at an incredibly low price; for the moment he appears, our sales cease, all the consumers turn to him, and a branch of French industry whose ramifications are innumerable is all at once reduced to complete stagnation. This rival, which is none other than the sun, is waging war on us so mercilessly that we suspect he is being stirred up by perfidious Albion (excellent diplomacy nowadays!), particularly because he has for that haughty island a respect that he does not show for us.
>
> We ask you to be so good as to pass a law requiring the closing of all windows, dormers, skylights, inside and outside shutters, curtains, casements, bull's-eyes, deadlights, and blinds—in short, all openings, holes, chinks, and fissures through which the light of the sun is wont to enter houses, to the detriment of the fair industries with which we are proud to say, we have endowed the country, a country that cannot, without betraying ingraditude, abandon us today to so unequal a combat.[5]

No doubt that such a law would increase the demand for candles and the services of candlemakers, but what would it do to the income of all Frenchmen?

4.6 FACTOR PRICE EQUALIZATION

There are several ways in which trade alters the distribution of income. Trade transfers income between producers and consumers, and it alters the relative incomes of regions of a country. Trade also changes the incomes of owners of factors of production. Trade alters factor incomes through its effect on factor prices. Just as trade tends to equalize product prices between countries, it also tends to equalize factor prices between trading countries. Given the factor endowments theory, trade increases the net demand for the relatively abundant factor in each trading country. Prices of the abundant factor increase and prices of the scarce factor decrease in each trading country.

The tendency for trade to equalize factor prices is shown with the assistance of an Edgeworth box diagram in Figure 4-5. Separate boxes are shown for each country, and the dimensions represent relative supplies of labor and

---

[5] "Perfidious Albion" is England, along with a typically French jibe at the English fog, which keeps the sun from interfering with artificial light in England as much as it does in France. During the 1840s, Franco-English relations were occasionally very tense. From Frederic Bastiat, *Economic Sophisms*, edited and translated by Arthur Goddard (New York: D. Van Nostrand, 1964).

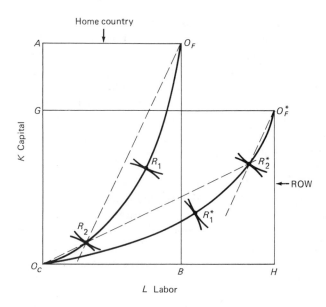

FIGURE 4-5   Trade and Factor Price Equalization

capital. The boxes are superimposed so that the countries have a common cloth origin (O_C), but different food origins (O_F, O_F^*). It is assumed that the home country has a relatively larger endowment of capital than ROW. The fact that the two contract curves $(O_C O_F$ and $O_C O_F^*)$ are bowed toward the labor axis indicate that cloth is the labor-intensive product in both countries. The slope of the contract curve represents the marginal rate of substitution between capital and labor. If firms choose least cost combinations of capital and labor, the marginal rate of substitution must equal the relative prices of labor and capital.

Assume that production functions are linear, homogeneous, and identical in both countries.[6] Relative factor prices are constant along any ray from the origin, such as $O_C R_1^* R_2^*$. In the absence of trade, the equilibrium points are R_1 in the home country and R_1^* in the rest of the world. The home country uses a greater ratio of capital to labor at R_1 than ROW does at R_1^* because of the relative cheapness of capital at home. Under free trade, home country food production expands, cloth production contracts, and equilibrium moves to R_2. Expansion of cloth production has increased the price of capital, as indicated by the lower ratio of capital to labor at R_2 than R_1. In ROW trade causes cloth production to expand from R_1^* to R_2^*. The relative price of labor, the abundant factor, increases. Since R_2 and R_2^* lie on the same ray from the cloth origin,

---

[6]Linear homogeneous functions exhibit constant returns to scale. Let $X = f(K, L)$ be a production function. It is linear homogeneous if $f(\lambda K, \lambda L) = \lambda f(k, L)$. See an intermediate textbook such as John P. Gould and Charles E. Ferguson, *Microeconomic Theory*, 5th ed. (Homewood, Ill.: Richard D. Irwin, 1980), Chap. 5.

factor intensities are the same in the cloth industry in both countries. Factor intensities are also equal in the food industry, since the rays from the food origin, $O_F R_2$ and $O_F^\star R_2^\star$, are parallel. Since trade equalizes factor intensities, it also equalizes factor prices in both countries. Partial equalization will occur if either country becomes completely specialized in one product.

Thus, international trade alters relative factor demands, factor intensities, and factor prices. International trade is a substitute for international factor mobility. Labor tends to migrate from low-wage to high-wage countries. This migration tends to lower wages in the country of immigration and raise the wages of those left behind in the country of emigration. Similarly, labor-abundant countries tend to export labor-intensive products, raising wages in the exporting country and lowering wages in the importing country.

The observed absence of complete equality of comparable factor prices is partly attributable to barriers to trade and migration. Completely free mobility of capital and labor or completely free trade may be sufficient to equalize factor prices in different countries. However, existing barriers to international migration and investment, as well as restrictive tariffs and quotas, interfere with factor price equalization.

There is also a measurement problem in determining the amount of factor price equalization that has occurred. The earnings of workers are partly a return to unskilled labor and partly a return on investment in human capital.[7] Most of the skills that result in high labor earnings are the result of an earlier investment in health, formal schooling, and on-the-job training. Because workers embody different amounts of human capital, one should not expect complete equalization of wages, even under free trade. The wages of malnourished, illiterate, unskilled workers in one country will not equal the wages of healthy electrical engineers in another country. Therefore, wages should be adjusted for differences in human capital. It is also possible that factor price equalization has not been satisfied because certain conditions such as identical production functions, constant returns to scale, or absence of factor intensity reversals have not been met.

Factor price equalization is not the same thing as income equalization. The income of a household or nation is equal to the price of the services of each factor of production (e.g., wages or land rental) times the quantity of each factor employed. Thus, even if factor prices were equal in all countries, per capita income could differ because of differences in the quantities of factors owned by residents. Countries with the same populations and different endowments of capital and land would have different per capita incomes. For example, both Kuwait and Ecuador are endowed with crude oil, which they sell for about the same price. However, per capita income is much higher in Kuwait because of that nation's much larger endowment of oil.

[7] T. W. Schultz, "Nobel Lecture: The Economics of Being Poor," *Journal of Political Economy*, August 1980.

An analogous issue is whether interregional trade has equalized factor prices and incomes within countries. There are no legal barriers to trade or factor mobility between the southern and northern United States, but there is an on-going debate about whether wages have been equalized for comparable workers.[8]

International trade alters the distribution of income by changing product and factor prices. If exports embody relatively large amounts of a country's abundant factor, trade tends to increase the income of the abundant factor and decrease the income of the scarce factor. In countries like Canada and Australia, where land is abundant, the opportunity to export agricultural products increases the incomes of landowners by increasing the demand for land and the rent on land. The English Corn Laws enhanced the incomes of English landlords while reducing the incomes of grain consumers. U.S. import quotas on dairy products enhance the incomes of midwestern dairy firms at the expense of consumers.

Regional interests played an important role in discussions of the nineteenth-century American tariff. The strongest protectionist pressure was in the North, where import-competing industries were concentrated. Important export industries were concentrated in the South, whose representatives espoused free trade. Regional trade issues continue to be important in the 1980s for the United States. The older industries of the North and East (e.g., automobiles and steel) face competitive pressure from imports and from expanding industry in the South and West. It is clear that trade can redistribute income between regions of a country. The redistribution of income raises the question of whether the regions or groups that gain from trade can compensate those who lose from trade.

The gains from trade shown in Figure 4-2 are net gains after the losses of some groups have been subtracted from the gains of others. Since there are net gains from trade, the gainers could potentially compensate the losers for all their losses due to trade, pay them a bonus, and still retain a net benefit. Suppose that in Figure 4-2 the values of the respective areas are

$$W + V + C = \$30 + \$30 + \$80 = \$140$$

The gross gain to home consumers would be $140, due to the effect of the price decrease from P_1 to P_2, attributable to imports. However, the price decline imposes a loss of $80 (area C) on domestic producers. Hence, area C represents a transfer of income from domestic producers to domestic consumers. The combined net national gain to producers and consumers is $60, the sum of areas W and V. Because of this net gain, those who benefit from trade could

---

[8] For a discussion of interregional wage equalization in the United States, see Don Bellante, "The North-South Differential and the Migration of Heterogeneous Labor," *American Economic Review*, March 1979; and Leonard G. Sahling and Sharon Smith, "Regional Wage Patterns: How Does New York Compare with the Rest of the Country?" *Quarterly Review*, Federal Reserve Bank of New York, Spring 1980.

potentially share the gains in such a way as to make everyone better off as a result of trade.

Since consumers gain $140 and producers lose $80, both groups would benefit if consumers compensated producers an amount more than $80 but less than $140. At one extreme, compensation of $81 would result in a net gain of $59 for consumers and $1 for producers. At the opposite extreme, compensation of $139 would leave consumers with a $1 gain and producers with a $59 gain. If compensation occurred, residents of the home country should unanimously favor free trade. In the absence of actual compensation, one may still consider the potential gains from trade.

One attempt to develop a formal scheme to compensate those adversely affected by trade is the U.S. Trade Adjustment Act of 1962. It originated following the Kennedy Round of multilateral tariff reductions. In the Kennedy Round, named for President John F. Kennedy, the United States agreed with other participating countries to mutually lower tariffs against each other. Both workers and firms were eligible for compensation, which would encourage resources to move out of the import-competing sector.

Production gains from trade depend on factor mobility. Compensation could be paid for (1) retraining benefits, (2) job relocation, and (3) cash supplements to unemployment insurance. The program was initially administered by the U.S. Tariff Commission (since renamed the International Trade Commission), and compensation was conditional on demonstrating that damage to workers or firms was primarily attributable to U.S. tariff reductions. The program was not active in its early years, and by 1969 all petitions for compensation had been rejected by the commission. Eligibility conditions were relaxed in 1974, and administration of the program was moved to the Department of Labor. Payments to injured parties increased, and, by 1980, total payments were $1.6 billion. Most of the payments were supplements to unemployment insurance going to workers in the automobile and related industries. Less than 3 percent of the payments have been used for retraining.

There is evidence that workers on trade adjustment assistance tend to be unemployed for longer periods than do those receiving standard unemployment insurance, raising the concern that the actual program has work-disincentive effects. In 1980, eligible workers could receive a maximum of nearly $14,000 for up to one year. The original aims of the program were to compensate people who were harmed by trade and to encourage workers to take jobs outside the import-competing sector. By 1981, the program was being criticized because (1) it had become expensive to taxpayers and (2) there was growing evidence that it discouraged workers from taking new jobs.[9]

[9]Two empirical studies of trade adjustment assistance are George R. Neumann, "Adjustment Assistance for Trade-Displaced Workers," in *International Trade and Finance: Readings*, Robert E. Baldwin and J. David Richardson, eds., 2nd ed. (Boston: Little, Brown, 1981); and J. David Richardson, "Trade Adjustment Assistance Under the U.S. Trade Act of 1974: An Analytical Examination and Worker Survey," in *Import Competition and Adjustment: Theory and Policy*, J. N. Bhagwati, ed. (Chicago: University of Chicago Press, 1982).

4.7 DISTRIBUTION OF GAINS
FROM TRADE
BETWEEN COUNTRIES

Trade generally benefits both trading countries, but the gains need not be equally divided. Figure 4-4 shows the gains from trade for both countries. At the free trade price of OP_2, the gains to the home country are represented by the area c (in panel B), which is the sum of the consumption (area b) and production (area a) gains in panel A. For ROW the total gains are equal to area d (in panel B), which is the sum of the consumption and production gains (areas e and f). The distribution of gains among the two countries is represented by the relative sizes of areas c and d, which depend on the slopes of the import supply and demand curves. In general, both countries benefit from trade, but there is one extreme case in which all the gains go to one country.

If one country is very small relative to its trading partner, trade will occur at the large country's prices. As a result, all gains will go to the small country. This case is shown in Figure 4-6, where the import supply curve facing the importing country is horizontal. This country may import any volume without affecting the price. Total gains to the small country are equal to the area of the triangle P_1BA. In general, the distribution of gains depends on the elasticities of import and export demand and supply (proportional to slopes of I^d and I^s), which depend on the shares of imports and exports and the domestic supply and demand elasticities.

The distribution of the gains from trade may be altered by changes in product prices. The terms of trade, which is the ratio of export prices to import prices, may be altered by many economic forces, including a change in market structure. One of the most dramatic changes has been the substantial increase in the relative price of oil since 1974, which has transferred many bil-

FIGURE 4-6   Gains from Trade When the Importer Is a Small Country

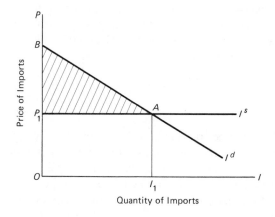

Quantity of Imports

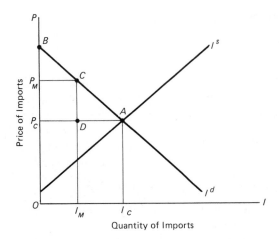

Quantity of Imports

FIGURE 4-7   Gains from Trade Under Competition and Monopoly

lion dollars of income from oil importers to oil exporters. The price increase was a result of transforming a competitive oil market into a monopolistic one, leaving consumers in the importing countries with no competition among oil suppliers. The Organization of Petroleum Exporting Countries became an effective cartel, which reduced the quantity of oil traded and raised its price.

Figure 4-7 shows that the gains to oil importing countries from trading in a competitive market (P_C and I_C) were equal to area AP_CB. With the monopoly price of P_M, the gains to importers are equal to the smaller area P_MBC. The resulting loss to consumers in the importing country is the area AP_CP_MC, which is partly a transfer to oil exporters (P_CP_MCD) and partly a deadweight loss that no one recoups (ADC). This loss is a result of consumers switching to inferior substitutes for oil because of the artificially high price. Thus, monopolization of trade reduces the total world gains from trade and redistributes the benefits in favor of exporters. Large exporting countries may also improve their terms of trade by imposing export taxes or export quotas. Similarly, large importing countries may improve their terms of trade by imposing tariffs or import quotas. Trade barriers will be analyzed in detail in Chapters 7 and 8, and monopoly will be considered in Chapter 10.

SUMMARY

Trade may be interpreted as indirect production. A country may either produce product X directly, or it may produce X indirectly by producing Y and trading it for X. As such, trade is a productive activity that increases the incomes of both trading countries. Earlier writers treated trade as unproductive in the sense that the gains of one partner were offset by the losses of the other partner. Many modern trade policies are based on the assumption that trade benefits only the exporting country. Although trade provides net benefits to both trading partners, it has harmful effects on some consumers, producers, factor owners, and regions. Trade is harmful to domestic producers of the importable product and domestic consumers of the exportable product. It is also harmful to owners of the scarce factor of production, which should be used extensively in the importable sector.

International trade tends to equalize factor prices as well as product prices. The money values of gains and losses can be measured in terms of consumer and producer surplus. If trade provides net national benefits, the gainers may potentially compensate the losers. Trade adjustment assistance is an attempt to reduce resistance to freer trade by compensating losers. However, there is some evidence that the program has delayed workers' adjustment to trade.

The benefits from trade may be shared unequally among countries. The distribution of benefits depends on country size, market structure, and other variables that alter the terms of trade. The present chapter has considered normative aspects of trade, such as the total gains and the distribution of the gains. Chapter 5 will discuss positive aspects of trade, specifically, theory and evidence of the commodity composition of trade.

REFERENCES

BASTIAT, FREDERIC. *Economic Sophisms.* New York: D. Van Nostrand, 1964. A collection of the author's popular nineteenth-century essays espousing free trade.

CLINE, WILLIAM R. "Imports and Consumer Prices: A Survey Analysis." In *International Trade and Finance: Readings*, Robert E. Baldwin and J. David Richardson, eds., 2nd ed., Boston: Little, Brown, 1981. An empirical estimate of the cost of protection to U.S. consumers.

CORDEN, W. M. *The Theory of Protection.* Oxford: Oxford University Press, 1971. Chapter 2 presents the gains from trade and losses from tariffs in terms of supply and demand curves.

DEWALD, WILLIAM G., ed. *The Impact of International Trade and Investment on Employment.* Washington, D.C.: U.S. Department of Labor, 1978. A compilation of empirical studies on trade and employment.

FINLEY, MURRAY. "Foreign Trade and United States Employment." In *International Trade and Finance: Readings*, Robert E. Baldwin and J. David Richardson, eds., 2nd ed., Boston: Little, Brown, 1981. A labor advocate's expression of the employment effects of trade.

HECKSCHER, ELI. *Mercantilism*, 2nd ed., 2 vols. London: George Allen and Unwin, 1955.

JOHNSON, D. Gale. "Comparative Advantage of United States Agriculture," in *International Trade and Finance: Readings*, Robert E. Baldwin and J. David Richardson, eds., 2nd ed. Boston: Little, Brown, 1981. A statement of the effect of trade on product and factor prices in U.S. agriculture.

KRAUSS, MELVYN B., and HARRY G. JOHNSON. *General Equilibrium Analysis: A Microeconomic Text*, Chap. 6. Chicago: Aldine, 1974. Appendix A presents the gains from trade in terms of supply and demand curves for traded goods.

MCCLOSKEY, D. N.   "Magnanimous Albion: Free Trade and British National Income." *Explorations in Economic History*, July 1980. A study of the Corn Laws emphasizing the monopsony power of Britain as an importer.

NEUMANN, GEORGE R.   "Adjustment Assistance for Trade—Displaced Workers." In *International Trade and Finance: Readings*, Robert E. Baldwin and J. David Richardson, eds., 2nd ed. Boston: Little, Brown, 1981. An empirical study of trade adjustment assistance.

RICHARDSON, J. DAVID.   "Trade Adjustment Assistance Under the U.S. Trade Act of 1974: An Analytical Examination." In *Import Competition and Adjustment: Theory and Policy*, J. N. Bhagwati, ed. (Chicago: University of Chicago Press, 1982). An empirical study of trade adjustment assistance stressing the changes in the 1974 law.

SAMUELSON, PAUL A.   "International Factor Price Equalization Once Again" (1949). In *Readings in International Economics*. Richard E. Caves and Harry G. Johnson, eds. Homewood, Ill.: Richard D. Irwin, 1968. A theoretical analysis of the conditions under which factor price equalization holds.

SCHULTZ, T. W.   "Nobel Lecture: The Economics of Being Poor." *Journal of Political Economy*, August 1980. A discussion of the importance of human capital.

SMITH, ADAM.   *An Inquiry into the Nature and Causes of the Wealth of Nations* (1776). New York: Random House/Modern Library Edition, 1937. Book I, Chapter I, presents a discussion of the division of labor.

STOLPER, WOLFGANG, and PAUL A. SAMUELSON. "Protection and Real Wages" (1941). In *Readings in the Theory of International Trade*, Howard S. Ellis and Lloyd A. Metzler, eds. Homewood, Ill.: Richard D. Irwin, 1950. A formal statement of the losses incurred by scarce factors as a result of trade.

VINER, JACOB.   *Studies in the Theory of International Trade*. London: George Allen and Unwin, 1937. A comprehensive study of the history of thought on international trade.

WILLIG, ROBERT.   "Consumer Surplus Without Apology." *American Economic Review*, September 1976. An advanced discussion of the use of surplus measures.

CHAPTER FIVE
POSITIVE THEORIES
OF TRADE

5.1. INTRODUCTION

This chapter presents the major theories that attempt to explain international trade in the real world. The analysis is positive economics in contrast to the normative economics of Chapter 4. Positive economics is an attempt to explain real-world behavior without passing moral judgment on it.

International trade occurs regularly, regardless of whether most people approve or disapprove of it. Positive theories attempt to explain the major economic determinants of trade. An example of a positive issue is whether trade is better explained by international differences in technology or differences in relative factor supplies. Normative economics considers an alternative set of issues, involving what the policies of households, firms, and governments ought to be. Whether a government should restrict imports is a normative question. To carry out normative analysis, one must measure and compare the benefits and cost of a given policy.

In Chapter 4 the benefits and costs of trade were expressed as areas under demand and supply curves for traded products. There are several positive aspects of trade, some of which have already been covered. This chapter will concentrate on the commodity composition of trade, which involves the determination of what products countries export and import. Some major features of the commodity composition of world and U.S. trade will be presented.

The earliest systematic explanation of trade was Ricardo's theory of comparative cost, based on differences in labor productivity. The factor endowments theory of Heckscher and Ohlin is an attempt to explain the source of differences in productivity. Empirical tests and extensions of the factor endowments theory will be considered. Empirical studies have not provided strong support for this theory in its simplest form, but all satisfactory empirical explanations of trade include factor endowments as one explanatory variable.

Several aspects of world trade require an explanation. The determination of the relative importance of international trade to various countries is one issue. Relative openness, which is commonly measured by the ratio of trade to the GNP, was considered in Chapter 2. A second question is what determines the direction of a country's trade? The determinants of the source of a country's imports and the destination of its exports was considered in Chapter 3. Many countries simultaneously import and export goods in the same product category. The importance of intraindustry trade was also considered in Chapter 3.

A fourth issue is whether trade will involve independent business firms or two divisions of the same firm. The growth of intrafirm trade, which is closely related to the development of multinational corporations, will be considered in Chapter 12. A final issue is the determination of the commodity composition of trade, which is the primary topic of this chapter.

The relative openness of economies varies considerably by country. As shown in Chapter 2, openness is more closely related to the size of countries than to per capita income. Since trade between regions substitutes for international trade, large countries tend to be less open than small countries.

Relative affluence does not explain trade. One can find high-income countries, such as Switzerland, that are quite open and others, such as the United States, that are relatively closed. Similarly, low-income, open economies, such as the Ivory Coast and Kenya, are offset by low-income, closed economies, such as India and Pakistan.

The direction of trade was considered in Chapter 3. The source of imports and the destination of exports depends partly on the products being traded. For example, one cannot import oil from a country that does not produce oil. The direction of trade depends heavily on transportation costs and the structure of trade barriers. It is difficult to ignore transport costs in explaining the large volume of trade among the United States, Canada, and Mexico. Similarly, the large trade volume between European Economic Community members is largely explained by low transport costs and the absence of tariffs. Intraindustry trade was also discussed in Chapter 3. Its existence is attributable to the broadness of product categories, the peculiarities of data collection, and product differentiation by business firms.

A fourth aspect of trade is intrafirm trade. It is international trade between two divisions of a single business firm. The development of intrafirm trade is closely related to the growth of multinational corporations. Precise data on the volume of intrafirm trade is not readily available, but rough estimates indicate that it is a significant portion of total trade for many countries, including the United States. Much of the interest in intrafirm trade stems from the incentives that firms have to behave differently when trading internally as compared to trading with independent firms.

Much of intrafirm trade is an attempt to appropriate the benefits of a firm's research and development expenditures. The object of research and development is to produce a superior product or a superior technique for producing a conventional product. It is in the interest of the firm to prevent rivals from copying its technology. Patents and copyrights are one way to protect information from rival producers, and intrafirm transactions are designed for the same purpose. IBM has persuaded many buyers that it offers a superior product. Whatever characteristics make the product unique are protected by trade among IBM divisions in various countries. Computers sold in Europe could be exported from the United States, but there may be a cost advantage (e.g., lower wages, taxes, or a favorable tariff on components) to producing at least part of the product in Europe. Thus, IBM would establish a plant in Europe (called direct investment) and export various inputs, including research and development, from its U.S. operations. This link between intrafirm trade and direct investment will be considered in more detail in Chapter 12.

A distinguishing feature of intrafirm trade is that for many products (e.g., components of IBM computers) there is no clearly defined market price. Therefore, the firm has some discretion in choosing prices to use for internal accounting purposes and for reporting to national governments. This intrafirm price is called a transfer price, and it may affect a firm's tariff liability or the amount of money the firm can legally take out of a country.

When IBM France imports from IBM U.S.A., it must pay the French tariff, which may be based on the reported value of the import. A lower transfer price would lower the firm's tariff obligation. Alternatively, France may have exchange controls that limit the amount of francs that firms can convert into foreign exchange. If IBM wants to repatriate profits to the United States, the firm can charge the French affiliate a higher transfer price for providing research and development services. Thus, transfer pricing may permit a capital flow that would not have occurred if the trading partners had been independent firms. The legal obligation of firms is to report a transfer price that is comparable to the price that would have been agreed on by two unrelated firms (the so-called "arm's-length price"). In practice, there may be no exactly comparable arm's length price, which gives the firm some freedom to select a price that is consistent with its private objectives. Intrafirm trade is important for many countries, and if economic conditions give most firms an incentive to distort the value of imports or exports in one direction, the reported trade statistics for the country could be substantially altered.

5.2 EMPIRICAL EVIDENCE ON THE COMMODITY COMPOSITION OF TRADE

The main purpose of this chapter is to explain the determination of the commodity composition of trade. Before considering the basic theories of trade, it will be instructive to consider some facts that the theories are designed to explain. What products enter international trade and what quantities of these products are traded? Table 1-3 in Chapter 1 shows world trade for four broad commodity groups (agriculture, ores and minerals, fuels, and manufactures) for the last 20 years. The main trends in trade have been (1) the steady decline in the relative importance of agriculture (32 percent to 16 percent), (2) the rise in the importance of manufactures (51 percent to 60 percent), and (3) the sharp increase in the importance of fuels, which began in 1974 and has persisted since. The decline of agricultural trade may be related to Engel's law, which says that the share of consumers' budgets that they devote to food declines with income. Growth of food demand has not kept up with growth of income per capita during this period. The increasing importance of manufactures trade is a continuation of a much longer trend. The greater prominence of trade in fuels is associated with a change in market structure whose permanence remains to be seen.

Data on the commodity composition of U.S. trade for 1979 was presented in Table 2-4. The largest export categories for those years were machinery and agricultural products. The remaining exports were rather evenly divided among the other categories. Petroleum was by far the largest import (28 percent), followed by consumer goods (15 percent) and automobiles (12 percent). It is interesting to consider how the composition of U.S. trade has changed over time and what forces have caused these changes. There has been a decrease in the U.S. share of world exports since 1950, especially in the U.S. share of automobile and steel exports. One explanation is that this is a movement back toward the normal situation that occurred before World War II.

An alternative explanation is that relative national factor supplies have changed in a way that has permanently altered the U.S. comparative advantage. Although the agricultural share of total world exports has declined, the agricultural share of total U.S. exports has remained steady at around 20 percent since 1954. (See Table 2-7.) The share of agricultural exports has remained constant, but the composition of agricultural exports has changed dramatically during this period. There has been a major shift from cotton and tobacco to grain and oil seeds (mainly soybeans).

Table 5-1 shows that in 1950 cotton plus tobacco were 44 percent of agricultural exports, whereas grain plus oil seeds were 35 percent. In 1979 cotton plus tobacco had declined to 10 percent, whereas the share of grain plus oil seeds had increased to 67 percent. During that same period, agricultural imports declined. The share of agriculture in total imports declined from nearly

TABLE 5-1 Commodity Composition of U.S. Agricultural Exports, 1950 vs. 1979

PRODUCT	PERCENTAGE OF AGRICULTURAL EXPORTS	
	1950	1979
Cotton plus tobacco	44%	10%
Grain	29	41
Oil seeds	6	26

Source: U.S. Department of Agriculture. *U.S. Foreign Agricultural Trade Statistical Report, 1979.* Washington, D.C.: U.S. Government Printing Office.

40 percent to less than 10 percent. Net agricultural exports (exports minus imports) have increased from approximately zero in 1954 to a $24 billion surplus in 1980. The increase in net exports suggests a growing U.S. comparative advantage in agriculture.

The other major changes in the pattern of U.S. trade have involved oil, automobiles, and steel. Oil was by far the most important U.S. import in 1980, but this was not always true. In 1980, petroleum was 32 percent of total U.S. imports, but in 1972, it was only 8 percent of the value of total imports. (See Table 2-5.) In the cases of automobiles and steel, the United States switched roles from net exporter to net importer.

World automobile trade is shown in Table 5-2 for the years 1963 and 1979. The main feature is the growth of the Japanese auto industry relative to Europe and North America. Auto production has also grown in developing countries, but mainly for home consumption. The percentage of industrial countries in total production fell from 91 percent to 84 percent, whereas the shares of developing countries rose from 2 percent to 7 percent and the share

TABLE 5-2 World Production and Exports of Automobiles, 1963 vs. 1979

REGION	1963		1979	
	PERCENTAGE OF WORLD PRODUCTION	PERCENTAGE OF WORLD EXPORTS	PERCENTAGE OF WORLD PRODUCTION	PERCENTAGE OF WORLD EXPORTS
Industrial countries	91%	91%	84%	93%
North America	46	21	30	21
Japan	6	3	22	18
Western Europe	39	68	32	54
Developing countries	2	0	7	1
Eastern trading area	4	—	7	—

Source: General Agreement on Tariffs and Trade, *International Trade, 1979/80* (Geneva, GATT, 1980).

of the Eastern trading area rose from 4 percent to 7 percent. Within the group of industrial countries, Japan's production share rose from 6 percent to 22 percent, while North America's production share declined by the same amount from 46 percent to 30 percent. Also, Western Europe's percentage of world production fell from 39 percent to 32 percent. World auto exports continue to be dominated by industrial countries, but Japan has increased in importance relative to Western Europe.

The industrial countries' percentage of world auto exports was 91 percent in 1963 and 93 percent in 1979. North America's share was constant at 21 percent, but Japan's share rose from 3 percent to 18 percent and Western Europe's share declined from 68 percent to 54 percent. These changes have brought about major adjustment problems for the U.S. and European auto industries. In response to declines in profits and employment, these industries have been granted import quotas and government subsidies. Similar developments have occurred in the world steel industry where Japan has expanded relative to the United States and Western Europe. The adjustment problems have resulted in protectionist measures such as the trigger price mechanism in the United States (a minimum import price) and import quotas.

5.3 RICARDIAN PRODUCTIVITY DIFFERENCES

The earliest systematic attempt to explain the commodity composition of trade was David Ricardo's theory of comparative cost. According to the theory, countries are expected to export products in which they have a comparative advantage and to import products for which they have a comparative disadvantage. Since comparative advantage is defined in terms of relative labor productivity, every country must have a comparative advantage in something. Labor productivity is measured by output per man-hour, and the theory predicts that the country with the highest labor productivity in an industry will export the product. Low-productivity countries will import the same product. The theory is extremely simple with modest data requirements.

Ricardo made little effort to explain why productivity might differ between countries. He referred to differences in climate and natural resources without offering a precise explanation. Even in its simple form the Ricardian theory has received some empirical support.[1] The idea has been applied to explain the export shares of two countries for a given product in terms of differ-

---

[1] See G. D. A. MacDougall, "British and American Exports: A Study Suggested by the Theory of Comparative Costs," *Economic Journal*, December 1951; Bela Balassa, "An Empirical Demonstration of Classical Comparative Cost Theory," *Review of Economics and Statistics*, August 1963; and Robert Stern, "British and American Productivity and Comparative Costs in International Trade," *Oxford Economic Papers*, October 1962.

ences in output per worker-hour in those countries. For example, if output per man-hour is large in the United States relative to output in the United Kingdom for a particular product, the U.S. export share for that same product in third-country markets should be large relative to the U.K. share. A shortcoming of the theory is that it does not explain why labor productivity differs between countries.

Looking back to the discussion in Chapter 2, the questions are, What causes the home country's (a_{LF}, a_{LC}) and ROW's $(a^{\star}_{LF}, a^{\star}_{LC})$ labor coefficients to differ? and What causes the slopes of the home country's and ROW's linear production possibilities curves to differ? In fact, labor is not the only factor of production, and its productivity depends not only on the quantity and quality of labor but also on the quantities of other factors of production and technology. Labor may be more productive in a country because of (1) superior technology, (2) an abundance of other factors, or (3) large amounts of human capital. Firms may control the quantity of other factors employed, and the amount of these factors used varies from one product to the next. An alternative theory that attempts to explain the source of productivity differences is the factor endowments theory.

5.4 FACTOR
ENDOWMENTS AND TRADE

The factor endowments theory was developed by the Swedish economists Eli Heckscher and Bertil Ohlin. The rudiments of the theory appeared in a 1919 paper by Heckscher, and Ohlin presented a more elaborate version in his 1933 book.[2] As does Ricardo's productivity theory, the factor endowments theory attempts to explain trade in terms of differences in cost. However, it goes beyond Ricardo by explaining cost differences in terms of countries' relative factor endowments. The simple version of the Heckscher-Ohlin theory assumes that all factors may be divided into capital and labor, each of which is homogeneous. Technology is assumed to be identical in each country. Factor intensities vary by product, but factor intensity reversals are assumed not to occur. Thus, if a product is labor intensive at one set of factor prices, it is labor intensive at all factor prices. Production functions are assumed to exhibit constant returns to scale. Demand conditions are assumed to be similar in trading countries. It is sufficient that preferences be identical and that the budget shares of products be the same at all income levels. Some barriers to trade are permitted, but they must not be biased toward the services of one factor of production.

It follows from these assumptions that countries will export products that

---

[2] Ohlin, a student of Heckscher, received the Nobel Prize in 1977 (shared with James Meade) for his contributions to trade theory. Heckscher, who also wrote a distinguished book on mercantilism, died before the Nobel Prize in economics was initiated.

employ large amounts of their relatively abundant factor and will import products that use large amounts of their relatively scarce factor. The factor endowments theory implies that knowledge of countries' factor supplies is sufficient to predict the commodity composition of trade. Since factor services are embodied in traded products, international trade may be interpreted as the exchange of the services of one's abundant factor for the services of one's scarce factor. Emphasizing the factor content of trade makes it clear that international trade substitutes for international mobility of factors of production.

A famous empirical test of the factor endowments theory was published by Wassily Leontief in 1953. He employed data on the factor content of U.S. exports and imports. Because of the surprising conclusions, his study has become known as the Leontief paradox. Since the United States is capital abundant relative to its trading partners, the theory predicts that U.S. exports will be more capital intensive than will U.S. imports. Leontief's empirical results showed just the opposite. He grouped all factors of production into either capital or labor and computed the factor content of exports and imports by using input-output tables.[3] The empirical results showed that, contrary to the factor endowments theory, U.S. imports were more capital intensive than were U.S. exports. Similar paradoxical results were found for other countries as well. Much subsequent work has been devoted to explaining these paradoxical findings.

The most general criticism of the simple theory and Leontief's test is that combining all factors of production into the two categories of labor and capital conceals much useful information about the factor content of trade. The category "labor" includes unskilled workers who sweep floors in textile factories as well as physicists whose research and development efforts contribute to exports of complex machinery. Economists distinguish among these diverse groups of workers in terms of their differences in human capital, the market value of their skills. Workers differ in skill and knowledge, and these differences are reflected in occupational wage and salary differences.

It has been widely observed that average wages are higher in U.S. export industries than in the U.S. import-competing sector. If all these workers were homogeneous, it would be paradoxical that exporting firms could pay higher wages and still compete with foreigners, who are paying lower wages. In fact, the workers are not alike, and the higher wages in the export sector reflect the higher endowment of human capital. The U.S. export sector employs more skilled workers, especially scientists and engineers, and spends more money on research and development than does the import-competing sector. Thus, empirical studies of the factor endowments theory would benefit from separating labor into at least two different categories. Subsequent studies have done that,[4] and the results show that the United States exports are skilled labor-intensive

---

[3] Leontief also received the Nobel Prize in economics for developing input-output analysis.

[4] See William Branson and N. Monoyios, "Factor Inputs in U.S. Trade," *Journal of International Economics*, May 1977; and Robert E. Baldwin, "Determinants of the Commodity Structure of U.S. Trade," *American Economic Review*, March 1971, reprinted in *International Trade and*

and U.S. imports are unskilled labor-intensive. Thus, the U.S. exports the services of skilled labor and imports the services of unskilled labor, but this information is lost when labor is treated as a single factor of production.

A similar problem arises with regard to treating capital as a single aggregate. Natural resources have been an important U.S. import, which is particularly true now because of petroleum. It may be useful to separate land or natural resources from other forms of capital, because land and capital appear to be complementary in the extractive industries (e.g., mining and petroleum) for which the United States is a major importer. The aggregation of land and other capital into a single unit makes U.S. imports look more capital intensive than they are. Empirical studies since Leontief have indicated that treating capital as a single unit biases the results in the direction of the Leontief paradox. The empirical work that divides both capital and labor into smaller components is consistent with an expanded version of the factor endowments theory. The United States imports the services of natural resources and exports the services of physical capital. An expanded factor endowments theory must include, as separate factors, unskilled labor, human capital, natural resources, and physical capital.

Another possible explanation for Leontief's results is that the U.S. tariff structure is biased against labor-intensive goods. U.S. tariffs reduce the total volume of imports, but they are more restrictive of goods that employ large amounts of labor. Thus, the tariff structure alters the commodity composition of imports away from labor-intensive goods. The factor endowments theory offers a prediction for a world of free trade or neutral tariffs. An empirical application of the theory should take into account the effect of tariff structure on the composition of trade. The effect of tariff structure should include nontariff barriers such as quotas and government procurement programs that discriminate against certain imports.

The preceding criticism relates to the proper measurement of labor, capital, and the tariff structure. A more fundamental criticism of factor endowments is that the theory itself may not generate a clear prediction about the factor intensity of trade. The argument is that a capital-abundant country may export labor-intensive goods because (1) demand is biased toward capital-intensive goods or (2) the technology may permit a factor intensity reversal. The capital-abundant country would be expected to export capital-intensive goods, but if consumer demand in that country were strongly biased toward capital-intensive goods, the country might still be a net importer of those goods.

Both supply and demand factors determine the pattern of trade, but factor endowments consider only supply. If demand were strongly biased toward the product that employed the abundant factor intensively, the prediction of factor endowments could be reversed. One could attempt to rescue the theory

Finance: Readings, Robert E. Baldwin and J. David Richardson, eds., 2nd ed. (Boston: Little, Brown, 1981).

by defining the abundant factor as the one used intensively in the exported good, but this reduces the theory to a tautology. If the theory is consistent with all possible observations about the factor content of trade, it is not very useful.

The second criticism concerns factor intensity reversals, which may permit a product to be labor intensive some of the time and capital intensive at other times. The capital-to-labor ratio actually employed in an industry depends on the technology and the price of capital relative to the price of labor. Depending on the technology, a product such as food could be capital intensive at one set of factor prices and labor intensive at another set of factor prices. If a factor intensity reversal occurred, a capital-abundant country might be a cloth exporter at one set of factor prices and a food exporter at another set of prices. The practical importance of factor intensity reversals depends on the technical properties of production functions, but it is not yet clear how important these are in the real world. Similarly, the demand reversal argument is logically correct, but it has not been demonstrated that such preferences are important in fact.

There is an argument that demand similarity is an important determinant of trade. It has been observed that much of international trade consists of industrial countries trading with each other and that these countries have similar income levels. If these income levels produce similar patterns of demand, then demand variables may provide a better explanation of this trade than do cost differences. However, it is not easy to evaluate this hypothesis because it is difficult to distinguish between (1) similar incomes and (2) geographical proximity. Most of the industrial countries are in Western Europe where incomes are similar, countries are geographically close, and tariffs are low. Two of the other major trading countries, the United States and Canada, have nearly identical incomes plus a long common border. Thus, the large volume of trade among industrial countries may be attributable to low transport costs.

5.5 TECHNOLOGY AND THE PRODUCT CYCLE

The simple factor endowments theory assumes that technology is the same in all countries. Thus, if factor prices are equal, the same factor proportions will be employed in both countries. However, if technology differed between countries, a country with superior technology might export a product that used its scarce factor intensively. For example, a capital-abundant country might export labor-intensive goods because the technological superiority would lower costs by more (smaller quantity of labor per unit of output) than the higher wage would raise costs. Trade based on differences in technology, rather than on differences in factor costs, is called technological gap trade. Since technology may be learned, a particular technological gap between two countries is a transitory phenomenon and explains trade for only a limited time period. Once the superior technology is transmitted to partner countries, trade should again be based on factor costs. Factor endowments might determine the long-run pattern of trade, whereas technological differences might determine transitory deviations from that trade pattern.

It has been argued that technological gap trade has been important for U.S. exports. The United States is well-endowed with human capital, which gives the country a comparative advantage in research and development of new products and lower-cost techniques for producing existing products. The product cycle is a particular hypothesis that involves the development of new products by the United States, and the resulting technological gap gives American firms a temporary advantage in exporting those goods. As knowledge of the new technology spreads to other countries, the gap narrows and U.S. exports are displaced by foreign production. The cycle is complete when all countries acquire the new technology, and trade is then determined by factor costs. Those countries possessing a comparative advantage in the product will ship it to the United States, displacing domestic production. Since the United States has a comparative advantage in research and development, a new innovation will set off a new product cycle. An implication of this hypothesis is that the United States should export relatively new products or existing products using new techniques.[5]

The effect of the product cycle on the pattern of trade of the innovating home country is shown in Figure 5-1. Before the invention of the product, the home economy is at point A, where production, consumption, and imports are all zero. The domestic supply curve X_1^s represents the introduction of the new product. The import demand curve I^d may be derived from the old demand curve (X_1^d) and the new supply curve. At the price O_2B, domestic production will equal domestic consumption and imports will be zero. At any price below O_2B (e.g., O_2P_3), the home country will be an importer of X_1, but at any price above O_2B, the home country will be a net exporter.

Home country imports are measured to the right of O_2, and exports are measured to left of O_2. Initially, let the home country be the only user of the new technology. Equilibrium will be at point C, where the world price is O_2P_1. The home country will be an exporter of $O_2I_1 = JK$ units, which corresponds to the excess of domestic production over consumption. This situation corresponds to the first stage in the product cycle.

Now let foreign producers partially adopt the new technology. As the new technology is adopted by ROW, the world price will fall in stages from P_1 to P_2 to P_3. Foreign production begins, and the increase in supply lowers the world price to O_2P_2. Foreign production displaces some home country exports, which fall to $O_2I_2 = MN$.

In the final stage, ROW completely adopts the new technology, which

---

[5] For a discussion of the product cycle, see Raymond Vernon, "International Investment and International Trade in the Product Cycle," *Quarterly Journal of Economics*, May 1966. Stephen Magee extends the idea to the substitution of synthetics for natural resources. See Stephen P. Magee, *International Trade* (Reading, Mass.: Addison-Wesley, 1980), Chaps. 3 and 4.

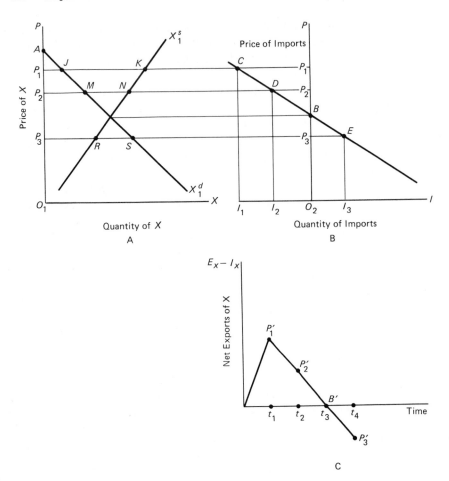

FIGURE 5-1   Technical Change and the Product Cycle

gives them a comparative advantage in X. The additional supply lowers the world price to $O_2 P_3$, which transforms the home country from an exporter of X to an importer of $O_2 I_3 = RS$ units. Following the innovation, the first two levels of exports ($O_2 I_1$ and $O_2 I_2$) represent technological gap trade, but the final level of imports ($O_2 I_3$) is based on differences in factor endowments when technology is the same in both countries.

The pattern of the home country's net exports of X is shown in panel C of Figure 5-1. At the initial price (P_1') following innovation, the country is a net exporter. As foreign adoption occurs at P_2', net exports decline. Finally, at P_3', the home country becomes a net importer of X. The exact pattern of trade over time depends on the frequency of innovation in the home country and the speed of adoption in the rest of the world.

Consider a numerical example in which technological change occurs but the new technology is adopted in stages. The innovation occurs in the home country, which gives residents a temporary cost advantage. Let the domestic demand and supply equations be the following:

$$X^d = 100 - 2P$$
$$X^s = 2P$$

The resulting import demand curve is

$$I^d = X^d - X^s = 100 - 2P - 2P$$
$$= 100 - 4P$$

If the initial price is $P = \$40$, the home country will export 60 units:

$$I^d = 100 - 4(40) = -60$$

Negative imports are to be interpreted as exports. This situation is equivalent to exports of $CP_1 = JK$ at price O_2P_1 in Figure 5-1. When ROW partially adopts the technology, the price falls (e.g., to $O_2P_2 = \$30$) and home exports fall to 20 units:

$$I^d = 100 - 4(30) = -20$$

Finally, when ROW completely adopts the technology, the price falls to $O_2P_3 = \$15$, and the home country becomes a net importer of 40 units:

$$I^d = 100 - 4(15) = 40$$

Thus, the home country completes the product cycle from net exporter to net importer.

Technological change may also be a way in which domestic production is substituted for imports. The United States has been an important importer of raw materials, but there have been some cases in which technological innovation has produced synthetic substitutes for imported raw materials. Synthetic rubber, industrial diamonds, and plastic are three examples of substitution. Similarly, the recent high prices of oil have provided a powerful incentive to develop a synthetic substitute. Import substitution as a result of technical change is shown in Figure 5-2. Define the product measured on the horizontal axis broadly enough to include both the natural resource and the synthetic substitute (e.g., natural rubber plus synthetic substitute). The initial equilibrium is at point A, where the import demand curve (I_1^d) has been derived from the initial domestic demand and supply curves (X_1^d and X_1^s). The price of X is O_2P_1 and the volume of imports is O_2I_1.

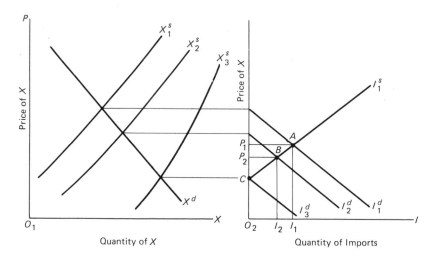

FIGURE 5-2   Induced Technical Change and Import Substitution

Let there be a technological innovation that lowers the cost of producing the domestic synthetic substitute. This change is shown by the new domestic supply (X_2^s) and the new import demand (I_2^d). The increased use of the synthetic product lowers the price to O_2P_2 and the quantity of imports falls to O_2I_2. If the innovation were large enough to lower costs to X_3^s, import demand would fall to I_3^d, the price would fall to O_2C, and imports would cease.

Of course, technological change is not a free good, and the amount of technological change available depends on the benefits and costs to those involved. The benefits take the form of a lower price or greater consumer surplus. The costs of innovation depend on technological possibilities, and the productivity of the research and development sector. The large stock of human capital in the United States may provide it with a comparative advantage in research and development, which may lower the cost of induced import substitution.

5.6 EXPLAINING CHANGES IN THE PATTERN OF U.S. TRADE

How can one explain changes in the pattern of U.S. trade following World War II? Theory suggests that one should consider changes in relative factor supplies, technology, and government policy. Another interpretation is that recent developments constitute a movement back toward an earlier pattern of trade that was interrupted by the Great Depression and World War II. William Branson has argued that the destruction brought about by World War II gave the United States an artificial and temporary comparative advantage in certain industrial products.[6] As Western Europe and Japan recovered from the war, the U.S. advantage disappeared. For example, the United States was a net importer of consumer goods every year from 1925 to 1937. The United States became a net exporter during the period from 1938 to 1958, but the country has been a net importer of consumer goods since 1959. While Branson stresses the long-run stability of U.S. comparative advantage, he does not deny that there have been significant changes. He acknowledges a growing comparative advantage in capital goods and chemicals and a growing comparative disadvantage in minerals, industrial supplies (including steel), and automobiles.

An alternative explanation of the U.S. trade pattern is a direct application of the factor endowments theory in a growing world economy. Since a country's comparative advantage is a function of its relative factor endowments, changes in factor supplies over time should alter comparative advantage, thus changing the structure of trade. Although the United States is a highly capital-abundant country, investment rates have been very low in recent years. Since annual investment is the addition to a nation's capital stock, a low investment rate means that the United States has become relatively less abundant in physical capital.

In the period from 1963 to 1975, the stocks of physical capital and skilled labor grew slowly in the United States relative to those of its trading partners, which caused a change in the comparative advantage of the U.S. export sector. In particular, physical capital and skilled labor grew very rapidly in Japan during this period, and this change in relative factor endowments made Japanese firms much more effective competitors.

On the import side, rapid accumulation of physical capital and semi-skilled labor by certain low-income countries has made these countries more competitive producers of goods in which the United States had a comparative disadvantage. The group of newly industrializing countries has become noticeably more competitive for certain products. If this interpretation is correct, several U.S. industries will not be able to avoid competitive problems unless there are major changes in investment rates for physical and human capital.

A third explanation stresses the domestic policies of the U.S. government and the export policies of foreign governments. The argument is that the entire set of domestic taxes and environmental and safety rules has raised costs, thereby altering the U.S. comparative advantage. These policies have affected some industries more than others, and advocates for the auto and steel industries have complained that they were severely hurt. Indeed, Chrysler Corporation based its plea for a federal loan guarantee in 1980 on the grounds that federal regulations had made them uncompetitive.

---

[6] William Branson presents a comprehensive survey of U.S. trade and investment in his "Trends in United States International Trade and Investment since World War II," which appears in Martin Feldstein, ed., *The American Economy in Transition* (Chicago: University of Chicago Press, 1980).

A related argument is that foreign governments subsidize their exports more than the U.S. government does. For example, the U.S. steel industry has repeatedly complained about the adverse effect of subsidized steel imports. However, this argument loses much of its force in the current regime of flexible exchange rates, in which currency values fluctuate according to supply and demand. An export subsidy by a foreign government would lower the price of its exports, but this effect would be offset by the appreciation of the exporter's currency relative to the U.S. dollar.

Some other variables that have affected U.S. trade are (1) the market structure for petroleum, (2) the increasing importance of service exports, and (3) the relationship between demand and income. In the case of petroleum, the transformation of a competitive market into a monopolistic one by OPEC has had a profound effect on world trade as well as on U.S. trade. Some of the direct effects of oil trade are obvious, but there are significant indirect effects as well. Because oil is an important input in many production processes, an increase in its price alters relative costs of importables, exportables, and nontraded goods. In addition to increasing the U.S. import bill, the price rise has increased the foreign earnings of American oil companies. These earnings show up as an increase in the value of U.S. service exports in the balance of payments.

The structure of trade discussed so far refers to merchandise trade, excluding services. However, services have become a larger share of the GNP, and are becoming a growing share of U.S. exports. Services are intangible items such as transport, travel, and factor income from abroad. The most important U.S. service export is foreign investment income. As a direct export of the services of capital, it is a substitute for exports of capital-intensive products.

From 1979 to 1981, the United States had large deficits in its merchandise trade, but these deficits were completely offset by net service exports. Thus, it is possible that the United States had a comparative disadvantage in merchandise trade and a comparative advantage in service exports. Finally, when income grows, demand for various products grows at different rates. There is evidence that the income elasticity of demand for imports into the United States is greater than the income elasticity of demand for U.S. exports by foreigners. Thus, as income per capita grows in the United States, there would be a tendency for U.S. imports to grow faster than U.S. exports, in the absence of relative price changes. In addition, the commodity composition of both imports and exports may change in response to income growth.

SUMMARY

This chapter has presented the major theories that attempt to explain the commodity composition of trade. It has also summarized empirical tests of the theories. There is some empirical support for Ricardo's hypothesis that trade is based on productivity differences. However, a major shortcoming of Ricardo's theory is that it does not explain the source of productivity differences.

The simple version of the Heckscher-Ohlin theory explains trade by international differences in supplies of capital and labor. The simple form of the theory ignores some important information. Empirical studies of U.S. trade have shown that it is important to distinguish between different kinds of labor and capital. The United States has exported the services of skilled labor and physical capital, while importing the services of unskilled labor and natural resources.

Technological differences have at least a transitory effect on the pattern of trade. U.S. import barriers have biased the composition of imports away from labor-intensive goods. Although these criticisms are damaging to the simple version of the Heckscher-Ohlin theory, they may all be incorporated into an expanded version of the theory. The modified theory explains trade in terms of relative supplies of skilled and unskilled labor, physical capital and natural resources, international differences in technology, and the structure of trade barriers.

REFERENCES

BALASSA, BELA. "An Empirical Demonstration of Classical Comparative Cost Theory." *Review of Economics and Statistics*, August 1963.

BALDWIN, ROBERT E. "Determinants of Trade and Foreign Investment: Further Evidence." *Review of Economics and Statistics*, February 1979. Uses recent data to confirm the major results of his 1971 study.

———. "Determinants of the Commodity Structure of U.S. Trade." *American Economic Review*, March 1971; reprinted in *International Trade and Finance: Readings*, Robert E. Baldwin and J. David Richardson, eds., 2nd ed. Boston: Little, Brown, 1981. A thorough empirical study of the determinants of the commodity composition of U.S. trade.

BECKER, GARY. *Human Capital.* New York: Columbia University Press, 1964. A thorough treatment of the concept of human capital.

BOWEN, HARRY. "Shifts in the International Distribution of Resources and Their Impact on U.S. Comparative Advantage." Paper presented to the annual meeting of the Southern Economic Association, Washington, D.C., November, 1980. An empirical study that explains changes in the pattern of U.S. trade by changes in relative factor supplies.

BRANSON, WILLIAM. "Trends in United States International Trade and Investment since World War II." In *The American Economy in Transition*, Martin Feldstein, ed. Chicago: University of Chicago Press, 1980. A comprehensive survey of recent developments in U.S. trade and investment.

———, and N. MONOYIOS. "Factor Inputs in U.S. Trade." *Journal of International Economics*, May 1977. Empirical study showing that U.S. exports are human capital intensive and imports are unskilled labor intensive.

GRUBEL, HERBERT, and P. J. LLOYD. *Intra-Industry Trade: The Theory and Measurement of International Trade in Differentiated Products.* New York: Halsted, 1975. A basic reference on the theory and facts concerning intraindustry trade.

HARKNESS, JON. "Factor Abundance and Comparative Advantage." *American Economic Review*, December 1978.

HECKSCHER, ELI.   "The Effect of Foreign Trade on the Distribution of Income."
Economisk Tidskrift, Vol. 21 (1919), pp. 497–512. Reprinted in *Readings in the
Theory of International Trade*, Howard Ellis and Lloyd Metzler, eds. Homewood,
Ill.: Richard D. Irwin, 1949. First statement of the fundamentals of the factor
endowments theory.

HOUTHAKKER, HENDRIK and STEPHEN P. MAGEE.   "Income and Price
Elasticities in World Trade." *Review of Economics and Statistics*, May 1969. An
empirical study of trade elasticities for several countries.

HUFBAUER, GARY.   "The Impact of National Characteristics and Technology on
the Commodity Composition of Trade in Manufactured Goods." In *The Technology Factor In International Trade*, Raymond Vernon, ed. New York: Columbia
University Press, 1970.

JOHNSON, HARRY G.   *Comparative Cost and Commercial Policy Theory for a Developing World Economy*. Stockholm: Almquist and Wiksell, 1968. A synthesis of
the basic theories of trade.

LEONTIEF, WASSILY.   "Domestic Production and Foreign Trade: The American
Position Re-examined." Proceedings of the American Philosophical Society, September 1953. Reprinted in *Readings in International Economics*, Richard E. Caves
and Harry G. Johnson, eds. Homewood, Ill.: Richard D. Irwin, 1968. The empirical study that came to be known as Leontief's paradox.

LINDER, STAFFAN B.   *An Essay on Trade and Transformation*. New York: John
Wiley, 1961. Emphasizes the effect of demand characteristics on trade.

MACDOUGALL, G. D. A.   "British and American Exports: A Study Suggested by
the Theory of Comparative Costs." *Economic Journal*, December 1951. Reprinted
in *Readings in International Economics*, Richard Caves and Harry G. Johnson, eds.
Homewood, Ill.: Richard D. Irwin, 1968. A pioneering empirical study of Ricardian comparative costs.

MAGEE, STEPHEN P.   *International Trade*. Reading, Mass.: Addison-Wesley, 1980.
Chapters 2 and 3 discuss the product cycle and apply the idea to the substitution
of synthetics for raw materials.

OHLIN, BERTIL.   *Interregional and International Trade*. Cambridge, Mass.: Harvard
University Press, 1933. An early formal statement of the factor endowments theory.

RICARDO, DAVID.   *Principles of Political Economy and Taxation* (1817). Volume 1
of Piero Sraffa, ed., *The Works and Correspondence of David Ricardo*. Cambridge:
Cambridge University Press, 1953.

STERN, ROBERT.   "British and American Productivity and Comparative Costs in
International Trade." *Oxford Economic Papers*, October 1962.

———.   "Testing Trade Theories." In *International Trade and Finance*, Peter B. Kenen, ed. Cambridge: Cambridge University Press, 1975. A survey of empirical
studies of the commodity composition of trade.

———, and KEITH MASKUS.   "Determinants of the Structure of U.S. Foreign
Trade." *Journal of International Economics*, May 1981.

VANEK, JARSOSLAV.   "The Natural Resource Content of Foreign Trade 1870–1955
and the Relative Abundance of Natural Resources in the United States." *Review
of Economics and Statistics*, May 1959. An empirical study of the importance of
natural resources in U.S. imports.

VERNON, RAYMOND.   "International Investment and International Trade in the
Product Cycle." *Quarterly Journal of Economics*, May 1966. Reprinted in *International Trade and Finance: Readings*, Robert E. Baldwin and J. David Richardson, eds., 2nd ed. Boston: Little, Brown, 1981. An early statement of the product cycle theory.

CHAPTER SIX
TRADE,
TRANSPORT COSTS,
AND MIDDLEMEN

6.1 INTRODUCTION

Until now the discussion of trade has abstracted from transport costs. The purpose of this chapter is to provide an explicit analysis of the effect of transport costs on international trade. In the absence of transport costs, trade will equalize the foreign and domestic prices of the same product. If 1 ounce of gold sells for $500 in London and $450 in New York, arbitragers have a powerful incentive to buy in New York for $450 and sell in London for $500. This spatial arbitrage adds to demand and raises the price in New York, and it adds to supply and lowers the price in London. The process will continue until the price is the same in both cities. Because arbitragers constantly monitor spatial price relationships and exploit profitable opportunities, such large price differentials in the real world should not be expected.

When the cost of transporting gold from New York to London is considered, arbitrage will not equalize prices. If transport costs are $10 per ounce, arbitrage will cease when the London price is $10 higher than the New York price. Any smaller price differential would be unprofitable for the trader, since he or she would spend more on transport costs than would be gained from the excess of the selling price over the buying price. Thus, in the presence of transport costs, trade tends to equalize prices, but the equalization is incomplete. By adding to total costs, transport costs reduce the volume of trade. Altering prices in both countries changes production, consumption, and the distribution of income. Because transport costs vary among products, the existence of transport costs alters relative prices and the commodity composition of trade.

Transport costs also affect the direction of trade. If an American firm decides to import copper, the choice between a Chilean source and a Zambian source depends, among other things, on transport costs. The fact that Canada and Mexico are two of the most important trading partners of the United States is largely a function of low transport costs.

The term "transport cost" refers to a number of distinct costs. The most obvious component is the cost of freight associated with ships, airplanes, railroad, pipelines, and other modes of transportation. The cost of loading and unloading, including waiting time, is another component. Damage from natural or human-created disasters is a cost that can be approximated by the cost of insurance.

Since transport costs create a divergence between the selling price in one country and the buying price in another country, the concept of transport costs can be generalized to include all the services of middlemen. Middlemen provide services such as storage, credit, and distribution in addition to transport. For example, Japanese importers buy their grain from large trading companies such as Mitsui or Cargill rather than trade directly with U.S. farmers. The difference between the price paid by importers and the price received by U.S. farmers is a measure of the services rendered by the trading company in its role as middleman. This marketing margin can be treated as a component of the generalized measure of transport costs.

The general concept of transport costs can be applied to the analysis of smuggling. Declaring a product to be illegal does not stop all trade in that product, but it does increase the cost of business in the same way as an increase in transport costs. The additional cost of illegal trade is related to the value of the penalty and the probability of being apprehended. Transport costs have been affected by the attempts of governments to protect transportation from international competition. Protective measures have included cargo preference laws, such as U.S. Jones Act. In addition there have been government sanctioned efforts to monopolize the airline and shipping markets.

6.2 THE NATURE
AND DEVELOPMENT
OF TRANSPORTATION

Transport costs include a variety of charges that cause the price of a product in the importing country to exceed its price in the exporting country. These charges include freight, loading, and insurance. Transportation comes in many forms, such as ships, airplanes, railroads, trucks, and pipelines. Electronic transmission of information is a significant recent innovation. Transport costs fluctuate widely over cycles, but there has been a definite downward trend for many years. The trend toward cheaper transport has been one of the main reasons for the growth in international trade. The increase in fuel costs since 1974 has been an important exception to the trend. The freight rate increases of the 1970s retarded trade by as much as the Kennedy Round tariff reductions of the 1960s increased trade.

Historical costs have declined because of new shipping routes and because of technological change in shipping. For example, Vasco DaGama's sailing around Africa opened new routes to the East, and the voyage of Columbus to America opened new routes to the West. The design of sailing ships improved substantially from the time of Leif Erickson to Columbus to the nineteenth-century clipper ships. The early steamships lowered costs further, and modern supertankers represent the latest shipping innovation.

Innovation in transport technology has been rapid in the past two centuries. Most products traded today are carried by steamships and trains invented in the nineteenth century or trucks and airplanes invented in the twentieth century. Transport costs are also reduced by improvements in navigation and construction of canals, bridges, pipelines, and tunnels.

The time that ships are in port being loaded and unloaded is an important cost, which has been reduced by the development of containerized ships. Loading costs are affected by labor costs, including unionization of longshoremen. Higher U.S. labor costs have led many U.S. shipowners to fly foreign flags on their vessels. National taxes and regulations also affect shipping costs, which affect the country of registration of ships. Some small countries, such as Liberia and Panama, have large merchant fleets flying their flags because they offer favorable conditions for shipowners. These "flags of convenience" have been important to both shippers and host countries, and in recent years roughly 10 percent of Liberia's national income has come from shipping fees. In 1980 some 2,500 ships flew the Liberian flag, but few of them ever touch that country's shores. About 10 percent of those ships are owned by American firms that are able to avoid more expensive U.S. labor that American registry would require.[1]

The most important seaborne traded item is petroleum, regardless of whether it is measured in volume or value. In 1965 crude petroleum and petroleum products comprised 52 percent of world shipping tonnage, and the share rose to 56 percent by 1974.[2] The sharp price increases in 1973 and 1974 and 1979 and 1980 increased the relative importance of petroleum trade even more. Most of the world's shipping capacity is registered in the high-income countries, although 25 percent fly the so-called "flags of convenience."[3] These ships are registered in low-income countries, even though they are owned primarily by Japanese and American firms.

[1] *The Wall Street Journal*, "American Firms With Ships Registered In Liberia Worry Over Effects of the Coup," April 4, 1980.

[2] See Alexander J. Yeats, *Trade Barriers Facing Developing Countries* (New York: St. Martins, 1979), Chap. 7.

[3] The practice of offering "flags of convenience" is called open registry. In addition to Liberia and Panama, the open-registry countries are Cyprus, Singapore, and Somalia. The majority of the members of the low-income countries that comprise the United Nations Conference on Trade and Development have openly opposed the practice of open registry in recent years.

The size of major merchant fleets is shown by nation in Table 6-1. The appearance of Liberia, Panama, and Singapore as having the first, sixth, and thirteenth largest fleets, respectively, shows the effect of flags of convenience. With that exception, the list is dominated by high-income countries. Included in the list with more than 20 million tons of capacity are Greece, Japan, the United Kingdom, Norway, the Soviet Union, and the United States. The ranking is slightly different by number of ships, but the same countries appear.

The amount of shipbuilding varies considerably from year to year, but Japan has been the largest shipbuilder in recent years. In 1978 the next largest shipbuilding nations (in order) were West Germany, Norway, Sweden, France, United Kingdom, Poland, Korea, and Brazil.

International trade is affected by domestic as well as international transportation. In some cases the cost of moving products from inland production sites to ports is greater than the cost of moving them between countries. In many cases it is more expensive to transport grain from the midwestern United States to Gulf ports than it is to ship the grain across the Atlantic Ocean. It follows that changes in domestic transportation can have a profound effect on international trade.

Domestic transport costs are particularly important for countries with large area, such as Canada. For example, Canada has been subsidizing rail rates for grain shipped from the interior to the Pacific Coast since the nineteenth century. As a result of the Crow's Nest Pass Agreement of 1897, the Canadian Pacific Railroad has agreed to ship all grain and flour at a fixed subsidized rate.

TABLE 6-1   Major Merchant Fleets, 1980

COUNTRY	WEIGHT (MILLIONS OF DEADWEIGHT TONS)
Liberia	159
Greece	64
Japan	61
United Kingdom	42
Norway	40
Panama	35
USSR	22
United States*	21
France	20
Italy	19
Spain	13
West Germany	13
Singapore	12
China	10

*Privately owned.

Source: Morgan Guaranty Survey, August 1982. New York: Morgan Guaranty Trust Company, p. 11.

As real costs have increased over time, the fixed rates have become a smaller fraction of total costs. For example, in 1982 grain could be shipped from Manitoba to Vancouver on the Pacific Coast at the subsidized rate of $0.16 per bushel. Grain shipped from Minot, North Dakota, cost up to $1.24 per bushel at rates existing in 1982. Even though the Crow's Nest Pass rate applies solely to transportation in Canada, it functions as an effective grain export subsidy. It has an indirect effect on the competitiveness of Canadian grain with grain from the United States, Australia, Argentina, and other exporting countries. It is an example of the international repercussions of domestic policy.

Transport costs are a natural trade barrier, whereas tariffs are a human-created barrier to trade. The historic decline in transport costs has stimulated trade at the same time that tariffs have discouraged trade. Because of the inverse relationship, Bastiat described tariffs as "negative railroads." Conversely, the unusual increase in transport costs in the 1970s offset some of the tariff reductions of the 1960s and 1970s. Specifically, the freight rate increases of the 1970s more than canceled the tariff reductions that followed the Kennedy Round of trade negotiations. For certain products, transport costs are a more important trade barrier than are tariffs. Transport costs can be compared with tariff rates by computing the ratio of the unit transport cost to the import price. Alexander Yeats computed this ratio for the products imported into the United States from developing countries in 1974.[4] The average transport cost was 12 percent, whereas the average tariff facing the same products was only 3 percent. Apparently exporters in developing countries would benefit more from transportation innovations than from tariff liberalization by the United States.

6.3 SUPPLY AND DEMAND ANALYSIS OF TRANSPORT COSTS

The effect of transport costs on trade is shown in Figure 6-1 in terms of supply and demand curves for imports. If transport costs are t per unit, the equilibrium price in the importing country (P) must exceed the price in the exporting country $(P^\star)$ by the amount of the transport costs:

$$P - P^\star = t$$

If transport costs are T_1T_2 per unit, the equilibrium prices are P_3 at home and P_4 in ROW. The price in the importing country is called the c.i.f. price (cost, insurance, and freight). The price in the exporting country is the f.o.b. price (free on board). The volume of trade is O_2I_3. The revenue paid to the trans-

---

[4] Yeats, *Trade Barriers Facing Developing Countries*, pp. 186–187.

TRANSPORT

FIGURE 6-1 The Effects of a Reduction in Transport Costs

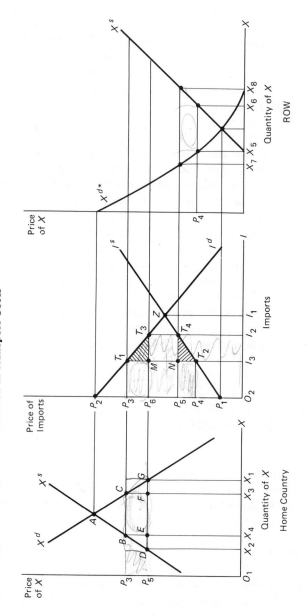

port industry is represented by the area of the rectangle $P_4P_3T_1T_2$. If trade were banned or transport costs were prohibitive, prices would be O_2P_2 at home and O_2P_1 in ROW. Thus, the effect of trade is to reduce the price differential from P_2P_1 to P_3P_4 without completely equalizing prices.

The economic effect of a reduction in transport costs can be seen in Figure 6-1. Let costs decrease from T_1T_2 to T_3T_4. The cost decrease will expand the volume of trade to O_2I_2 and reduce the price differential between the home country and ROW to $P_5P_6 = T_3T_4$. The price falls in the home country from P_3 to P_5 and rises in ROW from P_4 to P_6. Total revenue of the transport industry becomes $P_5P_6 = T_3T_4$, which may be greater or less than the initial total cost, depending on whether the elasticity of demand for transport services is greater or less than one. The beneficiaries of the cost decrease are consumers in the home country and producers in ROW. Conversely, lower transport costs are harmful to home country producers and ROW consumers.

The net gains to each country and the redistribution of income within each country can be seen with the aid of Figure 6-1. Consumers in the home country gain from lower transport costs because they buy a larger quantity of X at a lower price. This consumption gain is shown by the area of the triangle FCG. A second gain occurs because the home country can substitute lower-cost imports for domestic production of X. The additional imports release domestic resources to produce other products. This production gain is shown by the area DBE. The net gain to the home country is the area $MT_1T_3 = FCG + DBE$, in the center of the diagram. Using similar logic, it can be shown that area T_2NT_4 is the net gain to ROW from selling its export at a more favorable price. It is left to the reader to show that area T_2NT_4 is the sum of a production triangle related to $X^{s\star}$ and a consumption triangle related to $X^{d\star}$. The world gain from the transport innovation is the sum of the national gains $T_2NT_4 + MT_1T_3$. Alternatively, the net benefits of the additional imports (I_3I_2) can be viewed as the value of these imports to consumers (area $I_3T_1T_3I_2$) less the cost of producing them in ROW (the area $I_CT_2T_4I_2$) less the cost of transporting them (area NMT_3T_4):

$$\text{net benefits} = \begin{matrix}\text{consumption} \\ \text{gain}\end{matrix} - \begin{matrix}\text{production} \\ \text{cost}\end{matrix} - \begin{matrix}\text{transport} \\ \text{cost}\end{matrix}$$

$$T_2NT_4 + MT_1T_3 = \quad I_3T_1T_3I_2 \quad - \quad I_3T_2T_4I_2 \quad - NMT_3T_4$$

In addition to these net changes there will be a redistribution of income from producers to consumers of X in the home country and in the opposite direction in ROW. This redistribution occurs because cheaper imports force producers in the home country to sell each unit of X for P_5 instead of P_3. The money value of this income transfer is P_5P_3BD. Domestic producers lose part of the natural protection provided by transport costs. In ROW the opportunity to sell X abroad for a net price of $P_6(=P_5 - T_3T_4)$ forces the consumer price to rise to P_6 also. The reader can show the magnitude of the income transfer to producers in ROW. Even though lower transport costs provide net benefits for the world as a whole, producers of X at home and consumers in ROW are harmed. This illustrates the earlier point that all economic changes, no matter how beneficial, are harmful to someone. If by some miracle transport costs disappeared, the additional net benefits would be T_4T_3Z, but home producers and ROW consumers would be harmed even more.

6.4 A PROBLEM INVOLVING TRANSPORT COSTS

The precise economic effects of transport costs can be shown with the following problem. First, assume zero transport costs and the following import demand and supply equations:

$$I^d = 200 - 2P \quad \text{ED}$$
$$I^s = 8P \quad \text{ES}$$

The equilibrium price with free trade is

$$I^d = I^s$$
$$200 - 2P = 8P$$
$$P = 20 \quad \checkmark$$

The equilibrium volume of imports is

$$I^s = 12(20) = 240$$

Now suppose that transport costs become $4 per unit ($t = 4$). The price in the importing country (P) will exceed the price in the exporting country $(P\star)$ by the amount of the transport cost (t):

$$P - P\star = t$$

In this problem, rewrite the import supply equation to incorporate transport costs:

$$I^s = 8P\star = 8(P - t) = 8P - 32$$
$$I^d = I^s$$
$$200 - 2P = 8P - 32$$
$$P = \$23.20$$
$$P\star = P - T = \$23.20 - \$4.00 = \$19.20$$

The $4.00 transport cost causes the import price to rise to $23.20. In this case $3.20 or 80 percent of the transport cost is borne by the consumers in the importing country, and the remaining $0.80 or 20 percent is borne by foreign suppliers of imports. The import volume with transport costs is

$$I^s = 8(19.20) = 153.60$$

The total cost of transportation is $4.00 (153.60) = $614.40.

The results are summarized in Figure 6-2, where I_1^s and I_2^s are the import supply curves with and without transport costs, respectively. Transport costs per unit are shown by the vertical distance $CB = P_2P_3 = 4.00. The area P_3P_2CB represents total transport costs of $614.40. The area BCA represents the net loss to the world economy from reducing the volume of trade from 240 units of X to 153.60. This net loss is the difference between the gross loss to consumers of I_2CAI_1 and the resources saved by trading less, which is I_2BAI_1. Thus, world income is lower by the amount BCA than it would be if transport costs were zero.

Let technical change reduce transport costs from $4.00 per unit of X to $2.00. What will be the effect on prices and the volume of trade? The new import supply equation including transport costs will be

$$I^s = 8(P - t) = 8(P - 2) = 8P - 16$$

FIGURE 6-2   Transport Cost Problem

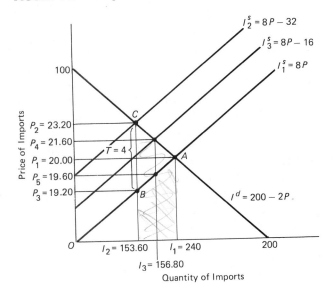

Quantity of Imports

Equilibrium occurs where import demand equals import supply:

$$200 - 2P = 8P - 16$$
$$P = \$21.60$$
$$P\star = P - t = \$21.60 - \$2.00 = \$19.60$$
$$I^s = 8(19.60) = 156.80$$

The \$2.00 decline in transport costs causes the price of X to fall by \$1.60 (\$23.20 − \$21.60) in the home country and rise by \$0.40 = \$19.60 − \$19.20 in ROW. The volume of imports increases by 156.80 − 153.60 = 3.20. Total payment to the transport industry falls to \$2.00(156.80) = \$313.60. The effects of a cost increase are symmetrical with those of a decrease. The benefits and costs of changes in transport costs depend on the slopes of I^d and I^s. A greater portion of transport cost increases will be borne by the import supplier, the more elastic (flatter) is import demand and the less elastic (steeper) is import supply. It is instructive to show that, if transport costs rise to \$100.00 (the vertical distance between the intercepts for I^d and I^s), trade will cease.

6.5 CARGO PREFERENCE AND PROTECTION OF DOMESTIC TRANSPORTATION

It is common practice for governments to protect the domestic shipping industry from foreign competition. Protection is often rationalized by appealing to national security considerations. Even Adam Smith, who was usually a staunch advocate of unfettered competition, advocated subsidies to the merchant marine. In defending the protectionist British navigation acts, he stated that "As defence, however, is of much more importance than opulence, the act of navigation is, perhaps, the wisest of all commercial regulations of England."[5]

Protection can either take the form of cargo preference or direct subsidies to production and operation of domestic transportation. Cargo preference is a government policy that preserves a portion of a nation's international trade for domestic shipping. An extreme form of cargo preference would require the use of domestic shipping for all international trade. Cargo preference may include any of the following requirements: (1) domestically produced ships, (2) domestic crews, and (3) domestic registration, which may specify crew size and salaries. Thus, cargo preference is an import quota on the use of transportation services. In its extreme form, it is an import embargo. As long as cargo preference is a binding constraint on trade, it has the effect of increasing transportation costs.

[5] Adam Smith, *Wealth of Nations* (New York: Random House/Modern Library Edition, 1936), p. 431.

Cargo preference has a long tradition in the United States, dating back to the British Navigation Acts of colonial times. The Navigation Acts contained many provisions, but the main ones required the use of British ships and British crews for all colonial trade. Since alternative shipping was available at lower cost, the Navigation Acts increased the cost of transportation for colonial importers and exporters. Thus, colonial importers paid a higher price for products, while colonial exporters earned a lower price. One of the first organized colonial protests involved Virginia tobacco growers who complained that the use of British ships lowered the net price they received for their product. Opposition to the Navigation Acts grew, and dissatisfaction with the acts is often listed as one of the proximate causes of the American Revolution.

Nevertheless, the United States has retained some features of cargo preference in its trade policies. The Jones Act requires the use of U.S. ships for all intracoastal trade. The act applies to all trade from one U.S. port to another, including Alaska and Hawaii. Since U.S. ships are considerably more costly than foreign ships, the restriction induces intracoastal shippers to seek alternative means of transportation. U.S.-flag ships are required by law to hire American crews, which result in labor costs that are at least double those in other countries.

The existence of the Jones Act magnified the impact of the congressional decision to ban oil exports from Alaska in 1974. It is potentially profitable to export Alaskan oil to Japan and import additional Mexican oil at Gulf Coast ports. Because of the export ban, Alaskan oil has been shipped to the Gulf Coast via the Panama Canal. By one estimate this pattern of trade has added $600 million per year in transport costs, partly due to the use of U.S. ships and crews.

It is not surprising that U.S. shipowners and maritime unions have lobbied actively to retain the export ban. In addition to the Jones Act, U.S. law requires the use of American ships for all military and civilian foreign aid shipments.[6] The latter includes all food shipments under Public Law 480. The largest recipient of food in recent years has been Egypt, and the additional cost of using American ships has not been negligible. In 1982 shipping wheat to Egypt on a U.S.-flag vessel cost $122 per ton, whereas a Greek ship could make the same trip for $30 per ton. The effect has been to reduce the real value of the aid per dollar spent by U.S. taxpayers. The shipping industry and maritime unions have regularly sought to extend cargo preference to additional trade. In 1974 Congress passed a bill requiring that a fixed percentage of all U.S. oil imports be carried on American ships. President Ford vetoed the bill, citing excessive consumer cost.

The U.S. government has attempted to protect the merchant marine in

---

[6] The 1904 Military Transportation Act required the use of U.S. ships to carry fodder for cavalry horses and other military supplies.

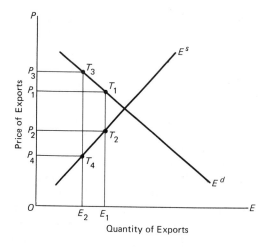

FIGURE 6-3   Effect of Higher Transport Costs on Exports

a variety of other ways, which sometimes conflict with each other. Presumably the object of cargo preference is to increase the size of the shipping industry. However, eligible shipping firms must employ American crews, use American-made ships, and carry American registry. All these restrictions increase costs, which make American shippers less competitive than they would have been. For example, the use of American crews makes labor costs at least double those of other nations, because crews are larger and salaries are the highest in the world. In 1950 40 percent of U.S. oceanborne foreign trade was carried by U.S.-flag vessels. By 1960 the share had declined to 11 percent, and by 1980 the U.S. fleet carried only 4 percent of U.S. trade.

The use of American-made ships also adds to cost. The Maritime Administration has estimated that comparable ships cost at least twice as much in U.S. shipyards as in Japan or Western Europe. As the incentive to invest in the U.S. fleet has declined, the average age of U.S. vessels has increased to 22 years compared with 12 years for other countries. Largely because of these additional costs of flying the American flag, approximately 500 U.S. owners register their ships in "flag of convenience" countries such as Liberia or Panama. Thus, an ironic result of shipping policy has been to make American registry an unattractive alternative. For the portion of trade that is carried by U.S. ships the cost is higher, the volume of trade is smaller, and the net price to exporters is lower.

Figure 6-3 shows the effect of using domestic ships when foreign ships would be cheaper. Paying the higher transport costs of T_3T_4 rather than T_1T_2 reduces export volume from E_1 to E_2 and lowers the net price to exporters from P_2 to P_4.

6.6 MONOPOLY POWER
IN TRANSPORTATION

Two conflicting sets of policies have characterized the international transportation sector. First, most governments have attempted to follow Adam Smith's advice and now subsidize the domestic transport sector. Second, most governments have tolerated or encouraged attempts to establish monopoly prices in transportation. Formal institutions have been developed to prevent price competition in shipping and airlines. Associations of shippers, called shipping conferences, exist for each major oceanic route. The International Air Transport Association (IATA) establishes minimum airfares on international flights, and it requests that national governments enforce the rates. Enforcement has been uneven, but in some cases governments have threatened to revoke landing rights from airlines that offered discount fares. West German courts have interpreted IATA minimum prices as binding under German law, and some travel agents have been prosecuted for providing discounts. In the case of shipping, the U.S. Federal Maritime Commission has levied fines against shippers for offering freight discounts. In an ironic decision in 1981 the Federal Maritime Commission fined a Soviet shipping line for granting rebates to American customers that resulted in "unnecessarily low" prices.[7]

In spite of persistent efforts to establish monopoly prices, success has been quite limited. Government transport subsidies have added to capacity, which has invited price cutting. Most international airlines are owned by governments, and they regularly lose money. For example, every country in Africa has its own airline, including the Royal Swazi National Airways, which has one plane. There is an inherent conflict between adding to transport capacity and maintaining minimum prices. A second problem is that the existence of so many countries makes it difficult to block entry on profitable routes. Some regularly scheduled airlines will not join IATA, and some regularly scheduled shippers will not join shipping conferences. The success of IATA has also been limited by its inability to prevent low-cost charter flights from encroaching on the business of regularly scheduled flights. As does the airline association, shipping conferences set rates only for regularly scheduled ships. Since they have no authority over the rates charged by tramp steamers that do not follow regular schedules, conferences have difficulty in setting minimum freight rates.

A final defense against monopoly freight rates is for large potential customers, such as Exxon, Cargill, and Mitsubishi, to buy and operate their own ships as many of them do. To the extent that monopoly freight rates do prevail, the economic effects on trade are the same as for any other increase in transport costs. Product prices rise in the importing country and fall in the exporting country, and the volume of trade declines.

[7] *The Wall Street Journal*, "Soviet Shipping Line to Pay Fine to U.S. to Settle Rebate Charge," April 2, 1981.

6.7 NATURAL DISASTER, WAR, AND EMBARGO

A product may be damaged in transit or it may never reach its destination because of disasters caused by nature or people. Such events are uncertain, but it is possible to make an objective estimate of the probabilities that unfortunate events occur. Information about the expected loss is used by insurance companies to determine insurance premiums. Marine insurance, first offered in Genoa, Italy, in the fourteenth century, was one of the first kinds of insurance to appear. Lloyds of London is famous for insuring people against unusual events, and its members began in business by offering marine insurance. Insurance is a common feature of international trade and the standard price quotation, c.i.f., refers to the fact that cost, insurance, and freight are included in the price. By purchasing insurance, a shipping company can convert an uncertain event into a known business cost. Premiums are based on the expected value of the damage, which is the money value of the damage done times the probability of the events' occurrence.

Suppose that for a certain shipping route the probability of disaster is 1 in 1,000, and when disaster occurs, the damage is $1 million. This means that no damage is expected on 999 trips and that damage of $1 million is expected on 1 trip. The expected value of the damage is $(0.001)(\$1 \text{ million}) = \$1,000$, and this amount will be included in the insurance premium. A shipper has the alternative of paying premiums to an insurance company or self-insuring by setting up a reserve fund. Thus, potential disasters affect international trade in the same way as ordinary transport costs; that is, they create a divergence between the product price in the importing country and the price in the exporting country. In commercial parlance, disasters add to the excess of the c.i.f. price, which includes insurance and freight, and the f.o.b. price, which does not.

In Figure 6-1, insurance can be treated as a kind of transport cost that affects distances such as T_1T_2 and T_3T_4. Ultimately, insurance affects the volume of trade and prices in the two trading countries. If a certain shipping route becomes less dangerous, the economic effects can be shown by reducing transport costs in Figure 6-1 from T_1T_2 to T_3T_4 or by reducing the value of t in the algebraic problem in Section 6.4. The combined transport and insurance costs can be expressed as a percentage or ad valorem rate to compare their trade-retarding effect with that of a tariff. For example, if the c.i.f. price is $120 and the f.o.b. price is $100, the percentage transport insurance cost is 20 percent.

In general, the rate (f) can be computed as

$$f = \frac{P_{c.i.f.}}{P_{f.o.b.}} - 1 = \frac{120}{100} - 1 = 0.20$$

It has been shown that for U.S. imports from low-income countries, the percentage transport cost was greater than the average tariff rate.

It is common to insure against natural disasters such as storms, but insurance is also available against certain human-created events such as theft. War can greatly increase the probability of shipping damage, but standard insurance contracts are not applicable during wartime. One reason for the difficulty of insuring against war is that actuaries have problems computing objective probabilities of damage. A second reason is the problem of moral hazard, which provides perverse incentives for the insured party. In insurance problems, moral hazard exists if insured parties have an incentive to change their behavior in such a way as to increase the probability of a claim. If the shipping firm is covered, it has an incentive to choose some shipping routes that are more dangerous (but perhaps quicker) than routes that would have been chosen in absence of insurance. Because of this problem, sometimes governments insure private ships during wartime.

Whether shippers can buy commercial insurance or whether they are forced to self-insure during wartime, the economic effects of war on trade can be analyzed as an increase in transport costs. Wars have had substantial effects on the pattern of trade, adversely affecting consumers in importing countries, producers in exporting countries, and the shipping industry. However, just as favorable events such as technical change necessarily harm someone, unfavorable events, such as war, necessarily benefit someone. Because war increases transport costs, it is beneficial to producers in importing countries and consumers in exporting countries.

Countries not involved in war may benefit from war because damage to their commercial rivals increases the demand for their services. If a neutral country can trade with both sides, the trade can be lucrative. Swiss traders have probably benefited from several European wars. U.S. traders attempted to benefit from the war between France and England in the early 1800s, but the combatants did not respect their neutrality. American ships were sunk and captured, and crews were impressed into the British Navy. In a deperate act to avoid war, President Jefferson ordered a total embargo on U.S. exports. As is true of all embargoes, it was difficult to enforce, and the conflict with England led to the War of 1812.

War is an uncertain event that interferes with international trade. Government economic policies such as tariffs and quotas add to uncertainty in the same way that war does. Whether a firm is prevented from importing an essential input by an unexpected import quota or an unexpected war, the economic impact on the firm is the same. The timing of tariffs and quotas is determined by the political process, which may be no more predictable than wars. As the U.S. government has come to use embargos as a regular instrument of its foreign economic policy, the uncertainty facing U.S. trading firms has increased. For example, the embargoes associated with the Soviet invasion of Afghanistan in 1980 and the construction of the Soviet natural gas pipeline in 1982 both involved abrogation of existing commercial contracts. In an attempt to prevent future nullification of outstanding contracts, exporting interests proposed a "contract sanctity law." It would prevent the president from abrogating existing contracts, but it would permit him to ban the signing of new contracts.

An exporter can be harmed by a surprise embargo, but commercial insurance against such an event is not available. For example, the Caterpillar Tractor Company supplied 85 percent of the Soviet market for large track-type tractors until 1978 when the Carter administration restricted export licenses. In 1982 a Japanese firm, Komatsu Ltd., supplied 85 percent of the market. Caterpillar claims that government policy caused it to lose $500 million in sales since 1978.[8]

Because the adverse effects of changes in government policy on trade are not insurable, they are more like war than natural disaster. The effects of tariffs are analyzed in Chapter 7, and quotas are considered in Chapter 8.

6.8 SMUGGLING

Smuggling is illegal trade. It is an ancient practice whose importance has not diminished over time. Because it is illegal, reliable data on the volume of trade are not available. However, there is sufficient indirect evidence to indicate that for certain products in certain countries smuggling is flourishing. Illegal trade can be explained by the same economic principles that explain legal trade. A ban on legal trade decreases the supply of the product in the importing country, which raises the price in that country relative to the exporting country. The price differential between countries makes smuggling profitable. Declaring certain trade to be illegal increases the cost of trade, but it does not eliminate trade.

An additional cost of illegal trade is the expected penalty associated with apprehension by legal authorities. The expected cost of apprehension can be approximated by the money value of the penalty times the probability of being captured. It is analogous to the cost of an uncertain natural disaster such as a storm. The probability of incurring this cost depends on the size of the budget of enforcement agencies, and it can be reduced by bribing law enforcement officials. It has been observed that, in certain countries with traditions of active smuggling, customs employees are willing to work for extremely low official salaries. Presumably they expect a salary supplement to be contributed by smugglers.

The probability of capture also depends on geographical factors. For example, the fact that Indonesia is a country of many islands with close neighbors facilitates smuggling. The cost of illegal trade may also be higher because additional real resources are required to keep operations secret. The sum of

---

[8] *The Wall Street Journal,* "Executives Say Pipeline Sanctions Won't Stall Soviets, Will Hurt U.S.," November 3, 1982.

these additional costs of illegal trade effectively shifts the legal import supply curve upward. Thus, illegality alters trade in the same way as transport costs. The source of illegality may be a law that bans all sales of a product, such as marijuana, opium, and cocaine in the United States. Alternatively, selling a product may be legal, but taxes or tariffs may be high enough to make tax evasion profitable. For example, coffee production is legal in East Africa, but high taxes have induced growers to smuggle part of the crop out of the country at a more favorable price.

Smuggling may take the form of underreporting the quantity of trade, the price of traded goods, or both. Some countries employ government marketing boards as the sole legal buyers of products such as coffee, peanuts, and grain. The boards effectively collect an export tax by paying domestic producers a low price and reselling the product abroad at a higher tax. The price differential is equivalent to a tax, but it invites domestic producers to circumvent the marketing board by smuggling. There is evidence that the volume of smuggling depends directly on the divergence between the world price and the board's buying price. In the late 1970s, the reported coffee exports of Uganda were extraordinarily small, while coffee exports from neighboring Kenya and Tanzania were extraordinarily large. At this time the Ugandan marketing board was offering a less favorable producer price than its neighbors. Independent observations confirmed the existence of large-scale smuggling out of Uganda.

Because smuggling is illegal, there are no reliable statistics on total trade volume, commodity composition of trade, direction of trade, or market prices. Therefore, analysts must rely on indirect evidence of smuggling activity. Richard Cooper compared the prices of products in Indonesia with the sum of the c.i.f. import prices and tariffs for comparable goods. He concluded that for certain products, the Indonesian prices were so low that the importer could not have paid the c.i.f. price plus the legal tariff. He inferred from the price relationships that smuggling occurred and that the pattern of smuggling followed economic incentives. Because of smuggling, domestic prices were artificially low, and the magnitude of the "artificial cheapness" was greater for products with higher tariff rates.[9]

The volume of illegal trade can also be estimated from the sample of smugglers who are apprehended by legal authorities. It appears from such evidence that illegal drugs are a significant import into the United States. Marijuana, opium, and cocaine appear to be the important products, and Latin America, Turkey, and Southeast Asia are said to be the dominant import suppliers. Mexico is an important source of marijuana imports. Coffee has traditionally been Colombia's major export, but it may have been surpassed in recent years by cocaine. Turkey and the Golden Triangle of Thailand, Burma, and Laos are reputed to be the source of most of the world's illegal opium.

---

[9]Richard Cooper, "Tariffs and Smuggling in Indonesia," in *Illegal Transactions in International Trade*, J. Bhagwati, ed. (Amsterdam: North-Holland, 1974).

Official statistics show the United States to be a net exporter of agricultural products, but if illegal drug imports were included in calculations, the United States may be a net agricultural importer.

An interesting economic question concerning drugs is what country would have a comparative advantage if production were legal everywhere? In the case of marijuana, what quantity of imports from Mexico and Colombia would be displaced by legal U.S. production? If the United States has a natural comparative advantage, the illegality of U.S. production serves as a subsidy to Mexican and Columbian growers. Regardless of comparative advantage, more vigorous enforcement of laws against U.S. drug production has the effect of stimulating drug imports and foreign production.

Figure 6-4 shows the effect of a more vigorous enforcement of the ban on U.S. production. X_1^s and I_1^d are the initial domestic supply and import demand curves. The world price is P_1 and the volume of imports is I_1. The policy of discouraging domestic production shifts domestic supply to X_2^s and import demand to I_2^d. The shortage of AB is eliminated by an increase in the world price to P_2 and an increase in import volume to I_2. Thus, imported drugs would serve as a partial substitute for the decreases in domestic production. An alternative policy is to enforce drug laws more vigorously at the borders. Increasing the difficulty of importing drugs would raise the price and encourage domestic production. In terms of Figure 6-4 the policy would shift the import supply curve (I_1^s) to the left, which would increase the price and stimulate domestic production.

A prudent law enforcement policy cannot ignore the interaction between domestic and foreign markets. It has been said that smuggling improves consumer welfare in the same way that free trade does. However, illegal traders

FIGURE 6-4   The Effect on Imports of Discouraging Domestic Production

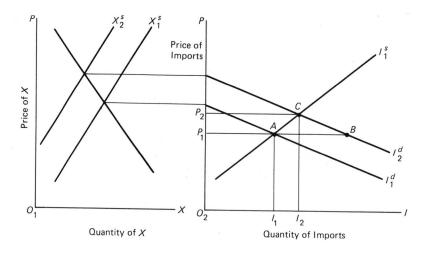

operate at a higher real cost than do comparable legal traders, and the government uses real resources enforcing the law. These additional economic costs of illegal trade must be weighed against the benefits of a larger trade volume before the net effect of smuggling on consumer welfare can be determined.

6.9 TRADING COMPANIES AS MIDDLEMEN

It is possible for ultimate consumers to buy products directly from producers, but more often consumers buy from some middleman. Transportation is one service provided by middlemen, who also provide storage, finance, and distribution services. Their compensation is sometimes called a marketing margin, which is measured by the excess of the selling price over the buying price. Competition narrows the marketing margin until it equals the cost of providing the services of middlemen. Because the services of middlemen contribute to the difference between the price in the importing country and the price in the exporting country, they can be analyzed as a kind of generalized transport cost. In addition to providing the standard services of domestic middlemen, firms dealing in international trade possess specialized knowledge about foreign currency markets and the legal aspects of customs procedures.

Trading companies that specialize in international trade have existed for centuries. Two of the early successful firms were the British and Dutch East India companies, which were prominent in the seventeenth century. Among modern trading companies, Japanese firms have tended to trade in a wide variety of products. Large Japanese trading companies, such as Mitsui, Mitsubishi, Itoh, Marubeni, and Sumitomo, have become world famous for providing a broad range of products and services. American trading companies have tended to specialize in a narrower range of products. Cargill and Continental have specialized in grain, whereas Phillipp Brothers (Phibro) has specialized in minerals.

One of the main services offered by middlemen is information, and it is easier to acquire current detailed information about one product market than about all products. In the case of grain, it is generally agreed that private grain companies have better information about the size and quality of crops and inventories in all countries than any national government or international agency. Because of economies of scale in acquiring information, successful companies tend to be large and few in number. For some time international grain trade has been dominated by Cargill, Continental, Bunge, Louis Dreyfus, and André.[10] Even some governments that have state marketing boards hire private grain companies to perform some of their marketing tasks.

---

[10] Dan Morgan's *Merchants of Grain* (New York: Viking, 1979) is a nontechnical account of the development of the private grain trading companies.

The services offered by middlemen are not obvious to the public, and producer and consumer groups have traditionally accused middlemen of appropriating a profit without performing a necessary service. The high degree of concentration of the international grain trade has also led critics to conclude that monopoly profits have been earned. The contention of extraordinary profits can be put to the test by "cutting out the middleman." If marketing margins of middlemen exceed the cost of providing services, producers can increase their profits by selling directly to consumers.

Producer cooperatives are an institution designed to eliminate middlemen. Cooperatives have been tried for a wide variety of agricultural products with mixed success. In the United States, cooperatives have been more successful with domestic marketing than with foreign sales. Foreign marketing may require more specialized knowledge about currency markets and foreign buying practices. A grain cooperative, Farmers Export Company, was founded in 1968 challenging the five big grain companies, and by 1977 it became the fifth largest U.S. grain exporter. However, it suffered a serious financial setback in 1980 (it lost $30 million), which forced it to follow a policy of retrenchment.

A Japanese firm, Zen-Noh, is the largest cooperative in the world, and it has become active in the grain trade. Mitsui and Mitsubishi have also become active in world grain trade through their American subsidiaries. All Japanese grain imports are handled by a state agency, which has led the foreign firms to accuse the Japanese government of giving preference to Japanese trading companies. In recent years eight large Japanese trading companies have been responsible for 60 percent of Japan's total imports. Ironically, Japanese trading companies have become some of the leading exporters of products from the United States. It has been estimated that subsidiaries of Mitsui and Mitsubishi handled nearly 10 percent of U.S. exports in 1980. If *Fortune* magazine's list of 50 leading exporting firms (see Chapter 10) included nonindustrial companies, Mitsui U.S.A. would have been the fourth largest U.S. exporter in 1980, following Boeing, General Motors, and General Electric.[11] Increased competition among middlemen lowers the marketing margin, which has the same effect on international trade as a reduction in transport costs.

SUMMARY

Transportation costs create a divergence between prices in the importing country and prices in the exporting country. This chapter has analyzed the effect of transport costs on the volume of trade and prices in both trading countries. Transport costs provide a kind of natural protection for producers in the importing country and consumers in the exporting country. Conversely, consumers in the importing country and producers in the exporting country are

---

[11] *The Wall Street Journal*, "Unlikely American Exporter: Japan," November 11, 1981.

adversely affected by transport costs. Costs vary because of changes in factor prices, technological change, discovery of new routes, and changes in market structure. Governments have tended to protect their transportation sectors from foreign competition, using national security as a rationale.

Cargo preference is a policy designed to increase the demand for the services of the national transportation sector. When taken by itself, cargo preference increases the profitability of domestic shipping. However, in the United States it has been combined with requirements that shippers employ American crews and purchase American made ships, which reduce the profitability of shipping. These costly conditions in the United States and elsewhere have led to the development of "flags of convenience" in countries such as Liberia and Panama.

There have been persistent efforts to monopolize international transportation through shippers' conferences and the International Air Transport Association, but success has been limited. Successful monopolization can be analyzed as an increase in transport costs.

Marine insurance permits trading firms to convert uncertain costs associated with disasters into known business costs. Less predictable events, such as war and adverse changes in government policy, are not normally covered by commercial insurance. The conditions of illegal trade can be analyzed as an increase in transport costs. Transportation and insurance are only two of the services provided by middlemen in international commerce. The entire set of services provided by trading companies can be analyzed as a kind of generalized cost of transportation.

REFERENCES

BENNATHAN, ESRA, and ALAN A. WALTERS. *The Economics of Ocean Freight Rates.* New York: Praeger, 1969. An assessment of the monopoly effects of liner conferences.

BHAGWATI, JAGDISH, ed. *Illegal Transactions in International Trade: Theory and Measurement.* Amsterdam: North-Holland, 1974. A collection of theoretical and empirical papers on smuggling.

Cargill Bulletin (Minneapolis). A monthly review of domestic and international agricultural trade. A discussion of the Crow's Nest Rate Agreement appears in the July 1982 issue.

COOPER, RICHARD N. "Tariffs and Smuggling in Indonesia," in *Illegal Transactions in International Trade: Theory and Measurement,* Jagdish Bhagwati, ed. Amsterdam: North-Holland, 1974. Empirical study of smuggling in Indonesia.

FINGER, J. N., and A. J. YEATS. "Effective Protection by Transport Costs and Tariffs: A Comparison of Magnitudes." *Quarterly Journal of Economics,* February 1976.

GOLD, EDGAR. *Maritime Transport: The Evolution of International Maritime Policy and Shipping Law.* Lexington, Mass.: D.C. Heath, 1981.

JANSSON, JAN, and DAN SHNEESON. "The Effective Protection Implicit in Liner Shipping Freight Rates." *Review of Economics and Statistics,* November 1978.

JANTSCHER, GERALD R. *Bread upon The Waters: Federal Aid to the Maritime Industries.* Washington, D.C.: The Brookings Institution, 1975. An analysis of government subsidies to the U.S. shipping industry.

MORGAN, DAN. *Merchants of Grain.* New York: Viking, 1979. A journalist's account of the development of the world's major grain trading countries.

NEFF, STEPHEN. "The U.N. Code of Conduct for Liner Conferences." *Journal of World Trade Law,* September–October 1980. A discussion of the practice of cargo preference.

NORTH, DOUGLAS. "Sources of Productivity Change in Ocean Shipping, 1600–1815." *Journal of Political Economy,* September 1968.

PATRICK, HUGH, and HENRY ROSOVSKY, eds. *Asia's New Giant: How the Japanese Economy Works.* Washington, D.C.: The Brookings Institution, 1976.

PIRENNE, HENRI. *Economic and Social History of Medieval Europe.* New York: Harcourt Brace, 1937. Discusses the importance of transportation for trade in medieval Europe.

PITT, MARK M. "Smuggling and Price Disparity." *Journal of International Economics,* November 1981. An analysis of smuggling using Indonesian data.

RICHTER, H. V. "Problems of Assessing Unrecorded Trade." *Bulletin of Indonesian Economic Studies,* Vol. 6, no. 1 (March 1970).

SIMKIN, C. G. F. "Indonesia's Unrecorded Trade." *Bulletin of Indonesian Economic Studies,* Vol. 6, no. 1 (March 1970).

WATERS, W. G. "Transport Costs and the Static Welfare Costs of Tariffs." *American Economic Review,* September 1974. Discusses the allocative effects of f.o.b. versus c.i.f. customs valuation.

YEATS, ALEXANDER J. *Trade Barriers Facing Developing Countries.* New York: St. Martins, 1979. Chapter 7 discusses the world transportation industry and its effect on low-income countries.

———. *Shipping and Development Policy: An Integrated Assessment,* New York: Praeger, 1981.

U.S. DEPARTMENT OF COMMERCE, MARITIME ADMINISTRATION. *Merchant Fleets of the World.* Washington, D.C.: U.S. Government Printing Office. A source of data on world shipping.

CHAPTER SEVEN
TARIFFS
AND EXPORT TAXES

7.1 INTRODUCTION

The gains from international trade, discussed in Chapter 4, accrue to both trading countries. Gains can be measured in terms of the concept of economic surplus, and they can be divided into production and consumption gains. Trade permits people to specialize in the production of what they do best, and it provides consumers with consumption opportunities that would not otherwise be available. The benefits from trade are reduced by the existence of transport costs, which are a natural trade barrier. The economic effects of transport costs are analyzed in Chapter 6. By increasing the cost of trade, transport costs raise prices in the importing country, lower prices in the exporting, and reduce the volume of trade. A tariff is a tax on imports. The economic effects of human-created trade barriers, such as tariffs, are similar to those of transport costs.

Both transport costs and tariffs reduce world income, but they provide benefits to particular groups in the exporting and importing countries. Because producers in importing countries benefit from tariffs, they have traditionally provided strong political support for tariffs and similar trade barriers. Since tariffs and transport costs have similar economic effects, it is anomalous that people have spent their time and other resources constructing ships, railroads, and bridges to facilitate trade, while others have negated these efforts by imposing tariffs that reduce trade. Because of their cost-increasing nature, the French economist Frederic Bastiat described tariffs as "negative railroads."

This chapter will investigate the effect of tariffs on the volume of trade and prices in importing and exporting countries. If the importing country is a small part of the world market, its tariff will affect domestic prices only. If the importing country is large, its tariff policy will alter foreign prices as well as domestic prices. The price changes induced by the tariff will alter both production and consumption. In contrast to transport costs, a tariff will generate revenue for the government of the importing country. Import quotas and other nontariff barriers are alternative devices for restricting trade. The relationship between these alternative protectionist instruments will be considered.

Tariffs bring about a pattern of trade contrary to the one prescribed by comparative advantage. The economic cost of tariff-induced distortions will be considered, and the history of tariff policy in the United States will be reviewed. Tariffs are as ancient as trade and so are the arguments that have been used to justify the imposition of tariffs. The standard arguments in favor of tariffs will be analyzed. Since tariffs are taxes on imports, the analysis of tariffs is applicable to other trade taxes. The analysis will be extended to the effects of export taxes and subsidies.

7.2 GENERAL ECONOMIC EFFECTS OF TARIFFS

Both tariffs and transport costs raise the cost of trade and reduce the volume of trade. A distinguishing feature is that tariffs generate revenue for the government, whereas transport costs provide revenue for firms providing transport services. From the perspective of the importer, both transport costs and tariffs are part of the cost of doing business. However, from the perspective of the economy as a whole, tariffs and transport costs differ in an important way. Tariff revenue is a transfer payment from the private sector to the government, which does not use real economic resources.[1] Conversely, transport costs represent the use of real economic resources that have alternative uses in the rest of the economy. If nature destroys a fleet of ships, the world economy is poorer. However, if a government loses tariff revenue, there is no comparable loss to the world economy. Another way to see the transfer aspect of a tariff is to compare the effects of an export tax and a tariff.

It will be shown in Section 7.16 that an export tax on a product levied by the exporting country has the same effect on trade as an equal rate tariff on the same product imposed by the importing country. The sole difference between the two policies is that the tax revenue accrues to the exporting country in one case and the importing country in the other case.

In addition to the revenue effect, tariffs alter the allocation of resources in the economy. Resource allocation refers to the assignment of land, labor, and capital to the production of various goods and services. By altering relative prices, tariffs attract resources to the import-competing sector from the rest of

---

[1] A possible exception, called rent seeking, will be considered in Section 7.13.

the economy. Since tariffs increase domestic prices of importable products, employment in the protected sector increases. Since labor is withdrawn from the exportable sector, tariffs do not increase total national employment. The distinction between the effect of tariffs on industry employment and national employment is often overlooked. Since importables and exportables employ factors in different proportions, tariffs alter relative factor demands and relative factor prices. The effect of trade on factor prices and the distribution of income was discussed in Chapter 4.

Tariffs adversely affect domestic consumers by raising the price of importables. Those consumers who continue to buy the importable at the higher price transfer income to domestic producers. Other consumers will switch to a product that was considered inferior to the importable at the initial price. Tariffs may also affect the competitive structure of the importable sector. By reducing foreign competition, tariffs may make it easier for domestic firms to form collusive arrangements. It has been said that free trade is the most effective anti-trust policy.

7.3 GENERAL CHARACTERISTICS OF TARIFFS

A tariff is a tax on an imported product.[2] It is equivalent to a sales tax from which domestically produced products are exempt. It is a discriminatory tax, with the location of production being the basis of discrimination. For example, a federal sales tax on automibiles is applicable to all cars sold in the United States, regardless of whether they were produced in the United States, Japan, or Germany. Conversely, a U.S. tariff is applicable only to automobiles produced in Japan, Germany, and other foreign countries. Therefore, a tariff provides an incentive to alter the location of production. Tariff revenue collected by the government (T) can be expressed as the product of the tariff rate per unit (t) and the base of the tariff (V_I):

$$T = tV_I$$

A specific tariff is one whose rate is a fixed amount of *money* per unit of the product. One property of a specific tariff is that the percentage rate is lower for more expensive goods within the product category. For example, if the tariff on all automobiles were $100, the percentage rate on a Rolls Royce would be less than the percentage rate on a Toyota. Thus, an apparently neutral spe-

---

[2] The term "tariff" is sometimes used in the generic sense to include all forms of import barriers. A third use of the term, unrelated to international trade, is that a tariff is a schedule of fees, especially for public utility rates.

cific tariff would reduce the relative price of more expensive products within a tariff category.

A second property of a specific tariff is that its real value is inversely related to the price level. Thus, inflation reduces the real value of a specific tariff. An ad valorem tariff is one whose rate is a fixed percentage of the value of the imported product. If the ad valorem tariff rate were 10 percent on all automobiles, the amount of money paid on a Rolls Royce would be greater than the amount of money paid on a Toyota. Also a general inflation of X percent that increased all prices, including those on automobiles, would increase tariff revenue by X percent, with no change in the real value of the tariff. Most tariffs are fixed either in terms of money (specific) or percentage of value (ad valorem), but some tariffs are variable. The most important contemporary example is the variable grain levy imposed by the European Economic Community (EEC). The object of the levy is to ensure a fixed domestic price $(\overline{P})$ that exceeds the world price $(P^\star)$. The variable import levy (t_v) is defined as the difference between the fixed domestic price and the world price that varies with supply and demand:

$$t_v = \overline{P} - P^\star$$

For example, let the domestic price be set at $6 per bushel and the world price at $5 per bushel. Importers must pay a tariff of $1 per bushel. If a large world crop causes the import price to fall to $4, the tariff automatically rises to $2. Thus, the tariff offsets any change in the world price, so that the domestic price remains constant. The system is symmetrical, so that if the world price rose to $6, the tariff would be zero. In principle, the tariff could become negative (import subsidy) at higher world prices. The variable levy makes the domestic price completely unresponsive to the world price. Since domestic demand and supply depend on the domestic price, EEC import demand is perfectly inelastic with respect to the foreign price of grain. The variable levy is an effective protective device, which has been heavily criticized by foreign grain suppliers.

The base of an ad valorem tariff is the value of the import, and there are several ways of determining customs valuation. Since a higher customs value increases the tariff, importing countries can use customs valuation as a protective device. Since a lower customs value reduces the tariff, firms that are able to declare a lower value for imports can reduce their tariff bill.

The f.o.b. (free on board) method of valuation uses the value of the product at the export point. The c.i.f. method (cost, insurance, and freight) uses value at the import point. The f.a.s. method (free alongside ship) excludes loading cost from the product's value.[3] For many years the United States used the

[3] A similar concept used in some British Commonwealth countries is f.a.q. (or free alongside quay). Unfortunately the same initials are sometimes used to mean fair average quality when referring to agricultural products.

American selling price method to value chemical imports. The method valued imported chemicals at the price of domestic substitutes, which were consistently more expensive than were imports. The practice was adopted in 1922 as a means of protecting the American chemical industry from German competition.[4] The practice was widely criticized by foreign governments, and it was abandoned following the Tokyo-Geneva Round of trade negotiations. Participants in the Tokyo-Geneva negotiations also agreed to attempt to standardize customs valuation practices.

The growth of multinational firms has caused a problem for customs officials. When one division of a firm imports from another division of the same firm, there may not be an objectively measurable market value for the product. Furthermore, the firm has an incentive to report a low transfer price on the invoice to reduce its tariff obligation. Thus, the level of a tariff may be altered by either a change in the tariff rate or a change in the base.

A uniform or nondiscriminatory tariff structure imposes the same tariff against a product regardless of its source. A nondiscriminatory tariff policy is also called the most favored nation principle, which is one of the basic tenets of the General Agreement on Tariffs and Trade (GATT). The GATT is both an international institution, with offices in Geneva, Switzerland, and an international agreement about trade policy. At the beginning of 1982, there were 87 members of GATT. GATT serves as a forum for resolving trade disputes, and it sponsors multilateral trade negotiations designed to reduce barriers to international trade. The most important examples of explicit discriminatory tariff structures are customs unions and the Generalized System of Preferences (GSP).

A customs union, such as the European Economic Community, is a group of countries that eliminates tariffs between members and erects a common tariff against nonmembers. The effects of a customs union will be considered in Chapter 8. The GSP is an agreement among most high-income countries to provide a preferential tariff for certain products exported by low-income countries. Thus, the GSP discriminates on the basis of income, whereas a customs union discriminates on the basis of union membership.

Tariff discrimination may also be based on political considerations. The United States generally adheres to nondiscriminatory tariff policy, except for trade with a small number of Communist countries. Goods from the Soviet Union, which has not been granted most favored nation status, face a higher U.S. tariff. In response to Soviet restrictions on the emigration of Jews, Congress passed the Jackson-Vanik amendment, which denies most favored nation status to countries that limit emigration. The People's Republic of China was granted most favored nation status in 1980. Poland received most favored nation status earlier, but the Reagan administration revoked it in 1982 in retaliation against military rule in Poland.

---

[4] See Kenneth Dam, *The GATT:* Law and International Economic Organization. Chicago: University of Chicago Press, 1970, Ch. 11.

Members of GATT have pledged to avoid discriminatory tariffs against other members, except for customs unions and the GSP. However, countries have achieved discrimination recently by imposing quotas, especially "voluntary" export restraints. It is also possible to achieve discrimination against a country, without naming the country, by constructing sufficiently narrow product categories. For example, the German tariff schedule of 1902 did not mention Switzerland, but it contained an especially high tariff against products from "brown or dappled cows reared at a level of at least 300 meters above sea level and passing at least one month in every summer at an altitude of at least 800 meters."

7.4 LEGAL ASPECTS OF TARIFFS

In most countries, the power to regulate international commerce is reserved for the national government. In the United States, the Constitution of 1789 forbids states from imposing tariffs and interfering with interstate commerce. Within the federal government, Congress was granted the exclusive right to impose tariffs and other taxes. This allocation of tariff authority to Congress is different from the system employed in many other countries, where the president or prime minister has some discretionary authority over tariffs. President Carter discovered this limitation on executive power when his attempt to levy a tariff on crude oil in early 1980 was found by a court to be unconstitutional. Congress has delegated limited authority to the president to negotiate mutual tariff reductions with other countries, but the resulting treaty must be ratified by Congress.

The Trade Agreements Act of 1934, which was renewed 11 times, authorized the president to negotiate tariff reductions with other countries. The act was an attempt to lower tariffs from the extremely high level of the Smoot-Hawley tariff of 1930. The Trade Agreement Act was based on two principles. First, tariff reductions should be mutual. Second, tariff cuts established in bilateral negotiations should be extended to all other trading partners. This practice became known as the most favored nation principle.

After World War II bilateral negotiations were replaced by multilateral negotiations under the auspices of GATT. The Havana Conference of 1947 proposed the creation of an ambitious International Trade Organization (ITO) that would promote cooperation in trade policy. The ITO was never ratified by the U.S. Congress, and GATT was created in 1948 as a substitute institution, which did not require congressional approval. Because GATT was less ambitious than the proposed ITO, U.S. participation was justified by the authority of the Trade Agreements Act.

The three basic principles of GATT are the following. First, trade barriers should follow the nondiscriminatory feature of the most favored nation principle. An explicit exception was made for customs unions. Second, protection should take the form of tariffs rather than quotas and other nontariff barriers. Exceptions were made for the protection of agriculture and balance-of-payments problems. Third, countries should resort to consultation to resolve international trade disputes. GATT has little enforcement power, and all three principles have been widely violated in recent years. The Kennedy Round of multilateral tariff negotiation (1962) and Tokyo-Geneva Round were both sponsored by GATT.

Prior to the adoption of the Constitution, the Articles of Confederation were the law of the land in the United States. The states were a loose confederation, and the Articles permitted individual states to levy tariffs on interstate trade. States did impose tariffs, and the practice was so damaging to commerce that the Annapolis Conference was called in 1786 to try to reform the tariff policies of states. Discussion moved well beyond commerce, and an outgrowth of the Conference was the Philadelphia Constitutional Convention of 1787.

Although the Constitution forbids states from levying tariffs, states sometimes impose implicit tariffs that remain in effect until they are challenged in court. The state of North Carolina has an excise tax on wine, which exempts wine produced by the small industry within the state. One observer noted that "it looks like a tariff and smells like a tariff, but it's not a tariff until a court says it is." In 1981 a federal court ruled that a Louisiana tax on natural gas passing through the state was an illegal tariff. In 1981 Canada had a serious legal dispute over whether the federal government or state governments had the authority to tax oil and other natural resources.

State health laws may be administered in a way that makes them an effective tariff. Some states ban milk sales from dairy farms that are not inspected by the state department of agriculture. If the inspection procedure discriminates against out-of-state farms, the policy interferes with trade. Another example of a state trade barrier is discriminatory procurement policy by state agencies. If administrators are instructed to buy products made in the state when others are cheaper, the policy is an effective tariff.

The Constitution explicitly forbids export taxes by the federal government. This restriction has not been a serious constraint on economic policy, since the economic effects of an export tax can be and have been achieved through an export quota. The export tax provision was part of a compromise designed to induce Southern states to ratify the Constitution. At the end of the eighteenth century, the Southern economy was a specialized producer of agricultural exports. Southern representatives feared that the new federal government might use export taxes as its main source of revenue. In fact, taxes on imports were the main source of federal government revenue until the twentieth century.

The constitutional ban on direct taxes prevented the use of an income tax, until the 16th Amendment in 1913 authorized an income tax. The income tax then replaced the tariff as the major source of federal revenue. An import subsidy is a negative tariff, that is, a payment by the government to buyers for each unit imported. Explicit import subsidies almost never occur, but they do exist in implicit form. When a state trading agency buys food at the world price and resells it domestically at a lower price, the difference between the prices constitutes an implicit import subsidy. Many governments such as Japan, Egypt, and Thailand have followed such policies.

Congress passes trade legislation, and the executive branch administers the law. Congress has authorized the president to negotiate lower tariffs, but it has imposed explicit limits on trade liberalization. The limits include the range of products on which tariffs may be reduced and the minimum acceptable tariff rate. In addition, if tariff reductions turn out to be more damaging to domestic industry than had been anticipated, the initial tariff can be reinstated. The entire set of restrictions on trade liberalization is called safeguards. Congress inserted safeguards into various revisions of the Trade Agreements Act.

The "peril point" provision required the president to submit to the Tariff Commission a list of products on which he intended to negotiate. He was required to specify a minimum tariff rate that would be necessary to avoid serious damage to each industry. The "peril point" provision was omitted from the 1962 Trade Expansion Act and subsequent legislation. The "national security clause" prevents tariff reductions on products that are essential for national defense. It also permits the withdrawal of previously negotiated trade concessions. The "escape clause" permits domestic firms to petition the International Trade Commission for relief from damage attributable to imports.

Prior to 1962 the usual form of relief was a higher tariff. The adjustment assistance program contained in the Trade expansion Act of 1962 was designed to substitute direct compensation of workers and firms for higher tariffs. The 1979 amendments to trade legislation encouraged the use of tariffs and quotas to enforce the safeguard mechanism. GATT rules also provide for safeguards, which should take the form of temporary, nondiscriminatory tariffs. GATT officials have denounced the use of "voluntary export restraints," which are discriminatory quotas. A related safeguard is the Anti-Dumping Law, which prohibits firms from selling in the United States at a lower price than they sell comparable products abroad. Injured parties can petition the International Trade Commission, which must determine whether dumping has occurred and whether serious injury to domestic firms has occurred. The Commission also hears cases related to domestic agricultural legislation. If imports interfere with the implementation of domestic agricultural policy, trade barriers can be imposed. For example, tobacco interests claimed in 1981 that imports were interfering with the domestic tobacco program that keeps prices artificially high. The Commission ruled that trade barriers were not warranted.

The Commission received a controversial case in 1981 involving alleged damage to the auto industry from imports. The Commission agreed with the U.S. auto industry's claim that they were harmed by imports but stated that the law permitting relief requires that imports be the primary source of damage. The industry's problems were considered to be primarily due to other conditions, such as fuel prices, consumer preferences, and recession. The Commission decided that auto import barriers were not justified. However, the industry received relief later in the form of a voluntary export restraint involving automobiles from Japan.

Because the Commission makes recommendations to the president that could be politically sensitive, Congress has tried to provide the agency with some independence. Presidents are free to ignore Commission recommendations, but they rarely do. There are six Commission members who are appointed by the president and approved by Congress. No more than three members can come from one political party, members can serve only one term, and the Commission budget is not subject to presidential review.

7.5 IMPORT QUOTAS

A tariff increases the cost of imports without directly limiting the quantity of imports. However, since the demand for imports depends on the cost, a tariff indirectly reduces the volume of imports. An import quota limits the quantity of imports without directly restricting the price of imports. However, since the price depends on the supply of imports, an import quota indirectly raises the price. Thus, tariffs and import quotas are alternative ways of achieving the same result. Every tariff has an equivalent quota in the sense that both result in the same price and quantity. Tariffs and quotas can be compared by computing tariff equivalent rates for quotas. Suppose that a quota results in a domestic price of \$125 and a foreign price of \$100. The tariff equivalent rate is $125/100 - 1 = 25\%$.

However, tariffs and quotas differ in other ways. For example, a decrease in the foreign price of an import will lead to an increase in import volume when there is a tariff, but not when there is an import quota. An import quota is a rule that limits imports of a product to a specified volume per period. The quota can be administered in several ways, but a common practice is to require an import license. Each license specifies the volume of imports permitted, and the total volume permitted should not exceed the import quota. The method used to allocate licenses to importers affects the distribution of income without changing the price or volume of imports. Licenses could be auctioned to the highest bidder.

It is more common for governments to give licenses to preferred importers, which provides incentives for political lobbying and bribery. As suggested by its name, a tariff quota combines the separate features of tariffs and quotas. Under a tariff quota there is a zero tariff rate (or a preferred rate) on all imports up to a certain volume $\overline{Q}$ and a tariff on all units beyond $\overline{Q}$. The European Economic Community employs tariff quotas as part of its tariff preference program for products imported from low-income countries. The economic effects of quotas will be analyzed in detail in Chapter 8.

7.6 OTHER NONTARIFF BARRIERS

A wide variety of other nontariff barriers to trade in addition to import quotas exist. Because of the success of multilateral trade negotiations in reducing the level of tariffs, nontariff barriers have become the major obstacle to international trade. GATT estimated that in 1980 40 to 50 percent of world trade was covered by some form of nontariff barrier. National government procurement policy that discriminates against foreign products constitutes an implicit tariff. For example, if the Department of Defense purchases a domestic product for $150 when a comparable import is available for $100, the policy is equivalent to a tariff of $(150 - 100)/100 = 50\%$.

Preference for domestic products may take subtle forms that are not easy to detect. Government agencies may deliberately choose product specifications that can be satisfied more easily by domestic firms. Government procurement policy has become more important for international trade as the size of the government sector has increased around the world. Minimum import prices are another nontariff trade barrier. The U.S. Anti-Dumping Law prohibits an import price that is less than the price of a comparable product in the exporting country. Dumping cases, which increased sharply after the trade law was amended in 1974, have included a wide range of products from steel and automobiles to mushrooms and Danish butter cookies.

The U.S. steel industry was protected by a minimum import price, popularly known as the "trigger price mechanism." The minimum import price was based on the cost of production in the exporting country. Thus, the U.S. Treasury was obliged to make regular estimates of the cost of producing various kinds of steel in Japan and Germany, which determined the minimum import price. Any price below the legal minimum price automatically "triggered" a compensating tariff. The trigger price mechanism broke down because it was difficult to administer. Foreign costs are inherently difficult to estimate, and importers found legal ways of circumventing the program. Steel importers established foreign affiliates that bought steel at low prices not covered by the trigger price mechanism. American firms then bought steel from their own affiliates at higher prices that satisfied the legal minimum. Thus, the multinational firm as a whole was able to import steel for less than the minimum price, even though the American affiliate paid more than the minimum.

Voluntary export restraints (VER) have become an increasingly important nontariff barrier. A VER is a quota on imports of a product from one country to another. It is usually discriminatory in the sense of applying only to certain supplying countries. It is initiated by the importing country. Exporters are induced to enforce the "voluntary" quota only because the alternative is a mandatory quota. Because exporters must collude on quantity to satisfy the VER, the arrangement makes it easier to collude on price as well. The higher price charged by foreign suppliers serves as partial compensation for the reduction in import volume. VERs have been applied to many products, including automobiles, steel, and textiles. Because they are discriminatory quotas, they violate the basic principles of GATT. If the arrangement includes all supplying countries, it is sometimes called an "orderly marketing agreement" (OMA). The Multi-Fiber Agreement, which regulates textiles trade, is a prominent example.

Since new ways of discriminating against imports are created daily, the range of potential nontariff barriers is endless. For example, the French government decreed in October 1982 that all legal documents accompanying imports must be translated into French. Nontariffs barriers were discussed at the Tokyo Round of GATT negotiations, but little agreement was reached. Future negotiation of nontariff barriers may extend the discussion to service trade (e.g., banking).

7.7 THE GEOMETRY OF TARIFFS

The economic effects of tariffs can be illustrated graphically using the import demand and supply curves introduced in Chapter 3. In Figure 7-1 the import

FIGURE 7-1 Tariff for a Small Country

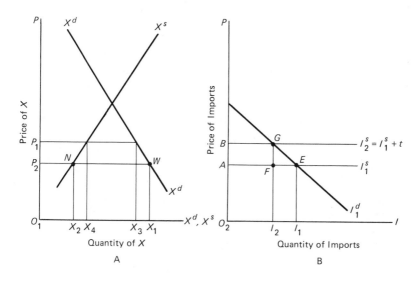

demand curve in panel B (I^d) is derived from the underlying domestic demand (X^d) and supply (X^s) curves in panel A. Specifically, import demand at each price (e.g., OP_1) is the horizontal distance $(NW = AE)$ between X^d and X^s. The importing country is assumed to be a small enough buyer on the world market that it cannot afford the world price. This small-country assumption implies that the import supply curve (I_1^s) is horizontal (i.e., infinitely elastic). The initial equilibrium is at point E where the amount importers want to buy equals the amount import suppliers want to sell $(O_2I_1 = AE)$. In the absence of transport costs and tariffs, the domestic price equals the foreign price $(O_2A = O_1P_1)$, domestic consumption is O_1X_1, domestic production is O_1X_2, and the difference $(X_2X_1 = O_2I_1)$ is imports.

Consider the effect of a specific tariff of t levied so that the import supply curve, including the tariff, becomes $I_2^s = I_1^s + t$. The upward shift of I^s indicates that suppliers now have higher costs, and at the initial price (O_1P_1), there is now an excess demand. Competition for the scarce product bids the price up to O_1P_2, where the market again clears. The tariff-inclusive or gross price paid by importers has risen by the full amount of the tariff (t), and the net price to the exporter has remained at OP_1.

In the small-country case, domestic residents cannot shift any of the tariff onto foreigners. If import suppliers could not receive at least OP_1 in this market, they would shift all their sales to other markets where they are paid OP_1. Empirically the small-country case is relevant for most countries and for most products. The volume of imports falls to O_2I_2, and tariff revenue is the area $ABGF$, which is the product of the tariff per unit (AB) and the volume of imports $(O_2I_2 = AF)$. Domestic consumption falls to O_1X_3, and domestic production rises to O_1X_4. The exact magnitude of these effects depends on the size of the tariff (t) and the slopes of X^d, X^s, and I^d, which are proportional to the elasticities of demand, supply, and imports. The effect of a tariff for a large country will be shown in Section 7.8.

Figure 7-1 shows the effect of a fixed tariff of AB per unit. The effect of a variable tariff can be shown in the same figure. Let the initial equilibrium be at point G, where the import supply curve is I_2^s and the initial tariff (t_v) is zero. The domestic price $(\overline{P} = O_2B)$ equals the world price $(P^\star)$, and the volume of imports is O_2I_2. This situation might represent the EEC's vairable grain levy. Now suppose that a large world grain crop shifts import supply downward from I_2^s to I_1^s. The new import supply curve implies that foreign grain traders are now offering unlimited amounts at a price of O_2A, and if the tariff remained constant at zero, the domestic grain price would have to fall to O_2A to make domestic grain competitive with imported grain. However, a decrease in the domestic price would violate the object of the variable levy, which is to insulate the domestic price from foreign disturbances. The variable levy is defined as the difference between the domestic and foreign prices:

$$t_v = \overline{P} - P^\star$$

Since the object is to keep the domestic price constant $(d\bar{P}=0)$, the tariff must change by the same amount as the world price, but in the opposite direction. Taking the total differential of the relationship yields

$$dt_v = d\bar{P} - dP^\star = -dP^\star$$

The tariff must increase by an amount equal to the decrease in the world price. In Figure 7-1 the world price falls by AB, so the tariff must rise by AB. Thus, the new tariff-inclusive import supply curve coincides with the initial supply curve I_2^s. Since the domestic price remains at O_2B_1, the volume of imports remains at O_2I_2. Because import volume was O_2I_2 at the world price of O_2B, and it remains O_2B at the lower world price of O_2A, the tariff-distorted import demand curve becomes a vertical line passing through I_2FG. Vertical demand implies that import demand is completely unresponsive to the world price, that is, elasticity of demand for imports of zero. Completely inelastic import demand occurs because domestic consumers and producers respond to changes in the domestic price $(\bar{P})$ that they pay and receive, and the variable levy prevents foreign price changes from being transmitted to domestic prices. This policy insulates the EEC from foreign disturbances such as a larger world crop, but it shifts all the adjustment onto other countries. Greater stability within the EEC is obtained at the expense of less stability in the rest of the world.

7.8 LARGE COUNTRIES AND THE TERMS OF TRADE

The terms "small country" and "large country" refer not to a country's area or population but rather to the collective influence of its residents on world prices. A small country is a price taker in import markets, and it can be represented by a horizontal supply of imports curve. Conversely, a large country is one whose purchases are so important that they affect the world price. This is represented by a positively sloped import supply curve, which implies that a large country can drive down the world price by curtailing its purchases. This case is shown in Figure 7-2.

Along import supply curve I_1^s, the price will be O_2A if O_2I_1 units are imported, but if imports are reduced to O_2I_3, the world price will fall to O_2D. The general term for market power on the part of a buyer is monopsony power, which is analogous to monopoly power by a seller. The important implication of monopsony for trade policy is that an importer can shift some of the burden of a tariff onto foreign suppliers by forcing them to accept a lower net price. This effect is called the terms of trade effect of a tariff, where terms of trade refers to the ratio of export prices to import prices. Since it is the ratio of prices received by residents as sellers to prices residents pay as buyers, changes in the terms of trade are sometimes used as a crude measure of changes in a coun-

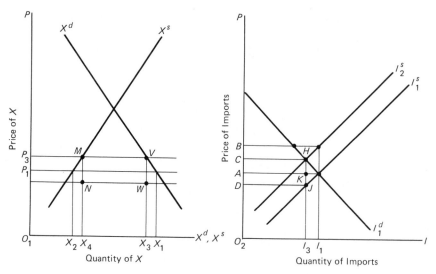

FIGURE 7-2   Tariff for a Large Country

try's welfare. An improvement in the terms of trade means that selling prices rise relative to buying prices. The measure is crude because it ignores quantities of exports and imports.

An analogous index is the parity ratio, which has been part of U.S. domestic agricultural policy for many years. It is the ratio of prices received by farmers to prices paid by farmers. Volatile conditions in the world in the 1970s brought about major changes in the terms of trade of the United States. Since the United States is a large net importer of crude oil, the sharp increase in oil prices in 1973 to 1979 and 1979 to 1980 substantially reduced the U.S. terms of trade. Conversely, the United States is the largest exporter of grain, and when grain prices rose sharply in 1974, the U.S. terms of trade improved. Of course, those countries importing both oil and grain suffered the biggest decline in their terms of trade during the period.

Consider the effect of a tariff imposed by a large country. Figure 7-2 shows that the effects are similar to the small-country case, except that the domestic rises by *less* than the tariff and the foreign price falls. In equilibrium the domestic price must exceed the foreign price by the amount of the tariff, so that the sum of the changes in foreign and domestic prices must equal the increase in the tariff:

$$dP - dP^\star = dt$$

For example, let the tariff increase by $dt = +\$1.00$. In the small-country case the foreign price cannot change $(dP^\star = 0)$, so that the domestic price must rise by the full amount of the tariff $(dP = dt = +\$1.00)$. But in the large-country case, the tariff will reduce import volume and lower the foreign price by, for example, $0.10, and the domestic price will rise by only $0.90. In this case the foreign seller is made to pay part of the tariff by accepting a lower price, and this benefit to domestic residents is called the terms of trade effect of a tariff. Notice that even though foreign sellers receive a lower net price, domestic consumers pay a higher price, and the terms of trade benefits all accrue to the government as greater tariff revenue.

In Figure 7-2 the tariff shifts the import supply curve from I_1^s to I_2^s, and $H\mathcal{J}$ is the amount of the tariff. Excess demand now exists at the initial price O_2A, and competition raises the tariff-inclusive price to $O_2C = O_1P_3 = I_3H$. Since the tariff is $H\mathcal{J}$, the net of tariff price retained by import suppliers is $I_3\mathcal{J}$, and the volume of imports is O_2I_3. Thus, the domestic price increase (HK) is less than the tariff $(H\mathcal{J})$, and the foreign price declines $(K\mathcal{J})$. Foreign suppliers could shift the entire tariff to domestic consumers if the gross price rose to O_2B $(dP = dt)$, but this price is not sustainable, because there is an excess supply at that price. Even though importers are legally obliged to pay the tariff, they will attempt to shift the tariff forward to consumers by charging a higher price or backward to suppliers by offering a lower price.

As in all cases of tax incidence, the ability of importers to shift the burden depends on market conditions. In particular, the extent to which foreign suppliers can be forced to accept a lower price depends on the collective monopsony power of domestic importers.

Monopsony power is reflected in the slope of the import supply curve, which is proportional to the elasticity of supply of imports.[5] In general, a more vertical import supply curve will result in a greater foreign price decrease for any given tariff. It will be shown in Chapter 8 that an import quota of O_2I_3 or a minimum import price of O_1P_3 would have the same effect on prices and trade volume as a tariff of $H\mathcal{J}$. Notice that consumers in all other countries would receive benefits from the lower foreign price. For example, a tariff on coffee by the United States would benefit coffee drinkers in Europe and all countries except the United States. It would be harmful to exporters in Brazil, Colombia, and all producing countries.

The analysis of terms of trade effects of a tariff can be extended to any policy that alters domestic supply and demand, since it necessarily alters import demand as well. For example, a tax on domestic production of the importable would shift X^s to the left and I^d to the right and increase the price paid to foreigners for imports. Thus, a tax on domestic production will worsen a large country's terms of trade.

---

[5] Specifically the slope of I^s is

$$\frac{dI^s}{dP} = \left(\frac{dI^s}{dP}\frac{P}{I^s}\right)\frac{I^s}{P} = \epsilon_{IP}\frac{I^s}{P}$$

7.9 ALGEBRAIC ANALYSIS
OF TARIFFS

Consider a problem involving the effect of a tariff in a large country. Let domestic demand be described by the equation $X^d = 90 - P$. Domestic supply is $X^s = 4P$. Since imports are the excess of domestic demand over domestic supply, the implicit import demand equation is

$$I^d = X^d - X^s = 90 - P - 4P = 90 - 5P$$

In a similar fashion the supply of imports could be derived from the underlying demand and supply equations for the rest of the world, and suppose that it is given by

$$I^s = 10P^\star$$

The world market clears where $I^d = I^s$ or

$$90 - 5P = 10P^\star$$
$$P = 6$$

At the world price $P = P^\star = 6$ import demand is

$$I^d = 90 - 5P = 90 - 5(6) = 60$$

Import supply is

$$I^s = 10P^\star = 10(6) = 60$$

This problem can be represented by Figure 7-3, where free trade equilibrium is at point E with $P = 6$ and $I = 60$. Now let a tariff of $2.00 per unit be imposed. In equilibrium with the tariff, the price in the importing country (P) must exceed the price in the exporting country $(P^\star)$ by the amount of the tariff: $P - P^\star = 6$. The price relevant to the exporter is the net of tariff price, $P^\star = P - t$. The import supply equation becomes $I_2^s = 10P^\star = 10(P - t) = 10(P - 2) = 10P - 20$.

In the posttariff equilibrium

$$I_2^s = I_1^d$$
$$10P - 20 = 90 - 5P$$
$$P = \$7.33$$

This price is paid by consumers and received by producers in the importing country. Thus, a $2.00-per-unit tariff raises the price by $1.33. Foreign sellers bear part of the tariff since $P^\star = P - 5$:

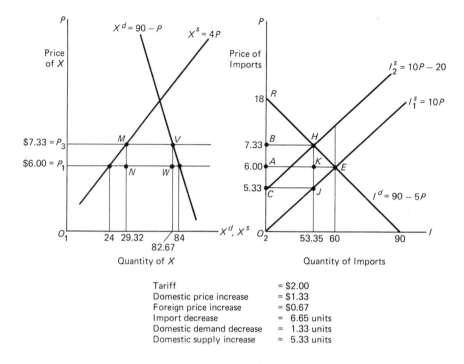

Tariff   = $2.00
Domestic price increase   = $1.33
Foreign price increase   = $0.67
Import decrease   = 6.65 units
Domestic demand decrease   = 1.33 units
Domestic supply increase   = 5.33 units

FIGURE 7-3   Results of Algebraic Problem

$$P^\star = \$5.33 = \$7.33 - \$2.00$$

Thus, the foreign price falls from $6.00 to $5.33.

The reduction in import volume can be computed from the import demand equations:

$$I^d = 90.00 - 5P = 90.00 - 5(7.33) = 53.35$$

This result can be verified by consulting the domestic demand and supply equations and showing that when $P = 7.33$,

$$X^d = 90.00 - 7.33 = 82.67$$
$$X^s = 4(7.33) = 29.32$$
$$I^d - X^d - X^s = 82.67 - 29.32 = 53.35$$

Thus, the $2.00 tariff raises the domestic price by $1.33, lowers the price paid to foreigners by $0.67, and reduces imports by 6.65 units as shown in Figure 7-3.

7.10 TARIFF REVENUE

In the case of a small country, all tariff revenue is paid by domestic residents. In the large-country case, part of the tariff is paid by foreigners. Government tariff revenue is the tariff rate times the tariff base:

$$T = tI = \$2.00(53.35) = \$106.70$$

The \$2.00-per-unit tariff is collected directly from importers, but \$1.33 per unit is shifted to consumers in the form of a higher price, and \$0.67 is shifted to foreign suppliers in the form of a lower net price. In this sense, one can say that of the \$106.70 of tariff revenue, domestic residents pay an additional \$70.96 = \$1.33(53.35) and foreign suppliers pay \$35.74 = \$0.67(53.35).

In Figure 7-3 the domestic share of the tariff burden is $ABHK = NMVW$, the foreign share is $CAKJ$, and total revenue is $CBHJ$. Foreign suppliers pay part of the tariff in the sense that they receive \$5.33 for each of the 53.35 units with the tariff. Without the tariff they would have received \$6.00 for each unit.

Notice that raising the tariff rate (t) does not necessarily raise tariff revenue (T), because a lower volume of imports results. The precise result depends on the slope of import demand, which is proportional to the elasticity of import demand. The possibility of the government's increasing its tax revenue by lowering the tax rate has received much popular attention in discussions of the Laffer curve.[6] In the tariff case, there are at least two tariff rates that result in zero revenue: a zero tariff and rate so high that trade ceases. The latter is called a prohibitive tariff, and in Figure 7-3 it is equal to O_2R, the distance between the intercepts of I^s and I^d on the price axis.

Since extremely high and extremely low tariff rates yield no revenue, there must be some intermediate rate that yields maximum tariff revenue. The maximum revenue tariff rate can be shown to be equal to half the distance between the I^s and I^d intercepts on the price axis.[7] In Figure 7-3, it is one-half of O_2R. This rate may be of interest to customs officials and the Treasury, but it carries no welfare significance for the economy as a whole. There is no reason to discourage international trade in order to finance government expenditures. It is traditional to distinguish two motives for tariffs: revenue and protection of domestic industry. There is a potential conflict between them, since the maximum protection is achieved by eliminating all imports, but such a policy would also eliminate all revenue. Significant conflicts between the revenue and protective motives occurred in the nineteenth-century United States, when the tariff was the major source of federal revenue.

---

[6] A Laffer curve is simply a graphical representation of tax revenue as a function of the tax rate.

[7] For a discussion of the maximum revenue tariff, see Richard Caves and Ronald Jones, *World Trade and Payments*, 3rd ed. (Boston: Little, Brown, 1980), Chap. 12.

7.11 PRODUCTION AND CONSUMPTION EFFECTS OF TARIFFS

The tariff encourages production and discourages consumption in the home country, and these effects can be seen in Figure 7-4. The domestic price increase from $6.00 to $7.33 increases production from 24.00 units to 29.32 units and decreases consumption from 84.00 units to 82.67 units. Imports, which equal domestic consumption minus domestic production, decrease by 6.65 units. Simultaneously the price decrease from $6.00 to $5.33 in the rest of the world increases consumption relative to production by $60.00 - 53.35 = 6.65$ units. In the home country these same production and consumption effects could have been achieved by domestic production and consumption taxes instead of a tariff.

In general, a tariff is equivalent to a consumption tax plus a production subsidy at the same rate. In this case the tariff causes domestic consumers to pay $1.33 more per unit than they would have paid with free trade. Since 82.67 units were bought, the additional consumer spending caused by the tariff was $1.33(82.67) = \$109.95$. At the same time domestic producers received $1.33

FIGURE 7-4   Production and Consumption Effects of a Tariff

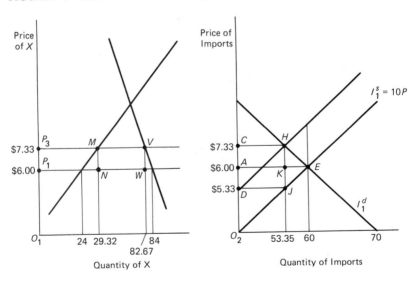

Tariff revenue = $DCHJ$ = $2.00 (53.35) = $106.70
Consumer share of tariff = $NMVW$ = $ACHK$ = $1.33 (53.35) = $70.96
Exporter share of tariff = $DAKJ$ = $0.67 (53.35) = $35.74
Production subsidy = MN = $1.33 (29.32) = $39.00
Consumption tax = VW = $1.33 (82.67) = $109.95

more per unit because of the tariff, and with production of 29.32 units, the additional producer revenue was $1.33(29.32) = $39.00. Thus, of the additional consumer expense of $109.95, $39.00 is transferred to domestic producers as an implicit production subsidy, and the remaining $70.95 goes to the government as tariff revenue. The government collects an additional $0.67(53.35) = $35.74 from foreign suppliers for total revenue of $70.95 + $35.74 = $106.70. The same result could have been accomplished with a consumption tax of $2.00 per unit and a production subsidy of $2.00. This would have raised the domestic price by $1.33 and lowered the foreign price by $0.67.

In terms of Figure 7-4 the consumption tax would raise revenue of $109.95, equal to area P_1P_3VW, and the production subsidy would cost $39.00, equal to area P_1P_3MN. The excess of consumption tax revenue over production subsidy payments is $109.95 - $39.00 = $70.95, which goes to the government (area $NMVW$ = area $ACHK$). In addition, the government collects $35.74 from foreign suppliers (area $DAKJ$) for total revenue of $106.70. Thus a tariff combines the effects of a consumption tax and a production subsidy. It follows that one could accomplish the allocative effects of a tariff without imposing one. One could also encourage domestic production through a subsidy without the consumption-depressing effects of a tariff. Similarly, one could discourage consumption through a tax without simultaneously encouraging domestic production as a tariff does.

The appropriate trade policy for a country depends on the object of trade policy. If maximum national income is the object, free trade tends to be the best policy. The main exception is the national optimum tariff, based on monopsony power, which is discussed in Chapter 10. If the goal is more domestic production than would occur under free trade, a production subsidy accomplishes the goal at a lower cost than does a tariff, because it avoids the unwanted consumption effect of a tariff. For example, if an industry is deemed essential for national defense, a production subsidy would provide the necessary encouragement without forcing consumers to pay an artificially high price. If the goal is to reduce consumption below what would occur under free trade, a consumption or sales tax is superior to a tariff because it avoids the unwanted production effect of a tariff. Notice that a tariff increases domestic production but a sales tax *decreases* it. Finally, it greater national self-sufficiency is the goal, a tariff is the best policy because it reduces import volume by simultaneously adding to production and subtracting from consumption.

7.12 U.S. ENERGY POLICY

U.S. energy policy can be analyzed in terms of consumption and production effects. From 1973 to 1981, price controls held the domestic price of crude oil far below the world price. Price controls also depressed the price of natural gas (a close substitute), and environmental restrictions made it difficult to expand the use of coal and nuclear energy. This cheap energy policy has encouraged consumption, discouraged domestic production, and increased the demand for imported crude oil. Because a tariff is equivalent to a consumption tax plus a production subsidy, these combined policies are equivalent to a negative tariff on crude oil.

It is ironic that during a period when three presidents and every Congress claimed "energy independence" as a high-priority national goal, the prevailing policy was a subsidy to crude oil imports. Crude oil prices were decontrolled in 1981 following enabling legislation in 1980. As a quid pro quo for oil price decontrol, Congress passed one of the largest tax increases in U.S. history in 1980. The tax was called a windfall profits tax, but it was a misnomer since it was a fixed amount of money per barrel of oil regardless of profits. This means that it was an effective sales tax, and its effect on oil imports depends on whether or not the decrease in oil consumption exceeds the decrease in domestic oil production. The U.S. cheap oil policy was justified in Congress as a way of protecting consumers from excessive profits of oil companies. The net effect has been to increase the demand for imported oil and reduce the elasticity of import demand. The magnitude of this effect was discussed in Chapter 3. Because the United States is a large country in the world oil market, its policy alters the terms of trade. By adding to the demand for crude oil, U.S. policymakers have unconsciously increased the price that the Organization of Petroleum Exporting Countries (OPEC) can charge customers. Perhaps one reason for OPEC's having been more successful than most cartels in history is that the largest buyer of its product pursued domestic policies that effectively subsidized oil imports.

7.13 COST
OF PROTECTION

The gains from trade were expressed in Chapter 3 in terms of an increase in consumer surplus. Since tariffs reduce the volume of trade, the cost of a tariff can be measured in terms of forgone consumer surplus. The cost of a tariff levied by a small country is shown in Figure 7-5. The cost of import quotas and other trade barriers can be analyzed in a similar fashion, as will be shown in Chapter 8.

Tariffs impose a net cost on the economy, because the loss incurred by consumers exceeds the income transferred to domestic producers and the government. The tariff causes the price to rise from O_1P_1 to O_1P_2, and the gross loss to consumers is the area $h + a + e + b$. From this area, h is transferred to domestic producers as a subsidy, and $e = f$ is transferred to the government as tariff revenue. The remaining area, $a + b = c$, is a deadweight loss to society in the sense that it is a loss to consumers without a corresponding gain to anyone

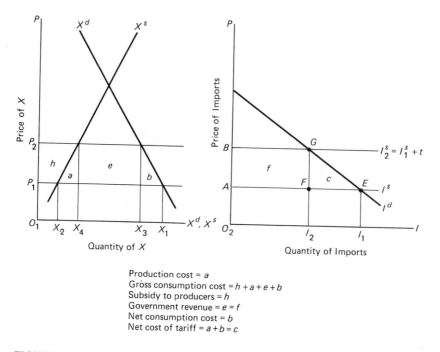

Production cost = a
Gross consumption cost = $h + a + e + b$
Subsidy to producers = h
Government revenue = $e = f$
Net consumption cost = b
Net cost of tariff = $a + b = c$

FIGURE 7-5   Cost of Trade Barriers for a Small Country

else. The area $a + b$ is the economic cost of a tariff, and it can be broken down into a production cost (a) and a consumption cost (b).

Area a measures the production cost, which is the excess of domestic marginal cost over the cost of importing X. It measures the consequence of violating comparative advantage by producing something at home that could be imported more cheaply. In Adam Smith's example, it is equivalent to the farmer making his own shoes when the shoemaker could make them for less. Area b measures forgone consumer surplus, the excess of marginal benefit from consumption over import cost. The total cost of the tariff depends on the height of the tariff and the slopes of the supply and demand curves. A large country can reduce the cost of a tariff by improving its terms of trade. This monopsony effect will be discussed in Chapter 10. A number of empirical studies have estimated the cost of tariffs[8] and other trade barriers for various countries. A recent study by the Federal Trade Commission estimated that the cost to the

[8] One of the more comprehensive studies appears in Stephen Magee, "The Welfare Effects of Restrictions on U.S. Trade," Brookings Papers on Economic Activity, 3:1972, pp. 645–707. A survey of empirical studies is W. M. Corden, "The Costs and Consequences of Protection: A Survey of Empirical Work," in *International Trade and Finance*, Peter B. Kenen, ed., (London: Cambridge University Press, 1975).

United States due to trade restrictions on color television sets, citizens' band radios, textiles, nonrubber shoes, and sugar was $2 billion per year.[9]

7.14 U.S. TARIFF HISTORY

Tariff policy was often a politically sensitive subject in the history of the United States. When the 13 colonies were still possessions of Great Britain, trade was heavily regulated by the British Navigation Acts. The acts were an instrument of mercantilism, whereby the colonies were regulated in an attempt to benefit the home country. A fundamental principle of mercantilism is the belief that a country benefits from exporting more than it imports. The principles of mercantilism were carried to an extreme by Jean Baptiste Colbert (1619–1683), the finance minister of Louis XIV of France, who imposed extensive import barriers, export subsidies, and controls over domestic trade.

The British mercantilist system that Adam Smith criticized was a less extreme form of the same economic system. Colonial opposition to the Navigation Acts was one of the factors leading to the Revolutionary War. All colonial trade was required to pass through Britain, and only British ships and crews could be legally used. Since the policy increased transportation costs, it had the effect of increasing prices paid by colonists for imports and decreasing prices received by colonists for exports. Enforcement of the trade restrictions was difficult for the British Navy, and smuggling was rampant.

Following independence, the Articles of Confederation became the legal foundation of tariff policy. The Articles provided little power for the central government, and states were permitted to impose tariffs on interstate trade. The Constitution of 1789 converted the United States into a customs union, which reserved tariff-making authority for the federal government. The new U.S. government inherited some of the mercantilistic policies of the British.

The first secretary of Treasury, Alexander Hamilton, was an early advocate of a protective tariff. In his 1791 *Report on Manufactures*, he advocated a tariff to promote infant industries. Because the protected industries were concentrated in the North, whereas the agricultural exporting sector was concentrated in the South, the early tariff debates took on a regional flavor. Northerners were protectionists, and Southerners supported freer trade. Some of the famous debates between Daniel Webster of New Hampshire and John C. Calhoun of South Carolina involved tariff policy. The interference with trade during the War of 1812 acted as a de facto tariff for the new country. The surge of import competition following that war led to strong protectionist pressures from the injured industries. The highly protectionist Tariff of Abominations

[9]The figures are from a staff report of the Federal Trade Commission reported by *The Wall Street Journal*, July 25, 1980.

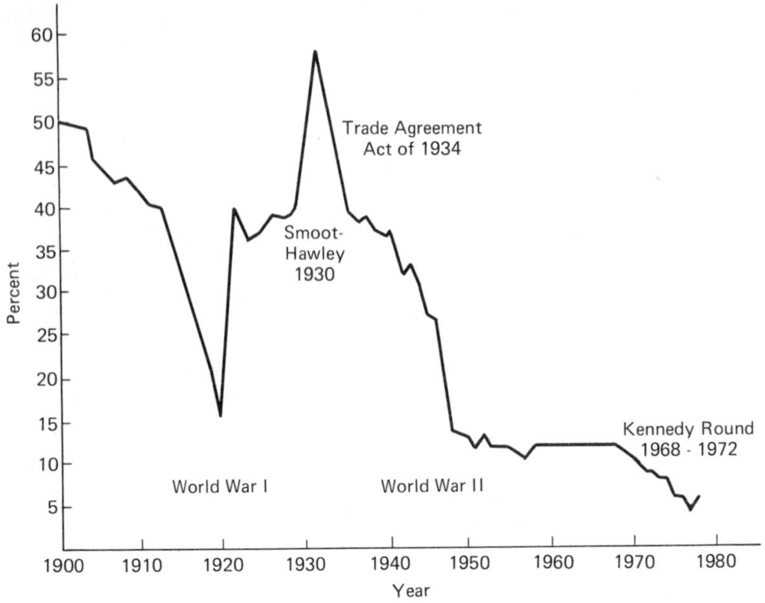

FIGURE 7-6   Average Tariff Rate in the United States, 1900–1980

Source: Historical Statistics of the United States (Washington, 1972); and Statistical Abstract of the United States (Washington, D.C.: Government Printing Office, various issues).

was passed in 1828 over the protest of Southern congressmen, including Calhoun. Opponents had employed the dangerous tactic of amending the bill in an attempt to make the tariff so high that a majority would vote against it. The tactic failed, and the bill became law. Backed by Calhoun's Nullification Doctrine, South Carolina threatened to refuse to collect the tariff in Charleston, but the promise of military action by President Andrew Jackson overcame the opposition. Regional aspects of the tariff controversy were one of several economic factors that led to the Civil War. Toward the end of the nineteenth century, tariff policy emerged again as a partisan national political issue. Democrats, such as Cleveland, supported freer trade, whereas Republicans, such as McKinley, advocated protectionism.

The average tariff rate has fluctuated considerably in the twentieth century, as shown in Figure 7-6. The average rate declined from 50 percent in 1900 to 15 percent at the end of World War I. The rate increased sharply in the 1920s, reaching a peak in 1930 with the Smoot-Hawley tariff. Passed during a period of massive unemployment, the Smoot-Hawley tariff was designed to increase jobs for Americans. Instead, other governments quickly retaliated by raising their own tariffs. The result was a decrease in the volume of world trade, which exacerbated unemployment and deepened the world depression.

The Trade Agreements Act of 1934 was the first of a series of attempts to reverse the protectionist effect of Smoot-Hawley. As Figure 7-6 shows, the average tariff rate in the United States has declined continuously since 1930. The Trade Agreements Act and subsequent revisions authorized the president to negotiate mutual tariff reductions with trading partners. Tariff reductions achieved in bilateral negotiations were extended to all trading partners according to the most favored nation principle. Following World War II, the General Agreement on Tariffs and Trade was founded with the object of avoiding the tariff warfare of the 1930s. The GATT sponsored multilateral tariff negotiations including the Kennedy Round and the Geneva-Tokyo Round. In conjunction with these conferences, the Congress passed the Trade Expansion Act of 1962 and the 1974 Trade Reform Act. As a result of these negotiations, U.S. tariffs have been reduced to the point where tariffs are a less serious obstacle to trade than are quotas and other nontariff barriers.

As shown in Figure 7-6, the average tariff rate is the lowest in the century. However, Congress has limited the executive's tariff-cutting authority by imposing various safeguards, such as the "peril point provision," the "escape clause," and the "national security clause." In addition, certain sensitive industries, such as textiles and agriculture, have been excluded from trade liberalization negotiations.

Although tariffs have been sharply reduced by negotiation, their effect on trade has been offset by an increase in the breadth and severity of quotas and other nontariff barriers. Mercantilist pressures remain strong, but tariffs are no longer the main instrument of protectionism. Labor unions, which once supported free trade, have become staunch advocates of protectionism. The AFL-CIO has sponsored legislation calling for restrictions on "local content" of products and trade policy "reciprocity." Local content, which has been advocated for automobiles, would require that X percent of all automobile components must be made in the United States. Advocates of reciprocity propose that the United States use commercial policy to retaliate against any country that restricts imports from the United States. According to one extreme interpretation of reciprocity, targets of retaliation would be any countries with large and persistent bilateral trade surpluses with the United States.

7.15 ARGUMENTS FOR TARIFFS

Many arguments in favor of tariffs have been offered, but nearly all of them fall into one of the following categories: (1) "scientific tariff" or fair trade, (2) national defense, (3) income redistribution, (4) employment, (5) optimum tariff, and (6) infant industry argument. Since the optimum tariff depends on monopoly power, it will be considered in Chapter 10. The infant industry argument depends on externalities, and it will be considered in Chapter 9.

The scientific tariff argument advocates a tariff just high enough to equalize domestic and foreign costs of production. The argument has been described as "scientific" because it provides a precise rule for determining the level of the tariff. Protectionists in the United States have recently stressed the "fair trade" version of this argument. They point out that a tariff is necessary to offset the unfair advantage foreigners have acquired as a result of lower wages or a favorable tax system. The argument is erroneous however, since people benefit from trade precisely because comparative costs differ. There may be a tariff high enough to induce some banana production in the United States, but such a policy would result in a net cost to residents of the United States. A tariff that would equalize costs would also eliminate the gains from trade.

According to the national defense argument, some minimum domestic production in excess of what would occur under free trade is essential to protect against an interruption of import supply. The source of interruption may be war or politically inspired embargoes, such as the oil embargo of the United States by several Arab countries in 1973 or the U.S. grain embargo of the USSR in 1980. The argument assumes that domestic production is more reliable than imports, and it contends that a tariff is the best way to protect against a supply interruption.

However, it has been shown that if the object of policy is to increase domestic production, a production subsidy is superior to a tariff. A production subsidy adds to domestic output yet avoids the consumption cost of a tariff. Another alternative that could have a lower cost than a tariff is a strategic stockpile, which is the traditional way that households and firms have hedged against uncertain supplies. However, there is reason for skepticism concerning the ability of government officials to manage a strategic stockpile. An appropriate time to release oil from the underground U.S. strategic reserve would have been during the shortage associated with the Iranian revolt of 1979. Unfortunately, the general in charge of the underground reserve had not yet installed pumps to bring the oil to the surface. A serious practical problem facing all these forms of protection is that it is difficult to agree on what products and what levels of output are essential for national defense.

According to the income distribution argument, the tariff is a convenient device for redistributing income toward factors of production employed heavily in the import-competing sector. If countries export products using large amounts of the abundant factor, tariffs would protect the scarce factor of production. In the United States, this factor would be unskilled labor. Even if one accepts redistribution of income toward the scarce factor as a legitimate national goal, it could be achieved at a lower cost by using an alternative fiscal device. A general income tax combined with a transfer would accomplish the goal without distorting international trade.

According to the employment argument, tariffs are a convenient way to preserve jobs for domestic workers. One interpretation of the early mercantilist literature is that a balance-of-trade surplus adds to domestic employment. The proponents of the Smoot-Hawley tariff predicted that their action would increase jobs in the United States. This argument has been made recently for the textile, shoe, steel, and automobile industries.

There are several problems with the argument. First, a tariff increases employment in the industry being protected, but it reduces employment in other sectors. Second, a tariff invites retaliation, which would reduce output and employment in the exportable sector. Finally, even if a tariff increased total national employment, other policies would do so at a lower cost. Specific labor market policy or aggregate demand policy would avoid the production and consumption effects of a tariff.

The object of a productive economy is to produce goods for consumption, and jobs are a means to this end. If creating jobs were an object itself, it would be prudent to create employment by burning books that describe modern technology, destroying machines, and permitting fertile land to remain idle. All these policies would reduce the total output from which the owners of labor, capital, and land are rewarded.

All these arguments have been repeated for centuries, and their durability comes from the fact that tariffs do provide economic benefits for their proponents. Advocates of tariffs are acting in their self-interest by attempting to restrict trade. The economic argument against tariffs is that for each $1 of benefits generated, costs of more than $1 are imposed on someone else. Thus, tariffs result in a net loss to society as a whole. Because of the net social loss, reconsider Bastiat's description of tariffs as "negative railroads."

7.16 EXPORT TAXES

The economic effect of taxing exports is perfectly analogous to a tariff. An export tax raises the cost of exporting and reduces the export volume. For a small country, the world price is unaffected, and the domestic price is lowered by the full amount of the tax. The effect can be seen in Figure 7-7 where the

FIGURE 7-7 Export Tax

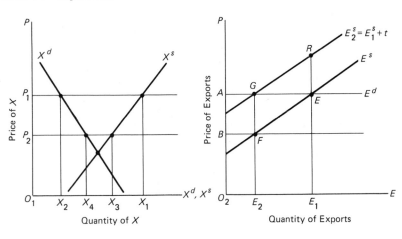

initial equilibrium is at point E. The price is $O_2A = O_1P_1$ and the volume of exports is O_2E_1. The export tax shifts export supply upward to E_2^s, reducing exports to O_2E_2. The domestic price falls to $O_2B = O_1P_2$, production falls to O_1X_3, and consumption increases to O_1X_4. In the large-country case, E^d would be negatively sloped, and the reader can show that the tax will cause a combination of a lower domestic price and a higher world price. Several countries with monopoly power for certain products have taxed exports in an attempt to improve their terms of trade. Brazil and Colombia have taxed coffee exports. Chile has taxed copper, and several countries have taxed oil exports. The application of export taxes is common in some countries, but they are unconstitutional in the United States. However, the same effects have been obtained by export quotas.

Explicit export taxes do exist, but implicit taxes are more common. Most OPEC governments market their oil through complicated arrangements that amount to an export tax. Since an export tax reduces the price to both domestic producers and consumers, it is equivalent to a tax on domestic production plus a subsidy to domestic consumption. In many OPEC countries, the producers being taxed are foreign oil companies. It is also common for governments in low-income countries to tax exports of primary products such as coffee and cocoa. The tax has been justified as a source of revenue and as a way to assert monopoly power in world markets. (See Chapter 10.) If the exporter is a large country, the reduction in export volume will cause the price to increase. The tax is sometimes implemented through a government marketing board. The board is decreed to be the sole legal exporter. It pays domestic producers less than the world price and resells the product at the world price. As was pointed out in Chapter 6, the disparity between the two prices creates an incentive for smuggling.

An alternative scheme for taxing exports is the practice of multiple exchange rates. The government declares two different legal exchange rates and requires that all trade in foreign currency must be with the government. If coffee is the product to be taxed, the government might declare a rate of 10 pesos per dollar for all other exports and 5 pesos per dollar for coffee exports. This unfavorable exchange rate for coffee transactions discourages coffee exports in the same way as an explicit tax on the commodity. It is difficult to enforce multiple exchange rates, since coffee exporters have an incentive to sell dollar earnings in the illegal market for more than 5 pesos. In countries practicing multiple exchange rates, black markets usually develop. American firms complain that certain laws and regulations hamper their exporting efforts. The Foreign Corrupt Practices Act of 1977 makes it illegal for U.S. firms and their agents to obtain sales by bribing foreign officials. If competing firms do not face the same penalties from their governments, the U.S. policy can be treated as an export tax.

7.17 EXPORT SUBSIDY

An export subsidy is analytically equivalent to a negative export tax. An export subsidy is a payment from the government to the seller for each unit of a product that is exported. The subsidy may be an explicit payment of money to the seller. An implicit subsidy may take many forms such as a reduction of ordinary taxes per unit of exports, or it may be subsidized credit that is available for export business only.

Until the middle of 1971, the U.S. Department of Agriculture paid explicit subsidies to grain companies that exported U.S. products. The program was justified as a way of developing foreign markets for U.S. products and as a way of offsetting artificially high domestic prices caused by the government's price support policy. The subsidy policy continued even after the Soviet Union began to purchase very large amounts of grain, and the incident has been called the Great Grain Robbery of 1971. The program was criticized on the grounds that U.S. taxpayers and consumers were subsidizing a few grain companies and Soviet consumers. The subsidy program was terminated after most of the large purchases were made.[10] Soviet consumers also benefit from subsidies on dairy exports from the European Economic Community, particularly the attempt to reduce the size of the infamous "mountain of butter."

U.S. dairy policy has also generated large surpluses of dairy products. In a desperate attempt to reduce the surplus, the U.S. Department of Agriculture shipped 100,000 tons of butter to New Zealand in 1981 at subsidized prices. Since New Zealand is the largest butter exporter in the world, the deal is comparable to "shipping coal to Newcastle." An artificially high domestic price plus an export subsidy have converted the EEC from a net grain importer to a net grain exporter.

Examples of implicit subsidies in the form of tax concessions are the U.S. Domestic International Sales Corporation (DISC) and European Economic Community export rebates on the value added tax. The DISC program permits American firms to set up a separate export division, and profits earned from exporting can be legally deferred for long periods. The value added tax is the major source of government revenue in Western Europe, and the fiscal system encourages sales in the export market by rebating to firms any value added taxes paid on products exported. The U.S. Export-Import Bank founded in 1934 encourages exports (but not imports in spite of its name) by making loans at less than market rates of interest. Eligible borrowers must be approved buyers of U.S. exports. Most governments have an agency that offers subsidized credit, and competition among governments in the form of export

---

[10] See Dan Morgan, *Merchants of Grain* (New York: Viking, 1979), Chap. 5, for an account of the incident.

subsidies has been extensive. One of the issues discussed at the Tokyo Round of tariff negotiations was a code for acceptable export subsidies, but no agreement was reached.

When the Reagan administration took office, there was some sentiment for abolishing the Export-Import Bank or sharply curtailing its lending. However, a curious export subsidy competition between the United States and Western European governments broke out in 1981, which enhanced the role of the Export-Import Bank. Because of the worldwide recession at the time, export subsidies were designed to increase domestic employment. Critics have charged that the Bank is wasteful for the same reason that tariffs are wasteful. Subsidized loans encourage high-cost production of exportables, which also imposes a loss on domestic consumers. The Bank also deals primarily with the exports of a few large corporations. More than 70 percent of its loans have gone to seven firms (including Boeing, Westinghouse, and General Electric), and more than 40 percent of the loans have been related to aircraft sales. Critics have called it Boeing's bank.

The effect of subsidy by a small country is analyzed in Figure 7-8. The initial equilibrium is at point E where the domestic price and the world price are $O_1P_1 = O_2A$ and the volume of exports is O_2E_1. A subsidy of $FG = ER$ per unit would shift the export supply curve downward to E_2^s. Because the exporting country is small, it faces a horizontal (infinitely elastic) demand curve, which implies that foreigners will buy the additional exports offered (EG) at the initial price. Exporters receive a net price of $O_1P_2 = O_2B$, which is the sum of the price paid by foreign consumer $(OP_1 = O_2A)$ and the subsidy check $(P_1P_2 = AB = FG)$ from the home government. The price increase leads ex-

FIGURE 7-8   Export Subsidy

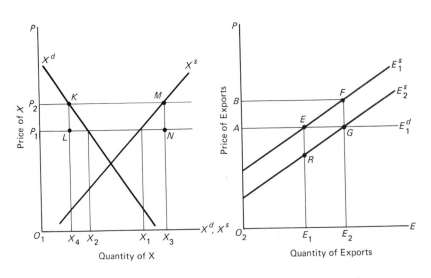

porters to switch sales from the domestic to the foreign market, which drives up the domestic price to O_1P_2. The increase in export colume is E_1E_2, which is the sum of an increase in domestic production (X_1X_3) and a decrease in domestic production (X_2X_4). The export subsidy is equivalent to a production subsidy at the rate of P_1P_2 per unit, which is partly paid by domestic consumers. Since the country is a net exporter, production exceeds consumption, and the tax revenue paid by consumers (area P_1P_2KL) is less than the total subsidy received by producers (area P_1P_2MN), and the difference (area $LKMN = ABJH$) is the net cost to the treasury. An export subsidy redistributes income away from domestic consumers and the taxpayers and in favor of domestic producers of product X.

The reader can analyze the effect of an export subsidy paid by a large country. Largeness implies a negatively sloped export demand curve instead of E_1^d. The subsidy will lower the world price and cause the domestic price to rise by less than in the small-country case. An export subsidy by a large country worsens its terms of trade.

SUMMARY

The effect of a tariff on trade is similar to that of transport costs. It raises the price in the importing country relative to the price in the exporting country, and it reduces the volume of trade. A difference is that transportation uses real economic resources, whereas a tariff is merely a transfer payment. The level of a tariff depends both on the rate and on the base of a tariff. The countries belonging to GATT have agreed to impose nondiscriminatory tariffs, against members except for customs unions, and the Generalized System of Preferences. In the United States, Congress retains the ultimate authority to determine tariffs, but it has delegated some authority to the president. Congress has protected its authority by precluding the president from negotiating tariff reductions against certain producers and by withdrawing tariff concessions if domestic industry is unduly harmed.

The effects of import quotas and other nontariff barriers are similar to those of tariffs. For a small country, the increase in the domestic price increases domestic production and decreases domestic consumption. A large country imposing a tariff will also experience an improvement in its terms of trade. A tariff transfers income to domestic producers, but it imposes net consumption and production losses on the domestic economy.

Some additional arguments in favor of tariffs have been considered, but tariffs accomplish the stated objective at a higher cost than do alternative policies. As a result of tariff negotiations since World War II, U.S. tariffs are at the lowest level in this century. However protection may not be so low, because of the widespread substitution of nontariff barriers for tariffs. Since a tariff is an import tax, the analysis of tariffs is directly applicable to the export taxes and subsidies.

REFERENCES

AFL-CIO. *The National Economy 1981.* New York: AFL-CIO, 1982. Contains the protectionist policy prescriptions of the AFL-CIO concerning international trade and investment.

BALDWIN, ROBERT E. *Nontariff Distortions of International Trade.* Washington, D.C.: The Brookings Institution, 1970. A comprehensive analysis of nontariff barriers to trade.

BASTIAT, FREDERIC. *Economic Sophisms* (1851). New York: D. Van Nostrand, 1964.

BHAGWATI, JAGDISH, and ANNE KRUEGER, eds. *Foreign Trade Regimes and Economic Development,* 11 vols. New York: National Bureau of Economic Research, 1974–78. A series of studies of trade policy of the following countries: Turkey, Ghana, Israel, Egypt, the Philippines, India, South Korea, Chile, Colombia. Volumes 10 and 11, by Krueger and Bhagwati, respectively, are surveys of the entire project.

BOYD, JOHN H. "Eximbank Lending: A Federal Program That Costs Too Much" *Quarterly Review,* Federal Reserve Bank of Minneapolis, Winter 1982. A cost-benefit study of the Bank's operations.

CLINE, WILLIAM R., ed. *Trade Policy in the 1980s.* Washington, D.C.: Institute for International Economics, 1983. A collection of papers that survey recent and likely future trade policy issues.

——, NOBORU KAWANABE, T. O. KRONJO, and THOMAS WILLIAMS. *Trade Negotiations in the Tokyo Round: A Quantititive Assessment.* Washington, D.C.: The Brookings Institution, 1978. An analysis of the effects of the Tokyo Round of tariff reductions.

CORDEN, W. M. *The Theory of Protection.* London: Oxford University Press, 1971.

——. *Trade Policy and Economic Welfare.* London: Oxford University Press, 1974.

——. "The Costs and Consequences of Protection: A Survey of Empirical Work." In *International Trade and Finance,* P. Kenen, ed. Cambridge: Cambridge University Press.

DAM, KENNETH. *The GATT: Law and International Economic Organization.* Chicago: University of Chicago Press, 1970.

DIEBOLD, WILLIAM, JR. *Industrial Policy as an International Issue.* New York: McGraw-Hill, 1980. Chapter 3 considers the issue of safeguards.

FRANK, CHARLES, JR. *Foreign Trade and Domestic Aid.* Washington, D.C.: The Brookings Institution, 1977. A study of the adjustment assistance program.

GOLT, S. *The GATT Negotiations 1973–79: The Closing Stage.* Washington, D.C.: National Planning Association, 1978. A survey of the Tokyo-Geneva negotiations.

GOLUB, STEPHEN, and J. M. FINGER. "The Processing of Primary Commodities: Effects of Developed Country Tariff Escalation and Developing Country Export Taxes." *Journal of Political Economy,* June 1979. Estimates the effect of tariffs and export taxes on processing of primary products in low-income countries.

HILLMAN, JORDAN JAY. *The Export-Import Bank at Work: Promotional Financing in the Public Sector.* Westport, Conn.: Greenwood Press, 1982. A study that stresses legal aspects of the bank's operations.

HUFBAUER, GARY C., and JOANNA SHELTON ERB. *Subsidies in International Trade,* Washington, D.C.: Institute for International Economics, 1983.

INSTITUTE FOR CONTEMPORARY STUDIES. *Tariffs, Quotas, and Trade: The Politics of Protectionism.* San Francisco: ICS, 1979.

JOHNSON, HARRY G. *Aspects of the Theory of Tariffs*. London: George Allen and Unwin, 1971. A collection of analytical papers on various aspects of tariffs.

KRUEGER, A. O. "The Political Economy of the Rent-Seeking Society." *American Economic Review*, June 1974. A presentation of the concept of rent seeking with an application to Turkey.

MAGEE, STEPHEN. "The Welfare Effects of Restrictions on U.S. Trade." *Brookings Papers on Economic Activity*. 3:1972, pp. 645–707.

MORGAN, DAN. *Merchants of Grain*. New York: Viking, 1979.

RATNER, SIDNEY. *The Tariff in American History*. New York: D. Van Nostrand, 1972.

RAY, EDWARD J. "The Determinants of Tariff and Non-Tariff Trade Restrictions in the United States." *Journal of Political Economy*, February 1981.

STERN, ROBERT. "Tariffs and Other Measures of Trade Control: A Survey of Recent Developments." *Journal of Economic Literature*, March 1973.

TAUSSIG, FRANK W. *The Tariff History of the United States*, 8th ed. New York: G. P. Putman, 1931. A classic study of U.S. tariff history.

THOMAS, R. KEITH. "The New U.S. Antidumping Law: Some Advice to Exporters." *Journal of World Trade Law*, July–August 1981.

U.S. GOVERNMENT PRINTING OFFICE. *The Tariff Schedule of the United States, Annotated*. Washington, D.C.: GPO, 1969. A list of U.S. tariff rates.

YEAGER, LELAND and DAVID G. TUERCK. *Foreign Trade and U.S. Policy*. New York: Praeger, 1976. A strong endorsement of free trade that systematically considers the arguments for protection.

CHAPTER EIGHT
QUOTAS
AND PREFERENTIAL
TRADE

8.1 INTRODUCTION

Tariffs and import quotas have some similar economic effects. Both forms of import barriers raise prices in the importing country, lower prices in the exporting country, and reduce the volume of trade. Both tariffs and quotas redistribute income from consumers to producers in the importing country. Both policies impose a net cost on the importing country. Unlike tariffs, however, import quotas generate no revenue for the government of the importing country. A second difference is that the volume of imports is more responsive to a change in economic conditions under a tariff than under an import quota.

This chapter will consider similarities and differences between tariffs and quotas in some detail. Import quotas appear in several forms. Some quotas are mandatory; others are described as "voluntary." Still other import barriers, such as a minimum import price or a variable levy, have the same effects on trade as a quota. The analysis will be extended to quotas on exports, which includes embargoes as a special case.

This chapter will also analyze preferential trade, which involves importers discriminating according to the source of import supply. Two important examples of prefential trade are customs unions and tariff preferences for low-income countries. The effect of preferential trade depends on whether the preferred supplier has higher or lower costs than alternative countries whose products are discriminated against.

The analysis of tariffs and quotas on final products can be extended to the case of tariffs and quotas on inputs. For example, a tariff on automobiles encourages domestic auto production. However, a tariff on steel, which is an essential input, will discourage domestic auto production. Thus, the protective effect on an industry depends on the entire tariff structure. The concept of the effective rate of protection is an attempt to measure the impact of the entire tariff structure.

The final topic of this chapter is the domestic and foreign determinants of international trade policy.

8.2 THE EFFECT OF AN IMPORT QUOTA

An import quota specifies the maximum legal volume of imports per period. If firms would have found it profitable to import less than the quota, then the quota has no effect during the period. The interesting case is where the quota is binding, that is, when firms would have imported more than the quota.

In Figure 8-1 the free trade equilibrium for a small country is at point M, where the price of X is $O_2A = O_1P_1$ and the volume of imports is $O_2I_1 = X_2X_1$. An import quota of more than O_2I_1 would not change anyone's economic behavior. However, a quota of O_2I_2, less than O_2I_1, will create a shortage of MN units of X at the price O_2A in the home country. The import demand curve with the quota becomes QRI_2, but with the tariff the import demand curve remains QRM.

The reason that the quota imposes a kink in the import demand curve at

FIGURE 8-1   Effect of an Import Quota

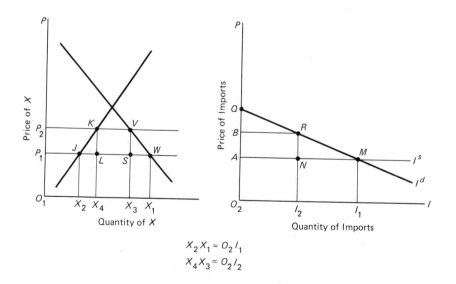

$$X_2X_1 = O_2I_1$$
$$X_4X_3 = O_2I_2$$

point R is that quantities greater than O_2I_2 are not permitted. Thus, import demand becomes vertical or perfectly inelastic at R. Even if suppliers gave the product away, no more than O_2I_2 could be legally imported. However, quantities less than the quota are permitted, which implies that import demand depends on price to the left of R.

The standard way to enforce the quota is through a system of import licenses. Importation without a license is illegal, and the total number of licenses issued by the government must be O_2I_2. The import supply curve shown, AI^s, is horizontal, indicating that the home country is too small to influence the foreign price of X. With the quota the foreign price would remain at O_2A, but the excess demand would cause the domestic price to rise to $O_2B = O_1P_2$. The volume of imports would decrease by I_1I_2. The decrease can be separated into consumption and production effects of the quota. Because of the higher domestic price, consumption falls by X_1X_3 and production increases by X_2X_4.

The effects of the quota of O_1I_2 on price and quantity of imports are the same as the effects of a tariff of AB per unit. However, a tariff would raise revenue of $ABRN$ for the government, but the quota need not. What happens to the equivalent of the tariff revenue depends on how the government distributes the import licenses. If the licenses are given to domestic importers at no cost, importers have the right to purchase X at the world price of O_2A and resell the product in the home country for O_2B. The right to import X would be valued at AB per unit, and the total value of all licenses would be $ABRN$. In this case the import quota transfers the equivalent of the tariff revenue to the holder of the import license.

If the licenses are negotiable, the license recipient can appropriate this revenue without importing the product. A secondary market for import licenses will emerge, and licenses will sell for AB per unit or a total of $ABRN$.

Alternatively, if the government auctioned import licenses to the highest bidder, the revenue would also be $ABRN$. The distribution of licenses has no direct effect on the price or volume of imports, but it alters the distribution of national income. One would expect various groups to try to persuade the government to give them the import licenses. The employment of real economic resources to attempt to acquire such revenue is called rent seeking. A study of the use of import licenses in Turkey indicated that rent seeking was a significant cost of the system.[1] Part of the labor and capital employed by lobbyists in capital cities is the cost of rent seeking. The U.S. oil import quota system that lasted from the Eisenhower administration until 1973 allocated licenses to oil refining companies in relation to their historical import shares.

Quotas differ from tariffs in terms of how revenue is distributed. Another difference is the elasticity of demand. With a tariff, the elasticity of the import demand curve (QRM) is still applicable to trade. With a quota, the elasticity of import demand is zero for all prices below O_2B. By reducing demand elasticity, quotas may encourage domestic monopoly.

[1] See Anne Krueger, "Some Economic Costs of Exchange Control: The Turkish Case," *Journal of Political Economy*, October 1966.

8.3 THE ECONOMIC COST
OF A QUOTA

The total economic cost of an import quota is similar to that of a tariff. In Figure 8-1 the net cost of the import quota to the home country is the area NRM, which is the sum of a consumption cost (SVW) and a production cost (JKL). In addition to the net cost, the quota transfers income of P_1P_2KJ from home consumers to home producers of X. Alternatively, the quota imposes a gross consumer loss of P_1P_2VW, but some of it is transferred to other domestic residents. Holders of import licenses receive $LKVS = ABRN$, and domestic producers receive P_1P_2KJ. The remaining area $JKL + SVW$ is the net cost to the home economy. The foreign price O_2A is assumed to be the result of competition among suppliers of imports. Conversely, if suppliers collude to raise the price to O_2B, their profits would rise by $ABRN$. Since this amount would be transferred abroad, the net cost to the home economy would be $ABRN + NRM$. Thus, the national cost of a quota depends on whether import supply is competitive or monopolistic. A characteristic of a voluntary export restraint is that it encourages import suppliers to collude on both quantity and price.

8.4 VOLUNTARY EXPORT
RESTRAINT

The preceding discussion has assumed that the import quota is a mandatory legal arrangement enforced by the importing country. Increasingly countries have restricted imports by inducing foreign suppliers to accept voluntary export restraints (VER). The term "voluntary" is a misnomer, because suppliers accept the arrangement under duress. It is described as an export restraint because it is enforced by the exporting country. VERs have been employed by the United States to restrict imports of several products, including automobiles, steel, textiles, and television sets.

Automobile imports from Japan were restrained in 1981. Steel imports from Japan and Europe were restrained from 1969 to 1975 and again in 1981. Imports of color television sets from Japan, Taiwan, and South Korea were restricted in 1977. Textile imports into the United States and Western Europe have been subject to quotas for many years. In 1957 Japanese exporters agreed to limit sales to the United States. In 1962 exporters from low-income countries accepted the Long-Term Arrangement on Cotton Textiles, which expired in 1973. The agreement was expanded in 1974 to include trade in cotton, wool, and synthetic fibers. It is known as the Multi-Fiber Arrangement, and it was renewed in 1977 and 1981. The arrangement provides a framework for regulating 80 percent of world textile trade, and it authorizes bilateral negotiations between importers and suppliers from low-income countries.

Table 8-1 shows that the dominant exporters are Hong Kong, South Ko-

TABLE 8-1   Net Trade in Textiles and Clothing, 1979*
         (in billions of dollars)

	TEXTILES	CLOTHING	TOTAL
West Germany	$-0.38	$-4.73	$-5.11
Italy	+1.82	+3.86	+5.68
The Netherlands	+0.10	-1.93	-1.83
United Kingdom	-0.78	-0.95	-1.73
Sweden	-0.53	-0.88	-1.41
United States	+1.07	-4.77	-3.70
Canada	-1.11	-0.56	-1.67
Japan	+1.97	-1.45	+0.52
Australia	-0.88	-0.30	-1.18
Hong Kong	-1.54	+3.60	+2.06
Korea	+1.37	+2.83	+4.20
India†	+0.73	+0.33	+1.06
USSR‡	-1.11	-1.88	-2.99

*GATT figures do not include Taiwan.

†1978.

‡1976.

Source: General Agreement on Tariffs and Trade, *International Trade, 1979/80* (Geneva: GATT, 1980).

rea, Taiwan, Italy, and the Peoples Republic of China.[2] The major net importers have been the United States, Canada, USSR, and Western Europe (except Italy). Notice that the United States and Japan import clothing and export textiles, whereas Hong Kong does the opposite.

GATT rules discourage the use of quotas, and VERs are a device for circumventing those rules. In particular, GATT rules prohibit the use of quotas unless an excessive volume of imports is caused by "prior tariff reductions." It appears that if imports are due to a change in comparative costs, quotas are not permissible. A second GATT rule is that when quotas are justified, they must be imposed in a nondiscriminatory manner. In the case of the U.S. automobile VER, the quota should apply to all auto imports, not just to Japanese. A final GATT rule is that the country imposing the quota must compensate the countries of import suppliers by lowering some other trade barrier. In the absence of compensation, the importing country may face retaliation against its exports. The VER is an attempt to avoid lowering other trade barriers and to avoid retaliation against U.S. exports. A political advantage for the president is that a VER does not require congressional approval.

A distinction is sometimes made between two kinds of quotas: (1) orderly marketing agreements (OMA) and (2) voluntary export restraints. OMAs are legal agreements between the governments of importing and exporting countries, and they usually include all of the major suppliers. VERs are agree-

[2]For details see Ann Vorce, "A Delicate New Weave," *Europe*, March–April 1982.

ments between the government of the importing country and business firms in the supplying country.

The distinction has some legal significance because firms participating in VERs may be subject to U.S. antitrust laws. Foreign suppliers could find themselves in the dilemma once faced by Swiss watchmakers. They were urged by the State Department to take collusive action to restrict watch shipments to the United States, but they were simultaneously threatened with antitrust prosecution by the Justice Department. OMAs face a different legal problem. Since they are agreements between governments, they appear to be mandatory, and mandatory quotas violate GATT. In the case of the VER on automobiles, the Reagan administration somehow finessed the two legal problems by claiming that the Japanese government unilaterally restrained auto exports to the United States.

A voluntary quota has the same effect on the domestic price and quantity of imports as does a mandatory quota. The difference is in the distribution of the tariff-equivalent revenue. In Figure 8-1 domestic residents (holders of import licenses or the government) receive the revenue if import suppliers sell at the competitive price O_2A, and foreigners receive the revenue if the collusive price O_2B prevails. A voluntary quota increases the probability of price collusion by suppliers. There are no licenses with a voluntary quota, so that suppliers must collude to be sure that aggregate sales do not exceed the quota. Since they must collude on quantities sold, it becomes easier for import suppliers to agree on a minimum price of O_2B rather than the competitive price of O_2A. If suppliers can enforce the minimum price of O_2B, their profits will increase by $ABRN$.

Notice that successful collusion requires price discrimination. Suppliers of X would have to sell at OA in the quota market and the competitive price of OB in all other markets. They must prevent arbitragers from buying in countries where the price is low and reselling in the high-price market. In spite of this problem, there is some evidence that suppliers have responded to U.S. voluntary import quotas by raising prices. The additional revenue may make foreign suppliers more willing to accept the quota policy. Alternatively, the government of import suppliers can appropriate the revenue by imposing an export tax of AB for each unit of X sold in this market. The same result could be achieved by an export quota of O_2I_2 to this market, with export licenses being auctioned to the highest bidder. The reason for the success of these policies is that the import quota makes import demand perfectly inelastic from I_2 to R. This means that the price can be increased to O_2B without losing any sales.

A VER may result in a deadweight loss relative to restricting imports by a tariff or a nondiscriminatory quota. Because a VER is a discriminatory quota, it will shift imports toward the high-cost source. Since the total cost of imports is minimum when the marginal cost is the same for all import suppliers, any divergence between marginal costs of suppliers will result in a deadweight loss.

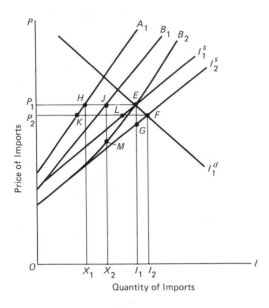

Quantity of Imports

FIGURE 8-2   Voluntary Export Restraint

Figure 8-2 shows the inefficiency associated with a VER. Curves A_1 and B_1 are the initial import supply and marginal cost curves of countries A and B. The initial aggregate import supply curve is I_1^s. The equilibrium is at E with price P_1 and total imports I_1. Imports from A are OX_1 and imports from B are OX_2. The marginal cost of importing from A (HX_1) equals the marginal cost of importing from B (JX_2).

Let an innovation occur in B, which shifts its import supply to B_2. Aggregate import supply shifts to I_2, price falls to P_2, and import volume rises to I_2. Imports from B increase from P_1J to P_2L, but imports from country A decrease from P_1H to P_2K.

Suppose that the importing country imposes a VER designed to limit imports to the initial level I_1. The desired level of total imports is accomplished by restricting B's sales to the initial level of OX_1. The problem with this arrangement is that the marginal cost of imports is lower in B (MX_2) than in A (HX_1). Thus, the total volume of imports (OI_1) is not being obtained at minimum cost. Total cost could be reduced by switching the source of some imports from A to B. Alternatively, if imports were restricted to OI_1 by a tariff of EG or a nondiscriminatory quota, the deadweight loss could be avoided. The problem could be avoided if the supplying countries changed the pattern of their trade. Suppose that B switched some of its shipments to a second import market and that A increased sales in the country imposing the VER on B. The deadweight loss would be avoided, but the home country would lose control over total imports and price.

8.5 APPLICATION
OF IMPORT QUOTAS

Rapid changes in industry structure tend to produce protectionism. Growth of the Japanese auto industry has threatened traditional producers in North America and Western Europe. Quotas against Japanese autos have been imposed on both continents.

Table 8-2 shows that between 1963 and 1979 Japan's share of world exports of road motor vehicles increased from 3 percent to 18 percent. During the same period, Western Europe's share declined from 68 percent to 54 percent.

Table 8-3 shows that Japan's share of world production rose from 6 percent to 22 percent, while North America's share declined from 46 percent to 30 percent. As a result of import competition, the United States negotiated a VER with Japan. The VER restricts the quantity of auto imports, but not the price. Since the imposition of the VER, the composition of imports from Japan has shifted toward more expensive models.

TABLE 8-2   Distribution of Exports of Road Motor Vehicles by Region,* Selected Years 1963–1979

	1963	1973	1978	1979
North America	21%	26%	23%	21%
Western Europe	68	54	51	54
Japan	3	12	19	18
Developing countries	0	1	1	1

*Australia, New Zealand, South Africa, and the Eastern trading area are not shown separately.
Source: General Agreement on Tariffs and Trade, *International Trade, 1979/80* (Geneva: GATT, 1980), p. 85.

TABLE 8-3   World Production of Road Motor Vehicles, Selected Years 1963–1979 (percentages of world output)

	1963	1973	1978	1979
Industrial countries	91%	88%	85%	84%
North America	46	35	33	30
Japan	6	18	20	22
Western Europe	39	35	32	32
Developing countries	2	5	6	7
Eastern trading area	4	6	7	7

Source: General Agreement on Tariffs and Trade, *International Trade, 1979/80* (Geneva: GATT, 1980), p. 83.

Sugar imports have been subject to quotas by the United States. Quotas were abandoned in 1974 and were replaced by a variable import fee. The fee was designed to maintain a target domestic price, and it resembled the variable grain levy of the European Economic Community. Import quotas were imposed again in 1982 under the protests of the Latin American countries that are the leading suppliers.

It was ironic that the quota was imposed soon after President Reagan proposed a Caribbean Basin aid program.[3] It is an example of a conflict between domestic political interests (sugar producers) and foreign policy interests. A similar conflict exists in the case of meat imports. Meat imports have been restricted for some time, the most recent legislation being the Meat Import Act of 1979. The act, which imposes mandatory quotas, adversely affects Australia, Canada, and New Zealand, the major suppliers. Australians complained that the United States was their only viable market, since the European Economic Community and Japan had already restricted meat imports from Australia. U.S. import quotas are not limited to products with a large domestic industry. Clothespins have been subject to an import quota since 1979 even though there are only three U.S. firms making the product. Most imported clothespins have come from Taiwan.

Other forms of import barriers have the effect of an import quota. For example, a monopoly state trading agency can impose a de facto import quota by choosing a quantity of imports that is smaller than the amount consumers would have chosen. Although such a buying policy is equivalent to an explicit quota, it would be difficult for an outside agency to detect. For example, the Japan Tobacco and Salt Corporation (JTS) is a government monopoly with exclusive control of the distribution of all tobacco products in Japan. American tobacco companies have complained that the JTS restricts foreign cigarette sales in a number of ways. Foreign cigarettes, which claim only 1 percent of the Japanese market, must be distributed by their chief competitor. Advertising of foreign cigarettes has been limited, and JTS employees have been accused of destroying material that promotes American cigarettes. Foreign cigarettes cannot be stocked in certain vending machines, and they can be sold through only 10 percent of the Japanese retailers licensed to sell tobacco products. In addition to these nontariff barriers, there is a tariff that causes foreign cigarettes to sell at retail prices 60 percent above those of Japanese cigarettes.[4]

An extreme case of a quota is an embargo. A boycott or import embargo can be thought of as an import quota of zero.[5] An embargo may apply to a particular product or a particular country. U.S. imports from Cuba have been

[3] See "Reagan's Caribbean Plan Is Coated with Sugar Quotas," *The Wall Street Journal,* July 20, 1982.

[4] For details see *The Wall Street Journal,* "How Japan Tries to Shut Out Foreign Goods," September 30, 1982.

[5] Charles Boycott was an English land agent whose Irish tenants "boycotted" him for charging excessive rents during the nineteenth-century potato famine.

forbidden since Fidel Castro gained power. Since the United States is one of the few countries to ban Cuban products, the main effect has been to change Cuba's trading partners without changing the total volume or composition of its trade.

The United States has imposed a series of export embargoes on grain trade with the USSR, the most recent case being January 1980 to April 1981. The object of an embargo is to inflict economic damage on a trading partner to achieve some political goal. The stated object was to retaliate for the Soviet invasion of Afghanistan. The embargo failed, as Soviet troops remained in Afghanistan throughout the period of the embargo. Success of an embargo depends on the country in question having considerable monopoly power as a buyer or seller. Otherwise, rivals will easily replace it as a trading partner.

International trade is competitive, and there are few products for which one country possesses significant monopoly power. The United States is the world's largest grain exporting country, but it is not the only exporter. Canada, Australia, and Argentina are all major grain exporters, and recently the EEC became a net exporter as well. The U.S. embargo was not very damaging, because the Soviets were able to substitute grain from other sources for U.S. grain. In addition to this substitution, there is evidence that some U.S. grain was shipped to third countries and reexported to the USSR.

The Export Administration Act of 1979 authorizes the president to restrain exports to Communist countries by requiring licenses. The licenses are administered by the Commerce Department's Bureau of East-West Trade and the Defense Department. The act was used to justify the embargo following the Soviet invasion of Afghanistan. An embargo is likely to be more effective if all buyers and sellers participate, since this arrangement would deny the victim the gains from trade. However, it is difficult to get full participation because no single government has an incentive to spend much on enforcement. The United Nations asked its members to cease all trade with Rhodesia (now Zimbabwe) from 1970 to 1980, but the apparent damage to the Rhodesian economy was minimal.

Quotas are also employed in bilateral trade agreements between governments. The United States and the USSR had a five-year trade agreement on grain (1977–1981 and renewed in 1983) that specified a permissible range for Soviet imports. The Soviets were required to buy a minimum quantity and prevented from buying more than a specified maximum without the permission of the U.S. secretary of Agriculture. The secretary was supposed to base his decision on domestic market conditions. In the case of 1980–1981 embargo, the United States had a bumper crop of grain, and the secretary had approved more exports than the maximum that was automatically permitted by the treaty. What the embargo did was to cancel this discretionary amount without violating the terms of the treaty. The United States has also signed bilateral grain agreements with China and Mexico. Argentina and the USSR signed a five-year agreement following the U.S. embargo.

Whether these agreements have any effect on the signatory countries depends on whether the volume of trade in absence of the agreements would have been different from the amount specified in the agreement. If not, they are a kind of nonbinding quota. They may provide some security to the two parties, although agreements are not always adhered to. They are analogous to long-term contracts between private firms. If the agreements are binding, they will change the pattern of world trade. Suppose that there is a small grain crop and that the agreements cause the United States to export more to the USSR, China, and Mexico and less to other countries than they would have. Since the world as a whole must adjust to the smaller crop, countries not covered by agreements must do more of the adjusting to the new conditions. Thus, bilateral agreements stabilize the volume of trade for countries covered, but they destabilize trade for other countries. Because countries not covered by agreements would be unable to buy as much grain as they otherwise would, prices would be pushed higher to eliminate excess demand. Thus, if bilateral agreements are binding, they destabilize quantities and prices for nonparticipants.

8.6 MINIMUM IMPORT PRICE

The United States has limited steel imports through the use of a so-called "trigger price mechanism." The mechanism specified a minimum price that foreign suppliers could charge for steel. The minimum price was supposed to be calculated by the Treasury Department based on the cost of producing steel in Japan, the lowest-cost producer. The effect of the policy can be shown in Figure 8-3.

FIGURE 8-3   Effect of a Minimum Import Price

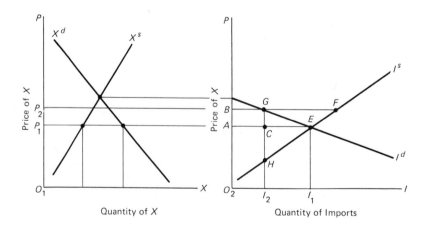

Let I^s be the competitive import supply curve. The policy is binding only if the legal minimum price is above the competitive import price O_2A. Let the trigger price be $O_2B > O_2A$. At the trigger price there is an excess supply of GF of the imported product. Since some sellers can not sell all they offer, some rationing scheme, such as first come, first served, must be followed. Those firms who succeed in selling receive AB per unit more than they would have, and the total transfer to these foreign firms is the area $ABGC$. The minimum import price has the same effect on prices and quantities as does a tariff of GH per unit or an import quota O_2I_2. However, the counterpart of the tariff revenue and the quota profit is appropriated by foreign suppliers.

A discriminatory procurement policy by the home government would have a similar effect. Suppose that with a nondiscriminatory purchasing policy domestic firms could not compete with imports at the price O_2A. If government agencies were instructed to buy domestic products that were offered for O_2B even though imports were available for less, this policy would be equivalent to an implicit tariff of GH. Discriminatory procurement policy would result in additional revenue of $BAGC$ for domestic firms, which would have accrued to the government in the case of a tariff.

8.7 THE EFFECT OF A QUOTA
WHEN SUPPLY
AND DEMAND
CONDITIONS CHANGE

It has been shown that for each tariff there exists an equivalent quota that results in the same price and volume of imports. Whether the equivalent of the tariff revenue goes to domestic importers, foreign exporters, or the government depends on how the quota is administered. Importers receive the revenue if licenses are given to them. The government appropriates the revenue if licenses are auctioned to the highest bidder, and foreign exporters receive it if they collude on price. Another difference between tariffs and quotas is the response of imports and prices to shifts in supply and demand.

Consider the effect an increase in import demand caused by either an increase in domestic demand or a decrease in domestic supply. This disturbance is represented in Figure 8-4 by a rightward shift in import demand from I_1^d to I_2^d. The cause of this change is a rightward shift in X^d or a leftward shift of X^s, which are not shown. With free trade the equilibrium is at point E, the intersection of I_1^s and I_1^d. The foreign and domestic prices are O_1P_1 and imports are O_1I_1. A tariff of P_1P_2 or an import quota of O_1I_2 would move the equilibrium of F where the domestic price is O_1P_2 (the foreign price would remain an O_1P_1) and the volume of imports would decline to O_1I_2.

From the equilibrium at point F, consider the effect of an increase in import demand in the two cases (1) with a tariff and (2) with an import quota.

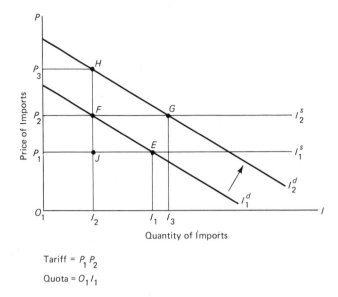

Tariff = $P_1 P_2$

Quota = $O_1 I_1$

FIGURE 8-4   Change in Import Demand with Tariff and Quota

In the tariff case the new equilibrium is at G where the price is O_1P_2 and volume of imports is O_1I_3. The increase in import demand has been satisfied by an increase in the quantity of imports (I_1I_3) without any change in import volume. Conversely, in the case of a quota of O_1I_2, the new equilibrium following a shift in import demand is point H. Here the price increases from P_2 to P_3 with no change in import volume. Indeed, the main feature of the quota is that imports cannot increase no matter what happens to supply or demand.

It follows that all adjustments to disturbances must take the form of price changes. With an import quota, there is no limit to the divergence between domestic and foreign prices. However, with a tariff, both prices and quantities change in response to supply and demand disturbances. Trade continues to be a link between domestic and foreign prices, and the domestic price cannot exceed the foreign price by more than the tariff $(P - P^\star = t)$. Therefore, the differential response to changes in import demand is an important difference between tariff and quotas. The same general conclusion holds for the case where the importer is a large country. The only difference is that foreign prices also rise, whereas domestic prices and imports do not rise as much.

The response to a shift in import supply is also different. In Figure 8-5, the free trade equilibrium is at point E. Either a tariff of FH or an import quota of O_1I_2 will move the equilibrium to point F, where the price is O_1P_2 and the import volume is O_1I_2. Now let import supply conditions change so that import supply including the tariff is I_3^s. This shift might have been caused by a large crop or technical change. With a tariff the price will fall to O_1P_3, and imports will increase to O_1I_3. Domestic consumers will benefit from the more favorable world supply conditions. With a quota, the import volume re-

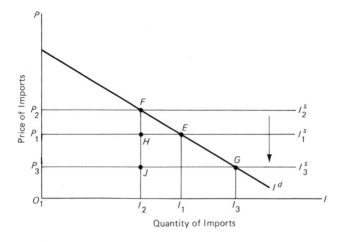

FIGURE 8-5   Change in Import Supply with Tariff and Quota

mains at O_1I_2, the foreign price falls to O_1P_3, and the domestic price remains at P_2. Just as with the shift in import demand, the quota keeps quantity constant and forces all the adjustment onto price. Even if foreign suppliers offered to give the product away, the volume of imports would not increase.

The relationship between tariffs and quotas can be generalized to show the effect of foreign and domestic disturbances on the domestic economy. A tariff permits the quantity of imports to vary, but an import quota does not. Consider the effects of a foreign disturbance to supply and demand compared with a domestic disturbance. Let the domestic disturbance be a decrease in X^s that shifts I^d to the right. This situation is shown in Figure 8-6. The price

FIGURE 8-6   Trade and Domestic Disturbance

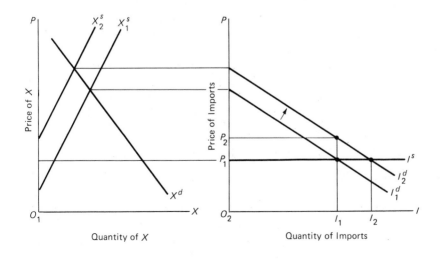

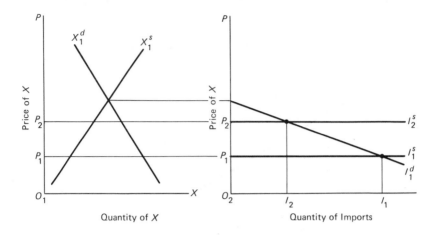

FIGURE 8-7   Trade and Foreign Disturbance

remains at O_2P_1 and import volume increases to O_2I_2. The variability of imports completely stabilizes the price in spite of the decrease in domestic supply. In this case, international trade acts as a buffer to cushion the effect of a domestic disturbance on price. Alternatively, if the volume of imports were fixed at OI_1 by a quota, the same domestic disturbance would have increased the price to P_2.

Conversely, let the source of the disturbance be foreign. Perhaps there is a decrease in the size of the foreign crop. This situation is shown in Figure 8-7. as a shift of import supply from I_1^s to I_2^s. The price will increase from P_1 to P_2 and the volume of imports will decrease from O_2I_1 to O_2I_2. In this case, prices will change in the home economy even though no disturbances have occurred there.

When disturbances originate abroad, international trade tends to destabilize domestic prices. For example, since 1970 average grain imports of the USSR have been large and imports have been highly variable. Because the main source of variability is the fluctuating size of the domestic crop, international trade has a stabilizing effect on grain consumption in the Soviet Union. Conversely, the United States is the main exporter, and disturbances in the USSR tend to destabilize prices in the United States. The U.S.-USSR bilateral grain agreement is an attempt to promote stability in the trade relationship.

8.8 VARIABLE LEVY

A variable import levy has some of the properties of an import quota. In particular, a variable levy causes import demand to be perfectly inelastic with respect to the world price. A quota possesses this property, but a fixed tariff

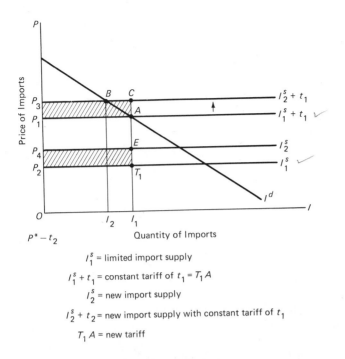

I_1^s = limited import supply

$I_1^s + t_1$ = constant tariff of $t_1 = T_1 A$

I_2^s = new import supply

$I_2^s + t_2$ = new import supply with constant tariff of t_1

$T_1 A$ = new tariff

FIGURE 8-8 **Variable Levy for Small Country**

does not. The case of a variable levy for a small country is shown in Figure 8-8. Let I_1^s represent import supply and, with a constant tariff of t_1, import supply becomes $I_1^s + t_1$. Equilibrium is at A with domestic price OP_1, foreign price OP_2, tariff of AT_1, and import volume OI_1. Let there be an increase in foreign cost that shifts supply from I_1^s to I_2^s. Foreign suppliers will now require a price of OP_4 per unit. If the tariff remained constant, the new tariff-inclusive import supply curve would be $I_2^s + t_1$. The equilibrium would be at B with domestic price OP_3, foreign price OP_4, and imports OI_2. Because the foreign price increase (P_2P_4) is passed onto domestic consumers (P_1P_3), the volume of imports declines by I_1I_2.

Alternatively, a variable levy is designed to keep the domestic price constant at OP_1. Thus, the upward shift of I^s (ET_1) must be offset by a lower tariff (CA). The new equilibrium with the variable levy is at A with a domestic price of OP_1 and import volume of OI_1. The cost increase does not change the domestic price or import volume, because the foreign price increase is exactly offset by the tariff decrease. The extra revenue of foreign suppliers $(P_2P_4ET_1)$ is equal to the tariff revenue reduction (P_1P_3CA). The home government has paid for the entire cost increase out of tariff revenue. This tariff policy provides an incentive for foreign suppliers to conspire to raise their price in the absence of a cost increase. With the variable levy the effective import demand curve becomes the vertical line $CAET_1$ instead of I^d.

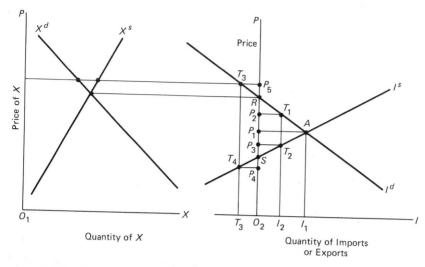

FIGURE 8-9   Transforming an Importer into an Exporter

In this respect, the variable levy is equivalent to an import quota. It stabilizes the volume of imports and insulates the home economy from foreign disturbances. Conversely, it forces the rest of the world economy to bear a larger share of adjustment to disturbances. Even though world supply is smaller in this case, the failure of the home economy to reduce imports forces other countries to reduce consumption by more than they would have with a constant tariff. The reader can show that in the large-country case, a variable levy causes a foreign supply decrease to result in a larger foreign price increase than would occur with a constant tariff.

If an importing country raises its tariff high enough, it can become an exporter. The EEC has done this with grain in the last few years. In Figure 8-9 equilibrium with free trade is at point A. A tariff of T_1T_2 raises the domestic price to O_2P_2 and lowers the foreign price to O_2P_3. If the tariff is raised to RS, all imports cease. If a subsidy of T_3T_4 is paid to domestic firms for exporting X, the country becomes a net exporter of O_2I_3 units (i.e., negative importer). Because of the subsidy policy, the world price falls to O_2P_4. Such a policy is naturally resented by producers in other exporting countries. In the case of grain, the United States, Canada, and Australia have protested the EEC policy.

8.9 EXPORT QUOTA

The effects of an export quota are similar to those of an import quota. An export quota is a rule limiting total exports of a product to a specified amount per period. The effects are shown in Figure 8-10. With free trade, the equilib-

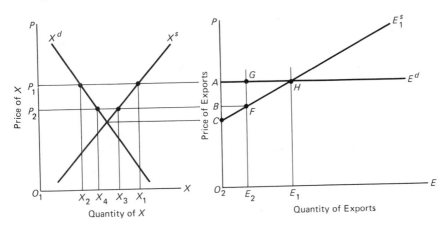

FIGURE 8-10   Effect of an Export Quota

rium is at H, where the foreign and domestic prices are O_2A and export volume is O_2E_1. If an export quota of $O_2E_2 = AG$ is imposed, the excess supply of exports (GH) will cause the domestic price to fall to O_2B. Since the home country is assumed to be small (E^d is horizontal), there is no effect on the world price. The decrease in the domestic price causes an increase in consumption (from O_1X_2 to O_1X_4) and a decrease in production (from O_1X_1 to O_1X_3). Since the foreign price is above the domestic price, any firm that is permitted to export can earn a pure profit or economic rent. The rent is AB per unit or a total of $BAGF$. The government could capture this area by requiring export licenses and auctioning them to the highest bidder. An export tax of AB per unit would also yield this revenue and have the same effect on prices and export volume. A difference between an export tax and a quota is that the export supply curve becomes perfectly inelastic at point F with a quota. With a tax, shifts in export supply or demand will increase export volume, but an export quota prevents an increase. An embargo is a kind of export quota, and a complete embargo is a quota of zero.

Perhaps the two most common justifications offered for quotas are (1) political considerations and (2) lower domestic prices. As a political device, quotas are considered to be a way of influencing foreign governments without resort to military action.[6] The United States imposed embargoes against Cuba, Rhodesia, the USSR, Poland, and Iran. Congress imposed an embargo against arms sales to Turkey (1974–1978) following the invasion of Cyprus. Occasionally, the International Longshoremen's Association has imposed its own embargo. However, its 17-month embargo of the USSR, which began in January 1980, was declared illegal by the Supreme Court.

<hr />

[6] Donald Losman has done an extensive study of embargoes, including that on the Rhodesian case. See Donald Losman, *International Economic Sanctions: The Cases of Cuba, Israel, and Rhodesia.* Albuquerque: University of New Mexico Press, 1979.

The problem with political embargoes is that foreign buyers have access to alternative suppliers and the home country gives up some gains from trade. With respect to the lower prices caused by the quota, domestic consumers benefit and domestic producers lose. Furthermore, the money value of the producer loss (area *BAHF* in Figure 8-10) exceeds the money value of the consumer gain *(BAGF)*. In recent years, the U.S. shoe industry has asked the government to limit exports of animal hides, and owners of sawmills have asked for restrictions on log exports to Japan. In both cases the petitioners argued that exports were causing domestic shortages. A final justification offered is that export quotas are a way for a nation's exporters to assert monopoly power. This issue is considered in Chapter 10.

8.10 PREFERENTIAL TRADE

The most favored nation principle of GATT prescribes a uniform tariff structure for all member countries. However, GATT authorizes discrimination in favor of certain trading partners when the countries are members of a customs union. A customs union is an agreement to eliminate tariffs among member countries and to erect a common external tariff. A free trade area consists of free trade among members, but each member country can impose its own tariff against nonmembers. The European Economic Community is the most important contemporary customs union. The original six members were West Germany, France, Italy, Belgium, The Netherlands, and Luxembourg. The United Kingdom, Denmark, and Ireland joined in 1973, and Greece became the tenth member in 1981. Spain and Portugal have applied for membership. The idea of a united Europe is very old, but concrete plans for economic integration began following the destruction of World War II.[7]

U.S. Secretary of State George Marshall's plan to aid European recovery led to the establishment of the Organization for European Economic Cooperation (OEEC) in 1948. The joint administration of Marshall Plan aid was the initial purpose of OEEC, which evolved into the Organization of Economic Cooperation and Development (OECD) located in Paris. The American agency that administered the Marshall Plan evolved into the Agency for International Development (AID). The European Coal and Steel Community was founded in 1951 with Jean Monnet as its first president. In 1957 the Treaty of Rome established the European Economic Community with six initial members. The elimination of internal tariffs and the erection of a common external tariff proceeded in stages that ended in 1968. Common agricultural policy regulations did not begin until 1962. In addition to trade between member states, the EEC

[7] For a detailed history of economic integration, see Fritz Machlup, *A History of Thought on Economic Integration* (New York: Columbia University Press, 1977).

has had preferential arrangements with other European countries, a large number of African countries, and most countries in the Mediterranean Basin. Before the enlargement of the EEC in 1973, the 18 former African colonies of France and Belgium retained the tariff preferences they had in colonial days. This arrangement was superseded by an agreement signed at Lomé, Togo, in 1975 (Lomé Convention) between the EEC and 50 low-income countries. The latter group included the 18 previous countries plus some British Commonwealth countries from Africa, the Caribbean, and the Pacific. The Lomé Convention was renewed in 1981. Thus, the European Economic Community is a large economic unit that is responsible for a substantial volume of preferential trade. Economic integration in the EEC has gone beyond tariff policy. Taxes have been standardized, there is free movement of capital and labor between member countries, there is an ambitious plan for monetary union, and in 1979 member states elected the first European Parliament.

The European Free Trade Area (EFTA) consists of seven countries: Austria, Switzerland, Norway, Sweden, Finland, Iceland, and Portugal. It began in 1959 as a group of countries that sought economic cooperation but would not accept the conditions of the EEC. The original group included the United Kingdom and Denmark. An industrial free trade agreement with the EEC in 1973 has encouraged trade between the two groups of countries. EEC exports to and imports from EFTA countries in 1981 were greater than EEC trade with either the United States or Japan. Thus, EFTA and EEC together comprise an industrial free trade zone that includes more than 300 million Europeans.

Other contemporary preferential trading arrangements have been less successful. The Council for Mutual Economic Assistance (CMEA or COMECON) is a group of Eastern European centrally planned countries.[8] Trade expansion has been hampered by inconvertible currencies, which has required countries to balance their bilateral trade. Preferential trading arrangements for East Africa, West Africa, Central America, and South America (Latin American Free Trade Area) were all proposed but never implemented. The five-nation Andean Common Market is still attempting to implement a plan for a free trade area, although several members are behind schedule in reducing tariffs against member countries. The original members, Colombia, Ecuador, Peru, Bolivia, and Chile, signed an agreement in 1969. Venezuela joined in 1974 and Chile dropped out in 1976. Australia and New Zealand proposed a free trade area in 1966. In 1982 they agreed to phase out all tariffs between them within five years. The U.S. Trade Agreements Act of 1979 called for investigating the possibilities of a North American common market. However, the governments of both Canada and Mexico quickly opposed the idea. There are many historical examples of preferential trade, such as the British Commonwealth and the German Zollverein. Modern nation-states can be thought of as customs unions that evolved from independent regional economic and political units.

[8] The members of CMEA are the USSR, Bulgaria, Czechoslovakia, Poland, Romania, Mongolia, and Cuba.

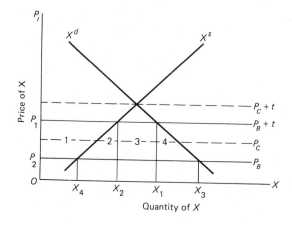

FIGURE 8-11   Customs Union and Trade Creation

When a customs union induces a country to substitute a low-cost supplier for a high-cost supplier, the result is called trade creation. The substitution of a high-cost supplier for a previously low-cost supplier is called trade diversion. These effects can be seen in Figure 8-11. Let B and C be trading partners of the home country.

B supplies the product at a lower price than country C would $(P_B < P_C)$. If the home country imposed a uniform tariff, B would again supply the home country. At the price $P_B + t$ the home country would consume OX_1, produce OX_2, and import X_1X_2 from B. Area 3 represents tariff revenue. The formation of a customs union between the home country and B (the low-cost supplier) means that the tariff against country B's goods becomes zero, whereas the tariff against the nonmember (C) remains at t per unit. The price of imports from B to the home country falls from $P_B + t$ to P_B, consumption rises to OX_3, domestic production falls to OX_4, and imports rise to X_3X_4. There is a net gain to home residents equal to the areas $2 + 4$. In addition, there is a transfer from the government to consumers (area 3) and from domestic producers to consumers (area 1). The source of the gain is that lower-cost production in B has displaced high-cost production in the home country. The gains from trade creation are simply the gains from freer trade.

The opposite case of trade diversion is shown in Figure 8-12. The difference is that the home country forms a customs union with country C, the higher-cost producer of imports. With a uniform tariff, the price would be $P_1 = P_B + t$ and B would be the source of imports. Home consumption, production, and imports would be OX_1, OX_2, and X_1X_2, respectively. When a customs union is formed with C, the price falls to $P_2 = P_C$. C becomes the supplier of imports, because it is the lower-cost source net of the discriminatory tariff, even though production costs are higher in C than in B. Home consumption rises to OX_3, production falls to OX_4, and imports rise to X_3X_4.

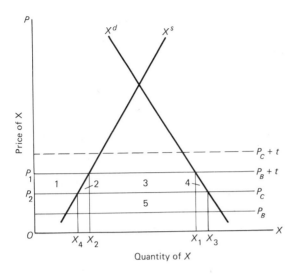

FIGURE 8-12   Trade Diversion

There are some trade creation gains equal to areas $2+4$. These gains are the result of some higher-cost home production being displaced by lower-cost production in partner country C. However, there is also a trade diversion loss equal to area 5, because higher-cost imports from C have displaced lower-cost imports from B. With the uniform tariff, areas $3+5$ were tariff revenue for the home country. With the trade-diverting customs union, area 3 remains tariff revenue, but area 5 becomes a payment to higher-cost producers in C, which was previously unnecessary. The net gain from the trade-diverting customs union is areas $2+4$ minus area 5, which could be either positive or negative. An example of trade diversion is the substitution of higher-cost French grain for lower-cost American grain in the United Kingdom after the United Kingdom joined the EEC.

Although formation of a customs union can either increase or decrease national welfare, some general statements can be made about customs unions. A net loss from a trade-diverting customs union is more likely (1) the less elastic are domestic supply and demand and (2) the larger the difference between the prices in countries B and C. In general, if the customs union includes the lowest-cost producer in the world, there can be no trade diversion. If no member produced the product before or after the creation of the customs union, there can be no trade diversion. If all members produced the product before the customs union, trade creation is likely, since some high-cost production will be reduced. If few members produced the product before the customs union and some imported from nonmembers, then trade diversion is likely. If trade between members was a large percentage of total trade prior to the union, trade diversion is less likely. In the case of the EEC, empirical studies indicate that trade creation has apparently exceeded trade diversion, and the largest single diversion has come from agriculture.

Another effect of a customs union is the development of "tariff factories." The term refers to the location of plants within the customs union that would not have been located there without the union. For example, in the absence of a customs union, a firm in the United States might export a product to France. The firm would face the same French tariff as a German firm. However, with the EEC a firm exporting from the United States is subject to the French tariff, but a German firm is not. To offset the disadvantage created by the customs union, the American firm might locate a plant somewhere inside the EEC. Such a "tariff factory" would be profitable if the saving from avoiding the tariff exceeds the additional cost of locating abroad. U.S. investment in Ireland increased after Ireland joined the Community in 1973. Thus, a tariff tends to encourage international factor mobility. Since international trade and factor mobility are substitutes, restricting trade encourages factor mobility.

8.11 TARIFF PREFERENCES FOR LOW-INCOME COUNTRIES

A customs union is the main exception to the GATT principle of nondiscriminatory tariffs. A second exception is tariff preferences for low-income countries known as the Generalized System of Preferences (GSP). Tariff preferences were proposed by the United Nations Conference on Trade and Development as a form of aid to low-income countries. Most members of OECD implemented preferences in the 1970s. The European Economic Community introduced preferences for 91 low-income countries in 1971, and U.S. preferences began in 1976. The system consists of a lower tariff against a list of eligible products coming from specified low-income countries. In the United States and Europe, a set of import-sensitive products, such as textiles, was eliminated from consideration. The U.S. Congress also made OPEC countries ineligible for tariff preferences.

The analysis of tariff preferences is the same as for a customs union except that the exporting countries do not reciprocate. The case of trade-diverting tariff preferences is shown in Figure 8-13. Let P_H be the price offered by a high-income supplier and P_L be the price offered by a low-income supplier. When a uniform tariff exists against all import suppliers, the domestic price will be P_1. With tariff preferences for the low-income country, the price will fall to P_2. Imports from the low-income country will replace those from the high-income country, and total imports rise from X_1X_2 to X_3X_4. The increase in total import causes trade creation gain (areas $2+4$), but the switch to a higher-cost supplier is a trade-diverting loss (area 5). The net effect on domestic welfare depends on these relative magnitudes.

Tariff preferences give rise to incentives for (1) capital mobility and (2)

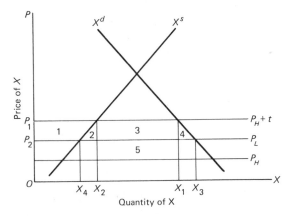

FIGURE 8-13   Tariff Preferences and Trade Diversion

collusion by exporters. The preferences are based on the country in which the product is produced, not the nationality of the firm's owners. Thus, a firm in a high-income country has an incentive to make a direct investment in a low-income country and export from that plant with the benefit of preferences. This is an example of a tariff factory. Collusion is profitable because exporters from high-income countries cannot compete at a price below $P_H + t$.

Suppose that $P_H + t = \$5 + \$5 = \$10$ and that $P_L = \$8$. Competition by low-income exporters would lead to a price of $8, but if they collude and sell for $9.99, they will retain the market and also earn a rent of $9.99 - \$8.00 = \$1.99$. An alternative to collusive pricing would be an export tax of $1.99 by all LDCs. The problem with either of these schemes is that if the importing country notices them, tariff preferences can be revoked.

An alternative to tariff preferences is nondiscriminatory tariff reduction in which low-income countries reciprocate. There is evidence that the attempt to substitute high-cost domestic production for low-cost imports has been a major barrier to economic development in the post–World War II period. (See Chapter 13.) Another alternative is for low-income countries to reduce export taxes. At least one study shows that export taxes levied by low-income countries reduce their trade by more than tariff preferences increase their trade.[9]

8.12 INPUT TARIFFS
AND EFFECTIVE RATES
OF PROTECTION

Domestic firms benefit from tariffs on products they produce, but they are harmed by tariffs on imported inputs they purchase. For example, producers of woolen textiles benefit from tariffs on wool textile products, but they are

---

[9] See Stephen S. Golub and J. M. Finger, "The Processing of Primary Commodities: Effects of Developed Country Tariff Escalation and Developing Country Export Taxes," *Journal of Political Economy*, June 1979.

harmed by a tariff on raw wool. It is useful to construct an index that measures the net effect of these two conflicting tariff forces on the domestic output of a product. The effective rate of protection is such an index, and it attempts to measure the net effect on a product's domestic value added of the entire tariff structure. The formula for the effective rate is

$$t_j^E = \frac{t_j^N - a_{ij}t_i}{1 - a_{ij}}$$

where t_j^N is the nominal tariff rate on output j, t_i is the nominal tariff rate on input i, and a_{ij} is the share of the ith input in value added of product j before the tariff. Value added is the value of the final product under free trade minus the value of imported inputs. The effective rate measures the percentage change in domestic value added for the jth product as a result of the tariff structure relative to what it would have been with free trade. Thus, a 50 percent effective tariff rate means that domestic value added for that product was 50 percent higher because of the tariff structure than it would have been with free trade.

Suppose that a desk using $50 of imported wood sells for $100 with free trade. If there is a 20 percent tariff on desks but none on wood, the effective rate of protection on desks is 40 percent:

$$t_j^E = \frac{0.20 - 0.50(0)}{1 - 0.50} = 0.40$$

Because $50 worth of wood is imported, the domestic value added of the desk industry is only $50, and the tariff of $20 is 40 percent of this amount. The domestic activity being protected is desk production rather than wood production. If the tariff is 20 percent on *both* desks and wood, the effective rate on desks is 20 percent:

$$t_j^E = \frac{0.20 - 0.50(0.20)}{0.50} = 0.20$$

If the tariff is 20 percent on wood and zero on desks, the effective rate of protection on desks is -20 percent:

$$t_j^E = \frac{0 - 0.50(0.20)}{0.50} = -0.20$$

A negative rate of effective protection indicates that domestic production of the product is lower with the current tariff structure than it would have been with free trade. In general, if the input and output tariff rates are equal, the nominal tariff rate equals the effective rate. If input rates are higher (lower) than output tariffs, the effective tariff on the output is greater (less) than the nominal rate on the output.

If tariff rates on final products exceed tariff rates on primary products, the relationship is called tariff escalation. Tariff escalation has been observed for many high-income countries, and several observations can be made. (1) Nominal rates tend to be higher for manufactured products than for semimanufactured products, and the latter are higher than for primary products. Magee's 1972 study showed the following effective rates for a sample of developed countries: manufactures 6 percent, semimanufactures 9 percent, and raw materials 10 percent.[10] The effect of tariff escalation is to discourage processing of raw materials in the producing countries. (2) A second observation on tariff structure is that less developed countries encourage import substitution by protecting capital goods production, but this punishes the manufacturing sector, which must pay more for capital goods. Agriculture has also been punished by having to pay more for machinery and fertilizer. (3) As can be seen from the foregoing example, an industry using imported inputs may suffer from negative protection. (4) By *cutting* tariffs on inputs, one can *raise* the average protective rate without changing the tariffs on final products. A current example of an effective rate below the nominal rate is the U.S. auto industry, which is suffering from the higher cost of steel caused by import barriers. Import quotas on inputs lower the effective protection for the final product. Domestic content laws are an example of an input quota. They reduce effective protection for auto assembly, while increasing protection for auto parts.

8.13 TRADE POLICY

In general the cost of a tariff or quota to consumers and producers exceeds the gain to import-competing producers and revenue collected by the government. Two possible exceptions are externalities and monopoly power, which will be discussed in Chapters 9 and 10, respectively. If tariffs impose a net cost on the residents of a country, those groups that are harmed by a tariff lose more than the value of the benefits received by gainers. Thus, the losers should be able to bribe the gainers to accept free trade.

The potential for compensation is shown in Figure 8-14. Let the extreme alternatives be free trade with price P_2 and a prohibitive tariff or quota with price P_1. Let the benefits from those who gain from free trade be $75, which can be represented by the area P_2P_1AB. Let the losses to import-competing producers be $50, which is shown by the area P_2P_1AC. The net gain to the nation of $25 is shown by the area ABC. For example, if the gainers from free trade paid $60 to the losers, everyone would be better off with free trade. After

---

[10] See Stephen Magee, "The Welfare Effects of Restrictions on U.S. Trade," *Brookings Papers on Economic Activity*, 3:1972.

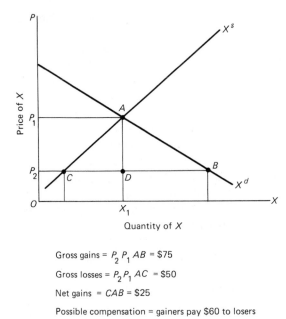

Gross gains = $P_2 P_1 AB$ = $75

Gross losses = $P_2 P_1 AC$ = $50

Net gains = CAB = $25

Possible compensation = gainers pay $60 to losers

Gainers' net gain = $70 − $60 = $15

Losers' net gain = $60 − $50 = $10

FIGURE 8-14   Compensating Those Who Are Harmed by Trade

compensation of $60, the original gainers would be $15 ($75 − $60) richer, and the initial losers would be $10 ($60 − $50) richer than with a tariff or quota. In general, the gainers should be willing to pay any amount less than $75 to retain free trade, and the losers should be willing to accept any amount greater than $50 to tolerate free trade.

Suppose that there are transactions costs associated with arranging compensation. Gainers and losers must be identified, gainers must be persuaded or compelled to participate, and money must be collected and distributed. This process uses real economic resources in addition to the compensation received by losers. If transactions costs are $30, successful compensation is not possible. If either gainers or losers paid the transactions cost, they would experience a net loss from the compensation scheme. Satisfactory compensation is not possible because the net gain to residents of $25 is less than transactions costs of $30.

Transactions costs will vary by product depending on the situations of consumers and producers. For example, the cost of mobilizing consumers harmed by a tariff would be smaller if there were 10 consumers who lost $1 million each than if there were 1 million consumers who lost $10 each. It has been argued that protectionist forces can organize a coalition against free trade at a lower cost if production is geographically concentrated and consumers are geographically separated. A related point is that the House of Representatives, whose members represent small geographical districts, appears to be more protectionist than the Senate. Senators representing individual states are more protectionist than the president, who represents the entire country.

There are two aspects of the distributive effects of trade. One involves redistribution of income between producers and consumers. A second involves redistribution between owners of factors of production. Empirical studies of U.S. commercial policy indicate that tariffs are higher for labor-intensive imports. Both nominal and effective rates of protection are positively related to the labor content of imports, and nontariff barriers are also biased toward labor-intensive imports.

Because trade legislation is passed by Congress and enforced by the executive branch, trade policy is necessarily political. Thus, understanding trade policy requires understanding how economic forces influence political behavior. Congress has played a more active role in formulating foreign economic policy, and the political interests of Congress do not always coincide with those of the president.

Because of these conflicting interests, a coherent foreign economic policy does not always emerge. Policy conflicts often exist between different agencies within the executive branch of the government. For example, the Defense Department and the State Department may favor an aggressive anti-Communist policy that would require restricting exports to the USSR. The Department of Agriculture may favor promising agricultural exports to the USSR to increase farm income. The Commerce Department may also favor promoting exports to improve the balance of trade and increase business profits. Policy conflicts between different political groups help to explain why the government promotes exports some of the time and prohibits exports at other times. At any given time, one government agency may be promoting trade while a different agency is discouraging trade. Inconsistent trade policies often result from these competing domestic political forces.

Analysts interested in the formation of trade policy have found it convenient to represent democracy as a process in which politicians compete for votes. Congress members can be assumed to determine their votes on trade legislation so as to maximize the probability of being elected. Therefore, votes on trade legislation can be influenced by economic interest groups in districts. Since knowledge of trade legislation is not costless to consumers and producers, this information will be acquired only if it is economically important to them. Consumers are affected by many products, but most consumers are not greatly affected by any single product. However, individual producers have a great interest in the products they produce.

Because of this asymmetry, producers are more knowledgeable about trade legislation affecting them than are consumers. The three U.S. firms that produce clothespins have considerable knowledge about the import quota, but few buyers of clothespins are aware that a quota exists. For the same reason, producers are more willing to spend money to influence the government, and it is easier for producers to form and enforce a coalition if the number of firms is small. It follows that oligopolistic industries have some advantage in forming political lobbies. Employees have a great interest in their own jobs. They have an interest in protectionist legislation that protects their jobs, even though the same legislation harms them as consumers. Labor unions are a prominent political institution, and they have become one of the strongest protectionist forces in Washington, D.C. The AFL-CIO once supported free trade, but as the United States became a net importer of industrial products such as steel and automobiles, it adopted a strong protectionist stance.

Robert Baldwin has had some success in explaining congressional voting on trade legislation by applying some of these basic economic ideas.[11] In particular, Congressmembers were found to be more likely to vote for protectionism (1) the larger the percentage of import sensitive industries in their districts and (2) the larger the campaign contribution they received from labor unions. The theory has some obvious and unsurprising implications (e.g., a Congressmember from Detroit will advocate restricting auto imports), but the framework may be useful in explaining some less obvious behavior as well.

A related policy question is whether the owners of capital and labor have common interests or conflicting interests in trade policy. The factor endowments theory of trade implies that a country will export products that employ its abundant factor intensively and import products that use the scarce factor intensively. By increasing the demand for the abundant factor, trade should increase its price and increase the incomes of owners of the abundant factor. Conversely, trade should be detrimental to owners of the scarce factor. This proposition is called the Stolper-Samuelson theorem, and it implies that owners of different factors of production have conflicting interests in trade policy. For example, if capital is the abundant factor, one would expect capital owners to promote free trade and labor to be protectionist.

However, Stephen Magee has produced evidence from particular industries indicating that representatives of capital and labor tend to take the same position on tariffs. For example, auto companies and the United Auto Workers have both pressed for auto import restrictions. The same situation is true in the U.S. steel industry and in textiles. Both labor and capital may be mobile in the long run with earnings that are equal in all uses. However, it may be useful to treat them as quasi-fixed in the short run with earnings differentials between industries. In that case, owners of both labor and capital have an incentive to lobby against imports that would reduce their earnings relative to that of comparable factors outside the import-competing sector.

[11] Robert E. Baldwin, "The Political Economy of Postwar United States Trade Policy," in Robert E. Baldwin and J. David Richardson, eds., *International Trade and Finance: Readings*, 2nd ed., Boston: Little, Brown, 1981.

The effect of trade on employment is an issue of great economic and political interest, and imports do destroy jobs in the import-competing sector. Trade necessarily expands employment in the export sector, but it is not easy to know what industries, skills, and regions will be affected. Workers in the import-competing sector have alternative employment opportunities, but not necessarily at the same wage or in the same town and industry. A well-functioning labor market is essential to receive the full benefits of international trade. However, international trade is not the only source of job turnover. There are daily changes in the general economy (e.g., new products, demographic changes) that affect labor demand far more than international trade. New technology, new machines, and international trade all produce net benefits even though they destroy particular jobs.

Trade policy can affect the distribution of income between producers and consumers and between owners of capital and labor within a country. It can also influence world income and the distribution of income between countries. Thus, the economic welfare of each country depends partly on the economic policies of its neighbors. Because of international interdependency, there is an interest in developing international institutions that resolve trade conflicts in an orderly way. All countries have an incentive to attempt to avoid a costly trade war of the type that occurred during the 1930s. One country can temporarily increase employment in the importable sector by imposing a tariff. However, the policy simultaneously reduces employment in the exportable sector in partner countries. Protectionism invites retaliation, and the net effect of a trade war is to reduce the volume of trade and the gains from trade. The General Agreement on Tariffs and Trade is a forum in which trade disputes may be discussed.

Under current rules GATT is not a court with the power to resolve trade disputes. GATT rules provide guidelines for resolving certain policy disputes, but GATT cannot impose solutions on interested parties. GATT sponsorship of multilateral trade negotiations has proven to be valuable, but the current problem of nontariff barriers does not lend itself so readily to the same kinds of negotiations. Quotas violate the basic principles of GATT, but their importance has grown rapidly. The tendency for countries to seek bilateral solutions to trade disputes violates the principle of nondiscrimination.

Another policy problem is the trend toward imposing political conditions on trade. The United States has increasingly resorted to trade embargoes in an attempt to influence the political and military policy of adversary countries. The attempt by the United States to persuade other countries to participate in embargoes has become an important source of international policy conflict.

The Reagan administration's 1982 embargo against equipment related to the Soviet natural gas pipeline was a dramatic example of policy conflict. The administration attempted to ban exports from the United States and exports from British, French, and German firms that had licensing agreements with the U.S. firm. Each of those governments instructed the firms to send the exports to the USSR according to the contract. This case is part of a broader problem of the extraterritorial application of U.S. law.

Another example occurred during the period when the U.S. prohibited trade with China. The U.S. government advised Canadian affiliates of American firms to avoid trade with China even though the official policy of the Canadian government was to promote Chinese trade. The systematic use of trade sanctions as a tool of foreign policy contrasts sharply to the views of Secretary of State Cordell Hull, who sponsored the Trade Agreements Act of 1934 and its successors: "I have never faltered, and I will never falter, in my belief that enduring peace and the welfare of nations are indissolubly connected with friendliness, fairness, equality, and the maximum practicable degree of freedom in international trade."[12]

SUMMARY

This chapter has analyzed the effects of import quotas. Quantitative restrictions have the same effect on prices and import volume as tariffs, but they have a different effect on revenue. Another difference is that tariffs permit imports to respond to changes in demand and supply, whereas quotas make import volume completely unresponsive. Voluntary export restraints have become a fashionable alternative to mandatory quotas. Other nontariff barriers such as minimum import prices and variable levies resemble quotas by making imports completely unresponsive to foreign prices. The analysis of import quotas is also applicable to export quotas, including the extreme case of an embargo.

The chapter also analyzed the economics of preferential trade. Because preferential trade contains both elements of freer trade and elements of protection, its effect on the income of members depends on the net effects of trade creation and trade diversion. In the case of the European Economic Community, trade creation appears to exceed trade diversion, except for the costly Common Agricultural Policy.

The analysis of tariffs and quotas on final products can be extended to restrictions on imported inputs by using the concept of the effective rate of protection. Because tariffs and quotas alter the distribution of income within and between countries, economic and political aspects of commercial policy are difficult to separate.

REFERENCES

ADAMS, WALTER et. al. *Tariffs, Quotas, and Trade: The Politics of Protectionism.* San Francisco: Institute for Contemporary Studies, 1979.

[12]Cordell Hull, *Economic Barriers to Peace* (New York: Woodrow Wilson Foundation, 1937), p. 14.

BALASSA, BELA, et al. *The Structure of Protection in Developing Countries.* Baltimore: Johns Hopkins University Press, 1971.

———, ed. *European Economic Integration.* Amsterdam: North-Holland, 1975.

BALDWIN, ROBERT E. *Non-Trade Distortions of International Trade.* Washington, D.C.: The Brookings Institution, 1970. A comprehensive study of nontariff barriers.

———. "The Political Economy of Postwar United States Trade Policy." In *International Trade and Finance: Readings,* Robert E. Baldwin and J. David Richardson, eds., 2nd ed. Boston: Little, Brown, 1981.

———, and TRACY MURRAY. "MFN Tariff Reductions and Developing Country Trade Benefits Under the GSP." *Economic Journal,* March 1977.

BERGSTEN, C. F. "On the Non-Equivalence of Import Quotas and 'Voluntary' Export Restraints." In *Toward a New World Trade Policy: The Maidenhead Papers,* C. F. Bergsten, ed. Lexington, Mass.: Heath, 1975.

———, R. O. KEOHANE, and J. S. NYE, JR. "International Economics and Politics: A Framework for Analysis." *International Organization,* Winter 1975.

BROCK, WILLIAM, and STEPHEN P. MAGEE. "The Economics of Special-Interest Politics: The Case of the Tariff." *American Economic Review,* May 1978. A study of the political economy of U.S. tariffs.

CARNOY, MARTIN. "A Welfare Analysis of Latin American Economic Union: Six Industrial Studies." *Journal of Political Economy,* July 1970.

CAVES, RICHARD E. "Economic Models of Political Choice: Canada's Tariff Structure." *Canadian Journal of Economics,* May 1976.

CLARK, DON. "The Protection of Unskilled Labor in the United States Manufacturing Industries: Further Evidence." *Journal of Political Economy,* December 1980. A study showing that U.S. nominal and effective tariff rates are positively related to the unskilled labor content of imports.

CLINE, WILLIAM R., and E. DELGADO, eds. *Economic Integration in Central America.* Washington, D.C.: The Brookings Institution, 1978.

———, N. KAWANABE, T. O. M. KRONSJO, and T. WILLIAMS. *Trade Negotiations in the Tokyo Round.* Washington, D.C.: The Brookings Institution, 1978.

COOPER, RICHARD N. *The Economics of Interdependence: Economic Policy in the Atlantic Community.* New York: McGraw-Hill, 1968.

CURZON, GERARD. *Multilateral Commercial Diplomacy.* London: Michael Joseph, 1965.

———, and VICTORIA CURZON. *Hidden Barriers to International Trade.* London: Trade Policy Research Centre, 1971.

DAM, KENNETH W. *The GATT: Law and International Economic Organization.* Chicago: University of Chicago Press, 1970. A study that considers legal, economic, and historical aspects of the General Agreement on Tariffs and Trade.

DESTLER, I. M. *Making Foreign Economic Policy.* Washington, D.C.: The Brookings Institution, 1980. A political scientist's assessment of the interaction between economic and political forces in the determination of U.S. foreign policy.

FIELEKE, NORMAN S. "Challenge and Response in the Automobile Industry." *New England Economic Review,* July–August 1981.

FINGER, J. M., H. K. HALL, and D. R. NELSON. "The Political Economy of Administered Protection." *American Economic Review,* June 1982. An empirical study of the use of nontariff barriers in the United States.

GOLUB, STEPHEN S., and J. M. FINGER. "The Processing of Primary Commodities: Effects of Developed Country Tariff Escalation and Developing Country Export Taxes." *Journal of Political Economy,* June 1979.

GRUBEL, HERBERT G. "Effective Protection: A Non-Specialist Guide to the Theory, Policy Implications, and Controversies." In *Effective Tariff Protection,* H. G.

Grubel and H. G. Johnson, eds. Geneva: General Agreement on Tariff and Trade, 1971.

GRUNWALD, JOSEPH, M. S. WIONEZEK, and MARTIN CARNOY. *Latin American Integration and U.S. Policy*, Washington, D.C.: The Brookings Institution, 1972.

HEWETT, ED A. "The Pipeline Connection: Issues for the Alliance." *Brookings Review*, Fall 1982. Discusses the use of embargoes in connection with the construction of the Soviet natural gas pipeline.

HUFBAUER, GARY C. *Economic Warfare: Sanctions in Support of National Foreign Policy Goals*. Washington, D.C.: Institute for International Economics, 1983.

JOHNSON, HARRY G. "The Gains from Freer Trade with Europe : An Estimate." *Manchester School of Economic and Social Studies*, September 1958.

JONES, KENT. "The Political Economy of Voluntary Export Restraint Agreements." Paper presented to the Annual Meeting of the Southern Economic Association, Atlanta, November 11, 1982.

KRAUSE, LAWRENCE B. *European Economic Integration and the United States*. Washington, D.C.: The Brookings Institution, 1968.

KRAUSS, MELVYN B., ed. *The Economics of Integration*. London: George Allen and Unwin, 1973.

LOSMAN, DONALD. *International Economic Sanctions: The Cases of Cuba, Israel, and Rhodesia*. Albuquerque: University of New Mexico Press, 1979.

LUTTRELL, CLIFTON R. "The Voluntary Automobile Import Agreement with Japan—More Protectionism." *Review*, Federal Reserve Bank of St. Louis, November 1981.

MACHLUP, FRITZ. *A History of Thought on Economic Integration*. New York: Columbia University Press, 1977. A detailed history of economic thought and experiments with economic integration.

PREEG, ERNEST H. *Traders and Diplomats*. Washington, D.C.: The Brookings Institution, 1970. Study of the Kennedy Round of trade negotiations.

RAY, EDWARD J. "The Determinants of Tariff and Non-Tariff Trade Restrictions in the United States." *Journal of Political Economy*, February 1981. An empirical study of the effect of U.S. tariffs on the commodity composition of U.S. imports.

RICHARDSON, J. DAVID. "Trade Adjustment Assistance Under the United States Trade Act of 1974: An Analytical Examination and Worker Survey." In *Import Competition and Response*, Jagdish Bhagwati, ed. Chicago: University of Chicago Press, 1982.

SAMPSON, GARY, and RICHARD SNAPE. "Effects of EEC's Variable Import Levies." *Journal of Political Economy*, October 1980.

SCHULTZ, GEORGE P., and KENNETH W. DAM. *Economic Policy Beyond the Headlines*. New York: W. W. Norton, 1977. A study of economic policy during the Nixon-Ford administrations.

SWANN, D. *The Economics of the Common Market*, 3rd ed. Baltimore: Penguin, 1975.

TAKACS, W.E. "The Non-equivalence of Tariffs, Import Quotas, and Voluntary Export Restraints." *Journal of International Economics*, February 1978.

VINER, JACOB. *The Customs Union Issue*. New York: Carnegie Endowment for International Peace, 1950. One of the earliest formal analyses of customs unions.

CHAPTER NINE
STATE TRADE
AND INDUSTRIAL POLICY

9.1 INTRODUCTION

Commercial policy consists of the set of policy instruments that directly alters international trade. Thus, tariffs and import quotas are components of commercial policy. Industrial policy is a broader concept that includes all government efforts to encourage certain domestic industries and discourage others. It includes tax policy, subsidies, and nationalization of industries. Because of the interdependence of industries, industrial policy that encourages a domestic industry may indirectly affect international trade. An example is the European Economic Community's attempt to aid its ailing steel industry, which indirectly reduces the demand for imported steel. This chapter will investigate the relationship between industrial policy and international trade.

Government agencies play an important role in all national economies, and state trade is an increasingly important component of international trade. State trade includes both government procurement policy and exports by state enterprises. Trade between Eastern and Western bloc nations is complicated by the frequent imposition of political conditions on trade. The effect of domestic tax policy on trade will be considered. Domestic sales taxes must be adjusted to account for imports and exports.

Since a tariff encourages domestic production and discourages domestic consumption, a set of domestic taxes can be found that will duplicate the effect of a tariff on resource allocation. Specifically, it will be shown that a tariff is equivalent to a tax on consumption plus a subsidy to production. The effect of a domestic production quota on import demand and export supply will also be shown.

Resource allocation may be distorted by the existence of external effects in production or consumption. The effect of externalities on trade will be examined in the context of the infant industry argument. Potential externality problems also exist with respect to the treatment of the oceans as international common property.

9.2 STATE TRADE

In many countries government agencies are directly involved in international trade. In the extreme case of centrally planned economies, government agencies are responsible for carrying out all international trade. It is more common for countries to limit state trade to certain critical products. Agricultural products, especially food, are frequently handled by state trade. In some countries, such as Japan, Mexico, and the Philippines, a government agency is the sole importer of food. In other cases, government marketing boards have been granted the monopoly right to export certain products. For example, Canada and Australia have had wheat marketing boards since the 1930s, and in 1977 and 1978 31 percent of world wheat trade involved state trade. During the colonial period, the British government used marketing boards as a way of taxing West African exports. Peasant producers were required to sell their crop to the marketing board for a fraction of the world price. After independence, the governments of Nigeria and Ghana have found it expedient to retain the boards as a source of revenue.

The excess of the world price over the price paid to domestic producers is a de facto export tax. Even in countries such as the United States, where there is little direct state trade, government procurement policy directly affects imports. As shown in Table 9-1, government expenditures are a large and growing percentage of gross domestic product in most countries.

Since most government agencies are biased toward domestic products, growth of the government sector has the effect of increasing the degree of protectionism in the world. Government agencies are actively involved in the production of goods such as energy, automobiles, steel, banking, and ships. Government agencies also directly influence exports of certain products. Military agencies play an important role in the sale of armaments in exporting countries, such as the United States, USSR, France, West Germany, and the United Kingdom. Political conditions are imposed on many products involved in East-West trade.

Consider the effect of a state agency that imports a product and resells it domestically. The Japan Food Agency usually resells food at a higher price than the import price, which is a policy equivalent to a tariff. Government agencies in low-income countries tend to resell food at a lower domestic price,

TABLE 9-1   Government Expenditures as a
Percentage of Gross Domestic
Product

	1973	1980
Canada	36%	40%
France	39	46
West Germany	41	46
Japan	25	32
The Netherlands	48	60
Sweden	46	63
United Kingdom	41	44
United States	32	33

Source: Bank for International Settlements, *Fifty-first Annual Report,* June 1981, p. 24.

which is equivalent to an import subsidy. The Philippines National Grains Authority and Mexico's CONASUPO have tended to keep food prices artificially low. Egypt's extensive consumption subsidies on flour, sugar, oil, and rice have led to dependence on imported food. Egyptian food subsidies in 1982 were $2.4 billion. For example, the subsidy on bread of $976 million exceeded the total income from the Suez Canal. The cost of the subsidy on corn, oil, and sugar of $497 million exceeded the total income from tourism. There is a general tendency for low-income countries, such as Egypt, to keep food prices artificially low, whereas high-income countries in North America and Western Europe tend to keep food prices artificially high.

Figure 9-1 shows the effect of a state agency in a small country that imports food and resells it at a loss. The horizontal import supply curve indicates

FIGURE 9-1   State Import Agency Resells at a Loss

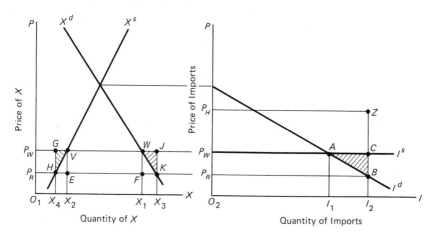

that the importer is a small country. The world price is P_W, and if the domestic price were also P_W, import demand would be $O_2I_1 = X_1X_2$. But if the agency's resale price is $P_R < P_W$, import demand is $O_2I_2 = X_3X_4$. The agency must buy O_2I_2 at the world price to avoid a domestic shortage. The agency's import bill will be $O_2P_WCI_2$, its revenue from reselling at home will be $O_2P_RBI_2$, and its net loss of P_RP_WCB must be financed by the treasury.

The effect of the "cheap food" policy is to increase consumption by X_3X_1, decrease domestic production by X_2X_4, and increase imports by I_2I_1. A common political justification of "cheap food" policy is that it encourages food consumption. However, an unavoidable consequence of depressing prices is to discourage domestic food production. The production cost of the policy is the area HGV, which is the excess of the cost of additional imports (X_4GVX_2) over the cost of producing that additional food at home (X_4HVX_2). There is also a net consumption cost, since the value of the additional food to consumers (X_1WKX_3) is less than the additional cost to the economy (X_1WJX_3). The total welfare cost of this policy is area $ABC = HGV + WJK$, which is the excess of the cost of imports over the national benefits from imports. If the importing country were a large one, the import supply curve would slope upward, and the policy of subsidizing food consumption would increase the world price of food.

Suppose that the world price fluctuates with world supply but that the agency tries to insulate the economy from foreign disturbances by fixing the price at P_R. If the world price rises to O_2P_H, the agency must import O_2I_2 to satisfy the difference between domestic demand O_1X_3 and domestic supply O_1X_4. The agency must lose $P_RP_HZB_2$, and the effective import demand curve becomes the vertical line $ZCBI_2$.

In general, any policy that attempts to insulate the economy by keeping domestic prices rigid in the face of changing foreign prices results in a perfectly inelastic import demand. Such a policy achieves domestic price stability, but only by destabilizing foreign prices. Insulating trade policies for grain were widely pursued outside the United States in the 1973–1974 period, when grain prices experienced their sharpest increase in this century. For example, the Japan Food Agency changed its normal tariff into an import subsidy. The agency bought at the high world price and resold grain at a loss.

A policy of reselling a product for less than the import price is an import subsidy or a negative tariff. The implicit negative tariff rate is determined by the excess of the import price over the domestic price. For example, if the world price is 100 and the domestic resale price is 80, the implicit tariff rate is

$$\frac{P - P^\star}{P^\star} = \frac{80 - 100}{100} = -20\%$$

The "cheap food" policies are examples of implicit negative tariffs. The imposition of a legal maximum domestic price for an importable is another example of a de facto negative tariff. From 1973 to 1981, the U.S. government established a legal maximum price for domestic crude oil. By depressing domestic oil production, the policy constituted an effective negative tariff on oil.

Figure 9-2 shows the effect of a legal maximum price on an importable product. In the absence of price controls, the world price equals the domestic price at P_1. Imports are I_1, the difference between consumption (X_1) and domestic production (X_2). If the maximum price were applied to both imports and domestic production, all imports would cease. At the maximum price P_m quantity demanded is X_1, quantity supplied by domestic firms is X_2, and imports are zero. Import suppliers will divert sales to other markets, where they will receive P_1. There will be a shortage of X_2X_1 in the home country. Alternatively, the legal maximum price may apply only to domestic production. U.S. price controls did not apply to imported oil. Since domestic producers cannot receive more than P_m, domestic supply is the constant amount $O_1X_2 = P_mF$.

For any world price of P_m or above, the domestic supply curve is the vertical line HF. The resulting import demand curve is $CBAI_1$. It coincides with the old import demand curve at prices below P_m, but it is steeper than I_1 at prices above P_m. The source of the greater steepness of import demand above P_m is that domestic supply does not respond to increase in the world price.

FIGURE 9-2   Legal Maximum Domestic Price

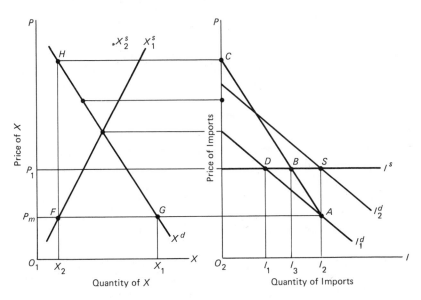

I_1 = unrestricted import demand

I_2 = Import demand with import subsidy of AS

$I_1^d ABC$ = Import demand with maximum domestic producer price

The effect of the minimum price policy is to shift the equilibrium from D to B, which represents an increase in import volume from I_1 to I_3.

In the United States, the stated object of the policy was to prevent domestic producers from obtaining windfall profits as a result of the international price increase. The result of the domestic price control policy was to *increase* the demand for imports and *decrease* the elasticity of import demand. The rightward shift of import demand from I_1 to $CBAI_1$ represents a kind of partial import subsidy. It was a partial subsidy because it lowered the price to domestic producers, but it permitted consumers to pay the world price for imports. A complete import subsidy would have also lowered the consumer price to P_m. It could be accomplished by a government subsidy to consumers of $P_1 P_m$ per unit. In the case of a full import subsidy, the import demand curve would be I_2. Equilibrium would be at S with import volume I_2. If the home country were large, a legal maximum price policy would also cause the terms of trade to deteriorate.

9.3 EAST-WEST TRADE
AND THE CMEA

The greater importance of state trade for the USSR, China, and Eastern European countries has reduced their trade with Western countries. Emphasis on central planning has reduced the importance of international trade for these economies and increased the proportion of trade occurring between CMEA members.

Table 9-2 shows the destination of exports and source of imports for seven Eastern European countries: USSR, Bulgaria, Czechoslovakia, East Germany, Hungary, Poland, and Romania. Bulgaria had the most trade with the USSR (55 percent of exports and imports). Romania experienced a major reduction in its trade with the USSR between 1965 and 1978. Exports to the USSR fell from 40 percent of total exports in 1965 to 18 percent in 1978, and imports from the USSR fell from 38 percent to 16 percent in the same period. For the other countries listed, trade with the USSR was 30 to 40 percent of total trade.

Several factors have reduced the importance of total international trade for these countries. First, the emphasis on central planning has caused leaders of these countries to view foreign trade as an economic disturbance that interferes with planning. Planners do not permit prices to allocate domestic resources, which makes it more difficult to have economic relations with market-oriented economies. The exchange rate between national currencies is an important price for most trading countries, but planners treat it as an arbitrary number. The official value of the ruble is not a price at which the demand for rubles equals the supply of rubles. There is usually an excess supply of rubles at the official price, but holders of surplus rubles are not permitted to sell them legally for goods or for currencies at a lower price.

TABLE 9-2 Trade of Eastern Europe and the USSR by Areas, 1965, 1977, and 1978 (shares in percentages)

	DESTINATION/ORIGIN											
	USSR			EASTERN EUROPE			DEVELOPED MARKET ECONOMIES			DEVELOPING AREAS		
REPORTING COUNTRY	1965	1977	1978	1965	1977	1978	1965	1977	1978	1965	1977	1978
Exports												
Bulgaria	52%	54%	55%	23%	22%	22%	18%	12%	10%	6%	11%	11%
Czechoslovakia	38	34	35	30	34	34	6	23	22	11	8	8
German Democratic Republic*	43	35	39	27	34	32	23	23	22	5	6	6
Hungary	35	36	37	31	30	29	25	24	24	8	9	9
Poland	35	32	34	24	25	24	31	33	33	8	9	8
Romania	40	19	18	24	22	23	27	34	36	7	21	17
Total Eastern Europe	40	34	36	27	29	28	24	25	25	8	10	9
USSR	x	x	x	56	46	48	20	30	28	18	21	21
Total Eastern Europe and the USSR	24	19	20	39	36	37	22	28	26	12	15	15
Imports												
Bulgaria	50	57	55	20	20	19	23	17	20	6	6	6
Czechoslovakia	36	34	35	32	32	32	22	26	26	9	7	5
German Democratic Republic*	43	36	36	25	29	29	26	28	28	5	6	6
Hungary	36	33	35	27	27	26	28	31	31	7	9	7
Poland	31	29	30	30	21	22	27	44	42	9	5	6
Romania	38	19	16	20	23	21	35	38	41	5	16	17
Total Eastern Europe	38	34	34	27	26	25	26	32	32	7	7	7
USSR	x	x	x	58	46	49	23	36	35	14	16	14
Total Eastern Europe and the USSR	23	20	20	40	34	35	25	34	33	10	11	10

*Including trade with the Federal Republic of Germany.

*Source: GATT. International Trade, 1978–79. Geneva, Table A12.

A currency with restrictions on its use is called an inconvertible currency, and the ruble and all the East European currencies are inconvertible. Inconvertibility makes a currency unattractive and hampers the trade of a country. One result of inconvertibility is that countries must achieve bilateral balance in their trade. For example, if Poland is a net exporter to the USSR, it cannot use the resulting rubles to pay for imports from Hungary. Instead, Poland must achieve bilateral balance with the USSR, Hungary, and other countries.

With a convertible currency, these bilateral balances would be irrelevant. This same problem of an excess supply of inconvertible currencies looks like a shortage of "hard" (convertible) currencies from the perspective of Eastern Europe. Several Communist countries have shown interest in achieving convertibility, and Yugoslavia, Romania, and China have joined the International Monetary Fund.

Another barrier to East-West trade is the low quality of Eastern exports, particularly consumer goods. The quality problem is partly a result of a system of rewarding workers on the basis of output quotas, which encourages workers to substitute quantity for quality. Trade is also hampered by restrictions on foreign investment from the West.

The problem of determining the appropriate prices has hampered trade between planned economies as well as with East-West trade. Planners have denied that current market prices are appropriate (because of monopoly power or externalities), but they have not succeeded in providing an agreeable alternative price for their own trade. The compromise adopted is to use some weighted average of past market prices. Naturally, if a market price rises rapidly, as in the case of oil, the compromise price is too low, and there tends to be a shortage of the product in the planned economies. For products with falling prices, there tends to be a surplus. In CMEA trade, countries try to be net buyers of products that are underpriced relative to the world market and net sellers of those that are overpriced, but obviously all countries cannot succeed. When world oil prices rose sharply in 1973 and 1974, the USSR had long-term agreements to sell oil to Eastern Europe at low prices. The agreements were abrogated by the USSR, and prices were increased gradually to the world level.

Politics continues to play an important role in East-West trade. The United States has tried to use "most favored nation status" to reward appropriate political behavior. China received this status in 1981, but the USSR did not. The status provides a nation with a lower tariff for its products and access to subsidized credit from the U.S. Export-Import Bank. In addition, all military and high-technology exports from the United States to Communist countries are licensed by the departments of Commerce or Defense.[1]

---

[1] OECD countries established the Coordinating Committee on Export Controls (COCOM) in 1950. It was designed to coordinate policies concerning exports of strategic products and credit terms with the East. U.S. export controls with the East have been more restrictive than COCOM.

Following the Soviet invasion of Afghanistan in January 1980, export licenses to the USSR became much more difficult to acquire, and some outstanding licenses were revoked. In addition, the United States imposed grain embargoes in 1974 and again in 1980. Exports of equipment related to the construction of the Soviet natural gas pipeline was the subject of an embargo in 1982. The United States has also had long-term embargoes against Cuba, North Korea, and North Vietnam. Politics has also affected international borrowing and lending.

One explanation of the origin of the Eurodollar market is that the USSR wanted to hold dollar accounts, but officials were afraid to hold them in the United States for fear of seizures. London banks were anxious to accommodate them, and the Eurodollar market was born. Competition in granting subsidized export credit to Eastern Europe was the basis of a dispute among Western allies in 1982.

One area of trade in which governments are particularly important is armaments. Government agencies are intimately involved in the production, purchasing, financing, and trade of armaments. To some extent armaments trade follows comparative advantage. The main exporters are high-income countries that tend to have a comparative advantage in other manufactured products (see Table 9-3). The main importers are low-income countries that have a comparative disadvantage in similar manufactured products. For the whole world in 1976, arms trade comprised 1.5 percent of total trade. For low-income countries, arms were 4.5 percent of imports and 0.3 percent of exports. For the group of high-income countries, arms were 2.0 percent of exports but only 0.5

TABLE 9-3   World Armaments Trade, 1976

	AMOUNT (MILLIONS OF DOLLARS)	AS A PERCENTAGE OF TRADE
Exports		
United States	5,206	5%
USSR	3,747	10
France	840	1
West Germany	656	1
United Kingdom	638	1
Imports		
Iran	1,450	10
Israel	947	16
Iraq	765	18
Libya	741	15
East Germany	504	4

Source: U.S. Arms Control and Disarmament Agency, *World Military Expenditures, 1967–76* (Washington, D.C.: USACDA, 1978) table VI, pp. 120–56.

percent of imports. However, politics also plays an important role in arms trade. Production and exports are subsidized, and the largest exporters of armaments for many years have been the United States and the Soviet Union. Only political allies are permitted to buy armaments that embody the latest technology.

Table 9-3 shows arms trade in terms of value and percentage of trade for the five largest exporters and importers in 1976. The United States exported more arms than did the USSR in value, but armaments were a larger percentage of total exports for the USSR. On the import side, oil wealth and Middle Eastern tensions partly explain the appearance of Iran, Libya, Israel, and Iraq. The ranking of arms importers has been more volatile over time than the ranking of arms exporters. In the latter case, the United States and the USSR have consistently been the leading exporters.

9.4 BORDER TAX ADJUSTMENTS AND TAXATION

In addition to state trade, governments influence trade through tax policies. Sales taxes are popular sources of revenue, and their effect on trade may depend on how the domestic tax treats imports and exports. The two general types of border tax adjustment are (1) the origin principle and (2) the destination principle. The origin principle applies the domestic tax to all goods originating in the country, so it taxes exports and exempts imports. The destination principle taxes all goods destined for the country, so it taxes imports and exempts exports. The European Economic Community relies heavily on a value added tax (VAT), which is a kind of sales tax levied on value added at each stage of the production process. The EEC also applies the destination principle, which permits it to rebate the VAT to its exporters. This practice looks like an export subsidy to foreign competitors, and it has provoked many complaints from American firms.

Instead of a value added tax, the U.S. federal government receives most of its revenue from personal and corporate income taxes. The General Agreement on Tariffs and Trade has a rule that permits indirect taxes such as VAT to be rebated to exporters. However, it does not permit direct taxes, such as income taxes, to be rebated.

The GATT rule is based on the questionable proposition that firms are able to shift indirect taxes but not direct taxes. For years American business executives have complained that GATT rules place them at a competitive disadvantage. Their proposal has been either to change the rule or adopt the VAT as the major U.S. tax. However, the possibility of using the tax system to obtain a competitive advantage has diminished with the practice of floating exchange rates. Tax rebates to exporters will be offset by currency appreciation.

If a country employs a VAT and switches from the origin principle to the destination principle, this is equivalent to changing its tariff structure. Switching from origin to destination means taxing imports that were previously untaxed and rebating taxes on exports that were previously taxed. This change is equivalent to raising all tariffs by the amount of the VAT and subsidizing all exports by the same amount. Thus, there are indirect ways of changing tariff rates.

Taxes can be imposed on factor services as well as on products. It has been observed that taxes on capital relative to labor are higher in the United States than in trading partners' countries. This tax policy has reduced the capital intensity of U.S. exports and operated as an implicit export tax.[2]

9.5 TARIFF-EQUIVALENT DOMESTIC TAXES AND SUBSIDIES

International trade is affected by domestic taxes as well as by tariffs and import quotas. The growing practice of using domestic taxes to protect domestic producers from import competition has been called "the new protectionism." A tariff can be thought of as a sales tax from which domestic producers are exempt. One can imagine the government collecting t for each unit of X sold and returning t per unit to domestic producers. Thus, a tariff is equivalent to a sales tax plus a production subsidy on the same product. This relationship is shown in Figure 9-3.

FIGURE 9-3   Tariff Equivalent Domestic Taxes

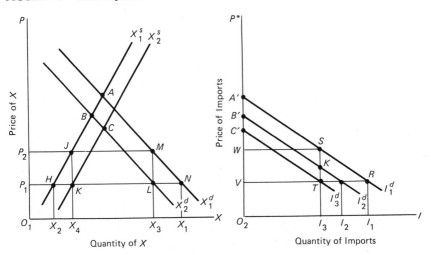

[2] An empirical study of U.S. domestic taxes and trade is John Whalley, "Discriminatory Features of Domestic Factor Tax Systems in a Goods Mobile-Factors Immobile Trade Model: An Empirical General Equilibrium Approach," *Journal of Political Economy*, December 1980.

The equilibrium with no taxes or tariff is at point R where the foreign and domestic prices are O_1P_1. Domestic production is O_1X_2, domestic consumption is O_1X_1, and imports are O_2I_1. Impose a sales tax of $AC = ML$. It can be represented by a downward shift of the demand curve from X_1^d to X_2^d and a downward shift of the import demand curve from I_1^d to I_2^d (by an amount SK). The net price received by producers remains at O_1P_1, and the consumer price rises to O_1P_2. The decrease in quantity demanded (X_1X_3) equals the decrease in imports (I_1I_2).

Now let the government also pay a subsidy of $AC = JK$ per unit to domestic producers. The subsidy causes the supply curve to shift down by $AC = JK$ and the import supply curve to shift down from I_2^d to I_3^d (by KT). Domestic production increases by X_2X_4, and imports fall by I_2I_3. The combined effect of the sales tax of AC and the production subsidy of AC is to reduce consumption by X_1X_3, increase domestic production by X_2X_4, and reduce imports by I_1I_3. A tariff of $ST = AC$ would have exactly the same economic effect. The economic cost of the tax plus subsidy is $HJK + LMN = TSR$, and the cost of the tariff is the same. The difference between the sales tax revenue (P_1P_2ML) and the production subsidy (P_1P_2JK) is equal to the tariff revenue $(VWST)$. In this case, a tariff of ST is equivalent to a sales tax of AC plus a production subsidy of AC.

It is possible to achieve the effects of a tariff by using solely domestic taxes and subsidies. Explicit sales taxes on products are common, but production subsidies are more likely to be implicit rather than explicit payments to firms. An implicit subsidy may take the form of exempting a firm from certain taxes or regulations, providing subsidized credit (e.g., the loan guarantee given to Chrysler Corporation), or compensating losses incurred by nationalized enterprises.

9.6 DOMESTIC PRODUCTION QUOTA AND EXPORT SUPPLY

A large country can improve its terms of trade by restricting exports through an export tax or an export quota. If the demand for exports is inelastic in that region, the effect is to increase export revenue. In Figure 9-4 exports can be restricted from E_1 to E_2 by an export tax of JK per unit or an export quota of O_2E_2. The result is to raise the export price from P_1 to P_2. An indirect way to accomplish this effect is to impose a domestic production quota on product X. A production quota of O_1X_3 will shift the domestic supply curve form X_1^s to X_2^s, shift the export supply curve from E_1^s to E_2^s, and raise the export price to P_3. The new export supply curve E_2^s is steeper than E_1^s, because domestic production cannot respond to higher prices. However, E_2^s is not vertical, because

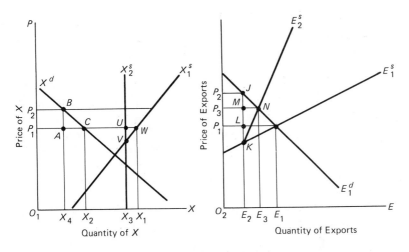

FIGURE 9-4   Domestic Production Quota and Export Supply

domestic consumption decreases at higher prices. Equilibrium with the domestic production quota is at N with price P_3 and export volume E_3.

Notice that the production quota raises both domestic and foreign prices. Conversely, an export quota could increase the foreign price and *decrease* the domestic price. One might expect domestic producers to prefer a production quota to an export quota, whereas domestic consumers would benefit more from an export quota.

An example of a domestic quota with a terms of trade effect is the tobacco allotment system in the United States. Tobacco growers are forbidden from marketing more than the quota assigned to them by the U.S. Department of Agriculture. Since the United States is the major tobacco exporter in the world, the program raises the world tobacco price. The empirical question is whether the program increases the foreign price by more than it decreases export volume. If it does, there will be a gain to the United States, which must be compared with the domestic production and consumption losses. The terms of trade gain is the area P_1P_3ML, which is the product of the price increase caused by the production quota (P_1P_3) times the decrease in export volume (E_2E_1). The domestic cost of the program is the consumption loss (ABC) plus the production loss (VUW). In a 1963 study, Paul R. Johnson found that the terms of trade gain exceeded the domestic loss, so that there was a net national gain.[3] Current figures indicate there is still a national gain even though the U.S. share of world tobacco exports has fallen.

[3]The 1963 results are summarized and current data are presented in Paul R. Johnson and Daniel Norton, "The Social Cost of the Tobacco Program Redux," *American Journal of Agricultural Economics*, February 1983.

9.7 INFANT
INDUSTRY ARGUMENT
AND DOMESTIC EXTERNALITIES

The infant industry argument is one of the oldest attempts to justify a tariff. Alexander Hamilton, the first secretary of the Treasury, employed the argument in his 1791 *Report on Manufactures*. Friedrich List also applied the idea to German industry in the nineteenth century. According to the argument, the newness of a domestic industry may cause costs to be temporarily high. If the infant industry is protected by a temporary tariff, domestic firms may learn how to compete with imports successfully. Thus, the infant industry argument acknowledges a temporary cost from protection, but it promises future benefits in the form of a healthy domestic industry. The test of whether the tariff is justified is whether the present value of future expected benefits exceeds the current costs of protection.

This same test is applicable to all investment problems. If future benefits exceed costs, private firms have an incentive to invest in learning by doing. Nearly all new business firms expect to lose money initially, so borrowing money to survive initial losses is common. If a poorly functioning loan market prevented firms from borrowing to finance profitable investments, the infant industry would not survive to maturity. In that case a tariff might result in more social benefits than costs, but elimination of the loan market distortion would be a superior solution.

A similar problem would arise if the industry's temporarily high costs were caused by poor labor skills. Acquisition of labor skills is a kind of investment in human capital. Workers could pay for the skill acquisition by accepting lower wages during the learning period. A problem could arise if legal minimum wages or labor union rules prevented wages low enough to finance the investment. In this case, skills would not be acquired, costs would not decline, and the infant industry would not grow up. Again a tariff might provide net benefits for the economy, but a superior solution would be to eliminate the labor market distortion at the source. Even if workers were free to accept low wages, the required wages may be below the subsistence level. To maintain a satisfactory standard of living, workers would have to borrow against future higher wages. A poorly functioning loan market could prevent such workers from getting credit. In that case, elimination of the loan market distortion would be superior to imposing a tariff.

In all these cases, a tariff is only a "second best solution" to economic problems. The optimal solution is to eliminate the labor or capital market distortion at its source. The same principle applies to other domestic distortions such as monopoly in product markets (e.g., cartels) or factor markets (e.g., labor unions). Although the infant industry argument is often used to justify tariff protection, there is reason to believe that it is abused. Industries with little potential for growth have been protected. In legitimate infant industries, costs should decline faster than in an average industry. Anne Krueger's study of infant industry protection in Turkey found no evidence that protected industries behaved this way.[4]

An issue related to the infant industry argument is the problem of domestic externalities and trade. That part of production cost that is borne by someone other than the firm producing the product is an external cost. For example, a firm's wage bill and cost of materials are internal or private costs. If the firm also pollutes the neighborhood, this is an external cost. The total cost to society is the sum of private and external cost, and it is called social cost. Society's resources are efficiently allocated when net social benefits from production are at a maximum, and this occurs where marginal social benefits equal marginal social costs. Marginal social cost exceeds marginal social benefit by the amount of external costs.

This relationship is shown in Figure 9-5, where X_1^s is the domestic supply curve, which measures the marginal private cost. X_2^s includes the external cost, and I^s is the import supply curve. The marginal social cost of acquiring X is X_2^s up to point F and the import supply curve at F. Thus, marginal social costs is the kinked curve O_1FGE. The demand curve is X^d, which measures the marginal social benefit. The social optimum is at the domestic output of O_1X_3, where marginal social costs equal marginal social benefit. The price is O_1P_1, consumption is O_1X_1, and imports are $O_2I_2 = X_1X_3$. In the presence of external costs competition will not yield this output. Instead, production will follow the supply curve X_1^s. At the price O_1P_1 production will be O_1X_2 with imports $O_2I_1 = X_1X_2$. Domestic production is excessive because the last unit of X cost JX_2 to produce at home when it could have been imported at a cost of

FIGURE 9-5   External Cost and Imports

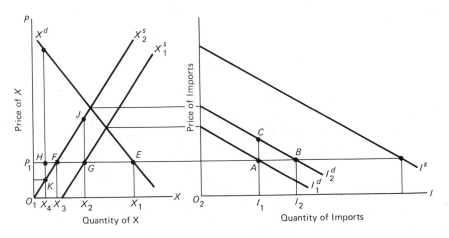

[4] Anne Krueger, "An Empirical Test of the Infant Industry Argument," *American Economic Review*, December 1982.

only GX_2. From society's point of view, it is a mistake, but private firms have no incentive to correct it. The private firms pay only GX_2, and the remaining external cost of JG is borne by someone else.

The welfare cost of this mistake is the area FJG. It measures the excess of domestic cost of X_3X_2 units over the cost of importing them. It would be eliminated if production were restrained to O_1X_3. In that case, imports of I_1I_2 would substitute for home production of X_3X_2. This solution could be achieved by a domestic production tax of JG per unit or a production quota of O_1X_3. Any arrangement that would force producers to bear the external cost of JG would yield the optimal output. However, it is possible for government regulation to discourage domestic production too much.

Suppose that the government imposes a production quota of O_1X_4, which is less than the optimum. The last unit would cost HX_4 to import but only KX_4 to produce at home. Compared with the optimum output O_1X_3, the cost of this mistake is the area KHF. In the diagram, the cost of excessive production in the presence of external cost (FJG) is greater than the cost of restraining production excessively (KHF). However, it is possible to restrain production so much that the cost of a production quota mistake would exceed the cost of tolerating the externality.

Why are some production costs borne directly by firms, whereas other costs are external to the firm? The explanation involves the legal assignment of property rights to factors of production. The law clearly assigns ownership of labor to workers themselves. Therefore, firms cannot employ labor without paying a wage that is acceptable to workers. Workers have a clear incentive to consider the marginal social cost of a particular job, which is the wage they could earn in the next best alternative. If jobs are dangerous, boring, or otherwise distasteful, workers have an incentive to avoid those jobs unless they offer premium pay. However, the law is less clear about who owns other factors of production such as air and water.

Factors lacking clearly defined individual owners are called common property resources. Property rights are important, because they permit people to exclude others from using resources without compensating the owner. If ownership is vague, firms have an incentive to use resources without compensating the owner. Since the implicit price for using resources is zero, they tend to be used excessively. The result is what is commonly called pollution.

One solution to the problem is to assign clear property rights to all resources, particularly air and water. Clear property rights would provide owners an economic incentive and a legal mechanism to transform external costs into private costs. The environmental movement of the 1970s increased the public's awareness of environmental problems. Many laws and regulations were passed in an attempt to remedy the problem. However, externality problems vary by industry, region, and country.

Most environmental regulations are uniform within the United States, but they vary by country. Variability of environmental rules across countries has the same effect on international trade as variability of factor endowments or taxes. More stringent rules increase production costs, increase imports, and decrease exports of the products affected. In the United States, the auto and steel industries have attributed their inability to compete with imports to government regulation. When Chrysler Corporation attempted to justify its loan guarantee request to Congress, it specifically mentioned the adverse effects of government regulation.

There are two kinds of issues concerning the effects of domestic regulation on trade. First are the positive questions of what industries are affected and what are the effects on costs, prices, and quantities. Second are the normative questions about whether a given set of regulations is desirable. One cannot necessarily conclude that regulation is undesirable simply because it increases imports or decreases exports. If regulation reduces external costs, it is desirable to substitute lower-cost imports for higher-cost (including previous external costs) domestic production. The domestic industry will oppose regulation, but there will be a net social benefit. An example of such an improvement would be a movement from O_1X_2 to O_1X_3 in Figure 9-3. However, one cannot conclude without empirical data that actual regulation has been beneficial. If regulation reduces domestic output below O_1X_2, it is suboptimal regulation. Furthermore, it is possible to reduce output so much that the situation is worse than no regulation at all.

9.8 INDUSTRIAL POLICY AND THE NEW PROTECTIONISM

All domestic policies that alter domestic demand and supply of importables and exportables have an indirect effect on international trade. The geometry of this relationship is obvious, since import demand and export supply are derived directly from domestic demand and supply. For example, an increase in the domestic cost of an importable will shift the domestic supply curve to the left and the import demand curve to the right.

It has been shown in Section 9.4 that the effects of a tariff can be accomplished indirectly by combining a production subsidy and a consumption tax. Governments are well aware of this relationship, and they use it in formulating economic policy. The increased use of domestic economic policy to protect industry from foreign competition has been called the "new protectionism." Industrial policy, which includes domestic policy as well as commercial policy, is replacing commercial policy as the primary instrument of protectionism. A protectionist industrial policy is one that uses taxes, subsidies, and regulation to reduce the demand for imports or increase the supply of exports. Production subsidies may take the form of direct money payments to firms, but it is more likely to take the form of preferential tax treatment, subsidized credit, or exemption from onerous regulation. Government enterprises, which are important in many countries, are subsidized by preferential tax treatment and access to credit as well as by direct payments from the treasury. In many cases industrial policy determines international trade policy for that product. In some cases, countries formulate explicit, coherent industrial policies that incorporate international trade. Japan's Ministry of International Trade and Industry (MITI) is often cited as a coordinating institution. In other cases, industrial policy is the result of the uncoordinated lobbying efforts of many individual representatives.

Most high-income countries have pursued domestic agricultural policies that result in prices that are artificially high. Import barriers or export subsidies are necessary to make domestic agricultural products competitive with foreign products. Because of these "high-price" domestic agricultural policies in Western Europe, North America, and Australia, international trade in agricultural products is one of the most heavily protected activities. The United States sought an exemption for agriculture in the GATT code. Import quotas on sugar, meat, and dairy products will not be lifted until Congress is willing to accept lower domestic prices for these products. The European Economic Community's highly protectionist Common Agricultural Policy has been excluded from all the multilateral tariff negotiations. The variable levy will not be abandoned until EEC politicians are willing to subject producers to lower farm prices.

Similar statements can be made about established manufacturing industries in high-income countries. Steel, automobiles, textiles, and shipbuilding have faced increasing competition from imports from low-income countries. Import barriers have been imposed, and they will not be removed until governments are prepared to accept lower prices and less employment in those sectors. Firms in the established sector seeking protection have been described as "senescent" industries. In the case of automobiles, some governments have responded to import competition by nationalizing all or part of the domestic sector. British Leyland, Volkswagen, Renault, and Alfa Romeo are state enterprises. The U.S. government loan guarantee to Chrysler led some observers to wonder whether nationalization would follow. Government activity in the steel industry has been extensive. The United States, which had been a traditional steel exporter, became a net steel importer in 1959. Net imports increased until steel imports were 19 percent of domestic consumption in 1981. EEC producers were the major U.S. supplier in 1959 (71 percent of imports), but the European share declined to 33 percent in 1981. The remaining import shares have been captured by Japan and a set of new exporters that includes Canada, Brazil, Korea, and Taiwan.

The result of import competition has been a series of trade barriers beginning with a voluntary export restraint in 1969. In Europe, governments have subsidized steel in several ways, including nationalization. British steel and other nationalized industries cost British taxpayers $7.5 billion in 1981. The justifi-

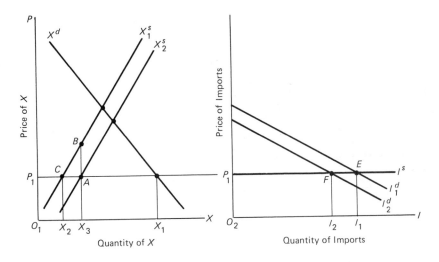

FIGURE 9-6 Production Subsidy and Trade

cation offered for the new protectionism is based on the traditional arguments for protectionism. In addition to the old rationale, Melvyn Krauss has observed that democratic governments have tended to offer new economic rights to their constituents.[5] These new rights include the right to a job in the current occupation, with the current employer, in the current location. If these rights conflict with comparative advantage, international trade will interfere with their realization. Governments have used industrial policy as an indirect means of restricting trade. An obvious and popular solution has been to subsidize an unprofitable firm in the senescent industry.

The effects of a production subsidy are shown in Figure 9-6. The free trade equilibrium is at the price of O_1P_1, where production is O_1X_2, consumption is O_1X_1, and imports are O_2I_1. The domestic supply curve is X_1^s, and the corresponding import demand curve is I_1^d. Let the government subsidize domestic firms by paying them directly or indirectly BA per unit. The subsidy shifts the supply curve to X_2^s and the import demand curve to I_2^d. Domestic firms now receive $X_3A = O_1P_1$ from consumers and BA from the government for a net price of X_3B. Because of this higher net price, production increases from O_1X_2 to O_1X_3 and imports decline to O_2I_2. Because the consumer price remains at O_1P_1, quantity demanded remains at O_1X_1. Without imposing a tariff or import quota, industrial policy has induced the substitution of X_2X_3 units of domestic production for I_1I_2 units of imports.

The policy has a net cost similar to the cost of a tariff or an import quota. The cost of the subsidy is the area CBA. It is the excess of the cost of domestic

[5] Melvin B. Krauss, *The New Protectionism: The Welfare State and International Trade* (New York: New York University Press, 1978).

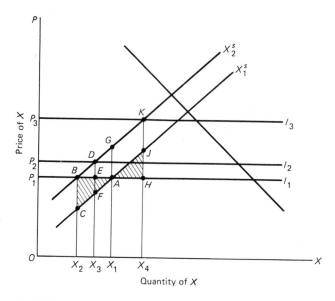

FIGURE 9-7   Domestic Distortions and Second Best

production (X_2CBX_3) over imports (X_2CAX_3). Production subsidies and tariffs are similar in that they both involve a production cost. They differ in that a tariff also has a consumption cost, but a production subsidy does not.

Not all domestic policy is protectionist. Cheap food and cheap oil policies have been offered as examples of implicit negative tariffs. Domestic environmental policies have been offered as examples of implicit production taxes. The effect of a production tax can be shown in Figure 9-7 by shifting X^s to the left and I^d to the right.

9.9 THE THEORY OF SECOND BEST

Barriers to international trade are sometimes offered as a solution to certain domestic economic problems. The main conclusion of the theory of second best is that if several distortions exist in the economy, adding one more distortion such as a tariff might improve welfare. An example might be a domestic industry that is heavily taxed or subject to discriminatory regulations, including tariffs on inputs. Barriers to steel imports raise the price of steel and increase the cost of producing automobiles in the United States. These distortions will result in suboptimal production of automobiles in the United States.

The situation is shown in Figure 9-7, where the domestic supply curve without taxes and regulation is X_1^s and supply with these distortions is X_2^s. The socially optimum output is OX_1, where the marginal cost of importing equals the marginal cost of domestic production (X_1A). With the domestic distortions, output will be OX_2, and the net cost of the distortions is the area CBA. It is the difference between the cost of importing the additional X_2X_1 units (X_2BAX_1) and the cost of producing them at home without the distortions (X_2CAX_1).

A small tariff can increase national welfare by increasing domestic output. A tariff of P_1P_2 will increase output to OX_3, which will reduce the cost of the domestic distortion from CBA to FEA. However, a large tariff will result in a larger cost than the initial distortion. A tariff of P_1P_3 will increase output to OX_4, where the marginal cost of domestic production (X_4J) exceeds the marginal cost of importing (X_4H). The total cost of the tariff distortion (AJH) exceeds the alternative cost of the domestic distortion. The optimal solution is to avoid the tariff and eliminate the domestic distortion directly. In this case, eliminating the domestic distortion would shift supply from X_2^s to X_1^s. With free trade the price would be P_1 and domestic output would be X_1. In general, in the case of multiple distortions, the optimal solution is to correct the problem at its source rather than from a distance.

9.10 INTERNATIONAL COMMON PROPERTY RESOURCES

Externalities present problems within national economies, but the problems are more difficult to resolve when more than one country is involved. The most serious problems involve the establishment of property rights to air and water. Negotiations over the right to use rivers or lakes usually involve a small number of countries (often two). Examples are Mexican-U.S. negotiations over the use of the Colorado River and Canadian-U.S. discussions of "acid rain." However, international discussions of the proper use of the oceans have involved many countries.

Several maritime countries were involved in an agreement to restrict whaling activity, and 158 nations participated in the United Nations Conference on the Law of the Seas (UNCLOS). The conference discussed many topics, including territorial waters and the right of passage through straits, but the most controversial subject was deep-sea mining. The conference adopted the position that the sea bed is a common property resource. In a famous speech in 1967, Ambassador Arvid Pardo of Malta declared that the resources on the ocean floor are the "common heritage of mankind." UNCLOS met from 1974 to 1982, and a treaty was adopted in spite of a negative vote by the United States. Private firms were given limited mining rights in conjunction with a new United Nations' enterprise. It has been known since 1873 that the ocean bed contains nodules of copper, cobalt, manganese, and nickel, but mining did not become economically feasible until the 1960s. Rich concentrations exist in the deep Pacific Ocean between Mexico and Hawaii, and four groups of North American firms have made preparations to begin mining.

The most controversial aspects of the treaty are (1) production quotas imposed on firms and (2) a requirement that the private firms sell their technology to the United Nations' enterprise. In addition the United States would have borne 25 percent of the cost of the United Nations enterprise. The stated purpose of the production quotas is to support present prices of metals and ensure that they are not lowered by output from the sea.

Not surprisingly, the condition imposing quotas was introduced by Canada and other countries where land-based mining is important. Supporters of the treaty described the alternatives as serving the interests of greedy miners versus the good of all mankind. Opponents of the treaty stated the alternatives as raising minerals to the surface for the good of mankind versus keeping them on the sea bed for the protection of land-based mining interests. The presence of so many transacting parties makes negotiation difficult. There is also a serious "free-rider problem" for all international agreements. In the case of the whaling agreement, all interested parties agreed to cease whaling, except for the two major whaling countries, Japan and Norway. The mining agreement will have little significance without the participation of the United States.

The common property resource problem is illustrated in Figure 9-8. It is sometimes called the "fishing problem," but it is applicable to other commonly owned resources as well. The competitive supply curve is X_1^s, when there are no restrictions on fishing. It includes all the private costs of fishing such as boats, fuel, and labor time. If the ocean is owned collectively, the arrangement is equivalent to no one owning it. No single fisherman has an incentive to conserve the stock of fish. If one fisherman reduces his catch in the current pe-

FIGURE 9-8   Common Property Resources

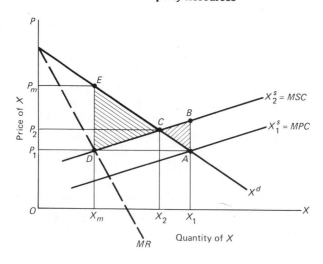

riod, there is no assurance that more fish will be avilable for him in the next
period. However, for the industry as a whole, the larger the catch in the current period, the smaller the stock available in the next period.

The depletion of the stock is a kind of external cost. It is a cost to society
of current fishing, but no single fisherman takes account of it. Therefore, the
marginal social cost curve (X_2^s) lies above the marginal private cost curve, the
difference being the external cost. The socially optimal quantity of fishing occurs at point C, where output is OX_2 and all costs are included in the price
OP_2. However, with no restrictions on fishing the equilibrium is at A, the intersection of the market demand and supply curves. The quantity of fishing
(OX_1) is excessive, and the price (OP_1) is below the optimum. Excessive fishing occurs because fishermen ignore some of the true costs of their activity (BA).
The cost to society of excessive fishing is the area CBA, which is the difference
between the additional social cost of X_1X_2 units (X_2CBX_1) and the additional
social benefits (X_2CAX_1). The socially optimal output could be induced by a
fishing tax of BA per unit, a fishing quota of OX_2, or the assignment of property rights in the ocean. In the last case, the depletion of the stock would reduce the value of the owner's property by an amount BA per unit. This amount
is a private cost to the owner, and he has an incentive to charge an equivalent
fee. Although some tax and some quota will be superior to unlimited fishing,
not all taxes and quotas will be.

Suppose that the government imposes a quota of OX_m instead of OX_1.
Since the marginal social benefit from another unit of fishing (EX_m) exceeds
the marginal social cost (DX_m) at X_m, too little fishing occurs. Here the net
cost to society of too little fishing is the area DEC, which is larger than the
area CBA. In this case, the damage from unlimited fishing is smaller than the
damage from a quota. The amount OX_m is the output that a monopolist would
choose if he had to pay the full social cost of his operation. Conservation is in
the interest of monopolists, but they will not necessarily choose the socially
optimal amount.

SUMMARY

State trading agencies can achieve the effects of tariffs and quotas through
their buying and selling policies. As the relative size of the government sector
increases, state trade acquires a larger role in international trade. Industrial policy
has important indirect effects on trade. Since subsidization of the importable
sector reduces the demand for imports, the policy has foreign as well as domestic economic effects.

Tax policy affects trade in several ways. A domestic sales tax system must
employ either the origin principle or the destination principle to account for
foreign trade. A combination of domestic taxes on production and consumption can be used to achieve the same economic effect of a trade tax. A domestic

production quota alters trade by changing import demand and export supply. Domestic externalities can affect trade, and their existence forms the basis of the traditional infant industry argument for tariff protection.

In the presence of a domestic distortion, a tariff might provide a net social benefit. However, elimination of the domestic distortion at the source would provide a larger net benefit. International common property problems, such as air and water, can be analyzed as externality problems.

REFERENCES

ADAMS, F. GERARD, and LAWRENCE R. KLEIN, eds. *Industrial Policies for Growth and Competitiveness.* Lexington, Mass.: D.C. Heath, 1982.

ALLEN, MARK. "The Structure and Reform of the Exchange and Payments Systems of Some East European Countries." International Monetary Fund *Staff Papers*, November 1976, pp. 718–739.

COOPER, RICHARD N. "The Oceans as a Source of Revenue." In Jagdish Bhagwati, ed., *The New International Economic Order: The North–South Debate.* Cambridge: MIT Press, 1977.

CORDEN, W. M. *Trade Policy and Economic Welfare.* Oxford: Clarendon Press, 1974. A comprehensive discussion of the interaction between domestic economic distortions and international trade.

CRANDALL, ROBERT W. *The U.S. Steel Industry in Recurrent Crisis: Policy Options in a Competitive World.* Washington, D.C.: The Brookings Institution, 1981. A study of the effect of import competition on the U.S. steel industry.

CURZON-PRICE, VICTORIA. *Industrial Policies in the European Community.* New York: St. Martins, 1981.

DIEBOLD, WILLIAM. *Industrial Policy as an International Issue.* New York: McGraw-Hill, 1980.

ECKERT, ROSS D. *The Enclosure of Ocean Resources: Economics and the Law of the Sea.* Stanford, Calif.: Hoover Institution Press, 1979.

FRIESEN, CONNIE. *The Political Economy of East–West Trade.* New York: Praeger, 1976.

GOLDMAN, MARSHALL. *The Enigma of Soviet Petroleum.* London: George Allen and Unwin 1980.

HEWETT, EDWARD A. *Foreign Trade Prices in the Council of Mutual Economic Assistance.* New York: Cambridge University Press, 1974.

HOLZMAN, FRANKLYN D. *International Trade Under Communism.* New York: Basic Books, 1976.

———. "Some Systematic Factors Contributing to the Convertible Currency Shortages of Centrally Planned Economies." *American Economic Review*, May 1979.

JOHNSON, D. GALE. *World Agriculture in Disarray.* London: Macmillan, 1973. A study stressing the relationship between domestic agricultural policy and international trade.

JOHNSON, HARRY G. "Optimal Trade Intervention in the Presence of Domestic Distortions." In *Trade, Growth, and the Balance of Payments*, Robert E. Baldwin, ed. Chicago: Rand McNally, 1965.

JOHNSON, PAUL R., and DANIEL NORTON. "The Social Cost of the Tobacco Program Redux." *American Journal of Agricultural Economics*, February 1983. An empirical study that incorporates the terms of trade effect of domestic production quotas.

KOSTECKI, M. M., ed. *State Trading in Market Economies.* London: Macmillan, 1981.
KRAUSS, MELVYN B. *The New Protectionism: The Welfare State and International Trade.* New York: New York University Press, 1978. Emphasizes the systematic relationship between modern industrial policy and protectionism.
KRUEGER, ANNE O. "An Empirical Test of the Infant Industry Argument." *American Economic Review,* December 1982. A study of Turkish commercial policy that fails to find infant industries growing up.
LAMONT, DOUGLAS F. *Foreign State Enterprises: A Threat to American Business.* New York: Basic Books, 1979.
LINDBECK, ASSAR. "Industrial Policy as an Issue in the Economic Environment." *The World Economy,* Vol. 4, no. 4 (1981).
LIST, FRIEDRICH. *National Systems of Political Economy.* New York: Longmans, Green, 1904. An early statement of the infant industry argument.
MCKINNON, RONALD I. *Money in International Exchange.* New York: Oxford University Press, 1979. Chapter 3 deals with the foreign trade of centrally planned economies.
MULLER, RONALD, and DAVID H. MOORE. "America's Blind Spot: Industrial Policy." *Challenge,* January–February 1982.
POLACHEK, SOLOMON. "Conflict and Trade." *Journal of Conflict Resolution,* March 1980.
RAPP, WILLIAM V. "Japan: Its Industrial Policies and Corporate Behavior." *Columbia Journal of World Business,* Spring 1977.
RENWICK, ROBIN. *Economic Sanctions.* Cambridge, Mass.: Harvard University Press, 1982. An historical study of the effects of sanctions against Germany, Japan, and Italy before World War II and more recent sanctions against Rhodesia and Cuba.
SANDLER, TODD, ed. *The Theory and Structures of International Political Economy.* Boulder, Colo.: Westview Press, 1980. A study of the relationship between international externalities and international institutions.
U.S. ARMS CONTROL AND DISARMAMENT AGENCY. *World Military Expenditures, 1967–76.* Washington, D.C.: USACDA, 1978. A source of data on world armaments production and trade.
VERNON, RAYMOND. "The Fragile Foundations of East–West Trade." *Foreign Affairs,* Summer 1979.
VERNON, RAYMOND, and YAIR AHARONI, eds. *State-Owned Enterprise in the Western Economies.* New York: St. Martins, 1981.
WACHTER, MICHAEL, and SUSAN WACHTER, eds. *Toward a New Industrial Policy.* Philadelphia: University of Pennsylvania Press, 1982.

CHAPTER TEN
TRADE AND MONOPOLY

10.1 INTRODUCTION

The discussion so far has assumed that trade occurs in competitive markets. In a competitive market, each individual buyer and seller is a price taker. Individual firms can increase the quantity sold without lowering the price. Individual buyers can increase purchases without causing prices to rise. Import demand curves and export supply curves of each country represent competitive behavior. The intersection of import demand and supply curves represents international competitive equilibrium.

This chapter will analyze the effect of monopoly on international trade. Monopoly power may exist either on the buying or selling side of the market. If a country's exporters have monopoly power, the price will be inversely related to the volume of exports. Hence, monopolists have an incentive to restrict export volume. Monopoly power on the part of buyers is called monopsony. If importers have monopsony power, the price will be an increasing function of the volume of imports. Hence, a monopsonist can buy at a more favorable price by reducing import volume.

Large countries with monopoly or monopsony power can improve their terms of trade by imposing trade barriers. If the national gain from trading at a more favorable price exceeds the loss from a smaller trade volume, the monopoly country can increase its national income. However, income in the rest of the world necessarily falls by a larger amount. Thus, monopoly is an inefficient form of industrial organization for the world as a whole.

Large-country exporters have the potential to raise national income by levying a "nationally optimal" tariff. The level of the export tax or tariff depends on the amount of monopoly power possessed by the country. The Organization of Petroleum Exporting Countries (OPEC), one of the most successful cartels in history, will be analyzed in connection with world petroleum trade.

Under certain conditions, price discrimination is more profitable for a monopolist than is a uniform price policy. Price discrimination will be analyzed in connection with the practice of dumping. International commodity agreements are an attempt by producer countries to use their collective market power to control the level or variability of their product prices. Experience with commodity agreements in the twentieth century will be analyzed, including the United Nations proposal for an integrated commodity program (ICP).

Monopoly power is sometimes confused with bigness. Firms can be large in terms of sales or assets owned without necessarily having monopoly power in a product market. A conventional measure of monopoly power is the excess of price over marginal cost of production, which depends on the absence of good substitutes for the seller's product. Thus, monopoly power depends on a seller's size relative to firms producing substitute products. It does not depend on size relative to unrelated firms. An example of the relevant size measure is the U.S. oil industry. The major oil companies are commonly referred to as "giants," and in one sense this is an accurate description.

Fortune magazine publishes an annual directory of the 500 largest U.S. industrial corporations. The firms are ranked according to the dollar value of sales and assets, and the 20 largest companies are listed in Table 10-1. The largest firm is Exxon, and 13 of the top 20 are oil companies. When the list is expanded to 50 companies, 20 of the 50 largest corporations are oil companies. Oil producers are giants relative to all other firms, but they cannot be giants relative to each other. More oil companies appear among the next 50 domestic firms, and the list does not include foreign firms. The monopoly power of any individual oil company is limited by the existence of so many rivals. Hence, bigness does not necessarily imply monopoly power.

Large firms tend to appear in certain industries, such as petroleum and automobiles, and where state enterprise is important. Table 10-2 shows the 20 largest industrial firms outside the U.S. according to the *Fortune* directory for 1981. Royal Dutch Shell and British Petroleum are the largest firms, and 7 of the first 8 are in petroleum. Six firms (Fiat, Volkswagenwerk, Daimler-Benz, Nissan, Renault, and Toyota) are in motor vehicles, and 4 (Philips, Siemens, Matsushita, and Hitachi) are in electronics. Many of these firms are at least partly state owned. In a separate list of the largest commercial banks outside the United States, 4 of the largest 5 are French (Caisse Nationale de Crédit Agricole, Banque Nationale de Paris, Credit Lyonnais, and Société Générale), and they have all been nationalized.

State trade can be a source of monopoly power, and it may present legal problems for antitrust policy. U.S. law does not treat state enterprise in the same way as private enterprise. A private lawsuit charging OPEC with violating U.S. antitrust law was dismissed on the grounds that the law did not apply

TABLE 10-1   Largest Industrial Corporations in the United States,
1982 (in billions of dollars)

COMPANY	SALES
Exxon (New York, New York)	$97.2
General Motors (Detroit, Michigan)	60.0
Mobil (New York, New York)	60.0
Texaco (Harrison, New York)	47.0
Ford Motor (Dearborn, Michigan)	37.1
IBM (Armonk, New York)	34.4
Standard Oil of California (San Francisco, California)	34.4
Dupont (E.I.) de Nemours (Wilmington, Delaware)	33.3
Gulf Oil (Pittsburgh, Pennsylvania)	28.4
Standard Oil of Indiana (Chicago, Illinois)	28.1
General Electric (Fairfield, Connecticut)	26.5
Atlantic Richfield (Los Angeles, California)	26.5
Shell Oil (Houston, Texas)	20.1
U.S. Steel (Pittsburgh, Pennsylvania)	18.4
Occidental Petroleum (Los Angeles, California)	18.2
IT&T (New York, New York)	16.0
Phillips Petroleum (Bartlesville, Oklahoma)	16.0
Sun Oil (Radner, Pennsylvania)	15.5
Tenneco (Houston, Texas)	15.2
United Technologies (Hartford, Connecticut)	13.6

Source: Fortune, May 2, 1983.

to government activity. Government enterprise is becoming increasingly important in most countries.

Table 10-3 shows the largest exporting firms in the United States in 1981. The importance of aircraft is apparent as Boeing is first, and General Electric, McDonnell Douglas, and United Technologies are among the top eight exporters. Aircraft sales are heavily influenced by government policy because much of the trade is either military aircraft, purchased by government-owned airlines, or financed by the Export-Import Bank.

The average size of firms in an industry is partly determined by technology. Economies of large-scale production are important for some products and negligible for others. Where economies of scale are important, the industry usually consists of a small number of large firms, each having some monopoly power. An alternative source of monopoly power is collusion among potentially competing firms. Firms have an incentive to collude, and, in the words of Adam Smith,

> People of the same trade rarely meet together, even for merriment and diversion, but the conversation ends in a conspiracy against the public, or in some contrivance to raise prices.[1]

[1] Adam Smith, *The Wealth of Nations* (New York: Random House/Modern Library Edition, 1936).

TABLE 10-2   Largest Industrial Corporations Outside the United States, 1981
(in billions of dollars)

COMPANY	COUNTRY	INDUSTRY	SALES
Royal Dutch Shell	Netherlands-U.K.	Petroleum	$82.3
British Petroleum	United Kingdom	Petroleum	52.2
ENI	Italy	Petroleum	29.4
Unilever	U.K.-Netherlands	Food	24.1
Francaise des Pétroles	France	Petroleum	22.8
Kuwait Petroleum	Kuwait	Petroleum	20.6
Elf-Aquitaine	France	Petroleum	19.7
Petroleos	Venezuela	Petroleum	19.7
Fiat	Italy	Autos	18.9
Petrobras	Brazil	Petroleum	18.9
Pemex	Mexico	Petroleum	18.8
Philips	Netherlands	Electronics	17.1
Volkswagenwerk	W. Germany	Autos	16.8
Daimler-Benz	W. Germany	Autos	16.3
Nissan	Japan	Autos	16.2
Renault	France	Autos	16.2
Siemens	Germany	Electronics	16.0
Matsushita	Japan	Electronics	15.7
Toyota	Japan	Autos	15.7
Hitachi	Japan	Electronics	15.5

Source: Fortune, August 23, 1982.

Whether attempted collusion will succeed depends partly on government policy toward monopoly. The most effective monopolies are those in which entry of new firms is restricted by government policy. Governments can employ their police power to restrict domestic competition, and foreign competition can be restrained by erecting import barriers. For this reason free trade has been called the most effective antitrust policy.

For many years the Justice Department has been concerned about the dominance of a few domestic firms in the automobile and steel industries. It is ironic that in the 1970s, when foreign competition increased, the U.S. government imposed trade barriers against competition from both automobile and steel imports. A similar situation exists in the textile industry where the Federal Trade Commission has forbidden mergers between domestic firms on antitrust grounds. At the same time the voluntary export restraints for textiles have reduced competition from foreign firms.

An interesting empirical question is whether the net effect of all government policies has been to increase or decrease the amount of monopoly power. In some cases, governments are more permissive about monopoly in foreign trade than in domestic trade. The Justice Department has granted antitrust immunity to oil companies in their dealings with OPEC governments. The Civil Aeronautics Board and the Federal Maritime Commission have cooperated with

TABLE 10-3   Leading Exporting Firms in the United States, 1981

COMPANY	PRODUCTS	VALUE OF EXPORTS (BILLIONS OF DOLLARS)	EXPORTS AS A PERCENTAGE OF SALES
Boeing	Aircraft	$6.1	62
General Motors	Autos	5.7	9
General Electric	Generating equipment	4.3	16
Ford	Autos	3.7	10
Caterpillar	Construction equipment	3.5	38
McDonnell Douglas	Aircraft	2.8	38
E. I. Dupont	Chemicals	2.6	12
United Technologies	Aircraft	2.6	19
IBM	Information system	1.9	6
Eastman Kodak	Photographic equipment	1.8	17
Westinghouse	Generating equipment	1.3	14
Signal Companies	Trucks, engines	1.2	23
Raytheon	Electronics	1.1	20
Union Carbide	Chemicals	1.1	11
Monsanto	Chemicals	1.0	15
International Harvester	Construction equipment	1.0	14
Hewlett-Packard	Electronics equipment	1.0	27
Weyerhaeuser	Wood products	0.9	21
Dow Chemical	Chemicals	0.9	8
Archer-Daniels-Midland	Soybeans, grain	0.9	25

Source: Fortune, August 9, 1982.

the International Air Transport Association and various shipping conferences in their attempts to fix airline and ocean shipping rates, respectively.

10.2 EXPORT CARTEL AND OPTIMUM MARKUP

Monopoly power may exist in international trade either because of a single large firm or because of a collusive agreement among smaller firms. If the producers in a country taken collectively constitute a large part of the world market for a product, it is in their interest to form a cartel. A cartel is an agreement among individual firms to behave as if they were separate plants of a single firm. The cartel policy yielding maximum profits is to choose the monopoly price and quantity determined by setting marginal revenue equal to marginal cost.

Equilibrium is shown in Figure 10-1 for the competitive and monopolistic alternatives. The competitive export supply curve (E^s) is derived from the domestic demand (X^d) and supply (X^s) curves as an excess supply. It can be interpreted as a collective marginal cost curve. The demand curve (E^d) for home

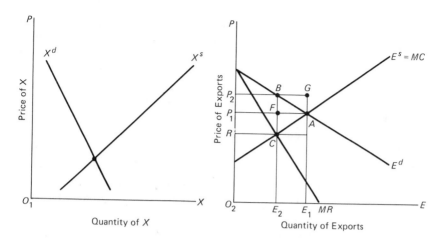

ROW loss = P_1P_2BF (higher cost) + FBA (lower volume)

Monopolist gain = P_1P_2BF (higher price) − CFA (smaller volume)

World loss = ROW loss − monopolist gain

$$= (P_1P_2BF + FBA) - (P_1P_2BF - CFA)$$

$$= FBA + CFA$$

FIGURE 10-1 Export Monopoly

country exports is negatively sloped, reflecting monopoly power of domestic sellers taken collectively.

However, if no individual firm possesses monopoly power and firms do not collude, the equilibrium will be at point A, the intersection of export supply and demand curves. The competitive price will be O_2P_1 and the volume of trade will be O_2E_1. Alternatively, if firms collude, the equilibrium is at the intersection of marginal revenue and marginal cost (C). The collusive or monopoly price is $O_2P_2 > O_2P_1$ and the export volume is $O_2E_2 < O_2E_1$. The monopoly benefits from the higher price per unit $(P_2 > P_1)$, but it loses from the smaller export volume $(E_2 < E_1)$. The total value of the benefit is the area P_1P_2BF, and the loss from smaller volume is the excess of competitive price over marginal cost (area CFA). Thus, the net benefit to the export monopolist is the area P_1P_2BF minus CFA. The rest of the world bears the cost of the higher export price and part of the cost of the smaller export volume. The cost to ROW of the higher cost is the area P_1P_2BF, and the cost of the smaller volume is FBA. The net world loss from monopoly is the difference between the ROW loss and the gain to the home country monopolist:

$$\text{world loss} = \text{ROW loss} - \text{monopolist gain}$$
$$= (P_1P_2BF + FBA) - (P_1P_2BF - CFA)$$
$$CBA = FBA + CFA$$

The world suffers a net loss from the export monopoly equal to the area CBA. However, the home country benefits from the monopoly price, which redistributes world income of $P_1 P_2 BF$ from ROW to the home country. Not everyone in ROW loses and not everyone in the home country gains. Notice that both domestic and foreign consumers pay the monopoly price, and foreign producers receive the same price as domestic firms. Producers in ROW gain and customers in the home country lose from the monopoly. In the case of oil, all non-OPEC producers (e.g., in the United States and the USSR) benefited from the monopoly price.

The most profitable price is the one for which marginal revenue equals marginal cost. The excess of the monopoly export price over cost can be expressed as an optimum markup over the marginal cost of production. The markup, expressed as a percentage $(P - MC/P)$, is derived from the monopoly equilibrium condition, $MC = MR$.

$$MC = MR$$
$$-MC = -MR = -P(1 + \frac{1}{\eta_f})$$
$$P - MC = P - P(1 + \frac{1}{\eta_f})$$
$$P - MC = P - P - \frac{P}{\eta_f}$$
$$\frac{P - MC}{P} = -\frac{1}{\eta_f} \quad \text{is the optimal markup}$$

The excess of price over marginal cost is inversely related to the elasticity of demand facing the firm, which is Abba Lerner's index of monopoly power. Thus, η_f would be small for a firm without good rivals, and the optimal markup would be relatively large.

The same excess demand expression applies to the demand facing a single firm and the demand for a country's exports:

$$\eta_f = \frac{1}{s}\eta - \frac{1-s}{s}\epsilon_0$$

In the case of export demand η is the elasticity of world demand for product X, s is the home country exporters' share of the world market for X, and ϵ_0 is the elasticity of supply of X by producers in the rest of the world. Thus, the optimal markup is greater (1) the larger the market share (s) of the home country exporters, (2) the smaller the elasticity of demand for the product, and (3) the smaller the elasticity of supply by other producers. The success of OPEC is partly attributable to a large initial market share, an inelastic demand for oil, and relatively unresponsive production in other countries.

10.3 ALTERNATIVE INSTITUTIONS FOR ACHIEVING THE MONOPOLY SOLUTION

A simple way to achieve the monopoly is collusion by private firms. In this case, the entire national gain is appropriated by owners of the firms. A possible problem is that individual firms have an incentive to be "free-riders" by selling at the cartel price without accepting the export volume restrictions of cartel members. A second possibility is state trade, which would legally preserve all export trade for a single government agency. In principle the state agency could choose the same price and export volume as a private cartel, but there is a question as to whether it would have the same profit orientation as the private cartel. In this case, the profit would go to the government. A third alternative is an optimum export tax, where the level of the tax is chosen to achieve the monopoly price and export volume. In Figure 10-1 the optimum tax would be BC per unit, which effectively shifts the export supply curve upward until it intersects export demand at point B. The world price would be O_2P_2 and the domestic price would fall to O_2R. The tax maximizes national income, but not tax revenue. The latter occurs where the tax is one-half the distance between the vertical intercepts of the E^s and E^d curves. In the United States, an export tax is forbidden by the constitution, but other countries use it frequently. A fourth alternative is an export quota of O_2E_2. The quota could be administered by requiring export licenses and issuing a total of O_2E_2 licenses. The quota would result in the same foreign (O_2P_2) and domestic prices (O_2R) as an export tax of BC per unit. The equivalent of the export tax revenue would be appropriated by exporting firms if licenses were given away, and it would accrue to the government if the licenses were auctioned.

These four alternative institutional arrangements are equivalent in the sense of yielding the same monopoly price to foreign buyers and the same volume of export. However, the arrangements result in quite different domestic income distributions. Domestic producers of the exportable would favor certain arrangements and oppose others. Domestic producers would benefit from a private cartel if they were also exporters. Additional cartel revenue for E_2 units would be P_1P_2BF. The government would appropriate this revenue with state trade. In the case of the export tax and the export quota, domestic producers receive a price of R, which is less than what they would have received (P_1) under competition. The government collects revenue of RP_2BC, but RP_1FC of it is paid by domestic producers. Even though the monopoly solution has the potential to increase national income, one would not expect domestic producers to favor state trade, an export tax, or an export quota. Since a partial embargo can be interpreted as an export quota, it is easy to see why American grain farmers have vigorously opposed grain embargoes.

10.4 OPEC AS A CARTEL

The Organization of Petroleum Exporting Countries is frequently viewed as the most successful cartel in the history of the world. The sharp increase in the relative price of crude oil in 1973 and 1974 can be interpreted as converting a competitive price such as OP_1 into a monopolistic price such as OP_2. OPEC is more complicated than a private cartel within a country, because many governments are involved. Although the organization was created by Iran, Iraq, Kuwait, Saudi Arabia, and Venezuela in 1960, it did not become an effective unit until 1973. Some prominent producers such as the USSR, United States, Mexico, China, and the United Kingdom are not members.

As Table 10-4 shows, four of the largest five producers of crude petroleum in 1982 were not OPEC members. Pricing policy is discussed at every meeting of OPEC ministers, but no explicit production or export quotas have been assigned. In some countries the oil companies have been nationalized, and the state-owned enterprises can be thought of as searching for the best markup over cost. Where foreign private firms continue to operate, one can think of the governments as searching for the optimum export tax.

The great success of OPEC distinguishes it from nearly all other historical cartels. There have been other successes, but they have been short lived. Subsequent attempts by other primary producers (e.g., bauxite) to emulate the behavior of OPEC have had limited success. There is no general agreement on what factors have contributed to the success of OPEC. Any explanation must include the factors that led to a rather inelastic demand for OPEC oil. These factors include a large initial market share for OPEC producers, a low short-run elasticity of demand for all crude oil, and a low elasticity of supply by non-OPEC producers. Nature has restricted oil supply to certain regions, and the total stock in each region is exhaustible. In spite of some political differences (e.g., war between Iran and Iraq), the major OPEC governments have formed a relatively cohesive political unit. The dominance of Saudi Arabia may have contributed to the cohesiveness of the group. Saudi Arabia's role in OPEC has been described as that of a dominant firm price leader.

One major factor that reduced the elasticity of demand for OPEC oil has been the pricing policies of non-OPEC governments, which reduced the supply response of their producers. The United States, the largest importer of crude oil, held the domestic oil price far below the world price from 1973 to 1981. U.S. domestic oil policy inadvertently added to net oil demand and reduced the elasticity of demand facing OPEC. Cooperation by the major demander permitted OPEC to charge a higher price than would otherwise have prevailed. Regardless of the reasons for its success, OPEC has achieved a transfer of billions of dollars from consumers to producers of oil.

The magnitude of the income transfers depends on the magnitude of the price increase and volume of oil trade. The price of oil imported into the United States is shown in Table 10-5. Column 1 shows the price in current dollars,

TABLE 10-4 **Major Producers of Crude Petroleum, 1974–1982**
(in millions of metric tons)

COUNTRY	1974	1975	1976	1977	1978	1979	1980	1981	1982
USSR	38.2	40.9	43.3	45.5	47.6	49.2	50.0	50.3	50.5
United States	36.1	34.4	33.4	33.8	35.7	35.1	35.4	35.2	35.6
Saudi Arabia	35.2	29.4	35.5	38.1	34.6	39.7	41.3	40.9	27.1
Mexico	2.5	3.1	3.4	4.1	5.2	6.2	7.7	9.6	11.5
China	N.A.	N.A.	7.2	7.8	8.7	8.8	8.8	8.4	8.5
Venezuela	13.0	10.2	10.0	9.8	9.5	10.3	9.6	9.3	8.3
Iran	25.1	22.3	24.6	23.6	21.9	12.8	6.1	5.5	8.2
United Kingdom	0	0.1	1.0	3.1	4.4	6.5	6.8	7.3	6.8
Indonesia	5.6	5.3	6.2	6.9	6.7	6.6	6.5	6.6	5.5
Nigeria	9.3	7.4	8.6	8.7	7.9	9.5	8.0	5.9	5.3
Canada	6.9	5.8	5.4	5.4	5.4	6.1	5.9	5.2	5.3
Libya	6.1	6.0	7.8	8.3	8.0	8.4	5.9	5.2	5.2
Kuwait	10.7	8.8	9.0	8.3	9.0	10.5	7.4	4.6	4.7
Iraq	8.1	9.3	9.4	10.2	10.5	14.0	7.1	4.7	3.5
							10.8	3.7	3.8

Source: United Nations, *Monthly Bulletin of Statistics.*

TABLE 10-5   Average Price per Barrel for Crude Petroleum and
Petroleum Products Imported into the United States,
1972–1980

YEAR	CURRENT DOLLARS	CONSUMER PRICE INDEX (1967 = 100)	CONSTANT 1967 DOLLARS
1972	$ 2.57	125.3	$ 2.05
1973	3.33	133.1	2.50
1974	11.01	147.7	7.45
1975	11.45	161.2	7.10
1976	12.14	170.5	7.12
1977	13.29	181.5	7.32
1978	13.29	195.4	6.80
1979	18.67	217.4	8.59
1980	30.46	246.6	12.35
1981	34.02	272.4	12.49
1982	31.26	289.1	10.81

Source: U.S. Department of Commerce, Survey of Current Business, March 1980 and March 1983.

column 2 shows the consumer price index, and column 3 (column 1 divided by column 2) shows the price in constant 1967 dollars. The three sharp increases occurred in 1974, 1979, and 1980. The 1974 price ($11.01) was more than three times the 1973 price ($3.33). The large dollar increases in 1979 and 1980 were smaller percentage increases than was that in 1974. Column 3 shows that the real price of oil fell in 1975 and remained below the 1974 peak of $7.45 until 1979. Both the nominal and real prices of oil fell during the glut of 1982.

The effect of the 1974 and 1979 price increases on the oil import bills of several major countries has been estimated by the General Agreement on Tariffs and Trade, and it is shown in Table 10-6. Column 1 shows the actual value of petroleum imports in 1973 and 1978 for each country. Column 2 shows the increment in the oil bill caused by the 1974 and 1979 price increases. For the United States, the 1974 increment in the oil bill was $19.6 billion, which was 19.8 percent of total U.S. imports, 1.1 percent of national income, and $93 per U.S. resident. The terms of trade effect was equivalent to a tax of $93 per person on all U.S. residents whose revenue was sent to oil explorers. The $19.6 billion transfer is equivalent to the area P_1P_2GA in Figure 10-1. It is the difference between the actual oil import bill in 1973 ($O_2P_1AE_1$) and the bill obtained by applying the 1974 price to the 1974 import volume.

The largest money increment occurred in the United States ($19.6 billion) followed by Japan ($14.0 billion) and Germany ($10.2 billion). The largest per capita increases occurred in Germany ($165), France ($148), Italy ($133), and Japan ($129). The per capita increase for Korea was only $21, but this was a larger percentage of national income than was that for any of the other listed countries. The size of the national income transfers was impressive. The decreases in real income per capita in some countries were as large as the annual income per capita in some other countries.

The oil price increases have been possible partly because of slow growth in oil production. Table 10-7 shows that since 1974 there has been no growth in OPEC production and slow growth outside of OPEC. The market share of OPEC producers reached its peak in 1974 at 55.5 percent and declined to 42.6 percent at the end of 1980. A falling market share has been characteristic of many of the earlier unsuccessful cartels, and this development has led to some optimism among oil consumers. The experience of individual producing countries has been highly variable.

Data for the eight largest producing countries from 1974 to 1980 were shown in Table 10-4. The largest production increase has come from the USSR. It has played the role of the classic "free-rider" by selling oil at the OPEC price while increasing output from 38.2 million tons in 1974 to 50.0 million tons in 1980. The other production increases have come from Saudi Arabia and two newer producers, Mexico and the United Kingdom. U.S. production in 1980 was still below the 1974 level. Notice the difference in behavior of Soviet and U.S. production during the period. In 1974 U.S. output was 95 percent of USSR output, but by 1980 it dropped to only 71 percent. The sharpest decline in national output came from Iran, which dropped from over 20 million tons to 12.8 million tons in 1979 and 6.1 million tons in 1980. Production was adversely affected by the Iranian revolution and the war with Iraq.

An alternative explanation of world oil prices has been offered by Ali Johany and others.[2] The hypothesis is that OPEC is not a cartel and that the world oil market is competitive. According to this explanation, the price increase since 1974 has been a competitive response to an increase in scarcity of world oil. If this were true, the disappearance of OPEC as an institution would have no effect on the price of oil.

The price increase in 1974 is explained by a change in property rights over oil. The threat of nationalization led foreign private oil companies to produce artificially large amounts before 1974. This speculative response to an expected loss of property rights contributed to an oil glut. Once OPEC governments acquired property rights from the private companies, they had an incentive to take into account future scarcity in determining present production. Since oil is storable, the marginal cost of selling a barrel today includes both the current production cost and the expected future price that could be obtained by storing the oil and selling in the future. Thus, the expectation of an increase in the future price would decrease current sales and increase the current price. However, this storage will occur only if the owner expects his or her property rights to continue in the future.

[2] See Ali Johany, *The Myth of the OPEC Cartel* (New York: Halsted, 1982).

TABLE 10-6 Indicators of the Possible Impact of the Price Increase of Imported Petroleum between 1973 and 1974 and 1978 and 1979 in Selected Countries

		VALUE OF IMPORTS OF PETROLEUM (BILLIONS)	INCREMENT DUE TO HIGHER PRICES (BILLIONS)	INCREMENT AS A PERCENTAGE OF IMPORTS OF GOODS AND SERVICES† (%)	INCREMENT AS A PERCENTAGE OF NATIONAL INCOME† (%)	INCREMENT PER CAPITA* AT CURRENT PRICES ($)	AT CONSTANT 1973 PRICES‡ ($)
United States	1973	$ 8.1	$19.6	19.8%	1.1%	$ 93	
	1978	41.8	16.7	7.3	0.9	76	$49
Japan	1973	6.7	14.0	31.4	4.0	129	
	1978	25.7	10.3	10.6	1.1	90	58
European Economic Community	1973	21.5	34.9	13.2	3.7	136	
	1978	68.1	27.2	4.9	1.4	105	67

Of which:							
West Germany	1973	5.7	10.2	14.4	3.3	165	67
	1978	16.1	6.4	4.1	1.0	104	
France	1973	3.9	7.7	16.4	3.6	148	63
	1978	13.3	5.3	5.2	1.2	99	
Italy	1973	3.6	7.3	21.6	5.9	133	54
	1978	12.0	4.8	7.2	1.7	85	
Brazil	1973	1.0	2.3	24.9	3.0	23	10
	1978	4.6	1.8	8.3	1.2	16	
Korea (Rep. of)	1973	0.3	0.7	15.1	5.8	21	15
	1978	2.3	0.9	4.8	2.1	24	

*The increments were calculated by applying the 1974 average import price increase to the 1973 volume, and a 40 percent price increase (the estimated average import price increase, 1979 over 1978, if there are no price changes in the second half of 1979) to the 1978 volume. Because of various lags, the average price increases are—in both instances—smaller than the increase in list prices of crude petroleum.

†The comparisons in the four right-hand columns are relative to actual imports and actual income in 1973 and 1978 respectively.

‡Calculated by dividing the 1978 figure in current prices by the increase in the United States wholesale price index between 1973 and 1978.

Sources: IMF, *International Financial Statistics;* UN, trade data tapes and *Monthly Bulletin of Statistics;* Eurostatistics, Data for short term economic analysis; national statistics.

Source: General Agreement on Tariffs and Trade, *International Trade, 1978–79* (Geneva: GATT, 1979), p. 13.

**TABLE 10-7   World Crude Oil Production, 1960–1980
(thousands barrels per day)**

	OPEC	GROWTH RATE*	REST OF WORLD	GROWTH RATE*	OPEC SHARE
1960	7,874		13,067		37.6%
1961	8,497		13,923		37.9
1962	9,954	10.8%	14,383	5.5%	40.9
1963	10,865		15,253		41.6
1964	12,082		16,081		42.9
1965	13,177		17,115		43.5
1966	14,217		18,693		43.2
1967	15,630	10.9	19,732	6.7	44.2
1968	17,660		20,983		45.7
1969	20,341		21,341		48.8
1970	22,134		23,692		48.3
1971	25,092		23,255		51.9
1972	26,711	8.5	24,070	1.5	52.6
1973	30,961		24,869		55.5
1974	30,683		25,192		54.9
1975	27,134	0.6	25,856	4.1	51.2
1976	30,711		26,684		53.5
1977	31,230		28,380		52.4
1978	29,800	−0.5	30,390	5.3	49.5
1979	30,928		31,472		49.6
1980†	26,743	−13.6	32,558	3.5	45.1
November 1979	30,770		32,370		48.7
		−21.8		−0.1	
November 1980	24,015		32,335		42.6

*Annual rates of change.

†Estimated for November and December.

Source: Federal Reserve Bank of St. Louis, Review, April 1981.

According to this competitive theory of the oil market, foreign private firms did not expect their property rights in oil to continue, but OPEC governments do. The competitive view stresses the long time horizon of planners in OPEC countries, but the expected life of a particular government (e.g., the government of the shah of Iran just prior to the revolution) is not necessarily longer than the expected duration of private claims to oil in OPEC countries. Thus, there is reason to doubt the increase in the incentive to conserve oil. The competitive view also has some trouble explaining the suddenness of the 1974 increase and the subsequent increases in 1979 and 1980.

Proponents of the competitive view can attribute some of the increase to U.S. pricing policy, and they can point to events in Iran (output fell from 21.9 million tons in 1978 to 6.1 million tons in 1980) and Iraq (decline from 14.0 million tons in 1979 to 10.8 million tons in 1980) as a cause of 1979 and 1980 increases. Regardless of whether the world oil market is better described as monopolistic or competitive, billions of dollars of wealth have been transferred to producing countries since 1974.

10.5 DUMPING AND PRICE DISCRIMINATION

Where conditions are appropriate, a monopolist can earn higher profits by engaging in price discrimination than by charging a uniform price to all buyers. Charging a lower price in one country than another is called dumping. The necessary conditions for price discrimination are (1) the existence of two separate groups of demanders and (2) the ability to separate the two groups. Import barriers are a convenient way to separate national markets in international trade. The profit-maximizing equilibrium for the price discriminating monopolist is to choose prices and quantities so that marginal revenue is the same in each national market and equal to the common marginal cost:

$$MR_1 = MR_2 = MC$$

Since marginal revenue can be expressed as

$$MR = P(1 + \frac{1}{\eta})$$
$$P_1(1 + \frac{1}{\eta_1}) = P_2(1 + \frac{1}{\eta_2}) = MC$$

it follows that if demand is less elastic in market 1 ($|\eta_1| < |\eta_2|$), P_1 should be greater than P_2. Japanese firms are often accused of dumping in the U.S. market. It would be profitable to do so if the elasticity of demand for a product were greater in the United States than in Japan, and if arbitragers could be prevented from reexporting from the United States to Japan. These conditions may be met because the permissive attitude of the Japanese government toward domestic cartels may reduce the demand elasticity in Japan. Import barriers at the Japanese border may prevent arbitrage. Persistent dumping, based on differences in national demand, is consistent with profit maximization. The lower price improves the terms of trade and benefits consumers in the importing country. Producers in the importing country are harmed, and their influence is responsible for antidumping laws that most countries have. Since prices are higher in the exporting country, one might expect consumers in that country to complain about dumping. In fact formal complaints nearly always come from producers in the importing country. This observation supports the proposition that producer groups are more effective in influencing trade policy than consumer groups. Japanese firms have been accused of violating the U.S. antidumping law more frequently than residents of any country. It is ironic that in 1982 the Japanese invoked their own 62-year-old law to protect domestic firms against "cheap" textile imports from South Korea and other Asian countries.

The United States has had an antidumping law since 1921, and GATT also has restrictions against dumping. Domestic firms are harmed by dumping, but they are also harmed by imports under free trade. Domestic consumers benefit from dumping relative to foreign consumers. The standard justification for antidumping laws is the same as for domestic laws against predatory pricing. Predatory pricing is a policy of pricing so far below cost that rival firms are driven out of business by the predatory firm. During the period of price war, consumers receive a temporary benefit. However, after the predator has destroyed his or her rivals, presumably he or she will raise the price to the monopoly level and exploit consumers. In the case of international trade, the predator is the foreign supplier, and his or her object is to exploit domestic consumers after first eliminating domestic producers. The entire justification for antidumping laws is questionable on both theoretical and empirical grounds. There may be better ways in which to achieve a monopoly (e.g., merger) than predation, and if the predator ever achieves a monopoly, he or she must prevent domestic firms from reentering the profitable industry. As an empirical matter, it is difficult to find any examples of firms that have achieved monopoly power as a result of predatory pricing.

In the United States, dumping was once defined as selling below cost (the relevant cost is rarely clear), but under the current law dumping is selling in the United States for less than the price of a comparable item in the supplier's country. Damaged parties can complain to the International Trade Commission and the commission makes nonbinding recommendations to the president. The commission can recommend a countervailing duty on the imported product retroactive to the day the complaint was filed. Critics of the law have complained that U.S. firms have an incentive to file frivolous complaints in the hope that the threat of a retroactive tariff may reduce imports. Since the 1974 Trade Act, the frequency of dumping cases has increased.[3] Some domestic firms that lose dumping cases are able to obtain relief from other sources. Both the U.S. auto and steel industries lost dumping cases but received voluntary export restraints.

Dumping associated with price discrimination and predatory pricing both require monopoly power by exporters. A separate phenomenon, known as sporadic dumping, is unrelated to monopoly. Sporadic dumping involves occasional sales abroad at prices below cost. What cost concept is relevant is not entirely clear, but presumably it is some measure of average cost. Thus, dumping could occur in a competitive export industry in the short run, provided that

[3] In the period 1975 to 1979, about 2 percent of U.S. manufactured imports have been granted tariff relief for either dumping or "unfair" subsidies. See J. M. Finger, H. K. Hall, and D. R. Nelson, "The Political Economy of Administered Protection," *American Economic Review*, June 1982.

marginal cost is less than average cost. This might occur, for example, for an agricultural product when there is a surprisingly large world crop. It is not profitable for private firms to sell for less than marginal cost unless the product is subsidized.

Unlike price discrimination, the practice of subsidizing exports is not motivated by profit considerations. The subsidy may be a direct payment of money per unit of exports, or it may be an indirect payment such as a subsidy to credit, insurance, or another input.

The subject of dumping and export subsidies has been a controversial one in recent years. Producers in importing countries refer to the practice as "unfair trade." U.S. law forbids a price that is "less than fair value." U.S. textile firms were accused of dumping synthetic textiles in Europe in 1980 because the price of an input, natural gas, was kept artificially low by the U.S. government. For many years, American businesspeople have objected to the GATT principle that permits the EEC to rebate value added taxes paid by community exporters, whereas the U.S. government cannot rebate corporate income taxes paid by U.S. firms. The GATT rule permits rebates for indirect taxes but not direct taxes. U.S. business groups have argued that this practice contributes to U.S. trade deficits and that it has led some groups to advocate the substitution of a value added tax for the corporate income tax.

Foreign aid is another example of dumping in the sense of selling below cost. U.S. food aid programs have been criticized because they discourage food production in recipient countries. Because price support programs for many agricultural products have kept domestic prices above world levels, U.S. and EEC governments have often resorted to export subsidies for commercial sales. Subsidized butter exports from the EEC to the USSR was opposed both by EEC consumers and rival dairy exporters.

A final example of dumping is state trade. It may be easier for state enterprises to subsidize exports because the firms are not expected to earn profits. State enterprises are often exempt from certain taxes and legal restrictions in their home country and the importing country. William Diebold has commented that

> Although private entrepreneurs are sure that they are more efficient than social-ized companies, they also feel that they are always at an unfair disadvantage in competing with socialized firms at home or abroad.[4]

10.6 NATIONAL OPTIMUM TARIFF

Just as there is a potential national gain from asserting the monopoly power of exporters, there is a potential gain to a large country on the import side. If a nation is large enough that its buyers have collective monopsony power, the

[4]William Diebold, *Industrial Policy as an International Issue* (New York: McGraw-Hill, 1980), p. 191.

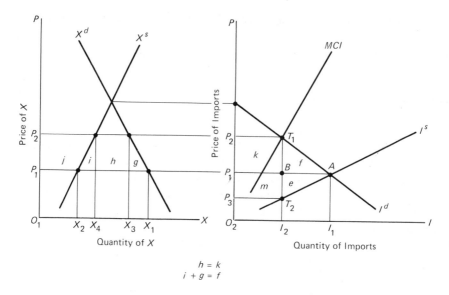

$$h = k$$
$$i + g = f$$

FIGURE 10-2   National Optimum Tariff

national welfare can be improved by judiciously reducing the volume of imports. Bigness as an importer implies an import supply curve with a positive slope, which means that the price importers pay increases with the volume of imports. The import supply curve can be interpreted as the average cost of imports, and the marginal cost of imports curve *(MCI)* must lie above it and be steeper (twice as steep for linear curves).[5] The optimal volume of imports for the nation is the quantity for which the marginal cost of imports equals the marginal benefit from imports, as measured by the import demand curve.

   In Figure 10-2 the competitive equilibrium is at point A, the intersection of import demand and import supply. The competitive price is O_2P_1 and the competitive quantity of imports is O_2I_1. If importers assert their monopsony power, the equilibrium is at point T_1, where the price paid to suppliers is O_2P_3 and the volume is O_2I_2. The decrease in the price paid to foreigners (P_1P_3) is the terms of trade effect of the tariff. This equilibrium could be reached by levying an optimum tariff of T_1T_2 per unit. The tariff would raise the price paid by domestic buyers to O_2P_2 and lower the price received by suppliers to

---

[5] The total cost of imports is the price paid to foreigners $(P^\star)$ times the volume of imports (I):

$$TCI = P^\star I$$

$$\frac{d(TCI)}{dI} = P^\star + \frac{I dP^\star}{dI} = P^\star(1 + \frac{I}{P^\star}\frac{dP^\star}{dI})$$

$$MCI = P^\star(1 + \frac{1}{\epsilon_{IP^\star}})$$

O_2P_3. The difference of $P_2P_3 = T_1T_2$ is the tariff per unit, and the area $P_3P_2T_1T_2$ is total tariff revenue. The domestic price increase raises domestic production from O_1X_2 to O_1X_4. The same result could be achieved without a tariff by forming a private importer's cartel or establishing a monopoly state importing agency. An import quota of O_2I_2 would bring about the same price and quantity as the tariff. The tariff-equivalent revenue would accrue to import licensees if licenses were given away, and the government would receive it if they were sold by auction. If an optimum tariff were imposed, foreign suppliers would receive the low price (P_3), but domestic consumers will pay the high price (P_2). Consumers do not benefit from an optimum tariff in their role as consumers. The benefits are appropriated by the government as tariff revenue, which may be substituted for other taxes.

Monopoly and monopsony are inefficient forms of market organization for the world as a whole. In this case the gain to the home country monopsonist is less than the loss to the rest of the world. The gross gain to the home country consists of the lower price paid to foreigners (area m in Figure 10-2) and the portion of tariff revenue paid by domestic consumers (area k). There is an offsetting loss due to a smaller import volume (area $f = i + g$) and the higher price paid by domestic consumers (area k). The net gain to the home country is $(m+k) - (k+f) = m - f$. Conversely, ROW loses because they receive a lower price (area m) and the volume of trade declines (area e). Thus, the net loss for the world as a whole is

ROW loss − Home gain
$m + e - [(m+k) - (k+f)]$
$m + e - (m-f) = e + f$

Notice that total tariff revenue is $k + m$. It can be divided into the portion that is paid by domestic consumers (area $k = h$) and the portion paid by foreign suppliers (area m). The home country loss from a smaller trade volume (area f) can be divided into a production loss (area i) and a consumption loss (area g). Area j represents a transfer of income from domestic consumers to domestic producers of importables.

The optimal tariff rate depends on the degree of a country's monopsony power in import markets. The nationally optimal volume of imports occurs where the marginal benefits from importing equal the marginal cost of importing:

$$MBI = MCI$$

Since MBI is measured by the price consumers are willing to pay (P) and $MCI = P^{\star}(1 + 1/\epsilon_{IP}^{\star})$,

$$P = P^{\star}\left(1 + \frac{1}{\epsilon_{IP^{\star}}}\right)$$

Since the domestic price is related to the foreign price according to:

$$P = (1+t)P^\star$$

the following equation holds:

$$P^\star(1 + \frac{1}{\epsilon_{IP^\star}}) = (1+t)P^\star$$

the nationally optimum tariff is

$$t = \frac{1}{\epsilon_{IP^\star}}$$

The optimum tariff rate is inversely related to the elasticity of supply of imports facing a country. The term $\frac{1}{\epsilon_{IP^\star}}$ is an index of a country's monopsony power. For a small country the elasticity of supply of imports is infinitely great (I^s is horizontal) and $\frac{1}{\epsilon_{IP^\star}} = 0$. Thus, the optimal tariff for a small country is zero. The optimum tariff rate depends on the degree of monopsony power just as the optimum export cartel markup or export tax depends on the degree of monopoly power possessed by a country's exporters. Since a large country's monopsony power might be different for different imports, the optimum tariff would be different for each product.

The optimal national tariff is not optimum for the world as a whole. Francis Edgeworth (1845–1926) was one of the early writers on the concept of an optimum tariff, and his comments on Bickerdike's discussion of tariffs bear repeating:

> Thus the direct use of the theory is likely to be small. But it is to be feared that its abuse will be considerable. It affords to unscrupulous advocates of vulgar protection a peculiarly specious pretext for introducing the thin edge of the fiscal wedge. Mr. Bickerdike may be compared to a scientist who, by a new analysis, has discovered that strychnine may be administered in small doses with prospect of advantage in one or two more cases than was previously known, the result of this discovery may be to render the drug more easily procurable by those whose intention . . . is not medicinal. . . . Let us admire the skill of the analyst, but label the subject of his investigation POISON.[6]

The nationally optimum tariff is not necessarily the actual tariff rate chosen by governments either. Several empirical studies of tariff policy have concluded that the theoretically optimal tariff was not a good predictor of actual

---

[6] Francis Y. Edgeworth, *Papers Relating to Political Economy*, Vol. II (1925). New York: Burt Franklin Reprint, 1970, pp. 365–66.

rates. Donald McCloskey studied British tariff policy following the repeal of the Corn Laws in 1846, and John James analyzed U.S. tariff policy just before the Civil War. Colin Carter and Andrew Schmitz considered whether the EEC's grain levy approximated an optimum tariff for that region. In all cases the actual tariff rate deviated substantially from the optimum tariff. Thus, the concept of the optimum tariff is an interesting application of the theory of monopsony, but it is not a good predictor of actual tariff policy, nor is it the best policy for the world as a whole.

The possibility of retaliation against one's own exports is one reason why the actual tariff may be different from the hypothetical optimum. Tariffs are a particular kind of regulation. The public interest theory predicts that benevolent policymakers will "do what is best for the country" regardless of their own self-interest. The economic theory of regulation predicts that the self-interest of policymakers will lead them to respond to the pressure of lobbyists. In the case of tariffs, domestic producers of import-competing goods should have an influence in determining tariff policy according to the economic theory. The economic theory would predict higher tariffs on products for which domestic production is important. Baldwin's study of tariff policy is consistent with this hypothesis. Conversely, the public interest theory would predict higher tariffs on products for which the home country has greater monopsony power.

To decide which theory has better predictive power, one must consider two situations that yield conflicting tariff predictions. If countries have large monopsony power but little domestic production, public interest theory predicts a high tariff whereas the economic theory predicts a low tariff. Coffee and bananas are imports for which the United States has some monopsony power but little domestic production. Tariffs on both products have been quite low. In some of the recent important protectionist cases, such as automobiles, steel, and textiles, the United States is a large producer and also possesses some monopsony power. In the extreme opposite case of no monopsony power and large domestic production, the public interest theory predicts a low tariff whereas the economic theory predicts a high tariff.

10.7 INTERNATIONAL COMMODITY AGREEMENTS

It has been shown that exporters can achieve a monopoly price in several ways. A cartel consisting of private firms or state agencies can restrict sales to keep price above marginal cost. The same result can be achieved by an appropriate export tax or quota. An international commodity agreement (ICA) is an arrangement between governments that is designed to achieve at least some of the economic effects of monopoly. Formal commodity agreements have been in effect for some products since the 1930s, and the idea has been actively promoted by United Nation's agencies in recent years. Some of the more prominent agreements have been for wheat, coffee, sugar, and tin, but many other primary products have been involved.[7]

One difficulty in evaluating ICAs is that the stated goals are often vague. Raising the average price of the product is one of the goals of nearly all the agreements. In this respect, ICAs have a characteristic of monopoly. Stabilization is another frequently stated goal, but it is not always clear what variable the ICA is designed to stabilize. In his study of ICAs, Alton Law found the following 11 variables that have been offered as stability goals: price, foreign exchange, earnings, quantities, producers' incomes, income from primary producing land, balance of payments, markets for industrial output, world trade, terms of trade, business cycles, and political stability.[8] Obviously some of the goals are incompatible, and others are not intended to be taken very seriously by their proponents.

Although vagueness of goals makes evaluation difficult, there is some agreement among economic analysts that ICAs have not been effective. The main reasons for failure have been lack of support by member countries and competition from alternative sources of supply. Increasing the price requires limiting production and exports. However, each individual country has an incentive to violate the limits, while letting other countries restrict sales. Frequent violations by member countries have resulted in price competition contrary to the agreement. In other cases when members have respected quotas, competition has come from nonmembers producing the same product or synthetics. The International Coffee Agreement had a successful period until the South American growers were faced with competition from African growers. A rubber agreement that began in 1922 successfully raised the price until the Great Depression and the invention of synthetic rubber during World War II.

The history of international wheat agreements represents some of the typical problems of ICAs. World wheat exports are highly concentrated among a few countries. In the crop year 1980–1981, the United States was responsible for 45 percent of world wheat exports. The United States and Canada combined had 63 percent, and when Australia was added, the group had 74 percent of world wheat exports. The potential for collusive pricing has not gone unnoticed, and the success of OPEC has heightened interest in an effective wheat agreement. The slogan "a bushel for a barrel" refers to a desire to reestablish the terms of trade between grain and oil that existed prior to 1973.

The first international wheat agreement was reached in 1933, after a period of prolonged surpluses. The agreement called for maintaining price by export quotas and acreage control. The agreement ended after one year when Argentina had a large crop and exceeded its export quota. Subsequent wheat agreements were signed in 1942, 1949, 1953, 1956, and 1967. A standard

[7] A list of products for which ICAs have been in effect appears in Alton Law, *International Commodity Agreements: Setting, Performance, and Prospects* (Lexington, Mass.: D. C. Heath, 1975).
[8] See ibid., p. 77.

interpretation of the experience is that prices remained within the specified range of the agreement when they were consistent with the goals of domestic agricultural policy in the United States and Canada. When domestic and international policy goals conflicted, the agreement was violated. The 1967 agreement became ineffective in 1971 when there was open violation of the minimum price.[9] The 1967 agreement had given a lower minimum price to Australia, because of its lower-quality wheat. During a period of favorable harvests in 1971, the quality of Australian wheat improved enough to eliminate any price differential based on market quotations. By selling wheat at the lower-quality minimum price, Australia lured customers away from the United States and Canada. Open violation of the minimum price followed. A rapid change in world wheat market conditions occurred, which raised prices in 1974 to the highest level since World War I. Extensive negotiations from 1974 to 1978 failed to bring about a new wheat agreement.

A fundamental barrier to an agreement is that the governments tend to keep domestic wheat prices artificially high as a way of subsidizing agriculture. The export market is a convenient device for disposing of the resulting surplus. Thus, there is a conflict between the domestic policy goal of promoting wheat exports and the ICA objective of curtailing exports. A final example of how difficult it is to achieve a common policy among wheat exporting countries is the U.S.-sponsored wheat embargo following the Soviet invasion of Afghanistan in 1980. The United States urged Canada, Australia, and Argentina to join in the embargo. Canada and Australia agreed not to seek an increase in their previous market shares. Argentina, which previously had little trade with the USSR, signed a five-year trade agreement promising virtually the entire crop to the Soviets.

10.8 THE NEW INTERNATIONAL ECONOMIC ORDER

Official attitudes toward international commodity agreements have varied over time. The Havana Conference of 1947, which recommended the creation of the International Trade Organization, produced a charter that clearly limited the scope of ICAs. A more favorable attitude toward ICAs developed within the United Nations, especially after the formation of the United Nations Conference on Trade and Development (UNCTAD) in 1964. The first meeting in Geneva was chaired by Raul Prebisch, a long-time proponent of the view that the terms of trade of primary products tend to decline. He considered ICAs to be a form of countervailing power that primary producing countries could use.

---

[9] For details, see Christopher P. Brown, *The Political and Social Economy of Commodity Control* (New York: Praeger, 1980), Chap. 1.

A bloc of low-income countries within UNCTAD[10] became a strong supporter of ICAs. A formal call for a new international economic order (NIEO) emerged from a series of UNCTAD meetings.

The NIEO contains many elements that are designed to redistribute income toward low-income countries, but its main feature is an ambitious international commodity agreement called the "integrated commodities program" (ICP). The basic features of the ICP are commodity agreements and buffer stocks for 10 basic ("core") commodities and more flexible arrangements for 8 other products.[11] The basic products are coffee, tea, cocoa, sugar, rubber, jute, hard fibers, cotton fiber and yarn, copper, and tin. Some opposition to the ICP is based on fundamental considerations, such as the substitution of monopoly for competition. Some opposition is based on details and financing of the buffer stock. The integrated program has not yet been implemented, but it remains a topic of lively discussion. The distribution of benefits would vary by country, and certain programs would harm certain countries.

Some of the support for the IPC derived from the success of OPEC, which was beneficial to Nigeria, Indonesia, and other oil exporters. However, OPEC had a devastating effect on India, Pakistan, Bangladesh, and other oil importers. The strongest economic criticism of the ICP is that monopolistic prices reduce the total world income that is available to distribute. One alternative to extending the scope of monopoly in world markets is to assist importers and exporters in low-income countries through a policy of freer trade. Exporters would benefit from greater access to foreign markets, and importers would benefit from buying at more favorable prices.

SUMMARY

Large countries can alter the prices received for exports and paid for imports by changing the volume of trade. Such countries are analogous to monopolistic or monopsonistic business firms. A country can assert its export monopoly power by a private cartel, state trade, an export tax, or an export quota. The success of the Organization of Petroleum Exporting Countries has raised the question of what characteristics distinguish OPEC from many less successful cartels. Price discrimination may be a profitable practice if the monopolistic seller can separate markets. The use of import barriers to segregate markets facilitates price discrimination in international trade. Antidumping laws are devices to protect domestic producers from import competition.

Large importing countries can improve their terms of trade by imposing nationally optimal tariffs. The height of an optimal tariff is inversely related to

[10] In 1968 the bloc was called the Group of 77, but by 1976 the number had grown to 117.

[11] For details, see Carmine Nappi, *Commodity Market Controls: A Historical View* (Lexington, Mass.: D. C. Heath, 1979), Chap. 6.

a country's monopsony power. However, the actual level of tariffs may be better explained by the importance of the import-competing sector of the home country. International commodity agreements can be interpreted as an attempt to achieve a monopoly price for certain primary products. Although most historical commodity agreements have achieved only limited success, the United Nations Conference on Trade and Development has proposed an ambitious integrated commodity program.

REFERENCES

ADELMAN, MORRIS. *The World Petroleum Market*. Baltimore: Johns Hopkins University Press, 1972.

——. "Politics, Economics, and World Oil." *American Economic Review*, May 1974.

BASEVI, GIORGI. "The Restrictive Effect of the U.S. Tariff and Its Welfare Value." *American Economic Review*, September 1968. An analysis of the terms of trade effect of the U.S. tariff structure.

BEHRMAN, JERE. *Development of the International Economic Order and Commodity Agreements*. Reading, Mass.: Addison-Wesley, 1978. A study of commodity market stability, commodity agreements, and the NIEO.

BHAGWATI, JAGDISH, ed. *The New International Economic Order: The North-South Debate*. Cambridge, Mass.: M.I.T. Press, 1977. A collection of papers evaluating aspects of the proposed NIEO.

BLAIR, JOHN. "Quinine: An International Cartel." In *Microeconomics: Selected Readings*, Edwin Mansfield, ed., 3rd ed. New York: W. W. Norton, 1979. A brief description of the quinine cartel.

BROWN, CHRISTOPHER P. *The Political and Social Economy of Commodity Control*. New York: Praeger, 1980. A study of commodity agreements stressing the recent role of UNCTAD.

CARTER, C., and ANDREW SCHMITZ. "Support Tariffs and Price Formation in the World Wheat Market." *American Journal of Agricultural Economics*, August 1979. A comparison of actual and hypothetical optimum tariffs on grain.

CAVES, RICHARD. "International Cartels and Monopolies in International Trade." In *International Economic Policy: Theory and Policy*, R. Dornbusch and J. Frenkel, eds. Baltimore: Johns Hopkins University Press, 1979.

CORDEN, W. M. *Trade Policy and Economic Welfare*. Oxford: Clarendon Press, 1974. Analysis of domestic distortions and trade, including chapters on second best, optimum tariff, and infant industries.

DIEBOLD, WILLIAM. *Industrial Policy as an International Issue*. New York: McGraw-Hill, 1980. Discusses monopoly and state trade in the context of industrial policy.

FINGER, J.M., H. K. HALL, and D. R. NELSON. "The Political Economy of Administered Protection." *American Economic Review*, June 1982. A study of countervailing duty, antidumping, and escape clause cases for the period 1975 to 1979.

GOLDMAN, MARSHALL. *The Enigma of Soviet Petroleum: Half Empty or Half Full*. Boston: George Allen and Unwin, 1980. Economic analysis of the Soviet oil industry.

JAMES, JOHN. "The Optimal Tariff in the Antebellum United States." *American Economic Review*, September 1981. A study showing that the actual U.S. tariff was below the nationally optimal tariff.

JOHANY, ALI D. *The Myth of the OPEC Cartel.* New York: Halsted, 1982. A denial that the world petroleum market is monopolistic.

JOHNSON, HARRY G. "Optimal Trade Intervention in the Presence of Domestic Distortions." In his *Aspects of the Theory of Tariffs.* London: George Allen and Unwin, 1971. An analysis of the "second best" argument for tariffs.

KALT, JOSEPH P. *The Economics and Politics of Oil: Federal Policy in the Post-Embargo Era.* Cambridge, Mass.: M.I.T. Press, 1981.

LAW, ALTON D. *International Commodity Agreements: Setting, Performance, and Prospects.* Lexington, Mass.: D. C. Heath, 1975. An extensive study of commodity agreements.

MCCLOSKEY, D.N. "Magnanimous Albion: Free Trade and British National Income." *Explorations in Economic History,* July 1980. An empirical study indicating that the British tariff was below the nationally optimal level in the nineteenth century.

MCNICOL, DAVID. *Commodity Agreements and Price Stabilization.* Lexington, Mass.: Lexington Books, 1978.

MEADE, JAMES E. *Trade and Welfare.* London: Oxford University Press, 1955. A modern classic on microeconomic aspects of trade and welfare.

MUTTI, JOHN. "Welfare Effects of Multilateral Tariff Reductions." *Southern Economic Journal,* January 1979. An attempt to calculate the terms of trade effects of the Kennedy Round tariff reductions.

NAPPI, CARMINE. *Commodity Market Controls: A Historical Review.* Lexington, Mass.: D. C. Heath, 1979. A study of commodity agreements stressing their historical development.

PINDYCK, ROBERT S. "The Cartelization of World Commodity Markets." *American Economic Review,* May 1979.

SAMPSON, ANTHONY. *The Seven Sisters.* New York: Viking, 1975. A descriptive history of the major international oil companies.

STOCKING, GEORGE W., and MYRON W. WATKINS. *Cartels in Action.* New York: Twentieth Century Fund, 1946. A study dealing with cartels before World War II.

U.S. DEPARTMENT OF ENERGY. *Monthly Energy Review,* Washington, D.C., monthly. A source of energy data.

VAN DUYNE, CARL. "Commodity Cartels and the Theory of Derived Demand." *Kyklos,* no. 3 (1975), pp. 597–611.

VERNON, RAYMOND, ed. *The Oil Crisis.* New York: W. W. Norton, 1976.

VINER, JACOB. *Dumping.* Chicago: University of Chicago Press, 1923. A classic contribution on the subject of dumping.

WARES, WILLIAM. *The Theory of Dumping and American Commercial Policy.* Lexington, Mass.: Lexington Books, 1977.

CHAPTER ELEVEN
INTERNATIONAL
LABOR MOBILITY

11.1 FACTOR MOBILITY
AS A SUBSTITUTE
FOR PRODUCT TRADE

An assumption of the basic theory of international trade is that factors of production are mobile between industries and regions of a country but that they are immobile between countries. Conversely, products are assumed to be mobile both within and between countries. International trade, which is product mobility, tends to substitute for international factor mobility. Trade tends to equalize both product prices and factor prices between countries. Since products have different capital and labor intensities, trade alters relative factor demands and factor prices. For example, U.S. imports of labor-intensive products from Mexico tend to equalize prices of those products in the two countries. At the same time, expansion of the labor-intensive sector increases wages in Mexico, while contraction of the labor-intensive sector in the United States lowers wages. Thus, product trade alters the structure of factor demand and equalizes wages. The imposition of trade barriers would interfere with both product price and factor price equalization. By increasing the wage disparity between countries, trade barriers would create a greater incentive for Mexican workers to migrate to the United States. In fact millions of Mexican workers have migrated in recent decades, and the relationship between protectionism and migration provides a partial explanation.

Figure 11-1 shows the effect of immigration on the demand for labor-intensive imports. Before migration domestic labor supply is L_1, the domestic

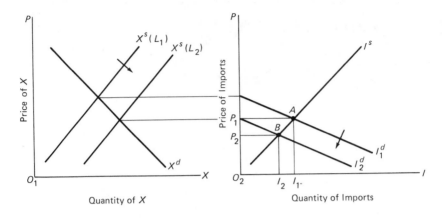

FIGURE 11-1   Immigration Substitutes for Labor-Intensive Imports

supply of the importable is X_1, and import demand is I_1^d. Equilibrium is at A with imports of O_2I_1. Immigration increases labor supply to L_2 and shifts the supply of the importable to X_2^s. The decrease in import demand to I_2^d yields the new equilibrium at B. Migration of labor has substituted for I_1I_2 units of imports.

Since trade and factor mobility are substitutes, one cannot make a satisfactory study of trade without also considering the mobility of labor and capital. The present chapter will analyze international migration of labor; Chapter 12 will consider international investment.

Migration has been an important source of population change in many countries. Immigration has been an important source of people for newly settled areas such as the United States, Canada, and Australia. Conversely, emigration has made areas such as Europe much less populous than they otherwise would have been. International migration continues to be important today for the United States, Western Europe, the Middle East, and Southeast Asia. Migration alters world comparative advantage by changing the factor endowments of both sending and receiving countries. In response to a change in comparative costs, the entire pattern of world trade changes. This chapter will analyze the effect of migration on the pattern of trade, product prices, and factor prices in both sending and receiving countries. Data on United States immigration will be presented.

Migration is induced by both economic and noneconomic considerations. Economic migration is induced by international wage differentials, and migration tends to equalize wages. Since the higher wages expected by migrants may not be realized until the future, migration is best analyzed as an investment decision. Domestic fiscal policy can influence migration by altering after-tax wages and the distribution of benefits from government programs.

Immigration quotas are the most common instrument used by governments to control migration. This chapter will discuss U.S. immigration policy, which permitted unrestricted immigration until the 1920s. Quotas established at that time restricted total immigration and the distribution of immigrants by the sending country. A 1965 revision of the law increased immigration from Latin America and Asia relative to Europe. The so-called "brain drain" of educated workers from low-income countries will be discussed in connection with U.S. policy.

Some countries have attempted to control migration by distinguishing between temporary and permanent migrants. The guest worker program in Europe and the earlier *bracero* program in the United States are examples. Just as tariffs and import quotas create an incentive for smuggling products, immigration barriers create an incentive for smuggling people. The number of illegal immigrants to the United States in recent years may have been as large as the number of legal arrivals. The problem of illegal migration between the United States and Mexico will be considered.

Two determinants of the commodity composition of trade are relative factor endowments and technology, and both are influenced by migration. The effect of immigration on relative factor endowments depends on whether immigrants bring capital with them. The receiving country will become more labor abundant if the labor-capital ratio of immigrants is greater than that of the initial population. Since capital may take the form of human capital as well as physical capital, immigration of highly skilled workers could have the effect of reducing a country's labor abundance.

It has been observed that U.S. exports are skilled labor (capital) intensive, whereas U.S. imports are unskilled labor intensive. If immigrants are unskilled, they should substitute for imports. If they are skilled workers, such as scientists and engineers, immigration should increase U.S. exports.

A second point related to human capital is that some skills are more easily transferred between countries than others. Because certain occupations are country specific, symphony conductors, ballet dancers, and unskilled laborers are more likely to migrate than are poets and lawyers. Some skills are transferable, but only after a period of adaptation. The present costs of transportation and forgone earnings must be weighed against future earnings in the receiving country. Thus, migration may be a prudent investment even if the initial wages in the receiving country are less than the wages in the sending country.

Barry Chiswick has presented data for several countries and time periods indicating that immigrants initially earn less than natives with comparable skills.[1] However, after they adapt to new economic and cultural conditions, their earnings eventually surpass those of comparable natives. In addition to altering factor proportions, migration may promote the international transmission of technology.

[1] Barry Chiswick, "The Economic Progress of Immigrants: Some Apparently Universal Patterns," in William Fellner, ed., *Contemporary Economic Problems, 1979*. Washington, D.C.: American Enterprise Institute, 1979.

11.2 MOTIVES
FOR MIGRATION

It is useful to distinguish between migrants who are motivated by better economic oportunities and those who move for noneconomic reasons such as war, religion, and politics. The economic migrants should be more productive in the receiving country, but the noneconomic migrants need not be. The latter group, commonly called refugees, may accept lower incomes to avoid noneconomic disadvantages in the sending country. The Overseas Development Council identified 16 million refugees in 1980, including large numbers of Vietnamese, Cambodians, Laotians, Palestinians, and Ethiopians. Therefore, economic migration is likely to increase world income for the same reasons that voluntary trade does, but the movement of refugees is not.

In addition to actual migrants, there may be many potential migrants every year who are prevented from moving by emigration barriers in their home countries or immigration restrictions abroad. A few countries, including the People's Republic of China, continue to restrict internal migration. Legal barriers that restrain potential migrants who would have been more productive abroad have the effect of reducing world income.

One situation that prompts immigration barriers occurs when foreigners become a significant fraction of the work force. Fear of foreign domination brought about immigration barriers in Switzerland and Kuwait. In 1982, native Kuwaitis comprised only 40 percent of the country's population of 1.5 million. International migration may be temporary as well as permanent. Seasonal workers in agriculture may follow harvests. Guest workers' migration may follow business cycles. Multinational firms may send executives abroad for temporary duty. Students may study abroad. In 1981, 312,000 foreign students studied in U.S. colleges and universities. They comprised 3 percent of the total student body and received 16 percent of the doctoral degrees.[2] However, not all students are temporary migrants. From 1960 to 1979, 53,000 Taiwanese students left home to study abroad but only 12 percent returned to Taiwan.[3]

11.3 U.S. MIGRATION
HISTORY

Apparently the first known Americans migrated from Asia via Alaska many centuries before Columbus arrived. These early immigrants, later called Indians by the Europeans, were probably motivated by better fishing and hunting

[2] The leading countries of origin in descending order were Iran, Taiwan, Nigeria, Canada, Japan, Venezuela, Saudi Arabia, Hong Kong, India, and Lebanon.

[3] See V. Kwok and H. Leland, "An Economic Model of the Brain Drain," *American Economic Review*, March 1982.

opportunities in America. If so, they were economic migrants, although they left no written records to confirm this explanation. Following the English settlements at Jamestown and Plymouth in the seventeenth century, many Europeans arrived for a variety of reasons. Many sought better economic opportunities; others fled political and religious persecution. Some migrants were prisoners, whose crimes ranged from murder to poverty. Many people financed the trip by becoming indentured servants, which permitted people without property to finance their migration. Lenders were promised a limited claim on the workers' labor services, but it was often difficult to enforce the terms of the contract.

Millions of Africans arrived as slaves. There is some evidence that slaves were more productive in America than in Africa; however, the productivity gain was appropriated by slave owners or consumers of labor-intensive products rather than by the involuntary migrants.[4] Legal importation of slaves into the United States ended in 1808, but smuggling of slaves continued until the end of domestic slavery in the 1860s. Until 1921 there were hardly any restrictions on immigration into the United States. The exceptions were a restriction against Chinese laborers in the 1880s, a "gentlemen's agreement" with the Japanese government that limited Japanese migration, and the ban on imports of slaves.[5]

Because of the vast flow of migrants, the United States has been described as the "melting pot" of the world. The net inflow of 24 million people from 1820 to 1914 is unmatched in world history. "By 1920, nineteenth century immigrants and their descendants had doubled the size of the American population compared with that which would have resulted from the colonial stock of 1790 alone."[6]

The total number of immigrants to the United States for the period 1820 to 1979 is shown in Table 11-1. Since the total population grew during the period, each immigrant represented a smaller portion of the population in later years. The numbers fluctuate with economic and political conditions in the United States and Europe, but a couple of periods stand out. Immigration was never more than 100,000 per year until the 1840s. It accelerated in the period 1851 to 1854, when it averaged more than 400,000 per year. This rate of immigration was not reached again until the 1880s. In the period 1880 to 1893, immigration averaged more than 500,000 per year. The largest influx of people in the history of the United States occurred in the decade prior to World War

---

[4] See Robert W. Fogel and Stanley Engerman, *Time on the Cross: The Economics of American Negro Slavery* (Boston: Little, Brown, 1974), for an economic analysis of slavery.

[5] The early attitude toward immigration was represented by the inscription on the Statue of Liberty: "Give me your tired, your poor, your huddled masses yearning to be free, the wretched refuse of your teeming shores. Send these, the homeless, the tempest-tost to me. I lift my lamp beside the golden door."

[6] Richard A. Easterlin, "American Population Since 1940," in *The American Economy in Transition*, Martin Feldstein, ed. (Chicago: University of Chicago Press, 1980), pp. 301–302.

TABLE 11-1   U.S. Immigration, 1820–1979
(thousands)

YEAR	NUMBER	YEAR	NUMBER	YEAR	NUMBER	YEAR	NUMBER
1820	10	1860	180	1900	449	1940	71
1821	12	1861	113	1901	438	1941	52
1822	9	1862	114	1902	649	1942	29
1823	8	1863	200	1903	857	1943	24
1824	10	1864	222	1904	813	1944	29
1825	13	1865	287	1905	1,026	1945	38
1826	14	1866	186	1906	1,101	1946	109
1827	22	1867	342	1907	1,285	1947	147
1828	30	1868	282	1908	783	1948	171
1829	25	1869	353	1909	752	1949	188
1830	25	1870	387	1910	1,042	1950	249
1831	24	1871	321	1911	879	1951	206
1832	54	1872	405	1912	838	1952	266
1833	60	1873	460	1913	1,198	1953	170
1834	68	1874	313	1914	1,218	1954	208
1835	49	1875	227	1915	327	1955	238
1836	81	1876	170	1916	299	1956	322
1837	85	1877	142	1917	295	1957	327
1838	45	1878	138	1918	111	1958	254
1839	75	1879	178	1919	141	1959	261
1840	92	1880	457	1920	430	1960	265
1841	88	1881	669	1921	805	1961	271
1842	111	1882	789	1922	310	1962	284
1843	57	1883	603	1923	523	1963	306
1844	85	1884	519	1924	707	1964	292
1845	120	1885	395	1925	294	1965	297
1846	159	1886	334	1926	304	1966	323
1847	239	1887	490	1927	335	1967	362
1848	229	1888	547	1928	307	1968	454
1849	300	1889	444	1929	280	1969	359
1850	315	1890	455	1930	242	1970	373
1851	409	1891	560	1931	97	1971	370
1852	397	1892	623	1932	36	1972	385
1853	401	1893	503	1933	23	1973	400
1854	460	1894	314	1934	29	1974	395
1855	230	1895	280	1935	35	1975	386
1856	224	1896	343	1936	36	1976	399
1857	272	1897	231	1937	50	1977	462
1858	145	1898	230	1938	68	1978	601
1859	156	1899	312	1939	83	1979	460

Source: U.S. Department of Commerce *Historical Statistics of the U.S., 1975,* and U.S. Department of Commerce *Statistical Abstract of the U.S.,* Washington, D.C.: U.S. Government Printing Office, 1980.

I. From 1905 to 1914, immigration averaged more than 1 million people per year. There was a sharp decline during the war, and subsequent immigration was limited by the quotas imposed in the 1920s.

The Quota Law of 1921 placed the first limit on the total number of immigrants. Legislation passed in 1924 and 1929 also imposed quotas by country of origin. Immigration virtually ceased in the 1930s, because of a decline in economic opportunities associated with the Great Depression. The 1965 amendments to the immigration law, which took effect in 1968, altered the national composition of migrants without changing the total number.

Table 11-2 shows the source of migrants for the period 1820 to 1978. Germany, Italy, Great Britain, and Ireland were the largest contributors, although the Irish share declined steadily over the period. The Scandinavian countries, Russia, and Italy had small shares at the beginning of the period, but they were major sources of migrants toward the end of the period. For the

TABLE 11-2   Source of U.S. Immigrants, 1820–1978

BY REGION

PERIOD	TOTAL (MILLIONS)	PERCENTAGE EUROPEAN	PERCENTAGE ASIAN	PERCENTAGE AMERICAN
1820–1978	48.7	74%	6%	19%
1961–1970	3.3	34	13	52
1971–1978	3.5	19	33	45

BY COUNTRY, 1850–1920

COUNTRY	TOTAL (MILLIONS)
Germany	7.0
Italy	5.3
Great Britain	4.9
Ireland	4.7
Austria-Hungary	4.3
Canada	4.1
USSR	3.4
Mexico	2.1
Sweden	1.3
Norway	0.9

Source: U.S. Department of Commerce *Statistical Abstract of the U.S.*, Washington, D.C.: U.S. Government Printing Office, 1980.

entire period, 74 percent of the immigrants were European, 19 percent were American, and 6 percent were Asian. However, the 1965 amendment reduced the percentage of Europeans sharply. From 1971 to 1978, the share of Europeans declined to 19 percent, whereas the percentage of Americans rose to 45 percent and Asians rose to 33 percent.[7] Many refugees fled Europe following World War II. Later the "brain drain" of well-educated people from low-income countries received much attention.

The most recent wave of migrants to the United States has been from Mexico, but the exact magnitude is not known because much of the movement has been illegal. Because some of the Mexican workers are temporary migrants and many who stay do not have permanent legal status, they have been compared with the guest workers of Europe. In addition to the economic migrants from Mexico, groups of refugees from Vietnam, Cuba, and Haiti have arrived recently. Even though recent immigration has been smaller than before World War I, it constituted 20 percent of the U.S. population increase in the 1970s. When illegal immigrants are included, the figure may be as high as 33 percent. The importance of immigration for population increase has been enhanced by the low U.S. birth rate. Although annual immigration has become relatively more important recently, the cumulative effect of the immigration quotas has been to reduce the share of foreign-born residents. The percentage of foreign-born residents of the United States dropped from 13 percent in 1920 to 5 percent in 1980.

11.4 MARGINAL PRODUCTIVITY ANALYSIS

Economic migrants leave home because their productivity is greater in the receiving country than it is in the sending country. Migration causes world income to rise because national income rises by more in the receiving country than it falls in the country of emigration. Migration also changes relative prices and the distribution of income in both countries. It changes the relative supplies of labor and capital in both the sending and receiving countries. As a result, it alters relative factor prices and the distribution of income. Labor becomes more abundant and the wage falls in the receiving country. At the same time, capital becomes scarce and its return rises. Migration has the opposite effect on capital and labor in the sending country. Product markets are also affected in both countries. Output of the labor-intensive product rises and its price falls in the country of immigration, with the opposite effects abroad.

The precise effects can be demonstrated in terms of the marginal pro-

---

[7] The main sources of legal immigrants from 1972 to 1976 in descending order were Mexico, the Philippines, Korea, Cuba, India, Taiwan, and the Dominican Republic. See U.S. Congress, Select Committee of Population, *Legal and Illegal Immigration to the United States*, Serial C, 95th Cong., 2nd sess., December 1978.

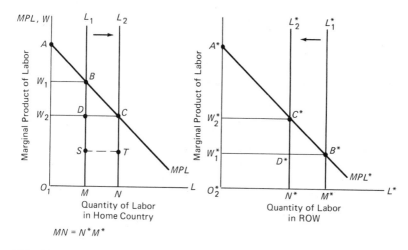

FIGURE 11-2 **Labor Migration to the Home Country**

ductivity of labor in each country, shown in Figure 11-2. The horizontal axes represent total labor employment in all industries at home and in ROW. The vertical axes measure the marginal product of labor *(MPL)* in each country. They represent the change in total output associated with a change in the quantity of labor, when capital and technology are held constant. Output represents an index or average of aggregate production in all industries. Aggregate output is conventionally measured by gross national product. The initial supply of labor in the home country is L_1M and the initial wage is O_1W_1. The wage bill or total labor income is O_1W_1BM. The remaining area under the *MPL* curve (W_1AB) is the income of owners of capital. Thus, the sum of these two areas $(O_1ABM = O_1W_1BM + W_1AB)$ represents gross national product.

An analogous situation exists in ROW where the comparable variables are marked with an asterisk. The wage is O_2*W_1* and labor income is O_2*W_1*B*M*. Capital income is W_1*A*B* and gross national product is $O_2*A*B*M*$. Since wages are initially higher in the home country, there is an incentive for workers to move from ROW to the home country. Let $MN = N*M*$ workers migrate to the home country so that the new labor supply curve becomes L_2N. The excess supply of labor at W_1 causes the wage to fall to W_2. Labor income becomes O_1W_2CN, and the income of the initial workers falls to O_1W_2DM from O_1W_1BD. Thus, the area W_2W_1BD represents a decrease in the income of native workers as a result of immigration. The income of immigrant workers rises from $N*D*B*M*$ to $MDCN$. Thus, the immigrants' gain from migration is the area $SDCT$. The income of capital owners rises to W_2AC in the home country. National income in the home country rises by $MBCN$ and falls in ROW by $N*C*B*M*$. World income rises by $SDCT$. Analogous effects on labor and capital occur in ROW. The net effect of migration is to increase world income and to redistribute income from labor to capital at home and from capital to labor abroad. Migration has the same effect on the distribution of income as does an increase in imports of labor-intensive products from ROW to the home country.

The analysis becomes more complicated if capital and labor migrate simultaneously. Skilled workers bring embodied human capital with them, and they may bring financial assets as well. The effect of the combined labor-capital mobility depends on the proportions in which the factors migrate. If the migration increases the labor-capital ratio in the receiving country, the effects are similar to those just discussed. However, if the migrants bring enough capital to reduce the labor-capital ratio in the receiving country, migration will have the opposite effects on the distribution of income. With regard to immigration policy, unskilled workers in the home country might welcome immigration of skilled workers while opposing immigration of unskilled workers. Some migration is permanent, but other movement is temporary or seasonal. Some agricultural workers follow the harvest season in different countries. Workers who explore for oil take their services all over the world without necessarily changing their permanent residence. Some prominent conductors are known to hold appointments with symphonies in several countries at the same time. The return of a temporary migrant simply reverses the initial economic effect.

Another complication is that migrants may embody technology. Information about technology is not a free good, and migration of skilled workers may be one way to transfer technology from one country to another. Individual firms try to protect technological secrets by patents, licensing, and internal security. Nevertheless, mobility of employees among firms tends to transfer technology. Sometimes governments have attempted to protect technological secrets by restricting exports of high-technology products. During the Industrial Revolution, England restricted exports of textile machinery, but this did not prevent people from emigrating with ideas. Samuel Slater and Francis Lowell are examples of those who successfully transferred textile technology from Old England to New England. For centuries, France has been exporting chefs, who embody both labor and culinary technology.

11.5 MIGRATION, TAXES, AND EXTERNALITIES

The foregoing discussion assumes that people move for economic reasons, which implies that their productivity is higher in the receiving country. It also ignores the effects of taxes and externalities in the two countries. However, the existence of income taxes with different national tax rates could induce workers to move toward the country where their productivity is lower, which would reduce world income. The reason for this possible perverse move is that a worker's contribution to output is measured by his or her gross marginal product (GMP), but labor supply behavior depends on the after-tax wage or net marginal product *(NMP)*. A country with higher labor productivity can discourage immigration by imposing a higher tax on labor. Employers would have to pay a higher gross wage to attract the same number of workers. In the extreme case where enough workers migrate to equalize after-tax wages, the equilibrium condition is

$$NMP = NMP^\star$$
$$W(1 - t) = W^\star(1 - t^\star)$$

If the tax rate is higher at home $(t > t^\star)$, the gross wage (W) and gross marginal product must also be greater at home. Thus, labor taxation discourages immigration and encourages emigration of workers. Favorable tax laws are one reason why many wealthy people have made Switzerland their permanent place of residence. It is also possible that relatively high U.S. taxes on capital have encouraged importation of labor-intensive products and immigration of labor.[8]

Taxes can be high enough to convert a labor importing country into a labor exporting country. Changing the direction of migration from high-productivity countries to low-productivity countries reduces world income. Suppose that labor is more productive at home than in ROW. This implies that the gross marginal product of labor and the wage will be greater at home:

$$GMP = W > GMP^\star = W^\star$$

In absence of taxation workers would move to the home country and world income would rise. Suppose that the gross marginal product is 16 at home and 10 in ROW. Let the home country impose a 50 percent tax $(t = 0.5)$ and ROW have a 10 percent tax on labor income $(t^\star = 0.1)$. The net marginal product of labor, $GMP(1 - t)$, at home will be 8, and in ROW it will be 9:

	Home	ROW
GMP	16	10
Tax rate (t)	0.5	0.1
$NMP = GMP(1 - t)$	8	9

After-tax earnings are greater in ROW, and workers will migrate in that direction, even though labor is more productive at home. The perverse migration occurs because the tax differential dominates the productivity difference.

The effect of taxation on migration can be seen in Figure 11-3. The initial labor supplies are O_1L_1 at home and $O_2L_1^\star$ in ROW. The gross wage is $O_1w_1 = 16$ at home and $O_2W_1^\star = 10$ in ROW. Without taxes migration would in-

[8] See John Whalley, "Discriminatory Features of Domestic Factor Tax Systems in a Goods Mobile-Factors Immobile Trade Model: An Empirical General Equilibrium Approach," *Journal of Political Economy*, December 1980.

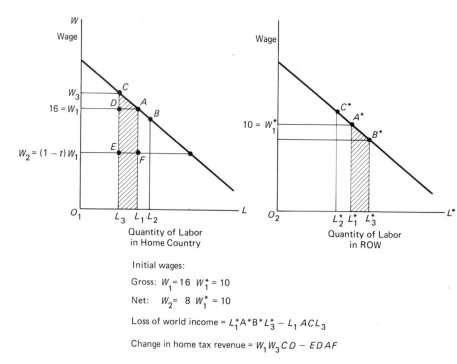

FIGURE 11-3   **Taxation and Perverse Migration**

crease the labor supply at home by $L_1 L_2$ and reduce it in ROW by $L_1^* L_2^*$. World income would rise because the area $L_1 ABL_2$ exceeds the area $L_1^* A^* C^* L_2^*$. However, the 50 percent tax at home lowers the NMP to $W_2 = 8$. $L_1 L_3$ workers move abroad, but world income falls because marginal productivity is greater at home. The magnitude of the decline in world income is measured by the difference between the decrease in national income at home $(L_1 ACL_3)$ and the increase in national income in ROW $(L_1^* A^* B^* L_3^*)$. Migration reduces world income in this case because differential taxation distorts incentives. An analogous situation with trade would occur if a country with a comparative advantage in labor-intensive products taxed those products so heavily that they became a net importer of those goods. It would become an exporter of capital-intensive products, and international trade would reduce world income. Such a perverse trade pattern would lead countries to specialize in what they did worst.

A similar perverse result is possible if workers generate external benefits to society that are different in the two countries. External benefits are benefits to society for which a worker is not compensated. If the research of a scientist is worth $14 to society when he is paid $10, the external benefit from his labor is $4. If the externalities are higher in the country where wages are lower, a perverse migration is possible. The worker's contribution is his marginal social product *(MSP)*, and the worker is paid his marginal private product *(MPP)*. The deviation between the two is his marginal external product *(MEP)*:

$$MEP = MSP - MPP$$

Suppose that a worker's productivity is the following:

	ROW	Home
$MPP = W$	10	12
MSP	14	13
MEB	4	1

The worker's total contribution to society is greater in ROW $(MSP^\star = 14 > MSP = 13)$, but he is only paid his private product, so he will migrate to the home country where he is paid more $(MPP = 12 > MPP^\star = 10)$. The reason for the socially perverse migration is the differential external benefit in ROW $(MEB^\star = 4 > MEB = 1)$. It would be in the interest of the ROW economy to internalize this external benefit by paying the worker for the externality that he generates. With sufficient compensation, he would remain in ROW, and world income would rise. A possible source of this problem is a government policy of setting maximum salaries for workers who can earn more abroad. Such policies contributed to a brain drain of scientists, engineers, and medical doctors from low-income countries that began in the 1960s.

11.6 MIGRATION AND WAGE EQUALIZATION

Migration tends to equalize wages between countries. One can imagine conditions under which wages would be completely equalized, but they are not met in the real world. There are several reasons for wage disparities, and the most obvious are legal barriers to immigration and emigration and the cost of transportation. Transport cost includes the cost of transporting the worker and the earnings forgone while searching for a job in the country of immigration. Learning the language and culture of the high-wage country is another form of transport cost that discourages migration. Thus, even if all workers were identical, unrestricted migration would not equalize wages.

Differences in skills or human capital are another important reason for wage differences across countries. It is not surprising that engineers in the United States earn more than laborers do in Mexico. Some skills are less easily transferred to a foreign country, and the specificity of those skills is a barrier to migration that is responsible for wage differentials. For example, Mexican baseball players can more readily transfer their skills to the United States than can Mexican lawyers.

A related point is that migration entails both costs and benefits, but the costs are mainly in the present and the benefits are mainly in the future. Thus, migration is a form of investment. The benefits are measured by the difference between foreign and domestic earnings $(w - w^\star)$ in each future period that the migrant works. The duration of the benefit stream depends on the expected work life of the migrant and his age. In fact, a disproportionate number of migrants are young people who expect a long stream of benefits. Conversely, an older worker might be unwilling to migrate even if he could earn higher wages in a foreign country. Age, combined with transport costs, discourages migration, and it serves as a barrier to wage equalization.

Consider the example of a worker who could earn more abroad but who must bear the cost of transporting herself and forgoing earnings for one period. The profitability of migration depends on the wage differential, the cost of migration, and future work life. Let the process involve three time periods, where the costs occur in the present, and the benefits come in two future periods. The costs are

$$w_0 - w_0^\star - TR$$

The benefits are the wage differential in each future period (indicated by a subscript):

$$(w - w^\star)_1 + (w - w^\star)_2$$

The formal investment problem is to calculate the net present value of the stream:

$$w_0 - w_0^\star - TR) + (w_1 - w_1^\star) + (w_2 - w_2^\star)$$

Let ROW wages be $w^\star = \$2$, home wages be $w = \$12$, and direct transport costs be $TR = \$8$. Let the interest rate the worker pays to borrow (or the rate she gives up if she uses her own savings) be $r = 0.05$, and assume that she cannot work while migrating ($w_0 = 0$ in the present). The net present value is

$$
\begin{aligned}
(w_0 - w_0^\star - TR)_0 &+ \frac{(w_1 - w_1^\star)}{1 + r} + \frac{w_2 - w_2^\star}{(1 + r)^2} \\
= (0 - 2 - 8) \quad &+ \frac{12 - 2}{1.05} + \frac{12 - 2}{1.10} = (-\$10.00 + \$18.61) = \$8.61
\end{aligned}
$$

Migration would be a profitable investment for such a worker. However, if the worker were older and expected to work in only one future time period ($w_2 = w_2^\star = 0$), the net present value would be -0.48, and the investment would not be profitable. Even though the older worker could earn higher wages abroad ($w = 12 > w^\star = 2$), she would not migrate because the present value of the earnings differential (9.52) is less than the cost of moving (10.00). Conversely, the younger worker with the same earnings potential would find it profitable to migrate. Thus, potential migrants need more information than simply current international wage differentials. Migration may be prudent even if the initial wage of the migrant is less than what was earned at home.

Suppose that a worker's skills are not readily transferred until he learns the language and customs of the receiving country. In the preceding example, let the initial wage in the receiving country be $w_1 = \$1 < w_1^* = 2$ and the subsequent wage be $w_2 = \$17$. The net present value is

$$-10 \ -0.95 + 13.64 = \ -10 + \frac{(-1)}{1.05} + \frac{(17-2)}{1.10} = \ +\$2.69$$

An observer who only looked at current wage differentials would have difficulty explaining why workers would move abroad to accept jobs for $1 when they could earn $2 at home. The situation is easily explained by the expected increase in future earnings ($w_2 = 17 > w_1 = 1$). This example is consistent with the findings of Barry Chiswick, who discovered a systematic increase in immigrants earnings as a function of the number of years of residence in the country.[9] The economic explanation is that it takes time to adapt one's skills to a new environment.

11.7 U.S. IMMIGRATION POLICY

Until 1921 there were few restrictions on immigration into the United States. The exceptions were the ban on importing slaves after 1808 and the restrictions on Chinese immigration in 1882 and Japanese immigration in 1907. Table 11-2 shows the source of immigrants to the United States from 1820 to 1978. All the legal slave imports occurred before then, and the immigration of free Africans has been negligible. A major change in immigration policy occurred in 1921 when quotas were imposed for total immigration and for each sending country. The national quotas were based on historical migration, which strongly favored migrants from Europe. The 1929 amendment based national quotas on the origins of residents revealed by the 1920 census. For the entire period, 74 percent of immigrants came from European countries. Thus, the quotas of the 1920s reduced the total number of immigrants, but it preserved the traditional pattern of immigration.

In 1965 the immigration laws were amended, and the earlier national quotas were replaced by regional quotas. The main effect was to increase the share of migrants from Asia and America and decrease the share from Europe. Greater

[9]Barry Chiswick, "The Economic Progress of Immigrants: Some Apparently Universal Patterns," in William Fellner, ed., *Contemporary Economic Problems, 1979*. Washington, D.C.: American Enterprise Institute, 1979.

preference was given to the reunification of families. Recent migrants have been well educated, and the large number of scientists, engineers, and medical doctors immigrating from low-income countries has led to some concern about the brain drain. This policy bias toward high human capital immigrants has been criticized in the same way as a tariff structure that favors exports of primary products to the United States. Both practices are said to have an unfavorable effect on low-income countries. Immigration laws have not changed since 1965, but the large volume of illegal immigrants has called into question the ability of the Immigration and Naturalization Service to enforce existing laws.

Product trade can be restricted either by a tariff or a quota, and in principle the same instruments could be used to restrict migration. In fact, quotas are nearly always used to restrict both immigration and emigration. As long as a quota is binding, it means that unsuccessful immigrants are willing to pay for the right to enter, and governments could auction entry rights to the highest bidder and appropriate the equivalent of tariff proceeds.[10] A similar practice could be used for emigrants. Such explicit money payments are generally considered to be inhumane, but two examples can be offered.

Concern about the unfairness of the brain drain has led Bhagwati and others to advocate a tax to be paid by migrants, collected in the country of immigration, and the proceeds returned to the country of emigration.[11] The justification is that migrants owe their native country for their education that was provided at below cost by taxpayers. The Soviet Union has also used the same logic to tax Jewish emigrants to Israel. Something like a tariff is sometimes paid by illegal immigrants when they hire specialists to smuggle them into the country and supply forged credentials. Some countries such as Australia, South Africa, and Israel have paid explicit subsidies to immigrants with certain characteristics.

If a tariff were used to regulate immigration, a tariff rate (including zero) could be chosen so as to admit any desired number of immigrants. With a tariff, everyone in the world who was willing to pay the fee could be admitted without regard for personal characteristics. Conversely, a quota requires a rule specifying who gets admitted to the country. Many rules have been used, and they often include controversial characteristics such as race, religion, nationality, occupation, kinship, and politics.

The United States has not actively regulated emigration, but some countries do. The Berlin Wall was built in 1961 to stem emigration from East Germany, and it remains as a symbol of an extreme policy toward migration. The USSR and China have restricted emigration and internal migration. The U.S. Congress responded to Soviet emigration policy by passing the Jackson-Vanik

---

[10] Indonesia has discouraged the employment of foreign workers by charging a fee for compulsory work permits. In June 1983 the fee was $400 per month paid by the employer. See "Work Permit Charges Quadruple in Indonesia," *Wall Street Journal*, June 2, 1983.

[11] See Jagdish Bhagwati, *Taxing the Brain Drain: A Proposal* (Amsterdam: North Holland, 1978).

amendment that denies most favored nation status to countries that restrict emigration. Cuba restricts emigration, but from time to time (e.g., 1980) the rules are relaxed and a surge of migration occurs. Exile was once a common punishment for certain crimes in Europe, and it provided many immigrants for America during the colonial period. The number of permanent emigrants from the United States is small, but many Americans work abroad temporarily. Whether American corporations staff their foreign operations with American nationals or foreigners depends to a certain extent on tax policy. The U.S. tax law was changed in 1981 so as to lower the total tax liability (foreign plus domestic) of Americans working abroad. Spokespeople for American corporations claimed that their foreign operations were being harmed by their inability to induce Americans to accept foreign assignments. A specific argument offered was that exports of U.S. multinational corporations would be greater with more American executives directing foreign operations.

11.8 THE BRAIN DRAIN

The brain drain became a political issue in the 1960s because it was alleged to have an unfavorable effect on the sending countries. The term refers to the migration of highly educated people from low-income countries to high-income countries such as the United States, Canada, Australia, and the United Kingdom. Canada and the United Kingdom were both receivers and senders of educated migrants, and the United States was the major ultimate destination. Many of the migrants were from low-income countries, especially in Asia, but more prosperous countries such as Switzerland, Norway, and The Netherlands were also net exporters of educated people. The skills of U.S. immigrants during the 1960s contrasted sharply to the skills of earlier immigrants.

In 1967, 35 percent of U.S. immigrants were classified as professional and entrepreneurial, whereas the comparable figure for the 1907–1923 period was 3 percent. In 1967, 11 percent were laborers, and in the 1907–1923 period, 51 percent were laborers. The number of professional and technical immigrants to the United States more than doubled between 1956 and 1967, and the proportion from low-income countries increased from 25 percent to 57 percent. The largest increase came from Asian countries, which were affected by the abolition of national quotas in 1965. Many of the migrants came as students who became permanent residents after earning their degrees. The ratio of people who came to the United States as students to total professional migrants in 1967 was 89 percent for Taiwan, 80 percent for Korea, 78 percent for India, and 71 percent for Iran. In Canada the number of professional immigrants was large relative to the number of Canadian college graduates in the same discipline. For the period 1953 to 1963, the figures were 141 percent for immigrant architects, 73 percent for engineers, and 53 percent for physicians.

The brain drain affected both receiving and sending countries, but the effect on countries of emigration has been more controversial. Has migration been a barrier to economic growth in sending countries, and if so, what policies can reduce the flow? There are several ways to assess the impact on countries of emigration. One can measure the effect of emigration on total income (GNP), income per capita, or the income of those left behind. An emigrant who produces anything useful has a marginal product greater than zero, and his or her exit necessarily reduces total national income. However, this does not imply that the remaining residents are poorer. The effect of emigration on per capita income depends on whether the migrant's initial income was above average. If it was, his or her exit will cause per capita income to fall. However, this does not imply that the per capita income of those left behind falls. Indeed, if the migrant has above-average income in the sending country and below-average income in the receiving country, per capita income will fall in *both* countries. This arithmetic result is consistent with an increase in world income that is expected when a worker moves toward a higher-productivity country.

The important economic impact on those left behind is the change in relative factor supplies. If labor emigrates without capital, wages should rise relative to the rental on capital in the sending country. However, if emigrants possess more than the average endowment of human capital, their exit may increase the relative scarcity of unskilled labor.

It is possible to induce perverse migration flows by differential tax policies, wage policies, or differential externalities as discussed. Perverse migration is the movement of workers from countries where their productivity is high to where it is low, because they are not compensated for their output. However, the problem can be controlled by the sending country. If valuable citizens are emigrating because of high tax burdens, the remaining residents can change the tax system to make residency more attractive to potential emigrants. The same principle applies to residents who may generate external benefits through "uncompensated leadership." If these external benefits are truly useful to other citizens, they should be willing to collectively compensate potential emigrants.

Two types of policies in sending countries contribute to the brain drain. First is the refusal to compensate workers as much as their foreign opportunity costs. Compensation may be limited by maximum salaries for certain occupations or by high taxes. In some countries, the government is the major employer of educated people, and it can influence emigration directly by its salary schedule for public employees. Limiting the compensation of professionals in low-income countries is usually justified in terms of domestic equity. If it results in the emigration of productive people, those people remaining must ask whether this is a reasonable price to pay for egalitarianism.

A second contributing policy is financing domestic education at the expense of taxpayers. If students paid for their own education (e.g., by loans), taxpayers would not lose their contribution when workers emigrate. Alternatively, governments could levy an emigration tax based on the public cost of education, but a similar Soviet policy has been heavily criticized as being inhumane.

11.9 THE ECONOMIC EXPERIENCE OF IMMIGRANTS TO THE UNITED STATES

Two possible goals of immigration policy are (1) to improve the economic productivity of the country and (2) to provide humanitarian relief for refugees. It is not always easy to distinguish economic migrants from refugees, but economic migrants can be expected to have higher earnings in the receiving country than comparable refugees.

Barry Chiswick has studied the economic experience of immigrants to the United States from various countries. He analyzed separately the experiences of the following groups: Chinese, Japanese, Filipinos, blacks, Cubans, Mexicans, and all other whites. The economic performance of each immigrant group was compared with that of comparable natives (same age, education, population) of the United States. Since skills are not immediately transferable between countries, an hypothesis is that immigrants will initially earn less than comparable natives, but the gap will decline with residence in the new country. A related hypothesis is that groups identifiable as refugees should show less improvement than economic migrants. Furthermore, if there is self-selection among economic migrants in favor of people with greater innate ability or work motivation, the immigrants can be expected to earn more than comparable natives after some period of adjustment.

Chiswick found empirical evidence to support these hypotheses for nearly every immigrant group.[12] U.S. immigrants initially earned less than did comparable natives. After a transition of 13 to 18 years, they earned the same incomes as natives, and eventually they earned more than native Americans. Similar results have been found for migrants to Canada, the United Kingdom, and Israel. The differential productivity of economic migrants relative to refugees may have implications for the 1965 amendments to the U.S. immigration law. The new law favors kinship relative to economic productivity in selecting immigrants. Thus, the new policy may satisfy the humanitarian goal of immigration policy at the expense of economic productivity.

11.10 EUROPEAN GUEST WORKERS

An important economic characteristic of the European Economic Community is unrestricted movement of labor among member countries. Within the initial community, large numbers of workers moved from low-wage countries such as

---

[12] The exception was Mexican immigrants, whose earnings remained below those of natives and other immigrants with comparable characteristics. See Barry R. Chiswick, "The Economic Progress of Immigrants: Some Apparently Universal Patterns" in *Contemporary Economics Problems, 1979*, William Fellner, ed. (Washington, AEI, 1979).

Italy to high-wage countries such as Germany. As the EEC expanded to include the United Kingdom, Denmark, Ireland, and Greece, the European labor market became more unified. In addition, some countries, especially Germany, have permitted migrants from nonmember countries such as Turkey, Yugoslavia, Spain, and Portugal to work temporarily as guest workers. The main difference between guest workers and immigrants is that guests are temporary residents and immigrants are permanent residents. Because of their permanent residence, immigrants have a stronger claim on public services such as unemployment compensation, pensions, and education. Immigrants usually bring families, but most guest workers leave their families behind. Some countries have sought to decrease the number of guests during recession and permit more during business expansion. A successful countercyclical immigration policy would shift some of the burden of unemployment onto foreigners.

The German guest worker program was the largest in Europe. German economic recovery from World War II first lured ethnic Germans from abroad. The construction of the Berlin Wall stopped the flow of workers from East Germany.

The first guest worker agreements were made with Greece, Spain, Yugoslavia, and Turkey in 1960 and 1961. The number of guest workers rose from 300,000 in 1960 to 2.5 million in 1972. The largest groups were Turks and Yugoslavs, who comprised 12 percent of the work force in 1972. The temporary status of guest workers was demonstrated during the recession of 1966, when 500,000 workers went home. However, later the guests acquired more permanent status. Employers sought to avoid some of the recruitment and training costs of shuttling temporary workers back and forth. Policy changes permitted migrants to remain in Germany, bring their families, and use public services. Recruitment of new migrants ended in 1973. Since then, the number of foreign workers has fallen to 2 million, but the number of nonworking dependents of migrants (2.5 million) exceeds the number of workers. The resulting claim on public services has created a political problem. The 1.4 million Turks with their linguistic and religious differences are a conspicuous minority in several large cities. Some of the economic benefits of the guest worker program are obvious. Access to cheaper labor contributed to Germany's prosperity during the period, and migrant workers' remittances were a major source of foreign exchange earnings for sending countries. However, the experience of Germany suggests that it may be difficult to prevent guest workers from becoming immigrants.

11.11 MEXICAN MIGRATION TO THE UNITED STATES

The recent increase in immigration of Mexican workers is explained by both supply and demand factors. The supply of migrants, often called "push factors," depends on population changes and job opportunities in Mexico. The demand for migrants, which summarizes the "pull factors," depends on wages and job opportunities in the United States.

Prior to World War II, the number of Mexican immigrants was not large, in spite of the absence of barriers.[13] From 1942 to 1964, the United States operated the *bracero* program, a legal system of importing workers from Mexico under contract. Several hundred thousand workers entered the country each year, primarily to work in agriculture. In the peak year of immigration in 1957, 450,000 workers entered. The number of illegal aliens apprehended by immigration authorities increased as soon as the program was terminated in 1964. Interestingly, the illegal immigrants apprehended by the Immigration and Naturalization Service have the same economic characteristics as the legal immigrants do. Because the immigration laws have not been enforced effectively, it has been said that the *bracero* program continued in fact even though it was legally terminated.

The volume of illegal immigrants increased sharply, although a precise number cannot be established. The Scheuer Committee Report of 1978 estimated the average annual flow of illegal immigrants as 300,000 per year, a number nearly as large as the flow of legal immigrants.[14] A lower estimate of 82,000 to 232,000 for the period 1970 to 1975 was obtained by Heer.[15] The number of deportable aliens apprehended by the Immigration and Naturalization Service rose from 87,000 in 1964 to nearly 900,000 in 1976. Law enforcement is made difficult by the length of the border and the limited budget of the Immigration and Naturalization Service.

A more fundamental problem is that there are strong economic incentives for migration to continue. Rapid population growth in Mexico stimulates immigration in the same way that rapid population growth in Southern and Eastern Europe stimulated migration to the United States prior to World War I. A low birth rate in the United States is a further stimulus. The large wage differential provides a powerful incentive for Mexican workers to move north and for U.S. employers to hire migrant workers. The fact that some illegal aliens return to the United States after being apprehended several times is a measure of the strength of the economic incentive. To some extent, importation of low-wage labor is a substitute for imports of labor-intensive products that would have been imported if the United States pursued a freer trade policy. An example is the production of winter vegetables in Florida and California, when they could be imported from Mexico at lower cost. Florida and California growers have successfully lobbied in favor of nontariff barriers for tomatoes, strawberries, and other vegetables. However, the same trade barriers that cause production to move from Mexico to the United States also provide an incentive for Mexican workers to move north of the border.

---

[13] See Easterlin, "American Population Since 1940."

[14] The Scheuer Report is a congressional document whose formal title is *Legal and Illegal Immigration to the United States*, Serial C, 95th Cong., 2nd sess., December 1978.

[15] David M. Heer, "What Is the Annual Net Flow of Undocumented Mexican Immigrants to the United States?" *Demography*, August 1979.

The early migrants were from rural Mexico, and they tended to return home after seasonal employment in U.S. agriculture. More recent arrivals from urban backgrounds are more likely to take nonagricultural jobs in northern cities. They are also more likely to bring families and become permanent residents of the United States. As were the earlier *braceros*, the illegal aliens are guest workers in the sense that no period of residence will make them eligible for citizenship. Since the workers' productivity is greater in the United States than it is in Mexico, migration increases the income of migrants and the world. Migration puts upward pressure on wages in Mexico, and immigrant remittances are a major source of foreign exchange for Mexico.

However, migration is controversial in the United States because it violates national laws and depresses wages of unskilled workers. Representatives of labor unions have claimed that employment of immigrants has reduced employment opportunities of their members. Proponents of stricter enforcement of the law have suggested penalizing employers of illegal aliens or requiring that all workers carry identification cards. Opposition has been expressed by employers and civil libertarians. The enforcement problem is analogous to the one involving smuggling of illegal drugs. In each case there is a powerful demand in the domestic economy, a ready supply outside the country, and high enforcement costs. In both cases, enforcement costs are higher because a large portion of the population considers the law improper. An alternative policy to importing Mexican workers directly is to import more labor-intensive products, which would improve job opportunities in Mexico.

11.12 MIGRATION AND DOMESTIC EGALITARIANISM

There is an inherent conflict between free migration and an egalitarian domestic policy. To the extent that residents of high-income countries tax themselves to provide a minimum income for poorer residents, this adds to the supply of immigrants and increases the domestic tax burden. Unless the working population is able and willing to provide a minimum income for much of the world, immigration must necessarily be restricted. Given the current notion of poverty, there is a large discrepancy between the poverty-level income in the United States (more than $4,000 per year) and the average level of income in many populous countries, such as India, Pakistan, Bangladesh, and Indonesia ($200 per person per year). Consequently, it would be impossible to have unrestricted immigration and a guaranteed minimum income. Conversely, with restrictive immigration, the gap between domestic and foreign income grows, which presents a different problem. In the case of the U.S.-Mexican border, economic circumstances have made the laws unenforceable. An analogous conflict exists in low-income countries between egalitarian domestic policies and free migration. If governments impose maximum salaries for skilled workers and professionals, those groups will tend to emigrate. The brain drain is partly a function of egalitarian policies in low-income countries.

SUMMARY

International migration is a substitute for international trade. Economic migration, as distinguished from the movement of refugees, can be expected to increase world income. Conversely, that portion of migration caused by war or political and religious persecution may reduce world income. Economic migration tends to transfer labor to areas where its marginal productivity is higher. Since migration is based on the after-tax or net marginal product of labor, it is possible for differential taxation to induce labor to move where its gross marginal product is lower.

More than 50 million immigrants have come to the United States, and they have had a profound economic effect. Because of restrictive legislation in the 1920s, U.S. immigration has never returned to the rate of 1 million people per year experienced in the years 1905 to 1914. The large volume of recent illegal immigration has made an accurate calculation difficult. However, the United States continues to accept more immigrants than any other country.

Recent migrants have been better educated than earlier arrivals, which has led to a controversy about brain drain. Some policies such as the European guest worker program and the U.S. *bracero* program were designed to admit workers on a temporary basis, but experience has shown that economic conditions make it difficult to prevent temporary migrants from becoming permanent residents.

There is an unavoidable conflict between free migration and domestic egalitarian policies. Policies in high-income countries that guarantee minimum incomes to residents stimulate immigration. Policies in low-income countries that limit the compensation of professional workers stimulate emigration. Participation in an open international economy provides many benefits, but it also limits the policy choices available to national governments.

REFERENCES

ABRAMS, ELLIOTT, and FRANKLIN ABRAMS.   "Immigration Policy—Who Gets in and Why?" *Public Interest*, No. 38 (Winter 1975). Changes in U.S. immigration brought about by the 1965 law.

ADAMS, WALTER.   *The Brain Drain*. New York: Macmillan, 1968.

BHAGWATI, JAGDISH.   *Taxing the Brain Drain: A Proposal*. Amsterdam: North-Holland, 1976.

———.   *The Brain Drain and Taxation: Theory and Empirical Evidence*. Amsterdam: North-Holland, 1976.

――――. "Taxing the Brain Drain." *Challenge*, July–August 1976. A popular presentation of the proposal to tax emigration.

BRIGGS, V. M.   "Mexican Workers in the United States Labor Market." *International Labor Review*, No. 5 (1975).

BUSTAMANTE, JORGE.   "Undocumented Immigration for Mexico: Research Report." *International Migration Review*, Spring 1977.

CHISWICK, BARRY.   "Sons of Immigrants. Are They at an Earnings Disadvantage?" *American Economic Review*, February 1977. A study concluding that sons of immigrants earn no less than comparable sons of native Americans.

――――. "The Effect of Americanization on the Earnings of Foreign-Born Men." *Journal of Political Economy*, October 1978. An empirical study of the earnings of immigrants.

――――. "Immigrants and Immigration Policy." In *Contemporary Economic Problems, 1978*, William Fellner, ed. Washington, D.C.: American Enterprise Institute, 1978. An economic analysis of U.S. immigration policy.

――――. "The Economic Progress of Immigrants: Some Apparently Universal Patterns." In *Contemporary Economics Problems*, Washington, D.C. American Enterprise Institute 1979, William Fellner, ed. An analysis of the earnings experience of different ethnic and racial immigrants to the United States.

――――, ed.   *The Gateway: U.S. Immigration Issues and Policies*. Washington, D.C.: American Enterprise Institute, 1982.

CURTIN, PHILIP.   *The Atlantic Slave Trade: A Census*. Madison: University of Wisconsin Press, 1969. An historical study of slave trade between Africa and America.

EASTERLIN, RICHARD A.   "American Population Since 1940." In *The American Economy in Transition*, Martin Feldstein, ed. Chicago: University of Chicago Press, 1980. Discusses immigration in the context of general demographic changes in the United States.

――――. "Immigration: Economic and Social Characteristics." In *Harvard Encyclopedia of American Ethnic Groups*. Cambridge, Mass.: Harvard University Press, 1980.

FOGEL, ROBERT, and STANLEY ENGERMAN.   *Time on the Cross: The Economics of American Negro Slavery*. Boston: Little, Brown, 1974.

GALENSON, WALTER.   *The International Labor Organization: An American View*. Madison: University of Wisconsin Press, 1981.

GRUBEL, HERBERT G., and A. D. SCOTT.   "The International Flow of Human Capital." *American Economic Review*, May 1966.

HAMADA, KOICHI.   "Taxing the Brain Drain: A Global Point of View." In *The New International Economic Order: The North-South Debate*, Jagdish Bhagwati, ed. Cambridge, Mass.: M.I.T. Press, 1977. An analysis of the worldwide efficiency of the brain drain tax.

HEER, DAVID M.   "What Is the Annual Net Flow of Undocumented Mexican Immigrants to the United States?" *Demography*, August 1979.

JENKINS, J. CRAIG.   "Push-Pull in Recent Mexican Migration to the U.S." *International Migration Review*, Spring 1977.

KWOK, V., and H. LELAND.   "An Economic Model of the Brain Drain." *American Economic Review*, March 1982. Advanced theoretical treatment stressing asymmetrical knowledge of workers in the native country and the country in which the worker studied.

LONG, JAMES.   "The Effect of Americanization on Earnings: Some Evidence for Women." *Journal of Political Economy*, June 1980. Extends the work of Chiswick to foreign-born and native women.

MARTIN, PHILIP L.   "Germany's Guestworkers." *Challenge*, July–August 1981. A discussion of Turkish workers in Germany.

————. "Select Commission Suggests Changes in Immigration Policy: A Review Essay." *Monthly Labor Review*, February 1982. Considers recent U.S. immigration policy.

MCNEILL, WILLIAM, and RUTH S. ADAMS. *Human Migration.* Bloomington: Indiana University Press, 1978. A general study of migration emphasizing noneconomic considerations.

PORTES, ALEJANDRO. "Illegal Mexican Migration to the United States." *International Migration Review*, Winter 1978. The entire issue is devoted to Mexican migration.

RYBCZYNSKI, T. M. "Factor Proportions and the Heckscher-Ohlin Theorem." *Economics*, November 1955. Reprinted in Richard E. Caves and Harry G. Johnson, eds., *Readings in International Economics*, Homewood, Ill.: Richard D. Irwin, 1968. Analyzes the effect on production of growth in the quantity of one factor of production.

SIMON, JULIAN L. "The Really Important Effects of Immigration on Natives Incomes." In *The Gateway: U. S. Immigration Issues and Policy*, Barry R. Chiswick, ed. Washington, D.C.: American Enterprise Institute, 1982.

THOMAS, BRINLEY. *Migration and Economic Growth.* rev. ed. Cambridge: Cambridge University Press, 1972. Comprehensive study of the economics of migration.

U.S. BUREAU OF THE CENSUS. "Estimates of the Population of the United States and Components of Change: 1940–78." *Current Population Reports*, Series P-25, no. 802. Washington, D.C.: U.S. Government Printing Office, May 1979.

U.S. CONGRESS, SELECT COMMITTEE OF POPULATION. *Legal and Illegal Immigration to the United States*, Serial C, 95th Congr., 2nd sess., December 1978. Commonly referred to as the Scheuer Committee Report.

WACHTER, MICHAEL L. "Second Thoughts About Illegal Immigrants." *Fortune*, May 1978.

CHAPTER TWELVE
INTERNATIONAL
CAPITAL MOBILITY

12.1 INTERNATIONAL INVESTMENT AS SUBSTITUTE FOR TRADE

Chapter 11 analyzed international labor migration. This chapter will extend the analysis of factor mobility to international investment. Many of the economic effects of labor and capital mobility are the same, but there are differences as well. For example, since the owner of capital need not migrate with his or her capital, nonpecuniary considerations may be less important for international investment than for international migration. A worker who could earn a higher income in country Z might not migrate there because of a despotic government in Z. However, the same worker might be willing to invest his or her capital in Z.

It was shown in Chapter 11 that migration substitutes for trade in labor-intensive products. Similarly, international investment substitutes for trade in capital-intensive products. This chapter will consider the various forms of capital flows. They may be bank loans, bonds, shares of corporations, or direct investment. The relationship between the balance-of-payments accounts of a country and capital flows will be considered. International investment changes the relative factor endowments in the source and host countries. Marginal productivity analysis will be used to show the effect on national incomes and relative factor prices in both countries.

If borrowing or lending countries are large, international investment may alter the national terms of trade. Terms of trade effects will be considered in the context of the transfer problem. Much of international investment consists of corporations' purchasing plant and equipment and operating enterprises abroad. Such direct investments by multinational firms will be analyzed. Some investors seek to balance their asset portfolios, and international investment is one way in which they can achieve portfolio diversification. The chapter will also consider the effect of taxation and quantitative restrictions on capital flows. The final section considers the effect of lending and foreign aid by national governments and international institutions.

Capital tends to flow toward countries where the return on capital is higher. By changing the relative scarcity of capital in both countries, international investment decreases the return on capital in the host country and increases the return in the source country. Thus, capital mobility tends to equalize the return on capital between countries in the same way that migration tends to equalize wages. It was shown in Chapter 4 that international trade tends to equalize prices of factors of production. Capital mobility and trade are alternative means of equalizing the return on capital.

Since capital mobility and trade are substitutes, an increase in barriers to trade would widen the international earnings differential on capital. A greater earnings differential would stimulate capital mobility. International investments that are induced by tariffs and import quotas are called tariff factories. Much of the foreign investment in the European Economic Community since the Treaty of Rome has been induced by the discriminatory tariff structure. For example, an American firm with a plant in any of the 10 EEC countries can export to the other 9 countries without facing a tariff. U.S. investment in Ireland increased immediately after Ireland joined the European Economic Community.

Some recent foreign investment in the United States has been induced by actual and anticipated barriers to the importation of road motor vehicles. Volkswagen began assembling cars at its Pennsylvania plant in 1978. Since then Nissan (producer of Datsuns), Honda, Daimler-Benz, Renault, Fiat, Deutz, and Volvo have made commitments to produce automobiles or trucks in the United States.[1]

In some cases, the creation of tariff factories is the deliberate goal of policymakers in the host country, but in other cases the emergence of tariff factories is a result that surprises government officials. In the case of automobiles and trucks the president of the United States, the Congress, and officials of the United Auto Workers union all urged Japanese firms to produce in the

---

[1] Nissan is producing trucks in Tennessee. Honda is producing cars in Ohio. Volkswagen has acquired a second plant site in Michigan to produce cars. Daimler-Benz began assembling trucks in Hampton, Virginia, in 1981. Renault, which acquired principal ownership of American Motors, began producing cars in the United States in 1982. A joint venture between Fiat and Germany's Deutz set up a facility in Pennsylvania in 1981 for marketing Ivesco trucks. Volvo acquired a plant in Virginia in which it plans to produce automobiles. For details, see "Restructuring of the World's Auto Industry," *International Letter*, Federal Reserve Bank of Chicago, March 1981.

United States. As a stimulus they simultaneously threatened to impose import quotas if investment did not occur. The clear object was to substitute Japanese investment for imports of Japanese cars and trucks. In other cases where tariff factories have been un unwanted result of trade policy, governments have had to restrict capital imports as well as product imports. The Mexican government has imposed extensive capital controls to prevent its high tariff policy from inducing a large volume of foreign (especially U.S.) direct investment in Mexico.

The relationship between trade and factor mobility is symmetrical. Just as trade barriers stimulate factor mobility, forces that increase factor mobility tend to decrease trade. If a country taxes the earnings of capital at a higher rate than trading partners do, capital exports will be stimulated. John Whalley has offered the hypothesis that differential taxes on capital in the United States stimulate capital outflows that substitute for exports of capital-intensive products from the United States.[2] It is the purpose of this chapter to investigate several aspects of the relationship between trade and international investment.

12.2 FORMS OF CAPITAL FLOWS

A capital inflow is the sale of an asset by a resident to a foreigner. The asset may be either a financial asset or a real asset, such as real estate or plant and equipment. The seller receives money that can be converted into real goods and services. The capital flow or loan permits residents of the borrowing country to collectively import more than they export by the amount of the loan. In the lending country, the real counterpart of the money loan is the excess of exports over imports. Thus, international investment is both a money flow and a transfer of real resources from one country to another.

The loan may be a promise to repay a fixed amount of money at a future date, such as a bond or a bank loan. In this case, the loan may be expressed in the currency of the lending country, the borrowing country, or a third country's currency. Alternatively, a loan may be a promise to pay a variable amount of money, such as a share in a corporation.

It is common to distinguish between portfolio investment and direct investment. A portfolio investment is the purchase of a financial asset that does not give the investor control of a business firm. The acquisition of a Deutsche mark bank account by an American and a loan by an American bank to a German firm are portfolio investments. The purchase of small amounts of shares (less than 10 percent of total shares) in Volkswagen is also a portfolio investment. Conversely, a direct investment is the purchase of a real asset such as

---

[2] John Whalley, "Discriminatory Features of Domestic Factor Tax Systems in a Goods Mobile–Factors Immobile Trade Model: An Empirical General Equilibrium Approach," *Journal of Political Economy*, December 1980.

real estate, plant, and equipment or shares that result in significant control (more than 10 percent of shares) in a corporation. The most important direct investments involve the operations of multinational corporations.

In addition to the distinction between portfolio and direct investment, it is common to separate private capital flows from government flows. Private flows are motivated by profit opportunities, but government flows appear to be motivated more by political influence and charity. Government capital is usually described as foreign aid. Bilateral aid is given directly by one government to another, and multilateral aid is given to an international institution, such as the World Bank, which allocates the aid to the ultimate recipient.

International investment can be expressed either as a flow per year or as a stock at a point in time. For example, during 1980 the net capital outflow from the United States was $27.7 billion. This figure is the difference between American purchases of foreign assets and foreign purchases of U.S. assets. At the end of 1980 the stock of net foreign assets held by American residents was $122.7 billion. This stock of assets was the result of capital outflows in 1980, 1979, and all previous years. The stock is called the net international investment position (or net foreign assets), and it is the sum of all previous capital outflows.

The net international investment position of the United States for 1977 to 1981 is shown in Table 12-1. Net foreign assets of $160.3 billion are the difference between U.S. assets abroad ($717.4 billion) and foreign assets in the United States ($557.1 billion). Since net foreign assets were $121.6 billion in

TABLE 12-1 International Investment Position of the United States, 1977–1981 (in billions of dollars)

	1977	1978	1979	1980	1981
Net international investment position of United States	$ 72.9	$ 76.2	$ 94.9	$121.6	$160.3
U.S. assets abroad	379.1	447.9	510.6	606.9	717.4
U.S. official reserve assets	19.3	18.7	19.0	26.8	30.1
Gold	11.7	11.7	11.2	11.2	11.2
SDRs	2.6	1.6	2.7	2.6	4.1
Reserve position, IMF	5.0	1.0	1.3	2.9	5.1
Foreign currency	0	4.4	3.8	10.1	9.8
Direct investment	146.0	162.7	187.9	215.6	227.3
Percentage of assets	30%	36%	37%	36%	32%
Foreign assets in United States	306.2	371.6	415.7	485.3	557.1
Foreign official assets	140.8	173.0	160.0	175.8	180.1
Percentage of assets	46%	47%	38%	36%	32%
Direct investment	34.6	42.5	54.5	68.4	89.8
Percentage of assets	11%	11%	13%	14%	16%

Source: U.S. Department of Commerce, *Survey of Current Business,* Washington: U.S. Government Printing Office, August 1982.

1980, the capital outflow in 1981 was $38.7 billion, the difference between net foreign assets in 1981 and 1980. Thus, the net capital outflow is computed as the difference between the net international investment position in any two years.

Since American residents have been net lenders for most of the twentieth century, the net international investment position of the United States has shown an upward trend. The position was negative in the nineteenth century when Americans were net borrowers. Since every dollar borrowed by someone must be loaned by someone else, the net position for all countries in the world must be zero. Notice that a small increase in net foreign assets in 1978 was followed by larger increases in 1979–1981. The figures are expressed in current dollars, so the later figures reflect less purchasing power than do the earlier ones. A country's total wealth is the sum of domestic assets and net foreign assets. Thus, an increase in a country's net foreign assets is favorable only if domestic investment would have yielded a smaller return than the observed foreign investment.

The table also shows the relative importance of direct investment. In 1981 direct investment abroad was $227.3 billion, or 32 percent of all U.S. assets abroad. The importance of direct investment declined from 37 percent in 1979. The table also permits us to compare foreign direct investment in the United States with direct investment by Americans abroad. Direct investment in the United States in 1981 was $89.8 billion, or 16 percent of total foreign assets in the United States. For many years foreign direct investment by Americans has been more important than has been direct investment in the United States. This relationship reflects the importance of American multinationals abroad. Conversely, foreign investment in the United States has been mainly portfolio investment. Foreign direct investment in the United States has been only 11 to 16 percent of total foreign investment in the United States. Portfolio investments of foreign governments at the end of 1981 were $180.1 billion, or 32 percent of total foreign investment. These foreign official assets reflect the key currency role of the dollar in international finance. Foreign governments use dollar reserves in an attempt to influence foreign exchange rates. In the five-year period 1977 to 1981, official assets of foreign governments have been more than twice as large as has been direct investment in the United States. The increase in official dollar holdings of $40 billion during a period when exchange rates were ostensibly floating has surprised many observers.

It is instructive to consider the distribution of U.S. direct investment abroad by industry and country group. Table 12-2 shows direct investment data for the 30-year period 1950 to 1979. The relative importance of direct investment in the foreign petroleum industry increased from 1950 (29 percent of total direct investment) to 1957 (36 percent) and declined sharply by 1979 (22 percent). In the same period, the share of manufacturing increased from 32 percent to 43 percent.

The geographical location also changed significantly during this period. In 1950 foreign direct investment was evenly divided between developed and

TABLE 12-2   Foreign Direct Investment by U.S. Residents, 1950–1979 (in billions of dollars)

	1950	1957	1966	1979
Total direct investment	$11.8	$25.4	$51.8	$192.6
Share by industry				
Petroleum	29%	36%	27%	22%
Manufacturing	32	32	40	43
Other	39	33	33	33
Share by country group				
Developed	48%	55%	68%	72%
Canada	30	35	30	21
Europe	15	17	32	42
Less developed	49	41	27	25
Latin America	39	32	19	19

Source: U.S. Department of Commerce, *Survey of Current Business*, Washington: U.S. Government Printing Office, February 1981.

less developed countries. However, by 1979, 72 percent of direct investment was in developed countries, whereas only 25 percent was in less developed countries. Within the country groups there was an increase in the importance of investment in Europe (15 percent in 1950 and 42 percent in 1979) and a decrease in the importance of Canada and Latin America.

The increased importance of Europe partly reflects the development of the European Economic Community as an effective customs union. The formation of the EEC made it profitable for some American firms to construct tariff factories in Europe rather than supply the market from U.S. plants. Income from direct investment is an important service export for the United States. For the three years ending in 1980, income from American direct investment was $25 billion, $38 billion, and $37 billion, respectively. Thus, in the last 30 years, U.S. direct investment has shifted (1) from petroleum to manufacturing, (2) from less developed to developed countries, and (3) from Canada and Latin America to Europe.

Although foreign direct investment in the United States is less important than is portfolio investment, it is not negligible. The distribution of direct investment in the United States by industry and area for 1978 to 1980 is shown in Table 12-3. Manufacturing is by far the most important sector, followed by trade and petroleum. Foreign purchases of real estate have received some attention, but they are only 4 percent of the total. Direct investors in the United States have come almost entirely from high-income countries. Investment from Canada, Europe, and Japan constituted nearly 90 percent of the total. Europe alone was the source of 69 percent of the investment. The most important single countries were the United Kingdom (18 percent), The Netherlands (24 percent), and Germany (10 percent). It is possible to conceal the residence of

TABLE 12-3   Foreign Direct Investment in the United States, 1978–1980 (in billions of dollars)

	1978	1979	1980
Total direct investment	42.5	54.5	65.5
By industry (percent)			
Manufacturing	41%	40%	37%
Trade	22	22	20
Petroleum	19	19	20
Insurance	7	7	8
Real estate	—	—	4
Other	13	10	12
By area (percent)			
Canada	15%	13%	15%
Europe	69	69	66
United Kingdom	18	18	17
France	5	4	4
West Germany	9	10	8
The Netherlands	24	24	25
Switzerland	7	6	6
Japan	6	7	6
Other	10	11	12
The Netherlands Antilles	6	6	7
OPEC	1	1	1

Source: U.S. Department of Commerce, Survey of Current Business, Washington, D.C.: U.S. Government Printing Office, August 1981, p. 42.

ultimate investors by the use of holding companies in third countries. The Netherlands Antilles, with 6 percent of total direct investment, contains a number of holding companies. Residents of OPEC countries were responsible for 1 percent of direct investment. This investment received considerable attention, because most of it was in real estate.

12.3 CAPITAL FLOWS AND THE BALANCE-OF-PAYMENTS ACCOUNTS

Information on international capital flows for the United States is presented quarterly in the balance-of-payments accounts, which appear in the Department of Commerce's Survey of Current Business. Because a credit and a debit are entered for each transaction, the accounting balance necessarily adds up to zero. The major components of the accounting balance are the following:

$$X_g - I_g + X_s - I_s - T - K - \dot{R} = 0$$

Here X_g and I_g are exports and imports of goods (also called merchandise), respectively. Examples are petroleum, wheat, and machinery. X_s and I_s are exports and imports of services. Examples are transportation, royalties and licenses, and investment income. T represents unrequited transfers sent abroad. Transfers may be either official government aid or private charity. K is the capital outflow per period or net lending to foreigners. It includes both direct and portfolio investment. $\dot{R}$ is the change in official monetary reserves per period.

The sum of the first five items is called the balance on current account (B_{ca}), which measures net lending to foreigners by all domestic residents:

$$B_{ca} = X_g - I_g + X_s - I_s - T = K + \dot{R}$$

Thus, there are two equivalent ways to measure the net lending of a country's residents to the rest of the world. Lending is equal to the private capital outflow (K) plus the increase in official monetary reserves $(\dot{R})$. Alternatively, lending is equal to the balance on current account. If residents of a country are net lenders, they must have a surplus $(B_{ca}>0)$ on current account. Lending means that residents are acquiring financial claims on the rest of the world $(K + \dot{R})$ in return for the sacrifice of currently produced goods and services $(B_{ca}>0)$. Conversely, a borrowing country must have a negative balance on current account.

There is a simple relationship between a country's balance on current account per period and its net international investment position (N_t). The net international investment position is a stock, which measures net foreign assets at a point in time. Since increases in net foreign assets are associated with current account surpluses, net foreign assets can be interpreted as the sum of all previous current account surpluses:

$$N_t = B_{t_0} + B_{t_1} + B_{t_2} + \cdots + B_t = \sum_{t_0}^{t} B_{ca}$$

The subscript t refers to the time period of the variable, where t is the current period and t_0 is the first historical observation. If balance-of-payments data were complete and accurate, the increase in net foreign assets would be exactly equal to the sum of capital outflows and the reserve increase:

$$dN_t = K + \dot{R}$$

Because some capital transactions are not reported, the Commerce Department reports a category called statistical discrepancy (formerly called errors and ommissions). In recent years, the statistical discrepancy (STAT) has been large enough to swamp the reported current account surplus. In 1980 the discrepancy was +$29.6 billion when the surplus was $3.7 billion. In 1979 the discrepancy was +$21.1 billion when the reported surplus was $1.4 billion.

A second measurement problem is that the value of net foreign assets can change without a change in the measured B_{ca}. An example would be an increase in the value of foreign real estate. It could occur because of an increase in the real productivity of property or a change in the exchange rate. The increase is taken into account by a separate item called valuation adjustment (VAL). In principle the situation could be handled by simultaneously increasing N and K, but in fact the accountants enter VAL as a separate item.

Table 12-4 shows U.S. data relating changes in net foreign assets and the balance on current account. In addition to the adjustments for $STAT$ and VAL, new allocations of Special Drawing Rights (a gift of newly created money from the International Monetary Fund) are entered as separate items instead of simply increasing R. With these adjustments the basic relationship is

$$dN_t = B_{ca} + SDR + STAT + VAL = (K + \dot{R}) + VAL$$

For example, in 1977 net foreign assets of Americans declined by $12.5 billion and the current account showed a deficit of $14.1 billion. The difference between the two was accounted for by statistical discrepancy and valuation adjustment. Since current account deficits and surpluses reflect borrowing and lending, they may be sustainable for long time periods. For example, during the period 1870 to 1914, the United Kingdom experienced a current account surplus in every year. For much of the nineteenth century, the United States experienced a current account deficit. Thus, a persistent deficit or surplus in the current account is not necessarily a signal that government policy must change.

TABLE 12-4   Changes in Net Foreign Assets and Balance on Current Account, 1976–1980
$d(NIIP) = B_{ca} + SDR + STAT + VAL = (K + \dot{R}) + VAL$
(in billions of dollars)

YEAR	d(NIIP)		B_{ca}	SDR	STAT	VAL		$K + \dot{R}$	VAL
1976	+9.5	=	+4.4	0	+10.4	−5.3	=	+14.8	−5.3
1977	−12.5	=	−14.1	0	−2.3	+4.0	=	−16.4	+4.0
1978	+6.2	=	−14.1	0	+11.4	+8.8	=	−2.7	+8.8
1979	+17.6	=	+1.4	+1.1	+21.1	−6.1	=	+23.7	−6.1
1980	+27.7	=	+3.7	+1.2	+29.6	−6.9	=	+34.5	−6.9

NIIP = net international investment position; SDR = new allocation of special drawing rights; STAT = statistical discrepancy; VAL = valuation adjustment.

Source: U.S. Department of Commerce, Survey of Current Business, Washington, D.C.: U.S. Government Printing Office, August 1981.

12.4 MARGINAL PRODUCTIVITY ANALYSIS

International capital mobility can be analyzed in the same way as can labor mobility. Figure 12-1, which shows the effects of capital mobility, is simply a relabeling of Figure 11-3. The marginal product of capital curve is drawn for a given technology and a given stock of labor. The diminishing marginal product of capital is sometimes referred to as a country's limited absorptive capacity. For the initial capital stock OM, the rental rate on capital is OR_1 per unit and capital income is OR_1BM. The residual area R_1AB is labor income. National income or gross domestic product is $OABM$. Let there be a capital inflow of MN. The excess supply of capital at R_1 drives the rental down to R_2. Capital income is now OR_2CN, and the income of initial capital owners is $OR_2DM<OR_1BM$. Thus, native capital owners have taken a capital loss of R_2R_1BD. However, labor income is now $AR_2C>AR_1B$, and native workers have taken a capital gain of R_2R_1BD. Thus, the area R_2R_1BD is an income transfer from home capital to home labor.

When foreign investment occurs, it is necessary to distinguish between gross domestic product (GDP) and gross national product (GNP). GDP is the value of output produced within a country. GNP is the value of income received by factor owners residing in a country. Following the investment, GDP is $OACN$, whereas GNP is smaller by the payments to foreign capitalists $MDCN$. The increase in gross domestic product is $MBCN$. Of this increase, ROW cap-

FIGURE 12-1 Effect of Capital Mobility on National Income and Its Distribution

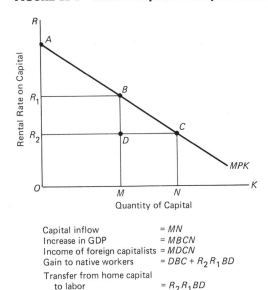

Capital inflow	$= MN$
Increase in GDP	$= MBCN$
Income of foreign capitalists	$= MDCN$
Gain to native workers	$= DBC + R_2R_1BD$
Transfer from home capital to labor	$= R_2R_1BD$
Increase in GNP	$= DBC$

italists receive $MDCN$, and home workers receive DBC. The investment income $(MDCN)$ will appear in the balance-of-payments accounts as a service export from ROW to the home country. The increase in gross national product is DBC. The reader can show that the opposite effects occur in the capital exporting country, ROW. Because capital becomes more scarce in ROW, the rental rises and the wage of labor falls. Thus, the beneficiaries of capital mobility are home country workers and ROW capitalists.

As long as capital moves toward the country where its productivity is higher, international investment must raise world income. Just as political motives may induce labor to move toward where its productivity is lower, political changes may also distort investment. Elections, revolutions, and wars may discourage investment in high-productivity areas.

Similar distortions may result from differential tax policy. If tax rates are higher in countries where the productivity of capital is higher, investment will be discouraged and capital outflows may also occur. Thus, differential national taxation could induce perverse international investment that would reduce world income. The appropriate tax concept is the general one that includes the threat of expropriation, foreign exchange controls, and unfavorable regulation. Marginal productivity analysis explains part of international investment, but it implies that capital should flow only from low-productivity countries to high-productivity countries rather than in both directions. An explanation of two-way investment requires a discussion of direct investment by multinational corporations, which will be considered in Section 12.6.

International investment tends to equalize the marginal productivity of capital across countries. International investment is a kind of arbitrage that equalizes capital productivity in the same way that migration tends to equalize wages and international trade tends to equalize product prices. The completeness of equalization is an important empirical question, but measurement is difficult because capital takes many different forms. Corporate bonds, government bonds, corporate stock, and real estate are substitute assets, but they are not perfect substitutes. Even within a country there is not a single interest rate for all assets.

In assessing the effects of international investment, it is important to use comparable assets. One extreme possibility is that capital mobility completely equalizes interest rates for comparable assets. This extreme case has two implications. The first is that domestic investment is unrelated to domestic saving. If domestic savers can lend abroad at a constant interest rate, any increase or decrease in domestic saving will result in an increase or decrease in foreign lending without a change in domestic investment.

This case is shown in Figure 12-2, where S and I represent domestic saving and investment and OR_1 is the single world interest rate. The line R_1CAB is effectively the rest of the world's perfectly elastic demand for the home country's savings. Along the initial savings curve, domestic saving is OS_1, domestic investment is OI_1, and foreign investment is I_1S_1. If the saving curve

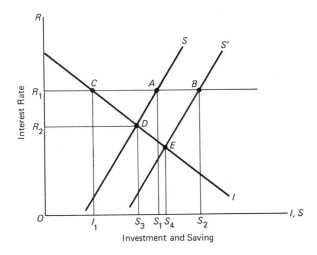

FIGURE 12-2   Effect of an Increase in Domestic Saving on Domestic Investment

shifts from S to S', domestic saving rises from OS_1 to OS_2, and foreign investment rises by an equal amount to I_1S_2. Domestic investment remains constant at OI_1. Thus, the entire increment to savings is sent abroad. In the opposite extreme case domestic and foreign interest rates would be unrelated. This case could be represented by the intersection of I and S at point D.

In the absence of foreign lending, domestic saving would equal domestic investment (OS_3). A shift in the savings curve to S' would bring about a new equilibrium at E. All the additional saving (S_3S_4) would be used for domestic investment. This case implies a high correlation between a country's domestic saving and its domestic investment. An empirical study by Feldstein and Horioka supports the latter view.[3] They argue that capital flows are limited by legal restrictions and investor risk preferences.

A second implication of perfect capital mobility is that an increase in domestic taxes on capital will be entirely shifted to workers. The incidence of a tax on capital is shown in Figure 12-3. First, let there be a fixed stock of capital and no capital mobility. With capital stock OK_1, the rental is OR_1, capital income is OR_1T_1K, and labor income is AR_1T_1. Let a tax on capital of T_1T_2 be levied. The pretax rental on capital remains at OR_1, and the posttax rental is OR_2. Gross capital income is OR_1TK_1, tax revenue is $R_2R_1T_1T_2$, and labor income remains AR_1T_1. In this case, owners of capital are unable to shift any of the tax to workers by lending abroad.

Conversely, if owners of capital have the opportunity to lend abroad at a constant rental rate OR_1, the entire domestic tax on capital will be shifted to workers. In the new equilibrium, investors must receive the same after-tax re-

[3] Martin Feldstein and Charles Horioka, "Domestic Saving and International Capital Flows," *Economic Journal*, June 1980.

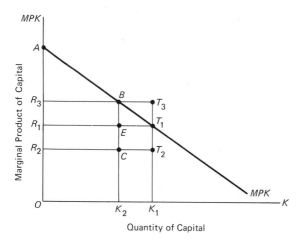

FIGURE 12-3   Incidence of a Domestic Tax on Capital

turn at home and abroad. This means that the domestic rental rate before taxes must rise to OR_3, so that the tax rate remains at OR_1. The line R_1ET_1 is effectively a perfectly elastic demand for home country capital by ROW. A capital outflow of K_2K_1 occurs, and gross domestic product falls by $K_2BT_1K_1$. Tax revenue is R_1R_3BE and capital income after taxes is $OR_1T_1K_1$, part of it coming from domestic investment (OR_1EK_2) and part of it coming from foreign investment $(K_2ET_1K_1)$. Labor income declines to AR_3B by the full amount of the capital tax. Thus, with perfect capital mobility, the entire burden of a tax on capital is shifted to workers. In intermediate cases where there is some capital mobility but not perfect capital mobility, the capital tax is shared by capitalists and workers. The opportunity of domestic owners of capital to invest abroad permits them to shift part of the burden of taxation onto workers.

12.5 INTERNATIONAL INVESTMENT AND THE TRANSFER PROBLEM

International lending occurs when home residents acquire a financial claim on ROW. However, borrowers seek command over goods and services, and a real transfer occurs only when the home country generates a surplus on current account equal to the financial transfer. The mechanism by which a financial transfer is converted into a real transfer of goods and services is called the transfer problem. The generation of a payments surplus may require a decrease in total spending at home and an increase in total spending abroad. Thus, monetary and fiscal policy are relevant to the transfer problem.

A policy concern is whether foreign lending reduces domestic employment by reducing total domestic spending. The AFL-CIO has complained in recent years that foreign investment by American firms has eliminated jobs for American workers. Since foreign investment stimulates imports, it does eliminate jobs in the import-competing sector. However, foreign investment also stimulates employment in the export sector without having any necessary effect on total employment in the whole economy.

If the lending country is a large country, its terms of trade may change as a consequence of investment. Since the home country's terms of trade may deteriorate because of a loan, the total cost of a $1 loan may be more than $1. The secondary burden of the transfer would consist of residents selling their exports for less and paying more for imports than before the loan. Whether or not the lending country's terms of trade deteriorate depends on consumers' propensities to spend on home- and foreign-produced products. The same transfer problem arises for unilateral transfers, such as foreign aid and war reparations payments. There was a famous discussion of German war reparations following World War I.[4] The specific question addressed was under what conditions could Germany's money payments to the Allies be transformed into a balance-of-payments surplus.

An obvious difference between lending and aid is that the former is expected to be repaid, but the latter is not. For a loan, the interest must be paid in every period, and the principal must eventually be repaid. The economic effect of debt repayment can be analyzed as a kind of reverse transfer. In this case the repaying country must generate a payments surplus and the lending country a payments deficit. In the balance-of-payments accounts, investment income is treated as an export of services by the lending country. Investment income has been a major service export for the United States, and in 1980 net investment income was $33 billion. This figure was comparable to total U.S. automobile imports ($27 billion) and all other consumer goods imports ($34 billion) in 1980. Because of this net foreign income, gross national product of the United States exceeds gross domestic product. This same $33 billion shows up as debt service (importing the services of capital) in the payments accounts of borrowing countries. Net investment income for the world must be zero. The burden of debt repayment of low-income countries and CMEA countries, which has received much attention in recent years, will be discussed in Section 12.9.

International investment may not affect total employment, but it does alter employment by industry. It also changes the distribution of national income by altering relative factor supplies. As was shown in Figure 12-1, capital imports reduce the rental on capital and redistribute income toward workers. Conversely, income is redistributed from workers to owners of capital in capital exporting countries. The effect of foreign investment on labor income ex-

[4] The famous exchange involved the British economist John Maynard Keynes and the Swedish economist Bertil Ohlin. Their arguments appear in Howard Ellis and Lloyd Metzler, eds., *Readings in the Theory of International Trade* (Homewood, Ill.: Richard D. Irwin, 1949).

plains, for example, why the AFL-CIO has opposed foreign investment by American firms, while favoring U.S. investment of foreign firms. Union spokespeople have also claimed that foreign investment by U.S. multinationals necessarily involves the export of technology. The Burke-Hartke Bill, which was sponsored by the AFL-CIO, was a formal proposal to restrict foreign investment and technological exports of U.S. firms. To the extent that U.S. exports depend on technological superiority, foreign investment may substitute for U.S. exports. However, firms are compensated for the export of technology through income from direct foreign investment and fees and royalties ($6 billion in 1980). Since these items appear as services in the balance-of-payments accounts, foreign investment may result in a substitution of service exports for merchandise exports without any effect on the current account.

12.6 MULTINATIONAL CORPORATIONS AND DIRECT INVESTMENT

Relative supplies of capital and labor alter the productivity of capital, and they are a determinant of international investment. However, if relative supplies were the only determinant of investment, each country would be either a capital exporter or a capital importer, but not both. If the marginal product of capital were greater in the rest of the world, the home country would be exclusively an exporter of capital. The observation that many countries simultaneously import and export capital leads to the search for other determinants of capital flows. Table 12-1 shows that at the end of 1980, U.S. residents owned $606.9 billion of assets abroad, while at the same time foreign assets in the United States were $485.3 billion. One explanation for the two-way flow of capital is that direct investment is a way for multinational firms to exploit their knowledge of a particular product. A second explanation is that investors may value stability of earnings as well as average earnings on capital, which leads investors to balance portfolios by making simultaneous investments in several countries.

A multinational corporation (MNC) is a firm with operations in more than one country. Multinationals are not completely new, but their importance increased greatly after World War II. The British East India Company was an important trading company that operated like a multinational in the seventeenth century. Today some of the more visible multinationals are in the automobile, petroleum, and grain industries. Exxon, Shell, General Motors, Volkswagen, and Cargill have worldwide operations. MNCs tend to be large firms, and they often operate in oligopolistic markets. It has been said that some MNCs are larger than nations. When countries and firms are ranked by either gross national product or gross annual sales, General Motors, Exxon, Ford, Shell, General Electric, IBM, Mobil, Chrysler, and Unilever rank among the 50 largest countries.[5] In a 1978 ranking of the 100 largest economic units in the world, 61 were countries and 39 were multinational firms. Specifically, General Motors is larger than Pakistan, South Africa, Indonesia, and many other large countries.

The main point about the enormity of certain firms is valid, but the comparison overstates the size of firms somewhat. GNP measures *net* value added by all firms in a country. For example, in computing the contribution of the auto industry to GNP, purchases of auto producers from other firms (e.g., steel, tires, textiles) are subtracted from gross sales. Thus, the net value added of large MNCs is smaller than gross sales, but the largest firms are still larger than many countries. The large size and power of some MNCs have led some observers to ask whether the corporations have reduced the sovereignty of nation-states. Multinational firms are largely, but not exclusively, from high-income countries. According to the 1981 *Fortune* magazine listing of the 100 largest industrial corporations in the world 45 were from the United States, 42 from Western Europe, and 8 were from Japan.

The growth of multinational corporations has political effects as well as economic effects. MNCs may alter the international political relations among host countries, source countries, and firms themselves. It is generally agreed that the growth of MNCs reduces the power of host country governments. However, there are two views concerning their effect on source country governments. According to the first view, the growth of MNCs has enhanced the power of source countries relative to that of host countries. Marxists, who hold this view, identify source country power with the interests of a narrow capitalist class. Non-Marxists, who agree that source country power increases, identify the additional power with the national security of the source country. In this view MNCs are a kind of modern mercantilistic institution through which the source country extends its power. An alternative view is that the growth of MNCs has reduced the power of both host country and source country governments.

Raymond Vernon expressed this view in his book, *Sovereignty at Bay.*[6] He looks on this development favorably for the international economy. Richard Barnet and Ronald E. Muller agree that MNCs reduce the power of both sets of governments, but they look unfavorably on this development. They argue in their book, *Global Reach,* that multinationals stifle competition and reduce income in both source and host countries.[7]

One possible reason for a loss of sovereignty is that some international trade involves firms trading with themselves. Intrafirm trade is international

[5] Sheldon W. Stahl, "The Multinational Corporation: A Controversial Force," *Monthly Review*, Federal Reserve Bank of Kansas City, January 1976. Data on the world's largest 100 economic units are compiled by the Conference Board. See *The Wall Street Journal*, May 7, 1980.

[6] Raymond Vernon, *Sovereignty at Bay*. New York: Basic Books, 1971.

[7] Richard J. Barnet and Ronald E. Muller, *Global Reach: The Power of the Multinational Corporations*. New York: Simon and Schuster, 1974.

trade between two divisions of a single firm. A significant fraction of U.S. trade is intrafirm trade of U.S. multinationals. Prices used to value intrafirm trade are called transfer prices. They may differ from market prices used in exchange between firms, which are sometimes called arm's-length prices. Valuation of trade is important because it may affect trade statistics, exchange control, or a firm's tariff or tax liabilities. A profit-motivated firm has an incentive to report a transfer price different from an arm's-length price if it can reduce tariff or tax liabilities or add to profits in any way.

Suppose that a foreign affiliate of an American firm is located in a country with higher tax rates than those in the United States. The firm has an incentive to report higher profits in the United States and lower profits abroad. It can be accomplished by valuing intrafirm trade at a transfer price above the arm's-length price. Production usually involves some joint costs such as research and development, and the firm has an incentive to assign a disproportionate share of the joint costs to the foreign affiliate. The allocation of joint costs also permits a firm to circumvent exchange controls. Foreign exchange controls are rules that restrict the conversion of domestic money into foreign money.

Suppose that exchange controls forbid a firm from repatriating profits to the home country. Assigning the affiliate in the host country a higher fraction of joint costs permits the firm to send profits home without reducing total profits. Pharmaceutical firms have been accused of allocating research and development costs in this fashion to avoid exchange controls in low-income countries.[8] Another example of the use of transfer pricing to circumvent controls is the U.S. trigger price mechanism for steel imports. The government specified a minimum import price for steel, say, $100. Foreign suppliers offered steel for a lower price, say, $90. Since it was illegal for U.S. firms to import steel for $90, some firms established foreign purchasing offices. The offices bought steel for $90 from foreign suppliers and resold to the home office for a transfer price of $100. The $10 difference would be repatriated as a profit. This practice violated the spirit of the price controls and led to the demise of the program in January 1982. Some of the same issues concerning transfer pricing exist for domestic firms with plants in different states. However, transfer pricing is more important for multinationals because of trade barriers between countries that do not exist between states, exchange controls, and larger tax differences between countries than between states.

One puzzling aspect of foreign direct investment is that, for many pairs of countries, investment occurs in both directions. This relationship is particularly true between the United States and Western Europe and between the United States and Canada. One explanation views direct investment as a way for a firm to appropriate economic benefits from superior technological knowl-

---

[8] See the study by Sanjaya Lall, "Transfer Pricing by Multinational Manufacturing Firms," *Oxford Bulletin of Economics and Statistics*, August 1973.

edge of a product. Technology is a particular kind of information, and firms produce information if they expect to appropriate the benefits from the information created. However, if rival firms are free to copy the new technology without compensating the creator, the latter has little incentive to engage in research. A peculiar characteristic of technological knowledge is that once it has been created, a second party can use that information without preventing the first party from using it. It is a characteristic of public goods. Indeed, use can be extended to any number of parties; that is, the marginal social cost is zero. This feature might suggest that information should be made freely available to everyone, but such a policy would discourage the production of new information. Thus, the dilemma is that if information use is encouraged by pricing it at its zero marginal social cost, private research would be discouraged. Conversely, if private firms extract a fee for technology, use of socially costless information is discouraged. This problem is called the appropriability problem.

One solution is for taxpayers to finance research and make it freely available. A problem with this solution in a closed economy is how to choose the kind of research to support. Furthermore, there is a free-rider problem for an open economy, since each country's taxpayers have an incentive to let other nations support research. A second solution is a legal system that grants a limited and temporary monopoly to the creator of an idea. Examples are patents, copyrights, and trade secrets that are protected by law. Direct investment by multinational firms is an attempt to appropriate the benefits of research and development expenditures by the firm.

It has been observed that multinational corporations tend to be large firms that produce relatively new products. The products tend to be differentiated and sold in relatively uncompetitive markets. These conditions permit firms to specialize in the production of certain kinds of information. For example, multinationals specialize in complicated technology rather than in simple technology that is easily copied. The technology is more appropriate for the skilled labor-abundant, high-income economies than unskilled labor-abundant economies. Otherwise the technology could be applied in low-income countries without compensating the firm.

Technology could be transferred between countries in several ways, and multinational firms specialize in the kind of information that is most easily transferred within the firm. Alternative means are private markets and government aid. Markets transfer information through the use of licenses and royalties. Most secrets can be kept only temporarily; hence multinationals tend to specialize in relatively new products. Secrets are easier to keep if there are few rivals, and multinationals tend to sell in less competitive markets. Economies of scale in research and development account for the large size of firms. Since research and development activity is a heavy user of skilled labor (especially scientists and engineers), the vast majority of firms engaged in foreign direct investment are located in high-income countries.

The appropriability theory associates foreign direct investment with the production of technological information and the sale of information that is embodied in new products.[9] This kind of investment is related to the notion of technological gap trade, in which a country's exports are based on technological superiority rather than lower factor costs. As the new technology spreads throughout the world, the initial exporter loses its cost advantage. Technological gap trade can be thought of as international trade in information.

12.7 PORTFOLIO BALANCE

Whether an investment is made in the home country or in various foreign countries depends on the average return expected on the various alternatives. In addition to the mean earnings on the investment, investors may also value stability of earnings. Thus, if two alternative investment portfolios offered the same mean earnings, the investor would prefer the portfolio with less volatile earnings. One way to reduce the variance of a portfolio's earnings, for a given mean, is to diversify the portfolio. In general the object is to choose assets for the portfolio whose earnings are not highly correlated with each other. Thus, there would be little effective diversification in a portfolio consisting entirely of shares in domestic steel corporations, whose earnings would be expected to rise and fall together. There are formal rules for selecting a minimum variance portfolio for given expected earnings.[10] In particular, information is needed about the variance and covariance in earnings of various firms.[11] Since some economic disturbances (e.g., taxes) are purely domestic, one might expect a lower correlation between earnings of foreign and domestic firms than between various domestic firms. Thus, an internationally diversified portfolio might be superior to a portfolio of exclusively domestic shares. There is evidence that during the 1970s Americans significantly increased their purchases of foreign stock, although purchases were heavily concentrated in Canadian, U.K., and Japanese shares. An alternative way to diversify is to purchase shares in U.S. multinationals that make foreign direct investments. The expectation is that fac-

---

[9] A fuller explanation is given by Stephen Magee, "Information and the Multinational Corporation: An Appropriability Theory of Direct Foreign Investment," in *The New International Economic Order: The North-South Debate*, Jagdish Bhagwati, ed. (Cambridge, Mass.: M.I.T. Press, 1977).

[10] Details are provided in William Sharpe, *Investments* (Englewood Cliffs, N.J.: Prentice-Hall, 1978).

[11] Variance is defined as $\text{var} = 1/n \sum_{i=1}^{n} (X_i - \overline{X})^2$, when n is the number of observations and $\overline{X}$ is the mean. Covariance between X and Y is defined as

$$\text{cov} = \frac{1}{n} \sum_{i=1}^{n} (X_i - \overline{X})(Y_i - \overline{Y})$$

where $\overline{X}$ and $\overline{Y}$ are the mean of the X's and Y's. Standard deviation is the square root of variance: $\text{SD} = \sqrt{\text{var}}$.

tors reducing domestic earnings of a corporation will not simultaneously reduce the firm's foreign earnings.

Data from 1970 to 1980 indicate that average earnings in the U.S. stock market were lower than were earnings in the six major foreign stock markets that accounted for 80 percent of U.S. investment. The earnings were based on dividends, capital gains, taxes, and exchange rate changes. During the same period, earnings in the United States were less volatile (lower standard deviation of earnings) than in any of the other countries. A diversified portfolio of both foreign and domestic stocks would have shown smaller variance for given mean earnings than strictly domestic or strictly foreign portfolios. An alternative to buying shares in foreign firms, namely, buying shares in U.S. multinationals, would have provided some advantage, but not nearly as much as buying foreign stock.[12] Thus, the desire to achieve internationally diversified portfolios is one explanation for two-way capital flows between pairs of countries.

However, there are some disadvantages of Americans purchasing foreign stock. The possibility of exchange controls means that U.S. investors might not be able to repatriate funds on demand. In addition, foreign stock exchanges have less stringent reporting requirements than do U.S. exchanges. Also, laws in some countries (e.g., Germany and Switzerland) permit employees to trade stock based on inside information.

12.8 CAPITAL CONTROLS AND TAXATION

International investment tends to equalize the earnings on capital. Conversely, barriers to capital mobility tend to increase the disparity in capital earnings and between countries. Some countries encourage capital exports, others discourage capital imports, and some discourage both. Controls may be taxes or quotas, including quotas of zero for certain industries or countries. The United States imposed controls on both direct investment and portfolio investment in the 1960s in an attempt to avoid devaluation of the dollar. The interest equalization tax (1963–1973) applied to foreign bonds issued in the United States. Quotas were applied to foreign direct investment by U.S. corporations from 1965 to 1973.

Most countries restrict capital movements, but today the United States is virtually free of capital controls.[13] Partly because of this freedom, the U.S. capital market is an attractive place for foreign investors. Many countries restrict foreign direct investment in certain strategic industries. Some countries, such as

---

[12] See the paper by Richard Abrams and Donald Kimball, "U.S. Investments in Foreign Equity Markets," *Economic Review*, Federal Reserve Bank of Kansas City, April 1981.

[13] A minor exception is that residents taking large amounts of currency out of the country must report the transaction to the government.

Mexico, permit foreign direct investment only as long as majority ownership in firms is held by domestic residents. A common justification offered is that extensive foreign ownership is incompatible with national sovereignty.

Governments have imposed many other conditions on foreign direct investment. Concern about job creation has led to conditions on domestic value added or local content. Rules may require that X percent of output must be exported. The foreign investor may be required to bring X percent of its own capital rather than borrow in the host country's capital market. The repatriation of capital by foreign firms may be limited, especially in the case of royalty payments. Expropriation of foreign-owned property can be interpreted as an extreme form of discriminatory tax on foreigners. Expropriation is not easy to identify since most host governments that nationalize property pay some compensation to the owners. The question is whether the compensation is related to the "fair market value" of the property. In some cases, foreign owners are treated no worse than domestic owners of nationalized property. When the Socialist government of François Mitterand implemented its nationalization program in 1981, it was more lenient toward foreign firms than toward French private firms. The threat of expropriation, which can be interpreted as the expectation of a future tax increase, may be a barrier to foreign investment. Some governments offer subsidized insurance against expropriation to their nationals. One of the main functions of the United States Overseas Private Investment Corporation (OPIC) is to insure foreign direct investment by American firms against expropriation risk.

U.S. policy has discouraged expropriation in several ways including cutting off foreign aid, voting against loans in international agencies, and denying trade preferences to countries expropriating U.S. firms' property. Occasionally, governments encourage capital flows through favorable tax treatment. However, many of these cases are merely tariff factories, in which a direct investment substitutes for imports. Foreign investments in the U.S. auto industry appear to be tariff factories.

Just as in the case of labor, capital flows can be affected by differential taxation. Let the productivity of capital be higher in ROW than at home. Capital will tend to flow to ROW, but a higher tax on capital in ROW will reduce the magnitude of the capital flow. Indeed, if the ROW tax rate on capital is high enough, capital will flow from ROW to the home country. Reversal of the direction of a factor movement was discussed in the case of labor in Chapter 11. If capital flows to the country where its gross marginal product is lower, world income will fall. In this connection, capital flows depend on the *expected* tax rate, which should be interpreted to include the expectation of expropriation. The United States taxes capital more heavily than Western Europe does. The United States relies heavily on the corporation income tax, whereas the major European tax is the value added tax. The result may be to encourage capital exports from the United States that substitute for exports of capital intensive products from the United States.

It was shown in Chapter 10 that a large country can improve its terms of trade by restricting product exports or imports. A similar possibility exists for a country that is a large supplier of capital to the world market. By restricting foreign investment by its residents, a country could increase the return on capital so as to increase national income. As do all monopoly schemes, the restriction would reduce foreign income by more than the increase in domestic income.[14]

12.9 GOVERNMENT CAPITAL

Government capital flows differ from private investment, because the profit motive is less important for government investment. Government flows usually involve a grant or a loan at a subsidized rate of interest. One can compute the grant equivalent of any subsized loan by comparing the terms of the concessional loan with the terms of a comparable commercial loan. If the market rate of interest for commercial loans is 10 percent, a country borrowing $100 million for one year will repay $110 million after one year. If that country is granted a 5 percent interest rate by a foreign government, it will repay $105 million at the end of one year. Since the same economic effect could have been achieved by a commercial loan at 10 percent plus a $5 million grant, one can say that the grant element in the concessional loan was $5 million.

A loan guarantee is an indirect form of aid, whose grant component can be similarly computed. If the donor government guarantees repayment of a private loan, the private market will lend at a lower interest rate. The difference between the ordinary market interest rate and the lower guaranteed rate is the grant element of the guarantee.

To say that government loans are not entirely based on profits does not imply that such loans are unconditional. Usually aid is sent only to friendly governments, and friends are expected to cooperate with the donor's foreign policy. One might say that private loans are based on a money return to the lender and that government aid is based on a political quid pro quo. Political conditions are naturally resented by recipients, and spokespeople for low-income countries tend to support multilateral aid through international institutions rather than bilateral aid. Conversely, taxpayers in donor countries tend to favor bilateral aid, which permits them to impose conditions directly.

In addition to political conditions, it is common for donors to insist that aid be spent in the donor country. Because of the condition that aid must be spent on domestic products, producers of exportables have provided strong political support for aid programs even when the recipients are not friendly

---

[14] An analysis of optimal foreign investment is G. D. A. MacDougall, "The Benefits and Costs of Private Investment from Abroad: A Theoretical Approach," *Economic Record*, March 1960.

countries. Thus, conservative American farmers have supported subsidized grain exports to the USSR, and conservative German industrialists have supported subsidized loans to the Soviets. If prices of the desired products are higher in the donor country, the condition has the effect of reducing the real value of the aid to the recipient. "Buy American" has been a condition of U.S. aid for many years. U.S. food aid programs have also had a requirement that U.S. ships transport the product. Since U.S. ships have higher costs, this condition reduces the real value of the aid to the recipient.

Most government capital flows are from high-income countries to low-income countries, and they are justified in donor countries as charitable contributions. In other cases, such as subsidized credit from OECD countries to CMEA countries, they are justified as mercantilistic export promotion policies. Although the volume of official aid to low-income countries is not negligible, it is smaller than the value of foreign private investment in the same countries.

Table 12-5 shows capital flows to developing countries from 1978 to 1980 as reported by the Organization for Economic Cooperation and Development (OECD) in Paris. The Development Assistance Committee (DAC) is a major group of donors within OECD. In 1980 the total net resource flows to developing countries were $82.0 billion. Official development assistance was $35.5 billion, and nonconcessional flows from the same DAC countries were $44.2 billion. Nonconcessional flows represent profit-motivated private investment.

In 1978 and 1979, private nonconcessional flows also exceeded official aid. Of the total development assistance of $33.5 billion in 1980, $26.7 billion came from DAC countries, $7.0 billion from OPEC countries, and $1.8 billion from the CMEA countries of Eastern Europe. The largest national donor was the United States, with $7.1 billion. Although U.S. total aid is largest, critics point out that gross national product is also largest in the United States. When aid is expressed as a percentage of GNP, the United States is one of the smaller donors.

TABLE 12-5 Capital Flows to Developing Countries, 1978–1980 (in billions of dollars)

	1978	1979	1980
Total net resource flows	$77.3	$83.0	$82.0
Official development assistance	25.6	30.4	35.5
DAC countries	20.0	22.4	26.7
OPEC countries	4.3	6.2	7.0
CMEA countries	1.3	1.8	1.8
United States		4.7	7.1
Grants by private voluntary agencies (DAC)	1.7	2.0	2.3
DAC nonconcessional flows	49.4	50.6	44.2

Source: International Monetary Fund, Survey, August 3, 1981.

TABLE 12-6   Official Development
Assistance (ODA),* 1980

COUNTRY	ODA/GNP (PERCENT)
DAC† total	0.37%
The Netherlands	0.99
Norway	0.82
Sweden	0.76
Denmark	0.72
France	0.62
West Germany	0.43
Japan	0.32
Canada	0.42
Italy	0.17
United Kingdom	0.34
United States	0.27

*ODA consists of grants (76 percent) plus subsidized loans.

†DAC is the Development Assistance Committee of the Organization for Economic Cooperation and Development.

Source: International Monetary Fund, *Survey*, August 3, 1981.

Table 12-6 shows official development assistance relative to GNP for the DAC countries. The Netherlands (0.99 percent), Norway (0.82 percent), Sweden (0.76 percent), and Denmark (0.72 percent) were large donors, while Italy (0.17 percent) and the United States (0.27 percent) were the relatively small donors. For all DAC countries, combined aid was 0.37 percent of GNP, far below the 0.70 percent target established by OECD.

Foreign aid has several different kinds of supporters in the United States. Perhaps the simplest justification for aid is altruism. There are also several arguments based on self-interest. The first is that in an interdependent world economy, economic growth in low-income countries promotes growth in the United States. The makers of foreign policy favor aid as a means of rewarding political allies and punishing enemies. State Department officials usually view aid as a nonviolent instrument for influencing other governments. Since the Vietnam war, U.S. policymakers have tended to substitute economic sanctions for military intervention. Finally, those firms and labor unions responsible for exporting products financed by aid form an effective lobby in Congress.

Total U.S. aid is shown in Table 12-7 for the period 1945 to 1979. Total assistance is divided into military grants, economic assistance, and aid to international financial institutions. In 1979, total aid was $7.7 billion, of which $6.2 was economic and $0.9 billion was military. Food aid, a component of economic aid, has been constantly within the range $1.0 billion to $1.5 billion since 1954. Most of the food has been shipped under the Food for Peace and

TABLE 12-7   U.S. Government Net Foreign Assistance, 1945–1979
(in billions of dollars)

PERIOD	TOTAL ASSISTANCE	MILITARY GRANTS	ECONOMIC AID	AID TO INTERNATIONAL FINANCIAL INSTITUTIONS*	FOOD COMPONENTS OF ECONOMIC AID
1945–49	$5.5	$0.3	$5.1	$0.1	
1950–54	5.1	2.5	2.6	0	
1955–59	4.8	2.4	2.3	0	$1.3
1960–64	4.7	1.6	3.0	0.1	1.5
1965–69	5.9	2.2	3.6	0.1	1.3
1970–74	7.1	3.3	3.5	0.3	1.0
1975	8.7	2.9	5.1	0.7	1.2
1976	7.9	1.3	5.5	1.1	1.1
1977	6.7	0.8	5.1	0.9	1.5
1978	8.0	0.8	6.3	0.9	1.5
1979	7.7	0.9	6.3	0.6	1.5

*African Development Fund, Asian Development Bank, Inter-American Development Bank, International Bank for Reconstruction and Development, International Development Association, and International Finance Corporation.

Source: Council of Economic Advisers, Economic Report of the President, 1981 (Washington, D.C.: U.S. Government Printing Office, 1981).

Public Law 480 programs. While the money value of food aid has been remarkably stable, food prices have been quite volatile. Thus, the quantity of food aid varied inversely with food prices. This relationship is consistent with the idea that the demand for goodwill or political influence by donor countries is inversely related to its price.

The volatility of the quantity of food aid is shown in Table 12-8. The mean quantity of aid for the entire 25-year period was 12.2 million metric tons. The maximum food aid occurred in 1962 when 19.2 million tons were shipped, and the minimum aid occurred in 1974 at 3.8 million tons. World food prices were depressed in 1962, and in 1974 they were at the highest level since World War I.

Critics of foreign aid programs have suggested some alternative policies. The form of aid could be changed from tied to untied aid and from loans to grants. Requiring that aid be spent in the donor country reduces the real value of the aid and makes it difficult to distinguish between aid to domestic exporters and aid to foreign governments. Substituting multilateral aid administered by international institutions for bilateral aid might reduce the conditions attached to aid. Recipients tend to favor such a change, whereas donors tend to oppose it. Conversion of loans to grants may reduce misunderstanding and avoid a debt repayment crisis. However, taxpayers in donor countries tend to favor loans.

If the object of aid is the promotion of economic growth, other policies

TABLE 12-8 U.S. Food Aid,* 1955–1979

YEAR	METRIC TONS (MILLIONS)	DOLLARS (BILLIONS)
1955	6.4	$ 0.8
1956	13.0	1.3
1957	17.5	1.9
1958	10.9	1.2
1959	12.8	1.2
1960	15.5	1.3
1961	18.2	1.5
1962	19.2	1.6
1963	17.5	1.5
1964	16.9	1.4
1965	18.5	1.6
1966	18.3	1.4
1967	14.1	1.3
1968	14.7	1.3
1969	10.1	1.0
1970	11.0	1.1
1971	10.2	1.1
1972	10.3	1.1
1973	7.7	1.0
1974	3.8	0.9
1975	5.3	1.2
1976	5.4	1.1
1977	8.7	1.5
1978	8.7	1.5
1979	8.1	1.5
Total	202.8	32.3
Mean	12.2	1.3

*Food aid is defined as U.S. agricultural exports under Public Law 480 and mutual security/AID programs. Data are reported by fiscal years.

Source: U.S. Department of Agriculture, *Foreign Agricultural Trade of the United States*, Washington, D.C.: U.S. Government Printing Office, November–December 1980.

may be more effective than aid. High-income countries could reduce import barriers against products from low-income countries. The General System of Preferences offers discriminatory tariffs, but it omits many sensitive labor-intensive products such as textiles. High-income countries could also liberalize their immigration laws. Low-income countries could reduce their own barriers to exports. The effective export taxes in low-income countries are so high that they reduce exports by more than the General System of Preferences increases them. Restrictions on foreign investment in low-income countries could be relaxed. Finally, pricing policies of low-income countries that discourage domestic production could be altered. The most obvious example is food, where low-price policies cause imports to displace domestic production.

Rapid growth of external debt has led to increasing concern about the debt service problems of low-income countries and Eastern European nations. Since borrowing can be a very useful practice, one cannot conclude that countries with larger external debt have more serious economic problems than do those with smaller debt. The profitability of a loan depends on the costs relative to the benefits, which indicate the ability of a country to repay a loan. An assessment of debt problems requires some measure of a country's debt service capacity. A loan used to finance productive investment would have different implications for debt service capacity than would a comparable loan used to finance current consumption. For example, a loan used to develop valuable mineral reserves would generate a larger debt service capacity than would one used to finance food imports. Some of the largest debtors are countries possessing the most promising investment opportunities. Other countries that have accumulated large debts have poor prospects of servicing the debt.

A popular explanation of the rise in external debt has been the oil price increases of 1973 thru 1974 and 1979 thru 1980 that led to increases in import bills of many countries. However, the size of external debt is not highly correlated with oil import bills. Some oil importers did become borrowers, but some major oil exporters such as Mexcio and Norway also borrowed extensively. Oil importers might be expected to borrow to finance a temporary decrease in real income, but not a decline in permanent income. Oil exporters might be expected to borrow to finance development of petroleum reserves. Potential debt difficulties can be divided into the problems of borrowers and lenders. Debt repayment requires the sacrifice of real resources that will be available if borrowed funds were used productively. The transfer problem was discussed earlier, and debt repayment can be analyzed as a reverse transfer. The borrowing country must generate a current account surplus to repay the loan. Even if past borrowing was used for unproductive purposes, it may be prudent to repay debt inherited from the past.

Default on past debt will restrict a borrower's future access to credit. Default will lead international lenders to incorporate a larger risk premium in determining the appropriate interest rate on future loans. Many governments defaulted on loans in the 1930s, when bonds were the form of most external debt. In recent years bank loans have replaced bonds as the most common form of external debt.

Although many countries have experienced debt problems, default has been rare since 1945. Cuba and Ghana are the only governments to repudiate their debt since 1960. However, debt rescheduling has become a substitute for default. Debt rescheduling consists of lengthening the maturity of a loan and adjusting other conditions such as the interest rate. Critics of debt reschedul-

TABLE 12-9   Eastern European Debt to the
West, 1970 vs. 1980
(in billions of dollars)

	1970	1980
Bulgaria	$0.7	$ 2.7
Czechoslovakia	0.6	3.4
East Germany	1.4	11.8
Hungary	0.6	7.0
Poland	1.1	21.9
Romania	1.6	9.0
USSR	1.0	9.6
COMECON banks	0.3	4.1
Total	$7.3	$69.5

Source: Reprinted by permission of *The Wall Street Journal,* © Dow Jones & Company, Inc., January 8, 1982. All Rights Reserved.

ing have described the practice as a poorly disguised default in which banks and debtors conceal bad loans. Proponents of rescheduling point out that outstanding debt is not written off and refinancing may occur at a higher interest rate.[15] Rescheduling requires negotiation between debtors and creditors, which may be easier to accomplish with bank loans than with earlier bond finance.

Between 1956 and 1982, there were 53 official debt reschedulings, and 22 since 1975. The external debt of low-income countries was approximately $500 billion in 1981. A rough index of debt service capacity is the ratio of debt service payments to exporters. Debt service payments were 15 percent of the exports of low-income countries in 1981, an increase from 12 percent in 1973. Brazil was the single largest borrower, with external debt of $57 billion, followed by Mexico, with external debt of $50 billion.

The debt of several Eastern European countries also increased rapidly from 1970 to 1980, as shown in Table 12-9. The collective debt of the CMEA countries increased by nearly 10-fold during the period. Poland was the largest single debtor in 1980, with external claims of $21.9 billion. The increase of more than $20.0 billion in Poland's debt was also the largest increase within the group. Other CMEA countries with large increases were East Germany ($10.4 billion), the USSR ($8.6 billion), and Romania ($7.4 billion). Polish debt repayment problems of 1981 and 1982 caused consternation both in Poland and in the West.

From the borrower's perspective the cost of debt repayment is the sacrifice of current real resources. Since default would make future borrowing more

---

[15] When Mexico rescheduled $20 billion in short-term loans in January 1983, the lending banks received a fee of $200 million and the interest rate was adjusted upward. See "Nations in Hock: Third World's Debts, Now Totaling $500 Billion, May Lead to Defaults and Bank Failures," *The New York Times,* January 10, 1983, p. 70.

difficult, the cost of default is the sacrifice of future resources. Lending countries also face a debt problem. Individual private banks lose income from bad loans, and some heavily exposed banks could fail.

At the end of 1979, the nine largest U.S. banks had $39 billion of loans outstanding to low-income countries. At the same time, the capital of the same banks was only $22 billion. Thus, if borrowers defaulted on just over half of the loans, the large banks would be insolvent. Some lenders had diversified portfolios, but certain banks had heavy commitments in particular countries. In 1980, New York's Citibank and Chase Manhattan earned 10 percent of their total income from Brazilian interest payments.[16] Because of the lenders' vulnerability, the banks have been described as "hostages" of the debtor nations. It has been said that if a government borrows $1 million from a bank and cannot repay, the government has a problem. If it borrows $1 billion and cannot repay, the bank has a problem.

In one sense the problem of bad loans is a common problem that commercial bankers have always faced. However, governmental involvement in international lending has been substantial, with one-third to one-half of all loans being insured by some government agency. Because of the heavy governmental commitment, debt problems have become matters of international economic policy. An additional concern of governments is the possibility that the failure of several large banks could bring on a financial panic of the kind that occurred during the Great Depression. Avoiding financial panics has been the traditional rationale for the "lender of last resort" function of central banks.

Most government loans and grants are made directly by one government to another government. In 1980, 72 percent of all official assistance was bilateral aid. In the case of such bilateral aid it is common for donor countries to impose economic or political conditions on the aid. Although conditional aid has appeal in donor countries, conditions reduce the real value of aid to recipient countries. The development of international agencies that administer aid is an attempt to reduce the stringency of conditions associated with bilateral aid.

The most important international institutions involved in lending are the International Bank for Reconstruction and Development (better known as the World Bank or IBRD) and the International Monetary Fund (IMF). Both institutions grew out of the same international conference at Bretton Woods, New Hampshire, in 1944. They are sister institutions located in Washington, D.C. By tradition the Fund is headed by a European, and the World Bank is headed by an American.

According to the traditional division of labor between the institutions, the Bank makes long-term loans to low-income countries, whereas the Fund makes short-term loans to member countries having balance-of-payments or exchange rate problems. The agencies are financed by donations from member

[16] *The Wall Street Journal*, January 28, 1981.

countries and loan guarantees. Because bonds are guaranteed by donor countries, the Bank can borrow at favorable interest rates in private capital markets. The Bank uses this borrowing privilege to lend money at less than commercial rates to eligible countries.

The initial purpose of the Bank was to promote redevelopment of countries damaged by World War II. Gradually, the Bank's main purpose became the economic development of low-income countries. Thus, high-income countries became ineligible to borrow.[17] The largest borrowers from the Bank have been Brazil, Mexico, Colombia, Korea, and India.

The World Bank also has a special agency, the International Development Association (IDA), that makes "soft loans" to the lowest-income countries. The terms of IDA loans are so favorable to borrowers (e.g., 50-year interest-free loans) that it is difficult to distinguish them from grants. IDA, which was founded in 1960, has a stricter means test than does the Bank in determining eligibility for loans. In 1980, 80 percent of IDA loans went to countries with per capita income below $410 per year. As economic growth occurs, certain countries become ineligible for IDA loans.[18] By 1982 a list of 27 "graduates" that had become too successful to borrow from IDA included Indonesia, South Korea, Tunisia, and Turkey. Because 42 percent of its $24.5 billion in loans has gone to India, IDA has been criticized as a one-customer bank. In 1982 the executive board of the Bank took steps to reduce the share of soft loans going to India. In addition, China, with a per capita income of $260 per year, may become eligible for IDA loans.

The prospect of China, with its population of 1 billion people, draining resources from India, Bangladesh, and other poor countries has concerned Bank officials. Both the Bank and the Fund impose economic conditions on loans, and the institutions are not free of political pressure. Nevertheless, the political power of a single donor country is less than what the donor would have had when administering bilateral aid. For example, the IMF made an unusual $5.8 billion loan to India in 1981 in spite of opposition by the United States. Also the conditions attached to IMF and IBRD loans are more likely to involve restrictions on economic policy (e.g., monetary and fiscal policy) rather than direct political considerations. In addition to the Bank[19] and the Fund, which operate at the world level, there are several regional institutions involved with multilateral aid including the Inter-American Development Bank, the African Development Fund, and the Asian Development Bank.

---

[17] In 1980 a country with per capita income exceeding $2,650 per year was ineligible for IBRD loans.

[18] The 1980 per capita income ceiling for eligibility for IDA loans was $730 per year. Some countries with lower incomes, including Indonesia, Egypt, and Thailand, were graduated because their creditworthiness reached a point where they could service loans on IBRD terms.

[19] The International Finance Corporation (IFC) is a small arm of the World Bank that makes loans to private firms.

SUMMARY

International investment is a form of factor mobility that can substitute for trade. Portfolio investment consists of international trade in financial assets. The investor expects to earn income without having a controlling interest in a foreign enterprise. Direct investment consists of a purchase of a real asset or controlling interest in a foreign firm. Most direct investment is carried out by multinational firms. Multinationals involved in intrafirm trade may have an incentive to charge transfer prices that differ from prices that would emerge in trade between unrelated firms.

Data on capital flows are presented in the capital account of the balance of payments. Since capital tends to flow toward countries where its productivity is higher, international investment tends to increase world income. Since investment changes relative factor supplies in both countries, it redistributes income toward labor in the host country and toward capital in the source country. Two-way direct investment flows are a commonly observed phenomenon. Direct investment is partly explained as an attempt by firms to appropriate the returns from information about new technology.

Government capital flows have economic effects similar to private flows, but they are usually associated with aid rather than with the profit motive. Aid may involve both elements of altruism and self-interest on the part of donors. The administration of multilateral aid by international agencies is an attempt to reach a compromise between recipients who prefer unconditional aid and national donors who prefer imposing conditions.

REFERENCES

ABRAMS, RICHARD K., and DONALD KIMBALL. "U.S. Investment in Foreign Equity Markets." *Economic Review*, Federal Reserve Bank of Kansas City, April 1981. Summarizes recent foreign portfolio investment by Americans.

ALIBER, ROBERT Z. *The International Money Game*, 4th ed. New York: Basic Books, 1983. Chapter 19, entitled "Optimal Bankrupts: Deadbeats on an International Treadmill," discusses debt problems.

BALDWIN, ROBERT, and J. DAVID RICHARDSON, eds. *International Trade and Finance: Readings*, 2nd ed. Boston: Little, Brown, 1981.

BARNET, RICHARD J., and RONALD E. MULLER. *Global Reach: The Power of the Multinational Corporations.* New York: Simon & Schuster, 1974. A critical view of MNCs emphasizing the loss of sovereignty of both source and host countries.

BERGSTEN, C. FRED, and LAWRENCE B. KRAUSE, eds. *World Politics and International Economics.* Washington, D.C.: The Brookings Institution, 1975. Collection of papers on the formation of international economic policy.

———, THOMAS HORST, and THEODORE H. MORAN. *American Multinationals and American Interests.* Washington, D.C.: The Brookings Institution, 1978. Comprehensive analysis of multinational firms.

BURKI, S. J., and NORMAN HICKS. "International Development Association in Retrospect." *Finance and Development*, December 1982. A brief summary of the activities of the World Bank's IDA affiliate.

CAVES, RICHARD E. "International Corporations: The Industrial Economics of Foreign Investment." *Economica* 1971. Reprinted in John Dunning, ed., *International Investment*. Baltimore: Penguin, 1972.

COHEN, BENJAMIN J. *The Question of Imperialism: The Political Economy of Dominance and Dependence.* New York: Basic Books, 1973. Discusses political and economic effects of international investment.

DUNNING, JOHN H., ed. *International Investment*. Baltimore: Penguin, 1972. A collection of papers on international investment.

EITEMAN, DAVID K., and ARUTHUR I. STONEHILL. *Multinational Business Finance*, 3rd ed. Reading, Mass.: Addison-Wesley, 1982.

FELDSTEIN, MARTIN, and CHARLES HORIOKA. "Domestic Saving and International Capital Flows." *Economic Journal*, June 1980. An empirical study of international investment and saving.

FIELEKE, NORMAN. *The Welfare Effects of Controls over Capital Exports from the United States.* Princeton studies in International Finance, No. 82. Princeton, N.J.: Princeton University Press, 1971. Empirical study of U.S. capital control.

————. "International Lending in Historical Perspective." *New England Economic Review*, November–December 1982. Compares international lending by industrial countries since World War II with nineteenth-century experience.

GRUBEL, HERBERT G. "Internationally Diversified Portfolios: Welfare Gains and Capital Flows." *American Economic Review*, December 1968. Empirical study of international portfolio investment.

HOOD, NEIL, and STEPHEN YOUNG. *The Economics of Multinational Enterprise.* London: Longman Group, 1979.

HYMER, STEPHEN. "The Efficiency Contradictions of Multinational Corporations." *American Economic Review*, May 1970, pp. 441–453. Reprinted in Robert E. Baldwin and J. David Richardson, eds., *International Trade and Finance: Readings*, 2nd ed. Boston: Little, Brown, 1981.

INTERNATIONAL MONETARY FUND AND WORLD BANK. *Finance and Development*, Washington, D.C. A quarterly publication reviewing activities of the Fund and the Bank.

JACQUILLAT, B., and BRUNO SOLNIK. "Multinationals Are Poor Tools for Diversification." In *International Financial Management*, Donald Lessard, ed. Boston: Warren, Gorham, and Lamont, 1970. A paper comparing purchasing foreign stock with shares in U.S. multinationals.

JOHNSON, HARRY G. "The Efficiency of the International Corporation." In *The International Corporation*, Charles Kindleberger, ed. Cambridge, Mass.: M.I.T. Press, 1970. Theoretical analysis of multinational firms.

KEYNES, JOHN M. "The German Transfer Problem." *Economic Journal*, March 1929. Reprinted in Howard Ellis and Lloyd Metzler, eds., *Readings in the Theory of International Trade.* Homewood, Ill.: Richard D. Irwin, 1949.

KINDLEBERGER, C. P., ed. *The International Corporation.* Cambridge, Mass.: M.I.T. Press, 1970. A collection of papers on multinational corporations.

KRAUSE, LAWRENCE B., and KENNETH W. DAM. *Federal Tax Treatment of Foreign Income.* Washington, D.C.: The Brookings Institution, 1964. Analyzes effect of domestic taxes on international investment.

LALL, SANJAYA. "Transfer Pricing by Multinational Manufacturing Firms." In *International Financial Management*, Donald R. Lessard, ed. Boston: Warren, Gorham, and Lamont, 1970. An empirical study of transfer pricing using Colombian data.

LEVY, HAIM, and MARSHALL SARNAT. "International Diversification of Investment Portfolios." *American Economic Review*, September 1970. An empirical study of portfolio diversification for the period 1951 to 1967.

MACDOUGALL, G. D. A.   "The Benefits and Costs of Private Investment from Abroad: A Theoretical Approach." *Economic Record*, March 1960. Reprinted in Richard E. Caves and Harry G. Johnson, eds., *Readings in International Economics*. Homewood, Ill.: Richard D. Irwin, 1968. Discusses the potential gains of a large country taxing capital exports.

MAGDOFF, HARRY.   *The Age of Imperialism*. New York: Modern Reader Paperbacks, 1969. A Marxist view of international investment.

MAGEE, STEPHEN P.   "Information and the Multinational Corporation: An Appropriability Theory of Direct Foreign Investment." In *The New International Economic Order: The North-South Debate*, Jagdish Bhagwati, ed. Cambridge, Mass.: M.I.T. Press, 1977. Interprets international investment as trade in information.

MUNDELL, ROBERT.   "International Trade and Factor Mobility." *American Economic Review*, June 1975. Reprinted in Richard E. Caves and Harry G. Johnson, eds., *Readings in International Economics*. Homewood, Ill.: Richard D. Irwin, 1968.

OHLIN, BERTIL.   "The Reparation Problem: A Discussion." *Economic Journal*, June 1929. Reprinted in Howard Ellis and Lloyd Metzler, eds., *Readings in the Theory of International Trade*. Homewood, Ill.: Richard D. Irwin, 1949.

REUBER, GRANT, et al.   *Private Foreign Investment in Development*. Oxford: Clarendon Press, 1973.

RUGMAN, ALAN.   *International Diversification and the Multinational Enterprise*. Lexington, Mass.: D. C. Heath, 1979.

SACHS, JEFFREY.   "LDC Debt in the 1980s: Risk and Reforms." National Bureau of Economic Research Working Paper, No. 861, February 1982. An economic and historical analysis of external debt problems.

SERVAN-SCHREIBER, JEAN-JACQUES.   *The American Challenge*. New York: Avon, 1969.

SHARPE, WILLIAM F.   *Investments*. Englewood Cliffs, N.J.: Prentice-Hall, 1978. A textbook that considers the advantages of portfolio diversification. International diversification is the subject of Chapter 20.

SIKORSKY, NILLY.   "The Origin and Construction of the Capital International Indices." *Columbia Journal of World Business*, Summer 1982. Capital International is an important source of world stock market data.

TAPLEY, MARK, and MARC SIMMONDS.   "International Diversification in the Nineteenth Century." *Columbia Journal of World Business*, Summer 1981. Description of nineteenth-century investment activity.

VERNON, RAYMOND.   "International Investment and International Trade in the Product Cycle." *Quarterly Journal of Economics*, Vol. 80 (1966), pp. 190–207.

———.   *Sovereignty at Bay*. New York: Basic Books, 1971. Argues that MNCs reduce the power of both source and host countries.

WELLS, LOUIS T., Jr.   *Third World Multinationals: The Rise of Foreign Investment from Developing Countries*. Cambridge, Mass.: M.I.T. Press, 1983.

CHAPTER THIRTEEN
TRADE AND ECONOMIC
GROWTH

13.1 INTRODUCTION

The discussion so far has assumed that national income is given in each trading country. The purpose of this chapter is to extend the analysis to economic growth. The relationship between international trade and economic growth is a complex one, and the two variables are probably simultaneously determined by more fundamental factors. Nevertheless, it is instructive to consider the ways in which trade affects economic growth and also the ways in which growth alters international trade. National income is distributed unevenly around the world, and the process of income growth is also uneven.

This chapter will consider ways in which different trade policies may alter growth. Trade policies that alter the national terms of trade can influence income growth. International commodity agreements have been proposed as a way in which primary producing countries can improve their terms of trade. Other trade policies are designed to alter the stability of prices without necessarily changing average prices. International buffer stocks have been proposed to reduce the variability of certain product prices.

The process of economic growth may alter the relative importance of trade. As income grows, demand may be biased toward either importables or exportables. If demand is biased toward importable products, trade will grow faster than national income. Supply considerations also influence the way in which growth affects the relative importance of trade. Since trade depends on factor endowments and the technology, the effect of growth depends on whether the source of growth is technical change, an increase in supply of the abundant factor, or an increase in supply of the scarce factor. Since large countries can alter their terms of trade, the source of economic growth will also determine whether a country's terms of trade will improve or worsen with growth.

13.2 NATIONAL INCOME , AND GROWTH

Prior to the Industrial Revolution, world income per capita was relatively stable. There has been a sustained growth in per capita income since that time, but world growth has occurred unevenly. The result of uneven income growth has been a highly variable income per capita across countries. The wealthiest countries are concentrated in North America and Western Europe, whereas the poorest countries lie mainly in Asia and Africa. Table 13-1 shows average income per capita by continent or region. In 1977 world average income per capita was $1,920. The average North American received an income of $8,710; the average European received $4,810. In contrast, the average African received $490, and the average Asian received $330 per person.

Table 13-1 also shows the distribution of world population and income as of 1977. A general feature is that North America and Europe have a small fraction of the world's people but most of the income. Conversely, Asia contains most of the people but produces a small fraction of the world's income. North America and Europe contained 19 percent of the world's population and produced 59 percent of world income. Asia contained 51 percent of world population but produced only 9 percent of world income. Africa is another rela-

TABLE 13-1   GNP per Capita by Region, 1977

REGION OR COUNTRY	GNP PER CAPITA (U.S. $)	GNP (U.S. $000 MILLIONS)	POPULATION MID-1977 (MILLIONS)	SHARE OF WORLD POPULATION	SHARE OF WORLD INCOME
North America	$8,710	$2,091	240	0.06	0.27
United States	8,750	1,897	218	0.05	0.24
Japan	6,510	737	113	0.03	0.09
Oceania	5,490	121	22	0.01	0.02
Europe, excluding USSR	4,810	2,504	521	0.13	0.32
USSR	3,330	861	259	0.06	0.11
Middle East	2,950	130	44	0.01	0.02
South America	1,360	308	227	0.06	0.04
Central America	1,120	129	115	0.03	0.02
Africa	490	209	426	0.11	0.03
Asia, excluding Japan and Middle East	330	689	2,080	0.51	0.09
World	1,920	$9,676	4,265		

Source: World Bank, *World Bank Atlas,* Washington, D.C., 1980.

tively poor continent, with 11 percent of the world's people and 3 percent of income. Japan stands out from the rest of Asia with 3 percent of the world's people and 9 percent of world income.

The continental averages conceal the variation across countries. For example, the Asian average includes relatively prosperous Singapore ($2,820) and Hong Kong ($2,620) and impoverished Bangladesh ($80). Per capita income arranged by country is shown in Table 13-2. With the exception of some specialized oil producers, the wealthiest countries are concentrated in North America and Western Europe. The national figures range from several countries with incomes of over $8,000 per year to a group of low-income countries with less than $300 per year. The latter group includes countries as large as India, Pakistan, and Bangladesh. The ranking of countries changes according to economic growth, which is shown in column 2 for the period 1970 to 1977. Some wealthy countries such as Switzerland and Sweden have experienced slow growth recently, and some poorer countries such as Brazil, Republic of China (Taiwan), and Korea have grown rapidly in recent years. The table also shows rapid growth by some high-income countries and slow growth by some low-income countries, which tends to increase the inequality of world income distribution. Extreme examples of the latter case are Ghana, Angola, Zaire, and Bangladesh, where income per capita declined. It will be shown that even if all countries grow at the same rate, the *difference* between incomes in rich and poor countries will increase.

Even though the table shows a continuous variation in income per capita, it has become customary to divide the world into two groups of countries. The higher-income group is usually called developed, advanced, or industrialized. The lower-income group is variously called underdeveloped, less developed, developing, or nonindustrialized. Sometimes the low-income group is called the Third World, to distinguish it from the richer capitalist and Communist countries. More recent terminology calls the newly rich oil exporters the Third World and the remaining poor countries the Fourth World. A set of newly industrialized countries (see Section 13.3) is sometimes distinguished from other low-income countries.

The grouping is usually done by international agencies or donor groups. The grouping is usually based on income, and the dividing line between rich and poor is necessarily arbitrary. The choice of names for the groups is a sensitive subject, because the namers would like to connote economic differences without also suggesting superiority or inferiority. This book will tend to use the terms high income and low income for the groups, except when referring to data published by international agencies.

There are many differences between the groups beside income per capita (e.g., life expectancy, literacy), but most of them are highly correlated with income. Because of the high correlation, knowledge of per capita income alone would also permit one to rank countries by life expectancy, literacy, and infant mortality. It should also be noted that average income per capita conceals var-

TABLE 13-2 GNP per Capita, 1977, and Average Annual Growth Rates, 1970–1977

COUNTRY	GNP PER CAPITA	
	AMOUNT 1977 (U.S. $)	REAL GROWTH RATE (%), 1970–77
Kuwait	$12,690	−0.9
Switzerland	11,080	0.1
Sweden	9,340	1.2
Denmark	9,160	2.3
United States	8,750	2.0
West Germany	8,620	2.2
Norway	8,570	3.9
Canada	8,350	3.4
Belgium	8,280	3.5
The Netherlands	7,710	2.2
France	7,500	3.1
Australia	7,290	1.6
Saudia Arabia	7,230	13.0
Libya	6,520	−4.5
Japan	6,510	3.6
Austria	6,450	3.8
Finland	6,190	2.8
German Democratic Republic	5,070	4.9
United Kingdom	4,540	1.6
New Zealand	4,480	0.9
Czechoslovakia	4,240	4.3
Israel	3,760	2.0
Italy	3,530	2.0
USSR	3,330	4.4
Poland	3,290	6.3
Spain	3,260	3.6
Hungary	3,100	5.1
Ireland	3,060	2.1
Greece	2,950	4.0
Bulgaria	2,830	5.7
Singapore	2,820	6.6
Venezuela	2,630	3.2
Hong Kong	2,620	5.8
Trinidad and Tobago	2,620	1.5
Puerto Rico	2,450	0.1
Yugoslavia	2,100	5.1
Argentina	1,870	1.8
Portugal	1,840	3.1
Iraq	1,570	7.1
Romania	1,530	9.9

COUNTRY	GNP PER CAPITA	
	AMOUNT 1977 (U.S. $)	REAL GROWTH RATE (%), 1970–77
Uruguay	1,450	1.3
Brazil	1,410	6.7
South Africa	1,400	1.1
Costa Rica	1,390	3.2
Chile	1,250	−1.8
Panama	1,200	−0.1
China, Republic of	1,180	5.5
Mexico	1,160	1.2
Algeria	1,140	2.1
Turkey	1,110	4.5
Jamaica	1,060	−2.0
Korea, Republic of	980	7.6
Malaysia	970	4.9
Jordan	940	6.5
Mongolia	870	1.6
Nicaragua	870	2.5
Syrian Arab Republic	860	6.1
Dominican Republic	840	4.6
Tunisia	840	6.5
Guatemala	830	3.3
Ecuador	820	6.1
Ivory Coast	770	1.1
Colombia	760	3.8
Cuba	750	−1.2
Paraguay	750	4.3
Peru	720	1.8
Korea, Democratic People's Republic of	680	5.3
Albania	660	4.1
Morocco	610	4.2
El Salvador	590	2.1
Nigeria	510	4.4
Bolivia	480	2.9
Philippines	460	3.7
Rhodesia	460	−0.1
Zambia	460	−0.2
Thailand	430	4.1
Honduras	420	0.0
China, People's Republic of	410	4.5
Liberia	410	1.1
Senegal	380	0.4
Ghana	370	−2.0
Egypt, Arab Republic of	340	5.2

TABLE 13-2   GNP per Capita, 1977, and Average Annual Growth Rates, 1970–1977

COUNTRY	GNP PER CAPITA	
	AMOUNT 1977 (U.S. $)	REAL GROWTH RATE (%), 1970–77
Sudan	330	2.5
Indonesia	320	5.7
Kenya	290	0.9
Angola	280	−3.4
Haiti	230	2.1
Tanzania	210	2.1
Zaire	210	−1.4
Pakistan	200	0.8
India	160	1.1
Burma	140	1.3
Ethiopia	110	0.2
Bangladesh	80	−0.2

Source: World Bank, World Bank Atlas, Washington, D.C., 1979.

iation in income within countries. Thus, the average American is wealthier than the average Pakistani, but there are many poor Americans and wealthy Pakistanis. Also, income is distributed less equally in low-income countries than in high-income countries.

High- and low-income countries differ in many ways other than income, although most of the differences are correlated with income. The economic and demographic differences between high- and low-income countries are shown in Table 13-3. In low-income countries, a larger percentage of GNP comes from the agricultural sector, and a larger percentage of the labor force is employed in agriculture. The relative unimportance of agriculture in high-income countries is the reason why international agencies refer to them as industrialized countries. Because agricultural production is correlated with low income, one is tempted to conclude that a policy of discouraging agricultural production in favor of manufacturing would increase national income. Indeed many governments of low-income countries have adopted policies that effectively discriminate against agricultural production. However, a counterargument is that agricultural innovation is a major source of economic growth. It follows that a policy of discouraging agriculture would stifle economic growth. In particular, policies that depress the relative prices of agricultural products would be counterproductive.

A related characteristic of low-income countries is that a smaller percentage of the population resides in urban areas. The birth rate is higher, the life

TABLE 13-3   Some Economic and Demographic Differences among High- and Low-Income Countries, 1960 vs. 1977

	1960	1977
Percentage of GDP from agriculture		
Industrialized	6.4%	3.8%
Developing	30.1	19.4
Percentage of labor force in agriculture		
Industrialized	21.4	12.8
Developing	62.0	53.9
Percentage of exports from fuels, minerals, and metals		
Industrialized	9.5	8.9
Developing	31.0	41.2
Percentage of population age 0–14 years		
Industrialized	27.0	24.6
Developing	41.6	42.3
Percentage of population urban		
Industrialized	65.1	71.8
Developing	21.2	26.4
Crude birth rate (per thousand)		
Industrialized	18.3	16.5
Developing	42.2	39.0
Life expectancy (years)		
Industrialized	68.9	71.8
Developing	46.9	51.3

Source: World Bank, *World Tables,* Washington, D.C., 1979.

expectancy is lower, and the population is younger in low-income countries. Exports are more concentrated in a smaller number of goods, and a larger percentage of the goods are primary products.

The income figures presented refer to gross national product (GNP) or gross domestic product (GDP). GNP measures the total value of goods and services produced by factors owned by residents of a country. For example, GNP of the United States includes rent on land in the United States and rent on American-owned land in Canada. GDP measures the value of goods and services produced within a country's borders. Thus, rent on American-owned land in Canada is part of U.S. GNP and Canadian GDP. Differences between a country's GNP and GDP may be caused by foreign investment or by workers temporarily employed abroad. Countries such as Turkey, Egypt, and Yugoslavia are exporters of labor services, and the European Economic Community and the Persian Gulf countries are importers of labor. If a worker becomes a permanent migrant, his or her income becomes part of the GNP of the country of immigration. For the world as a whole, the sum of all countries' GNP must equal the sum of all countries' GDP.

GNP and GDP are not perfect measures of national income. They measure the value of goods that are sold in markets, but they do not include household activity. Thus, the value of the output of self-sufficient farmers and housewives is not included in GNP or GDP. If the omitted sectors had the same importance over time and across countries, GNP figures would still be useful for comparative purposes. However, the nonmarket sector is larger in low-income countries, which causes the relative income of low-income countries to be understated. The relative size of the nonmarket sector has also declined over time in nearly all countries. A second source of distortion in relative incomes is the use of market exchange rates to convert one country's GNP into the currency of another country. This relationship will be discussed in some detail in Chapter 16. The main point is that the use of market exchange rates as a conversion factor understates the incomes of low-income countries. Even after correcting for these two sources of bias, it remains true that average income in the poorest countries is far below average income in the richer countries.

In making international income comparisons, it is important to recognize that equal rates of income growth will *increase* the initial difference between per capita income levels. It follows that a lower-income country must grow at a more rapid rate to preserve the initial income difference. This arithmetical point is illustrated in Table 13-4.

Let countries A and B have initial income levels of $1,000 and $100, respectively, in period t. The initial money income difference is $900, and A's income is 10 times B's income. If income in both countries grows at 5 percent per year, in period $t+1$ the money income levels will be $1,050 and $105. In period $t+1$, the income difference increases to $945, but the ratio of the income levels remains 10 to 1. For the money income difference to remain constant at $900 in period $t+1$, income in B would have to be $150. Thus, income would have had to grow at a rate of 50 percent in B, given the initial income difference and a 5 percent growth rate in A. After 16 periods of equal

TABLE 13-4 Income Levels and Income Growth*

INCOME MEASURE	PERIOD t	PERIOD $t+1$	PERIOD $t+2$	PERIOD $t+16$
Income of $A(Y_A)$	$1,000	$1,050	$1,102.50	$2,182.87
Income of $B(Y_B)$	100	105	110.25	218.287
$Y_A - Y_B$	900	945	992.25	1,963.98
Y_A/Y_B	10	10	10	10

*Income is assumed to grow at the same rate of 5 percent in each country ($g_A = g_B = 5\%$) and $Y_{t+n} = Y_t(1+g)^n$.

TABLE 13-5   Growth of Income and Population, 1950–1977
            (average annual growth rates)

	1950–60	1960–65	1965–70	1970–77
Population				
Developing countries	2.2%	2.4%	2.5%	2.4%
Industrialized countries	1.2	1.2	0.9	0.8
Gross domestic product				
Developing countries	4.9	5.6	6.4	5.7
Industrialized countries	3.8	5.3	4.9	3.2
Gross domestic product per capita				
Developing countries	2.7	3.1	3.8	3.2
Industrialized countries	2.5	4.0	4.0	2.4

Source: World Bank, *World Tables,* Washington, D.C., 1979.

growth at 5 percent, the money income difference would increase to $1,963.98, but *A*'s income would remain 10 times *B*'s income. Thus, equal growth rates between rich and poor countries implies an increasing gap between money incomes.

There has been a tendency for both income and population to grow more rapidly in low-income countries. Table 13-5 shows rates of growth of gross domestic product and population for the period 1950 to 1977. GDP grew more rapidly in developing countries in each of the four subperiods. In the last period, GDP grew at a 5.7 percent rate in developing countries and 3.2 percent in industrialized countries. However, population also grew more rapidly in developing countries in each subperiod, and in the 1970s population grew three times as fast in developing countries. Consequently, growth rates of gross domestic product per capita were not significantly different in the two country groups. Again, the average growth rate for the group conceals differences among members. For some low-income countries, including Brazil, Taiwan, Korea, Hong Kong, and Singapore, income per capita grew at more than 5 percent per year from 1970 to 1977 (see Table 13-1.) During the same period, income per capita fell in several low-income countries.

The purpose of this chapter is to investigate the relationship between international trade and economic growth. A traditional argument is that dynamic gains from trade and specialization promote economic growth. Thus, a free trade policy would be favorable toward growth. A contrary argument is that trade has retarded growth by leading to excessive dependence by some countries, and it has served as a transmitter of foreign economic disturbances. Free trade may be inimical toward growth. The next section will consider the effect of trade policy on economic growth. Beginning in Section 13.5, the effect of economic growth on trade will be considered. Depending on the source of economic growth, the importance of the international trade sector of an economy may increase as a result of growth.

13.3 TRADE POLICY
AND GROWTH

At the time Adam Smith wrote *Wealth of Nations* (1776), most governments placed heavy restrictions on foreign and domestic trade. Smith was highly critical of mercantilism, a popular policy of the time. Mercantilists believed that countries would be wealthier and would generate more employment if they exported more goods than they imported. They advocated achieving an export surplus by discouraging imports and encouraging exports. Presumably a trade surplus would increase the national stock of gold, which they identified as wealth. An extreme proponent of mercantilism was Jean Baptist Colbert (1619–1683), the economic minister of Louis XIV of France, who recommended that nothing be imported if it could be produced domestically (presumably at any cost). Colbert imposed an extensive set of regulations designed to substitute French production for foreign production regardless of the cost difference. The doctrine that exports add to the strength of a nation's economy, while imports contribute to weakness, has many modern supporters among policymakers and popular writers.

As many colonies achieved political independence following World War II, they also sought economic independence. During the colonial period, the colonies became heavily dependent on trade with colonial countries. A popular policy among newly independent nations was to substitute domestic production for imports. After 30 years of experience, there is now a growing concensus that import substitution has been a costly policy.

The postwar experience of many low-income countries with import substitution has been analyzed in a multivolume study for the National Bureau of Economic Research.[1] The general conclusion is that many resources employed in import substitution would have contributed more to economic growth by producing for export. In contrast to the import substitution policies of most low-income countries, a set of newly industrializing countries[2] has experienced rapid economic growth while following freer trade policies. This set includes Brazil, Hong Kong, Singapore, Taiwan, and Korea.

Taiwan is a striking example of export-based growth. During the period 1952 to 1980, Taiwanese real income grew at 9 percent per year, one of the

---

[1] The project includes separate volumes on 10 countries: Turkey, Ghana, Israel, Egypt, Philippines, India, South Korea, Chile, Colombia, and Brazil. There are two survey volumes: Jagdish Bhagwati, *Foreign Trade Regimes and Economic Development: Anatomy and Consequences of Exchange Control Regimes*, and Anne Krueger, *Foreign Trade Regimes and Economic Development: Liberalization Attempts and Consequences* (Cambridge, Mass.: Ballinger, 1978).

[2] Some agencies treat the newly industrialized countries (NICs) as a separate category. One grouping of NICs includes South Korea, Taiwan, Hong Kong, and Singapore (the Gang of Four); Brazil; Mexico; Argentina; and India. The OECD also includes Greece, Portugal, Spain, and Yugoslavia. See Louis Turner and Neil McMullen, *The Newly Industrializing Countries: Trade and Adjustment* (London: George Allen and Unwin, 1982), Chap. 1.

fastest rates in the world. The island is small with few natural resources. In the late 1940s, there was rapid inflation and little economic growth. Less than 10 percent of exports were industrial products. The national foreign trade policy switched from import substitution to export promotion. Production concentrated on labor-intensive products that used simple technology. Exports grew rapidly, and by 1980 Taiwan was the world's twentieth largest trading nation and the eighth largest trading partner of the United States. More than 90 percent of exports were manufactured goods. In 1980 the population of 17 million had a per capita income of $2,280. It remains to be seen whether the experience of Taiwan and the NICs is applicable to other low-income countries. The success of their export-based growth depends on their access to markets in high-income countries.

Import substitution requires the use of tariffs and quotas to make import substitution privately profitable. The widespread use of quotas has called attention to the practice of "rent seeking" as a cost of protection in addition to the ordinary production and consumption cost. A quota generates no tariff revenue, but the equivalent of the revenue becomes a profit or rent to the holder of import licenses. Since a license permits an importer to buy a product at the lower world price and resell at the higher domestic price, licenses have economic value (see Chapter 8). Domestic firms have an incentive to compete for licenses by employing real economic resources. The use of real economic resources to bid for licenses, called rent seeking, is part of the real cost of protection. Thus, the cost of protection includes not only the triangles under the domestic demand and supply curves, but the equivalent of the tariff revenue as well. Anne Krueger attempted to measure rent seeking in her study of commercial policy in Turkey. She estimated the cost of rent seeking to be 15 percent of GNP in 1968.[3]

It has been observed that agriculture is relatively more important in low-income countries. Agricultural output is a larger fraction of GNP, agricultural employment is a larger fraction of total employment, and food expenditures are a larger fraction of the average consumer's budget in low-income countries. This observation has led some policymakers to associate agriculture with backwardness. Consequently, a widespread policy in low-income countries is to discourage domestic agricultural production. A result has been a lower level of agricultural exports or a higher level of agricultural imports than would otherwise occur.

A number of policies have been used to discourage production, including export taxes, legal maximum prices, and tariffs on agricultural inputs (e.g., fertilizer). The effect of these policies is summarized by the effective rate of protection, which tends to be low or negative for agriculture in low-income

---

[3] Anne Krueger, "The Political Economy of a Rent-Seeking Society," *American Economic Review*, June 1974.

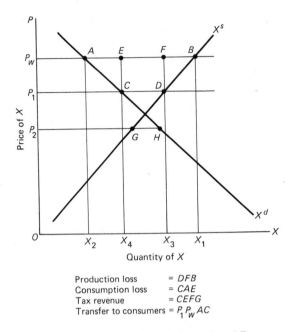

Production loss   = DFB
Consumption loss   = CAE
Tax revenue   = CEFG
Transfer to consumers = $P_1 P_W AC$

FIGURE 13-1   Effective Tax on Agricultural Exports

countries. In a study by Lutz and Scandizzo, effective rates were found to be negative in nearly 90 percent of the cases studied.[4] This policy amounts to a substantial de facto export tax for countries that would naturally export agricultural products. The effect for a small country is shown in Figure 13-1.

With free trade the domestic price would equal the world price OP_W. Production would be OX_1, domestic consumption OX_2, and exports would be X_1X_2. An export tax of P_WP_1 lowers the home price to OP_1, which lowers production of OX_3, raises domestic consumption to OX_4, and reduces exports to X_4X_3. The net loss to the country is the production loss DFB plus the consumption loss CAE. The two domestic transfers are the government's tax revenue $CEFD$ and a transfer to consumers of P_1P_WEC. An extreme application of low price policies can convert an exporter into a net importer.

In Figure 13-1 a domestic price of OP_2 would result in net imports of GH. For example, in the 1970s Pakistan imported an average of 1.3 million metric tons of wheat when it followed low price policies. Alternatively, Lutz and Scandizzo estimated that at world prices Pakistan would have been a net *exporter* of 1.2 million tons. The "cheap food" policies of low-income countries contrast to policies in high-income countries, where food prices have been kept

[4]The countries studied were Argentina, Egypt, Kenya, Pakistan, Portugal, Thailand, and Yugoslavia. The products were wheat, maize (corn), beef, rice, cotton, coffee, sugar cane, olive oil, rubber, and pork. See Ernst Lutz and Pasquale Scandizzo, "Price Distortions in Developing Countries: A Bias Against Agriculture," *European Review of Agricultural Economics*, Vol. 7, no. 1 (1980).

higher than they would have been under free trade. It is puzzling that the political process has led to artificially low food prices where income is low and artificially high prices in high-income countries. Two observed differences between the country groups that might explain the policies are (1) the budget share for food is higher in low-income countries and (2) urban consumers have a disproportionate amount of political power in low-income countries. The effect of price policy can be seen by comparing low-income countries that have similar climate, history, and agricultural potential. Since 1960 "agricultural production has increased twice as fast in Cameroon and Liberia as it has in neighboring Guinea and Ghana, and four times as fast in Tunisia and Colombia as in Morocco and Peru."[5]

A persistent issue is whether the trade policies of high-income countries are systematically biased against the economic growth of low-income countries. There is evidence of tariff escalation by high-income countries that discourages processing of raw materials. High-income countries have also imposed quotas against labor-intensive products, such as textiles and apparel. This argument has been expressed by various United Nations agencies, and a formal political bloc of low-income countries has developed. The group can be traced back to the 1955 conference of developing countries at Bandung, Indonesia.

In 1964 the First United Nations Conference on Trade and Development (UNCTAD) was held. UNCTAD became a formal institution within the United Nations, and the participating countries are called the Group of 77. One of the early proposals of the group was the Generalized System of Preferences, a set of preferential tariffs of products exported by low-income countries. All the major high-income countries granted tariff preferences, including the United States in 1976. In 1974 UNCTAD made a formal plea for a new international economic order. The proposal contains many components, but the main items are (1) an elaborate international commodity agreement with a buffer stock, (2) generalized debt relief, and (3) freer transfer of technology.[6] International commodity agreements were discussed in Chapter 10, and buffer stocks will be analyzed in Section 13.5.

13.4 TERMS OF TRADE AND GROWTH

A country's real income and its rate of growth can be affected by the prices it pays for imports and the prices it receives for exports. The terms of trade of a nation is defined as the ratio of export prices to import prices, and it can influ-

[5] Harry E. Walters, "Agriculture and Development," *Finance and Development*, September 1982, p. 9.

[6] The proposal has generated a large literature. See, for example, Rachel McCulloch, *Economic and Political Issues in the New International Economic Order*, Original Paper 22, International Institute for Economic Research, July 1979; or J. N. Bhagwati, ed., *The New International Economic Order: The North-South Debate* (Cambridge, Mass.: M.I.T. Press, 1977).

ence growth of real income. Since the terms of trade is a ratio of two price indices, it is not unique. The export and import indices are averages whose precise value depends on the weights assigned to each imported and exported good. The general form of a terms of trade index is

$$T = \frac{P^E}{P^I} = \frac{w_1 P_1^E + w_2 P_2^E + \cdots + w_n P_n^E}{v_1 P_1^I + v_2 P_2^I + \cdots + v_n P_n^I}$$

The export price index P^E is the weighted average of individual export prices, where the w's are the quantity weights. Similarly, P^I is the import price index, and the v's are the import quantity weights. A Laspeyres-type index would use for weights the actual quantities of exports and imports from some base year. Since the terms of trade is the ratio of prices received by residents to prices paid by residents, changes in the index are sometimes interpreted as a crude measure of changes in a country's welfare. The parity index published by the Department of Agriculture is an analogous index that attempts to measure changes in the welfare of farmers.

The terms of trade provides some useful information about welfare, but it is sometimes misleading because it fails to incorporate quantity changes. For example, a decrease in an export price reduces national welfare, other things constant. However, suppose that the cause of the price decrease is a technological innovation that lowers the cost of the export. The lower cost might increase the quantity of exports enough to dominate the decrease in the price of exports. National welfare may rise in spite of a decline in the term of trade. A similar argument applies to a rise in the price of imports. If it is caused by rapid economic growth that increases import demand, the rise in import volume may dominate the increase in price. Again, national welfare may improve in spite of a decline in the terms of trade. Thus, some caution must be exercised in interpreting changes in the terms of trade. Dramatic changes in national terms of trade occurred in 1973 and 1974 and again in 1979 and 1980 as a result of sharp increases in the price of oil. The magnitude of these changes was presented in Chapter 10. The issue of relevance to this chapter is whether the process of economic growth systematically alters the terms of trade.

Raoul Prebisch of the United Nations Economic Commission for Latin America put forth the hypothesis that the terms of trade of primary producing countries would decline secularly.[7] Some initial empirical support for the hypothesis was presented, but the results are sensitive to the time period studied. For example, if the base period is the Korean Conflict, when primary prices were high, subsequent periods show a decline in the terms of trade of primary producers. The pattern changes when a longer time period is considered. In particular, when one includes the oil price increases of the 1970s, the terms of

---

[7] Raoul Prebisch, *Towards a New Trade Policy for Development*. New York: United Nations, 1964.

TABLE 13-6   **Terms of Trade of the United States, 1770–1968**
(1913 = 100)

PERIOD	TERMS OF TRADE	PERIOD	TERMS OF TRADE
1770–1775	39	1879–1888	97
1784–1792	51	1889–1898	90
1789–1798	58	1899–1908	97
1799–1808	66	1909–1918	108
1809–1818	60	1919–1928	111
1819–1828	65	1929–1938	130
1829–1838	79	1939–1948	130
1839–1848	77	1944–1953	113
1849–1858	90	1954–1963	103
1859–1868	80	1964–1968	111
1869–1878	87		

Source: Lance Davis et al., *American Economic Growth: An Economist's History of the United States.* New York: Harper and Row, 1972, p. 566.

trade for primary producers become favorable. The economic history of the United States until World War II is roughly consistent with Prebisch's thesis. As the United States grew, manufacturing became more important and the terms of trade improved.

Table 13-6 shows the U.S. terms of trade from 1770 to 1968, with the terms of trade index equal to 100 for the base period of 1913. The U.S. terms of trade improved rather steadily from 39 in the period in 1775 to 130 in the period ending in 1938. However, the terms of trade have declined since then, and there is no reason to believe that the earlier U.S. experience is representative of the experience of other countries. Whether terms of trade are grouped according to developed versus developing countries or primary products versus manufactured products, recent evidence does not appear to support Prebisch.

Table 13-7 shows that the terms of trade of developed countries were quite stable from 1960 through 1973. They declined to 87 in 1974 and remained near that level since then. The column for developing countries shows the opposite experience, and the magnitude of the terms of trade improvement was larger. Of course, much of the change in 1974 was attributable to oil, and column 3 shows the terms of trade of developing countries when fuel prices are eliminated. Removing fuel does eliminate the improvement in the terms of trade of developing countries, but it does not support the hypothesis of a decline in the terms of trade. The final column expresses the terms of trade by product categories instead of country groups. Even for the period 1960 to 1972, there was no clear tendency for primary product prices to decline relative to manufactured prices. In 1973 ratio increased from 103 to 113 and in 1974 it rose to 169.

The only safe conclusion appears to be that primary producers benefit

TABLE 13-7   Terms of Trade of Developed and Developing Countries, Selected Years 1960–1977 (1970 = 100)

YEAR	DEVELOPED COUNTRIES	DEVELOPING COUNTRIES	DEVELOPING COUNTRIES LESS FUELS	PRIMARY PRODUCTS RELATIVE TO MANUFACTURED
1960	99	102	98	111
1963	100	99	95	106
1965	100	98	96	104
1969	100	101	102	102
1970	100	100	100	100
1971	100	100	91	102
1972	100	99	90	103
1973	98	107	97	113
1974	87	154	102	169
1975	91	140	85	154
1976	89	145	92	163
1977	88	152	102	163

Source: United Nations, *Yearbook of International Trade Statistics*, New York, 1978, p. 82.

from price changes during some periods and suffer in other periods. Price changes occur because of shifts in supply and demand, and there is no inherent reason to believe that one of the forces will dominate. Although there is no clear trend in primary product prices, they are quite sensitive to world business cycles. A broad index of primary product prices declined sharply during the recession of 1981 to 1982.

A final point concerns the relationship between the income level of a country and primary exports. Primary product exports are relatively more important for low-income countries, but high-income countries are important exporters of certain primary products. Wheat is an important example, whose main exporters are the United States, Canada, and Australia. It is also one of the primary products whose price shows a secular decline.

Since the terms of trade measure the price received by an exporter relative to the price paid by an importer, one might expect a change to favor the exporter or the importer, but not both. However, because of transport costs and other trade barriers, the c.i.f. price in the importing country is different from the f.o.b. price in the exporting country. It follows that a decrease in transport costs will improve the terms of trade of both exporting and importing countries. In fact, transport costs had been falling for many years until 1974. If terms of trade indices were broad enough to include transport costs, the terms of trade would decline for countries specializing in shipping services.

Private firms producing the same product tend to form trade associations that promote the product and provide information to members. Sometimes the trade associations collude on price and quantity, in which case they are an effective cartel. In international trade, governments of countries that specialize in certain products have tended to collaborate in an attempt to promote their product. One form of collaboration is an international commodity agreement, discussed in Chapter 10. Agreements have existed for many primary products, such as wheat, coffee, tin, sugar, cocoa, bauxite, rubber, and copper, and OPEC can be thought of as a kind of international commodity agreement. Among the many stated objectives of commodity agreements are an increase in the average price of the commodity and an increase in price stability. To raise the price, the agreement must control the production of exports of member countries. The common device for attempting to stabilize prices is a buffer stock. The price-increasing aspect of commodity agreements can be analyzed using the theory of cartels presented in Chapter 10.

With the major exception of OPEC, most commodity agreements have been notably unsuccessful in raising prices. Each member taken separately has an incentive to be a "free-rider." Consequently, countries have tended to export more than the amount specified by the agreement, and the resulting surplus has brought prices down. The history of the various international wheat agreements has been fairly typical. The first agreement, in 1933, specified export quotas and minimum prices for member countries, but it was widely violated within a year after it was signed. When world wheat crops were small, prices were about the agreement's minimum, but in large crop years, exports were promoted and the agreed minimum prices were violated. In spite of the failure of commodity agreements to achieve the stated goals, an elaborate commodity agreement called the integrated program for commodities is a basic component of the proposal for a new international economic order.

13.5 PRICE FLUCTUATION AND GROWTH

The terms of trade measures the average level of prices received by and paid by a country's traders. Trade and economic growth may also be affected by the variability of prices. Thus, even if there is no trend in a country's terms of trade, fluctuating prices for imports and exports may present economic problems. Product price instability is frequently mentioned as a potential barrier to growth in low-income countries. Primary product prices tend to be less stable than other prices, partly because of their sensitivity to business cycles. Alternating periods of business expansion and recession induce large changes in the demand for primary products.

As shown in Table 13-8, low-income countries are specialized exporters of primary products. As the table shows there are many countries that receive as much as 70 percent of total export revenue from only three products. Algeria, Libya, Saudi Arabia, and Uganda received in excess of 95 percent of

TABLE 13-8   Export Concentration of Low-Income Countries, 1978

COUNTRY	PERCENTAGE OF TOTAL EXPORTS	PRODUCTS
Algeria	95%	Petroleum, wine
Angola	80	Petroleum, coffee
Bolivia	85	Tin, copper, petroleum
Burma	75	Rice, wood
Chile	82	Copper, iron ore, fodder
Colombia	63	Coffee, cotton
Dominican Republic	77	Sugar, cocoa, pig iron
Gambia	91	Peanuts, vegetable oil
Ghana	89	Coca, wood, aluminum
Guyana	80	Sugar, bauxite, rice
Ivory Coast	78	Coffee, cocoa, wood
Liberia	91	Iron ore, rubber, coffee
Libya	99	Petroleum
Saudi Arabia	99	Petroleum
Somalia	85	Cattle, fruit, hides
Sri Lanka	68	Tea, rubber, gems
Uganda	95	Coffee, cotton, copper
Zaire	71	Copper, coffee, gems
Zambia	90	Copper, zinc

Source: United Nations, Yearbook of International Trade Statistics, New York, 1979.

export revenue from no more than three products. The high degree of export concentration implies that a change in one or two product prices could create a large disturbance in a national economy. Favorable prices could bring about an economic boom, and unfavorable prices could lead to severe economic hardship. Whether fluctuating prices of primary products significantly retard economic growth is ultimately an empirical question, but it is easier to understand the problem if certain relationships are clarified.

Export prices are different from export revenue, and variability of prices does not imply variability of revenue. If low export quantities are associated with high export prices and vice versa, unstable prices may be associated with stable export revenue. Whether revenue is destabilized by price changes depends on the source of demand and supply shifts and the elasticities of demand and supply of the product. For example, if a specialized exporter tends to have a small crop in years when other exporters also have small crops, the price will be unusually high. The product price increase will offset the quantity decrease, and export revenue will be stabilized. Thus, more information is needed before one can conclude that unstable prices cause unstable export revenue.

An additional consideration is that the welfare of citizens depends on consumption rather than on export revenue or national income. For heavily specialized countries, certain exports may constitute a large fraction of national income, and destabilizing export revenue may also destabilize income. However, an uneven national income stream need not imply an uneven consumption stream. An even national consumption pattern can be achieved by lending abroad during periods of above-average income and borrowing during periods of below average income. Converting an uneven income stream into a stable consumption stream does depend upon the country's having access to the international capital market. Barriers to private lending can be supplemented by loans from governmental agencies. For example, the International Monetary Fund makes loans to countries with fluctuating national income.

A number of empirical studies have considered the relationship between primary product prices and economic growth, and much of the work is summarized in a book by MacBean.[8] It appears that primary product prices have been particularly volatile, but volatile prices have not systematically retarded economic growth. However, there is sufficient concern about volatile prices, and several actual and proposed commodity agreements include facilities designed to stabilize prices. The Common Fund of UNCTAD's integrated proposal for commodities is a prominent example of a buffer stock.

Consider the problem of an economy confronted by fluctuating prices. Two alternative means of stabilizing prices are a buffer stock and international trade. For purposes of comparison, first consider the problem of a closed economy. A buffer stock is an inventory policy designed to stabilize some product price. Let the buffer stock be a government agency whose goal is to stabilize the price at its average level. Although the government agency is not profit motivated, it will need the same information to carry out its task as a profit-motivated private speculator. To operate the stock, the manager must have both money and an inventory of the product in question. At the target price the inventory manager must buy the product when there is an excess supply and sell the product when there is an excess demand. Whether the fund can succeed depends on the price chosen, the size of the inventory, and the financial resources of the fund.

The problem is illustrated in Figure 13-2. Let demand be stable and let supply fluctuate, perhaps due to the weather. X^d is the stable demand curve and X_A^s is the average supply curve, the mean of X_L^s and X_S^s. In years when the smaller supply occurs, the price is P_S, and when the supply is larger, the price is P_L. In absence of a buffer stock the price will fluctuate between P_L and P_S as shown in panel B of the diagram. The object of the buffer stock is to stabilize the price at its average level, P_A. When the larger supply, X_L^s, prevails, there is an excess supply of AB at the price OP_A, and the stock must purchase this amount. In years of smaller supply, X_S^s, there is an excess demand of CA at the price OP_A, and the buffer stock must sell this amount from inventories. The net effect of the operation is to substitute fluctuation in the

[8] A. I. MacBean, *Export Instability and Economic Development* (London: George Allen and Unwin, 1966).

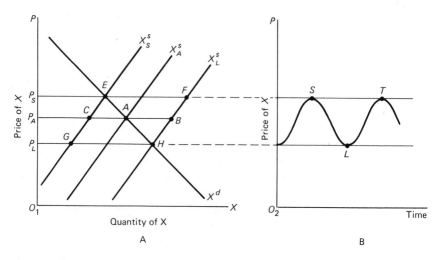

FIGURE 13-2   Buffer Stock for a Closed Economy

quantity of the stock's inventory for fluctuation in the market price. If the leftward and rightward shifts X^s are equal in magnitude $(CA = AB)$ and occur with equal frequency, purchases by the buffer stock in some periods will equal sales in other periods. In the long run, the inventory will be constant. Most international commodity agreements include a buffer stock arrangement.

There are some problems associated with a buffer stock, the first of which is the cost of storage. Storage costs include the cost of physical facilities and forgone interest. To earn enough revenue to meet these costs, the fund must permit enough price fluctuation so it can sell the product for more than its purchase price. A more fundamental problem is that the manager of the stock must be able to identify the long-run average price, which requires knowledge of the frequency and magnitude of supply shifts. Thus, the manager must have some ability to forecast variables such as weather, wars, technical change, and business cycles, which are the sources of supply shifts. If the manager attempts to stabilize the wrong price, he or she will either run out of money or deplete the inventory.

For example, if the manager attempts to stabilize the price at P_S, the market would clear in years of small supply, but the stock would buy EF in large supply years. The inventory would increase until the fund ran out of money. Conversely, if the manager chose to peg the price at P_L, the market would clear in years of large supply, and the fund would sell GH in small supply years. Since the fund would be a net seller of X without ever buying any X, its inventory would eventually be exhausted. Thus, accurate forecasting of supply and demand is an important condition for a buffer stock. Successful stabilization also depends on a satisfactory inventory level and financial resources. A manager could forecast supply shifts accurately, but the scheme would fail if resources were insufficient.

Consider the following example of fluctuating supply. Half the time, supply is

$$X_1^s = 200 + 2P$$

Half the time, supply is

$$X_2^s = 2P$$

Demand is stable at

$$X^d = 400 - 2P$$

The alternative equilibrium prices are

$$X_1^s = X^d$$
$$200 + 2P_1 = 400 - 2P_1$$
$$P_1 = 50$$
$$X_2^s = X^d$$
$$2P_2 = 400 - 2P_2$$
$$P_2 = 100$$

Thus, prices would fluctuate between \$50 and \$100. If a buffer stock manager had information about these demand and supply equations, he or she could compute the average supply $(X_A^s = 100 + 2P)$ and the average price $(P_A = 75)$. At a stable price of \$75, quantity demanded would be

$$X^d = 400 - 2(75) = 250$$

each year. Quantity supplied would be either

$$X_1^s = 200 + 2(75) = 350$$

or

$$X_2^s = 2(75) = 150$$

The fund would buy 100 units in large supply years and sell 100 units in small supply years. However, suppose that the manager underestimates the average price to be \$60. In this case, the fund would sell 160 units half the time and buy 40 units half the time. The net sales of the fund would deplete the stock. The reader can show that an attempt to stabilize the price at above \$75 would cause the fund to be a net buyer of X and its monetary resources would be depleted.

The relationship between the buffer stock and private speculation must

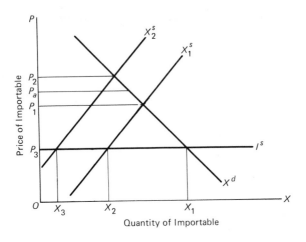

FIGURE 13-3   Trade and Price Stability: Disturbances Originate at Home

be considered. If speculators observe the pattern of prices shown in Figure 13-2, they have an incentive to buy the product at points such as L and sell it at points such as S and T. The addition of speculative demand at points such as L will raise the price, and the addition of speculative supply at points such as S will lower the price. The net effect of well-informed speculation would be to stabilize the price in the same way as a buffer stock. Private speculation would reduce the range of price fluctuation until the bid-ask differential is just equal to storage costs. Speculation would achieve price stabilization even if speculators were solely concerned about private profits. Similarly, a successful buffer stock manager would earn profits from buying at low prices and selling at high prices even if he or she were solely concerned about price stability.

FIGURE 13-4   Trade and Price Stability: Disturbances Originate Abroad

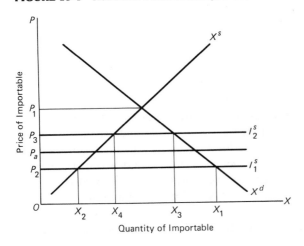

A prerequisite for the success of either one is that they be well informed in the sense of accurately forecasting the long-run average price. An important empirical question about commodity markets is whether government agencies or private speculators have better market information. Since government stockpiling substitutes for private inventories, a government buffer stock does not necessarily increase total inventories. This point is sometimes ignored in discussions of world food stocks. If an additional ton of food stored by government agencies merely reduces private inventories by 1 ton, the program will not add to price stability.

In a closed economy, domestic supply fluctuation can be offset either by private speculation or a government buffer stock. Price stabilization can be achieved by private or public inventory holding. International trade can also influence product price stability. Trade may stabilize or destabilize domestic prices depending on the source of market disturbances. For example, consider a small country whose domestic supply fluctuates. A free trade policy would stabilize the domestic price by permitting the quantity of imports to vary so as to offset the change in domestic supply.[9]

The case of variable domestic supply with free trade is shown in Figure 13-3, where X_1^s and X_2^s are the fluctuating domestic supply curves. In the absence of trade, the price would fluctuate between P_2 and P_1, with an average price of P_a. With trade, the import supply curve is I^s and the price is stable at P_3. When domestic supply is X_1^s imports are X_2X_1. When supply falls to X_2^s, imports increase to X_3X_1. When the source of the supply disturbance is domestic, international trade has a stabilizing effect on the domestic price. Alternatively, suppose that the disturbance originates in the rest of the world.

This case is shown in Figure 13-4. X^s is the stable domestic supply and P_1 is the stable domestic price that would prevail in absence of trade. I_1^s and I_2^s are the fluctuating import supply curves and P_2 and P_3 are the resulting prices when the home country engages in trade. P_3 is the average price with trade, and it is below the domestic price in the absence of trade. In the case where disturbances originate abroad, international trade destabilizes the domestic price. Nevertheless, trade may still be a preferable policy to no trade, since the average price is lower.

The stabilizing or destabilizing effect of trade has been discussed in connection with wheat trade between the United States and the USSR. Wheat supply has been extremely unstable in the USSR, because much wheat land is in areas with volatile weather. Until 1971 the USSR was not a major wheat importer. In 1971 a decision was made to use the international market to offset changes in domestic supply. Since then, the USSR has been a large importer on the average, but imports have been highly variable. The net effect of the post-1971 import policy has been to stabilize the USSR market and destabilize wheat prices in the rest of the world. The United States is the largest exporter of wheat and

---

[9]Price stability would also occur with a constant tariff but not with a quota or a variable levy.

variable world wheat prices have destabilized U.S. wheat prices. At the same time the presence of the USSR as a wheat importer has increased the variability of wheat prices, it has increased the average price received by U.S. exporters. Concern about price stability led to the five-year trade agreement between the two countries that began in 1976 and specified minimum and maximum quantities of grain that could be traded.

When all economic disturbances occur at home, international trade stabilizes prices. When all disturbances originate abroad, trade is a source of price instability. The most interesting empirical cases are those in which disturbances originate both at home and abroad. To assess the role of trade in those intermediate cases, it is necessary to know the relative frequency and magnitude of domestic and foreign disturbances. Since the rest of the world consists of many countries in different parts of the globe, information about the correlation between disturbances in different foreign countries is also useful. The rest of the world could be subject to frequent shocks, but if small supplies in some countries occurred at the same time as large supplies occurred in other countries, the rest of the world would be a stable trading partner. The rest of the world could be thought of as a kind of diversified portfolio. Engaging in international trade with a stable trading partner would add to price stability in the home country. By imparting price stability, trade would function as a substitute for domestic inventories. In periods of small domestic supply, the home country could increase imports instead of reducing domestic inventories. The stabilization advantages to the home country come from stability of the rest of the world as an economic unit. They do not require that all individual countries in the rest of the world be stable.

D. Gale Johnson and associates have studied the substitution possibilities between world grain reserves and freer international trade.[10] Supply variability is not perfectly correlated across countries of the world. Small crops in some countries coincide with large crops in other countries. They concluded that freer trade would be an effective substitute for larger world inventories of grain. However, trade acts as a stabilizing force only if countries permit the volume of imports and exports to respond to economic conditions. The imposition of import and export quotas reduces the stabilization effect of trade and is equivalent to reducing the effective size of world inventories.

The widespread use of insulating trade policies by importing and exporting nations exacerbated the "world food crisis" of 1974. The initial excess demand for grain raised world prices, but the major importing and exporting countries refused to permit domestic grain prices to respond to external conditions. Consequently, import demand was greater and export supply was smaller than they would have been in absence of insulating policies. All the major im-

---

[10] D. Gale Johnson, "Increased Stability of Grain Supplies in Developing Countries: Optimal Carryovers and Insurance" in Jagdish N. Bhagwati, ed., *The New International Economic Order: the North-South Debate.* Cambridge, Mass.: M.I.T. Press, 1977.

porting countries, including Japan, the European Economic Community, India, the USSR, and China, used government policy to stimulate import demand. At the same time Canada, Australia, and Argentina explicitly limited grain exports. The United States was the only major grain exporter to refrain from imposing trade restrictions. The result of these trade policies was to make world grain inventories less adequate than they otherwise would have been. Because of the instability that was partly induced by trade policies in the rest of the world, prices were destabilized in the United States. Thus, international trade has the potential to produce economic stability or instability. Variable weather could be a natural source of instability. Insulating trade policies of other countries could be a government-sponsored source of instability.

13.6 ECONOMIC GROWTH, DEMAND, AND TRADE

Thus far the chapter has considered the effect of trade and trade policy on economic growth. The remainder of the chapter analyzes the effect of economic growth on the relative importance of trade. Will the forces of economic growth increase the interdependence among nations? The importance of international trade to a country is conventionally measured by the ratio of imports or exports to GNP. If imports are significantly different from exports, the average of the two can be compared with GNP as a measure of openness.

Table 1-1 (in Chapter 1) shows that the importance of trade varies substantially across countries. As national income grows, consumers can afford to buy more of all goods, including importables and exportables. The relative rates of growth of import demand and income are measured by the income elasticity of demand for imports. If the elasticity is greater than 1, the import share will increase with economic growth.

In Figure 13-5 let point A be the initial consumption point on consumption possibilities line B_1. The line shows all the combinations of exportable and importable goods that are available to consumers at the initial income level. Economic growth shifts the consumption line to B_2, and the new consumption point will depend on consumer preferences. Line OAH is a reference line along which the budget shares for goods E and I remain constant. At point H, the percentage increase in income (AH/OA) is equal to the percentage increase in demand for E (E_2E_1/OE_1) and I (I_2I_1/OI_1). Thus, between A and H, both income elasticities of demand are equal to 1.

Of course, growth in demand may be biased toward either importables or exportables. If the demand for importables grows faster than income does, the share of imports will increase. Since the weighted average of all income elasticities must be 1, if the income elasticity for importables is greater than 1, the elasticity for exportables must be less than 1. In this case, the new consumption point would be southeast of H on B_2 (e.g., at F). The relative share

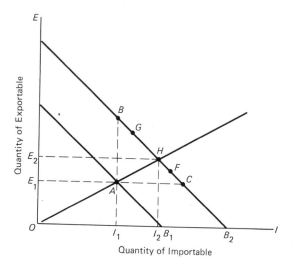

FIGURE 13-5   Demand Growth and Trade

of imports would increase. Conversely, an income elasticity of less than 1 for imports would decrease the importance of trade (e.g., at point G). If the importable is an inferior good, the new consumption point will be northwest of B. Any of the demand growth patterns is possible, and it is conventional to divide the cases according to whether they are neutral or biased toward or against trade. Point H represents neutral growth of demand, and points between H and C are called protrade biased. Points southeast of C are called ultra-protrade biased, because the demand for importables grows so much that the demand for exportables falls (E is inferior).

If demand growth is biased toward exportables, trade will become less important. More exportables will be consumed at home and less will be exported. Points between H and B are called antitrade biased, and points northwest of B are called ultra-antitrade biased. In the latter case, importables are an inferior good. Thus, even if relative prices remained constant, economic growth could alter the pattern of demand and change the relative importance of international trade.

The same point can be expressed in terms of supply and demand curves. Figure 13-6 shows domestic demand and supply, import demand, and export supply. Growth in demand for importables shifts X_1^d to the right to X_2^d, and this movement shifts the demand for imports (I_1^d) to the right to I_2^d. The magnitude of the rightward shift in both curves depends on the growth of income and the elasticity of demand for imports. The larger the shift of import demand, the greater the protrade bias of economic growth. The lower portion of the diagram shows the effect of income growth on the demand for exportable goods. Demand shifts from Y_1^d to Y_2^d, which causes the supply of exports to

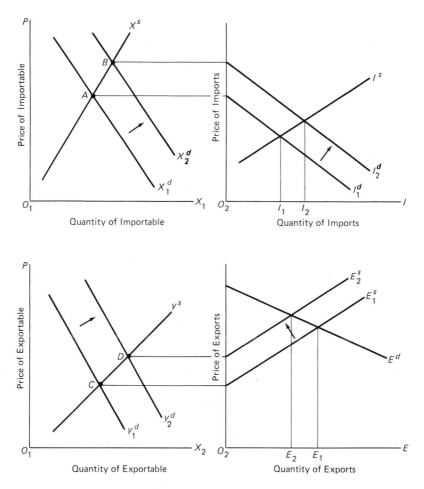

FIGURE 13-6   Income Growth and Demand

shift to the *left*. Because more of the exportable is consumed at home, less is available for the export market. The greater the income elasticity of demand for the exportable, the greater the leftward shift of export supply. The leftward shift of E^s indicates an antitrade bias to economic growth.

Any of the cases shown is theoretically possible, but knowledge of the commodity composition of a country's imports and exports helps to determine the likely magnitude of income elasticities. Houthakker and Magee studied U.S. trade and estimated that the income elasticity of demand for U.S. exports was less than the U.S. income elasticity of demand for imports.[11] It follows that if

[11] Hendrik Houthakker and Stephen Magee, "Income and Price Elasticities in World Trade," *Review of Economics and Statistics*, May 1969.

TABLE 13-9   Commodity Composition of U.S. Agricultural
Exports, 1926–1980

PERIOD	FOOD	FEED	RAW MATERIALS*
1926–30	39%	5%	56%
1931–35	30	3	67
1936–40	33	8	59
1941–45	78	2	20
1946–50	60	9	31
1951–55	49	13	38
1956–60	51	16	33
1961–65	53	23	24
1966–70	49	30	21
1971–75	49	35	16
1976–80	45	38	17

*Cotton and tobacco make up most of this category.
Source: U.S. Department of Agriculture, Foreign Agricultural Trade of the U.S.,
Washington, D.C.: U.S. Government Printing Office, September–October 1981,
p. 90.

income in the United States grew at the same rate as in the rest of the world, the demand for imports would grow faster than would foreign demand for exports. The result would be a protrade bias, whose immediate effect would be a balance-of-trade deficit under fixed exchange rates or a currency depreciation under floating exchange rates.

It is well known that the demand for food grows less rapidly than income. Ernst Engel discovered this relationship in ninteenth-century Europe, and it remains true in the twentieth century. This relationship would give growth a protrade bias for a food exporter such as the United States and an antitrade bias for a food importer. Largely because of the slow growth in demand the agricultural share of world trade has fallen steadily from 32 percent in 1960 to 16 percent in 1979.

At the same time, the composition of agricultural trade has changed considerably. There has been a shift away from agricultural raw materials (e.g., rubber, jute, cotton, and tobacco) toward food (e.g., wheat) and feed (e.g., corn and soybeans). This change in the composition of agricultural trade has been particularly pronounced for the United States.

Table 13-9 shows the growth in importance of food and feed relative to agricultural raw materials from 1926 to 1980. In the period 1926 to 1930, food and feed were 39 percent and 5 percent of U.S. agricultural exports, respectively, while in the period ending 1980 the shares were 45 percent and 38 percent. At the same time, raw materials declined in importance from 56 percent in the period ending 1930 to 17 percent in the period ending 1980. Food exports jumped sharply during and immediately after World War II. The rapid growth in feed demand reflects the high income elasticity of demand for meat.

Most of the growth in demand for food has come from low-income countries, and most of the growth in feed demand has come from high-income countries.

13.7 FACTOR ACCUMULATION AND SUPPLY

The sources of economic growth can be divided into technological change and increases in supplies of factors of production. Growth can be represented by a shift in a nation's production possibilities curve away from the origin. Changes in factor supplies alter prices of factors of production. Since products use factors in different proportions, changes in factor prices alter the relative costs of producing different products. In this way factor accumulation causes economic growth and alters the nation's comparative advantage. The change in the composition of the country's production and trade depends on which factor is growing more rapidly. According to the factor endowments theory, the country should export goods using large amounts of its abundant factor. Whether factor accumulation is protrade or antitrade biased depends on whether the abundant or the scarce factor is growing more rapidly. If the supply of the abundant factor grows faster, the relative cost of the exportable will decline, and the supply of exports will increase.

The upper portion of Figure 13-7 shows the effect of growth of the abundant factor on domestic supply and export supply. The supply of the exportable shifts from Y_1^s to Y_2^s, which causes the supply of exports to shift from E_1^s to E_2^s. Because of the increase in export supply, the volume of trade increases from E_1 to E_2. Growth of the abundant factor increases the volume of trade. The effect of growth of the scarce factor is shown in the lower portion of the diagram. The importable product should use large amounts of the scarce factor. The supply of the importable shifts from X_1^s to X_2^s, which reduces the demand for imports from I_1^d to I_2^d. The volume of imports declines from I_1 to I_2 as factor accumulation substitutes for trade.[12] Thus, factor accumulation increases or decreases the importance of trade for a country according to whether it causes the nation's factor proportions to approach or diverge from those of its trading partners.

Factor accumulation may be the result of domestic forces or international factor mobility. Domestic forces such as population growth, change in labor force participation, or saving may alter the supplies of factors of production. International migration and investment may also change factor supplies. If factor mobility is based on economic motives, factors should move to the country where their productivity is higher. This would lead countries to import their

[12] In addition to increasing output in the sector that employs that factor intensively, factor accumulation will reduce output in the remaining sector of the economy. See T. M. Rybczynski, "Factor Endowment and Relative Commodity Prices," *Economica*, November 1955.

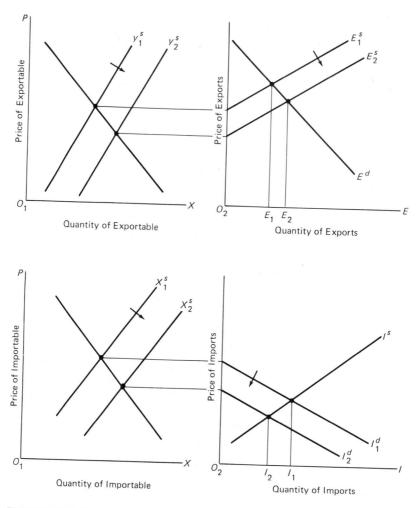

FIGURE 13-7   Factor Accumulation in the Exportable or Importable Sectors

scarce factor and export their abundant factor of production. This pattern of factor mobility would decrease imports and exports and make a country less dependent on international trade. The case of Mexican labor migration to the United States appears to be an example of labor emigration substituting for exports of labor-intensive products from Mexico. Conversely, world population trends tend to increase the importance of international trade.

Table 13-10 shows that population has been growing more rapidly in low-income countries since 1950. From 1970 to 1977 population grew three times as fast in developing countries as in industrialized countries. Table 13-11 shows the level of population and its rate of growth for individual countries. Countries where labor was initially the scarce factor (e.g., the United States, West

TABLE 13-10 Population in 1978 and Population Growth Rate, 1970–1978

COUNTRY	POPULATION 1978 (MILLIONS)	POPULATION GROWTH RATE, 1970–78
China	952.2	1.6%
India	643.9	2.0
USSR	261.0	0.9
United States	218.5	0.8
Indonesia	136.0	1.8
Brazil	119.5	2.9
Japan	114.9	1.2
Bangladesh	84.7	2.8
Nigeria	80.6	2.5
Pakistan	76.1	2.9
Mexico	65.4	3.3
West Germany	61.3	0.1
Italy	56.7	0.7
United Kingdom	55.8	0.1
France	53.3	0.6
Vietnam	51.7	3.1
Philippines	46.6	2.7
Thailand	44.5	2.8
Turkey	43.1	2.5
Egypt	39.9	2.2
Spain	37.1	1.1
South Korea	36.6	2.0
Iran	35.8	3.0
Poland	35.0	0.9
Burma	32.2	2.2
Ethiopia	31.0	2.5
South Africa	27.7	2.7
Zaire	26.8	2.7
Argentina	26.4	1.3
Colombia	25.6	2.3
Canada	23.5	1.3
Yugoslavia	22.0	0.9
Romania	21.9	0.9
Morocco	18.9	2.9
Algeria	17.6	3.2
Sudan	17.4	2.7
North Korea	17.1	2.6
Tanzania	17.0	3.4
Peru	16.8	2.8
East Germany	16.7	−0.2
Czechoslovakia	15.1	0.7
Kenya	14.7	3.4

TABLE 13-10   Population in 1978 and Population Growth Rate, 1970–1978

COUNTRY	POPULATION 1978 (MILLIONS)	POPULATION GROWTH RATE, 1970–78
Afghanistan	14.6	2.2
Sri Lanka	14.3	1.7
Australia	14.2	1.6
Venezuela	14.0	3.4
The Netherlands	13.9	0.8
Nepal	13.6	2.3
Malaysia	13.3	2.7
Uganda	12.4	3.0
Iraq	12.2	3.4
Ghana	11.0	3.1
Chile	10.7	1.7
Hungary	10.7	0.7
World	4,160.0	

Source: World Bank, World Bank Atlas, Washington, 1980.

Germany, Italy, and the United Kingdom) have had slow population growth. Population grew at less than 1 percent per year in those countries. Conversely, countries where labor was initially the abundant factor have had more rapid population growth. Population has grown at more than 2 percent in nearly all low-income countries. In Mexico, Kenya, Venezuela, and Iraq, it has grown at more than 3 percent per year. This pattern increases the comparative advantage of low-income countries in labor-intensive products.

TABLE 13-11   Trade-Income Ratios* for Selected Countries, 1875–1975

PERIOD	GREAT BRITAIN	ITALY	SWEDEN	NORWAY	DENMARK	TOTAL	UNITED STATES
1875–1884	49.0%	19.5%	39.3%	36.3%	47.7%	38.4%	
1885–1894	46.2	18.0	44.2	40.2	48.0	39.3	
1895–1904	42.3	19.8	42.2	44.0	52.0	40.1	
1905–1914	48.6	23.4	40.3	48.6	57.6	43.7	
1915–1924	41.5	25.7	38.5	49.7	55.1	40.3	12.4%
1925–1934	35.4	19.0	32.5	38.0	53.4	35.7	7.7
1935–1944	23.1	13.5	26.4	34.5	35.4	26.7	6.8
1945–1954	32.3	18.2	33.7	43.9	39.0	33.8	7.4
1955–1964	31.5	20.0	37.9	46.2	48.5	36.8	7.1
1965–1975	35.2	30.4	42.1	52.2	47.9	41.6	10.2

*Exports plus imports divided by GNP.

Source: Sven Grassman, "Long-Term Trends in Openness of National Economies," Oxford Economic Papers, March 1980.

13.8 TECHNICAL CHANGE AND GROWTH

Technical change is a second source of economic growth. It permits more output to be produced with constant factor supplies. Technical change can be represented by rightward shifts of the production possibilitives curve or the supply curves for importables and exportables. The exact nature of the shift depends on (1) the industry in which technical change occurs and (2) whether technical change is biased toward saving a particular factor of production. If technical change occurs more rapidly in the exportable sector, it will reduce the relative cost of exports and increase the importance of trade.

The upper portion of Figure 13-8 shows the effect of technical change in

FIGURE 13-8   Technical Change in the Exportable or Importable Sector

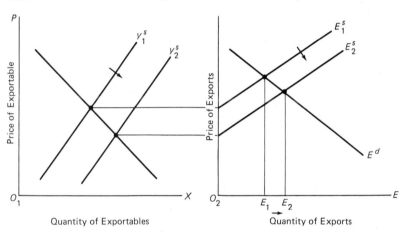

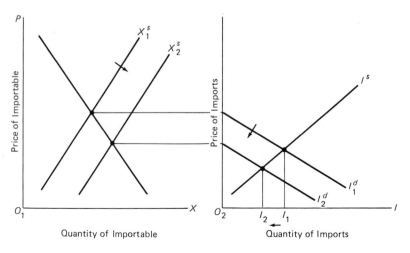

the exportable sector. The domestic supply curve (Y_1^s) and export supply curve (E_1^s) shift to the right and the volume of exports increases from E_1 to E_2. The lower portion of the same figure shows the opposition case of technical change in the import-competing sector. The domestic supply curve shifts to the right, $(X_1^s$ to $X_2^s)$ import demand shifts to the left $(I_1^d$ to $I_2^d)$, and the volume of imports declines from I_1 to I_2. Thus, technical change increases the volume of trade if it occurs in the exportable sector and decreases trade if the innovation occurs in the importable sector.

Technical change reduces the number of inputs necessary to produce a given output, but it may save on the use of some inputs more than others. Technical change is factor neutral if it reduces the necessary quantities of capital and labor in the same proportion. Neutral change is equivalent to increasing the effective quantities of capital and labor in the same proportions. Even if technical change is factor neutral, it will alter a country's comparative advantage if it occurs at different rates in different industries. Technical change is factor biased if it changes factor proportions at the initial factor prices. It is labor saving if it increases the labor-capital ratio and capital saving if it increases the capital-labor ratio.

The effect of factor-biased technical change on trade depends on whether it is biased toward the abundant or the scarce factor. Bias toward the abundant factor would cause a greater increase in the effective supply of that factor. The supply of the exportable and the supply of exports would shift to the right, increasing the volume of trade. If technical change is biased toward the scarce factor, there will be a greater increase in the effective supply of that factor, and the country's factor endowments will become more like those of the rest of the world. The supply of importables will shift to the right, the demand for imports will shift to the left, and the volume of imports will increase.

Technical change is not costless, and it is not entirely a random process. It is an attempt to reduce costs through expenditures on research and development. Thus, technical change may be induced by factor costs. Technical change that saves the scarce and expensive factor of production may be more profitable, and innovations may be biased in this direction. To the extent that technical change is biased toward saving the scarce factor, domestic production would substitute for imports and the importance of trade would decline. Evidence from the work of Hufbauer and Magee indicates that the development of synthetics in the United States has substituted for imports of raw materials.[13] The Carter administration's program to subsidize research on synthetic fuels was an explicit attempt to substitute synthetics for imported crude oil.

---

[13] Gary Hufbauer, *Synthetic Materials and the Theory of International Trade*. Cambridge, Mass.: Harvard University Press, 1966. Stephen P. Magee and Norman I. Robins. "The Raw Material Product Cycle" in Lawrence Krause and Hugh Patrick, eds., *Mineral Resources in the Pacific Area*. San Francisco: Federal Reserve Bank of San Francisco, 1978.

13.9 EVIDENCE ON ECONOMIC GROWTH AND THE IMPORTANCE OF TRADE

Does the process of economic growth tend to increase the importance of international trade? This chapter has shown how changes in demand, technology, and factor accumulation may increase or decrease the importance of international trade. When empirical data on trade and national income are consulted, it is difficult to find significant changes in the trade relationship. A safe statement is that there have been no clear trends in the last century in the relative importance of international trade.

International trade is more important now than it was before the Industrial Revolution, but industrialization has not brought about a continuous increase in the importance of trade. Trade increased in importance for certain periods and certain countries, but the opposite was true for other periods and countries. Much has been said and written about the increasing interdependence of the world in recent years. Trade has become more important when the last decade is compared with the period immediately after World War II. However, if the comparison is made over the last century, trade appears to be no more important now than it was then.

Some data compiled by Sven Grassman on trends in openness are shown in Table 13-11. They cover the period 1875 to 1975 for five Western European countries and the United States. Trade is the sum of exports and imports, and it is expressed as a percentage of GNP. For all countries trade increased in importance during the period ending 1975 relative to the previous decade. Trade increased even more dramatically when the last period is compared with the decades ending in 1944 or 1954. For the total of five European countries, the trade-income ratio increased from 26.7 percent in 1944 to 33.8 percent in 1954 to 36.8 percent in 1964 to 41.6 percent in 1975. However, when the last two decades are compared with the period 1875 to 1884, the secular growth in the importance of trade is less clear.

For the group of five countries, trade was more important in 1975 (41.6 percent) than in 1884 (38.4 percent), but it was more important in 1884 than in 1964, 1954, 1944, and 1934. Trade tends to decline during war and depression. The trade-income ratio increased steadily to 43.7 percent until World War I (1914). It declined sharply during World Wars I and II and the Great Depression, reaching a low of 26.7 percent in the decade ending 1944. The ratio increased in each successive decade, but by 1975 it had still not returned to the peak reached in 1914 (43.7 percent). The experience was different for different countries, but it is difficult to reject the hypothesis that there is no long-term trend in the openness of economies. This hypothesis does not deny that there are economic determinants of the size of the trade sector. Instead it implies that the protrade-biased changes in demand, supply, commercial policy, and transport costs have been approximately offset by other antitrade-biased changes in the same variables.

13.10 LARGE COUNTRIES, GROWTH, AND THE TERMS OF TRADE

The terms of trade of small countries change because of changes in conditions in the rest of the world. However, for large countries, domestic changes that bring about economic growth will also change the nation's terms of trade. Specifically, those forces that increase import demand or export supply will increase the volume of trade and cause the terms of trade to deteriorate.

The case of economic growth with declining terms of trade is shown in Figure 13-9. In the upper portion of the diagram, the initial equilibrium is at A, the intersection of I_1^d and I_1^s. Let economic growth increase import demand to I_2^d. Import demand might shift because of a high income elasticity of demand for the importable or because of rapid growth in output of the exportable good that reduced output of the importables. The terms of trade of the large country would decline as the price of imports would increase to P_2. Since economic growth initiated the change, deterioration of the terms of trade does not necessarily reduce national income. Given the nation's monopsony power as a buyer of imports, the rise in the price of imports could be avoided by imposing a barrier to imports, such as an optimal tariff.

The analogous situation for exports is shown in the lower portion of Figure 13-9. The initial equilibrium is at point A, the intersection of E_1^d and E_1^s. Let economic growth increase the supply of exports to E_2^s. The shift might be caused by a low income elasticity of demand for the exportable, technical change in the exportable sector, or accumulation of the abundant factor. The large country's terms of trade will deteriorate as the price of exports falls from P_1 to P_2. If export demand is inelastic, total export revenue will decrease, and it is possible for national income to decline.

The anomalous possibility of economic growth reducing the welfare of residents has been named "immiserizing" or "damnifying" growth. World income and income in the rest of the world would rise, but domestic income would fall due to the deterioration of the terms of trade. The home country could always avoid this outcome by restraining exports, for example, with an optimum export tax. Although immiserizing growth is a theoretical possibility, there is no empirical evidence to indicate that it is an important real world phenomenon.

An alternative possibility is that economic growth will improve a large country's terms of trade. Improvement will occur if the volume of trade declines either through a decrease in the demand for imports or a decrease in the supply of exports. This case can be seen in Figure 13-9 by reversing the previous analysis. In the upper portion of the diagram, the initial equilibrium is at B and import demand declines from I_2^d to I_1^d. This might occur because of

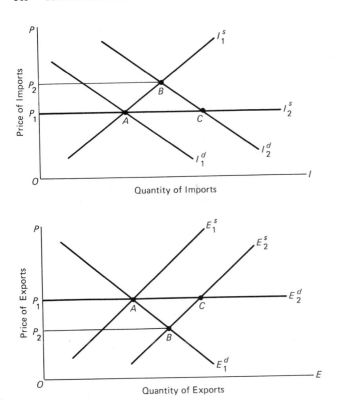

FIGURE 13-9   Growth and Declining Terms of Trade for a Large Country

technical change in the importable sector or accumulation of the scarce factor. The net effect is a decrease in the price of imports from P_2 to P_1 and an improvement in the terms of trade. Alternatively, the terms of trade may improve as a result of a decrease in the supply of exports. This might occur as a result of a high income elasticity of demand for the exportable or rapid growth in production of the importable that reduced exportable output. This case can be shown in the lower portion of Figure 13-9 by interpreting point B as the initial equilibrium. The decrease in export supply from E_2^s to E_1^s will increase the price of exports from P_2 to P_1 and improve the country's terms of trade. In general, economic growth that decreases the volume of trade will improve the terms of trade, and growth that increases trade volume will cause the terms of trade to deteriorate.

SUMMARY

Income per capita and rates of economic growth vary widely across countries. Some of the differences can be explained by different national experiences with international trade. Governments have attempted to use trade policy to promote national economic growth or to promote particular sectors of the economy. Modern policies of import substitution resemble mercantilistic policies that prevailed prior to the Industrial Revolution.

Changes in the international terms of trade can influence economic growth, and commodity agreements are an attempt by exporting countries to improve their terms of trade. International trade can stabilize product prices as an alternative to a buffer stock or private speculation.

Just as trade and trade policies can influence economic growth, growth can also affect trade. If domestic demand is biased toward importable products, growth will increase the relative importance of trade. Economic growth is brought about by increases in supplies of factors of production and technological change. In general, if the growing country becomes less similar to the rest of the world, trade will grow faster than income. Faster growth in the supply of the abundant factor and greater technical change in the exportable sector will be pro-trade biased. Alternatively, faster accumulation of the scarce factor and greater technical change in the importable sector will be biased against trade.

The trade-income ratio was larger in recent years than it was after World War II, but there is no pronounced trend over the last 100 years. Growth may alter the terms of trade of large countries. Growth that substitutes for trade tends to improve the terms of trade.

REFERENCES

BALASSA, BELA, et al. *The Structure of Protection in Developing Countries.* Baltimore: Johns Hopkins University Press, 1971.

BALE, MALCOLM, and ERNST LUTZ. "Price Distortions in Agriculture and Their Effects: An International Comparison." *American Journal of Agricultural Economics,* February 1981.

BEHRMAN, JERE. *Development, the International Economic Order, and Commodity Agreements.* Reading, Mass.: Addison-Wesley, 1978.

BHAGWATI, JAGDISH. *Foreign Trade Regimes and Economic Development: Anatomy and Consequences of Exchange Control Regimes.* Cambridge, Mass.: Ballinger, 1978. Summarizes 10 country studies of import substitution policies in low-income countries.

CLINE, WILLIAM R., ed. *Policy Alternatives for a New International Economic Order.* New York: Praeger, 1979.

GRASSMAN, SVEN. "Long-Term Trends in Openness of National Economies." *Oxford Economic Papers,* March 1980. Considers trends in the openness of Western countries over the last century.

HECKSCHER, ELI F. *Mercantilism,* Vols. 1–2, rev. 2nd ed. London: George Allen and Unwin, 1955. Classic economic study of mercantilism.

HUFBAUER, GARY. *Synthetic Materials and the Theory of International Trade.* Cambridge, Mass.: Harvard University Press, 1966.

INTERNATIONAL MONETARY FUND. *International Financial Statistics,* Washington, D.C., monthly. Contains data on commodity prices and terms of trade.

JOHNSON, D. GALE. "Increased Stability of Grain Supplies in Developing Countries: Optimal Carryovers and Insurance." In *The New International Economic Order: The North-South Debate,* Jagdish N. Bhagwati, ed. Cambridge, Mass.: M.I.T. Press, 1977. Discusses the substitutability of freer trade and inventories of grain.

JOHNSON, HARRY G. *Economic Policies Toward Less Developed Countries.* New York: Praeger, 1967. Discusses a variety of trade problems of low-income countries.

――――. "Trade and Growth: A Geometrical Exposition." *Journal of International Economics,* February 1971. A theoretical analysis of trade and economic growth.

――――. "Tariffs and Economic Development: Some Theoretical Issues." In *Aspects of the Theory of Tariffs,* Harry G. Johnson, ed. London: George Allen and Unwin, 1971.

KRUEGER, ANNE. "The Political Economy of a Rent-Seeking Society." *American Economic Review,* June 1974. Development of the rent-seeking concept with an application to import licenses in Turkey.

――――. *Foreign Trade Regimes and Economic Development: Liberalization Attempts and Consequences.* Cambridge: National Bureau of Economic Research, 1978. Survey of the 10-country study of import substitution in low-income countries.

――――. "Trade Policy as an Input to Development." *American Economic Review,* May 1980. Stresses the favorable effect of export growth on income growth.

LITTLE, IAN, TIBOR SCITOVSKY, and MAURICE SCOTT. *Industry and Trade in Some Developing Countries: A Comparative Study.* London: Oxford University Press, 1970. Country studies comprising OECD's industry and trade project.

LUTZ, ERNST, and PASQUALE SCANDIZZO. "Price Distortions in Developing Countries: A Bias Against Agriculture." *European Review of Agricultural Economics,* Vol. 7, no. 1 (1980).

MACBEAN, A. I. *Export Instability and Economic Development.* London: George Allen and Unwin, 1966. Survey of the literature on price instability and economic growth.

――――, and D. NGUYEN. "Commodity Concentration and Export Earnings Instability: A Mathematical Analysis." *Economic Journal,* June 1980.

MAGEE, STEPHEN P., and NORMAN I. ROBINS. "The Raw Material Product Cycle." In *Mineral Resources in the Pacific Area,* Lawrence Krause and Hugh Patrick, eds. San Francisco: Federal Reserve Bank of San Francisco, 1978. Discusses the substitution of synthetic materials for natural resource imports.

MCCULLOCH, RACHEL. *Economic and Political Issues in the New International Economic Order,* Original Paper 22. Los Angeles: International Institute for Economic Research, July 1979.

MEIER, GERALD M. *Leading Issues in Economic Development,* 3rd ed. New York: Oxford, 1976. A collection of articles on economic problems of low-income countries.

PREBISCH, RAOUL. *Towards a New Trade Policy for Development.* New York: United Nations, 1964. Discusses the tendency of the terms of trade of primary producers to decline.

RYBCZYNSKI, T. M. "Factor Endowment and Relative Commodity Prices." *Economica,* November 1955. Reprinted in Richard E. Caves and Harry G. Johnson, eds. *Readings in International Economics,* Homewood, Ill.: Richard D. Irwin, 1968.

SCHULTZ, T. W. "Nobel Lecture: The Economics of Being Poor." *Journal of Political Economy,* August 1980. Discusses the tendency of low-income countries to underprice agricultural products.

SPRAOS, JOHN. "The Statistical Debate on the Net Barter Terms of Trade Between Primary Commodities and Manufacturers." *Economic Journal,* March 1980. An empirical study of changes in the terms of trade.

TURNER, LOUIS, and NEIL MCMULLEN. *The Newly Industrializing Countries: Trade and Adjustment.* London: George Allen and Unwin, 1982. A collection of papers on countries and industries affected by development of newly industrializing countries.

WORLD BANK. *World Tables.* Washington, D.C.: World Bank, 1979. Presents detailed economic and demographic data for most of the world's countries.

CHAPTER FOURTEEN
FOREIGN EXCHANGE
MARKET INSTITUTIONS

14.1 INTRODUCTION

Part I of the book has analyzed international trade while abstracting from the role of money. For certain kinds of problems, such abstraction is appropriate, since money is merely "a veil" that conceals more fundamental forces. Ultimately, supply depends on technology and factor supplies, demand depends on preferences and real income, and the interaction of supply and demand determines relative prices. However, nearly all contracts are expressed in terms of money, and there are many important economic questions related to the determination of money prices, inflation, and exchange rates.

Part II of the book concentrates on monetary aspects of international trade. The subject, sometimes called international finance, emphasizes financial markets in an open economy. Chapter 14 introduces the foreign exchange market and some important institutions. Chapter 15 derives the demand and supply of foreign exchange from their underlying determinants. International economic data are presented in the balance-of-payments accounts, which are discussed in Chapter 16. Some problems of individual business firms under floating exchange rates are considered in Chapter 17. Some economywide problems under floating exchange rates are analyzed in Chapter 18. Basic models of exchange rate determination are presented in Chapter 19.

Two extreme exchange rate regimes are (1) freely floating rates, where the rates vary continuously, and (2) permanently fixed rates, where the rates never vary. Chapter 20 analyzes a permanently fixed rate system, the most important example of which is the gold standard. Chapter 21 discusses the adjustable peg system, an important compromise between fixed and floating rate systems. Chapter 22 examines the international transmission of inflation.

This chapter will consider the nature of money and foreign exchange. Money transactions have displaced barter in all national economies. The economic importance of money is undeniable, but financial innovation has made it more difficult for policymakers and analysts to agree on an appropriate empirical definition of money. The development of interest-bearing checking accounts and money market mutual funds has made it more difficult to define the domestic money stock. The development of Eurodollars and other external currencies has made it difficult to determine the appropriate world money stock.

In examining the nature of the foreign exchange market, the market can be divided into the spot and forward markets. The forward market for foreign currency has expanded considerably since most countries in the world abandoned fixed exchange rates in 1973. The determinants of spot and forward exchange rates will be considered. The foreign exchange market processes information about currencies. The concept of an informationally efficient market will be discussed. Disturbances to the foreign exchange market will create disequilibrium. Alternative exchange market adjustment mechanisms will be considered, including exchange rate adjustment, aggregate demand adjustment, changes in monetary reserves, and direct trade controls. The chapter will also discuss the evolution of the international monetary system.

An exchange rate is the price of foreign money in terms of domestic money. Although most currency exchange rates have been floating since 1973, periods of floating rates have been extremely rare in international monetary history. At the suggestion of Secretary of Treasury Alexander Hamilton, the United States adopted fixed exchange rates in 1789. Fixed rates between national currencies were accomplished indirectly by adopting the system of bimetallism. Bimetallism fixes the price of gold and silver in terms of domestic money, which also fixes the price of each foreign money that is linked to gold or silver. With the exception of the Greenback period associated with the Civil War, the United States has operated with fixed rates throughout its history. Nevertheless, floating is a logical outcome of the evolution from monetary systems based on metal to paper money standards. Under metallic standards, governments have little freedom to carry out discretionary monetary policy, since the quantity of money is determined by discoveries of gold and silver.

Governments have achieved greater independence for monetary policy by abandoning various features of a metallic standard. The dollar was made inconvertible into silver at the end of the nineteenth century. The dollar was made inconvertible into gold for Americans in 1933. Dollar inconvertibility for foreign governments became a fact in 1968, and inconvertibility was formally acknowledged in 1973. As national governments increasingly directed monetary policy to domestic objectives, it became impossible to sustain fixed exchange rates. Governments used monetary policy to try to achieve domestic employment goals that were incompatible with balance-of-payments equilibrium. The world adopted floating exchange rates in 1973 as the result of unconscious evolution rather than as a result of some grand design. There was much opposition to the adoption of floating rates by government officials, businesspeople, and officials of the International Monetary Fund. Floating rates may be abandoned in the future, but a fixed rate system is viable only if national central banks sacrifice some monetary autonomy.

14.2 THE NATURE OF MONEY

Since foreign exchange is simply foreign money, it is appropriate to review the nature of money. The traditional functions of money are (1) unit of account (also called numeraire), (2) medium of exchange, and (3) store of value. The unit of account is the asset in terms of which prices are expressed. Thus, dollars are a unit of account when invoices, loans, and wages are expressed as a fixed number of dollars. A medium of exchange is an asset that is used for making payments. Usually the same asset serves simultaneously as a unit of account and a medium of exchange. However, the functions are logically separable, and sometimes different assets are used. For example, in some inflation-prone countries, contracts may be expressed as a fixed number of dollars, but payment would be made in an equivalent amount of local currency. Thus, the dollar would serve as the unit of account, and local currency would function as the medium of exchange.

The store of value function of money is also performed by many other assets (e.g., bonds, housing, copper). Whether money is a more stable store of value depends on the rate of inflation (decrease in purchasing power of money) relative to the frequency and magnitude of shifts in demand and supply in individual markets. In the absence of inflation, money is the most stable store of value, but when the expected inflation rate is highly variable, people substitute other assets for money. In an international context, loss of confidence in domestic money may lead residents to acquire foreign money. The substitution of foreign money for domestic money is called currency substitution.

Demanders value money for its purchasing power over real goods and services. The real demand for money can be expressed as the nominal quantity of money (M) demanded relative to the average price level (P) of goods and services. Thus, if the demand for money is $50 at the initial price level, money demand will be $100 if all prices of goods and services double. The price of goods in terms of money is variable, and it is inversely related to the price of money in terms of goods $(P_{gm} = 1/P_{mg})$. If the price of a machine is $50, the price of money in terms of machines is 0.02 machines per dollar. An increase in the price of machines to $100 decreases the machine price of money to 0.01 machines per dollar. The same reciprocal relationship holds for currency exchange rates. The price of pounds sterling in terms of dollars is the reciprocal of the price of dollars in terms of pounds. Inflation is a general rise in money prices, which implies that the price or value of money in terms of goods decreases.

Money prices of goods nearly tripled in the United States between 1967 and 1982. It follows that the same collection of goods that cost $1.00 in 1967 cost nearly $3.00 in 1982. Alternatively, $1.00 in currency or $1.00 deposited in a checking account would buy one-third as many goods in 1982 as it bought in 1967.

Money is the traditional unit of account, and it is convenient to express all prices in terms of money. However, demand and supply depend on relative prices rather than on money prices. The demand for Chevrolets depends not only on the money price of Chevrolets but also on the prices of Fords, Toyotas, and gasoline as well as household income. If the money price of Chevrolets doubles, the effect on Chevrolet demand depends on what happens to other prices and money income. If they are constant, the relative or real price of Chevrolets has increased, and quantity demanded will decline according to the law of demand. However, if all other prices and money income also double, the demand for Chevrolets would not change. Similarly, the quantity supplied by business firms depends on relative prices, not on money prices.

Because of the ultimate importance of relative prices, money and money prices are sometimes described as "a veil." All the prices discussed in Part I of this book have been relative or real prices. Sometimes the subject matter of Chapters 1 through 13 is called the real or barter theory of international trade.

Trade can exist without money by directly bartering goods against other goods. A common problem with barter is the requirement of a "double coincidence of wants." A trader must find someone who simultaneously wants to buy the product he wants to sell and wants to sell the product he wants to buy. The use of money saves real economic resources by reducing the number of prices that must be considered and by reducing the number of transactions that must be carried out. Because money reduces information costs, growth in the use of money is closely related to the growth of trade.

Economic agents specialize in production in order to trade a surplus of some goods for other goods they wish to consume. Specialized producers need information about the demands of other households. At the same time, consumers need information about the supplies of other households and firms. The use of money facilitates the dissemination of economic information. A given volume of trade can be carried out at lower cost by using money than through barter. All national economies have evolved away from barter economies to the use of money. The widespread use of money persists throughout the world in spite of vast political, social, and economic differences among countries.

Various revolutionary movements, including Russian Communists, have advocated the abolition of money. However, those who have gained control of governments have found money to be too useful to banish. Eastern European governments have not abolished money, but they have fixed money prices at levels that result in excess demand for some goods and excess supply of other goods including money. As a result of this practice, some government agencies have engaged in barter transactions with other firms and other countries.

Some prominent barter arrangements have been concluded between Eastern European governments and private Western firms. For example, in 1982 McDonnell Douglas traded airplanes to Yugoslavia for canned hams, and General Electric traded turbines for a variety of Romanian goods. The U.S. government sent nonfat dried milk to Jamaica for bauxite. Vienna has become the geographical center for barter transactions, which are also called countertrade. In countries in which prices adjust to clear markets, barter has been abandoned as an inefficient form of trade.[1]

The observation that people find money to be useful is hardly a controversial one. However, it is more difficult to reach agreement on the precise empirical definition of money. At one point in history, only coins made of precious metal were considered to be money. Later paper currency became generally accepted as well. Commercial bank deposits, convertible into currency on demand, became a good substitute for currency and coin.[2]

From 1933 to 1981, U.S. banking law made a sharp distinction between demand deposits (checking accounts) and time deposits (saving accounts). Checks could be written only against demand deposits at commercial banks. Thus, demand deposits performed the medium of exchange function of money, but time deposits did not. A common narrow definition of money was currency plus demand deposits. A traditional broad definition of money was currency plus demand deposits plus time deposits. A second legal distinction was the prohibition of interest payments on demand deposits. It follows that banks could not compensate depositors for increases in bond interest rates. These two distinctions were eliminated by changes in the banking laws in 1980.[3]

The new law permits many types of financial institutions to offer checking accounts, and it permits interest payment on checking accounts. The Federal Reserve now uses the term "checkable deposits" for all accounts offering check-writing privileges. Checkable deposits include all of the old demand deposits plus some of the old time deposits. The Federal Reserve Board offers a number of money supply measures that are published monthly in the *Federal Reserve Bulletin*.

The current definition of narrow money (M_1) is currency (C) plus demand deposits (D) plus other checkable deposits (OCD) plus traveler's checks:

$$M_1 = C + D + OCD + TC = \$442.1 \text{ billion (end of 1981)}$$

---

[1] An exception is the use of barter to avoid the payment of income tax.

[2] The famous Currency School-Banking School controversy in nineteenth-century England involved the question of whether bank deposits were money. See Jacob Viner, *Studies in the Theory of International Trade* (London: George Allen and Unwin, 1937).

[3] For a discussion of the historical development of the banking law, see Robert Craig West, "The Depository Institutions Deregulation Act of 1980: A Historical Perspective," *Economic Review*, Federal Reserve Bank of Kansas City, February 1982.

A broader definition (M_2) includes (M_1) plus savings deposits (S) plus small time deposits (ST) plus money market mutual funds $(MMMF)$ plus two smaller items (O):[4]

$$M_2 = M_1 + S + ST + MMMF + O = \$1,842.2 \text{ billion (end of 1981)}$$

Even broader monetary totals are also available.

Money is important because it is the major explanatory variable in prominent theories of inflation and exchange rate determination. The problem is in choosing an empirical measure to associate with the theoretical concept of money. There is an unchanging theoretical concept of money, but the proper empirical measure depends on monetary technology. As monetary innovations occur, the appropriate empirical measure gets broader. The definition of money is important for international economics because foreign exchange is foreign money.

14.3 NATIONAL AND WORLD MONEY

Because of technical change in the production of money and money substitutes, the appropriate empirical measure changes over time. The choice of a proper monetary total by economic analysts depends on the purpose of analysis and on the availability of data. If the object of economic analysis is to predict the rate of inflation, one should choose a monetary total that is most closely related to inflation. Currency might be the best total for 1840, but M_1 or M_2 might be more appropriate for the 1980s. A more practical point is that monetary data are collected and reported by governments, and some monetary totals that are potentially useful may not be available for some countries.

There are more than 180 countries in the world, and nearly every country has its own money. The number of world monies has been increasing as colonies become independent countries. A minor offset to this trend is the formation of monetary unions, such as the arrangement between Belgium and Luxembourg.

The European Economic Community has an ambitious plan to replace the national currencies of member states with a common European currency. The plan began with an attempt to reduce the variability of exchange rates between member currencies, but it is considerably behind schedule. The union of the 13 colonies into the United States of America with a single currency is

---

[4]The remaining two items (O) are overnight repurchase agreements and overnight Eurodollars at Caribbean branches of U.S. banks. At the end of 1981, the components of M_1 and their relative shares were:

$$M_1 = C + D + OCD + TC$$
$$440.8 = 123.1 + 236.4 + 77.0 + 4.3$$
$$1 = 0.28 + 0.54 + 0.17 + 0.01$$

a monetary union. The subject of monetary union will be considered in more detail in Chapter 20. Data on national and world money supplies are published monthly by the International Monetary Fund in its *International Financial Statistics*. The IMF publishes a narrow definition of money similar to the M_1 total for the United States. It also presents a total for quasi-money, which includes various time and savings deposits. The sum of the totals for money and quasi-money is roughly comparable to the U.S. M_2. Because of legal and institutional differences between monetary systems, national monetary figures reported to the IMF may not be strictly comparable. Nevertheless, the IMF reports a series on the world money supply. It is obtained by expressing each national money supply in dollars by multiplying by the dollar exchange rate and adding the dollar values of the national monies.

The world money supply can be written as

$$M^W = \Pi_{1\$}M^1 + \Pi_{2\$}M^2 + \cdots + \Pi_{n\$}M^n + M^{U.S.}$$

Here M^i is the money supply of the ith country expressed in national units, and $\Pi_{i\$}$ is the price of the ith currency in terms of dollars. Thus, the world money supply can be changed by a change in national money supplies or a change in exchange rates. For example, an increase in country 2's money supply or an increase in the dollar price of 2's currency will increase the world money supply. Data on the world money supply, which appear in Chapter 22, have been used in an attempt to explain the world rate of inflation.

One problem with the previous concept of world money is that it excludes external or Eurocurrencies. The U.K. money supply includes all the pound deposits at banks in the United Kingdom, and the U.S. money supply includes the dollar deposits at banks in the United States. However, pound deposits at banks outside the United Kingdom and dollar deposits at banks outside the United States (except some deposits at Caribbean banks) are not included in the U.K. money supply, the U.S. money supply, or any other country's money supply. Deposits denominated in currency other than the domestic money of the country in which the bank is located are called external currency or Eurocurrency. The most important external currency is the U.S. dollar, and Europe (especially London) is the geographical center of the market.

A Eurodollar is a dollar deposit at a bank located outside the United States. The bank may be foreign owned or a branch of an American-owned bank. Since other external currencies are traded and the market has spread throughout the world, the term Eurodollar no longer describes the market accurately. A generic term for the activity is the external currency market. The market has grown rapidly since 1960, and it has spread from Europe to the Middle East, Asia, and the Caribbean.

Some figures on the size of the Eurocurrency market for the period 1973 to 1981 are shown in Table 14-1. The stock of Eurodollars is larger than the

TABLE 14-1   Eurodollar Market, 1973–1981
            (in billions of dollars)

YEAR	EURODOLLARS	NONBANKS	HELD BY CENTRAL BANKS	HELD BY OTHER BANKS	SHARE OF TOTAL EURO-CURRENCIES	U.S. MONEY SUPPLY
1973	$ 315	$ 55	$ 40	$ 220	74%	$270.5
1974	395	80	60	255	76	282.9
1975	485	90	65	330	78	295.2
1976	595	115	80	400	80	313.5
1977	740	145	100	495	76	338.5
1978	950	190	115	645	74	361.1
1979	1,220	255	150	815	72	388.8
1980	1,515	325	150	1,040	74	417.0
1981	1,800	415	130	1,255	75	428.4

Source: *International Economic Conditions*, Federal Reserve Bank of St. Louis, October 25, 1982; and Council of Economic Advisers, *Economic Report of the President* (Washington, D.C.: U.S. Government Printing Office, 1982).

U.S. money stock, and it has grown more rapidly. Although the dollar is not the only Eurocurrency, it is by far the most important one. The dollar share of all Eurocurrencies remained between 70 and 80 percent during the entire period. Omitting Eurocurrencies from the world money supply may be a serious omission, but the stock of Eurocurrencies is not measured as accurately as is national money. These Eurocurrency figures are obtained from a small sample of banks that voluntarily report to the Bank for International Settlements in Basel, Switzerland. As the table shows, many of the deposits are held by banks. In national statistics, the deposit figures reported are for net deposits, that is, deposits after interbank deposits have been subtracted. For 1981, according to the table, $1,255 billion of the $1,800 billion were interbank deposits. Thus, net deposits were far smaller than gross deposits. Unfortunately, the size of interbank deposits is not known for many banks, and this makes it impossible to calculate an accurate figure for net deposits.

There has been considerable interest in trying to explain the development of the Eurodollar market. One explanation for the origin of the market is that Soviet banks wanted to hold dollar deposits to facilitate trade with the West. However, they preferred to deal with banks outside the legal control of the U.S. government. In the event of a political dispute, presumably the U.S. government could seize Soviet deposits in the United States but not dollar deposits at European banks.[5]

Apparently the main reason for growth of the market is differential reg-

[5] The amount of security provided by the European location of banks may have been exaggerated. In the U.S.-Iranian dispute following the seizure of American hostages in Tehran, some dollar deposits of the Iranian government in Europe were frozen.

ulation that provides a cost advantage to banks located abroad. Banks in the United States are required to hold noninterest-bearing reserves against deposits. Required reserves are a cost of operating a bank in the United States that varies directly with market interest rates. Since there are no required reserves against dollar deposits outside the United States, there is a cost advantage to locating abroad.

Banks are subject to the laws of countries in which they operate, and the United Kingdom and other host governments have the authority to impose Eurodollar reserve requirements. They have chosen not to. In most cases, host governments impose reserve requirements against local currency deposits (e.g., pound sterling accounts in the United Kingdom), but not against Eurodollars. In the United Kingdom, the government has explicitly encouraged the activities of Eurodollar banks. Central bankers have expressed concern about the lack of regulation of the Eurodollar market, but they are aware of the geographical mobility of the activity. It has been said that if one country imposes costly regulations on Eurodollar banks, the activity will simply move to a more favorable country. A branch office need not be an expensive operation. In Nassau in the Bahama Islands, some branch offices consist of part of a room, a secretary, and a part-time accountant. All important paperwork is done at the home office in another country.

A second regulatory advantage of the Eurodollar market is the absence of restrictions on deposit interest rates. For many years the United States has had a legal maximum interest rate (Regulation Q) that banks could pay depositors. When interest rates on competing financial assets rise above the legal maximum, U.S. banks lose deposits to other domestic financial institutions or to foreign banks. Eurodollars are a good substitute for these restricted U.S. deposits. Eurodollar banks deal only in large deposits, and because of the European competition, the Federal Reserve has exempted large deposits from Regulation Q. Small depositors cannot place their money in Eurodollars directly, but they can circumvent Regulation Q by depositing their funds in money market mutual funds. By pooling the money of many small depositors, the funds have been able to acquire large certificates of deposit issued by U.S. and Eurodollar banks and pay depositors interest rates above the Regulation Q maximum.

The Federal Reserve has recently shown an awareness that differential regulation moves banking activity abroad. A new set of rules is designed to lure some Eurodollar banking back to the United States.[6] Beginning December 1981 banks in the United States could set up "international banking facilities" (IBFs) that would have some of the advantages of Eurodollar banks. The IBFs need not be a separate office but merely a separate set of books. By August 1982 American banks with IBFs attracted deposits of $142 billion.

---

[6] For details see *The Wall Street Journal*, "Banks Can Do Euromart Business in U.S. after Free Trade Zone Starts Thursday," November 30, 1981.

The main advantages are that deposits of IBFs are not subject to U.S. interest rate ceilings or reserve requirements. The main disadvantages for banks are (1) they cannot accept deposits from or make loans to U.S. residents, (2) deposits must stay on the books for at least two days, and (3) banks cannot issue negotiable instruments. A disadvantage of Eurodollars to the depositor is that, unlike deposits in the United States, Eurodollar deposits are not insured. A second problem is the possibility of exchange controls, which would restrict conversion of dollars into local currency. Dollar depositors in Mexico were adversely affected by the combination of peso devaluation plus exchange control in 1982. The peso was devalued from approximately 30 pesos per dollar to more than 100 pesos per dollar, but the Mexican government prevented dollar depositors from converting into pesos at the new rate.

14.4 FOREIGN EXCHANGE INSTITUTIONS

From the perspective of any single country, foreign exchange is simply all foreign money. Since there are many foreign currencies, they can only be added by converting them to a common currency by using a set of exchange rates. The stock of foreign exchange at any point in time is the world money stock minus the domestic money stock. The volume of foreign exchange transactions can also be expressed as a flow per unit time. Thus, the stock of pounds sterling on December 31, 1981 is quite different from the volume of pounds sterling traded during the month of December 1981. The distinction between stock and flow measures is common in economics, and it is applicable to all durable assets, financial and real. For example, the stock of gold in the world at the end of 1981 was many times the flow of newly mined gold in 1981.

The foreign exchange market is the market in which the currencies of the world are traded. As are most organized markets, the foreign exchange market is not merely a geographical location but, rather, a systematic means of communication among traders all over the world. Financial institutions in New York, London, and Zurich play an important role in the market, but traders in Singapore, Tokyo, Cairo, Rio de Janeiro, and other cities are closely linked with financial conditions outside their countries.

The foreign exchange market is an integrated world market, and one measure of the degree of integration is the variation in the price of a given currency around the world. What is the difference between the price of pounds sterling in New York, London, and Zurich at any given time? In an integrated market the price difference should not exceed the transaction cost of buying pounds in one city and selling pounds in another. Conversely, if geographical markets were not linked, there would be no reason for the price of pounds in one city to be related to the price in another city. In fact, these exchange rates are closely related because banks employ foreign exchange specialists who constantly monitor geographical price differences. If discrepancies are discovered, they immediately buy where the currency is cheap and simultaneously sell where it is expensive. The result of the simultaneous purchase and sale is a riskless profit, and the operation is called spatial arbitrage. As arbitragers add to the demand where the price was low, the price rises. As arbitragers add to the supply where the price was high, the price falls. Thus, spatial arbitrage reduces geographical price differences until they are equal to the cost of carrying out transactions.

Information is not a free good and transactions costs include the expense of maintaining a complex communication network around the world. Institutions that specialize in international banking must develop an effective communications system, which is subject to economies of large-scale production. Firms that trade foreign exchange infrequently tend to deal with the specialists.

There are many participants in the foreign exchange market. The ultimate buyers and sellers of foreign exchange are importers and exporters of goods and services. Importers who need to make payments in foreign exchange could buy it directly from exporters who have just earned it, but they usually deal with financial intermediaries, such as commercial banks. The large international banks trade regularly in 12 to 15 major currencies. The banks "maintain a position" in these currencies in the sense that they are prepared to quote a buying and selling price for each currency. The buying price is called the bid price, and the selling price is called the offer or ask price. Whether a currency is traded regularly depends on the country's importance in international trade and the severity of the exchange controls on the currency.

Exchange controls are legal restrictions on the use of the currency by the holder. A common restriction is that holders of a currency can convert it into foreign exchange only at the central bank. This restriction precludes trading that currency in the private foreign exchange market. Currencies subject to severe exchange controls are called inconvertible, and they are not widely traded on the foreign exchange market. Most of the IMF's more than 140 members have inconvertible currencies.

International banks exchange currencies at two levels. At the retail level, they deal with importers and exporters of goods and services who are the ultimate demanders and suppliers. At the wholesale level, they trade with other banks. In the United States, banks have found it convenient to deal with each other through another intermediary, the foreign exchange broker. There are six major brokers in New York who provide information to banks and preserve the anonymity of bank traders.

Trade between U.S. and foreign banks is usually carried out without the services of a broker. The foreign exchange market does not have a single geographical meeting place, although activity is more concentrated in some locations than others. The City of London and Wall Street in New York City are traditional centers of international banking. Since the advent of floating exchange rates, currencies have been increasingly traded on commodity markets, such as the International Monetary Market of the Chicago Mercantile Exchange. Most trade takes place over the telephone or through the telex, which does not require that participants gather in the same location. There are fixed opening and closing times applicable to most transactions for each time zone (e.g., traditional banking hours), but because of geographical time differences, there is no single time limit that applies to the entire world market.

Government institutions are sometimes important participants in the foreign exchange market. Central banks are the most active government agencies, but treasuries or finance ministries are sometimes involved. In the United States, the Federal Reserve Bank of New York implements the foreign exchange policy of the Federal Reserve System. The Exchange Stabilization Fund of the Treasury is responsible for that agency's foreign exchange activity. The foreign exchange operations of both the Federal Reserve and the Treasury are reported in the *Quarterly Review* of the Federal Reserve Bank of New York. Reports include the volume of purchases and sales of various currencies, borrowing and lending, and foreign exchange profits and losses.

The amount of government intervention in the market depends on (1) the goals of government policy and (2) the volatility of the market. If the government attempts to fix the exchange rate, it must operate a kind of buffer stock in foreign exchange, analogous to the inventory policy described in Chapter 13. If there is a private excess demand, the central bank must supply foreign exchange from its reserves. If there is an excess supply, the central bank must be a net buyer of foreign currency.

Since 1973 most countries have abandoned strictly fixed exchange rates. Instead, most countries have adopted a policy of managed floating, for which governments occasionally intervene to influence rates. It is difficult to generalize about actual intervention policy under the managed float. Some governments have intervened more than under fixed rates, while others have rarely intervened. The United States intervened frequently during the Carter administration, but during the Reagan administration intervention nearly ceased. For example, during a six-month period in 1981, the United States did not intervene once in currency markets. By contrast, other IMF members spent $30 billion of reserves in currency market intervention. Since the Federal Reserve holds both gold and U.S. Treasury securities for the accounts of foreign central banks, the trading desk of the New York Fed does intervene as agent for other central banks.

The effect of government intervention on the foreign exchange market remains an open question. The stated policy of central banks is to stabilize rates and provide for "orderly markets." Critics say that central bankers can successfully stabilize markets only if they have better information about currency markets than private banks do. The substantial losses of central banks on currency operations are interpreted by critics as evidence that central banks are poorly informed.

The ability of a government to defend an exchange rate depends on the size of its inventory of reserves. Governments supplement owned reserves by borrowing foreign exchange from other central banks. The Federal Reserve has negotiated an extensive "swap" arrangement with other central banks. Each participant has agreed to extend a line of credit to other central banks. The loan is called a swap because the borrowing central bank buys the foreign exchange (with domestic money) and agrees to resell it at a specified future date at the price prevailing on that date. The lending central bank agrees to invest in a Treasury security of the borrowing country during the swap period. Because of its policy of nonintervention in currency markets, the Reagan administration has not activated the swap network.

International institutions also influence the foreign exchange market. The International Monetary Fund makes loans to member countries with balance-of-payments or exchange rate problems. The Fund has more than 140 members, including some Eastern European Communist countries. Yugoslavia, Romania, and Hungary are members, and Poland applied for membership in 1982. Poland had been a member from 1946 to 1950 when it withdrew. Members typically use the proceeds from Fund loans to buy back their currencies to prevent them from depreciating. The IMF has also created its own money, called special drawing rights, which members can use to defend currency exchange rates.

Another international institution that influences the foreign exchange market is the Bank for International Settlements (BIS). The BIS, which is often described as the central bankers' bank, was founded in Basel, Switzerland, in 1930 to help European governments collect war reparations from Germany. A group of 29 central bankers sit on the board of directors. The BIS makes short-term loans to central banks, which are similar to those made by the Fund, but the Bank is known for its flexibility. In 1982 the BIS negotiated a $2 billion loan for Mexico in 48 hours. The Bank also serves as a central bankers' forum. The Banks' board of directors has 10 regular meetings per year at which monetary cooperation is discussed. The BIS manages the European Economic Community's currency stabilization system and gathers the most comprehensive statistics on international banking.

The foreign exchange market can be divided into the spot and forward markets. The spot or cash market is the market in which the price is determined in the present and delivery and payment also occur in the present. According to current practice, delivery and payment occur within two days after agreement for a spot transaction. The forward market is the market in which the price is determined in the present, but delivery and payment occur at a specified future date. Notice that since both delivery and payment are deferred, no credit is extended in a forward transaction. Credit is extended if delivery precedes payment. Most transactions are in the spot market, but forward market activity has grown rapidly since 1973.

Although forward transactions have grown in importance, they are not a new idea. One observer has traced forward transactions back to the papal court of Avignon in the thirteenth century.[7] There is a separate market and a separate exchange rate for each forward period. Common quotations are available for 30 days, 60 days, 90 days, 180 days, and 1 year forward. Daily forward rates appear in *The Wall Street Journal* in the table on foreign exchange. (See Table 14-2 taken from the *Journal*.) The futures market is closely related to the forward market. Standardized contracts for the major currencies are traded on the New York and Chicago commodity markets.[8] Forward markets will be analyzed in detail in Chapter 17.

14.5 FOREIGN EXCHANGE RATES

An exchange rate is conventionally defined as the price of some foreign currency in terms of domestic (Π_{FD}) currency. That definition seems natural to most people, since it uses domestic money as the unit of account. Occasionally (especially in the United Kingdom), the exchange rate is defined as the price of domestic currency in terms of some foreign currency (Π_{DF}). Since the second rate is the reciprocal of the first ($\Pi_{DF} = 1/\Pi_{FD}$), the same information is conveyed. Because the term is used in both senses, the meaning of the expression "increase or decrease in the exchange rate" is sometimes ambiguous. Whether the domestic money increases or decreases in value must sometimes be determined from the context of the discussion.

Devaluation, or depreciation,[9] of the home currency means that it loses value. It implies that Π_{FD} increases and Π_{DF} decreases. For example, if the price of the pound sterling rises from $\Pi_{£\$} = \$2.00$ to $\Pi_{£\$} = \$2.50$, the dollar has depreciated. Simultaneously, the pound has increased in value, which is called an appreciation or revaluation upward. Since $\Pi_{£\$} = 1/\Pi_{\$£}$, the price of the dollar has gone from $\Pi_{\$£} = £0.50$ to $\Pi_{\$£} = £0.40$. It would be ambiguous to describe this situation as an increase in the exchange rate, since $\Pi_{£\$}$ went up and $\Pi_{\$£}$ went down. No matter which exchange rate definition is used, the dollar depreciated and the pound appreciated.

Daily exchange rates for the major currencies are reported in *The Wall Street Journal*, and an historical sample is shown in Table 14-2. Notice that

---

[7] See Paul Einzig, *The History of Foreign Exchange* (New York: St. Martins, 1962), p. x.

[8] The International Monetary Market of the Chicago Mercantile Exchange offers futures contracts in the following currencies: Swiss francs, German marks, French francs, British pounds, Dutch guilders, Canadian dollars, Mexican pesos, and Japanese yen.

[9] In the absence of a gold standard, there is no meaningful distinction between devaluation and depreciation. With a gold standard, devaluation refers to an increase in the price of gold in terms of domestic money, without any necessary change in exchange rates. Depreciation refers to an increase in the price of foreign exchange in terms of domestic money without any necessary change in the gold price. For example, if all countries doubled the price of gold, all currencies would be devalued without any depreciation.

TABLE 14-2   Exchange Rates

Foreign Exchange

Wednesday, September 21, 1983
The New York foreign exchange selling rates below apply to trading among banks in amounts of $1 million and more, as quoted at 3 p.m. Eastern time by Bankers Trust Co. Retail transactions provide fewer units of foreign currency per dollar.

Country	U.S. $ equiv. Wed.	U.S. $ equiv. Tues.	Currency per U.S. $ Wed.	Currency per U.S. $ Tues.
Argentina (Peso)	.08368	.08368	11.95	11.95
Australia (Dollar)	.8920	.8906	1.1210	1.1228
Austria (Schilling)	.0533	.05344	18.75	18.71
Belgium (Franc)				
Commercial rate	.01875	.01862	53.82	53.68
Financial rate	.01828	.01839	54.68	54.35
Brazil (Cruzeiro)	.00143	.00143	701.	701.
Britain (Pound)	1.5032	1.5065	.6652	.6638
30-Day Forward	1.5033	1.5067	.6651	.6637
90-Day Forward	1.5045	1.5077	.6646	.6632
180-Day Forward	1.5063	1.5096	.6638	.6624
Canada (Dollar)	.8115	.8111	1.2323	1.2329
30-Day Forward	.8120	.8115	1.2315	1.2322
90-Day Forward	.8126	.8123	1.2306	1.2310
180-Day Forward	.8134	.8131	1.2293	1.2298
Chile (Official rate)	.01237	.01237	80.86	80.86
China (Yuan)	.5045	.5050	1.9822	1.9802
Colombia (Peso)	.01216	.01216	82.20	82.20
Denmark (Krone)	.1043	.10452	9.5875	9.5670
Ecuador (Sucre)				
Official rate	.02052	.02052	48.73	48.73
Floating rate	.01119	.01119	89.35	89.35
Finland (Markka)	.1756	.1760	5.6940	5.6820
France (Franc)	.1238	.1236	8.0725	8.0900
30-Day Forward	.1236	.1233	8.0910	8.1090
90-Day Forward	.1225	.1222	8.1575	8.1775
180-Day Forward	.1206	.1202	8.2915	8.3200
Greece (Drachma)	.01076	.01075	92.95	93.00
Hong Kong (Dollar)	.1218	.1210	8.2100	8.2600
India (Rupee)	.0981	.0981	10.19	10.19
Indonesia (Rupiah)	.00102	.00102	985.	985.
Ireland (Punt)	1.1758	1.1780	.8505	.8489
Israel (Shekel)	.01733	.01733	57.70	57.70
Italy (Lira)	.000625	.000626	1601.25	1597.
Japan (Yen)	.004124	.004123	242.47	242.50
30-Day Forward	.004132	.004133	242.00	241.95
90-Day Forward	.004153	.004154	240.75	240.73
180-Day Forward	.004186	.004186	238.88	238.86
Lebanon (Pound)	.20408	.20408	4.90	4.90
Malaysia (Ringgit)	.4255	.4259	2.3500	2.3480
Mexico (Peso)				
Floating rate	.00672	.00668	148.75	149.50
Netherlands (Guilder)	.3351	.3353	2.9840	2.9825
New Zealand (Dollar)	.6560	.6545	1.5244	1.5278
Norway (Krone)	.1349	.13504	7.4120	7.4050
Pakistan (Rupee)	.07547	.07547	13.25	13.25
Peru (Sol)	.000489	.00489	2043.50	2043.50
Philippines (Peso)	.09085	.09085	11.007	11.007
Portugal (Escudo)	.008054	.00806	124.15	124.05
Saudi Arabia (Riyal)	.28735	.28735	3.48	3.48
Singapore (Dollar)	.4671	.4677	2.1410	2.1380
South Africa (Rand)	.9055	.9045	1.1043	1.1055
South Korea (Won)	.001266	.001266	789.80	789.80
Spain (Peseta)	.00657	.0066	152.00	151.30
Sweden (Krona)	.1268	.1271	7.8850	7.8675
Switzerland (Franc)	.4619	.4618	2.1650	2.1650
30-Day Forward	.4640	.4640	2.1551	2.1550
90-Day Forward	.4679	.4679	2.1370	2.1370
180-Day Forward	.4738	.4738	2.1106	2.1107
Taiwan (Dollar)	.0249	.0249	40.15	40.15
Thailand (Baht)	.04346	.04346	23.01	23.01
Uruguay (New Peso)				
Financial	.02788	.02788	35.87	35.87
Venezuela (Bolivar)				
Official rate	.23256	.23256	4.30	4.30
Floating rate	.07519	.07519	13.30	13.30
W. Germany (Mark)	.3749	.3744	2.6670	2.6705
30-Day Forward	.3763	.3758	2.6574	2.6608
90-Day Forward	.3787	.3783	2.6403	2.6434
180-Day Forward	.3822	.3817	2.6164	2.6196
SDR	1.05162	1.05248	.950916	.950133

Special Drawing Rights are based on exchange rates for the U.S., West German, British, French and Japanese currencies. Source: International Monetary Fund.
z-Not quoted.

$\Pi_{F\$}$ is shown in the first two columns and that $\Pi_{\$F}$ is shown in the last two columns. Forward rates for some currencies and some maturities are presented. The rates shown apply to wholesale transactions (at least \$1 million) between banks. Tourists trading smaller amounts receive less favorable rates.

If there are n currencies in the world, there will be $n - 1$ exchange rates in terms of each national money. Thus, there will be $n - 1$ dollar exchange rates, $n - 1$ pound exchange rates, and so on:

Dollar rates: $\Pi_{1\$}, \Pi_{2\$}, \ldots, \Pi_{n\$}$
Pound rates: $\Pi_{1\pounds}, \Pi_{2\pounds}, \ldots, \Pi_{n\pounds}$

In fact n is more than 100, and people involved in international trade are rarely interested in all exchange rates for a given currency.

It is common to ask what happened to the dollar on a given day, and the precise answer is that it probably appreciated in terms of some currencies, depreciated relative to others, and remained constant in terms of some of them. It is convenient to summarize this information by using some average or index. Since our experience with floating exchange rates is still relatively new, there is no consensus as to what average or index is most useful. The problem is analogous to the problem of constructing the consumer price index to measure the average change in prices. Some products are more important than others, and the index should incorporate this information.

In the case of the CPI, housing is more important to consumers than is salt, so that a 10 percent increase in housing prices and a 10 percent decrease in the price of salt should not average out to no change in the cost of living. The relative importance of products is represented by assigning differential weights in the index. For the CPI, the weights for various products are based on budget shares of those products obtained from sample surveys of households. A standard index number problem is that budget shares depend on relative prices, and one can choose budget shares either before a price change occurred or after the change occurred.[10]

A similar problem exists in the construction of an exchange rate index. If some currencies are more important than others, what is the appropriate set of weights? In U.S. trade, the Canadian dollar is more important than is the Danish kroner, but how much more important? An exchange rate index for the U.S. dollar can be expressed as

$$\Pi_{F\$} = w_1\Pi_{1\$} + w_2\Pi_{2\$} + \cdots + w_n\Pi_{n\$}$$

The most commonly used indexes have assigned weights (w_i) based on each country's importance in world trade. The next problem is whether to compute trade shares based on total world trade, trade with some subset of important

[10] A Laspeyres price index uses base period weights; a Paasche price index uses current period weights.

TABLE 14-3 U.S. Dollar Exchange Rates, 1973–1982 (cents per unit)

COUNTRY	MARCH 1973	1974	1975	1976	1977	1978	1979	1980	1981	1982
Belgium	2.5377	2.7158	2.5311	2.7483	2.9608	3.3637	3.5423	3.1543	2.6115	2.1843
Canada	100.33	101.19	98.627	98.204	91.132	84.763	85.471	83.560	84.382	81.011
France	22.191	22.109	22.428	20.055	20.844	23.178	24.614	21.925	17.502	15.199
West Germany	35.548	40.816	38.144	41.965	46.499	53.217	57.671	50.769	44.862	41.186
Italy	.17600	.15179	.14645	.11521	.11416	.11863	.12329	.10704	.08392	.07380
Japan	.38190	.33288	.32715	.33933	.41491	.51038	.41613	.47747	.44843	.40150
The Netherlands	34.834	39.331	37.234	40.240	42.955	49.120	52.092	46.730	40.435	37.427
Sweden	22.582	23.897	22.685	24.051	21.044	22.808	23.935	22.722	18.049	15.914
Switzerland	31.084	38.442	37.970	40.823	48.168	59.703	62.542	56.022	55.098	49.196
United Kingdom	247.24	232.94	202.21	167.84	185.46	198.61	220.07	234.60	190.25	174.80
Trade-weighted average*	100.00	101.38	98.46	105.58	103.29	92.39	88.09	87.39	102.94	116.57
Dollars per SDR†	$1.192	$1.203	$1.214	$1.155	$1.168	$1.252	$1.292	$1.302	$1.179	$1.104

*An SDR (special drawing right) is a composite currency consisting of fixed amounts of five national currencies.

†The Federal Reserve Board's trade-weighted average measures the exchange value of the dollar against the Group of Ten plus Switzerland.

Source: International Monetary Fund, *International Financial Statistics Yearbook* and Federal Reserve System, *Federal Reserve Bulletin,* Washington, D.C., various periods.

countries, or bilateral trade with the United States. The trade-weighted dollar, computed by the Morgan Guaranty Trust, uses bilateral weights in trade with the United States.[11] Because of the importance of Canadian-U.S. trade, 40 percent of the weight in this index is assigned to the Canadian dollar. The Federal Reserve Board computes a trade-weighted dollar index that gives less weight to the Canadian dollar. The index appears in the *Federal Reserve Bulletin*, and each country's weight is determined by its share in the multilateral trade of the Group of Ten countries plus Switzerland.

A third exchange rate index is the value of a currency in terms of special drawing rights (SDRs). SDRs are a currency first issued by the International Monetary Fund in 1970. The characteristics of SDRs have changed over time, but since January 1981, an SDR consisted of fixed quantities of U.S. dollars, British pounds, German marks, French francs, and Japanese yen.[12]

Initially, SDRs were traded only among central banks, but in recent years the IMF has encouraged the use of SDRs as a private unit of account. Because it consists of fixed amounts of five currencies, the SDR is sometimes described as a "currency basket." It is an asset that permits an investor to diversify his or her currency holdings. Because the value of the SDR is market determined, it can be used as an index to measure changes in the value of a currency against the average of the five component currencies. The value of the dollar in terms of SDRs is shown in Table 14-3. The row labeled "Dollars per SDR" shows the dollar price of an SDR from 1973 through 1982. The Federal Reserve Board's trade-weighted average value of the dollar, which is shown in the previous row, is inversely related to the dollar price of an SDR. The dollar depreciated in 1974 and 1975 (more dollars were required to buy an SDR), and it appreciated sharply in 1976 to $1.155. The dollar depreciated continuously for the next four years, from $1.155 in 1976 to $1.302 in 1980. It appreciated to $1.179 in 1981, a movement that continued through most of 1982. It reached $1.04 in late 1982 before depreciating to $1.10 by the end of the year. Since the SDR is based on five prominent currencies and its value is published daily (e.g., in *The Wall Street Journal*), it is a convenient foreign exchange index. Other indexes are used as well, but most of them are rather highly correlated with the SDR and each other.

---

[11] The Morgan Guaranty Index is a trade-weighted average of the dollar's value against 15 other currencies. For example, the March 12, 1982, value of the dollar was 6.3 percent above the December 18, 1971 value (after the first devaluation of the 1970s) and 12.6 percent above the February 15, 1973 value (after the second devaluation). The index is reported daily in *The Wall Street Journal*.

[12] Specifically, the 1981 SDR consisted of

0.54	U.S. Dollars
0.46	Deutsche marks
0.74	French francs
.34	Japanese yen
0.071	Pounds sterling

14.6 SUPPLY
AND DEMAND
FOR FOREIGN EXCHANGE

We have discussed the nature of foreign exchange and some problems related to measuring the exchange rate. The next question is, What determines the exchange rate and the volume of currency traded? The market for foreign exchange can be examined by using supply and demand analysis. To make the problem manageable, treat all foreign currencies as a single aggregate called foreign exchange. This composite currency (F) is analogous to an SDR, and its quantity per unit time is shown on the horizontal axis of Figure 14-1. Let Π represent the price of foreign exchange in terms of domestic money. It can be interpreted as an index or average price of the component currencies. As in all markets, the equilibrium point is E, where the quantity of foreign exchange demanded equals the quantity of foreign exchange supplied. The equilibrium exchange rate is Π_1. The behavior of the system out of equilibrium depends on whether the national central bank follows a fixed or flexible exchange rate system.

Suppose that a policy of freely floating exchange rates is followed. The price of foreign exchange would be determined by the same forces of private demand and supply as any other price. If the initial exchange rate is $O\Pi_2$, quantity demanded is OF_2 and quantity supplied is OF_3. The excess demand of F_3F_2 will cause the price to rise from $O\Pi_2$ to $O\Pi_1$. This increase in the price of foreign exchange is called a depreciation of the home currency or an appreciation of foreign exchange.

FIGURE 14-1 Foreign Exchange Market

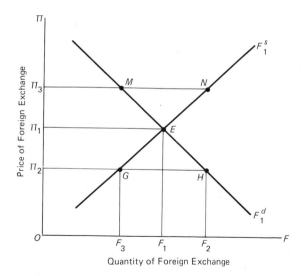

Quantity of Foreign Exchange

Notice that the amount of depreciation ($\Pi_2\Pi_1$) necessary to eliminate a given excess demand (GH) depends on the slopes of supply (F^s) and demand (F^d), which are proportional to supply and demand elasticities. Frequently depreciations are expressed as percentage changes, and in this case it is $\Pi_1\Pi_2/O\Pi_2$. Conversely, if the initial rate is $O\Pi_3$, there is an excess supply of MN units. This surplus of foreign exchange will cause the price to fall to $O\Pi_1$. This percentage change of $\Pi_3\Pi_1/O\Pi_3$ is called an appreciation of the home currency.

Under freely floating exchange rates, private bankers will automatically adjust exchange rates up and down to eliminate discrepancies between quantity demanded and quantity supplied. Freely floating means that central banks never attempt to push the price up by buying foreign exchange or push the price down by selling foreign exchange. U.S. policy in the first two years of the Reagan administration approximated a free float. Most countries have operated systems of floating rates since March 1973, but they have not been free floats. Because of frequent government intervention, these policies are called managed floats.[13] Because some central banks have been accused of deliberately cheapening their currencies to obtain a competitive advantage for their exporters, managed floating has been called "dirty floating."

The extreme opposite of floating is a permanently fixed exchange rate. In Figure 14-1 if $O\Pi_2$ were the fixed exchange rate, the excess demand for foreign exchange (GH) would have to be eliminated by something other than currency depreciation. One possibility is a foreign exchange buffer stock that would sell GH from its inventory for domestic money. Notice that since foreign exchange is measured on the horizontal axis and the price of foreign exchange is measured on the vertical axis, the amount of domestic money bought is the area of the rectangle F_3GHF_2. As shown in Chapter 13, a buffer stock sale of GH would succeed only if Π_2 were temporarily below its long-run average. If GH were a permanent excess demand for foreign exchange, the buffer stock would run out of reserves. The only other alternative to currency depreciation is to pursue a domestic policy that will shift foreign exchange demand to the left or supply to the right. Before considering these policies, we must consider the determinants of the supply and demand for foreign exchange.

14.7 DETERMINANTS
OF FOREIGN EXCHANGE
SUPPLY AND DEMAND

The demand and supply curves for foreign exchange are derived from the underlying demand and supply curves for imports and exports of goods and ser-

[13] According to the *1981 Annual Report* of the International Monetary Fund, "The principal purpose of official intervention in exchange markets is to reduce short-run exchange rate fluctuations, or smooth medium-term movements in exchange rates, through the purchase of foreign ex-

vices. It is convenient to think of the demanders of imported goods and services as the demanders of foreign exchange. Importers must obtain foreign currency to fulfill contracts denominated in foreign exchange. The set of importers includes buyers of merchandise (e.g., crude oil and automobiles) and tourists who travel abroad. Importers of financial assets include residents making direct and portfolio investments abroad. For example, American corporations purchasing plants abroad or foreign currency bonds are demanders of foreign exchange. American firms that are repaying foreign currency loans are also foreign exchange demanders. It is convenient to think of foreign exchange suppliers as the domestic residents who export goods and services. Exports include merchandise (e.g., machinery, airplanes, grain) and services such as tourist expenditures in the home country. Among the sources of supply of foreign exchange are foreign direct investment in the home country, purchases of domestic financial assets by foreigners, and income from previous foreign investment.

Net investment income has become an extremely important service export for the United States ($32.8 billion in 1980). Notice that foreign investment adds to the demand for foreign exchange, but income from previous investment adds to foreign exchange supply. Thus, expenditures by an American firm for oil exploration in the North Sea add to foreign exchange demand, but profits from those activities returned to the United States add to foreign exchange supply. A typical exporter receiving payment in foreign exchange would want to convert those earnings into domestic money. A typical domestic importer would want to acquire foreign exchange to make the payment.

In principle, importers could buy their foreign exchange directly from the exporters who earn it. However, most firms have found banks to be a convenient financial intermediary in the foreign exchange market. Thus, exporters sell foreign exchange to banks and importers buy foreign exchange from banks. Banks earn income by offering to buy currency for less than their selling rate, and the spread between buying and selling rates (bid-offer) depends on the degree of competition among banks. The supply and demand curves for foreign exchange are drawn for fixed values of important economic variables, except for the price and quantity of foreign exchange. When one of the other variables changes, one of the curves shifts. Among the important domestic economic variables whose value is constant along the demand curve for foreign exchange are (1) real GNP, (2) the money price level, (3) the stock of domestic money, (4) nominal interest rates, (5) tariffs and other trade barriers, and (6) the expected future exchange rate. The same variables for the rest of the world are held constant along the foreign exchange supply curve. The next section will discuss the effect of disturbances to the foreign exchange market.

---

change when the home currency tends to appreciate and the sale of foreign exchange when the home currency tends to depreciate" p. 47.

14.8 RESPONSE OF THE FOREIGN EXCHANGE MARKET TO DISTURBANCES

A change in value of one of the underlying variable shifts the supply or demand curve, which brings about an excess demand or supply at the initial exchange rate. Under floating exchange rates, the foreign exchange market will adjust to the disturbance by a change in price. Under fixed exchange rates, the initial price can be maintained only by inducing a compensating change in one of the underlying determinants of the curves. Consider the effect of an increase in domestic real GNP. Assuming that imports are normal goods, income growth will shift the foreign exchange demand curve to the right. The size of the shift depends on the magnitude of income growth and the income elasticity of demand for imports.

Figure 14-2 shows the initial equilibrium at E being disturbed by a rightward shift from F_1^d to F_2^d. The excess demand of EG can be eliminated by a price increase to Π_2, a central bank sale of reserves of EG, or a policy-induced shift of F^d or F^s. An increase in the domestic money supply will also shift the F^d curve to the right. Since domestic and foreign money are substitutes, an increase in the stock of domestic money will increase the quantity of foreign money demanded at each exchange rate. An increase in the general price level at home will make imports relatively cheaper and shift F^d to the right. A decrease in domestic interest rates (for a given price level) will increase the demand for foreign exchange by making foreign securities relatively more attrac-

FIGURE 14-2   Disturbances in the Foreign Exchange Market

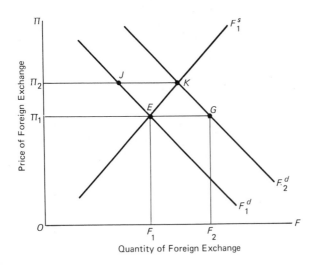

Quantity of Foreign Exchange

tive. More stringent trade barriers imposed by the home country will reduce import demand and the demand for foreign exchange.

Expectations about future prices have a direct impact on present prices. If new information leads traders to expect the home currency to depreciate in the future, the current demand for foreign exchange will increase. This shift of F^d occurs because the present price is considered to be relatively cheap. Changes in the corresponding foreign variables will cause the supply curve of foreign exchange to shift.

14.9 EXPECTATIONS AND FOREIGN EXCHANGE MARKET EFFICIENCY

Expectations about the future play an important role in the determination of foreign exchange rates. Changes in market expectations explain much of the volatility of exchange rates that has occurred since the advent of floating in 1973. Both foreign exchange and equities are traded on organized markets, and these markets process information about the assets. It is appropriate to consider how efficiently markets acquire and interpret information.

One interpretation of an efficient market is that it incorporates all available information in current asset prices. For example, the announcement of an oil discovery will increase the value of a country's currency before any oil is pumped out of the ground. Traders would act on good news about a currency by trying to buy it, and this market optimism would bid up the price until the currency was no longer a bargain. Similarly, bad news would lead the market to discount a currency. If markets efficiently process information, current prices will reflect all relevant information, and all past prices will be irrelevant to future events. In particular, past exchange rates will be useless in predicting future exchange rates. For example, if a currency depreciated for five straight days, this information on past weakness would have no forecasting value in an efficient market. The relevant weakness for traders is future weakness, and the expectation of future depreciation should lower the current value below what it otherwise would have been.

One implication of efficient markets is that the advice to "borrow weak currencies and lend strong currencies" is not very helpful. If other market participants have the same expectations about exchange rates, any expected capital gains from holding strong currencies will be offset by a premium built into the current price of the currency. An implication of efficient foreign exchange and bond markets is that the expected rate of depreciation of the home currency will equal the difference between foreign and domestic nominal interest rates. Prudent investors will hold assets in a currency they expect to depreciate only if they are compensated by a premium interest rate. Conversely, the expected capital loss on weak currencies will be offset by a discount in terms of current price.

However, if markets are not efficient processors of information, the pattern of past prices may reveal some trading strategy that would result in extraordinary profits. For example, the observation that a currency depreciated for five consecutive days might indicate in an inefficient market that it will depreciate on the sixth day. A strategy of selling that currency at the end of the fifth day and buying it at a lower price at the end of the sixth day might yield pure profits. The information efficiency of the foreign exchange market will be considered in more detail in Chapter 17.

14.10 FOREIGN EXCHANGE MARKET ADJUSTMENT MECHANISM

The equilibrium exchange rate is determined by the intersection of supply and demand. A disturbance to the foreign exchange market will shift one of the curves, causing an excess demand or supply at the initial exchange rate. There are a limited number of ways in which the disequilibrium can be eliminated, and the process is called the foreign exchange market adjustment mechanism. In accounting terminology it is called the balance-of-payments adjustment process. The alternative adjustment mechanisms are (1) exchange rate adjustment, (2) change in aggregate demand, (3) change in foreign exchange reserves, and (4) adjustment of trade controls.

In terms of Figure 14-2, let a disturbance shift demand from F_1^d to F_2^d. The excess demand of EG at Π_1 must be eliminated by one of the four adjustment mechanisms. With mechanism 1 the exchange rate would rise to Π_2. Mechanisms 2 and 3 would require the use of aggregate demand policy and commercial policy, respectively, to shift F_2^d back to F_1^d. With mechanism 3 the excess demand of EG would be satisfied by the sale of foreign exchange from reserves.

Each of these alternatives has disadvantages for policymakers, but it is important to recognize that these are the only alternatives. There is no costless adjustment process. If a government refuses to let the exchange rate adjust, it must employ aggregate demand or commercial policy to adjust the foreign exchange market. Thus, a cost of fixed exchange rates is that policymakers lose some control over aggregate demand and commercial policy. Floating exchange rates were reluctantly adopted in 1973 after it became clear that the restrictions on other policies necessary to sustain fixed rates were excessive.

14.11 AGGREGATE DEMAND POLICY

The use of exchange rate adjustment to eliminate excess demand has already been discussed. An alternative is the use of monetary and fiscal policy to alter the aggregate demand for goods and services. Aggregate demand refers to the total demand for goods and services in the economy at various price levels. Aggregate demand depends on the money stock and the government budget. Increases in the money supply or government spending increase aggregate demand, the demand for imports, and the demand for foreign exchange. In Figure 14-2, the excess demand of EG at Π_1 could be eliminated by reducing the money supply enough to shift F_2^d back to F_1^d. In this case, central bank policy would be determined by external economic conditions.

A dilemma is that the use of monetary policy for external purposes may conflict with domestic economic goals such as price level stability or full employment. For example, if a country with an excess demand for foreign exchange also were in a recession, a reduction in the money supply would bring about adjustment in the exchange market while exacerbating the recession. The foreign exchange market intervention necessary to fix the exchange rate automatically reduces the money supply. The central bank must sell foreign exchange reserves and buy an equivalent amount of domestic currency at the fixed exchange rate. Since the domestic money purchased is taken out of circulation, the money supply automatically contracts. The obligation to maintain a fixed exchange rate imposes discipline on the central bank, which is an important feature of the fixed rate system. If the central bank creates too much money, it will be forced to buy the money back through its foreign exchange operations. The government sells EF of foreign exchange for F_1EGF_2 of domestic money.

Proponents of fixed rates praise this feature as an anti-inflation mechanism. Critics stress that the discipline gives the central bank too little freedom to achieve domestic policy goals. Since the foreign trade sector in the United States is relatively small, it has been said that the automatic mechanism amounts to "letting the tail wag the dog." A particularly sensitive issue is that monetary contraction induced by the foreign exchange market may cause temporary unemployment. The automatic tendency for the money supply to contract when there is a shortage of foreign exchange is a characteristic of all fixed exchange rate systems, including the gold standard.

David Hume (1711–1776), the Scottish economist and philosopher, was one of the first analysts to write about the automatic adjustment mechanism. Under a gold standard, gold is money. Hume described the adjustment of the gold stock to external conditions as the price-specie flow mechanism. Gold standard adjustment will be analyzed in more detail in Chapter 20.

14.12 BUFFER STOCK, FOREIGN EXCHANGE RESERVES, AND STERILIZATION

A third policy can be used to deal with certain kinds of disturbances to the foreign exchange market. Temporary shifts in supply and demand can be offset by a buffer stock in foreign exchange. The principles of a buffer stock, which were presented in Chapter 13, are applicable to currency markets as well as to commodity markets. It was shown there that price could be stabilized by offsetting fluctuations in commodity supply by purchases and sales from the buffer stock. The price chosen to be fixed must be the average price. If any other price is chosen, the policy will fail, because the buffer stock will run out of the commodity or money. A buffer stock in foreign exchange reserves can be used to stabilize the exchange rate in face of temporary shifts in supply and demand. However, it can only offset random shocks that would not otherwise change the average exchange rate.

If there are fundamental disturbances that would change the long-run average exchange rate, a buffer stock could not be used to maintain a fixed rate. For example, if random fluctuations in the weather shifted the export supply curve and the foreign exchange supply curve back and forth, a buffer stock in foreign currency would stabilize the exchange rate. An inventory of foreign exchange would be an alternative to a buffer stock in the exported product. However, if a fundamental change permanently eliminated part of the export market, a buffer stock could not maintain the exchange rate. An example of a fundamental change would be the substitution of synthetic rubber for natural rubber. Natural rubber exporters could not successfully defend a fixed exchange rate with foreign exchange reserves.

The world monetary system that prevailed from 1946 to 1973 was based on the concept of a buffer stock. The system is called the adjustable peg or the Bretton Woods system. The term adjustable peg means that the price of foreign exchange remains fixed (pegged) for temporary disturbances, but the price is adjusted for permanent disturbances. The International Monetary Fund, which administered the system, was an outgrowth of the Bretton Woods (New Hampshire) Conference of 1944. The Fund used the terms "temporary" and "fundamental disequilibrium" to distinguish the two situations. A basic practical problem is that policymakers had great difficulty distinguishing the two cases in fact.

When there is an excess demand for foreign exchange, the buffer stock will sell foreign exchange from its reserves. The buffer stock accepts payment in domestic currency, which is withdrawn from the domestic money supply. As discussed in the previous section, the monetary contraction reduces aggregate demand, which shifts F^d to the left in Figure 14-2. Without an additional operation, a buffer stock would be identical to the use of aggregate demand.

To distinguish the two policies, the money supply must be held constant. This can be accomplished by a sterilizing or offsetting open market operation. The domestic money that was purchased with foreign exchange must be returned to circulation by selling an equal amount of domestic money for domestic bonds. The process is called sterilization or offsetting because the object is to break the link between reserves and the money supply. A shortcoming of the policy is that it does not eliminate the source of the excess demand. In terms of Figure 14-2, it does not shift F_2^d to the left. Therefore, the policy is best suited to deal with temporary shortages, such as those caused by a crop failure or a dock strike.

The mechanism is the same as that in the previous section except that foreign exchange intervention must be accompanied by offsetting open market operations. In terms of Figure 14-2, with initial curves F_2^d and F_1^s, there is an excess demand of EG at $O\Pi_1$. The central bank sells EG of foreign currency and buys F_1EGF_2 of domestic money. The contractionary effect of this foreign exchange operation can be seen in the consolidated balance sheet of the central bank.

Assets can be decomposed into domestic (D) and foreign (R), and monetary liabilities are called the monetary base:

$$D + R = M_b$$

In the case of the Federal Reserve, D consists primarily of bonds issued by the Treasury, and R consists of the dollar value of foreign exchange reserves $(\Pi_F F)$, gold $(\Pi_G G)$, and the dollar value of special drawing rights $(\Pi_S S)$ issued by the IMF. Under floating exchange rates, these reserve values are a function of market prices:

$$R = \Pi_F F + \Pi_G G + \Pi_S S$$

The monetary base is currency held by the public and at commercial banks plus commercial bank deposits at Federal Reserve banks. Under a system of fractional reserve banking, the money supply (M) is some multiple of the monetary base:

$$M = m M_b$$

Thus the money supply can be expressed as a function of the central bank's domestic and foreign assets:

$$D + R = \frac{1}{m} M$$

An excess demand for foreign exchange that is met by a sale of reserves for domestic money by the central bank reduces R, M_b, and M. The process is symmetrical, so that if the initial exchange rate were $O\Pi_2$ in Figure 14-2, there would be an excess supply of foreign exchange of JK units. The central bank would acquire JK units of foreign currency and pay with newly created domestic money increasing R, M_b, and M.

The Federal Reserve can prevent this effect on money by engaging in offsetting open market operations. Open market operations are the exchange of domestic assets in the form of government bonds (D) for money. An open market purchase of bonds is paid for with newly created money, so it increases the money supply. Conversely, an open market sale of bonds decreases the money supply. An open market operation is the most common way of changing the money supply, and these operations are carried out every trading day by the Federal Reserve Bank of New York. In the case of an excess demand for foreign exchange, we have seen that the money supply tends to contract automatically. The central bank can sterilize this reserve flow by an offsetting open market purchase of bonds. The amount of outstanding bonds to purchase (D) with newly created base money (M_b) should be just large enough to offset the monetary contraction caused by the decline in reserves. These asset quantities can be expressed in terms of changes (d) per unit time (t):

$$\frac{dD}{dt} + \frac{dR}{dt} = \frac{dM_b}{dt}$$

The sum of the changes in domestic assets and foreign assets per unit time equals the change in the monetary base. The initial shortage of foreign exchange determines the size of the reserve loss.

In Figure 14-2, the reserve loss at $O\Pi_1$ is $EG = F_1F_2$ in terms of foreign currency or the area F_1EGF_2 in terms of domestic currency. Thus dR/dt is negative and equals F_1EGF_2. The foreign exchange intervention reduces the monetary base by this amount:

$$\frac{dR}{dt} = \frac{dM_b}{dt}$$

To restore the monetary base to its initial level $(dM_b/dt = 0)$ requires an offsetting open market operation so that

$$\frac{dD}{dt} = -\frac{dR}{dt}$$

The net effect of these combined operations is to (1) keep the exchange rate constant, (2) sterilize the effect of reserve changes on the money supply, and (3) cause the central bank to substitute domestic assets for foreign assets in its portfolio. Since the initial stock of monetary reserves is limited, sterilization can be applied only in the case of temporary shortages of foreign exchange.

14.13 DIRECT TRADE CONTROLS

The fourth and final way to eliminate an excess demand for foreign exchange is for the government to impose direct controls on trade and payments. The controls may be tariffs or quotas on imported goods, or they may be exchange controls that restrict either the amount of foreign currency that may be purchased by residents or the way in which the currency may be spent. Currencies subject to exchange controls are called inconvertible currencies. The United States limited foreign portfolio investment in 1963 and direct investment in 1965, but all exchange controls were ended in 1973. The use of exchange controls has a long history. In Tudor England, foreign exporters were required to spend sterling proceeds on English goods within a specified time period.[14]

Exchange controls may also be used to separate groups of demanders of foreign exchange who may face multiple exchange rates. An increase in trade controls shifts the foreign exchange demand curve to the left. The required magnitude of the controls depends on the size of the excess demand. An increase in foreign controls against the home country's products would be represented by a leftward shift in the foreign exchange supply curve. The problem with trade controls as an adjustment mechanism is that they distort the pattern of trade in a way that reduces the national income. The cost of trade controls was discussed in Chapters 7 and 8.

14.14 THE EVOLUTION OF THE INTERNATIONAL MONETARY SYSTEM

The United States followed a policy of fixed exchange rates from the beginning of its history. An exception was the Greenback period during and immediately after the Civil War. From 1870 until World War I, the major Western countries were on the gold standard. Exchange rates were rigidly fixed, and excess demands for foreign exchange were eliminated primarily by automatic changes in monetary reserves and money supplies. Convertibility into gold and fixed rates were abandoned during World War I, and several countries followed floating exchange rates during the 1920s. Fixed rates were abandoned again during the Great Depression, when the U.S. dollar was devalued in 1933 from $20 per ounce of gold to $35. World War II disrupted patterns of international trade, and in 1944 a conference was held at Bretton Woods, New Hampshire, that was aimed at returning to some form of fixed exchange rate system.

The result of the conference was a compromise monetary system of mainly fixed or pegged exchange rates, in which countries would have the option of changing the exchange rate if the excess demand for foreign exchange was fundamental. Because of these periodic adjustments of the exchange rate, the system has been called the adjustable peg. The International Monetary Fund, located in Washington, D.C., was established in 1946 to administer the system. Fixed exchange rates were the foundation of the system, and floating violated the charter of the Fund. The adjustable peg system prevailed from 1946 to 1973.

---

[14] Einzig, *The History of Foreign Exchange*, p. 160.

By 1973 economic events had forced most major countries to adopt floating rates. Acknowledging that most major members were violating the charter, the IMF amended the charter at a 1976 Jamaica meeting to permit floating exchange rates. Because of frequent government intervention, the system since 1973 is commonly described as a managed float. Floating exchange rates will be analyzed in Chapters 17 and 18. The gold standard and permanently fixed rates will be considered in Chapter 20. The adjustable peg, a compromise system, will be analyzed in Chapter 21.

SUMMARY

There are many currencies in the world, and their exchange rates can be explained in terms of supply and demand analysis. The foreign exchange market is regularly subjected to disturbances that result in excess demand or supply. There are only four ways to eliminate the excess demand: (1) exchange rate adjustment, (2) monetary reserve adjustment, (3) change in aggregate demand, and (4) direct controls on trade and payments. All these alternatives have disadvantages, but this predicament is simply a special case of the principle that every action has a cost. The problem is to find the least cost solution.

Some form of fixed exchange rate system prevailed for most of the Western countries from about 1870 to 1973 with interruptions for the Great Depression and the two World Wars. During this period, the adjustment process involved mainly reserve adjustments, aggregate demand policy, and trade controls. Adjustment under fixed exchange rates became more difficult as governments increasingly directed aggregate demand policy toward domestic goals. Greater international integration of financial markets and greater disparities in national demand policies made reserve adjustments inadequate to maintain fixed rates. The use of direct trade controls became more common.

Economic events brought about the system of managed floating that began in 1973. A system of floating rates raises microeconomic questions about uncertainty for individual business firms and macroeconomic issues about inflation and real output. Under managed floating the exchange rate has become a more prominent adjustment mechanism. However, frequent intervention by central banks means that some of the features of the fixed rate system have been retained.

REFERENCES

ALIBER, ROBERT Z., ed. *The International Market for Foreign Exchange*. New York: Praeger, 1969. A collection of analytical and descriptive papers on the foreign exchange market.
——. *The International Money Game*, 4th ed. New York: Basic Books, 1983. Analysis of international financial institutions.

BANK FOR INTERNATIONAL SETTLEMENTS. *Annual Reports.* Basel: BIS, annually. Provides surveys of developments in Eurocurrency markets.
BERNAUER, KENNETH. "Asian Dollar Market." Federal Reserve Bank of San Francisco, *Economic Review.* Winter 1983.
CHICAGO MERCANTILE EXCHANGE. *International Monetary Market Yearbook.* Chicago: CME, annually. Includes data on futures prices of major currencies.
Columbia Journal of World Business. Entire Winter 1981 issue is devoted to international banking.
CONINX, RAYMOND G. F. *Foreign Exchange Today.* New York: John Wiley, 1978.
DUFEY, GUNTER, and IAN GIDDY. *The International Money Market.* Englewood Cliffs, N.J.: Prentice-Hall, 1978. Comprehensive analysis of the Eurocurrency market.
EINZIG, PAUL. *A Textbook on Foreign Exchange.* London: Macmillan, 1961.
———. *The History of Foreign Exchange.* New York: St. Martins, 1962. Traces the historical development of foreign exchange institutions.
Euromoney, London, monthly. Provides current information on international banking and finance. For example, the June 1982 issue lists the 500 largest banks in the world.
GRASSMAN, SVEN. *Exchange Reserves and the Financial Structure of Foreign Trade.* Lexington, Mass.: Lexington Books, 1973. Reports on a survey of the foreign exchange practices of Swedish firms.
HABERLER, GOTTFRIED. "The Market for Foreign Exchange and the Stability of the Balance of Payments: A Theoretical Analysis." *Kyklos* 1949. Reprinted in Richard Cooper, ed., *International Finance.* Baltimore: Penguin, 1969.
HODJERA, ZORAN. "The Asian Currency Market: Singapore as a Regional Financial Center." International Monetary Fund *Staff Papers,* June 1978, pp. 221–253.
HOLMES, ALAN and FRANCIS SCHOTT. *The New York Foreign Exchange Market.* New York: Federal Reserve Bank of New York, 1965.
KEY, SYDNEY J. "International Banking Facilities." *Federal Reserve Bulletin,* October 1982. Report on the early experience with banking laws that make it easier for U.S. banks to compete with Eurodollar banks.
KUBARYCH, R.M. *Foreign Exchange Markets in the United States.* New York: Federal Reserve Bank of New York, 1978. Description of foreign exchange market institutions.
LIETAER, B. A. *Financial Management of Foreign Exchange.* Cambridge, Mass.: M.I.T. Press, 1971.
MACHLUP, FRITZ. "The Theory of Foreign Exchanges." In *Readings in the Theory of International Trade,* Howard S. Ellis and Lloyd A. Metzler, eds. Homewood, Ill.: Richard D. Irwin, 1949. Classic analysis of the foreign exchange market.
MACBEAN, A. I. and P. N. SNOWDEN. *International Institutions in Trade and Finance.* Winchester, Mass.: Allen and Unwin, 1981.
McKINNON, RONALD I. *Money in International Exchange: The Convertible Currency System.* New York: Oxford University Press, 1979. Chapter 9 is on the Eurocurrency market.
PICK, FRANZ. *Pick's Currency Yearbook.* New York: Pick Publishing Corporation, annually. Provides extensive data on black market exchange rates.
REVEY, PATRICIA A. "Evolution and Growth of the United States Foreign Exchange Market." *Quarterly Review,* Federal Reserve Bank of New York, Autumn 1981. Describes recent practices in the U.S. foreign currency market.
RIEHL, HEINZ, and RITA M. RODRIGUEZ. *Foreign Exchange Markets: A Guide to Foreign Currency Operations.* New York: McGraw-Hill, 1977. A description of foreign exchange market institutions.
RODRIGUEZ, RITA, and E. EUGENE CARTER. *International Financial Management,* 2nd ed. Englewood Cliffs, N.J.: Prentice-Hall, 1979.

RUTLEDGE, JOHN. "An Economist's View of the Foreign Exchange Market: Report on Interviews with West Coast Foreign Exchange Dealers." In *International Trade and Finance: Readings,* Robert E. Baldwin and J. David Richardson, eds., 2nd ed. Boston: Little, Brown, 1981.

SAMPSON, ANTHONY. *The Money Lenders: Bankers and a World in Turmoil.* New York: Viking, 1982.

SOBOL, DOROTHY MEADOW. "The SDR in Private International Finance." *Quarterly Review,* Federal Reserve Bank of New York, Vol. 6, no. 4 (Winter 1981–1982).

YEAGER, LELAND. *International Monetary Relations: Theory, History, and Policy,* 2nd ed. New York: Harper & Row, 1976. Chapters 15 through 32 describe the evolution of the international monetary system.

CHAPTER FIFTEEN
ANALYSIS
OF THE FOREIGN
EXCHANGE MARKET

15.1 FOREIGN EXCHANGE, IMPORTS, AND EXPORTS

It was shown in Chapter 14 that supply and demand analysis can be applied to the foreign exchange market. Supply and demand is called partial equilibrium because the analysis considers a single market in isolation. An advantage of partial equilibrium is that it is a standard analytical tool whose application to other problems is well known. A possible disadvantage is that some important interdependencies between foreign exchange and other markets may be ignored. Foreign exchange and product markets are closely related. Since importers are the ultimate demanders of foreign exchange, the demand for foreign exchange can be derived from the demand for imports. Since exporters are the ultimate suppliers of foreign currency, the supply of foreign exchange can be derived from the supply of exports. The details of the derivation will be given in the paragraphs that follow.

The demand and supply of foreign exchange depend on exports and imports of goods and services. Export supply depends on domestic conditions in the market for the exportable product. Import demand depends on conditions in the domestic market for the importable. Thus, this chapter will emphasize the interdependence between product markets and the foreign exchange market. In addition to product trade, the effect of international capital flows on the exchange market will be considered. The effect of the domestic money supply on the foreign exchange market will be shown. Some useful economic functions performed by the foreign exchange market will be considered, in-

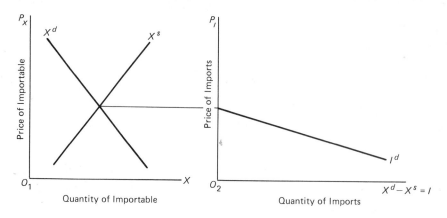

FIGURE 15-1   Import Demand for the Importable Product

cluding clearing, credit, arbitrage, hedging, and speculation. Different international monetary regimes are sometimes distinguished according to the nature of government intervention in the exchange market. Freely floating exchange rates and permanently fixed rates are two extreme monetary regimes. They will be analyzed, as will the compromise systems of the adjustable peg and managed floating.

Let there be two goods, X and Y, produced at home and in the rest of the world. Product X is the importable and Y is the exportable for the home country. The exchange rate depends on conditions in markets for goods, bonds, and money. However, given the money supply, and capital flows, information about conditions of demand and supply for X and Y determine the demand and supply for foreign exchange by the home country. Figure 15-1 shows the derivation of import demand for X from the domestic demand and supply curves for the importable. Specifically, import demand is defined as the excess demand for the importable product by home country residents:

$$I^d(P) = X^d(P) - X^s(P)$$

It was shown earlier that import demand is more elastic than is the demand for the importable. It follows that I^d must be more horizontal than X^d. Since importers are residents of the home country, their demand depends on prices expressed in home currency. Import supply comes from ROW, and its derivation is shown in Figure 15-2. Since import suppliers are residents of ROW, the relevant price is expressed in ROW currency. Specifically, import supply is

$$I^s(P^\star) = \overset{\star}{X^s}(P^\star) - \overset{\star}{X^d}(P^\star)$$

Import supply to the home country is the excess supply of product X by ROW. Derivation of import supply from conditions in ROW is shown in Figure 15-

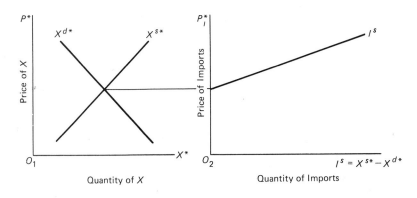

FIGURE 15-2   Import Supply from the Rest of the World

2. Arbitrage between the home and ROW markets will equate the prices of X when they are expressed in the same currency. The home currency equivalent of the ROW price is ΠP^*, and the equilibrium condtion is

$$P_I = \Pi P_I^*$$

For example, let wheat sell for 2 pounds sterling per bushel in London when the price of sterling is $2 per pound. The dollar-equivalent price of wheat in London is $4 per bushel. Arbitragers will compare this price with the dollar price in the United States. If the prices differ, a riskless profit can be earned by simultaneously buying at the low price and selling at the high price. Equalization of prices in different geographical markets is sometimes called the law of one price or absolute purchasing power parity.

Figure 15-3 shows that equilibrium in the market for imports can be expressed either as a function of home currency or as foreign currency prices. At the initial exchange rate Π_1, equilibrium is at A in terms of domestic prices and A' in terms of foreign currency prices. The two prices are linked by the equilibrium condition, and the volume of trade is the same in either case (OI_1).

The upper portion of the diagram shows import supply by ROW as a function of home currency prices. Import supply actually depends on ROW prices, but ROW prices can be translated into home prices at a given exchange rate. Thus, I^s is drawn for a given value of Π, and it shifts when the exchange rate changes. Specifically, an increase in Π (depreciation of home currency) causes I^s to shift upward because, at each home currency price, the import supplier receives less ROW currency. The lower portion of the diagram shows import demand by home residents as a function of the ROW currency price. The position of I^d is drawn for a given exchange rate. If Π increases, I^d shifts downward. At each value of P^* the increase in Π increases the price of imports expressed in home money.

It is important to distinguish between the home and foreign currency prices because they move in opposite directions when the exchange rate changes. For

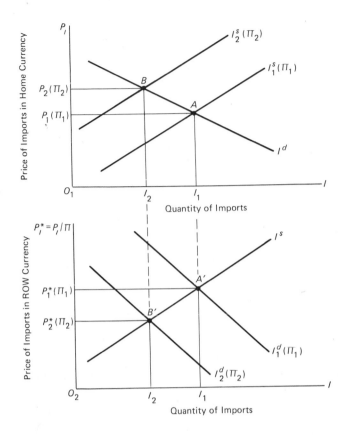

FIGURE 15-3   Equilibrium in Terms of Domestic and Foreign Currency Prices

example when the home currency depreciates from Π_1 to Π_2, the home currency price of imports *rises* from P_1 to P_2 and the foreign currency price *falls* from P_1^* to P_2^*.

It follows from the equilibrium condition that price changes must satisfy the following relationship:

$$\frac{dP_I}{P_I} = \frac{d\Pi}{\Pi} + \frac{dP_I^*}{P_I^*}$$

The percentage change in the home currency price of imports equals the percentage change in the exchange rate plus the percentage change in the foreign currency price. If the home country is small, the latter term will be zero.

A similar relationship holds for the home country's exportable good, Y. Figure 15-4 shows the derivation of the home country's export supply curve from the domestic demand and supply of exportable Y. The lower portion of the diagram shows the derivation of ROW's demand for exports of Y as a func-

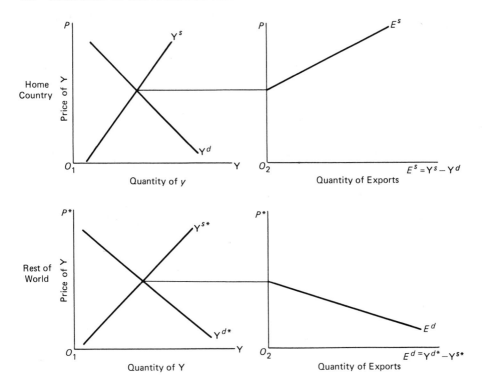

FIGURE 15-4   Export Supply and Demand

tion of prices expressed in ROW currency. Equilibrium in the export market occurs where the quantity demanded by ROW equals the quantity supplied by the home country.

Equilibrium can be expressed either as a function of domestic or foreign prices, as shown in Figure 15-5. As a function of domestic prices, export demand can be drawn for a given exchange rate. Equilibrium at the initial exchange rate Π_1 is at A. As Π increases from Π_1 to Π_2 E^d shifts upward, since foreign currency prices are lower at each home currency price. The lower portion of the diagram shows home export supply as a function of foreign currency prices. When Π increases from Π_1 to Π_2 E^s shifts downward, since P increases for each level of $P^\star$. A devaluation of the home currency increases the home currency price of exports from P_1 to P_2 and decreases the foreign currency price of exports from $P_1^\star$ to $P_2^\star$.

It follows from the equilibrium condition $(P_E = \Pi P_E^\star)$ that

$$\frac{dP_E}{P_E} = \frac{d\Pi}{\Pi} + \frac{dP_E^\star}{P_E^\star}$$

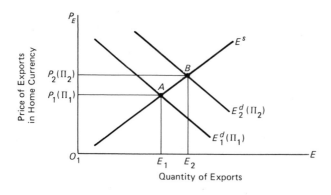

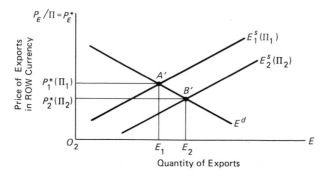

FIGURE 15-5   Export Equilibrium in Terms of Domestic and Foreign Prices

For example a 10 percent devaluation might raise home currency prices by 8 percent and lower foreign currency prices by 2 percent. However, if the devaluing country were small, domestic currency prices would rise by the same percentage as the exchange rate.

15.2 FOREIGN EXCHANGE DEMAND AND SUPPLY

Foreign exchange may be demanded (1) to pay for imported goods and services, (2) to finance capital outflows, or (3) to finance government intervention. It will be assumed in this chapter that only the demand for goods and services depends on the exchange rate. Capital flows and government intervention are assumed for the moment to be determined by other variables. The possibility of capital flows that respond to the exchange rate will be considered later. It follows that the demand for foreign exchange can be derived directly from the demand for imports. The demand for foreign exchange is simply the volume of imports multiplied by the foreign currency price:

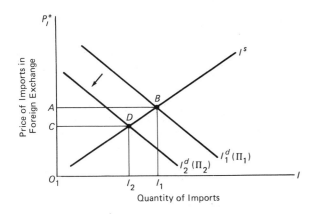

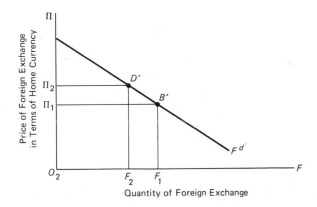

FIGURE 15-6   Import Demand and Foreign Exchange Demand

$$F^d(\Pi) = P_I^\star I$$

The quantity of foreign exchange demanded at each exchange rate is equal to total expenditure on imports expressed in foreign currency.

Figure 15-6 shows the demand curve for foreign exchange and the demand curve for imports. Import demand is shown as a function of the foreign currency price, which shifts downward when the home currency depreciates. At the initial exchange rate Π_1, the import demand is I_1^d, the import price is O_1A, and the volume of imports is OI_1. Total expenditure on imports is the area of the rectangle O_1ABI_1. This area is plotted in the lower portion of the diagram as the horizontal distance O_2F_1. It is simultaneously total expenditure on imports at the exchange rate Π_1 and the quantity of foreign exchange demanded at Π_1.

Let the home currency depreciate to Π_2. Import demand shifts downward to I_2^d. The foreign currency price of imports falls to O_1C, and the volume of imports falls to O_1I_2. Since both price and quantity fall, total expenditure on imports decreases to the area O_1CDI_2. This area is represented in the lower diagram by the horizontal distance O_2F_2, which is necessarily less than O_1F_1. Thus, depreciation of the home currency from Π_1 to Π_2 necessarily reduces the quantity of foreign exchange demanded.

As the diagram indicates, the magnitude of the decrease depends on (1) the slope of I^s and (2) the shift of I^d. The former reflects the elasticity of supply of imports (ϵ_I), and the latter reflects the elasticity of import demand (η_I). More precisely, the elasticity of demand for foreign exchange with respect to Π can be expressed as[1]

$$\eta_{F\Pi} = \frac{\eta_I(1+\epsilon_I)}{\epsilon_I - \eta_I}$$

If the importing country is a small country, ϵ_I is infinitely great and the I^s curve is horizontal. The foreign currency price of imports $(P_I^\star)$ is beyond the control of the home country and the relationship becomes simpler. The equation can be rewritten to emphasize the effect of large values for ϵ_I:

$$\eta_{F\Pi} = \frac{(\eta_I/\epsilon_I) + \eta_I}{1 - (\eta_I/\epsilon_I)}$$

As ϵ_I becomes infinitely great, $\eta_{F\Pi}$ approaches η_I. Thus, for small countries the elasticity of demand for foreign exchange depends only on the elasticity of demand for imports.

The supply of foreign exchange can be derived in an analogous fashion. The supply of foreign exchange is equal to the value of exports expressed in foreign currency:

$$F^s(\Pi) = P_E^\star E$$

Figure 15-7 shows the demand and supply of exports and the supply of foreign exchange. At the initial exchange rate Π_1, export supply is E_1^s. Equilibrium is at A, the price of exports is O_1B, and the volume of exports is O_1E_1. Total revenue from exports is O_1BAE_1, which is equal to the horizontal distance O_2F_1 in the lower portion of the diagram. If the home currency depreciates to Π_2, export supply shifts to E_2^s. At each foreign currency price, home exporters receive more home currency. The excess supply of exports (AC) is eliminated by a price decrease to O_1G. Export volume increases to O_1E_2. Total revenue from exports rises if the percentage increase in export volume (E_1E_2)

[1]A derivation of the basic relationships appears in Robert Stern, *The Balance of Payments* (Chicago: Aldine, 1973), Chap. 2 appendix.

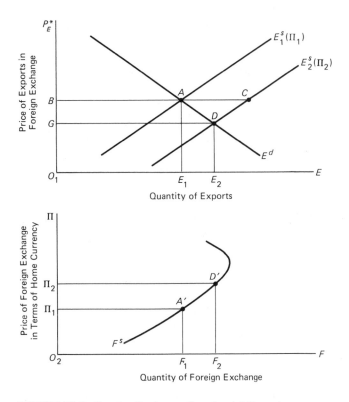

FIGURE 15-7   Foreign Exchange Supply and Exports

exceeds the percentage decrease in price *(GB)*. In this case the area O_1GDE_2 will be greater than the area O_1BAE_1. In the lower diagram, the foreign exchange supply curve has a positive slope between Π_1 and Π_2. Whether export revenue and foreign exchange supply increase following depreciation depends on the slope of the export demand curve between A and D. If export demand is elastic, total revenue and export supply will increase. However, if export demand is inelastic, revenue and foreign exchange supply will decrease. The foreign exchange supply curve will bend backward and take a negative slope.

In terms of Figure 15-7 the elasticity of supply and foreign exchange depends on (1) the slope of export demand and (2) the horizontal shift of export supply. The exact relationship is the following:

$$\epsilon_{F\Pi} = \frac{\epsilon_E(1 + \eta_E)}{\eta_E - \epsilon_E}$$

The elasticity of supply of foreign exchange with respect to Π depends on the elasticity of supply of exports and the elasticity of demand for exports in ROW. Since the denominator is always negative, the sign of the ratio depends on the sign of the numerator. It is also negative and ϵ_{FII} is positive if η_E is greater than 1 in absolute value. Thus, if export demand is elastic, the elasticity of supply of foreign exchange is greater than zero. Conversely, if η_E is less than 1 in absolute value, ϵ_{FII} is negative.

A well-known microeconomic principle is that firms have an incentive to avoid operating where demand is inelastic. It is not in the interest of the country's exporters to operate where export demand is inelastic, since the marginal revenue from exporting is negative. The country has an incentive to reduce export volume through private collusion, an export tax, or an export quota (see Chapter 10) to the point where export demand is elastic. To the extent that exports are restricted to the elastic range of demand, the negatively sloped portion of the foreign exchange supply is not relevant.

A second reason why the backward-bending portion of the foreign exchange supply curve may not be important is in the case of the small country. As a price taker in export markets, a small country faces an infinitely elastic export demand. The importance of export demand can be seen by rewriting the equation for ϵ_{FII}:

$$\epsilon_{FII} = \frac{(\epsilon_E/\eta_E) + \epsilon_E}{1 - (\epsilon_E/\eta_E)}$$

As the country becomes smaller, η_E increases, and in the limit $\epsilon_{FII} = \epsilon_E$. For a small country, the elasticity of foreign exchange supply depends only on the elasticity of export supply, which is necessarily positive. In this case, the "backward-bending problem" cannot occur. It can occur only for large countries whose exporters operate where export demand is inelastic.

The exchange rate is affected by monetary variables such as the home and foreign money supplies. The previous analysis indicates that it is also affected by all the real variables that influence the markets for importables and exportables. Those real forces, considered in Part I of the book, include technology, factor supplies, consumer preferences, transport costs, commercial policy, and market structure.

Since foreign exchange demand depends on import demand, anything that increases import demand will cause an excess demand for foreign currency. An example is economic growth combined with a high income elasticity of demand for the importable good (X). Alternatively, technological innovation that increases the supply of the importable will reduce the demand for imports and reduce the demand for foreign exchange. Any force that increases the supply of exports will increase the supply of foreign exchange and appreciate the currency. Technological innovation in the exportable sector (Y) is an example of such a change. Conversely, income growth combined with a high income elasticity of demand for the exportable would reduce export supply and depreciate the home currency. Knowledge of these general principles permits one to analyze the impact of any real economic disturbance on the exchange rate.

It has been shown how the demand and supply of foreign exchange can be derived from the underlying conditions in the markets for goods X and Y. The basic relationships can be illustrated with an algebraic example. Let the home country be a small country with known equations of demand and supply for X and Y. The prices of X and Y in foreign currency $(P_X^\star, P_Y^\star)$ are given. Conditions in the home market for X are the following:

$$X^d = 100 - 2P$$
$$X^s = 8P$$

It follows that import demand for X is:

$$I^d = X^d - X^s = 100 - 2P - 8P = 100 - 10P$$

Because the home country is small, import supply is infinitely elastic at the world price. The given world price of X in foreign currency is

$$P_I^\star = F1$$

The conditions in the Y market are

$$Y^d = 100 - 4P$$
$$Y^s = 16P$$

It follows that export supply is

$$E^s = 16P - (100 - 4P) = 20P - 100$$

Because it is a small country, the demand for the home country's exports is also infinitely elastic at the world price:

$$P_E^\star = F2$$

Thus, relative prices of X and Y in ROW are

$$\frac{P_Y^\star}{P_X^\star} = \frac{P_E^\star}{P_I^\star} = \frac{F2}{F1}$$

Foreign exchange demand is derived directly from the value of imports:

$$
\begin{aligned}
F^d = I^d P_I^\star &= (100 - 10P_I)P_I^\star = (100 - 10P_I^\star\Pi)P_I^\star \\
&= 100P_I^\star - 10\Pi P_I^\star \\
&= 100(1) - 10\Pi(1)^2 = 100 - 10\Pi
\end{aligned}
$$

Foreign exchange supply is obtained from the value of exports:

$$F^s = E^s P_E^\star = (-100 + 20P_E)P_E^\star = (-100 + 20\Pi P_E^\star)P_E^\star$$
$$= -100P_E^\star + 20\Pi(P_E^\star)^2$$
$$= (-100)(2) + 20\Pi(2)^2 = -200 + 80\Pi$$

The foreign exchange market is in equilibrium when

$$F^d = F^s$$
$$100 - 10\Pi = -200 + 80\Pi$$
$$\Pi = \frac{300}{90} = 3.33$$
$$F^d = 100 - 10(3.33) = 66.67$$

At the exchange rate $\Pi = 3.33$, the domestic currency value of the foreign exchange traded is

$$\Pi F^d = (3.33)(66.67) = 222.01$$

Given the exchange rate and world prices, domestic prices are

$$P_I = \Pi P_I = (3.33)(1) = 3.33$$
$$P_E = \Pi P_E^\star = 3.33(2) = 6.67$$

From these domestic currency prices, the quantity and value of imports and exports can be determined:

$$I^d = 100 - 10P = 100 - 10(3.33) = 66.67$$

The value of imports is

$$V_I^\star = P_I^\star I = (1)(66.67) = 66.67$$

$$V_I = P_I I = (3.33)(66.67) = 222.01$$

The volume of exports is

$$E^s = 20P - 100 = 20(6.67) - 100$$
$$= 133.40 - 100 = 33.40$$

And the value of exports is

$$V_E^\star = P_E^\star E = 2(33.40) = 66.80$$
$$V_E = P_E E = (6.67)(33.40) = 222.8$$

Thus, for the small open economy facing prices of $P_X^\star = F1$ and $P_Y^\star = F2$, the foreign exchange market clears at a price of 3.33, and the X and Y markets clear at prices of $P_X = 3.33$ and $P_Y = 6.67$. For a small country with given foreign currency prices, demand and supply conditions for traded goods determine domestic currency prices and the exchange rate.

15.3 THE MONEY MARKET AND THE FOREIGN EXCHANGE MARKET

In addition to the real variables discussed in the previous section, the exchange rate is affected by monetary variables such as the money supply, money demand, and inflation. The foreign exchange demand curve is drawn for a given money stock and a given domestic price level. Demand also depends on the current expectation of the future money supply and price levels. The arrival of news about future monetary conditions can alter the current exchange rate even if current exports and imports are constant. Domestic monetary expansion increases the demand for foreign exchange and shifts F^d to the right. The foreign exchange supply curve is drawn for a given money stock in ROW. Monetary expansion abroad shifts F^s to the right, causing the home currency to appreciate. Differential inflation is another force that affects the foreign exchange market.

Suppose that a financial innovation reduces the demand for money at home. For a given money supply, the price level will rise. Higher money prices make home goods less competitive, causing foreign exchange demand to shift to the right. Thus, domestic inflation tends to weaken the home currency. Financial innovation that raises the price level abroad shifts foreign exchange supply to the right. Thus, foreign inflation strengthens the home currency. Notice that it is differential national inflation that alters exchange rates. High or low inflation rates that are the same in both countries should not alter currency exchange rates. The purchasing power parity theory emphasizes the effect of differential inflation on the exchange rate. The monetary theory of the exchange rate stresses the effects of money supply and money demand. Both theories will be presented in Chapter 17.

15.4 CAPITAL FLOWS

International capital flows are another determinant of the exchange rate. Let K represent net capital outflows from the home country, the difference between gross outflows and gross inflows. Suppose that the amount of K is independent of the exchange rate. K can be added to import demand to determine the total demand for foreign exchange:

$$F^d = F_I^d + K$$

Here K includes all capital outflows whether they are private or government, portfolio or direct, or long term or short term. The balance-of-payments accounts separate transfers (gifts) from profit-motivated lending, but no such distinction is made here. Suppose that initially there is no net capital outflow from the home country.

This situation is shown in Figure 15-8, where the initial equilibrium is at point A. A new capital outflow will shift the foreign exchange demand from F_I^d to $F^d + K$. The excess demand for foreign exchange of AB at Π_1 will be eliminated by a depreciation of the home currency to Π_2. A new capital outflow will induce a currency depreciation whose magnitude depends on (1) the size of the capital flow (horizontal shift of F^d) and (2) the slopes of F^d and F^s. The latter are proportional to η_{FII} and ϵ_{FII}, which depend on η_I, ϵ_I, ϵ_E, and η_E.

Prior to the capital flow, the value of imports equaled the value of exports. The currency depreciation will increase foreign exchange supplied and decreased foreign exchange demanded. The value of exports will increase and the value of imports will decrease. In the new equilibrium at C, the excess of exports over imports (balance-of-trade surplus) equals the capital outflow. The desired financial transfer of AB has been converted into a real transfer of $DC = AB$. At $O\Pi_2$ the value of exports is OF_2, the value of imports is OF_3, and the capital outflow is $F_3F_2 = DC$. Thus, a floating exchange rate induces a trade surplus equal to the capital outflow. Alternatively, with a fixed exchange rate, some other policy is necessary to generate the trade surplus.

FIGURE 15-8   Capital Outflow and the Foreign Exchange Market

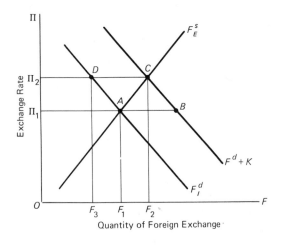

15.5 FUNCTIONS OF THE FOREIGN EXCHANGE MARKET

The economic functions performed by the foreign exchange market can be divided into clearing, arbitrage, credit, hedging, and speculation.

A market is said to clear when the desires of potential buyers are reconciled with those of potential sellers. A simple clearing mechanism is for price to adjust until quantity demanded equals quantity supplied. A freely floating exchange rate is a clearing mechanism in the foreign exchange market. Clearing means that foreign exchange demanded for all purposes equals total foreign exchange supplied. In the presence of capital flows, it does not necessarily mean that the value of exports equals the value of imports. When the foreign exchange market clears, there is no reason to expect individual components of demand to equal individual components of supply. K represents net demand for foreign exchange by capital exporters.

The market equilibrium condition can be stated as an equality between foreign exchange demanded by all importers plus net capital outflows and foreign exchange supplied by all exporters:

$$F_I^d + K = F_E^s$$

As long as there is net lending, the demand by importers will differ from the supply by exporters.

Unbalanced trade is consistent with foreign exchange market equilibrium. For much of the ninteenth century, for example, the United States experienced trade deficits combined with capital inflows. In addition, there is no reason to expect the foreign exchange demanded by a particular category of importers to equal the foreign exchange earned by exporters in the same product category. A nation's food imports need not equal its food exports. If a nation is a net food importer, it must be a net exporter of another product or a net borrower if the foreign exchange market is to clear. The pattern of a country's net imports and exports of individual products depends on comparative advantage. Sometimes governments announce policy goals of eliminating particular deficits, such as food, energy, or tourism, when the net benefits of the policy are far from obvious. Advocates of protectionism in the United States have recently called attention to the automobile and steel trade deficits.

The proposition that market clearing depends on total demand and supply rather than individual components also applies to trade between many countries. All foreign exchange markets can clear without there being bilateral balance in trade between any two countries. Overall balance or clearing simply requires countries to offset deficits with certain trading partners against surpluses (including capital flows) with other countries. Thus, U.S. deficits with Japan or the group of OPEC countries may be consistent with long-run equilibrium in currency markets.

In U.S. congressional discussions of trade legislation, the word "reciprocity" has played a prominent role. Some discussants cited the large U.S. trade deficit with Japan as evidence of discrimination against U.S. exports. They propose to reciprocate by restricting Japanese imports into the United States. The implicit and erroneous assumption is that trade should be balanced on a country-by-country basis. Such a condition is unnecessary when foreign exchange markets clear. If bilateral balance were required, the condition would seriously reduce trade. The Eastern European CMEA countries have had inconvertible currencies without market clearing for many years. The resulting bilateral balance requirement has been a major trade barrier that has led some countries (Romania, Yugoslavia, Hungary, and Poland) to seek convertibility and membership in the IMF.

Arbitrage is a second function of the foreign exchange market. Spatial arbitrage links the prices of the same currency in geographically separated markets. For example, if the dollar-pound exchange rate were $2.40 in New York and $2.42 in London, arbitragers would buy pounds in New York and sell in London. The excess demand for pounds in New York would raise the price, and the excess supply in London would lower the price until the exchange rates were equal. Since specialized banks scrutinize the market for geographical discrepancies, large price differences are rarely observed.

However, if legal trade is blocked by exchange controls, discrepancies may arise. In the same example, if the U.S. government forbids conversion of dollars into pounds at a price above $2.40 and prevents arbitrage, two prices will persist. Some black market activity will emerge in which American residents buy pounds for $2.40 in the United States, take the pounds abroad illegally, and sell them for $2.42. Currency smuggling would tend to equalize exchange rates. Black markets are common for currencies subject to exchange control including multiple exchange rates. Data on black market exchange rates is provided in Franz Pick's annual *Currency Yearbook*. Since American laws apply only to residents of the United States, U.S. exchange controls could not prevent dollar-pound arbitrage in any other part of the world.

Strictly speaking, currency arbitrage is the simultaneous purchase and sale of the same currency at two different prices. In contrast to speculation, it is a riskless operation. Speculation consists of buying (selling) at a price and expecting to sell (buy) later at a higher (lower) price. Because the future price is unknown, speculation is risky. Arbitrage involves trading at a known price differential at a given time. Successful spatial arbitrage requires discovering price differentials quickly and acting on them. Profits depend on the cost of acquiring information and the cost of transacting. Because of economies of scale in collecting information about currencies, large banks are the primary spatial arbitragers. Transactions costs consist of the difference between buying (bid) and selling (ask) prices for currencies. Furthermore, the bid-ask spread will be different for different forms of currency (paper currency, traveler's checks, etc.).

Triangular arbitrage is the use of three currencies to purchase one of them at a low price and sell it at a higher price. The technique applies the idea that the prices of currency A in terms of currencies B and C establish an indirect or cross-price (Π_{CB}^I) between B and C. The arbitrager then compares the direct and indirect prices.

$$\Pi_{CB}^I = \frac{\Pi_{AB}}{\Pi_{AC}}$$

For example, if the following prices for currency A prevailed,

$$\Pi_{AB} = B10$$
$$\Pi_{AC} = C2$$

an indirect price of 5 units of B is available to potential buyers of currency C. The indirect trade is accomplished by (1) selling 10 units of B for 1 unit of A and (2) converting the unit of A into 2 units of C. Thus, the indirect price of C is $B5$:

$$\Pi_{CB}^I = \frac{\Pi_{AB}}{\Pi_{AC}} = \frac{B10}{C2} = B5$$

The options available can be summarized by the following diagram. An economic agent can convert B into C directly by moving clockwise, or C can be acquired indirectly through A by moving counterclockwise. In equilibrium a clockwise trade should have the same price as a counterclockwise trade.

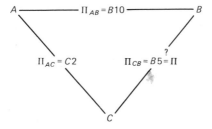

Direct exchange rates between B and C are regularly quoted by banks. If the direct rate differs from the indirect rate, triangular arbitragers can earn a riskless profit by buying at the low price and simultaneously selling at the high price. A discrepancy between direct and indirect rates is called disparate cross-rates. In foreign exchange market equilibrium, the direct rate equals the indirect rate. The general principle applies to an arbitrarily large number of currencies. The indirect price of the ith currency in terms of the jth currency is

$$\Pi_{ij}^I = \frac{\Pi_{kj}}{\Pi_{ki}}$$

If two countries (*i* and *j*) seek fixed exchange rates between their currencies, fixity can be accomplished indirectly if each country fixes the price of a third currency (*k*). Private triangular arbitrage will establish equality between direct and indirect rates. An example of this relationship is the gold standard. Each participating government fixed the price of gold in terms of its national money. Fixed exchange rates between currencies was assured by triangular arbitragers. Another example is the adjustable peg system established at Bretton Woods. Each participating government (except the United States) fixed the price of dollars in terms of home currency. Triangular arbitragers ensured that fixed exchange rate for all nondollar currencies would result.

The foreign exchange market performs a credit function by providing a link between national credit markets. Bonds are promises to repay a fixed amount of a given currency on a specified future date. The foreign exchange market permits agents to borrow in one country (sell bonds denominated in one currency) and lend in another country (buy bonds in a different currency). Thus, the foreign exchange market contributes to the international equalization of interest rates through a kind of interest arbitrage. Traditionally, this process involved banks located in different countries. However, the essence of Eurodollars and other external currencies is that a single bank will deal in both domestic and foreign currencies. For example, London banks offer the opportunity to borrow or lend in either pounds or dollars. The result of borrowers seeking lower interest rates and lenders seeking higher rates is a tendency to bring the dollar and pound rates together. Thus, the development of external currency markets tightens the link between interest rates in different currencies.

Hedging is a fourth function of the foreign exchange market. In general, hedging is a transaction designed to reduce uncertainty. Uncertainty about future exchange rates can be reduced by operations in the spot or forward exchange markets. Measuring a firm's exposure to foreign exchange risk has become an important problem under floating exchange rates. An accounting measure of a firm's exposure to exchange rate changes is its net assets in a given currency. A firm whose assets equal liabilities in a currency is said to have a closed position in that currency. Inequality between assets and liabilities is an open position. The position is long if there are net assets and short if there are net liabilities.

Let $A^\star$ represent assets in a foreign currency and $L^\star$ represent liabilities in the same currency. Net assets can be written as

$$N = (A^\star - L^\star)\Pi$$

If the value of $A^\star$ and $L^\star$ can be taken as given by outstanding contracts, the effect of an exchange rate change on the domestic currency value of foreign assets is

$$dN = (A^\star - L^\star)d\Pi$$

A firm with net foreign assets $(A^\star > L^\star)$ will receive a capital gain if the home currency depreciates (i.e., foreign currency appreciates). Conversely, a firm with net foreign liabilities would experience a capital loss from depreciation of home money. A firm with a closed position would not be exposed to exchange risk $(dN = 0)$, because a rate change would result in exactly offsetting gains and losses for the firm. In this context, hedging can be interpreted as converting an initial open position into a closed position by an appropriate spot or forward operation.

Consider the following example of a hedging operation. Suppose that an American importer agrees to buy Volkswagens for 1 million marks to be paid in 90 days. The current spot price of marks is $0.50 per mark, but the spot rate in 90 days is unknown. The firm has net liabilities in marks:

$$N = (A^\star - L^\star)\Pi$$
$$-\$500,000 = (0 - DM1,000,000)(\$0.50)$$

If the dollar depreciates (mark appreciates) to $0.60, the dollar value of the mark liability rises to $-\$600,000$. The capital loss is $dN = (-DM1,000,000)(+\$0.10) = -\$100,000$. Alternatively, if the dollar appreciates (mark depreciates) to $0.40 per mark, the dollar value of the mark liability falls to $400,000.

The firm can eliminate uncertainty about the dollar value of the mark liability by hedging through the spot or forward market. A spot hedge is accomplished by buying DM1 million at the current spot price and investing them in Germany for 90 days. An alternative forward hedge involves buying DM1 million at the current forward rate for delivery in 90 days. In both cases, the firm converts an open position (short) in marks into a closed position. Either the spot or the forward purchase provides the firm with DM1 million asset to offset its DM1 million mark liability. A firm with a short position in foreign exchange can hedge explicitly by buying foreign exchange. A firm with an initial long position can hedge explicitly by selling foreign currency.

It will be shown in Chapter 17 that foreign exchange and credit markets provide an implicit hedge against depreciation. In the preceding example, a firm choosing not to hedge explicitly would be protected against depreciation by a premium of home interest rates over foreign rates. A domestic interest premium would raise the cost of a spot hedge. Similarly, if the home currency were expected to depreciate, the forward price of marks would exceed the spot price. This forward premium raises the cost of a forward hedge. The question of whether the firm should hedge explicitly depends on whether markets incorporate the expected depreciation of the home currency.

For a fully anticipated depreciation, the expected change in the spot rate should equal the home-foreign interest differential and the forward premium:

$$\frac{dS^E}{S} = i - i^\star = \frac{F - S}{S}$$

It will be useful to use S to represent the spot exchange rate and F to represent the forward exchange rate. The spot rate S is equivalent to the previous term Π. An important empirical question is whether markets accurately forecast currency depreciation. The relationship between exchange rates and interest rates will be considered in more detail in later chapters.

Speculation is the final function performed by the foreign exchange market. In contrast to hedging, speculation is the deliberate transformation of a closed position in foreign exchange to an open position. The speculator forecasts future exchange rates and seeks a capital gain equal to the difference between his or her forecast and actual market rates.

Suppose that the current spot rate is $2.00 and that a speculator expects the price to rise to $2.10 in the next period. A spot speculator will buy foreign exchange for $2.00 and expect to sell it later for $2.10. The expected capital gain is

$$S_{t+1}^{E} - S_t = \$2.10 - \$2.00 = +\$0.10$$

Since the speculator must pay for the foreign exchange in the present period and invest it abroad until $t+1$, interest of $i - i^\star$ must be forgone. The expected capital gain net of interest costs is

$$\frac{S_{t+1}^{E} - S_t}{S_t} - (i - i^\star)$$

An alternative to spot speculation is to buy foreign exchange in the forward market. Suppose that the current price of foreign exchange to be delivered at $t+1$ is $2.00. The speculator would buy a forward contract for delivery at $t+1$ expecting to resell for $2.10 at $t+1$. The expected capital gain is

$$S_{t+1}^{E} - F_{t+1} = \$2.10 - \$2.00 = \$0.10$$

The forward contract is simultaneously an asset denominated in foreign currency and a promise to pay domestic money. The speculator has a long position in foreign exchange and a short position in domestic money. This position is commonly described as "selling the home currency short" or "going long" in foreign exchange. Speculative profits depend on two things. First, depreciation must occur so that the speculator can sell the foreign currency for $2.10. Second, the depreciation must be a surprise to other market participants. Otherwise, the forward rate would be bid up to $2.10, and profit opportunities would disappear. Thus, successful speculation requires that speculators forecast more accurately than the market.

15.6 EXCHANGE RATE REGIMES AND GOVERNMENT INTERVENTION

Exchange rate regimes can be distinguished according to the amount of government intervention. Freely floating rates and permanently fixed rates are the two extreme systems. With freely floating rates, the government does not intervene, and the price changes continuously to clear the market. There is no need for the government to hold foreign exchange reserves. Each day there is a high probability of a price change, but sufficient foreign exchange is always available to buyers at that price. Under permanently fixed rates, the government must be the residual buyer or seller of foreign exchange at the fixed rate. On a given day, the probability of a price change is zero, but there may be uncertainty about the availability of foreign exchange. Uncertainty may arise because some form of nonprice rationing must be substituted for price rationing.

Most of the exchange rate regimes observed in the real world have been some compromise lying between these two extremes. Under compromise systems, rates would change some of the time but not all the time. Under the adjustable peg system that prevailed from 1946 to 1973, there is an official fixed rate that is changed infrequently. A managed float is a system of mainly floating rates, but governments frequently intervene to influence the rate. Most countries have followed a managed float since 1973. Alternative exchange rate regimes can be represented by the following continuum:

Permanently ——————— Adjustable ——————— Managed ——————— Freely
    fixed   peg   float   floating
    rates   rates

In some cases the distinctions are not clear. If the exchange rate is changed very frequently under an adjustable peg, it cannot be distinguished from a managed float. If it is changed very rarely, it cannot be distinguished from permanently fixed rates. The historical gold standard is an example of fixed rates over an extended period. The implicit fixed rates between the dollars of the 50 United States are another example of extremely fixed rates.

The effect of government intervention in the foreign exchange market can be shown in Figure 15-9. The initial equilibrium is at point A where the exchange rate is π_1. Let foreign exchange demand increase to F_2^d, causing an excess demand of AB at π_1. Under permanently fixed rates, the government would enter the market and supply AB units of foreign exchange or eliminate the excess demand in some other way (e.g., trade controls). Under floating rates, the price would rise to π_2 without government intervention. In the case of an adjustable peg, intervention would depend on whether the shift to F_2^d were

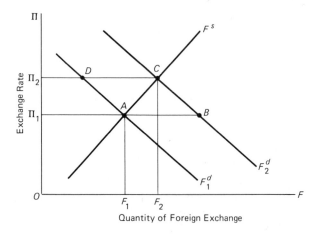

FIGURE 15-9   Government Intervention in the Foreign Exchange Market

considered by the government to be temporary or permanent (fundamental disequilibrium).

The rules for intervention are probably least clear under a managed float. Central bankers commonly state their objective to be "stabilizing the market" or avoiding "disorderly markets." Successful stabilization requires some forecasting ability, and whether stabilization efforts succeed remains an empirical question. One test of successful stabilization is whether the agency earns profits from its activities. Profits would be earned by buying when prices are low relative to the mean and selling when they are high relative to the mean and adding to demand when prices are low and adding to supply when they are high stabilized prices. From this perspective, one can judge the stabilization activities of central banks under the managed float since 1973.

An empirical study by Dean Taylor attempted to determine whether central bank intervention in the 1970s stabilized or destabilized the foreign exchange market.[2] He analyzed the foreign exchange intervention activities of the central banks of nine major countries including the United States. Since central banks employ accounting practices that tend to conceal foreign exchange losses, part of the study was simply fact-finding.

Taylor reported that in the 1970s the major banks suffered losses of $12 billion. These losses are large relative to the better publicized losses of state enterprises such as the British Steel Corporation or various national airlines. Whether these losses are large or small, random or systematic, they must be compared with some standard. Presumably the money was lost as a result of trading rules that central bankers designed to stabilize the market. The actual

---

[2] See Dean Taylor's paper, "Official Intervention in the Foreign Exchange Market, or Bet Against the Central Bank," *Journal of Political Economy*, April 1982. The losses by central banks may also cause problems for economic analysts. Government destabilization may give the appearance that private currency markets are inefficient processors of information when they are not.

behavior of banks was compared with the hypothetical losses that would have occurred if central banks had employed a random process to intervene in exchange markets. The actual losses were found to be larger than those that could have reasonably occurred by chance. Even though central banks intended to stabilize markets, they systematically seemed to destabilize them.

A possible explanation for the anomaly is that central banks tend to resist changes in equilibrium exchange rates. Foreign exchange demand and supply curves shift, but the authorities either do not perceive the shift or they interpret it as temporary. They buy or sell foreign reserves in an attempt to defend the initial rate. When they later realize that the equilibrium rate has changed, they reverse the initial transaction at the new exchange rate.

Central banks appear to respond to market changes with a lag. The situation can be shown in Figure 15-9. The initial equilibrium is at A with the exchange rate π_1. A shift of the foreign exchange demand curve from F_2^d to F_2^d is not perceived by the central bank. The bank attempts to defend exchange rate π_1 by selling AB of foreign exchange. Later, when bank officials realize that the equilibrium rate has increased to π_2, they buy foreign reserves (possibly to repay a loan). As a result of selling currency at low prices (π_1) and buying at higher prices (π_1), the bank loses money. Although the motives are different, such a policy is equivalent to the behavior of a poorly informed speculator. If this hypothesis is correct, currency exchange rates would be more stable under freely floating rates than under a managed float. The managed float remains a relatively new institution, and a full understanding of the effect of government intervention requires more experience and analysis.[3]

SUMMARY

The demand and supply of foreign exchange are determined by both monetary and real forces. The monetary forces include current money demand and supply as well as current expectations about future monetary magnitudes. These monetary variables will be studied in more detail in Chapter 19. The real determinants of the exchange rate are the demands and supplies of traded goods and services.

The demand for foreign exchange can be derived from the demand and supply of imports. Foreign exchange supply can be derived from the demand and supply of exports.

The foreign exchange market performs several economic functions. If the foreign exchange market clears, balanced trade for individual products and with individual countries is unnecessary. Several forms of arbitrage are carried out by market participants including spatial arbitrage, interest arbitrage, and tri-

---

[3] For other attempts to interpret the recent experience with managed floating, see the studies by Michael Mussa, *The Role of Official Intervention*, Occasional paper 6 (New York: Group of 30, 1981); and Victor Argy, *Exchange-Rate Management in Theory and Practice* (Princeton, N.J.: Princeton University Press, 1982).

angular arbitrage. Both the hedging and speculative functions are related to uncertainty about future exchange rates. Government agencies can play an important role in the foreign exchange market.

Exchange rate regimes can be defined in terms of the amount of government intervention. Under the two extreme systems of freely floating and permanently fixed rates, government policy is clearly defined. Under the two compromise systems, the adjustable peg and managed floating, there is uncertainty about when the government will intervene. A major empirical question is whether actual intervention has stabilized or destabilized currency markets.

REFERENCES

ARGY, VICTOR. *Exchange-Rate Management in Theory and Practice*, Princeton Studies in International Finance, Princeton, N.J.: No. 50. Princeton University Press, 1982. Empirical study of foreign exchange market intervention.

DORNBUSCH, RUDIGER. "Exchange Rates and Fiscal Policy in a Popular Model of International Trade." *American Economic Review*, December 1975. Analyzes the interaction between the foreign exchange market and the underlying monetary and fiscal policy.

HABERLER, GOTTFRIED. "The Market for Foreign Exchange and the Stability of the Balance of Payments: A Theoretical Analysis." *Kyklos* 1949. Reprinted in Richard N. Cooper, ed., *International Finance*, Baltimore: Penguin, 1969. Analysis stressing the effect of devaluation on the terms of trade and the balance of payments.

INTERNATIONAL MONETARY FUND. *Annual Report on Exchange Restrictions*, Washington, D.C., annually. Regular compilation of foreign exchange restrictions of member countries.

MACHLUP, FRITZ. "The Theory of Foreign Exchanges." *Economica*, 1939, 1940. Reprinted in Howard S. Ellis and Lloyd A. Metzler, eds., *Readings in the Theory of International Trade*. Homewood, Ill.: Richard D. Irwin, 1949. Classic analysis of the foreign exchange market.

MALKIEL, BURTON. *A Random Walk Down Wall Street*. New York: W. W. Norton, 1975. A popular discussion of the efficiency of financial markets stressing the stock market.

MUSSA, MICHAEL. *The Role of Official Intervention*, Occasional paper 6. New York: Group of 30, 1981. Survey of theoretical and empirical work on official intervention.

PICK, FRANZ. *Pick's Currency Yearbook*. New York: Pick Publishing Corporation, annually. Source of data on black market exchange rates.

QUIRK, PETER. "Exchange Rate Policy in Japan: Leaning Against the Wind." International Monetary Fund *Staff Papers*, No. 3 (1977). Empirical study of Japanese exchange market intervention policy.

STERN, ROBERT M. *The Balance of Payments*. Chicago: Aldine, 1973. Chapter 2 and its appendix presents an advanced analysis of the foreign exchange market.

TAYLOR, DEAN. "Official Intervention in the Foreign Exchange Market, or Bet Against the Central Bank." *Journal of Political Economy*, April 1982. Empirical study of the effectiveness of government intervention in foreign exchange markets.

CHAPTER SIXTEEN
BALANCE-OF-PAYMENTS
ACCOUNTS

16.1 INTRODUCTION

Much information about a country's international trade and investment is presented in balance-of-payments accounts. This chapter will present the basic characteristics of the accounts and relate them to the foreign exchange market. Because of the nature of the accounting framework, the balance of payments is always in balance when all transactions are included. Various partial balances will be presented, which differ according to which international transactions are omitted. The merchandise balance and the balance on current account are two of the better known partial balances.

The world balance of payments can be constructed as the sum of all the national balances. The balance of payments measures flows of trade and investment per period, which can be related to a nation's stock of net foreign assets. U.S. historical data will be used to illustrate the balance-of-payments concepts. The relationship between balance-of-payments deficits and the excess demand for foreign exchange will be considered. If deficits measure excess demand, they may be useful in forecasting exchange rates. The relationship between the money supply and the balance of payments will also be discussed.

The balance of payments of a nation is a systematic record of transactions between residents of the country and residents of the rest of the world. More specifically, it refers to the difference between receipts and payments during a given period. The term "balance of payments" entered the English literature during the mercantilist period. Because mercantilists associated a gold inflow with an increase in wealth, they described an excess of receipts over payments as a "favorable balance." The opposite case was described as an "unfavorable balance." Gradually the more neutral terms "surplus" and "deficit" were adopted. However, popular users continue to associate surpluses with national virtue and deficits with national vice.

All major governments regularly publish balance-of-payments data. The U.S. Department of Commerce publishes quarterly and annual data in the *Survey of Current Business*.[1] Data on merchandise trade come from the customs accounts, and customs records provide some of the earliest economic data. Excellent customs data are available for England for the fourteenth and fifteenth centuries.[2]

The balance of payments is intended to be a comprehensive statement of receipts and payments, but because of errors in measurement and reporting, some distortions occur. There are some random errors of measurement, but there are also systematic errors associated with illegal transactions. For example, it is widely believed that illegal drugs are a major U.S. import, but they do not appear as a payment in the official accounts. In spite of measurement error, the balance-of-payments accounts may be a useful source of economic data. In particular, they may provide evidence about the market for foreign exchange.

16.2 THE ACCOUNTING BALANCE

Since the accounts are based on double-entry bookkeeping, a credit and a debit must be entered for each transaction. It follows that the accounting balance (total receipts minus total payments) is necessarily equal to zero. This tautology is sometimes given the name "Cournot's law."[3]

As shown in Chapter 12, the accounting balance can be written as

$$B_A = (E_g - I_g) + (E_s - I_s) - T - K - \frac{dR}{dt} = 0$$

E_g and I_g are the values of exports and imports of goods (merchandise), E_s and I_s are exports and imports of services, and T refers to unrequited transfers from residents to foreigners. The term T includes both private gifts and official government aid. K measures the net capital outflow from the home country; alternatively, K can be interpreted as net lending to foreigners. Compensation

---

[1] The March issue of each year contains data for the previous calendar year.

[2] Annual data by port city, ship, and merchandise are available. See M. M. Postan, *Medieval Trade and Finance* (London: Cambridge University Press, 1973), Chap. 9.

[3] Augustin Cournot (1801–1877) was a French economist best known for his contribution to the theory of monopoly.

for foreign lending takes the form of net foreign assets. As discussed in Chapter 12, lending is classified as direct or portfolio depending on the form of the asset acquired. The term dR/dt is the change per period in the monetary reserves of the central bank.

The variables are defined so that the accounting balance necessarily adds up to zero. However, it is possible to construct various partial balances that do not sum to zero by omitting certain transactions. For example, it is possible to consider a surplus or deficit in the merchandise balance, which considers only the first two items in the equation. Because of measurement error, empirical balance-of-payments accounts rarely sum to zero. Logical consistency is preserved by adding a balancing item that the Department of Commerce calls "statistical discrepancy"[4] (formerly errors and omissions). The sum of the reported items and "statistical discrepancy" is zero in the reported accounts.

16.3 PARTIAL BALANCES

There is no single measure of the balance of payments. Any number of different partial balances may be constructed by assembling components of the accounting balance. It is possible to have a deficit in one partial balance and simultaneously experience a surplus in a different partial balance. For example, in recent years the United States has experienced deficits in the merchandise balance and surpluses in the current account.

Much confusion can be avoided by specifying what partial balance is being used. The U.S. government once designated an official measure of "the balance of payments," but that practice has been abandoned. Prior to 1965 the Commerce Department designated the net liquidity balance as the official measure. Following a recommendation of the Bernstein Committee, the official settlements balance was adopted as the official measure in June 1965. Major changes in the world monetary system, such as floating exchange rates, made the official settlements measure obsolete. Following the report of another ad hoc committee (the Advisory Committee on Presentation of Balance of Payments Statistics), the Commerce Department abandoned the concept of an official balance-of-payments measure in June 1976.[5]

The current practice of the Commerce Department is to present in the *Survey of Current Business* all the data that are necessary to compute any of the partial balances. Since different partial balances often show different results,

[4] The 1982 statistical discrepancy for the United States was + $41.9 billion. Commerce Department officials have attributed most of the discrepancy to unreported capital inflows. The reported merchandise balance for 1982 was − $36.3 billion. See *Survey of Current Business*, March 1983.

[5] See the June 1976 *Survey of Current Business* for a discussion of the current presentation. The issues considered by the Advisory Committee are discussed by Robert Stern et al., *The Presentation of the U.S. Balance of Payments: A Symposium*, Princeton Studies in International Finance, No. 123 (Princeton, N.J.: Princeton University Press, August 1977).

the department has adopted a position of neutrality concerning which measure is most relevant to policy questions. The following partial balances are most frequently employed.

Merchandise Balance

$$B_g = E_g - I_g$$

The most frequently cited partial balance is the merchandise balance (B_g), which is also called the balance of trade.[6] A surplus in the merchandise balance has been an important policy goal of traditional and modern mercantilists. Merchandise trade includes all goods that pass through customs, and data are available on a monthly basis. The merchandise balance is sometimes mistakenly interpreted to be a kind of national profit or loss measure. Following a misleading analogy with a firm's income statement, a deficit in merchandise trade is sometimes interpreted as national loss ("red ink"). The analogy is misleading because of the significant differences between business firms and countries, which will be discussed in Section 16.9

The method of valuing goods is relevant to the measurement of the merchandise balance. The value of imported goods will be smaller if they are measured f.o.b. or f.a.s. (free alongside ship) rather than c.i.f. In this case, the cost of transport and insurance will appear as a service import rather than as a merchandise import. In 1980 the United States changed the valuation of imports from the f.a.s. method to the c.i.f. method. However, exports continue to be valued f.a.s. This change in the method of valuing imports is an example of a change that increases merchandise imports and decreases service imports without changing the value of total imports of goods and services. The U.S. merchandise balance showed a surplus every year from 1894 to 1970. However, since 1977 (see Table 16-1) there have been regular annual deficits of approximately $30 billion per year.

Balance on Goods and Services

$$B_{gs} = (E_g - I_g) + (E_s - I_s)$$

The balance on goods and services simply adds service trade to the merchandise balance. There is no justification for excluding service trade from a measure of international transactions. Services add to GNP in the same way

---

[6] Because the accounting balance must equal zero, an equivalent measure of the merchandise balance is

$$B_g = -(E^s - I^s) + T + K + \frac{dR}{dt}$$

**TABLE 16-1 U.S. Current Account Transactions, 1970–1982
(in billions of dollars)**

YEAR	MERCHANDISE BALANCE (B_g)	SERVICE BALANCE (B_s)	NET INVESTMENT INCOME	UNILATERAL TRANSFERS (T)	CURRENT ACCOUNT BALANCE (B_{ca})
1970	$ 2.6	$ 3.0	$ 6.2	$ -3.3	$ 2.3
1971	-2.3	4.5	7.3	-3.7	-1.4
1972	-6.4	4.5	8.2	-3.9	-5.8
1973	0.9	10.1	12.2	-3.9	7.1
1974	-5.3	14.7	15.5	-7.2	2.1
1975	9.0	13.8	12.8	-4.6	18.3
1976	-9.3	18.7	16.0	-5.0	4.4
1977	-30.8	21.4	18.0	-4.6	-14.1
1978	-33.8	24.8	21.4	-5.1	-14.1
1979	-27.3	34.4	33.5	-5.6	1.4
1980	-25.3	36.1	32.8	-7.1	3.7
1981	-27.8	41.2	36.8	-6.8	6.6
1982	-36.3	+36.0	+28.7	-7.9	-8.1

Source: U.S. Department of Commerce, Survey of Current Business, November 1982, p. 30.

that goods do. Service imports add to foreign exchange demand and service exports add to foreign exchange supply in the same way that goods do. Service trade is important for the United States, and in recent years it has shown an increasing surplus.

Table 16-1 shows a $41.2 billion surplus in service trade in 1981, most of which is investment income. Thus, the merchandise balance and the service balance have tended to offset each other in recent years. Large merchandise deficits have been offset by larger service surpluses. The result has been small surpluses in the balance on goods and services. The more narrowly one defines a partial balance, the more it tells about a country's comparative advantage in a particular product, and the less it tells about total trade for the country. A merchandise deficit combined with service surplus may reflect a comparative disadvantage in producing goods and a comparative advantage in service trade.

The main internationally traded services are transportation, tourism, royalties and licenses, and income from foreign investment. Income from royalties and licenses represents a return on earlier expenditures on research and development. Investment income is a return on exports of capital services, which is an alternative to exporting capital-intensive products. Labor income of people working temporarily abroad (not emigrants) is a service export. It is a major source of income for countries such as Egypt, Yugoslavia, and Mexico.

Because of international mobility of capital and labor, it is necessary to distinguish between gross national product (GNP) and gross domestic product

(GDP). GNP is the total income of all factor owners permanently residing in a country, including their income from foreign activities. GDP is the total value of goods and services produced within the borders of a country, regardless of whether factors producing the income are owned by permanent residents or foreigners. Thus, the difference between GNP and GDP is net factor income from abroad (FA):

$$GNP - GDP = FA$$

Factor income from abroad includes both investment income and labor income from abroad, which appear as exports of services (E^s) in the balance-of-payments accounts. Because the United States is a net capital exporter, the ratio of GNP to GDP in 1980 was 1.02. For Canada, which is a net capital importer, the same ratio was 0.97 in 1980. The ratios of GNP to GDP changed substantially for specialized oil exporters between 1973 and 1980. Consider the cases of Saudi Arabia and Kuwait:

	1973	1980
Saudi Arabia	0.74	1.01
Kuwait	0.76	1.03

In 1973 GNP was approximately 75 percent of GDP in both countries. By 1980 income from investment abroad was so large that GNP exceeded GDP in both countries. For the world as a whole the two income measures must be equal. In the national income accounts, the item "net exports" is measured by the balance on goods and services.

Gross national product (Y) is defined as the value of all goods and services produced by residents of a country in a given period:

$$Y = C + I_n + G + E_{gs} - I_{gs}$$

C, I_n, and G are total spending per period on consumption and investment goods by private agents and the government. They include spending on both domestically produced goods and imports. Imports (I_{gs}) are not part of GNP, and double-counting is avoided by subtracting them explicitly. Since exports (E_{gs}) are produced at home, they are part of GNP, and they are added explicitly. Thus, GNP can be thought of as the value of production or income of domestic residents per period. Because of lending and gifts, it is possible for total expenditure of residents to differ from total income.

Gross national expenditure, sometimes called total absorption, is defined as

$$E = C + I_n + G$$

It is total spending by residents on all goods, regardless of their origin.

It follows that the balance on goods and services is the difference between gross national product and gross national expenditure:[7]

$$Y - E = (C + I_n + G + E_{gs} - I_{gs}) - (C + I_n + G)$$
$$= E_{gs} - I_{gs} = B_{gs}$$

Reducing a deficit in the goods and services balance requires reducing total spending relative to total income. The absorption approach to balance-of-payments analysis begins with this identity from the national income accounts.

Balance on Current Account

$$B_{ca} = (E_g - I_g) + (E_s - I_s) - T$$

The balance on current account equals the goods and services balance minus transfers. It measures net lending by residents. The excess of receipts for exports over payments for imports and gifts is equal to the increase in financial assets. Because it measures the increase in private and government claims against the rest of the world, the current account balance is sometimes called the net worth balance.

A current account deficit means that residents are borrowing from the rest of the world. Whether a current account deficit is harmful or beneficial to a country depends on the benefits of borrowing relative to the costs. One cannot say in general that deficits are always harmful or always beneficial. In the United States, the current account was usually in deficit before 1874 and usually in surplus from then until 1970. Even though Americans were net borrowers in the first period and net lenders in the second period, there is no significant difference between economic growth rates in the two periods.

Monetary Reserve Balance

$$B_R = (X_g - I_g) + (X_s - I_s) - T - K$$

The monetary reserve balance (also called the overall balance) is simply the change in monetary reserves per period. Because the accounting balance

---

[7] There are three equivalent ways of expressing the balance on goods and services:

a. $B_{gs} = E_{gs} - I_{gs} = K + T + \dfrac{dR}{dt}$

b. The difference between gross national product and gross national expenditure:

$B_{gs} = Y - (C + I_n - G)$

c. The difference between domestic saving and domestic investment:

$B_{gs} = (S_{pd} + S_g) - I_{pd}$

where S_{pd} and S_g are private domestic saving and government saving, respectively. I_{pd} is private domestic investment.

must be satisfied, an equivalent expression for the monetary reserve balance is the difference between present period reserves and previous period reserves. The monetary reserve stock at any time is simply the sum of the reserve balances in all previous periods:

$$R_t = B_{R,t-1} + B_{R,t-2} + \cdots + B_{R,t-m}$$

where m represents the number of previous periods in which reserves were reported. The reserve balance is important because it provides a link between the foreign exchange market and the domestic money supply.

The stock of foreign reserves (R) is a component of the monetary base:

$$R + D = M_b$$

R and D are the foreign and domestic components, respectively, of the central bank's assets. The monetary base in the United States is total currency plus member bank deposits at Federal Reserve banks. The monetary base is the primary determinant of the domestic money supply.

Changes in monetary reserves change the monetary base and the money supply:

$$\frac{dR}{dt} + \frac{dD}{dt} = \frac{dM_b}{dt}$$

Thus, the monetary reserve balance indicates the effect of international transactions on the domestic money supply:

$$B_R + \frac{dD}{dt} = \frac{dM_b}{dt}$$

For example, a \$1 billion current account deficit accompanied by a \$1 billion capital inflow will not affect monetary reserves or the monetary base:

$$B_R = B_{ca} - T - K = \frac{dR}{dt}$$
$$0 = -1 - (0) - (-1) = 0$$

However, the same current account deficit without the capital flow will lead to a loss of reserves and a \$1 billion decrease in the monetary base.

In analyzing the effect of a balance-of-payments deficit on the money supply, the appropriate partial balance is the monetary reserve balance. A deficit in the monetary reserve balance will be associated with a decrease in the monetary base. However, deficits in other balance-of-payments measures (e.g., merchandise balance or current account) are not necessarily associated with monetary contraction. In particular, deficits in the merchandise balance of the

United States since 1977 have not been associated with decreases in the money supply. Whether balance-of-payments deficits alter the money supply depends on the amount of government intervention in the foreign exchange market. Under the managed float, intervention has been frequent. The same relationship also applies to payments surpluses.

Other partial balances that have been used in the past are the basic balance, net liquidity balance, and the official settlements balance. They all modify the balance on current account by including some capital flows but not others. The basic balance distinguishes between long-term and short-term capital. Net liquidity distinguishes between liquid and illiquid assets. The official settlements balance, also known as the balance on official reserve transactions, distinguishes between private and government capital flows.[8] Its formal definition is

$$B_{os} = \frac{dR}{dt} - \frac{dF_g}{dt}$$

The official settlements surplus of the home country is equal to the increase in home reserves minus the increase in home country liquid liabilities to foreign governments (F_g). This balance has relevance only to countries whose money is used as a reserve currency. For all other countries, F_g and dF_g/dt are zero, and the official settlements balance is equivalent to the monetary reserve balance. The empirical relevance of B_{os} is limited to the United States and, to a lesser extent, the United Kingdom and Germany. Prior to 1976, U.S. officials interpreted the B_{os} deficit as a measure of the increase in potential claims on U.S. reserves.

16.4 THE WORLD
BALANCE OF PAYMENTS

For a single country, the accounting balance necessarily adds up to zero, but partial balances (e.g., current account) do not. For the world as a whole, the accounting balance is zero, and each partial balance must be zero when summed over all countries. Thus, the world merchandise balance (B_g^w) and the world current account (B_{ca}^w) must add up to zero:

$$B_g^w = B_g^1 + B_g^2 + \cdots + B_g^n = 0$$
$$B_{ca}^w = B_{ca}^1 + B_{ca}^2 + \cdots + B_{ca}^n = 0$$

The superscripts refer to countries, and a term such as B_g^2 refers to the merchandise balance of country 2.

[8] For more details on payments concepts, see Charles Kindleberger's paper, "Measuring Equilibrium in the Balance of Payments," *Journal of Political Economy*, November 1969.

An implication of this "adding up" property is that one country's deficit is another country's surplus. Since the world remains a closed economy, it is logically impossible for the world as a whole to experience a deficit or a surplus. While theoretical world balances must sum to zero, the actual published balances rarely do. For example, the International Monetary Fund reported that the world experienced a current account deficit of $14 billion in 1980.[9] The discrepancies are due to faulty reporting and inconsistent accounting practices between countries. For example, if country A reports its imports from country B using c.i.f. value (including transport cost and insurance), and country B reports its exports to A using f.o.b. value (excluding transport and insurance), world merchandise imports will not equal world merchandise exports. In this case, the inconsistent accounting practices will result in a reported merchandise deficit for the world. Prior to 1980 the United States reported both exports and imports using f.a.s. value, but imports are now valued by the c.i.f. method.

In contrast to the other partial balances, the world monetary reserve balance is not equal to zero. Instead, it is equal to the net increase in world monetary reserves:

$$B_R^w = B_R^1 + B_R^2 + \cdots + B_R^n = \frac{dR^w}{dt}$$

The asymmetry is a result of the conventional practice of excluding monetary authorities from the accounting system. If monetary authorities were included, their deficit would equal the increase in world reserves. As reported by the International Monetary Fund, there are three sources of monetary reserves: (1) gold (R_G); (2) IMF money, which consists of special drawing rights and reserve positions in the fund (R_S); and (3) foreign exchange, which consists of mostly dollars (R_F). The dollar value of world reserves at any time can be expressed as

$$R^w = R_G + R_S + R_F$$

The world monetary reserve balance in a given year is equal to the increase in the value of monetary gold plus the increase in the value of IMF money plus the increase in the value of foreign exchange held by central banks:

$$B_R^w = \frac{dR^w}{dt} = \frac{dR_G^w}{dt} + \frac{dR_S^w}{dt} + \frac{dR_F^w}{dt}$$

Notice that the world reserve balance depends on changes in the value of reserves, which can change because of a change in the quantities of gold, SDRs,

[9] In its *1981 Annual Report* (p. 20), the Fund reported that the current account deficits of industrial countries ($44.1 billion) and less developed countries ($82.1 billion) exceeded the surpluses of oil exporters ($112.2 billion) by $14.0 billion.

and foreign exchange or because of a change in prices of these assets. For example, the physical gold stock has not changed much in the last 10 years, but the price has fluctuated substantially. In 1971 the official gold price was $35 per ounce. It increased sharply and reached a peak of near $900 in 1980. By the end of 1981, the gold price had fallen to near $300.

Notice that foreign exchange reserves are defined as *gross* rather than net reserves. For example, if the German central bank acquires dollars and the U.S. central bank acquires marks, the additional liabilities of each bank are not subtracted from their additional assets. If foreign exchange reserves were defined net of a nation's liabilities to foreigners, world foreign currency reserves would be zero, and the change in those reserves would also be zero. Because of Eurodollars and other external currencies, reported net foreign exchange reserves may not be zero. Some central banks hold Eurodollar deposits that are an asset to the holder, but they will not be reported as a liability of the United States or any other country.

16.5 BALANCE
ON CURRENT ACCOUNT
AND NET FOREIGN ASSETS

All the partial balances measure flows of receipts and expenditures per unit time. The balance on current account measures the flow of net lending by residents per period. Flow measures can be interpreted as changes in stocks during the same period. The current account balance can be interpreted as the change in net foreign assets held by residents.

Define net foreign assets of the home country (N) as the difference between claims against foreigners (A_f) and liabilities to foreigners (L_f):

$$N = A_f - L_f$$

The current account balance can be expressed as

$$B_{ca} = K + \frac{dR}{dt} = \frac{dN}{dt} = \frac{dA_f}{dt} - \frac{dL_f}{dt}$$

Thus, a country with a current account surplus is necessarily increasing its net foreign assets.

This general relationship was discussed in Chapter 12. It was shown there that the published B_{ca} is not exactly equal to $K + dR/dt$ because of statistical discrepancies and valuation adjustment. Table 12-4 shows the empirical relationships for 1976 to 1980, and it is reproduced as Table 16-2. When the variables are accurately measured, the balance on current account should be exactly equal to the change in net foreign assets. Unfortunately, the statistical discrepancy has been substantial in certain years, particularly in 1979 ($+$\$21.1

TABLE 16-2   Changes in Net Foreign Assets and Balance on Current Account, 1976–1980

$$d(NIIP) = B_{ca} + SDR + STAT + VAL = (K + \frac{dR}{dt}) + VAL$$

(in billions of dollars)

YEAR	d(NIIP)		B_{ca}	SDR	STAT	VAL		$K + \frac{dR}{dt}$	VAL
1976	+9.5	=	+4.4	0	+10.4	−5.3	=	+14.8	−5.3
1977	−12.5	=	−14.1	0	−2.3	+4.0	=	−16.4	+4.0
1978	+6.2	=	−14.1	0	+11.4	+8.8	=	−2.7	+8.8
1979	+17.6	=	+1.4	+1.1	+21.1	−6.1	=	+23.7	−6.1
1980	+27.7	=	+3.7	+1.2	+29.6	−6.9	=	+34.5	−6.9

NIIP = net international investment position; SDR = new allocation of special drawing rights; STAT = statistical discrepancy; VAL = valuation adjustment.

Source: U.S. Department of Commerce, Survey of Current Business, August 1981, p. 53.

billion) and 1980 (+$29.6 billion). In four of the five years, the current account and net foreign assets moved in the same direction, but in 1978 they moved in opposite directions. Because of a statistical discrepancy and valuation adjustment of +$20.2 billion, net foreign assets rose by $6.2 billion whereas the current account showed a deficit of $14.1 billion.

The stock of net foreign assets of the United States is shown in Table 16-3, which is a reproduction of Table 12-1. In 1981 claims of Americans against foreigners were $717.4 billion and foreign claims against U.S. residents were $557.1 billion. Net foreign assets in 1981 were $160.3 billion. This figure can be contrasted to the 1914 figure of −$4 billion. Net foreign assets are also called net international investment position. The current account balance is the change in net foreign assets:

$$B_{ca,t} = \frac{dN}{dt} = N_t - N_{t-1}$$

Net foreign assets at time t are equal to net assets in the previous period plus the current account balance in period t:

$$N_t = N_{t-1} + B_{ca,t}$$

Since N_{t-1} and N in all earlier periods can be expressed as the sum of the current B_{ca} and the previous period's N, the general relationship between net foreign assets and the current account is

$$N_t = B_{ca,t} + B_{ca,t-1} + B_{ca,t-2} + \cdots + B_{ca,t-m}$$

Net foreign assets at time t can be interpreted as the sum of all previous current account surpluses. The equation shows current assets of one country

TABLE 16-3   International Investment Position of the United States, 1977–1981 (in billions of dollars)

	1977	1978	1979	1980	1981
Net international investment					
position of United States	$ 72.9	76.2	94.9	121.6	160.3
U.S. assets abroad	379.1	447.9	510.6	606.9	717.4
U.S. official reserve assets	19.3	18.7	19.0	26.8	30.1
Gold	11.7	11.7	11.2	11.2	11.2
SDRs	2.6	1.6	2.7	2.6	4.1
Reserve position IMF	5.0	1.0	1.3	2.9	5.1
Foreign currency	0	4.4	3.8	10.1	9.8
Direct investment	146.0	162.7	187.9	215.6	227.3
Percentage of assets	39%	36%	37%	36%	32%
Foreign assets in United States	306.2	371.6	415.7	485.3	557.1
Foreign official assets	140.8	173.0	160.0	175.8	180.1
Percentage of assets	46%	47%	38%	36%	32%
Direct investment	34.6	42.5	54.5	68.4	89.8
Percentage of assets	11%	11%	13%	14%	16%

Source: U.S. Department of Commerce, Survey of Current Business, August 1982, p. 53.

as a function of its historical accumulation. There is also a restriction on net foreign assets of all countries at a point in time. Since there must be a debtor for each creditor, net foreign assets for the world as a whole must be zero. Thus, in 1981 the net foreign assets of the world excluding the United States were − $160.3 billion.

16.6 TERMS OF TRADE AND THE GROSS NATIONAL PRODUCT

The balance on goods and services is a component of gross national product. GNP (Y) can be expressed as

$$Y = C + I_n + G + V_E - V_I$$

The components of GNP are the money values of consumption, investment, government expenditure, exports, and imports, respectively. The term $V_E - V_I$ is called net exports, and it is measured by the balance on goods and services. Real GNP is equal to money GNP divided by an appropriate price index. In computing real GNP, the Department of Commerce obtains real net exports by dividing the value of exports and the value of imports by separate price indices. Thus, in the national income accounts of the United States, the real net exports are

$$\frac{V_E}{P_E} - \frac{V_I}{P_I} = \frac{P_E E}{P_E} - \frac{P_I I}{P_I} = E - I$$

Because of this procedure, real exports and real GNP are not affected by changes in the terms of trade. Since P_E and P_I enter both numerator and denominator, changes in these prices cannot affect measured real GNP. This is a shortcoming of the procedure, because an increase in import prices (given P_E) reduces the command over real goods and services of domestic residents. In fact a decline in the terms of trade has been a major problem for the United States in recent years. The behavior of the U.S. terms of trade is shown in column 6 of Table 16-4 for the period 1960 to 1980. The terms of trade declined continuously from 106.4 in 1969 (1972 = 100) to 72.7 in 1980, largely because of oil price increases. The diminished command over real goods and services of the average American is not fully reflected in the official GNP figures.

Edward Denison has proposed revising the GNP series to incorporate the

TABLE 16-4   Terms of Trade, Net Exports, and Real GNP, 1960–1980 (in billions of dollars, 1972 = 100)

YEAR	REAL EXPORTS GNP	REAL IMPORTS GNP	NET IMPORTS GNP	COMMAND	TERMS OF TRADE	RATIO OF GNP TO COMMAND GNP
1960	$ 38.4	$ 30.7	$ 7.7	$ 7.2	98.8	0.9993
1961	39.3	30.9	8.5	8.8	100.8	1.0044
1962	41.8	34.3	7.5	8.6	102.4	1.0013
1963	44.8	35.4	9.4	10.1	101.5	1.0008
1964	50.3	37.5	12.8	13.1	100.5	1.0003
1965	51.7	41.6	10.1	11.3	102.2	1.0012
1966	54.4	47.9	6.5	8.2	103.1	1.0018
1967	56.7	51.3	5.4	7.9	104.5	1.0025
1968	61.2	59.3	1.9	5.2	105.4	1.0032
1969	65.0	64.1	0.9	5.0	106.4	1.0038
1970	70.5	66.6	3.9	7.5	105.2	1.0033
1971	71.0	69.3	1.6	4.4	104.0	1.0025
1972	77.5	76.7	0.7	0.7	100.0	1.0000
1973	97.3	81.8	15.5	12.2	96.6	0.9973
1974	108.5	80.7	27.8	8.1	81.8	0.9842
1975	103.6	71.4	32.2	14.9	83.3	0.9860
1976	110.1	84.7	25.4	7.4	83.7	0.9862
1977	113.2	91.3	21.9	−2.1	78.8	0.9825
1978	127.5	103.0	24.6	−0.3	80.6	0.9827
1979	146.9	109.2	37.7	5.5	78.0	0.9782
1980	161.1	109.1	52.0	8.0	72.7	0.9703

Source: U.S. Department of Commerce, *Survey of Current Business*, May 1981, p. 20.

terms of trade effect.[10] The official and revised figures (shown as "Command") for net exports are shown in Table 16-4. For example, the official real net exports were $52.0 billion in 1980 ($= 161.1 - 109.1$). This figure was obtained by dividing nominal exports by export prices and nominal imports by import prices. Denison proposes to incorporate the terms of trade effect by dividing both exports and imports by import prices:

$$\frac{V_E - V_I}{P_I} = \frac{P_E E}{P_I} - \frac{P_I I}{P_I} = (\frac{P_E}{P_I})E - I$$

The term in parentheses P_E/P_I is the terms of trade effect, and an increase in P_I will reduce real net exports and real GNP. The magnitude of the terms of trade adjustment is substantial for recent years. For example, the official net exports were $52.0 billion in 1980, but after the adjustment, they were only $8.0 billion. Thus, real GNP adjusted for command over goods and services was $44.0 billion less than official GNP. For the entire period 1969 to 1980, the annual growth rate for official real GNP was 2.84 percent, and the adjusted growth rate was 2.53 percent. Denison computed the two real GNP series for the entire period 1929 to 1980, but discrepancies were important only since 1969.

16.7 THE BALANCE
OF PAYMENTS
OF THE UNITED STATES

Balance-of-payments data for the United States for the postwar years are presented in Table 16-5. The merchandise balance was in surplus every year until 1971. The sizable deficits that have occurred since 1977 have been the subject of much discussion. When a longer time period is considered, the recent merchandise deficits are even more striking. For the period 1894 to 1970, the United States had a merchandise surplus every year. One explanation of the change from surplus to deficit attributes the deficits to macroeconomic policy, whereas an alternative explanation attributes them to a fundamental change in comparative advantage.

The current account, which includes service trade and transfers, has been more variable than has the merchandise balance been. In several years the merchandise balance and the current account have had opposite signs. In the last six years given, the merchandise balance has shown large deficits, but the current account has shown surpluses in four of those six years. The differences between the two partial balances are shown in Table 16-1.

Service trade and unilateral transfers are included in the current account but not in the merchandise balance. Transfers have been in the neighborhood

[10] Edward Denison, "International Transactions in Measures of the Nation's Production," *Survey of Current Business*, May 1981.

TABLE 16-5   U.S. Merchandise Balance and Current Account, 1946–1982
(in billions of dollars)

YEAR	MERCHANDISE BALANCE	CURRENT ACCOUNT	YEAR	MERCHANDISE BALANCE	CURRENT ACCOUNT
1946	$ 6.7	$ 4.9	1965	$ 5.0	$ 5.4
1947	10.1	9.0	1966	3.8	3.1
1948	5.7	2.4	1967	3.8	2.6
1949	5.3	0.8	1968	0.6	0.6
1950	1.1	−1.8	1969	0.6	0.4
1951	3.1	0.8	1970	2.6	2.3
1952	2.6	0.6	1971	−2.3	−1.4
1953	1.4	−1.3	1972	−6.4	−5.8
1954	2.6	0.2	1973	0.9	7.1
1955	2.9	0.4	1974	−5.3	2.1
1956	4.8	2.7	1975	9.0	18.3
1957	6.3	4.8	1976	−9.3	4.4
1958	3.5	0.8	1977	−30.9	−14.1
1959	1.1	−1.3	1978	−33.8	14.3
1960	4.9	2.8	1979	−29.5	−0.8
1961	5.6	3.8	1980	−25.3	3.7
1962	4.5	3.4	1981	−27.8	6.6
1963	5.2	4.4	1982	−36.3	−8.1
1964	6.8	6.8			

Source: Council of Economic Advisers, *Economic Report of the President, 1981;* and U.S. Department of Commerce, *Survey of Current Business,* March 1983, p. 53.

of $5 billion to $7 billion in the last six years. However, the surplus on service trade has increased from $3.0 billion in 1970, to $18.7 billion in 1976, and to $41.2 billion in 1982. Thus, the divergent behavior of the merchandise and current account balances can be explained by the differences between merchandise and service trade.

The major component of service exports is investment income, which rose from $6.2 billion in 1970 to $16.0 billion in 1976 to $36.8 billion in 1982. A major share of investment income comes from direct investment in petroleum. Table 16-6 shows that income from direct investment was $36.8 billion in 1980 and that 35 percent of it came from petroleum.

Thus, the high oil prices since 1973 affected the United States in two different ways. By increasing the value of oil imports, higher oil prices increased the merchandise deficit. At the same time the higher prices also increased the earnings of American oil companies abroad, which increased the value of investment income and service exports. Thus, oil price changes altered the composition of the current account between merchandise and services, but it may not have had a large effect on the current account balance.

Table 16-7 shows the components of U.S. service trade in 1970 and 1980.

TABLE 16-6   U.S. Direct Investment Income Receipts, 1970–1980
(in billions of dollars)

YEAR	INVEST- MENT INCOME	DIRECT INVEST- MENT	SHARE OF PETROLEUM	SHARE OF MANUFAC- TURING	SHARE WESTERN EUROPE	SHARE LATIN AMERICA
1970	$11.7	$ 8.2	30%	38%	29%	17%
1971	12.7	9.2	31	38	30	16
1972	14.8	10.9	28	43	33	14
1973	21.8	16.5	35	40	35	15
1974	27.6	19.2	36	35	30	16
1975	25.4	16.6	29	36	30	19
1976	29.3	19.0	27	38	32	18
1977	32.2	19.7	27	34	37	19
1978	43.3	25.5	24	39	41	19
1979	66.7	38.3	35	34	45	17
1980	75.9	36.8	35	31	44	19

Source: U.S. Department of Commerce, Survey of Current Business, November 1981, p. 42.

Most items were stable over the decade. The major changes were an increase in net royalties from $2.2 billion to $6.1 billion and a major increase in net investment income from $6.2 billion to $32.7 billion. From a long-run perspective, the merchandise balance moved to deficit in the 1970s, the service balance moved to a large surplus in the 1970s, but the current account is not significantly different from that in the past.

There has been an attempt to identify stages in the historical development of the balance of payments of the United States. Similar stages have been identified for the United Kingdom, and it has been suggested that all countries

TABLE 16-7   U.S. Service Transactions, 1970 and 1980
(in billions of dollars)

	1970			1980		
	EXPORTS	IMPORTS	NET	EXPORTS	IMPORTS	NET
U.S. government transactions	$ 1.8	$ 5.6	$ -3.8	$ 8.6	$12.5	$ -3.9
Travel	2.3	4.0	-1.7	10.1	10.4	-0.3
Passenger fares	0.5	1.2	-0.7	2.6	3.6	-1.0
Transportation	3.1	2.8	0.3	11.4	10.9	0.5
Royalties and fees	2.3	0.2	2.2	6.9	0.8	6.1
Miscellaneous	1.3	0.8	0.5	5.2	3.2	2.0
Investment income	11.7	5.5	6.2	75.9	43.2	32.7
Total	$23.0	$20.1	$ 3.0	$120.7	$84.6	$ 36.1

Source: U.S. Department of Commerce, Survey of Current Business, November 1981, p. 31.

will pass through the same stages.[11] The general idea is that at low levels of per capita income, countries will be debtors and, at higher income levels, they will be creditors. The concept of stages implies current account deficits at low-income and current account surpluses at high-income levels.

Investment income is a component of service trade that alters the current account. In the initial balance-of-payments stage, income is low, and the merchandise trade and the current account show deficits. Borrowing to finance the deficits makes the country a debtor. As income rises, the merchandise balance turns to a surplus. Interest payments on previous debt (negative investment income) offset the merchandise deficit, so that the current account is in balance. In the third stage, the country continues to have a merchandise surplus, but it also becomes a net lender. Surpluses in both merchandise and services imply a current account surplus. In the fourth stage, the merchandise balance turns to deficit. Service trade remains in surplus because of investment income and the current account is in approximate balance. The stages can be briefly summarized:

Stage	B_g	B_s	B_{ca}
1	−	−	−
2	+	−	0
3	+	+	+
4	−	+	0

The stages are roughly consistent with U.S. balance-of-payments history. Recent U.S. experience is consistent with stage 4. The stages are also consistent with British economic history. However, there is no strong empirical support for the stages idea from other countries. A fundamental weakness of the idea is that it does not provide an economic explanation of why countries should move from one stage to another. Another problem is that countries must be distributed among the various stages so as to satisfy the condition that the world current account balance be zero. If all countries were in the same stage, creditors could not be matched with debtors.

A detailed presentation of the U.S. balance of payments for 1980 and 1981 is shown in Table 16-8. It contains the major components already discussed, and it provides much more detail about transactions. Balance-of-payments data for the United States appear quarterly in the *Survey of Current Business*. The major subdivisions are exports of goods and services (line 1), imports of goods and services (line 17), unilateral transfers (line 33), U.S. assets abroad (line 37), foreign assets in the United States (line 56), and statistical discrepancy (line 75). The difference between U.S. assets abroad and foreign assets in the United States is the net capital outflow, $K + dR/dt$. The data presented in Table 16-8 for 1981 can be arranged in terms of the accounting balance:

---

[11] A paper by Nadav Halevi discusses the stages in more detail and provides an empirical analysis; see his "An Empirical Test of the Balance of Payments Stages Hypothesis," *Journal of International Economics*, February 1971.

TABLE 16-8   U.S. International Transactions, 1981–1982
(millions of dollars)

LINE	(CREDITS; DEBITS)	1981	1982
1	Exports of goods and services	372,892	350,088
2	Merchandise, adjusted, excluding military	236,254	211,013
3	Transfers under U.S. military agency sales contracts	9,747	12,615
4	Travel	12,168	11,392
5	Passenger fares	2,991	2,980
6	Other transportation	12,168	11,994
7	Fees and royalties from affiliated foreigners	5,867	5,596
8	Fees and royalties from unaffiliated foreigners	1,386	1,510
9	Other private services	5,940	6,651
10	U.S. government miscellaneous services	426	436
	Receipts of income on U.S. assets abroad:		
11	Direct investment	31,873	23,657
12	Interest, dividends, and earnings of unincorporated affiliates	18,894	16,611
13	Reinvested earnings of incorporated affiliates	12,978	7,046
14	Other private receipts	50,407	58,112
15	U.S. government receipts	3,665	4,132
16	Transfers of goods and services under U.S. military grant programs, net	602	514
17	Imports of goods and services	−361,813	−350,313
18	Merchandise, adjusted, excluding military	−264,143	−247,344
19	Direct defense expenditures	−11,288	−11,975
20	Travel	−11,460	−12,347
21	Passenger fares	−4,487	−4,772
22	Other transportation	−11,611	−10,580
23	Fees and royalties to affiliated foreigners	−429	−25
24	Fees and royalties to unaffiliated foreigners	−264	−274
25	Private payments for other services	−3,294	−3,533
26	U.S. government payments for miscellaneous services	−1,930	−2,282
	Payments of income on foreign assets in the United States:		
27	Direct investment	−7,808	−5,602
28	Interest, dividends, and earnings of unincorporated affiliates	−3,708	−4,502
29	Reinvested earnings of incorporated affiliates	−4,099	−1,100
30	Other private payments	−28,352	−33,622
31	U.S. government payments	−16,748	−17,957
32	U.S. military grants of goods and services, net	−602	−514
33	Unilateral transfers (excluding military grants of goods and services), net	−6,608	−7,868
34	U.S. government grants (excluding military grants of goods and services)	−4,504	−5,413
35	U.S. government pensions and other transfers	−1,459	−1,484
36	Private remittances and other transfers	−645	−971
37	U.S. assets abroad, net (increase/capital outflow (−))	−109,294	−118,265
38	U.S. official reserve assets, net	−5,175	−4,965
39	Gold	(*)	—
40	Special drawing rights	−1,824	−1,371
41	Reserve position in the International Monetary Fund	−2,491	−2,552
42	Foreign currencies	−861	−1,041

TABLE 16-8   U.S. International Transactions, 1981–1982
(millions of dollars)

LINE	(CREDITS; DEBITS)	1981	1982
43	U.S. government assets, other than official reserve assets, net	−5,137	−5,766
44	U.S. loans and other long-term assets	−9,710	−10,123
45	Repayments on U.S. loans	4,370	4,326
46	U.S. foreign currency holdings and U.S. short-term assets, net	204	32
47	U.S. private assets, net	−98,982	−107,535
48	Direct investment	−8,691	2,198
49	Equity and intercompany accounts	4,287	9,244
50	Reinvested earnings of incorporated affiliates	−12,978	−7,046
51	Foreign securities	−5,429	−7,772
	U.S. claims on unaffiliated foreigners reported by U.S. nonbanking concerns:		
52	Long-term		
53	Short-term	−331	n.a.
	U.S. claims reported by U.S. banks, not included elsewhere:		
54	Long term		
55	Short-term	−84,531	−106,711
56	Foreign assets in the United States, net (increase/capital inflow (+))	77,921	84,494
57	Foreign official assets in the United States, net	4,785	3,043
58	U.S. government securities	6,272	5,046
59	U.S. Treasury securities	4,983	5,716
60	Other	1,289	−670
61	Other U.S. government liabilities	−69	−12
62	U.S. liabilities reported by U.S. banks, not included elsewhere	−4,083	−1,713
63	Other foreign official assets	2,665	−278
64	Other foreign assets in the United States, net	73,136	81,451
65	Direct investment	21,301	9,424
66	Equity and intercompany accounts	17,201	8,325
67	Reinvested earnings of incorporated affiliates	4,099	1,100
68	U.S. treasury securities	2,932	6,945
69	U.S. securities other than U.S. Treasury securities	7,109	5,973
	U.S. liabilities to unaffiliated foreigners reported by U.S. nonbanking concerns:		
70	Long-term		
71	Short-term	532	n.a.
	U.S. liabilities reported by U.S. Banks, not included elsewhere:		
72	Long-term		
73	Short-term	41,262	62,869
74	Allocations of special drawing rights	1,093	—
75	Statistical discrepancy (sum of above items with sign reversed)	25,809	41,864
75a	*Of which* seasonal adjustment discrepancy	—	—

LINE	(CREDITS; DEBITS)	1981	1982
	Memoranda:		
76	Balance on merchandise trade (lines 2 and 18)	−27,889	−36,331
77	Balance on goods and services (lines 1 and 17)	11,079	−225
78	Balance on goods, services, and remittances (lines 77, 35, and 36)	8,975	−2,680
79	Balance on current account (lines 77 and 33)	4,471	−8,093
	Transactions in U.S. official reserve assets in foreign official assets in the United States:		
80	Increase (−) in U.S. official reserve assets, net (line 38)	−5,175	−4,965
81	Increase (+) in foreign official assets in the United States (line 57 less line 61)	4,854	3,055

Source: U.S. Department of Commerce, *Survey of Current Business,* March 1983, p. 51.

$$B_g + B_s - T - K + \frac{dR}{dt} + SD = 0$$

$$-27.8 + 41.1 - 6.8 - 32.2 + 24.6 = 0$$

The merchandise, service, and transfer items can be collected as the balance on current account:

$$B_{ca} - K + \frac{dR}{dt} + SD = 0$$

$$+6.6 - 32.2 + 24.6 = 0$$

In 1981 the United States experienced a $6.6 billion current account surplus and a measured capital outflow (private plus government) of $32.2 billion. Logical consistency requires that the transactions add up to zero, which implies a statistical discrepancy of $24.6 billion. The current account surplus implies net lending by Americans of $6.6 billion and an increase in net foreign assets (ignoring valuation adjustment) of that amount.

The current account surplus can be broken down into its three main components. The merchandise balance showed a $27.8 billion deficit, the service balance showed a surplus of $41.1 billion, and there was a deficit in unilateral transfers of $6.8 billion. Some partial balances shown at the bottom as memoranda include balance on merchandise trade (line 76), balance on goods and services (line 77), and balance on current account (line 79). Detailed information about components of merchandise trade appears in a separate table of the *Survey of Current Business* (not shown).

The important components of service exports include receipts of income on U.S. assets abroad (line 11), travel (line 4), passenger fares and transportation (lines 5 and 6), and fees and royalties (lines 7 and 8). Changes in U.S. monetary reserves are shown on line 38, and the components of the reserve change appear on lines 39 through 42. Gross capital flows, divided into government and private capital, are shown on lines 43, 47, 57, and 64.

TABLE 16-9   U.S. Balance of Payments by Region, 1981
(in billions of dollars)

	MERCHANDISE BALANCE (B_g)	CURRENT ACCOUNT BALANCE (B_{ca})
Western Europe	+12.3	+8.0
Eastern Europe	+2.9	+3.5
Canada	−1.0	+7.3
Latin America	+3.7	+23.2
Japan	−15.8	−13.3
Australia, New Zealand, S. Africa	+3.4	+6.3
Other Asia and Africa	−32.3	−26.5
Other	0	−1.3
World	−27.8	+6.6

Source: U.S. Department of Commerce, Survey of Current Business, March 1982, p. 49.

The figures just noted refer to U.S. trade with all the rest of the world. The data can be decomposed to show U.S. trade with various regions and countries of the world. Some regional balances are shown in Table 16-9 for the merchandise balance and the balance on current account. The sum of the merchandise balances with all the regions must add up to the total merchandise balance of −$27.8 billion. The deficit of $15.8 billion with Japan received much attention from American protectionists. The deficit of $32.3 billion with Other Asia and Africa was largely related to oil trade. The United States experienced a large surplus of $12.3 billion with Western Europe. Similarly, the total current account balance of +$6.6 billion must equal the sum of the regional balances. The pattern is similar to the one for the merchandise balance.

There were large deficits with Japan and Other Asia and Africa and a surplus with Western Europe. One noticeable difference between the merchandise balance and the curent account is the much larger current account surplus with Latin America. The difference between the $23.2 billion surplus on current account and the $3.7 billion merchandise surplus is largely attributable to investment income of the United States.

16.8 THE BALANCE
OF PAYMENTS
AND THE FOREIGN
EXCHANGE MARKET

The balance of payments is a system of accounts, and it is important to consider the relationship between the accounting magnitudes and the real-world magnitudes in the foreign exchange market. Is it legitimate to say that a

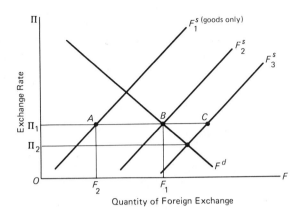

FIGURE 16-1   Foreign Exchange Market and Deficit in Merchandise Balance

balance-of-payments deficit causes the home currency to depreciate and a payments surplus causes the currency to appreciate? This is a popular interpretation of balance-of-payments figures. Since there are several different partial balances, which of the balances is related to the exchange rate?

Presumably a payments deficit would cause depreciation only if it led to an excess demand for foreign exchange. However, a merchandise deficit does not necessarily imply an excess demand, since it may be offset by a surplus in service trade or capital flows.

As shown, the United States had a merchandise deficit in 1981 and a larger service surplus. The current account was in surplus, and the dollar appreciated substantially in 1981. In that case, the merchandise balance was a poor indicator of conditions in the foreign exchange market. This situation is shown in Figure 16-1.

The term F^d is the total demand for foreign exchange. F_1^s is the supply of foreign exchange earned by exporters of merchandise. If merchandise trade were the only source of supply of foreign exchange, there would be an excess demand of AB at the exchange rate Π_1. This excess demand would correspond to a merchandise deficit. Let F_2^s represent the supply of foreign exchange coming from both merchandise and service exports. Given this total foreign exchange supply curve, the market is in equilibrium at Π_1. There is a merchandise deficit of AB, which is offset by a service surplus of AB. The currency has no tendency to depreciate. Finally, the situation of the United States in 1981 can be shown using the supply curve F_3^s. At Π_1 there is a merchandise deficit of AB and a larger service surplus of AC. Because of the excess supply of BC, the home currency appreciates to Π_2. If the merchandise balance were interpreted as a measure of excess demand, it would lead to the expectation of currency depreciation when appreciation actually occurs. A speculator or a central bank using this incorrect information would lose money.

It is also possible for the current account balance to be a misleading indicator of excess demand. A current account deficit may be offset by a larger capital inflow. If the current account were interpreted as an indicator of excess demand, it would lead people to expect depreciation of the home currency. However, the omitted capital inflow would add enough to foreign exchange supply to cause the currency to appreciate. This situation can also be illustrated in Figure 16-1.

The term F^d represents total demand for foreign exchange. F_1^s now represents supply coming from goods, services, and unilateral transfers. AB measures the current account deficit. F_3^s represents total foreign exchange supply, including capital inflows. When total demand and supply are considered, there is an excess supply of BC and the currency appreciates. The main conclusion is that partial measures of the balance of payments may not be a good indicator of market conditions, because they omit sources of foreign exchange supply and demand that may be important.

Because of this problem, broader balance-of-payments measures are probably more reliable than are narrow ones. The broadest of the partial balances is the monetary reserve balance, which includes all private demands and supplies. If measured properly, it would indicate the private excess demand for foreign exchange. Implicit in this interpretation is that governments only intervene in currency markets to maintain the exchange rate. If this were true, government sales or purchases of foreign exchange in any period would be exactly equal to the private excess demand or supply. This situation is shown in Figure 16-2.

The term F_P^d is the total private demand for foreign exchange; F_P^s is the total private supply of foreign exchange. There is a private excess demand of AB at Π_1. If the government entered the market only to fix the exchange rate, the government supply would equal private excess demand of AB.

When the government is strictly the residual buyer or seller, the monetary reserve balance is exactly equal to the private excess demand. However, governments may deal in foreign exchange for many purposes other than exchange rate pegging. Chapter 10 discussed state trade, which has become increasingly important. Thus, government agencies may buy foreign exchange to pay for imports or sell it in connection with exporting. Governments are also heavily involved in borrowing and lending through the foreign exchange market. In this case, the monetary reserve balance, which includes private transactions only, will not be an accurate measure of excess demand for foreign exchange.

In Figure 16-2, let F_{P+G}^s represent total supply by private and government traders, except for the government's exchange rate pegging operations. Thus, F_{P+G}^s would include foreign exchange earned by exports of the state oil company but not pegging activities of the central bank. At the exchange rate Π_1, the monetary reserve balance would show a deficit of AB equal to the pri-

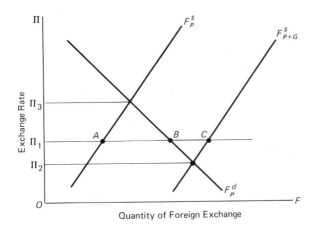

FIGURE 16-2   Monetary Reserve Balance and the Foreign Exchange Market

vate excess demand. If private excess demand also equaled total excess demand, one would expect a depreciation. However, the total market includes government commercial activity, and it shows an excess supply of BC. The home currency would appreciate to Π_2 in spite of a surplus in the monetary reserve balance. Alternatively, if the exchange rate were pegged, the central bank would acquire BC of reserves in spite of the deficit on monetary reserve account.

In principle, the reserve balance could be defined to include all transactions except the rate pegging operations of the central bank. This would require separating the commercial activities and the rate pegging operations of the government. Because of the accounting practices of many governments, it is difficult to make this empirical distinction. The accounting balance is the most complete measure, but it is always equal to zero by definition. It conveys the information that the quantity of foreign exchange bought always equals the quantity sold, which is true, but not very useful.

No single balance-of-payments concept is a perfect measure of the excess demand for foreign exchange. However, broader measures are less likely to omit important supplies and demands than are narrow measures. An important empirical question is whether the best of the imperfect measures is helpful in forecasting exchange rates. A popular view of exchange markets is that balance-of-payments deficits cause a currency to depreciate. If this were true, balance-of-payments data might be useful in forecasting exchange rates. The announcement of the latest balance-of-payments figures might have a predictable effect on exchange rates. Business firms are willing to pay for foreign exchange information, and forecasting rates has become a competitive business. At least one of the successful foreign exchange advisory services employs a balance-of-payments variable in its exchange rate forecasting equation.[12] However, if foreign exchange markets efficiently process information, past balance-of-payments data should not alter future exchange rates.

All relevant information contained in past balance-of-payments data should be built into current exchange rates. For example, if a past payments deficit correctly indicated an excess demand for foreign exchange, the currency should have depreciated immediately. Hence, the current price of foreign exchange should already be high enough to reflect that information. The past data should have no value in forecasting future exchange rates.

A separate question is whether the announcement of new balance-of-payments figures alters exchange rates. Most balance-of-payments figures are published quarterly with a lag. Thus, the figures for the fourth quarter of 1981 are not published until March 1982. An exception is the merchandise balance, which is available monthly. A problem, as noted, is that the merchandise balance is the narrowest measure and omits several important components of foreign exchange supply and demand.

Because of the time lag, the announced balance-of-payments figures contain both old and new information. Foreign exchange markets process information daily, which means that the old information should already be built into exchange rates on the day of the announcement. Only the new information should alter prices. Hence, balance-of-payments "news" should affect current exchange rates, but some payments information should have no effect.

Let B^U represent the "news" or unexpected balance of payments. It is the difference between the actual reported balance (B) and the expected balance (B^E), which contains the old information:

$$B^U_t = B_t - B^E_t$$

If the foreign exchange market efficiently processes information, the current exchange rate should depend on the unexpected portion of the balance-of-payments figures:

$$\Pi_t = f(B^U_t) = f(B_t - B^E_t)$$

Since the variables B^U_t and B^E_t are not directly observable, the hypothesis is not operational until the variables are assigned empirical counterparts.

In his empirical work, Dornbusch has used as a proxy for the expected balance the forecasts of the balance of payments issued by the OECD in Paris.[13]

---

[12] Richard Levich reports that the Predex Service includes a lagged value of the curent account in its equation; see his "Analyzing the Accuracy of Foreign Exchange Advisory Services: Theory and Evidence," in *Exchange Risk and Exposure*, R. Levich and C. Wihlborg, eds. (Lexington, Mass.: D.C. Heath, 1980).

[13] See the paper by Rudiger Dornbusch, "Exchange Rate Economics: Where Do We Stand?" *Brookings Papers on Economic Activity*, 1980:1.

He found empirical support for the hypothesis that only balance-of-payments "news" alters exchange rates. For example, suppose that a food importing country has a drought that damages domestic crops. As the information spreads, the demand for imported food and foreign exchange will increase. The home currency will depreciate before balance-of-payments figures are announced. People will expect the drought to cause a balance-of-payments deficit. If the payments figures announced later show a deficit exactly equal to the one that people expected, the announcement will have no effect on exchange rates. The market had already discounted this information. If the announced deficit is larger than the expected deficit $(B > B^E)$, the home currency will depreciate. However, if the announced deficit is smaller than expected, the currency will appreciate. The announcement that the drought was less severe than expected is good news for the home currency.

16.9 THE BALANCE OF PAYMENTS AND THE MONEY SUPPLY

Is there a direct link between the balance of payments and the domestic money supply? Can one conclude that money will flow out of a country that experiences a balance-of-payments deficit? The questions cannot be answered without more information. Specifically, the answer depends on which balance of payments measure is used and whether the exchange rate is fixed or floating.

In one extreme case, freely floating exchange rates, the money supply is unrelated to any measure of the balance of payments. In general, the stock of monetary reserves is the link between the money supply and the balance of payments:

$$\frac{dM_b}{dt} = \frac{dD}{dt} + \frac{dR}{dt} = \frac{dD}{dt} + B_R$$

Growth in the money supply depends on growth in the monetary base (M_b). The base depends on domestic open market purchases plus purchases of foreign exchange reserves. The reserve balance is the partial balance that measures reserve changes. By definition of freely floating rates, reserves do not vary, and the reserve balance is always zero. The current account must equal capital outflows, but it has no effect on the money supply. The merchandise balance can take on any value under floating rates, but it has no effect on the money supply.

In the opposite extreme case of permanently fixed rates, the reserve balance is a direct determinant of the monetary base and the money supply. It can be said that a central bank loses its monetary independence under fixed exchange rates. David Hume stressed the relationship between the balance of payments and the money supply under fixed exchange rates. He argued that the trade surpluses advocated by mercantilists would be self-correcting because of monetary expansion. The statement must be qualified because of the possibility of sterilized intervention, which breaks the link between reserve changes and money changes. However, the scope for sterilized intervention is extremely limited in modern economies.

Monetary reserves do flow out of the country when there is a deficit in the monetary reserve balance, and the domestic money supply contracts. Deficits in other partial balances do not necessarily imply a reserve loss or monetary contraction. For example, a country with a merchandise deficit and an equal service surplus would not lose reserves or money. Similarly, a country with a current account deficit and an equal capital inflow would not experience a decline in reserves or money supply. In all the intermediate cases where the central bank intervenes some of the time but not all of the time, the money supply will be affected by the reserve balance. None of the other partial balances systematically alters the money supply.

16.10 MERCANTILISM

Mercantilism is a complex set of beliefs about how to regulate a national economy.[14] Mercantilists advocated strict regulation of domestic and foreign trade. One of their important prescriptions for this chapter is that government policy should be directed toward achieving a balance-of-trade surplus. Since mercantilist writers lived before Adam Smith in a time when service trade was unimportant, they did not distinguish between the merchandise balance and the current account. As has been shown, however, this distinction is quite important today for many countries, especially the United States.

The old proposition that trade deficits are bad for a country and trade surpluses are good remains a popular idea today. Adam Smith and David Hume strongly criticized mercantilist doctrines in the eighteenth century, and economists ever since that time have tried to convince practical people that trade surpluses are not necessarily beneficial to a nation. Mercantilists tried to rationalize trade surpluses on the grounds that (1) they would add to the nation's stock of gold and (2) they would increase national employment. Mercantilists confused gold, which served as money, with real wealth. Hume argued that a trade surplus would increase the money supply and the price level, which would in turn induce a trade deficit.

A more fundamental point is that money is ultimately desired for its

---

[14] For a more detailed discussion of mercantilism see Jacob Viner's *Studies in the Theory of International Trade* (London: George Allen and Unwin, 1937), Chaps. 1 and 2; and Eli Heckscher's two-volume *Mercantilism*, rev. 2nd ed. (London: George Allen and Unwin, 1955).

451 BALANCE-OF-PAYMENTS ACCOUNTS

command over real goods and services. Utility or satisfaction comes from consuming goods and services that are bought with money. A trade surplus involves giving up current goods and services for money. Thus, the mercantilist goal of acquiring gold is a confusion of means and ends. A more charitable interpretation of the mercantilist argument is that surpluses on current account add to net foreign assets, a form of wealth.

However, the return on foreign lending associated with the surplus must be compared with the return on alternative domestic lending. One cannot say, in general, that foreign lending always has a higher rate of return than does domestic lending. Thus, one cannot say that trade surpluses are preferable to trade deficits. It was probably wise for Americans to be net borrowers in the early nineteenth century and net lenders for most of the twentieth century.

The wisdom of trade surpluses depends on economic conditions at home and abroad. Consider a country with an elastic demand for imported oil. If a competitive world oil market becomes monopolistic, the price will rise and expenditure on imported oil will decline (percentage volume decrease exceeds percentage price increase). Other things being equal the country's balance of trade will turn to surplus. A misleading mercantilistic interpretation of the event is that the country benefited from the price change. In fact, the real purchasing power of residents has declined. Furthermore, if the monopoly is destroyed, the price will fall, a trade deficit will occur, and the residents will benefit.

A second mercantilistic rationale for advocating surpluses is that they might add to total employment. Export expansion adds to foreign demand for domestic labor. Substituting domestic production for imports adds to domestic demand for domestic labor. By restricting imports and promoting exports, a country can "export its unemployment." The argument has several problems. First, trading partners will not be anxious to "import unemployment." Protectionist policies are likely to provoke retaliation as they did in the Great Depression. The American Smoot-Hawley tariff was quickly followed by European protectionism. If all countries restrict trade, world trade volume declines, and all countries lose.

A second problem follows from the condition that the world balance of payments must be zero. Some countries can achieve surpluses but all countries cannot. If all nations follow mercantilist policies, some must fail, and their attempts to achieve surpluses will reduce the gains from trade. A third objection to using trade policy to increase employment is that trade does not affect total employment in the long run. Export expansion and import substitution alter employment by industry, but not total employment in the long-run. Trade surpluses and deficits can have a transitory effect on total employment, but only by accepting unfortunate side effects. Short-run employment problems are better dealt with by increasing aggregate demand through monetary and fiscal policy without distorting foreign trade.

SUMMARY

Much useful information about international trade and investment is recorded in the balance-of-payments. The accounting balance, which includes all transactions, is necessarily equal to zero. By omitting certain transactions, partial balances, such as the merchandise balance and the balance on current account, can be constructed. It is meaningful to discuss deficits and surpluses in partial balances, but they should be interpreted with caution.

Balance-of-payments deficits are sometimes interpreted as measuring the excess demand for foreign exchange. None of the partial balances measures it precisely, but the monetary reserve balance is the closest proxy. An accurate proxy would indicate the amount of monetary contraction under fixed exchange rates or the excess demand that must be eliminated by depreciation under floating rates.

Because the world is a closed economy, it is not possible for all countries simultaneously to experience payments deficits or surpluses. Large merchandise deficits for the United States in recent years contrasted sharply to the surpluses of the rest of the twentieth century. At the same time large surpluses in service trade have left the U.S. current account in approximate balance. An important tenet of mercantilist thought is that balance-of-trade surpluses are beneficial to a country. However, surpluses may be beneficial or harmful depending on the cause of the surplus. Consulting the balance-of-payments accounts is not a substitute for economic analysis.

REFERENCES

DENISON, EDWARD. "International Transactions in Measures of the Nation's Production." *Survey of Current Business*, May 1981. An attempt to measure the terms of trade effect for the United States.

DORNBUSCH, RUDIGER. "Exchange Rate Economics: Where Do We Stand?" *Brookings Papers on Economic Activity*, 1:1980.

HALEVI, NADAV. "An Empirical Test of the Balance of Payments Stages Hypothesis." *Journal of International Economics*, February 1971. Presents data on the stages hypothesis.

HECKSCHER, ELI. *Mercantilism* (1931), 2 vols., rev. 2nd ed. London: George Allen and Unwin, 1955.

HUME, DAVID. "Of the Balance of Trade." In *David Hume: Writings on Economics*, Eugene Rotwein ed., Madison: University of Wisconsin Press, 1970. Statement of the price-specie flow mechanism.

INTERNATIONAL MONETARY FUND. *Annual Report, 1981*, Washington, D.C., annually. Concise source of recent international economic information.

———. *Balance of Payments Yearbook*, Washington, D.C., annually. Contains detailed balance-of-payments data for member countries using a standard format.

KEMP, DONALD S. "Balance of Payments Concepts—What Do They Really Mean?" *Review*, Federal Reserve Bank of St. Louis, July 1975.

KINDLEBERGER, CHARLES. "Measuring Equilibrium in the Balance of Payments." *Journal of Political Economy*, November 1969. Reprinted in Kindleberger, *International Money: A Collection of Essays.* London: George Allen and Unwin, 1981. Discussion of various balance-of-payments concepts.

LEVICH, RICHARD.   "Analyzing the Accuracy of Foreign Exchange Advisory Services: Theory and Evidence." In *Exchange Risk and Exposure*, R. Levich and C. Wihlborg eds., Lexington, Mass.: D. C. Heath, 1980. Discusses the use of balance-of-payments data in forecasting exchange rates.

MEADE, JAMES.   *The Balance of Payments.* New York: Oxford University Press, 1951. Prominent analysis of balance-of-payments issues.

MEIER, GERALD.   *International Economics: The Theory of Policy.* New York: Oxford University Press, 1980. Chapter 13 contains a discussion of two-gap analysis.

MUNDELL, ROBERT.   *International Economics.* New York: Macmillan, 1968. Chapter 10 covers conceptual balance-of-payments issues.

POSTAN, M. M.   *Medieval Trade and Finance.* London: Cambridge University Press, 1973. Presents and discusses early customs data.

SACHS, JEFFREY.   "The Current Account and Macroeconomic Adjustment." *Brookings Papers on Economic Activity*, 1: 1981. Economic analysis of the determinants of the current discount balance.

SCHMIDT, WILSON E.   *The U.S. Balance of Payments and the Sinking Dollar.* New York: New York University Press, 1979. An analysis of the U.S. balance of payments and foreign exchange markets.

SIKORSKY, NILLY.   "The Origin and Construction of the Capital International Indices." *The Columbia Journal of World Business*, Summer 1982. Capital International is an important source of world stock market data.

STERN, ROBERT, et al.   *The Presentation of the U.S. Balance of Payments: A Symposium*, Princeton Studies in International Finance, No. 123. Princeton, N.J.: Princeton University Press, August 1977. Discusses the abandonment of an official balance-of-payments measure.

U.S. DEPARTMENT OF COMMERCE.   *Survey of Current Business*, Washington, D.C., monthly. The March issue contains annual balance-of-payments data for the previous calendar year.

VINER, JACOB.   *Studies in the Theory of International Trade.* London: George Allen and Unwin, 1937. Chapters 1 and 2 discuss mercantilist views on the balance of payments.

WILLIAMSON, JEFFREY.   *American Growth and the Balance of Payments.* Chapel Hill: University of North Carolina Press, 1964. Analysis of historical development of U.S. balance of payments.

YEAGER, LELAND, and DAVID G. TUERCK.   *Foreign Trade and U.S. Policy.* New York: Praeger, 1976. Chapter 6 discusses the balance of payments, money, and employment.

CHAPTER SEVENTEEN
FLOATING
EXCHANGE RATES
AND FOREIGN EXCHANGE
RISK

17.1 INTRODUCTION

Floating exchange rates will be the topic of Chapters 17 and 18. Chapter 17 will concentrate on foreign exchange risk as it affects individual business firms. Chapter 18 will emphasize the effect of floating on currency markets and the general economy. The limited historical experience with floating rates will be examined. The nature of foreign exchange risk and hedging opportunities will be considered. The determination of exchange rate expectations will be discussed in conjunction with speculation and hedging. A distinction will be made between accounting exposure and economic exposure to foreign exchange risk. The market will be analyzed in terms of the interest rate parity theory. The floating exchange rate system has made it more valuable for business firms to forecast future exchange rates. The use of alternative forecasting techniques, including the forward exchange rate, will be discussed.

17.2 THE HISTORICAL EXPERIENCE WITH FLOATING EXCHANGE RATES

Most countries of the world have experienced some form of floating exchange rates since 1973. In most cases, governments have attempted to manage the float, but there has been considerable variability of rates.

Table 17-1 reproduces some annual exchange rates that were shown in Table 14-3. In addition to the annual variation in rates, there has been considerable monthly, weekly, and even daily exchange rate fluctuation. Some groups of countries have formed currency blocs within which exchange rates are stable. However, exchange rates between bloc members and the rest of the world have remained floating. Most members of the European Economic Community[1] have joined the European monetary system, and a de facto dollar system has emerged. Thus, even those countries that have pegged their national currencies to some key currency have experienced considerable exchange rate variability.

The period since 1973 is the longest peacetime experiment with worldwide floating exchange rates. A few individual countries have had extended experiments with floating rates. The Austro-Hungarian gulden floated from 1879 to 1892. Canada permitted its currency to float from 1950 to 1961. Lebanon and Peru also experimented with floating rates following World War II. However, those cases were isolated national experiments in the context of fixed exchange rates for the world as a whole.

In other historical examples, floating rates were associated with wartime finance. Because of the high correlation between war and inflation, a popular view is that floating exchange rates are a cause of inflation.[2] The wartime experiences often involved the transitory substitution of paper money for commodity money. When wars were terminated, convertibility of money and fixed exchange rates were restored.

During the French Revolution, paper money *(assignats)* was substituted for gold. A large enough quantity of *assignats* was printed to cause inflation and currency depreciation. During the American Revolutionary War paper continental money was associated with inflation and depreciation. The phrase "not worth a continental" indicated the high rate of expected depreciation. During the Napoleonic wars, the pound depreciated after the British declared paper money inconvertible into gold. After the U.S. government issued paper greenbacks during the Civil War, prices rose and the dollar depreciated. Following World War I Germany experienced hyperinflation and severe currency depreciation. England and France also experienced inflation and floating rates following the war.

Because of the historical association between inflation and floating rates, the idea of basing a peacetime international monetary system on floating was not a popular one. One crude interpretation of the earlier episodes is that floating causes inflation by pushing up import prices. An alternative interpretation concedes that monetary expansion is necessary for inflation and that it is more

---

[1] The United Kingdom has not yet joined the European monetary system, which means that the pound floats against the other EEC currencies. In addition, there have been frequent discrete changes in exchange rates among EMS members.

[2] A more accurate interpretation is that both inflation and floating rates have been caused by the monetary and fiscal policies that have traditionally been employed to finance wars.

TABLE 17-1 U.S. Dollar Exchange Rates, 1973–1982 (cents per unit)

COUNTRY	MARCH 1973	1974	1975	1976	1977	1978	1979	1980	1981	1982
Belgium	2.5377	2.7158	2.5311	2.7483	2.9608	3.3637	3.5423	3.1543	2.6115	2.1843
Canada	100.33	101.19	98.627	98.204	91.132	84.763	85.471	83.560	84.382	81.011
France	22.191	22.109	22.428	20.055	20.844	23.178	24.614	21.925	17.502	15.199
West Germany	35.548	40.816	38.144	41.965	46.499	53.217	57.671	50.769	44.862	41.186
Italy	.17600	.15179	.14645	.11521	.11416	.11863	.12329	.10704	.08392	.07380
Japan	.38190	.33288	.32715	.33933	.41491	.51038	.41613	.47747	.44843	.40150
The Netherlands	34.834	39.331	37.234	40.240	42.955	49.120	52.092	46.730	40.435	37.427
Sweden	22.582	23.897	22.685	24.051	21.044	22.808	23.935	22.722	18.049	15.914
Switzerland	31.084	38.442	37.970	40.823	48.168	59.703	62.542	56.022	55.098	49.196
United Kingdom	247.24	232.94	202.21	167.84	185.46	198.61	220.07	234.60	190.25	174.80
Trade-weighted average*	100.00	101.38	98.46	105.58	103.29	92.39	88.09	87.39	102.94	116.57
Dollars per SDR†	$1.192	$1.203	$1.214	$1.155	$1.168	$1.252	$1.292	$1.302	$1.179	$1.104

* An SDR (special drawing right) is a composite currency consisting of fixed amounts of five national currencies.

† The Federal Reserve Board's trade-weighted average measures the exchange value of the dollar against the Group of Ten plus Switzerland.

Source: International Monetary Fund, *International Financial Statistics Yearbook* and Federal Reserve System, *Federal Reserve Bulletin*, Washington, D.C., various periods.

likely to occur under floating rates. According to this view, the obligation to maintain fixed rates acts as a kind of monetary constitution (it has also been described as an "anchor") that restrains the central bank.

In addition to their concern about inflation, critics pointed out that exchange rate uncertainty might reduce the volume of international trade. Exchange rate risk might be an additional business cost that would deter some firms from importing and exporting. Thus, the two traditional arguments against floating rates were that (1) they were inflationary and (2) they reduced the volume of world trade. Economists were skeptical of the efficacy of floating rates, and for many years Milton Friedman's 1953 essay, "The Case for Flexible Exchange Rates," was one of the few published pieces[3] favoring floating. Most businesspeople and government officials were even more strongly opposed to floating than the economists were.

In spite of this formidable opposition, the world adopted floating rates in 1973. The move was not the result of a conscious plan. Economic events forced policymakers to adopt floating rates. Eventually, floating was found to be expedient because of the increased cost of defending fixed rates. The viability of fixed rates declined as national monetary and fiscal policies became increasingly diverse and international capital markets became increasingly integrated. The experience since 1973 has not convinced everyone of the superiority of floating rates. However, it has provided some valuable empirical evidence about the economic effects of exchange rate uncertainty. Chapter 18 will consider the relationship between inflation and floating.

17.3 BUSINESS FIRMS AND FOREIGN EXCHANGE RISK

The profits of a firm depend on revenue and cost expressed in domestic currency. A firm engaged in international trade may have outstanding contracts to receive or pay foreign exchange. Profits can be written as

$$\rho = R - C = SR^\star - SC^\star = S(R^\star - C^\star)$$

The domestic currency value of profits is ρ. $R^\star$ *and* $C^\star$ are revenue and cost denominated in foreign currency and S is the spot exchange rate. A change in the exchange rate will confer a windfall gain or loss on the firm.

Whether the firm gains or loses depends on the direction of the currency change and the firm's initial position in foreign exchange. If the firm had net revenue ($R^\star > C^\star$) in foreign currency initially, it would gain from depreciation of the home currency (appreciation of foreign money). For example, the firm

---

[3] In his 1924 *Tract on Monetary Reform*, John Maynard Keynes advocated widening the gold points, which is a limited form of floating rates. Lloyd Mints, one of Friedman's mentors, was another early proponent of floating.

might be an American exporter of grain to Germany with net revenue of 1,000 marks. At the initial exchange rate of $0.50 per mark, the expected profit is $500. If the dollar depreciates to $0.60, the firm will earn $600. If the firm had net costs in foreign exchange, it would lose from depreciation. Because exchange rate changes cannot be known in advance, the possibility of change adds to uncertainty in international trade. If the added uncertainty increases business costs, floating exchange rates may inhibit international trade. Since the gains from trade are proportional to the volume of trade, floating exchange rates may reduce real income.

What is the mechanism by which floating rates may reduce trade? Floating may increase exchange rate uncertainty, but other kinds of uncertainty may be greater under fixed rates. In fact fixed rates were often defended by quotas. Thus, the increased quantity uncertainty (unavailability of foreign exchange) under fixed rates must be compared with the price uncertainty of floating rates. In fact, fixed rates were never permanently fixed, and changes that did occur tended to be large. On a given day, firms would have to compare (1) a high probability of a small price change under floating with (2) a small probability of a large price change under fixed rates. Because of the continuous nature of price changes under floating, it may be easier for firms to hedge against them. If floating exchange rates decrease the volume of trade, they must either increase costs or increase the variability of profits. If managers or investors are risk averse, increased variance of profits may decrease trade even if average profits are constant.

Exchange rate flexibility can be a source of business risk. However, firms and investors encounter many kinds of business risk in their purely domestic operations. As a consequence, a number of economic institutions have developed to deal with the problem of risk. The insurance industry and the stock market are obvious examples. Investors have the option of buying bonds, which promise a fixed amount of money, or stocks, which promise an unknown amount of money. By altering the composition of their portfolios, investors can acquire as much or as little risk as they desire. Organized forward and futures markets provide a way of dealing with uncertain prices of factors of production or final products. Some of the same institutions can also deal with foreign exchange risk, and some new institutions have developed as well.

In any international transaction the contract can either be expressed in the home country's currency, the partner country's currency, or some third country currency (so-called "vehicle" currency). The choice of invoice currency depends upon economic conditions, and it can be used to alter the incidence of foreign exchange risk.

Once the invoice currency has been determined, the firm has several ways of hedging against exchange risk. For example, if the firm has foreign currency liabilities due at time $t+1$, it can buy foreign exchange at t and invest abroad until $t+1$. Alternatively, it can buy foreign currency in the forward market for delivery at $t+1$. In addition to these explicit hedges, markets provide an automatic or implicit hedge by adapting to expected changes in exchange rates. For example, a firm holding assets in a foreign currency will experience a loss if that currency depreciates. However, if the depreciation were anticipated, the foreign currency asset would pay an interest rate premium over the domestic rate to compensate for the expected depreciation.

Economic institutions develop in response to market demand. During the gold standard and adjustable peg periods, some forward markets existed for major currencies, but there was not much activity. Since exchange rates have begun to float, the volume of forward trade has increased in traditional markets, and new forward exchange activity has emerged. For example, foreign currency futures are now traded on the traditional commodity markets of New York and Chicago. The International Monetary Market, a division of the Chicago Mercantile Exchange, is an entirely new operation that offers opportunities to hedge, arbitrage, and speculate in foreign exchange. It would not have existed without floating rates. In addition, the London International Financial Futures Exchange began trading currency futures contracts in late 1982.

17.4 PRICE EXPECTATIONS IN THE FOREIGN EXCHANGE MARKET

The foreign exchange market incorporates information about current supply and demand and expectations about future supply and demand. A weak currency is one that market participants expect to lose value in the future. If economic agents act on their expectations, they will sell the weak currency, expecting to buy it back later for less. Attempts to sell the weak currency will lower its present value. Thus, current expectations about a future depreciation are built into the present price. Expectations affect all prices including spot and forward exchange rates and domestic and foreign interest rates. Of course, expectations may be incorrect, and an expected depreciation may never occur. Market prices will incorporate expectations, but they will not provide perfect forecasts of future realized prices. However, no forecasts are perfect, and an important empirical question is whether market forecasts are more accurate than other forecasts.

Consider an example of spot speculation. The current spot exchange rate is $2.00 per pound, and speculators expect the price of pounds to rise to $2.20 in the next period. The spot speculator would buy pounds for $2.00 and sell in the next period for $2.20 for an expected gain of $0.20 per pound or 10 percent of the spot price:

$$\text{expected gain} = \frac{S_{t+1}^E - S_t}{S_t} = \frac{\$2.20 - \$2.00}{\$2.00} = +10\%$$

However, the speculator must get his or her dollars from somewhere, which requires borrowing at the U.S. interest rate i. The U.S. interest rate is the appropriate cost whether one borrows explicitly or gives up interest on one's own funds. Since the speculator buys pounds at time t and sells at time $t+1$, he or she must invest in the United Kingdom for one period at the rate $i^\star$. Thus, the interest cost of spot speculation is the difference between forgone interest at home and interest earned abroad:

$$\text{interest cost} = i - i^\star$$

The net realized gain from spot speculation is the difference between the capital gain and the interest cost:

$$\frac{S_{t+1} - S_t}{S_t} - (i - i^\star)$$

In this example the spot speculation will be profitable if the domestic interest is less than 10 percentage points above the foreign rate. However, if dollar depreciation is generally expected in the market, dollar interest rates will be above pound interest rates. Competition from speculators, all trying to carry out the same transactions, will eliminate profits. All speculators will attempt to borrow in the United States, and the excess demand for funds will raise U.S. interest rates. All will attempt to buy pounds spot, which will raise the spot price. All will attempt to lend in the United Kingdom, and the excess supply of funds will lower interest rates there. In equilibrium expected profits will be zero, as expected depreciation will equal the interest differential.[4]

$$\frac{S_{t+1}^E - S_t}{S_t} = \frac{dS^E}{dt} = i - i^\star$$

The expected rate of depreciation of the dollar is equal to the difference between U.S. and U.K. interest rates. The market tends to provide an interest premium $(i - i^\star)$ that is equal to the expected devaluation. In this example where the dollar is expected to depreciate by 10 percent, interest rates in the United States would be 10 percentage points higher than would those in the United Kingdom. The speculator should gain from the price change, but he or she would lose an equal amount because of borrowing at a high rate and lending at a low rate.

International business firms are sometimes advised to borrow in countries with weak currencies and lend in countries with strong currencies. The

[4]This relationship is sometimes called the Fisher condition for an open economy. It is named after Irving Fisher (1867–1947) who stressed that the expected inflation rate (dP^E/P) is the difference between nominal and real (r) interest rates: $dP^E/P = i - r$. Fisher applied the concept to an open economy in his *Theory of Interest* (1930) (New York: Kelley, 1955).

advice is prudent only if the "weakness" and "strength" have not been incorporated into market prices. If market prices reflect the information, the policy is not profitable. The actual gain from spot speculation is

$$\frac{dS}{S} - (i - i^\star)$$

"Weakness" can be interpreted as expected depreciation, and it is built into market prices according to

$$\frac{dS^E}{s} = i - i^\star$$

Thus, the actual gain can be rewritten as

$$\frac{dS}{S} - \frac{dS^E}{S} = \frac{dS^U}{S}$$

The speculator gains if actual depreciation exceeds the rate that was expected by the market. This latter residual can be called the unexpected (S^U) depreciation rate. It cannot be known in advance, and it is analogous to balance-of-payments "news" discussed in Chapter 16. It is prudent to borrow weak currencies only if they turn out to be weaker than the market expected them to be. If the market expects 10 percent depreciation (and builds it into interest rates) and if 10 percent actually occurs, speculation is not profitable. If the market expects 10 percent and 12 percent occurs, speculation is profitable. Finally, if the market expects 10 percent and actual depreciation is only 8 percent, a spot speculator will lose money. The loss from borrowing at higher interest rates exceeds the exchange rate gain. In general, if actual exchange rate changes are equal to expected changes, there will be neither speculative gains nor losses. Speculative gains depend on speculators' forecasting actual changes more accurately than the market does.

A possible source of superior forecasts would be inside information. Certain central bank or treasury officials might have relevant information that is not yet available to the market. If they used the information to speculate, they might earn speculative profits. Usually, employees are forbidden to trade on inside information. A second problem is that central banks lost billions of dollars in the 1970s due to exchange market intervention in spite of their access to inside information. It should be clear that a private analyst with a superior forecast can earn speculative profits. However, if his or her forecasting technique becomes generally known (e.g., sells advisory services), prices will change and profits will disappear.

The forward market would also tend to incorporate expected depreciation. In the same situation where the spot rate is expected to rise from \$2.00

to \$2.10, let the initial forward rate for delivery at $t+1$ be \$2.00. Forward speculators have an incentive to buy at the forward rate of \$2.00, which is known at time t, and sell spot at $t+1$ for \$2.20. The actual gain will be

$$S_{t+1} - F_{t+1}$$

Of course, S_{t+1} is not known at time t, and the expected gain at time t is

$$S_{t+1}^E - F_{t+1} = \$2.20 - \$2.00 = \$0.20$$

The expected percentage gain is

$$\frac{S_{t+1} - F_{t+1}}{S_t} = \frac{\$2.20 - \$2.00}{\$2.00} = +10\%$$

Profit opportunities depend on speculators' ability to buy at a forward price that is below the expected future spot price. However, if the dollar is generally expected to depreciate, all speculators will be trying to buy forward. The excess demand will cause the forward price to rise until it equals the expected spot price.[5] In equilibrium,

$$F_{t+1} = S_{t+1}^E = \$2.20$$

In percentage terms the expected depreciation of the dollar (appreciation of the pound) will equal the forward premium on the pound (discount on the dollar):[6]

$$\frac{S_{t+1}^E - S_t}{S_t} = \frac{dS^E}{S_t} = \frac{F_{t+1} - S_{t+1}^E}{S_t}$$

The speculative gain from the 10 percent depreciation of the dollar would be fully offset by the 10 percent premium paid for forward pounds. The actual realized gain from forward speculation is

$$S_{t+1} - F_{t+1}$$

----

[5] If speculators require special compensation for bearing risk, the maximum forward price they pay will be less than S_{t+1}^E. The difference can be interpreted as a risk premium.

[6] Forward contracts extending further into the future will incorporate expectations about subsequent depreciation:

$$\frac{dS_{t+1}}{S_{t+1}} = \frac{F_{t+2} - F_{t+1}}{F_{t+1}}$$

Expected depreciation in the next period will be given by the percentage difference between the forward rates for delivery at times $t+2$ and $t+1$. In general, the term structure of forward rates can be used to forecast subsequent spot rates. See Gunter Dufey and Ian H. Giddy, *The International Money Market* (Englewood Cliffs, N.J.: Prentice-Hall, 1978), Chap. 2.

which can be written in percentage terms as

$$\frac{S_{t+1}-S_t}{S_t} - \frac{F_{t+1}-S_t}{S_t}$$

The term on the right is the forward premium, which is equal to the expected depreciation of the dollar. Thus, realized profits are equal to the difference between actual depreciation and expected depreciation:

$$\frac{dS}{S_t} - \frac{dS^E}{S_t}$$

This same relationship holds for spot speculation. Successful speculation requires not only an accurate exchange rate forecast, but it requires one that is more accurate than the market forecast. In this case, an accurate forecast of a 10 percent devaluation would yield no profits if the market expected the devaluation. Success depends on an unexpected devaluation.

An important empirical question is whether the forward exchange rate provides a good forecast of subsequent spot rates. Forecast bias is one relevant property to consider. An unbiased forecast is one whose average error is zero. Forecasts may be too high for certain dates and too low for other dates, but on the average unbiased forecast errors must be zero. Lack of bias would be an important property for firms dealing in foreign trade on a daily basis over an extended period. If the firm planned its transactions based on the forward rate, it could ignore daily exchange rate fluctuations. Any exchange rate losses on a given day would be offset by gains on another day. Unfortunately the empirical studies of forward rate bias have had mixed results. Another relevant property of forecasts is the magnitude of the absolute error. Since errors can be positive or negative, the average algebraic error can be zero, whether the average absolute error is large or small.

Consider the following two series of forecast errors for the forward exchange rate:

Series	$t+1$	$t+2$	$t+3$	$t+4$
$(S-F)^A$	+1	−1	+1	−1
$(S-F)^B$	+10	−10	+10	−10

Both series A and series B are unbiased, since the average algebraic error is zero. However, series A is more accurate, because the average absolute error ($=1$) is less than the average absolute error for B ($=10$). Empirical evidence continues to accumulate. Forecasts were more accurate when exchange rates floated in the 1920s than in the 1970s. Forecasts of the near future have been more accurate than those of the distant future.

The final point concerning expectations and the exchange rate is the relationship between domestic and foreign inflation. In the home economy the nominal interest rate is equal to the real inflation rate plus the expected rate of inflation:

$$i = r + \frac{dP^E}{P}$$

A similar relationship exists in ROW:

$$i^\star = r^\star + \frac{dP^{\star E}}{P^\star}$$

If international capital mobility equalizes real rates of interest at home and abroad, the following relationship holds:

$$r = r^\star$$
$$i - \frac{dP^E}{P^E} = i^\star - \frac{dP^{\star E}}{P^\star}$$
$$i - i^\star = \frac{dP^E}{P^E} - \frac{dP^{\star E}}{P^\star}$$

The difference between nominal interest rates at home and abroad represents the expected difference between future domestic and foreign inflation rates. If capital controls prevent equalization of real interest rates, this relationship will provide a biased forecast of expected inflation differentials. Interest differentials between the United States and Canada might provide better information about expected inflation than would similar data for the United States and Italy.

17.5 EXPOSURE TO FOREIGN EXCHANGE RISK

It is important to measure the extent of a firm's exposure to foreign exchange risk. A firm's accounting position in foreign exchange was discussed in Chapter 15. An accounting position in a currency is determined by a firm's net assets in that currency. Positive net assets (a long position in foreign exchange) imply that a firm will benefit from depreciation of the home currency. Conversely, a firm with net liabilities (short position) in a foreign currency will be harmed by a depreciation of home money. A firm's accounting exposure to exchange rate changes is readily obtained by calculating its net foreign assets in each currency. However, a firm's accounting exposure is not necessarily equal to its economic exposure.

The concept of economic exposure includes accounting exposure plus any other systematic changes associated with exchange rate changes. Firms with open accounting positions may have closed economic positions. In particular, firms suffering accounting losses from exchange rate changes may be systematically compensated by market forces. If the compensation is sufficient, firms apparently exposed to exchange risk may actually be in a closed economic position. For example, Section 17.3 showed that an expected depreciation of the foreign currency will lead to an interest rate premium abroad. A firm that borrows at home and lends to its foreign customers will suffer an accounting loss if the foreign currency depreciates. However, if the foreign depreciation were expected, the foreign interest rate would be proportionately higher than the domestic interest rate. If the firm's foreign exchange loss is offset by a gain in interest earned, its open accounting position is simultaneously a closed economic position. The firm has neither gained nor lost from the exchange rate change.

To measure economic exposure of foreign assets, one must distinguish between financial and real assets. Financial assets are those whose value is fixed in foreign currency. Examples are bonds, bank loans, and accounts receivable. Since they are fixed in terms of foreign money, they increase in domestic value when the home currency depreciates. Let $N^\star$ be the fixed foreign currency assets of a firm. The change in the domestic currency value of the assets as a result of home depreciation is

$$\frac{dS}{S} N^\star$$

A firm with net foreign assets implicitly gives up the domestic interest rate to earn the foreign interest rate. The interest gain from holding assets abroad is the differential

$$(i^\star - i)N^\star$$

The net economic exposure of foreign assets to foreign depreciation is the sum of the two components:

$$E_F = \frac{dS}{S} N^\star + (i^\star - i)N^\star$$
$$= [\frac{dS}{S} + (i^\star - i)]N^\star$$

E_F measures the loss to home residents from depreciation of the foreign currency.

Whether the firm is exposed to foreign exchange risk depends on whether the exchange rate change is expected. If it is expected, the change will be built into the interest differential, and the firm will be in a closed position. For example, let the foreign currency depreciate (home appreciates) by 3 percent. The home currency value of net foreign assets will decline. However, if the change were anticipated, foreign interest rates would be three percentage points above domestic rates (e.g., $i^\star - i = 0.10 - 0.07 = +0.03$). The firm's exchange rate loss would be fully offset by a gain in interest. Thus, the firm's economic exposure depends on the exchange rate change being unexpected by the market. For all expected currency changes, markets provide an automatic hedge for business firms.

A firm's economic exposure is slightly different for real assets. The money value of real assets is variable according to economic conditions. In particular, prices of real assets can respond to exchange rate changes. Examples of real assets are land, plant and equipment, and inventories. If a firm owns real assets abroad, depreciation of the foreign currency will reduce the home currency value of the assets. However, if foreign currency prices of the real assets rise in proportion to the foreign devaluation, the firm will not be exposed to exchange risk.

Let $A^\star$ be the foreign currency value of real assets evaluated at historical cost. The decrease in the domestic currency value of real assets resulting from devaluation of the foreign currency is

$$\frac{dS}{S}A^\star$$

The increase in the foreign currency value of real assets following foreign devaluation is

$$\frac{dP^\star}{P^\star}A^\star$$

The net economic exposure of real assets is the sum of the two components:

$$E_R = \frac{dS}{S}A^\star + \frac{dP^\star}{P^\star}A^\star = \left(\frac{dS}{S} + \frac{dP^\star}{P^\star}\right)A^\star$$

E_R is the loss to home resident owners of real assets abroad resulting from depreciation of foreign currency. A depreciation of the foreign currency means that dS is negative.

Why should $P^\star$ rise in conjunction with devaluation? Arbitrage should equate domestic and foreign currency prices when expressed in the same currency:

$$P = SP^\star$$

The percentage changes must be

$$\frac{dP}{P} = \frac{dS}{S} + \frac{dP^\star}{P^\star}$$

If the foreign country is small, its devaluation will not alter home currency prices $dP = O$. It follows that

$$\frac{dS}{S} = -\frac{dP^\star}{P^\star}$$

The general relationship between inflation and depreciation is called purchasing power parity (PPP), and it will be analyzed in more detail in the next chapter. The main conclusion here is that if PPP holds, real assets abroad are not exposed to foreign exchange risk. For example, if the foreign currency depreciates by 10 percent ($dS/S = -10\%$), the prices of real assets abroad will rise by 10 percent ($dP^\star/P^\star = +10\%$), and the home currency value will not be affected. Thus, the economic exposure of real assets becomes an empirical question of how accurate is PPP as a theory of the exchange rate. It has been established that PPP is more accurate over longer time periods than short periods.

To the extent that interest rates adjust to protect foreign financial assets and prices adjust to protect foreign real assets, markets provide firms with an automatic hedge against currency changes. However, if these market adjustments are incomplete, firms can hedge against the residual economic exposure by explicit transactions in the spot and forward markets. For example, firms with net foreign liabilities can borrow at home and lend abroad or buy foreign exchange in the forward market. In fact managers are not completely free to decide whether explicit hedging is prudent. Legal considerations may compel a firm to adopt a closed accounting position even if it results in an open economic position.

The Financial Accounting Standards Board is an American institution with some authority over how U.S. firms report foreign currency gains and losses. The board attempted to mollify critics of its controversial Rule No. 8 by changing foreign currency regulations in 1981. Businesspeople complained that Rule No. 8 forced them into unnecessary hedging transactions, which made reported earnings of firms more volatile than they otherwise would have been.[7]

---

[7] For a detailed discussion of Rule No. 8, see E. Raymond Simpson, "Financial Reporting in a Time of Volatile Exchange Rates," Financial Accounting Standards Board, 1982.

17.6 THE FORWARD
MARKET

Forward transactions are one device by which firms can hedge against foreign exchange risk. Since the advent of floating rates in 1973, the volume of forward transactions has increased substantially. In addition, trading of currencies has been made more convenient by the development of futures trading in the major currencies on organized commodity markets.

Although forward markets and futures markets perform the same basic function, they provide slightly different specialized services. Forward transactions are usually carried out through banks, and futures transactions usually involve organized commodity exchanges, such as the Chicago Mercantile Exchange. In general, banks are able to tailor the characteristics of a forward contract to the desires of individual customers. In determining characteristics of currency futures contracts, commodity exchanges seek standardized contracts to ensure an active secondary market. Contract size refers to the number of units of foreign exchange specified. In a forward transaction with a bank, any size contract is possible. With futures contracts there is a single uniform size contract such as 1 million German marks or Swiss francs.

In dealing with banks about the maturity of forward contracts, firms can arrange any acceptable date. Futures contracts mature on a single date (often the fifteenth) each month. Firms desiring unusually long maturities are probably better served by banks.

Futures traders must deposit a margin or security deposit with a broker as a guarantee that they can fulfill contracts. If the trader's equity declines because of an adverse movement in the exchange rate, the required deposit will increase ("margin call"). Because banks reserve forward exchange opportunities to their better customers, they require no explicit margin deposit.

Futures contracts are available only in those national currencies that are traded in large volume. The International Monetary Market offers contracts in the following eight currencies: Swiss francs, German marks, French francs, British pounds, Dutch guilders, Canadian dollars, Mexican pesos, and Japanese yen.

Despite these institutional differences the forward currency market and the currency futures markets are closely related. Arbitrage between the two markets tends to keep exchange rates in line. For example, the price of a futures contract for a specified currency to be delivered in a given month (fifteenth day) should equal the forward price of the same currency maturing same day. Because of these similarities between forward and futures markets, they will be treated as being analytically equivalent. Two of the more active centers of currency futures trade are the International Monetary Market of the Chicago Mercantile Exchange and the American Board of Trade in New York.

An important economic question is what determines the relationship between the spot and forward exchange rates. The relationship is partly determined by the actions of covered interest arbitragers. First, consider the process of uncovered interest arbitrage. Suppose that interest rates on comparable assets are 5 percent at home (United States) and 10 percent abroad (United Kingdom) and the spot exchange rate is $S_t = \$2.00$ per pound. An investment of \$2.00 in the United States would yield $\$2.00(1 + 0.05) = \$2.10$ at time $t + 1$. Alternatively the investor could buy pounds spot, invest in the United Kingdom for one period, and convert the pound earnings into dollars at $t + 1$. If the exchange rate does not change, the investor will end up with

$$\$2.00(\tfrac{1}{2})(1 + 0.10)(2) = \$2.20$$

It appears that the foreign investment is more lucrative. However, the spot exchange rate at $t + 1$ is unknown, and it may move against the investor.

Suppose that the pound sterling depreciates to \$1.80 at $t + 1$. The £1.1 will now be worth only $\$1.80(1.1) = \$1.98$. The investor would have been better off keeping his or her money at home under a pillow.

Because investors compare home and foreign interest rates, the process is called interest arbitrage. It is called uncovered arbitrage because the firm has an open position (long) in foreign exchange. In general, the relative returns from home and foreign investment of $\$I$ can be written as

$$I(1 + i) \gtrless I(\tfrac{1}{S_t})(1 + i^\star)S_{t+1}$$

The left-hand side is the value of the investment in the home country. The right-hand side shows the value of (1) buying $\$I$ worth of pounds at the spot rate S_t, (2) investing the pound proceeds in the United Kingdom at the rate $i^\star$, and (3) converting the pound earnings into dollars at the spot exchange rate S_{t+1}. The investor has an open position because S_{t+1} is not known at time t. The investor gains from increases in S_{t+1} (appreciation of the pound) and loses from decreases in S_{t+1}. There exists a hypothetical value of S_{t+1} that would equate domestic and foreign earnings. In this example, the investor would be indifferent between home and foreign investment if $S_{t+1} = \$1.909$.

Hedging in the forward market will permit the investor to close his or her position. In this case, hedging is called cover, and the entire process is called covered interest arbitrage. Suppose that the forward rate for delivery at $t + 1$ is $F_{t+1} = \$2.00$. The investor would agree at time t to sell £1.1 forward at the price $F_{t+1} = \$2.00$ for delivery at $t + 1$. Since the investor now has a pound liability (obligation to deliver £1.1) to offset the pound asset, his or her position is now closed. Any subsequent change in the exchange rate will not affect the investor's wealth. If the pound depreciates to \$1.80, the dollar value of pound earnings will again fall by \$0.20 per pound. However, the pounds that the investor has agreed to deliver for \$2.00 at $t + 1$ can be purchased spot for \$1.80. This capital gain of \$0.20 from the forward transaction exactly offsets the capital loss on the pound earnings. Covered interest arbitrage eliminates exchange rate uncertainty. Indeed, in this example investors can earn riskless profits by borrowing at home for 5 percent, buying pounds spot for $2.00, investing abroad at 10 percent, and selling pounds forward for $2.00.

When covered interest arbitrage is employed, the choice between domestic and foreign investment is the following:

$$I(1+i) \gtrless I(\frac{1}{S_t})(1+i^\star)F_{t+1}$$

Notice that in this expression the known forward rate (F_{t+1}) replaces the unknown future spot rate (S_{t+1}^E). In the example, the relationship is

$2.00(1.05)<$2.00(\frac{1}{2})(1.10)2$
$2.10<$2.20

The existence of riskless profits implies disequilibrium. All arbitagers will want to borrow in the United States, buy pounds spot, lend in the United Kingdom, and sell pounds forward. The resulting excess demands and supplies will cause prices to change. In the simple case where only the forward rate adjusts, the excess supply will cause the price to fall until profits disappear. The equilibrium forward rate will be $1.909. Market equilibrium is established when the return from domestic investment equals the covered return from foreign investment:

$$I(1+i) = I(\frac{1}{S})(1+i^\star)F$$
$2.00(1.05) = $2.00(\frac{1}{2})(1.10)($1.909)$
$2.10 = $2.10

Given domestic and foreign interest rates covered interest arbitrage determines the relationship between spot and forward exchange rates.

17.7 INTEREST RATE PARITY THEORY

Strictly speaking, interest rates and exchange rates are determined simultaneously. As an approximation the interest rate parity theory can be thought of as a theory of the forward exchange rate, given the spot rate and interest rates. It has been shown that covered interest arbitragers are indifferent between domestic and foreign investment if the following relationship holds:

$$1+i = \frac{F_{t+1}}{S_t}(1+i^\star)$$

All characteristics of bonds, such as default risk, must be comparable. The term F_{t+1} is the forward exchange rate with the same maturity as the bonds. This equilibrium condition can be rewritten as

$$\frac{F}{S} = \frac{1+i}{1+i^\star}$$

One can see from inspection that if the interest rate is higher at home, the forward rate will exceed the spot rate. It is conventional to express the forward premium on foreign exchange as a percentage of the spot rate:

$$PR = \frac{F-S}{S} = \frac{F}{S} - 1$$

Substituting from above yields

$$1 + PR = \frac{F}{S} = \frac{1+i}{1+i^\star}$$

$$PR = \frac{1+i}{1+i^\star} - 1$$

$$= \frac{1+i}{1+i^\star} - \frac{1+i^\star}{1+i^\star}$$

$$= \frac{i-i^\star}{1+i^\star}$$

This expression is the exact statement of the interest rate parity theory. It says that the premium of the forward rate over the spot rate is equal to the difference between home and foreign interest rates divided by 1 plus the foreign interest rate.

It is more common to state the approximate version of the theory:

$$PR = i - i^\star$$

It is approximately true because $1 + i^\star$ approaches one as $i^\star$ becomes smaller. The phrase interest rate parity refers to equality between the forward premium and the interest rate differential. Covered interest arbitrage equalizes real interest rates at home and abroad, but not nominal rates. Alternatively, one can say that nominal interest rates, net of cover, are equalized.

$$i = i^\star + \frac{F-S}{S}$$

The forward premium is the cost of cover, and the entire expression on the right-hand side can be thought of as the foreign interest rate net of the cost of cover.

Using numbers from the previous example, the equilibrium forward rate should be below the spot rate. The attempt by investors to earn the higher U.K. interest rate will lead to forward sales of pounds, which will drive the forward price of pounds to a discount. Specifically, the forward premium (negative for discount) will be

$$\frac{F-S}{S} = \frac{1.901 - 2.000}{2.000} = -\frac{0.091}{2} = -0.046$$

In general there will be a forward discount on the currency in the high interest rate country. Information about relative interest rates should provide a forecast of the forward premium. It is conventional to express interest rates and forward premiums on an annual basis. If the maturity of the bonds and forward contracts is different from a year, the following adjustment must be made to convert the premium to an annual basis:

$$\frac{F-S}{S} \left(\frac{12}{\text{no. months forward}} \right)$$

In the earlier example, if the bonds matured in six months, the annual forward premium would be

$$\frac{F-S}{S} = \left(\frac{1.909 - 2.000}{2} \right) \frac{12}{6} = -0.091$$

A geometrical summary of the approximate version of interest rate parity is shown in Figure 17-1. The algebraic forward premium is measured along the horizontal axis. A positive premium is indicated to the right of the origin, and a negative premium (discount) is shown to the left of the origin. The algebraic interest differential is measured along the vertical axis. For example, point A represents a situation in which home interest rates are five percentage points below foreign rates, and the forward exchange rate is equal to the spot rate. A 45-degree interest parity line represents market equilibrium, where the forward premium equals the interest differential. The theory predicts that all empirical observations should lie on the line.

Point E is an equilibrium where foreign interest rates are 5 percent above domestic rates, and the forward rate is at a 5 percent discount relative to the spot rate. At E there is no incentive for additional arbitrage. Point A represents the same 5 percent interest differential with no forward premium. It is not an equilibrium, since investors can earn a riskless profit by sending funds abroad. They will earn a 5 percent interest differential without losing anything from a forward discount. For all points below and to the right of the IRP line, there is an incentive to send funds abroad. In region 3b, the interest gain exceeds the forward discount. In region 1a, it is profitable to send funds abroad

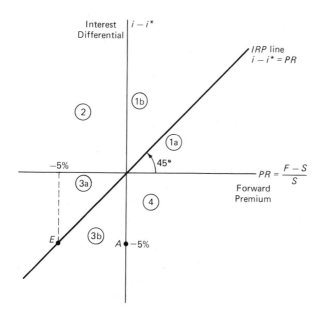

FIGURE 17-1   Interest Rate Parity and the Forward Rate

even though interest rates are higher at home. Investors are able to sell their foreign currency at a premium in the forward market, and the forward premium exceeds the interest loss. In region 4, an investor sending funds abroad gains from both a higher foreign interest rate and a premium in the forward market. One is unlikely to observe points in region 4, because they represent peculiar expectations. Foreign interest rates are above domestic rates, but the foreign currency is expected to appreciate. Points above and to the left of the *IRP* line complete the taxonomy. It is left to the reader to show why it is profitable to send funds to the home country in regions 3a, 2, and 1b.

The financial pages of some newspapers report forward exchange information by using phrases such as "in favor of New York" or "in favor of London." In the present context the phrase "in favor of ROW" would simply be the difference:

$$\frac{F-S}{S} - (i - i^\star)$$

It refers to a point below and to the right of the *IRP* line.

The interest rate parity theory in its simplest form must be qualified. Covered interest arbitrage involves transactions costs because brokers must be compensated for trading spot and forward currency and borrowing and lending. Generally, transactions costs prevent complete equalization of prices. In this case, transactions costs prevent complete equalization of covered interest rates.

In the presence of transactions costs, the interest parity line becomes a band whose width is determined by the cost of transacting. Observing points within the band is consistent with the theory, since small deviations from parity add more to transactions cost than they do to revenue. An empirical study of Frenkel and Levich supported the general proposition.[8]

A more fundamental qualification is that domestic and foreign bonds may not be perfect substitutes, and real interest rates may not be equalized. A basic assumption of *IRP* is that investors are indifferent between domestic and foreign bonds. The possibility of exchange control is one reason for investors to view foreign bonds as being different from domestic bonds. An investor may contract to sell his or her foreign exchange proceeds forward, but if the foreign government imposes exchange controls, the contract may be abrogated. Imposition of exchange controls can convert an apparently closed position in foreign exchange into an open position. The possibility of exchange controls is an element of country risk,[9] which includes unfavorable changes in regulation and taxation. Aliber has suggested that, in applying interest rate parity to U.S. dollars and pounds sterling, Paris market data should be used.[10] Eurodollar and Europound interest rates would be comparable because both are external currencies in Paris. This comparison would control for country risk. An implication of exchange control is that the supply of covered interest arbitrage funds may not be perfectly elastic. One would expect *IRP* to be more accurate for currencies for which exchange control is not a common practice. A related point is that investors will choose an optimal portfolio of money, domestic bonds, and foreign bonds. They may be unwilling to acquire additional foreign bonds through covered interest arbitrage without additional compensation. Any limitation on the supply of arbitrage funds permits the possibility of a deviation from interest rate parity.

17.8 FORECASTING EXCHANGE RATES

In a regime of floating exchange rates, information about future rates is important to many business firms. Some firms make internal exchange rate forecasts. Others consult banks or specialized foreign exchange advisory services. The forward exchange market provides a low-cost forecast that can be compared with those from other sources. Richard Levich has studied the relative

[8] Jacob Frenkel and Richard Levich, "Covered Interest Arbitrage: Unexploited Profits?" *Journal of Political Economy*, April 1975.

[9] A variety of advisory services offer to assess the political risk associated with investing in various countries. The available services include Haner's Business Risk Environment Index, Business International's Country Assessment System, and Frost and Sullivan's World Political Risk Forecasts.

[10] Robert Z. Aliber, *Exchange Risk and Corporate International Finance*. New York: Halsted, 1978.

accuracy of the forward rate and the forecasts of foreign exchange advisory services.[11] The forward rate compares quite favorably with alternative forecasts, and it is available at virtually no cost. If this were generally true, subscribers would either be making mistakes, or they would be paying largely for other services rendered.

Exchange rate forecasts may be made in many different ways. Analysts may construct formal econometric models, including variables such as inflation rates, money supply, and interest rates. So-called "judgmental forecasts" are an extreme alternative. Some practitioners with experience in trading foreign currency will render forecasts based on their personal implicit models. It is common for advisory services to combine a formal (it may be only one equation) model with an expert's judgment. No matter how elaborate a formal model may be, it necessarily omits certain variables that may be relevant. The judgment of a well-informed analyst may provide a way of incorporating the missing information. Another class of models omits economic variables entirely. Statistical time-series analysis attempts to forecast future exchange rates solely on the basis of past exchange rates.

The only relevant information is a time series of exchange rates:

$$S_{t+1} = f(S_t, S_{t-1}, \ldots, S_{t-n})$$

The hypothesis is that the pattern of price changes that occurred in the past will be repeated in the future. Analysts may use formal statistical techniques, or they may use the informal practices of chartists. Chartists plot historical exchange rates and search for patterns that may have forecasting value.

All forecasts, regardless of their source, face the problem that efficient markets incorporate all relevant information into current prices. If market participants have access to the same information (including the forecasts) as forecasters do, all that information should be built into the present price.

One implication of an efficient market is that past price information should have no forecasting value. There is a direct conflict between time-series analysis, which emphasizes the importance of past prices, and the hypothesis of an efficient foreign exchange market. The recent period of floating rates has provided useful empirical data for scholars who are actively studying this relationship.

One approach to testing for market efficiency is to devise a mechanical trading rule that would tell an agent when to buy and sell a currency. The object of the rule is to employ past exchange rate information to earn profits. One class of rules is a k percent rule that advises one to sell a currency when its price has fallen k percent below its previous peak and buy the currency when its price has risen k percent above its previous trough. If such a rule

[11]Richard Levich, "On the Efficiency of Markets for Foreign Exchange," in Rudiger Dornbusch and Jacob Frenkel, eds., *International Economic Policy: Theory and Evidence.* Baltimore: Johns Hopkins University Press, 1979.

were successful, it would indicate that the foreign exchange market had been ignoring some relevant information in pricing foreign exchange. A problem with the test is that one can construct a rule that would have been successful if it had been employed in the past. However, the same rule will not necessarily be successful in the future.

There are two extreme views of the role of speculators in the foreign exchange market. According to the first view, private speculators are well-informed, dispassionate people who efficiently process information. They buy foreign exchange when the price is low and sell when the price is high. The dual effect is simultaneously to stabilize currency markets and earn profits for speculators. Some adherents of this first view also point to the destabilizing role of government intervention under the managed float.

Central bank foreign exchange losses are cited as evidence of antisocial behavior. Central bankers may be poorly informed or poorly motivated, or perhaps political goals conflict with economic goals. It is not uncommon for political leaders and central bankers to blame private speculators for depreciation of their currencies (the infamous "gnomes of Zurich" are a familiar scapegoat) while they carry out expansionary monetary and fiscal policies at home. According to this first view, private speculators ameliorate the economic damage done by unfortunate government intervention.

A second view of private speculators is that they are poorly informed, emotional people whose actions amplify the natural fluctuations of the exchange rate. Speculators are described as following "animal spirits" rather than logic. As a substitute for rational analysis, they are said to follow "bandwagon psychology." In contrast to the mischief of private speculators, central banks are viewed as a source of stability. Central bank intervention is described as "leaning against the wind" or providing "orderly markets." This second view considers government intervention to be a necessary offset to the destabilizing behavior of private speculators. Several prominent officials[12] criticized the U.S. policy of free floating since April 1981 as an irresponsible act that surrendered exchange rates to the whims of private speculators. Both views of private speculation have been overstated here to highlight the differences. As more evidence about floating accumulates, it will become easier to analyze the effects of speculation.

A more moderate interpretation has been offered by McKinnon: "Thus, the problem seems not to be one of excessive destabilizing speculation, but rather one of the absence of speculation over time horizons longer than a day or two."[13] From a broader perspective, the price of foreign exchange and its volatility depend partly on conditions beyond the foreign exchange market. Foreign exchange rates cannot remain stable, regardless of the nature of speculation, if

[12] Public critics include President Mitterrand of France; H. Johannes Witteveen, former managing director of the IMF; and Robert V. Roosa, former Undersecretary of the Treasury.

[13] R. McKinnon, *Money in International Exchange* (New York: Oxford University Press, 1979), p. 156.

the underlying monetary and fiscal policies are volatile. This point will be pursued further in Chapter 18.

SUMMARY

The worldwide experiment with floating exchange rates since 1973 has included more countries for a longer time period than has any previous experience. One traditional criticism of floating is that exchange rate uncertainty would reduce the volume of world trade by adding to business costs. Since 1973 rates have been more volatile than they had been and perhaps more volatile than most observers expected them to be. However, there has been no apparent decline in trade that can be attributed to floating rates. Firms have adapted to new circumstances by explicitly or implicitly hedging against currency changes. Spot hedges can be carried out using foreign and domestic credit markets. Forward transactions provide an alternative form of explicit hedge. In addition the tendency for markets to incorporate expected exchange rate changes into current prices provides firms with an automatic or implicit hedge.

A country with a weak currency will tend to have an interest rate premium, and its currency will sell at a discount in the forward market. The interest rate parity theory explains the forward discount on a currency in terms of the international interest rate differential. The accuracy of interest rate parity depends largely on the behavior of covered interest arbitragers. Forecasting future exchange rates has become an important activity, and forward rates provide a benchmark by which other forecasts can be measured. Both private speculation and central bank intervention have the potential to stabilize or destabilize foreign currency markets. The relative contributions of the two activities to market stability remain an unresolved empirical issue.

REFERENCES

ALIBER, ROBERT Z. "The Firms Under Fixed and Flexible Exchange Rates." *Scandinavian Journal of Economics*, No. 2 (1976).
————. *Exchange Risk and Corporate International Finance.* New York: Halsted, 1978. Comprehensive analysis of foreign exchange risk faced by firms involved in international trade.
BARON, DAVID, and ROBERT FORSYTHE. "Models of the Firm and the Level of Trade." *American Economic Review*, September 1979. Analyzes the effect of uncertainty on the volume of trade.
BILSON, JOHN, F. O. "Recent Developments in Monetary Models of Exchange Rate Determination." International Monetary Fund *Staff Papers*, June 1979. Analyzes some aspects of foreign exchange market efficiency.
CHICAGO MERCANTILE EXCHANGE. *International Monetary Market Yearbook*, Chicago, annually. Includes data on futures prices of major currencies.
DOOLEY, MICHAEL, and PETER ISARD. "Capital Controls, Political Risk, and

Deviations from Interest Rate Parity." *Journal of Political Economy*, April 1980. A study of the effects of German capital controls on interest rate parity.

DORNBUSCH, RUDIGER.   "Exchange Rate Economics: Where Do We Stand?" *Brookings Papers on Economics Activity*, 1: 1980. Survey of recent work on exchange rate determination.

DUFEY, GUNTER.   "Forecasting Foreign Exchange Rates: A Pedagogical Note." *Columbia Journal of World Business*, Summer 1981. A brief survey of forecasting problems.

————, and IAN H. GIDDY.   *The International Money Market*. Englewood Cliffs, N.J.: Prentice-Hall, 1978. Chapter 2 surveys the literature on exchange rate expectations.

EITEMAN, DAVID, and ARTHUR STONEHILL.   *Multinational Business Finance*, 3rd ed. Reading, Mass.: Addison-Wesley, 1982. Chapters 5 and 6 deal with exchange risk.

FIELEKE, NORMAN S.   "Foreign Exchange Speculation by U.S. Firms: Some New Evidence." *New England Economic Review*, March–April 1979.

FISHER, IRVING.   *The Theory of Interest* (1930). New York: Kelley, 1955. Chapter 19 considers the relationship between interest rates and expected depreciation.

FRENKEL, JACOB.   "Flexible Exchange Rates, Prices, and the Role of 'News': Lessons from the 1970s." *Journal of Political Economy*, August 1981. Emphasizes the effect of unexpected changes on exchange rates.

————, and RICHARD LEVICH.   "Covered Interest Arbitrage: Unexploited Profits?" *Journal of Political Economy*, April 1975. Discusses the effects of transactions cost on interest rate parity.

————, and MICHAEL MUSSA.   "The Efficiency of the Foreign Exchange Market and Measures of Turbulence." *American Economic Review*, May 1980. Considers whether floating exchange rates have been excessively volatile since 1973.

FRIEDMAN, MILTON.   "The Case for Flexible Exchange Rates." In Friedman, *Essays in Positive Economics*. Chicago: University of Chicago Press, 1953. An analytical essay favoring floating at a time when that position was quite unpopular.

————, and ANNA JACOBSON SCHWARTZ.   *A Monetary History of the United States*. Princeton, N.J.: Princeton University Press, 1963. The section on the Greenback period deals with the floating dollar.

GRASSMAN, SVEN.   "A Fundamental Symmetry in International Payment Patterns." *Journal of International Economics*, May 1973. Presents data on the determination of invoice currencies.

GRUBEL, HERBERT.   *Forward Exchange, Speculation and the International Flow of Capital*. Stanford, California: Stanford University Press, 1966. A theoretical and empirical analysis of forward markets.

JACQUE, LAURENT.   *Management of Foreign Exchange: Theory and Praxis*. Lexington, Mass.: Lexington Books, 1978. Advanced textbook on techniques used by firms to deal with exchange risk.

————.   "Management of Foreign Exchange Risk: A Review Article." *Journal of International Business Studies*, Spring–Summer 1981. A survey of the literature on foreign exchange risk.

LESSARD, DONALD, ED.   *International Financial Management: Theory and Applications*. Boston: Warren, Gorham, and Lamont, 1979. Collection of papers related to international financial problems faced by business firms.

LEVICH, RICHARD.   "On the Efficiency of Markets for Foreign Exchange." In *International Economic Policy: Theory and Evidence*, R. Dornbusch and J. Frenkel eds. Baltimore: Johns Hopkins University Press, 1979. Analyzes various aspects of the efficiency of foreign exchange markets.

————, and C. WIHLBORG, eds. *Exchange Risk and Exposure.* Lexington, Mass.: D.C. Heath, 1980.

LOGUE, D. and G. OLDFIELD. "Managing Foreign Assets When Foreign Exchange Markets Are Efficient." In *International Financial Management: Theory Applications,* Donald Lessard, ed. Boston: Warren, Gorham, and Lamont, 1979.

MAGEE, STEPHEN, and RAMESH RAO. "Vehicle and Nonvehicle Currencies in International Trade." *American Economic Review,* May 1980. Discusses the determinants of the currency in which invoices are expressed.

NURKSE, RAGNAR. *International Currency Experience.* Geneva: League of Nations, 1944. A study of the interwar period stressing the unfavorable effects of floating exchange rates.

RODRIGUEZ, RITA, and E. EUGENE CARTER. *International Financial Management,* 2nd ed. Englewood Cliffs, N.J.: Prentice-Hall, 1979. Chapters 6 through 9 deal with foreign exchange problems of business firms.

SIMPSON, E. RAYMOND. "Financial Reporting in a Time of Volatile Exchange Rates." Financial Accounting Standards Board, 1981. Discusses FASB Rule No. 8.

WESTERFIELD, J. M. "An Examination of Foreign Exchange Risk Under Fixed and Floating Rate Regimes." *Journal of International Economics,* May 1977. An empirical study of foreign currency risk.

WIHLBORG, CLAS. *Currency Risks in International Financial Markets.* Princeton Studies in International Finance, No. 44, December 1978. Survey of literature on exchange risk faced by business firms.

WONNACOTT, PAUL. *The Floating Canadian Dollar: Exchange Flexibility and Monetary Independence.* Washington, D.C.: American Enterprise Institute, 1972. Analysis of the Canadian experience with floating from 1950 to 1962 and since 1970.

YEAGER, LELAND. *International Monetary Relations: Theory, History, and Policy,* 2nd ed. New York: Harper & Row, 1976. Contains a section on historical experience with floating exchange rates.

CHAPTER EIGHTEEN
FLOATING, THE FOREIGN EXCHANGE MARKET, AND THE GENERAL ECONOMY

18.1 INTRODUCTION

This chapter will analyze the relationship between the foreign exchange market under floating rates and the general economy. The concept of a stable foreign exchange market will be discussed. It will be shown that the question of exchange market stability is related to the question of whether the balance of trade improves following currency devaluation. Market stability conditions will be expressed in terms of elasticities of demand and supply for exports and imports. The effect of exchange rate changes on domestic and foreign currency prices of exports and imports will be shown. The effect of exchange rate changes on the terms of trade will be considered. The relationship between exchange rate changes and domestic taxes will be considered. In particular, it will be shown that devaluation is equivalent to a tax on consumption of importables plus a production subsidy.

The response of the trade balance to devaluation has been popularly described by a "J" curve. The J curve can be interpreted as a hypothesis that the balance of trade improves following devaluation, but only after an initial deterioration.

The relationship between devaluation and inflation will be considered. In addition to a possible effect on domestic inflation, floating rates may alter the transmission of inflation between countries. Transmission of external economic disturbances under fixed and floating rates will be considered. The final topic will be the formation of currency blocs within which rates are fixed and between which exchange rates float.

18.2 STABILITY OF THE
FOREIGN EXCHANGE RATE

Prior to the adoption of floating rates, there was concern about the stability of floating exchange rates. Moderate critics predicted considerable volatility of rates, and extreme critics denied that any equilibrium price would be established. Nearly a decade of experience with floating has convinced most observers that equilibrium exchange rates do exist. Currency markets clear on a daily basis without prices approaching zero or infinity. However, some observers have concluded that exchange rates have been more volatile than they ought to be.

The amount of price change in any market depends on the frequency and magnitude of outside disturbances and the elasticities of demand and supply in the market. Before one can determine whether observed exchange rate changes have been excessive, one must first determine what constitutes a normal amount of rate variability. Specifically, one should consider the elasticities of supply and demand for foreign exchange and the sources of disturbance to the foreign exchange market. If disturbances are frequent enough or large enough, exchange rates will be volatile even if elasticities are large. To determine the normal amount of exchange rate fluctuation, one must consider the interaction between the foreign exchange market and the general economy of which it is a part. If the general economy is turbulent, one cannot expect a stable exchange rate.

It is apparent from discussions about exchange rate stability that the term "stability" is used in several different senses. Some confusion will be avoided if the purely semantic issues are resolved first. One should distinguish between the economic concept of dynamic instability and the popular notion of volatility. A market is dynamically unstable if it fails to return to equilibrium following a disturbance. Thus, a stable market will be characterized by volatile prices, provided that it is subjected to large and/or frequent outside disturbances. Price volatility refers to changes that are large or frequent relative to some notion of normal price behavior. Thus, exchange rates may be described as volatile relative to previous exchange rate behavior or relative to prices in other markets. International financial experience since 1973 has shown exchange rates to be more volatile than in the past, but foreign exchange markets have been dynamically stable.

Consider the possible sources of dynamic instability of the foreign exchange market or any other market. Figure 18-1 shows a dynamically unstable market. Under Walrasian assumptions, a price will rise whenever there is an excess demand and fall whenever there is an excess supply. Since the demand curve in Figure 18-1 has a positive slope and the supply curve has a negative slope, a price that is pushed above P_1 will rise indefinitely. At P_2 there is an excess demand of BC, which will raise the price farther from equilibrium. Similarly, if the price is displaced below equilibrium, it will not return. At P_3 there is an excess supply of DE, which will lower the price and move it further

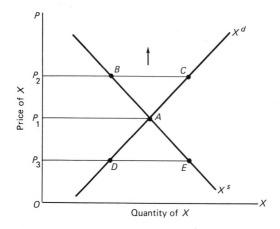

FIGURE 18-1   Dynamically Unstable Market

from equilibrium. It is apparent that the source of dynamic instability in this example is that both supply and demand curves have perverse slopes.

However, dynamic instability can also occur in less extreme cases, as shown in Figure 18-2. The demand curve has the conventional negative slope, while two alternative negatively sloped supply curves are shown. Supply curve X_1^s is more vertical than is X_1^d, while supply curve X_2^s is less vertical than is the demand curve. The situation with the supply curve X_2^s is dynamically unstable. A price rise from P_1 to P_2 will generate an excess demand of DC, which will push the price further from equilibrium. Thus, instability can occur when only one curve has a perverse slope.

If the demand curve has the conventional negative slope but the slope of the supply curve is more negative, the market is unstable. However, a nega-

FIGURE 18-2   Market Stability and Alternative Backward-Bonding Supply Curves

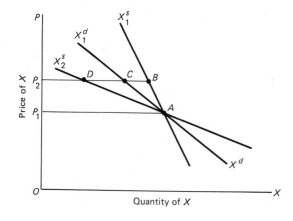

tively sloped or backward-bending supply curve does not guarantee instability. If the market supply curve is X_1^s instead of X_2^s, the market will be stable. In that case, a price rise to P_2 will generate an excess supply of CB, which will cause the price to return to P_1. Thus, the factor that determines dynamic stability is whether the supply curve is more negative than the slope of the demand curve. The possibility of a backward-bending foreign exchange supply curve based on an inelastic export demand was discussed in Chapter 15 and will be considered in the paragraphs that follow.

One source of dynamic instability is that either one or both curves have unconventional slopes. A possible alternative source of instability is unrelated to slopes of curves. Markets may be unstable if expected prices are highly responsive to actual prices. In particular, a market will be dynamically unstable if an actual price change of k percent induces a change in the expected price of more than k percent. The expectation of a price increase will shift the demand curve to the right as consumers attempt to avoid the price increase. The relationship can be summarized by using the concept of the elasticity of expectations $(\eta_{P_E P})$:

$$N_{P_E P} = \frac{dP^E / P_E}{dP / P}$$

A market will be unstable if the elasticity of expectations is greater than 1. Highly elastic price expectations are sometimes described as "bandwagon psychology."

If the price rises, people expect it to rise even more. The effect of elastic expectations is shown in Figure 18-3. The initial equilibrium at A is disturbed by a shift of supply from X_1^s to X_2^s. With unitary price expectations the new

FIGURE 18-3   Elastic Price Expectations and Instability

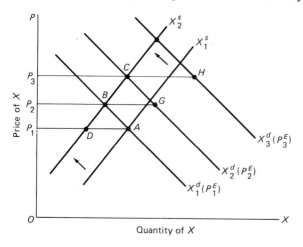

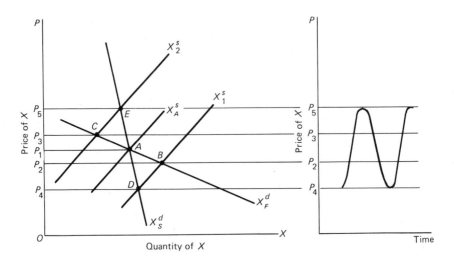

FIGURE 18-4   Inelastic Demand and Price Volatility

equilibrium would be at point B. The increase in the actual price from P_1 to P_2 would induce an equal increase in the expected price. Elastic price expectations mean that the actual price increase from P_1 to P_2 induces a greater increase in the expected price. Because of the new price expectation, the demand curve shifts to X_2^d, creating an excess demand of BG at P_2. The actual price increase to P_3 would induce a larger increase in the expected price, and the demand curve would shift to X_3^d.

Currency exchange rates may be volatile even if foreign exchange markets are dynamically stable. Price volatility may occur either because foreign exchange demand and supply are inelastic or because of significant outside disturbances to the market.

The effect of inelastic demand on price volatility is shown in Figure 18-4. Let supply fluctuate between X_1^s and X_2^s, with X_A^s as the average supply. X_F^d is the flatter or more elastic demand curve at point A. If X_F^d is the demand curve, the price will fluctuate between P_2 and P_3. However, if demand is represented by the steeper curve X_s^d, the price will fluctuate between P_4 and P_5. The greater range of price fluctuation ($P_4P_5 > P_2P_3$) can be attributed to inelastic demand. Inelastic supply curves would also contribute to price volatility. Attributing exchange rate fluctuation to inelastic demand and supply has been called "elasticity pessimism."

An alternative source of price volatility would be large or frequent shifts of supply and demand curves, regardless of the slopes and elasticities of the curves. The foreign exchange market may be shocked by real forces involving supply and demand for imports, or it may be disturbed by macroeconomic variables such as monetary and fiscal policy.

As seen in Figure 18-4 inelastic demand and supply will amplify the effect of a market disturbance. The notion of elasticity pessimism and the occurrence of frequent outside shocks are complementary explanations of exchange rate volatility. The last decade has been characterized by highly erratic monetary and fiscal policy, which has not been coordinated across countries. Because of the resulting shifts in foreign exchange supply and demand curves, it may have been difficult to have less fluctuation of exchange rates under any set of foreign exchange elasticities. It would have been particularly difficult to have maintained fixed exchange rates in the face of divergent monetary and fiscal policies.

18.3 THE ELASTICITIES APPROACH TO THE EXCHANGE RATE

The economic impact of exchange rate fluctuations depends on the effect on prices of traded goods and services and the volume of trade. To separate relative price changes from inflation one must distinguish between the nominal (Π) and real (Π_R) exchange rates. The real rate between two currencies is the nominal rate adjusted for relative inflation rates:

$$\frac{d\Pi_R}{\Pi} = \frac{d\Pi}{\Pi} - (\frac{dP}{P} - \frac{dP^\star}{P^\star})$$

The domestic and foreign inflation rates are dP/P and $dP^\star/P^\star$, respectively.

   Suppose that inflation is 10 percent at home and 6 percent in ROW. If the nominal exchange rate depreciates by 4 percent, the real exchange rate will not change. The differential inflation of 4 percent would make foreign products more attractive to home residents, but the 4 percent depreciation would just offset the price differential. Without a change in the real exchange rate, there is no incentive for exports or imports to change. However, a nominal depreciation of more than 4 percent would raise the prices of importables and exportables relative to those of nontraded goods. By altering relative prices, the real depreciation induces domestic firms to produce more traded goods and domestic consumers to buy less. The result of producing more traded goods and consuming less is a larger volume of net exports. The neutral effect of devaluation equal to differential inflation can be shown in terms of nominal prices.

   Let the initial price of X be £2 in the United Kingdom when the exchange rate is $2 per pound. The price of X in the United States will be $4.

$$P = \Pi P^\star$$
$4.00 = $2.00 (£2)
$4.40 = $2.20 (£2)

Let there be 10 percent inflation in the United States and none in the United Kingdom. If the exchange rate adjusts for differential inflation, the rate will be $2.20 per pound when X sells for $4.40. The real price of X to U.S. consumers and producers has not been altered by inflation plus currency depreciation. The pound price of X has not been changed by appreciation of the pound. U.K. consumers must pay $0.40 more per unit of X, but each pound will buy $0.20 more (gain $0.40 on a £2 item). Thus, U.K. consumers experience a $0.40 loss per unit of X due to U.S. inflation that is just offset by a $0.40 gain per unit of X from the exchange rate change. A nominal exchange rate change without a change in the real rate will not alter the pattern of trade.

The nominal exchange rate depends on the demand and supply of foreign exchange. Assume that the general price level is constant at home and abroad. It follows that changes in the nominal exchange rate can also be interpreted as changes in the real rate. It was shown in Chapter 15 that foreign exchange demand and supply can be derived from the underlying markets for importables and exportables. The elasticity of demand for foreign exchange (η_{FII}) depends on the elasticity of demand for imports (η_I) and the elasticity of supply of imports (ϵ_I):[1]

$$\eta_{FII} = \frac{\eta_I(1+\epsilon_I)}{\epsilon_I - \eta_I}$$

For small countries, the elasticity of supply of imports is infinitely great, and the expression reduces to

$$\eta_{FII} = \eta_I$$

The elasticity of supply of foreign exchange (ϵ_{FII}) generally depends on the elasticity of supply of imports (ϵ_I) and the elasticity of demand for imports (η_I):

$$\epsilon_{FII} = \frac{\epsilon_E(1+\eta_E)}{\eta_E - \epsilon_E}$$

Since a small exporting country faces an infinitely elastic demand for its product, the expression simplifies to

$$\epsilon_{FII} = \epsilon_E$$

These expressions can be used to determine the dynamic stability of the foreign exchange market. Specifically, if the price of foreign exchange increases will the excess demand for foreign exchange decrease? When capital flows are

[1] For a derivation of the basic relationships, see Robert Stern, *The Balance of Payments* (Chicago: Aldine, 1973). Chap. 2 and appendix or Miltiades Chacholiades, *International Monetary Theory and Policy*, New York: McGraw-Hill, 1978.

unresponsive to the exchange rate, the question is equivalent to the question of whether currency depreciation will reduce the balance-of-trade deficit. As shown in Figure 18-2, the foreign exchange market will be stable if the foreign exchange supply curve is less negatively sloped than the foreign exchange demand curve. The condition is automatically satisfied if the demand curve is negatively sloped and the supply curve is positively sloped. The condition is also satisfied if the supply curve bends backward, provided that it is not too negative. Specifically, the slope of the supply curve must exceed the slope of the demand curve:

$$\frac{dF^s}{d\Pi} > \frac{dF^d}{d\Pi}$$

The same condition can be written in elasticity form:[2]

$$\epsilon_{F\Pi} > \eta_{F\Pi}$$

Using these expressions, the condition can be written in terms of export and import elasticities:

$$\frac{\epsilon_E \eta_E + \epsilon_E}{\eta_E - \epsilon_E} > \frac{\eta_I \epsilon_I + \eta_I}{\epsilon_I - \eta_I}$$

The terms can be rearranged to obtain the more conventional expression:

$$1 + \eta_E + \eta_I < \frac{\eta_E \eta_I}{\epsilon_E \epsilon_I}(1 + \epsilon_I + \epsilon_E)$$

The stability of the foreign exchange market depends on the magnitudes of the four trade elasticities. The demand elasticities are negative and the supply elasticities are positive. It follows that the right-hand side (RHS) of the inequality is positive, since it is the product of two positive terms. The stability condition is automatically satisfied if the left-hand side is negative, which occurs when

$$|\eta_E| + |\eta_I| > 1$$

The sum of the demand elasticities exceeding 1 is called the Marshall-Lerner condition, and it is a sufficient condition for market stability. It is satisfied if either demand elasticity exceeds 1 by itself. The magnitude of η_E pro-

---

[2] Since

$$\epsilon_{F\Pi} = \frac{dF^s}{d\Pi}\frac{\Pi}{F} \quad \text{and} \quad \eta_{F\Pi} = \frac{dF^d}{d\Pi}\frac{\Pi}{F}$$

vides information about the country's monopoly power in export markets. Since inelastic demand implies negative marginal revenue, it is in the interest of a prudent monopolist to avoid this region. As long as this region is avoided, the foreign exchange market will be stable. The Marshall-Lerner condition is not necessary for stability.

The stability condition remains satisfied when the left-hand side (LHS) is negative, provided that it is not too negative. For example, let $\eta_E = \eta_I = -0.4$ and RHS $= +0.3$. The market is stable since LHS $= +0.2 <$ RHS $= +0.3$. Satisfying the elasticity condition ensures that the foreign exchange market is dynamically stable in the sense that the supply curve is either positively sloped or less negative than the demand curve. Satisfying this condition does not rule out instability attributable to elastic exchange rate expectations. Neither does it rule out volatile exchange rates due to inelastic demand and supply or large and frequent outside disturbances.

18.4 THE EXCHANGE RATE, PRODUCT PRICES, AND THE VOLUME OF TRADE

International trade is affected by changes in the real exchange rate. To separate real exchange rate changes from the effects of inflation, assume that the general price level is held constant by appropriate monetary and fiscal policy.[3] An exchange rate change will influence trade by altering prices of traded goods relative to nontraded goods. It was shown in Chapter 15 that depreciation of the home currency will raise the prices of importable and exportable goods expressed in home currency. Unless the country is small, depreciation will also lower prices of traded goods expressed in foreign currency. The relationship between currency depreciation and import prices is shown in Figure 18-5.

Panel A shows the volume of imports as a function of domestic currency prices, and panel B below shows imports as a function of foreign currency prices. The distinction between prices expressed in the two national monies is crucial, because prices move in opposite directions. The equilibrium at the initial exchange rate at domestic prices is at point A. Depreciation of the home currency to Π_2 shifts the import supply curve to $I_2^s(\Pi_2)$. At a given home currency price, as measured on the vertical axis, the foreign currency price is lower, and consequently foreigners are less willing to supply imports. At the new equilibrium point B, the price is higher and the volume of imports is lower.

Because of this price increase, it is commonly said that currency devaluation adds to inflationary pressure. The statement confuses relative prices and

[3] See Rudiger Dornbusch, "Exchange Rates and Fiscal Policy in a Popular Model of International Trade," *American Economic Review*, December 1975, for a discussion of the appropriate macroeconomic policy.

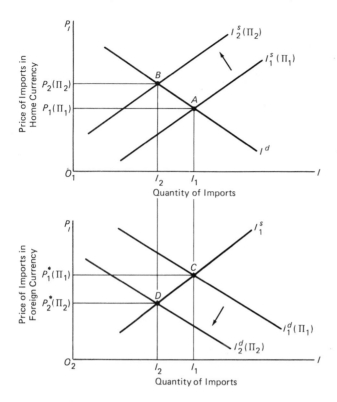

FIGURE 18-5 Devaluation and Imports

the general price level. However, the general price level can be constant only if monetary and fiscal policy are used to reduce prices of nontraded goods. Notice that the effect of devaluation on the value of imports $(V_I = P_I I)$ expressed in domestic currency is uncertain. In panel A the question is whether the area of the rectangle $O_1 P_1 A I_1$ is greater than that of $O_1 P_2 B I_2$. Devaluation will decrease the domestic currency value of imports if the elasticity of demand for imports is greater than 1.

Panel B shows the comparable relationship in foreign currency. The initial equilibrium is at point C on I_1^d. Devaluation shifts the demand curve to I_2^d. For a given foreign currency price, as shown on the vertical axis, the domestic currency price of imports is higher. Consequently, domestic buyers reduce their import demand. The new equilibrium is at point D, where the price is $P_2^\star$ and the import volume is I_2. Notice that the decrease in $P_I^\star$ increases residents' command over imports (i.e., improves the terms of trade).

Since devaluation lowers both the foreign currency price and the volume of imports, it necessarily reduces the foreign currency value of imports $(V_I^\star = P_I^\star I)$. In panel B the area $O_2 P_2^\star D I_2$ is necessarily smaller than is the area $O_2 P_1^\star C I_1$. The two diagrams must show the same decrease in imports, $I_2 I_1$.

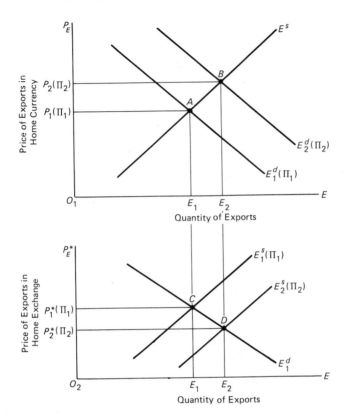

FIGURE 18-6   Devaluation and Exports

Devaluation raises the domestic currency price of imports and lowers the foreign currency price of imports, and the difference between the percentage changes must equal the percentage devaluation:

$$\frac{dP_I}{P_I} - \frac{dP_I^{\star}}{P_I^{\star}} = \frac{d\Pi}{\Pi}$$

The impact of devaluation on exports is shown in Figure 18-6. The initial equilibrium is at A. Devaluation shifts export demand from E_1^d to E_2^d. At each domestic price of exports, as shown on the vertical axis, the foreign currency price falls. Consequently, foreigners increase their demand for exports.

At the new equilibrium point B, the domestic currency price has increased $(P_2 > P_1)$, and the volume of exports has increased $(E_2 > E_1)$. Since both price and quantity of exports increase, the domestic currency value of exports $(V_E = P_E E)$ necessarily increases. The area $O_1 P_2 B E_2$ exceeds the area $O_1 P_1 A E_1$. The effect of devaluation in terms of foreign currency is shown in panel B of Figure 18-6. From initial equilibrium at point C, devaluation shifts the export supply curve from E_1^s to E_2^s. At each foreign currency price, domestic export suppliers receive more home currency. As export supply increases, the foreign currency price decreases and the volume of exports increases. The decline in the export price contributes to a worsening of the terms of trade, whose magnitude depends on the shift in E^s and the elasticity of export demand along E^d. Because of the price decrease, the effect of depreciation on the foreign exchange value of exports is uncertain.

The question is whether the area of the rectangle $O_2P_2^*DE_2$ exceeds $O_2P_1^*CE_1$. The answer depends on the elasticity of export demand (η_E). If η_E is greater than 1 in absolute value, depreciation will increase the value of exports. Conversely, a decline in export value requires that exporters be operating in the inelastic region of demand. Recall that the elasticity of supply of foreign exchange depends on the elasticity of demand for exports. It was also shown that $|\eta_E| > 1$ is sufficient, but not necessary, for exchange market stability.

The combined effect of depreciation on imports and exports is the effect on the balance of trade. If the foreign exchange market is stable, depreciation will reduce the excess demand for foreign exchange. It is equivalent to decreasing the balance-of-trade deficit expressed in foreign currency. Figure 18-7 shows the relationship between the balance of trade and market stability under the assumption that capital flows are unresponsive to exchange rate changes.

The term F^d represents foreign exchange demanded by importers, and F^s represents foreign exchange supplied by exporters. The currency is devalued from Π_1 to Π_2. Panel A shows the conventional case in which the market is stable, and devaluation reduces an initial trade deficit. Since most countries are small in the sense of lacking market power, this is the most important case in fact. Smallness means that the elasticity of demand for exports is infinitely great, which implies that F^s slopes upward. The deficit measured in foreign exchange is

$$B^\star = V_E^\star - V_I^\star$$

The change in the balance is

$$dB^\star = dV_E^\star - dV_I^\star = F_2F_4 - (-F_3F_1)$$

The deficit declines as foreign exchange supplied by exporters increases by F_2F_4 and foreign exchange demanded by importers declines by F_3F_1.

Panel B shows the case in which the foreign exchange supply curve bends backward, but it remains less negative than F^d. The foreign exchange supply curve bends backward, because the demand for exports is inelastic. The market is stable, and devaluation improves the trade balance. Devaluation from π_1 to π_2 reduces the initial deficit from AB to CD. The deficit declines because the demand for foreign exchange by importers declines by more than the supply by exporters falls:

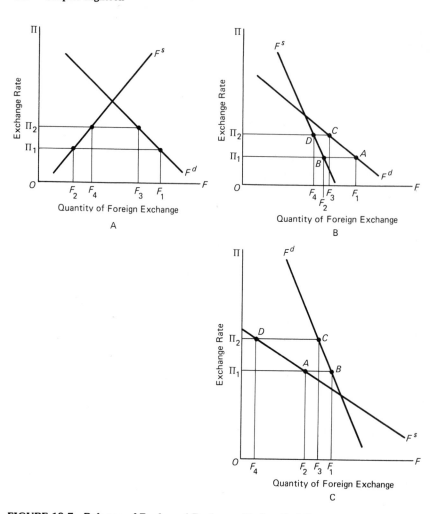

FIGURE 18-7   Balance of Trade and Exchange Market Stability

$$dB^\star = F_2F_4 - (F_1F_3)$$

Panel C shows the unstable case, in which depreciation increases the trade deficit. At the exchange rate Π_1 there is a deficit of AB. A devaluation to Π_2 increases the excess demand to DC. Because of the relative slopes of F^d and F^s, the demand for foreign exchange by importers falls by less (F_1F_3) than the decrease in foreign exchange supply by exporters (F_2F_4). The steepness of F^d is partly caused by inelastic demand for imports.

18.5 DEVALUATION
AND THE TERMS OF TRADE

Currency devaluation may alter the terms of trade of large countries. Since small countries are price takers in import and export markets, they cannot alter their terms of trade through domestic policies. Changes in terms of trade are imposed on them by the rest of the world. As shown, devaluation by large countries will decrease foreign currency prices of both exports and imports. Since the term of trade is defined as the ratio of export prices to import prices expressed in the same currency, the direction of change caused by devaluation is uncertain without more information:

$$TT = \frac{P_E^\star}{P_I^\star} = \frac{\Pi P_E^\star}{\Pi P_I^\star} = \frac{P_E}{P_I}$$

The terms of trade can be expressed either as a function of foreign currency prices or of domestic currency prices, but prices should not be mixed. Consider the following common but misleading statement about the effects of devaluation. "Devaluation improves the trade balance by making exports cheaper and imports more expensive." The statement appears to say that residents receive less for exports and pay more for imports, which implies a deterioration of the terms of trade. However, the correct interpretation is that $P_E^\star$ falls (P_E rises) and P_I rises ($P_I^\star$ falls), but the ratio of $P_E^\star$ to P_I is not the terms of trade. The information needed is whether $P_E^\star$ falls by more than $P_I^\star$ falls. Alternatively, does P_E rise by more than P_I? For a large country, devaluation worsens the terms of trade on the export side and improves them on the import side. Information about the relative magnitude of these effects is needed.

The two effects represent the relative monopoly and monopsony power of the nation's exporters and importers. Since devaluation induces more exports, it lowers the foreign currency price and tends to "spoil" the monopolized market. The price declines more as monopoly power increases, which can be summarized by the elasticity of export demand (η_E). Since devaluation reduces import volume, it reduces the price. The magnitude of the price decrease depends on the degree of monopsony, which can be summarized by the elasticity of import supply (ϵ_I).

One can say roughly that the terms of trade will deteriorate following devaluation if the country's monopoly power in export markets exceeds its monopsony power in import markets. Concern about the adverse terms of trade effects of devaluation is common in countries that are specialized exporters. In such cases, it is not uncommon to combine devaluation and an export tax. The export tax is designed to ameliorate the decline in the foreign currency price of exports.

One can derive a more precise condition under which devaluation will worsen the terms of trade. TT will deteriorate if the product of the supply elasticities exceeds the product of the demand elasticities:

$$\epsilon_E \epsilon_I > \eta_E \eta_I$$

The condition for terms of trade deterioration can be obtained by calculating the separate effects of devaluation on export and import prices. The inverse relationship between the exchange rate and the foreign currency price of exports is given by

$$\frac{dP_E^\star}{P_E^\star} = \frac{\epsilon_E}{\epsilon_E - \eta_E} \frac{d\Pi}{\Pi}$$

A comparable expression for the import market is

$$\frac{dP_I^\star}{P_I^\star} = \frac{\eta_I}{\epsilon_I - \eta_I} \frac{d\Pi}{\Pi}$$

The change in the terms of trade is given by the difference between the price changes:

$$\frac{dP_E^\star}{P_E^\star} - \frac{dP_I^\star}{P_I^\star}$$

It is left to the reader to show that the change in the terms of trade is equal to

$$\frac{\eta_I \eta_E - \epsilon_I \epsilon_E}{(\epsilon_I - \eta_I)(\epsilon_E - \eta_E)}$$

Since the denominator is necessarily positive, the terms of the trade will deteriorate only if $\epsilon_I \epsilon_E > \eta_I \eta_E$. An intuitive explanation is that deterioration occurs when import prices fall less than export prices. The inverse of ϵ_I is an index of monopsony power, and $P_I^\star$ will fall less the larger is ϵ_I. In the extreme case of infinitely great ϵ_I, $P_I^\star$ does not fall at all. Thus, the less monopsony power a country has, the less terms of trade benefit it gets from devaluation. On the export side, the inverse of η_E is an index of monopoly power. The smaller the η_E, the greater the monopoly power and the more export prices fall after devaluation. Thus, large values of ϵ_I and small values of η_E are associated with declining terms of trade. This condition for declining terms of trade is related to the condition for market stability.

The market is *unstable* if

$$1 + \eta_E + \eta_I > \frac{\eta_E \eta_I}{\epsilon_E \epsilon_I}(1 + \epsilon_E + \epsilon_I)$$

The LHS is necessarily less than 1 (since η's are negative), and the RHS term $(1 + \epsilon_E + \epsilon_I)$ is greater than 1. The only way the LHS can exceed the RHS is for the expression

$$\frac{\eta_E \eta_I}{\epsilon_E \epsilon_I} < 1$$

Slightly rewritten, this is precisely the condition necessary for devaluation to worsen the terms of trade. Thus, one can conclude that deterioration of the terms of trade is a necessary condition for market instability.

18.6 DEVALUATION AND EQUIVALENT TAXES

The economic effects of tariffs and export taxes were analyzed in Chapters 7 and 8. By altering relative prices, real exchange rate changes alter international trade in the same way as taxes on trade. It was shown that devaluation raises the domestic currency price of imports. In this respect, devaluation has the same effect as an across-the-board tariff on all imported goods and services at the same percentage rate. The two policies are equivalent in the sense that they have the same effect on prices, consumption, production, and the volume of trade. A difference is that a tariff earns revenue but devaluation does not. Both a tariff and a depreciation can be represented by shifting the import supply curve to the left (see Figures 7-2 and 18-5), which raises the domestic currency price and reduces import volume. Currency depreciation also raises export prices, and in this respect it is analogous to an export subsidy.

The effects of an export subsidy are reproduced in Figure 18-8. The initial equilibrium is at point A, where the price is P_1 and the volume of exports is E_1. An export subsidy of AB will shift the export supply curve to E_2^s, which lowers the foreign price to P_2 and increases the volume to E_2. The net price

FIGURE 18-8 Export Subsidy and Devaluation

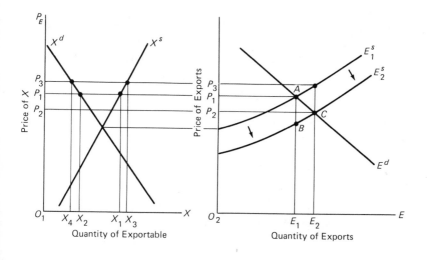

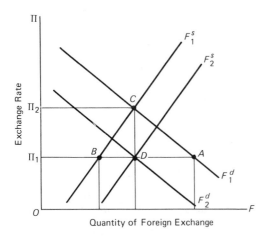

FIGURE 18-9   Equivalence of Devaluation and Tariff Plus Export Subsidy

received by exporters of X is P_3, which is equal to P_2 plus the subsidy of AB. Since firms have the option of exporting X or selling it at home, the domestic price must also be P_3. The increase in exports induced by the subsidy (E_1E_2) is equal to the increase in domestic production (X_1X_3) plus the decrease in domestic consumption (X_2X_4).

It was shown that currency depreciation also raises domestic currency prices of exports, lowers foreign prices, and increases the volume of exports. Devaluation has the same effect as an across-the-board subsidy on all exports of goods and services at the same percentage rate. A difference is that the subsidy requires revenue but the devaluation does not. The combined effect of a k percent devaluation on exports and imports is equal to a k percent tariff on all imports plus a k percent subsidy on all exports.[4] The equivalence of the two effects is shown in Figure 18-9.

With initial foreign exchange demand and supply curves F_1^d and F_1^s, an excess demand for foreign exchange of AB at Π_1 can be eliminated by devaluation to Π_2. Alternatively, a tariff will reduce demand to F_2^d, and an export subsidy will increase foreign exchange supply to F_2^s. Thus, two alternative equilibria are point D with the tariff and export subsidy and point C without them.

The argument is symmetrical, so that a currency appreciation is equivalent to an import subsidy plus an export tax. The relationship can be summarized as follows:

$$\text{Dev} = \text{Tariff} + \text{ExpSub}$$
$$\text{Apprec} = \text{ImpSub} + \text{ExpTax}$$

---

[4]To be strictly equivalent to devaluation, the tariff and export subsidy must apply to capital flows as well as goods and services.

Import competing firms and exporters are protected by devaluation because they receive higher prices. Some governments are accused of deliberately undervaluing their currencies ("competitive devaluation") in an attempt to promote exports and discourage imports. Allegations of this practice inspired the term "dirty float" as a derogatory description of a managed float. Conversely, real appreciation has an adverse effect on import-competing firms and exporters.

Recall that a tax on trade is equivalent to a pair of taxes on production and consumption. Specifically, a tariff is equal to a consumption tax plus a production subsidy. An export subsidy is equal to a consumption tax on the exportable plus a production subsidy. Thus, a real currency devaluation is equivalent to a set of purely domestic taxes and subsidies:

$$\text{Dev} = (\text{ConsTax} + \text{ProdSub})_I + (\text{ConsTax} + \text{ProdSub})_E$$

It follows that currency devaluation can be accomplished indirectly through the fiscal system.

One can also devalue indirectly by changing the system of border tax adjustment. Domestic sales taxes such as the value added tax must employ a border tax adjustment for imports and exports. (See the earlier discussion in Section 9.3.) Under the origin principle, exports are taxed but imports are not. Under the destination principle, imports are taxed but exports are not. If a country switches from the origin principle to the destination principle, the currency has been effectively devalued. The switch involves taxing imports that were previously untaxed and rebating taxes on exports that were previously taxed. This combined tariff plus export subsidy is equivalent to currency devaluation.

18.7 CURRENCY CONTRACTING AND THE J CURVE

It is sometimes observed that currency devaluation causes the trade balance to deteriorate before it improves. When the trade balance is plotted as a function of time, its path may resemble the letter J. One can rationalize this pattern by appealing to the proposition that elasticities are greater in the long run than in the short run. Demand for a country's exports may be elastic in the long run and inelastic in the short run. As a result, foreign exchange supply may be positively sloped in the long run and sufficiently negatively sloped in the short run. The short-run effect of devaluation may be to reduce the value of exports by more than it reduces the value of imports. Currency contracting is a related consideration. Whether export and import contracts are expressed in domestic or foreign currency may alter the immediate effect of devaluation and the shape of the J curve.

The currency contract period is defined as a period so short that the quantities of exports and imports are fixed and the prices are fixed in either foreign or domestic currency. The change in the foreign currency value of the trade balance is related to foreign exchange market stability, and it can be expressed as

$$B^\star = V_E^\star - V_I^\star = P_E^\star E - P_I^\star I$$

Since E and I are fixed in the currency contracting period, the effect of devaluation on the trade balance depends on what happens to prices.

$$dB^\star = dP_E^\star E - dP_I^\star I$$

If contracts are expressed in foreign currency, devaluation has no effect on $P_E^\star$, $P_I^\star$, or $B^\star$. If contracts are expressed in domestic currency, prices will fall in terms of foreign money. The currency denomination of contracts is an empirical question, and there are four extreme logical possibilities: (1) both imports and exports are expressed in foreign currency, (2) both are in domestic currency, (3) imports are in foreign currency and exports are in domestic currency, and (4) imports are in domestic currency and exports are in foreign currency. A necessary condition for devaluation to worsen the balance of trade in currency contract period is that import contracts be expressed in foreign currency. This implies that devaluation will not lower the foreign currency value of imports $(dP_I^\star = O)$. If in addition export prices are expressed in domestic currency, the trade balance will necessarily deteriorate:[5]

$$dB^\star = EdP_E^\star - IdP_I^\star = Ed(\frac{1}{\Pi}) < 0$$

In this case, devaluation causes the trade balance to deteriorate because exporters earn less foreign exchange without importers earning more. In some cases, contracts are expressed in vehicle currencies, which are different from those of the exporter and importer. In fact the U.S. dollar is an important vehicle currency. This complicates the analysis, because both traders are subject to exchange risk and the trade balance could improve in terms of one foreign currency while deteriorating in terms of the other. Over a longer time period, contract prices will also respond to devaluation. One can then ask how much of a devaluation will be "passed through" to foreign consumers of exports and imports in the form of lower foreign currency prices. Finally, quantities will respond to prices, and one can investigate the magnitudes of the export and import elasticities.

---

[5] The foreign currency price of exports is $P_E^\star = 1/\Pi/(P_E)$. The effect of devaluation is $dP_E^\star = P_E d(1/\Pi) = 0$.

The idea of currency contracting also applies to capital flows. If a firm borrows abroad, and the loan is expressed in foreign currency, it will suffer a capital loss if the home currency depreciates. If the loan were fixed in domestic currency, the foreign lender would suffer a loss measured in foreign currency. To the extent that the depreciation was expected by market participants, the home currency interest rate would exceed the foreign currency interest rate. Thus, the domestic borrower or the foreign lender would receive some indirect compensation.

One of the immediate reasons given for the failure of Laker Airways in 1982 was depreciation of the pound. The firm had borrowed a large amount of dollars, and the weakening of the pound increased the pound cost of repaying the dollar liability. Freddie Laker stated publicly that the dollar loan looked attractive because the interest rate was so low relative to pound interest rates. Perhaps credit markets anticipated the depreciation of the pound better than Laker did.

18.8 DEVALUATION, INFLATION, AND THE VICIOUS CIRCLE

Since historical currency depreciation has been highly correlated with inflation, it is sometimes argued that depreciation causes inflation. The alleged inflation mechanism is that depreciation raises the domestic currency prices of both importables and exportables, which brings about a kind of cost-push inflation. By making home exports and imports less competitive, inflation induces further depreciation of the currency. The process of depreciation-inflation-depreciation is sometimes described as a "vicious circle." The corresponding process for strong and less inflationary countries is called a "virtuous circle."

An extreme example of this interpretation is the claim that the German hyperinflation of the 1920s was caused by depreciation of the mark. This explanation has the same weakness of all cost-push theories of inflation; namely, it ignores the demand for money. A stable demand for real money balances will attenuate any inflationary pressure that is not accompanied by an increase in the money supply. If prices of traded goods rise because of currency depreciation, there will be an offsetting deflationary pressure coming from an excess demand for money. The only way to sustain the inflationary pressure is for the central bank to accommodate the excess money demand by creating more money. However, if an increase in the money supply is a necessary component of the vicious circle, one cannot distinguish exchange rate cost-push inflation from any other type that is a result of expansionary money policy.

The effect of devaluation on inflation depends on what happens to variables outside the foreign exchange market. Specifically, the effect depends on what happens to aggregate demand and the money supply. The general price level can be expressed as a weighted average of the prices of traded and non-traded goods:

$$P = w_T P_T + w_N P_N$$

The budget shares, w_T and w_N are constant for a Laspeyres-type consumer price index. Two possible monetary policies in response to devaluation are (1) a constant price level (P) and (2) a constant price of nontraded goods. To maintain a constant price level in the face of an increase in the price of traded goods, the money supply must be held constant so as to lower the price of nontraded goods. The magnitude of the price decrease depends on the size of the increase for traded goods adjusted for the relative importance of the two classes of goods in consumer budgets.[6] In this case, the relative price of traded goods would rise without an increase in the average price level.

An alternative policy of stabilizing the price of nontraded goods would permit some monetary accommodation. If the money supply increases enough to hold P_N constant, the average price level will increase by an amount equal to the increase in traded goods prices, adjusted for their importance in the index.[7]

One cannot determine the effect of currency depreciation on the price level without specifying the nature of monetary policy. Suppose that an economy is subject to real disturbances (e.g., increase in import prices) that are accommodated by the central bank. Currency depreciation will be correlated with inflation even though it is not the ultimate cause of inflation. There is some evidence that under floating rates the variance of inflation rates across countries has increased. This observation could be explained by real disturbances with uneven effects across countries combined with monetary accommodation by central banks.

A further problem with the concept of a vicious circle is that it fails to explain fluctuations in exchange rates. The vicious circle implies that once a currency moves in a certain direction, it will continue in that direction indefinitely. However, most currencies fluctuate in fact. Why, for example, did the U.S. dollar appreciate in 1981, 1982, and 1983 after nearly a decade of depreciation?

18.9 TRANSMISSION OF EXTERNAL DISTURBANCES

One can distinguish two issues concerning the effect of floating exchange rates on the interdependence of countries. The first is whether exchange rate uncer-

[6] A stable price requires:
$$dP = w_T dP_T + w_N dP_N = 0$$
$$dP_N = -\frac{w_T}{w_N} dP_T$$

[7] If $dP_N = 0$, then $dP = w_T dP_T$.

tainty interferes with the international division of labor by reducing the volume of trade. Decreasing interdependence in this sense would reduce world income. A second issue concerns the effect of floating on the average inflation rate for the world and the dispersion of national inflation rates around the world average.

A traditional argument made by men such as Jacob Viner and Lionel Robbins is that floating rates would bring about more inflation by encouraging more expansionary monetary policy.[8] Data on inflation rates since 1973 is not inconsistent with that hypothesis. The average world inflation rate has been greater since floating, and the acceleration of inflation has been very widespread. For example, in the decade of the 1960s, 29 percent of the countries of the world had inflation rates in excess of 5 percent. In the decade of the 1970s, the comparable figure was 100 percent. Also in the 1960s, 10 percent of the countries of the world had inflation rates greater than 10 percent per year. The comparable figure for the decade of the 1970s was 55 percent. In 1980, 80 percent of the countries had inflation rates exceeding 10 percent. However, one cannot conclude that floating was the cause of inflation. Both floating and inflation may have been caused by more fundamental forces.

A second part of the inflation issue is whether national inflation rates have become more dispersed with floating rates. Obligatory foreign exchange market intervention links national money supplies and inflation rates under a fixed rate system. The automatic link between national money supplies is broken under freely floating rates. Central banks are freer to pursue independent monetary policy with greater variability in national inflation rates.

An additional hypothesis is that inflation rates will be more variable under a floating rate regime. Some evidence providing mild support for the hypothesis is presented in Table 18-1, which shows the dispersion of inflation rates around the mean for the period 1950 to 1980. Dispersion of inflation is measured by the standard deviation (s.d.) and the coefficient of variation (c.v.). The latter is an attempt to standardize for the increase in the average inflation rate. As measured by the standard deviation, world inflation appears more variable in the later years. The s.d. was 12.3 in the 1950s and 7.5 in the 1960s, and it increased to 17.5 in the period 1970 to 1974. As of 1980, the standard deviation of inflation rates had not fallen below 20.

Of the three country groups, the set of non-oil developing countries had the greatest standard deviation in each period. Thus, the figures on standard deviation tend to support the hypothesis of greater variability of inflation under floating rates. However, the picture is not as clear when the coefficient of variation is used to measure dispersion. It is simply the s.d. divided by the mean. Since average inflation increased during this period, use of c.v. is an attempt to adjust for the change. When the c.v. is used to measure dispersion,

[8] Jacob Viner, *Studies in the Theory of International Trade.* London: George Allen and Unwin, 1937, Chapter 4, and Viner, "Some International Aspects of Economic Stabilization," in L. D. White, ed., *The State of the Social Sciences.* Chicago: University of Chicago Press, 1956. See also Lionel Robbins, *The Economist in the Twentieth Century.* London: Macmillan, 1954.

TABLE 18-1   Dispersion of Inflation Rates, 1950–1980
(percent per year)

PERIOD	WORLD	INDUSTRIAL COUNTRIES	OIL EXPORTING COUNTRIES	NON-OIL DEVELOPING COUNTRIES
1950–59				
s.d.	12.3	1.6	3.4	16.1
c.v.	1.8	0.4	1.1	1.7
1960–69				
s.d.	7.5	2.0	1.0	8.9
c.v.	1.5	0.5	0.5	1.6
1970–74				
s.d.	17.5	3.0	5.4	20.1
c.v.	1.4	0.3	0.7	1.4
1975–79				
s.d.	23.8	7.5	3.9	27.0
c.v.	1.5	0.7	0.3	1.5
1979				
s.d.	21.0	9.1	6.3	23.2
c.v.	1.2	0.9	0.6	1.2
1980				
s.d.	20.8	10.5	7.6	22.8
c.v.	1.0	0.8	0.6	1.0

s.d. = the standard deviation; c.v. = the coefficient of variation, s.d. divided by the mean.
Source: International Monetary Fund, Survey, December 14, 1981, p. 388.

there is no evidence of an increase under floating rates. The figures of 1.8 for the 1950s and 1.5 for the 1960s were followed by 1.4 for 1970–1974, 1.5 for 1975–1979, 1.2 for 1979, and 1.0 for 1980. The only country group that is consistent with the hypothesis of greater variability is the set of industrial countries. It is possible that they are the only group that has effectively changed from fixed rates to floating rates.

Under the Bretton Woods system the exchange rates of developing countries were adjusted more frequently. Under the managed float, many of their currencies are effectively pegged to certain key currencies such as the dollar. Thus, the exchange rate regime may not have changed much for them. For industrial countries the coefficient of variation was 0.4 in the 1950s, 0.5 in the 1960s, and 0.3 from 1970 to 1974. The c.v. increased to 0.7 in the late 1970s, to 0.9 in 1979, and to 0.8 in 1980. Thus, there is some evidence for greater monetary independence under floating, but it depends on how variability is measured and what set of countries is considered.

Dispersion of national inflation rates depends on dispersion of national money supplies. It has been hypothesized that countries will have greater monetary independence under floating rates. Under fixed exchange rates, the money supply is determined by relative growth of nominal GNP at home and abroad. If inflation and growth in nominal GNP are excessive at home, monetary reserves and the money supply decline. Conversely, if inflation is low relative to that of trading partners and money GNP grows slowly, monetary reserves and the money supply will increase. The empirical implication is that under fixed exchange rates, changes in money GNP will precede changes in the money supply. In a limited sense, one can say that changes in GNP cause "changes in the money supply." However, under floating, one would not expect changes in GNP to induce changes in money. An hypothesis is that the timing of the relationship between money and GNP should be different under fixed and floating rates. Greater monetary dependence is expected under fixed rates than under floating rates. There is some evidence to support the hypothesis for the United Kingdom.[9]

According to the preceding argument, floating should insulate countries from certain foreign disturbances because it breaks the link between national money supplies. In particular, such monetary disturbances as inflation should not be transmitted as readily. However, the phenomenon of currency substitution may prevent the insulation from being complete. The direct substitution of foreign money for domestic money is currency substitution. It is analogous to the substitution of foreign goods for domestic goods in trade and foreign bonds for domestic bonds as part of international investment.

Many business firms hold cash balances in both foreign and domestic money, the proportions depending on economic conditions. An expected depreciation of the home currency will induce the substitution of foreign money for domestic money, which will amplify the initial depreciation. Currency substitution permits the transmission of inflation between countries under floating rates even though each central bank controls its national money supply. For example, let there be monetary expansion and inflation in ROW under floating exchange rates. As long as foreign and domestic money are substitutes, some of the new foreign money will be acquired by domestic residents. Because of the additional foreign cash balances, the demand for domestic money will decrease. Without any increase in the domestic money supply, the excess supply of money will cause the domestic price level to rise.

A kind of imported inflation is possible even with floating exchange rates. The magnitude of the domestic price increase depends on the money supply increase abroad and the degree of substitution between the two monies. In the logical extreme case of perfect money substitutes, a one-unit increase in foreign money has the same effect on the domestic price level as does a one-unit increase in domestic money. In this case the central bank would lose control over the price level, even though it retained control over domestic money. In

---

[9]See the paper by Bluford Putnam and D. S. Wilford, "Money, Income, and Causality in the U.S. and the U.K.," *American Economic Review*, June 1973.

addition there would be no equilibrium exchange rate between the currencies.

There is empirical evidence for the existence of currency substitution, but not for perfect substitution. For example, a study by Miles estimated an elasticity of substitution between the U.S. and Canadian dollars of $+5.$[10] One reason why foreign and domestic money are imperfect substitutes is the possibility of exchange control. For example, in the absence of restrictions, a firm can use either a dollar account in the United States or a franc account in France to pay for imports. However, if the French government imposes exchange controls, the franc loses some of its liquidity and becomes an imperfect substitute for the dollar. The significance of currency substitution is that the demand for domestic money can be influenced by foreign economic conditions, even under floating exchange rates. Because of induced changes in the demand for domestic money, the price level can change without a change in the domestic money supply.

Floating exchange rates insulate the domestic money supply from the foreign money supply, but they cannot insulate money demand from foreign influences. In addition they cannot prevent domestic interest rates from responding to foreign rates. A central bank's control over domestic interest rates depends on the degree of capital mobility between countries, not on whether exchange rates are fixed or floating. For example, if domestic and foreign bonds are good substitutes, real interest rates will move in unison whether fixed or floating exchange rates prevail.

Some central bankers have complained that they have less monetary independence than they expected under floating rates. Floating has permitted more independence or control over monetary reserves and the domestic money supply. Without interfering with international capital flows, a system of floating rates cannot confer greater control over interest rates. Increased integration of world capital markets, including the development of external currency markets, has reduced the authority of central banks. Thus, interest rates provide another channel through which foreign disturbances can influence the domestic economy under floating exchange rates.

18.10 CURRENCY BLOCS
AND THE MANAGED FLOAT

A currency bloc or currency area is a set of currencies for which fixed rates are maintained between members and floating rates prevail with respect to nonmembers. If a currency bloc becomes permanent, it is a monetary union. The 50 United States of America are a monetary union. One New York dollar regularly exchanges for one North Carolina dollar, and the probability of deval-

[10] Marc Miles. "Currency Substitution, Flexible Exchange Rates, and Monetary Independence," *American Economic Review*, June 1978.

uation by any one state is negligible. Most members of the European Economic Community have participated in a currency bloc, whose ultimate object is monetary union. However, exchange rate changes between members have been more frequent than planned. For example, the French franc was devalued twice within a year after the Mitterrand government took power.

What determines the number of currency blocs in the world? One extreme possibility would be a single world currency. All exchange rates would be permanently fixed, and national currencies would lose their separate identities. Greater certainty and lower transactions costs would be immediate advantages of a single currency. At the opposite extreme each country could maintain floating exchange rates against others. The advantages of greater monetary independence must be weighed against greater exchange rate uncertainty and transactions costs. In intermediate cases, countries form currency blocs characterized by fixed rates within each bloc and floating between. For example, let there be three countries, A, B, and C. If all three joined a currency bloc, there would be a single world currency. At the opposite extreme, each could float against the other two. A third possibility is a bloc of any two (A and B, B and C, or A and C) that would float against the third currency.

How to form these currency blocs is an important theoretical and practical question. Each country has to decide which currency bloc, if any, to join. A useful theory could provide guidance in selecting a currency bloc. For example, it has been suggested that factor mobility is useful within a currency bloc. Another suggestion is that a highly open economy would benefit from forming a currency bloc with its major trading partners. Instead of trying to derive the economic characteristics of an optimum currency bloc, Heller did an empirical study of the economic determinants of fixed and floating exchange rates. He concluded that countries were more likely to choose floating rates (1) the larger the country in terms of GNP, (2) the less open the economy, (3) the greater the deviation of national inflation from world inflation, and (4) the greater the country's financial integration with the rest of the world.[11]

One extreme exchange rate policy is to join a currency bloc and maintain permanently fixed rates within and freely floating rates between blocs. Since the exchange rate would respond to all disturbances, the source and duration of exchange market disturbances would be irrelevant to exchange rate policy. It would not matter whether disturbances originate at home or abroad, in the money market or the goods market, or whether they are permanent or transitory. In all cases, the exchange rate would float. In the opposite extreme case of permanently fixed rates, the source and duration of disturbances would also be irrelevant for policy purposes. The exchange rate would always remain fixed. An alternative mixed policy is the managed float. Governments respond to certain kinds of disturbances by changing the exchange rate, but they respond to other disturbances by buying or selling reserves.

[11] For details of the study see H. Robert Heller, "Determinants of Exchange Rate Practices," *Journal of Money, Credit, and Banking*, August 1978.

There are both positive and normative questions about a managed float that remain unanswered. Some positive questions are (1) What rules have central banks used in implementing exchange rate policy? and (2) What have been the effects of intervention policy on the market? The specific question of whether central banks have stabilized or destabilized the market has been addressed. On the normative side, people have attempted to determine the characteristics of an optimal managed float. One suggestion is that whether the exchange rate should change in response to a disturbance should depend on the source of the disturbance. Specifically, it depends on whether a disturbance originates in the money market, the goods market, or the foreign exchange market. For example, if all disturbances originate in the money market, fixed rates are optimal. If an increase in the money supply causes an excess demand for foreign exchange, the problem is automatically solved if the central bank sells reserves for domestic money. This line of analysis may prove to be useful, but it imposes a large information cost on the central bank managing the float. Detecting the sources of economic disturbances is not a simple task.

Operating a managed float requires some policy coordination among central banks. Uncoordinated policies may lead to conflict, because there is only one independent exchange rate between two currencies. If the German government tried to increase the value of the mark against the dollar and the U.S. government tried to increase the value of the dollar against the mark, they could not both succeed. Inconsistent intervention could be avoided by coordination. Even if there were agreement about the desired exchange rate, a decision must be made about which central bank will intervene.

Suppose that both banks agree that the mark should depreciate by a certain amount relative to the market rate. The desired depreciation could be accomplished either by the U.S. selling marks for dollars or by the German central bank doing the same thing. Following the U.S. decision to implement a free float in April 1981, several European governments complained that they were carrying out intervention that should have been carried out by the United States.[12] Central banks make some attempt to coordinate intervention policies.

There are several institutions in which governments attempt to coordinate general economic policies. European central bankers have 10 regular meetings per year at the Bank for International Settlements. The Organization for Economic Cooperation and Development (OECD) is a second example, and the annual economic summit conferences held since 1974 are a third.[13] In ad-

[12] At the Versailles Economic Summit Conference of June 1982, the French government criticized the United States for not intervening to prevent the dollar from appreciating. In the case of the dollar-franc rate, this would have required buying francs and selling dollars, which was carried out by the French central bank. One week after the conference, the franc was devalued. The French bank sold dollar reserves for 6.27 francs per dollar, which turned out to be worth more than 6.50 francs per dollar after the devaluation. In this case, the choice of intervening country determined who took the capital loss.

[13] The 24 members of the OECD, which is based in Paris, are: Australia, Austria, Belgium, Canada, Denmark, Finland, France, West Germany, Greece, Iceland, Ireland, Italy, Japan, Lux-

dition to coordination between national governments, the International Monetary Fund has attempted to devise some broad guidelines for appropriate exchange market intervention. One general idea is that governments should not resist basic trends in rates, but they may intervene to reduce the variance around trend.

Many alternative rules have been proposed, including some that specify an appropriate quantity of reserves to be held by the central bank. For example, Robert Triffin and Donald B. Marsh have authored a "fork proposal" that would require each country to state a target reserve level.[14] Actual reserve holdings would be permitted to vary within a fixed range around the target. Once reserves fell to the minimum level, the currency would depreciate. If they rose to the maximum level, the currency would appreciate. This system of limited reserve fluctuation is analogous to the Bretton Woods system, which permitted limited exchange rate fluctuation around the par value, beyond which reserves must change.

SUMMARY

A system of floating exchange rates is viable only if the market is stable. It is important to distinguish among several meanings of the term "stability." The foreign exchange market may be dynamically unstable if the supply and demand curves have perverse slopes. The market may be volatile if supply and demand curves have conventional slopes but are inelastic. The market may be dynamically unstable regardless of slopes provided that exchange rate expectations are elastic. Finally, the foreign exchange market may be dynamically stable but volatile if outside disturbances are frequent and large. Specifically, divergent national monetary and fiscal policies have been a major disturbance since 1973.

Because elasticities are greater in the long run, the ultimate response of the trade balance to devaluation will be greater than the immediate effect. Devaluation may improve or worsen the terms of trade depending on the magnitude of the trade elasticities. Because it changes relative prices, a change in the real exchange rate is equivalent to taxing or subsidizing imports and exports. The effect of devaluation on inflation depends on the underlying monetary pol-

embourg, Netherlands, New Zealand, Norway, Portugal, Spain, Sweden, Switzerland, Turkey, United Kingdom, and the United States. The OECD was founded in 1961 as the successor to the Organization for European Economic Cooperation (OEEC), which was established in 1948. Participants in the annual economic summit conferences have been the United States, Canada, Japan, the United Kingdom, West Germany, France, and Italy.

[14]Donald B. Marsh, "The Fixed-Reserve Standard: A Proposal to Reverse Bretton Woods," in George N. Halm, ed., *Approaches to Greater Flexibility of Exchange Rates: The Burgenstock Papers*. Princeton: Princeton University Press, 1970. Robert Triffin. *Gold and the Dollar Crisis: Yesterday and Tomorrow*. Essays in International Finance Number 132. Princeton: Princeton University Press, December 1978.

icy. Floating exchange rates insulate the money supply from foreign disturbances but not money demand or interest rates. Average inflation in the world
has been greater under floating rates, but it is difficult to determine the direction of causation. Many countries have opted for currency blocs, which imply
fixed rates against some countries and floating rates against others. Most countries have employed a managed float, but the actual rules employed and the
optimal rules for intervention are not yet fully understood.

REFERENCES

ARGY, VICTOR. *Exchange Rate Management in Theory and Practice*, Princeton Studies in International Finance, No. 50. Princeton, N.J.: Princeton University Press,
1982. Empirical study of foreign exchange market intervention.

ARTUS, JACQUES, and JOHN H. YOUNG. "Fixed and Flexible Exchange Rates:
A Renewal of the Debate." International Monetary Fund *Staff Papers*, Decem-
ber 1979. Reprinted in *International Trade and Finance: Readings*, Robert E.
Baldwin and J. David Richardson, eds., 2nd ed. Boston: Little, Brown, 1981.

BERGSTEN, C. FRED. "The Villain Is an Over-valued Dollar." *Challenge*, March–
April 1982. An essay contending that the dollar is not properly valued in currency markets.

BLACK, STANLEY W. *Floating Exchange Rates and National Economic Policy*. New
Haven, Conn.: Yale University Press, 1977. A comparative study of macroeconomic policy under floating exchange rates.

BOYER, RUSSELL. "Optimal Foreign Exchange Market Intervention." *Journal of
Political Economy*, December 1978. A theoretical argument that intervention should
depend on the source of exchange market disturbances.

COOPER, RICHARD, et al., eds. *The International Monetary System Under Flexible
Exchange Rates*. Cambridge, Mass.: Ballinger, 1982. Collection of papers on the
recent experience with floating exchange rates.

DORNBUSCH, RUDIGER. "Exchange Rates and Fiscal Policy in a Popular Model
of International Trade." *American Economic Review*, December 1975.

DREYER, JACOB S., GOTTFRIED HABERLER, and THOMAS D. WILLETT,
eds. *Exchange Rate Flexibility*. Washington, D.C.: American Enterprise Institute, 1978.

FEDERAL RESERVE BANK OF BOSTON. *Managed Exchange Rate Flexibility: The
Recent Experience*, 1978. Proceedings of a conference on managed floating.

FRENKEL, JACOB A. "Flexible Exchange Rates, Prices, and the Role of 'News':
Lessons from the 1970s." *Journal of Political Economy*, August 1981. Stresses the
effect of unanticipated events on exchange rates.

————, and MICHAEL MUSSA. "The Efficiency of Foreign Exchange Markets and
Measures of Turbulence." *American Economic Review*, May 1980. Stresses that
foreign exchange markets have not been more volatile than domestic asset markets.

GIRTON, LANCE, and DON ROPER. "Theory and Implications of Currency Substitution." *Journal of Money, Credit, and Banking*, February 1981. Statement of
the theory of currency substitution.

HELLER, H. ROBERT. "Determinants of Exchange Rate Practices." *Journal of
Money, Credit, and Banking*, August 1978. Empirical study of the determinants
of fixed and floating exchange rates.

HERIN, JAN, ASSAR LINDBECK, and JOHAN MYHRMAN, eds.   *Flexible Exchange Rates and Stabilization Policy.* London: Macmillan, 1977.

HOUTHAKKER, HENDRIK, and STEPHEN MAGEE.   "Income and Price Elasticities in World Trade." *Review of Economics and Statistics,* May 1969. Empirical study of import demand elasticities.

LEAMER, EDWARD, and ROBERT STERN.   *Quantitative International Economics.* Boston: Allyn & Bacon, 1970. A survey of the empirical literature on international economics.

LERNER, ABBA.   *The Economics of Control.* London: Macmillan, 1944.

MAGEE, STEPHEN.   "Currency Contracts, Pass-Through, and Devaluation." *Brookings Papers on Economic Activity,* 1:1973. An attempt to explain the J curve.

MARSH, DONALD B.   "The Fixed Reserve Standard: A Proposal to Reverse Bretton Woods." In *Approaches to Greater Flexibility of Exchange Ratio,* George N. Halm, ed. Princeton, N.J.: Princeton University Press, 1970. A proposal based on limited variability of foreign exchange reserves.

MARSHALL, ALFRED.   *Money, Credit, and Commerce.* London: Macmillan, 1923. An early statement of the Marshall-Lerner condition.

MCKINNON, RONALD I.   "Optimum Currency Areas." *American Economic Review,* September 1963. Discussion of the characteristics of an optimum currency area.

MILES, MARC.   "Currency Substitution, Flexible Exchange Rates, and Monetary Independence." *American Economic Review,* June 1978. An empirical study of the substitutability between U.S. and Canadian dollars.

MUSSA, MICHAEL.   *The Role of Official Intervention,* Occasional paper 6. New York: Group of 30, 1981. Survey of theoretical and empirical work on official intervention.

PUTNAM, BLUFORD, and D. S. WILFORD.   "Money, Income, and Causality in the U.S. and the U.K." *American Economic Review,* June 1978. Empirical study of the monetary independence of the United States and the United Kingdom.

SOHMEN, EGON.   *Flexible Exchange Rate,* revised edition. Chicago: University of Chicago Press, 1969. Analysis and advocacy of floating exchange rates.

STERN, ROBERT.   *The Balance of Payments.* Chicago: Aldine, 1973. Advanced textbook on international finance.

TAYLOR, DEAN.   "Official Intervention in the Foreign Exchange Market, or Bet Against the Central Bank." *Journal of Political Economy,* April 1982. Empirical study of the profitability and effectiveness of government intervention in foreign exchange markets.

WILLETT, T. D. and EDWARD TOWER.   *The Theory of Optimum Currency Areas and Exchange Rate Flexibility,* Special papers in International Economics, No. 11. Princeton, N.J.: Princeton University Press, 1976. Survey of the literature on optimum currency areas.

CHAPTER NINETEEN
EXCHANGE RATE
DETERMINATION

19.1 INTRODUCTION

The previous chapters analyzed exchange rates in terms of the supply and demand for foreign exchange. That analysis is correct as far as it goes, but it deemphasizes the relationship between the foreign currency market and the rest of the economy. This chapter focuses on the general determinants of the exchange rate that lie behind supply and demand curves for foreign exchange. The analysis presented here does not necessarily conflict with the use of elasticity concepts discussed earlier, but it sacrifices some detail to stress market interdependence.

The foreign exchange market is closely related to other markets, and an attempt to study it in isolation may be misleading. For example, in a dynamically stable foreign exchange market, the degree of exchange rate fluctuation depends on the slopes of curves and the frequency and magnitude of shifts of the curves. The determinants of the slopes of foreign exchange demand and supply curves were analyzed in Chapter 18. The present chapter will discuss the nature of outside disturbances that impinge on the foreign exchange market and shift the demand and supply curves for foreign exchange. If these shocks are large enough or frequent enough, the exchange rate will be volatile no matter how elastic foreign exchange demand and supply curves are.

The first explanation of exchange rates to be considered is the purchasing power parity theory (PPP). Absolute PPP attempts to explain the money exchange rate, whereas relative PPP attempts to explain percentage changes in the rate. The concept of PPP can be used to show how the use of market exchange rates can distort national income comparisons.

This chapter will also consider the monetary approach to the exchange rate that is an attempt to overcome some deficiencies of PPP in explaining short-run movements in exchange rates. The monetary approach focuses on the money market, whereas PPP stresses arbitrage between national commodity markets. A third approach to the exchange rate stresses real economic variables that enter through the current account balance. The final approach considered in this chapter is based on imperfect substitutability between domestic and foreign bonds. Changes in relative bond supplies between countries will alter real interest rate differentials and exchange rates. Theories of the exchange rate that emphasize the money and bond markets, rather than the goods market, are called asset market approaches.

19.2 ABSOLUTE PURCHASING POWER PARITY

The oldest and simplest theory of the spot exchange rate is purchasing power parity. It explains the exchange rate in terms of the relative purchasing power of domestic and foreign money over a comparable bundle of goods. The simple idea is that if it takes twice as much domestic money as foreign money to buy a comparable set of goods, a unit of foreign money possesses twice as much purchasing power. There will be a parity between the purchasing power of the two currencies and the rate of exchange when two units of domestic money exchange for one unit of foreign money.

This relationship is called the absolute version of the PPP theory, and it can be formally stated as

$$\Pi = \frac{P}{P^\star}$$

P and $P^\star$ are the domestic and foreign currency prices of a comparable set of goods. In this example, if it takes 20 units of domestic currency to buy a bundle of goods and 10 units of foreign currency to buy the same bundle, the exchange rate should be 2 units of domestic money per unit of foreign money.

The economic mechanism behind the equality is spatial arbitrage. Traders will compare the domestic currency price (P) with the domestic currency equivalent price abroad $(\Pi P^\star)$. If the prices differ, arbitragers will add to demand in the low-price market and add to supply in the high-price market until the difference is eliminated. For example, suppose that the price of a good is $2 at home and 1 unit of foreign exchange abroad and that the exchange rate is $1.80 per pound. Traders will buy abroad at $1.80 and sell at home for $2.00.

The upward pressure on the foreign price and the downward pressure on the home price will continue until the prices are equal.

Absolute PPP is applicable to the idea of the real exchange rate (Π_R). The real exchange rate is defined as the nominal exchange rate divided by the ratio of PPP prices:

$$\Pi_R = \frac{\Pi}{P/P^\star}$$

When absolute PPP holds, the real exchange rate is equal to unity. Thus, the real exchange rate is a way of representing deviations from PPP. For example, a real devaluation can be accomplished either by an increase in Π at constant prices or by a decrease in P relative to $P^\star$ at a constant nominal exchange rate. Let the initial equilibrium be $\Pi = \$2$, $P = \$2$, $P^\star = F1$. A real devaluation of 10 percent is accomplished if Π increases to $2.20 when prices are constant:

$$\Pi_R = \frac{2.20}{2/1} = 1.1$$

The same real devaluation occurs if the foreign price rises to 1.1 while the nominal exchange rate is constant:

$$\Pi_R = \frac{2.00}{2/1.1} = \frac{2}{1.818} = 1.1$$

Foreign inflation is a substitute for home devaluation. In international policy conferences, it is not uncommon for countries with weak currencies to urge their trading partners to increase aggregate demand (an oblique reference to inflation) as an alternative to their own devaluation. The final method of accomplishing a real devaluation is deflation of the home price to $1.818, given the foreign price and nominal exchange rate:

$$\Pi_R = \frac{2.00}{1.818} = 1.1$$

Domestic price deflation is an alternative to explicit devaluation of the nominal exchange rate. The economic effects of devaluation can be accomplished even in a system of fixed nominal exchange rates. A common use of PPP is to determine what nominal devaluation is necessary to offset a real appreciation brought about by an excess of domestic inflation over foreign inflation.

Suppose that the domestic price rises from $2.00 to $2.20. This requires a nominal exchange rate that will return the real exchange rate to its initial value of unity:

$$\Pi_R = 1 = \frac{\Pi}{2.20/1} = 2.20$$

The real exchange rate relationship can be expressed in terms of percentage changes: [1]

$$\frac{d\Pi_R}{\Pi_R} = \frac{d\Pi}{\Pi} - \left(\frac{dP}{P} - \frac{dP^\star}{P^\star}\right)$$

As shown in Chapter 18 the so-called "elasticities approach" is an attempt to explain the economic effects of changes in the real exchange rate. Conversely, a change in the nominal exchange rate that just offsets the difference between domestic and foreign inflation should have no real economic effects.

An assumption of absolute PPP is that prices are completely equalized by trade. This relationship is sometimes given the imposing title of the law of one price. Since price equalization depends on free trade, barriers to trade are a source of price discrepancies. Transportation costs, tariffs, quotas, and exchange controls are barriers that prevent home currency prices from being equal to the domestic currency equivalent of foreign prices.

Let t represent the money cost of transport or trade barriers per unit of X. If the home country is a net importer, the equilibrium relationship is

$$P = (1+t)\Pi P^\star$$

The home currency price will exceed the foreign price by an amount equal to the trade barrier. The simple version of PPP that ignores trade barriers would provide an incorrect forecast of the market exchange rate. The true exchange rate should be

$$\Pi = \frac{P}{P^\star(1+t)} < \frac{P}{P^\star}$$

Suppose that $P = \$2$, $P^\star = 1$, and $t = 0.10$:

$$\Pi = \frac{2.00}{1(1+0.10)} = 1.818 < 2$$

---

[1] The relationship can be expressed in percentage changes by taking the logarithmic derivative:

$$\log \Pi_R = \log \Pi - \log \frac{P}{P^\star}$$
$$\log \Pi_R = \log \Pi - (\log P - \log P^\star)$$
$$\frac{d\Pi_R}{\Pi_R} = \frac{d\Pi}{\Pi} - (\frac{dP}{P} - \frac{dP^\star}{P^\star})$$

By ignoring the trade barrier one would predict an exchange rate of $2.000 while the actual rate was only $1.818. The error would lead to understating systematically the value (overstating the price of foreign exchange) of the home currency. In principle, one could incorporate the value of trade barriers into an augmented version of absolute PPP, but the computational cost would be substantial.

19.3 RELATIVE PURCHASING POWER PARITY

A common practical alternative is to employ relative PPP, which simply expresses the relationship in terms of percentage changes:

$$\log \Pi = \log P - \log P^\star$$
$$\frac{d\Pi}{\Pi} = \frac{dP}{P} - \frac{dP^\star}{P^\star}$$

The percentage change in the nominal exchange rate is predicted to be equal to the difference between the domestic and foreign inflation rates. Notice it is not inflation per se that causes depreciation, but more inflation than one's trading partner. If the home country experiences 10 percent inflation while ROW has 3 percent, the home currency will depreciate by 7 percent. However, if both countries have 10 percent inflation, the exchange rate will remain constant. Indeed, if the home country has 10 percent inflation while ROW has 12 percent, the home currency will *appreciate* by 2 percent. The main implication of relative PPP is that exchange rate behavior is determined by *relative* inflation rates. It is not world inflation that causes fluctuation of exchange rates but rather divergent rates of inflation. At a more fundamental level, it is not expansionary monetary and fiscal policy that causes fluctuating exchange rates but rather divergent monetary and fiscal policies.

According to PPP, if all countries pursued monetary-fiscal policies that generated 50 percent inflation per year, no exchange rates would change. Greater international coordination of aggregate demand policies would result in more stable exchange rates even under a free float. A problem for coordination is that it is not easy to agree on what the average world inflation rate ought to be.

Purchasing power parity can be expressed in terms of the supply and demand for foreign exchange. The domestic and foreign price levels determine the positions of F^d and F^s. In Figure 19-1, the initial equilibrium is at A along F_1^d and F_1^s. First, let there be domestic inflation without foreign inflation. The new domestic price level P_2 shifts demand from F_1^d to F_2^d, and the new equilibrium is at B with exchange rate Π_2. Suppose that at the same time the for-

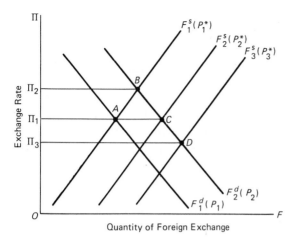

FIGURE 19-1   Inflation and the Exchange Rate

eign price level rises by the same percentage to $P_2^\star$. Since home exports are more competitive, foreign exchange supply shifts from F_1^s to F_2^s. Because of equal foreign and domestic inflation, the new equilibrium at C is at an unchanged exchange rate Π_1. The third possibility is that the rate of foreign inflation exceeds the rate of domestic inflation. The foreign price level $(P_3^\star)$ represents the greater foreign inflation, and it causes the supply curve to shift to F_3^s. The equilibrium at D represents an appreciation of the home currency in spite of domestic inflation. The example illustrates the proposition that exchange rate behavior depends on relative inflation.

Purchasing power parity is an old theory that dates back in the English literature at least to the bullionist controversy in England during the Napoleonic wars. There was an earlier Swedish bullionist controversy (1755–1765) in which a rudimentary PPP was stated by Pehr Niclas Christiernin of Uppsala. The British government suspended convertibility of the pound into gold during the wars, and the pound prices of gold and foreign currency increased. The bullionists, including Ricardo, Wheatley, and Thornton, attributed the pound depreciation to differential inflation in England caused by wartime finance. Thus, the English bullionists were proponents of purchasing power parity.

The antibullionists denied the relevance of inflation, citing particular items of the balance of payments. They stressed capital outflows to finance the war on the Continent and extraordinary imports of war-related raw materials. The arguments made by both sides have been repeated on many later occasions of currency weakness. Critics of governments tend to use the bullionist argument attributing depreciation to inflation brought about by aggregate demand policy. Supporters of governments tend to take the antibullionist line by attributing currency weakness to special components of the balance of payments. Examples commonly used are dock strikes, small crops, foreign speculators, and foreign business cycles.

The PPP issue reemerged as a result of the inflation during and immediately following World War I. Many countries that had abandoned fixed exchange rates during the war sought to reestablish fixed rates after the war. Since countries had experienced different rates of inflation, the problem was how to determine a new set of equilibrium rates. The Swedish economist Gustav Cassel (1886–1945) proposed that new rates be determined by relative inflation rates since the initial equilibrium. He is generally credited with being the originator of the formal PPP theory.

The theory of PPP has several well-known shortcomings. The first is the existence of a class of goods that does not enter international trade. Whether goods are traded or not depends on transport costs and trade barriers, which are high for certain natural resources and labor services. For example, the cost of hiring a maid or a barber might vary considerably between countries because of labor immobility. Commodity arbitrage will equalize prices of internationally traded goods but not for the set of nontraded goods.

This problem raises the question of which prices enter the indexes P and $P^\star$ that are relevant to PPP. Provided that some nontraded goods enter the indexes, complete equalization is not to be expected. If an index of traded goods is used to determine the exchange rate, it will not be representative. Winston Churchill used an index of traded goods to determine the U.K. exchange rate after World War I. Keynes criticized him for overvaluing the pound, which depressed the economy throughout the 1920s.

The existence of transport costs and tariffs for traded goods presents a smaller problem. Prices will be equalized net of transport costs or tariffs, so that the relative form of PPP can be written as

$$\frac{d\Pi}{\Pi} = \frac{dP}{P} - \frac{dP^\star}{P^\star} - \frac{d(1+t)}{1+t}$$

There have been periods when trade barriers have been relatively stable, and the error from ignoring the final term would be small. During periods of significant changes in trade barriers, these charges can be included in calculations.

PPP does not account for international capital flows that are unrelated to inflation. For example, a discovery of a mineral might induce capital inflows that would strengthen a currency. The appreciation in the host country and the depreciation in the capital exporting country would be unrelated to relative inflation rates. This point was made by the English antibullionists.

A more general criticism is that PPP relies solely on monetary variables, to the exclusion of all real variables. Product demand, technical change, factor accumulation, and market structure are implicitly treated as if they have no effect on the exchange rate. Would not the formation of OPEC lead to appreciation for oil exporters and depreciation for oil importers regardless of inflation rates? Would not the invention of synthetic rubber lead to depreciation in natural rubber exporting countries?

PPP excludes many potentially relevant economic variables, which has led to the criticism that it is too simple as a theory of the exchange rate. However, in one sense, simplicity is its virtue. Data requirements are small, and it is easy to calculate. However, the greatest virtue of PPP is that it has been roughly consistent with the broad pattern of historical experience. Countries with higher inflation rates over extended periods have experienced currency depreciation.

Predictions have been more accurate in the long run than in the short run. Perhaps the many real variables that are excluded by PPP offset each other in the long run. For example, some kinds of technical change strengthen a currency, while others weaken it. Over long periods, there is no reason to expect one kind of innovation to dominate the other. PPP has been more accurate when inflation differentials have been large rather than small. PPP has performed well during hyperinflations, perhaps because monetary changes dominate real changes. PPP is not a complete theory of exchange rate determination, but a more comprehensive theory cannot ignore the basic monetary elements of purchasing power parity.

The results of several studies of floating exchange rates in the 1920s have been favorable to PPP. Similar studies of the accuracy of PPP in the 1970s have found less favorable results. Exchange rates in the 1970s were volatile, and spot exchange rates were not accurately predicted by forward rates or international interst rate differentials. It follows that most rate fluctuations have been caused by "news" that, by its very nature, is unpredictable. It has been observed that foreign exchange rates behave more like asset prices than commodity prices.

Asset markets, such as the stock market, incorporate new information rapidly, and their prices adjust continuously to clear the market. Stock prices have been observed to follow a random walk, and there is some evidence that foreign exchange rates do as well. Commodity prices, such as the consumer price index, move sluggishly in response to economic disturbances. The consumer price index exhibits serial correlation, which implies that future changes can be partly predicted by past changes. Because of the different patterns of change of P, $P^{\star}$, and Π, deviations from PPP are to be expected. The 1970s were years of divergent monetary and fiscal policies and major real disturbances.

If exchange rates respond quickly to new information and commodity prices respond sluggishly, deviations from PPP will result. It is not easy to interpret deviations from PPP. Some observers interpret deviations from PPP as an economic mistake that ought to be corrected by policymakers. It is sometimes said that exchange rates have been more volatile than the underlying economic forces would justify. The reference to "underlying economic forces" usually means relative inflation rates, that is, PPP.

It has been proposed that central banks use PPP as a guide in determining its foreign exchange market intervention policy. A PPP rule might say that if a currency depreciates by more than the difference between home and foreign inflation, its central bank should buy the currency. The rule would be symmetrical for appreciation. A problem with such a rule is that real disturbances occur that are neglected by PPP. If an oil importing country suddenly faces a monopoly price, its currency will tend to depreciate by more than PPP would indicate. If the disturbance is permanent, an attempt to support the PPP exchange rate will send the wrong signals to the economy. The fundamental problem with using PPP as a guide to intervention is that it provides information about monetary disturbances to the exchange market but not real disturbances. Evidence from the 1970s indicates that many of the disturbances were real.[2] A formidable practical problem is the difficulty of identifying the sources of disturbances on a daily basis.

19.4 PURCHASING POWER PARITY AND NATIONAL INCOME COMPARISONS

The concept of purchasing power parity has been employed as a guide in making income comparisons between different countries. To compare the average income of residents of two countries, one must express the incomes in a common currency. It is not meaningful to compare lira income with dollar income unless one knows how many lire a dollar is worth. The most common practice is to translate one country's income into the other by using the market exchange rate between the two currencies. It has been shown that the practice of using market exchange rates produces a biased income comparison. The bias arises because market exchange rates are influenced only by the prices of internationally traded goods. National income or GNP measures purchasing power over a broader set of goods, including nontraded goods. For example, the services of maids enter the national income of both Italy and the United States. However, those services have no direct impact on the lira-dollar exchange rate.

To determine the effect of market exchange rates on national income comparisons, one must first establish the relationship between the market exchange rate and the purchasing power parity exchange rate. Bela Balassa first

---

[2] A study by Charles Pigott concluded that most of the disturbances were real. See "The Influence of Real Factors on Exchange Rates," *Economic Review*, Federal Reserve Bank of San Francisco, Fall 1981.

studied this relationship in the 1960s, and his work has been extended in some recent work by the World Bank.[3]

Consider an example taken from Balassa's work. The market exchange rate between the dollar and the lira observed in 1960 was L620 per dollar. What was the comparable PPP exchange rate? A PPP rate would be the number of lire necessary to buy the same bundle of goods in Italy that could be bought for $1.00 in the United States. The same bundle of goods must be priced in both countries, but which bundle? One could use the bundle of goods purchased by the typical American or the one bought by the typical Italian. Even if consumer preferences are identical, bundles can be expected to differ because of differences in relative prices in the two countries. Two different PPP exchange rates would result. The problem is analogous to whether base year or current year weights should be employed in constructing a price index. The PPP rate using the Italian (think of Italy as the home country) bundle of goods is

$$\Pi_P^I = \frac{P}{P^\star} = \frac{\Sigma PQ}{\Sigma P^\star Q} = \frac{\Sigma P_I Q_I}{\Sigma P_U Q_I}$$

The exchange rate resulting from the U.S. bundle is

$$\Pi_P^U = \frac{P}{P^\star} = \frac{\Sigma PQ^\star}{\Sigma P^\star Q^\star} = \frac{\Sigma P_I Q_U}{\Sigma P_U Q_U}$$

The index obtained by pricing the Italian bundle at both Italian and U.S. prices was

$$\Pi_P^I = L330$$

In 1960 it cost L330 to buy the goods bought by an average Italian that would have cost $1.00 in the United States. The PPP index gotten by pricing the U.S. bundle is

$$\Pi_P^U = L574$$

It took L574 to buy the goods bought by an average American that would have cost $1 in the United States. The lira showed greater purchasing power over the Italian bundle of goods than it did over the American bundle. Consumers

[3] Balassa's first paper was in 1964; see Bela Balassa, "The Purchasing Power Parity Doctrine: A Reappraisal," *Journal of Political Economy*, December 1964. A recent World Bank study is by Irving Kravis, Robert Summers, and Alan Heston, *World Product and Income: International Comparisons of Gross Product and Purchasing Power* (Baltimore: Johns Hopkins University Press, 1975).

were rewarded for "doing in Rome as the Romans do." At least part of the discrepancy is attributable to the substitution effect induced by relative price differences between the two countries. Because some goods are not traded, relative prices are different. Consumers in each country substitute toward goods that are relatively cheap in their country, that is, relatively expensive in the other country. Since labor is relatively cheap in Italy, the Italian bundle (Q_I) contains more labor-intensive goods than does the U.S. bundle. Since the Italian bundle is relatively cheaper in Italy, the lira exhibits greater purchasing power (L330 per dollar) when the Italian bundle is priced in both countries. Of the two PPP indices, $\Pi_P^I = L330$ is an upper bound on the purchasing power of the lira and $\Pi_P^U = L574$ is a lower bound on the purchasing power of the lira. Since there is no clear choice between the two, it has become conventional to use the (geometrical) mean as the PPP index. In this case the mean is

$$\Pi_P = L435 < \Pi_M = L620$$

The PPP index shows greater purchasing power for the lira than the market exchange rate. If the PPP index were used as a forecast of the lira-dollar rate, it would systematically overstate the value of the lira (understate the price of dollars in lire). What is the source of the bias? The market exchange rate is influenced only by the prices of internationally traded goods. The national income bundles used to calculate PPP include both traded and nontraded goods. The set of nontraded goods, which tends to be labor intensive, is relatively cheaper in Italy. The purchasing power of the lira over these relatively cheap nontraded goods is incorporated into the PPP index, but it is ignored by the market exchange rate.

If the exchange rate bias were unique to the U.S.-Italy case, it would not be of great interest. However, the bias is systematically related to per capita income. In comparing countries with the United States, the exchange rate bias is greater the lower the per capita income of the second country. The reason for the relationship is that wages are positively correlated with income per capita. Thus, the relative cheapness of labor-intensive nontraded goods is greater in low-income countries. One would expect a greater bias between India and the United States than between Italy and the United States.

Because the market exchange rate is biased, using it to translate one country's national income into another country's currency introduces a distortion. The exchange rate bias is greater the lower the income of the country in question. In the Italian-U.S. example, using the market exchange rate to translate Italian GNP into dollars would yield a lower income for Italy than using the PPP exchange rate. To convert Italian income in lire into dollars at the market exchange rate requires the price of lire in dollars, which is the reciprocal of the price already given:

$$\Pi_{L\$}{}^M = \frac{1}{\Pi_{\$L}M} = \frac{1}{620} = \$0.0016$$

The comparable PPP rate would be

$$\Pi_{L\$}{}^P = \frac{1}{\Pi_{\$L}P} = \frac{1}{435} = \$0.0023$$

The dollar value of Italian income will be greater when translated at the PPP exchange rate ($0.0023) than at the market rate ($0.0016):

$$\Pi^P_{L\$}Y^I = (\$0.0023)Y^I > \Pi^M_{L\$}Y_I = (\$0.0016)Y^I$$

Exchange rate bias exists at all income levels, but it increases as per capita income declines. Irving Kravis and others at the World Bank have estimated the magnitude of the bias, and some results for 1970 are presented in Table 19-1. After the adjustment is made, the poorer countries do not look as poor as they did, but significant income differences remain. The adjustment is largest in the case of India. Using market exchange rates Indian GDP per capita was 2.3 percent of U.S. income. After adjusting for PPP, the percentage increased to 7.1 percent. Thus, the Indian percentage more than tripled. The Colombian percentage more than doubled (from 7.1 to 15.9), and the Kenyan percentage nearly doubled (3.2 to 5.7). The increase is smaller at higher income levels, and in the case of France, the percentage increases by a factor of 1.15 (from 65.1 to 75.0).

A related income comparison issue has emerged in recent years. As the dollar depreciated from 1971 to 1980, the per capita incomes of several West-

TABLE 19-1   Gross Domestic Product per Capita as
Percentage of United States GDP, 1970

COUNTRY	USING MARKET EXCHANGE RATE	USING PPP
Kenya	3.2%	5.7%
India	2.3	7.1
Colombia	7.1	15.9
Hungary	33.6	40.3
Italy	37.0	45.8
United Kingdom	47.7	60.3
Japan	40.3	61.5
West Germany	61.6	74.7
France	65.1	75.0

Source: World Bank, *Finance and Development,* Washington, D.C., September 1975.

TABLE 19-2   1980 GNP Comparison

	CONVERTED BY MARKET EXCHANGE RATES	CONVERTED BY PPP
United States	$11,364	$11,364
West Germany	13,305	9,428
France	12,136	9,040
The Netherlands	11,855	8,614
Japan	8,905	8,464
United Kingdom	9,335	7,629
Italy	6,906	7,202

ern European countries rose above the U.S. level when translated into dollars at market exchange rates. Some analysts have argued that when purchasing power parity comparisons are made, U.S. income per capita remained higher.[4] In particular, a study by OECD[5] showed that U.S. per capita income was below that of West Germany, France, and The Netherlands when market exchange rates were used to convert all income into U.S. dollars (see Table 19-2).

However, when income was converted using PPP, income in the United States was higher than that in any European country. The magnitude of the adjustment can be seen by considering West Germany, the highest-income European country. At market exchange rates, German income was about $2,000 per year higher than U.S. income, but using PPP conversion, U.S. income was about $2,000 per year higher. The large magnitude of the difference underscores the fact that an apparently simple comparison of economic measures is in fact complex.

19.5 MONETARY APPROACH TO THE EXCHANGE RATE

It has been observed that PPP explains exchange rates more accurately in the long run than the short run. It is believed that the disparity is due to the short-run rigidity of product prices. The monetary approach to the exchange rate is an attempt to overcome this short-run problem by substituting the monetary determinants of the price level for prices themselves. Instead of explaining the

[4]Both Jai-Hoon Yang (1978), "Comparing Per Capita Output Internationally: Has the United States Been Overtaken?" *Review*, Federal Reserve Bank of St. Louis, May 1978 and Robin Marris (1981, citing the study by Kravis, Heston, and Summers) Robin Marris, "Is EC Really Richer Than US?" *Europe*, March/April 1981, conclude that U.S. income remained higher after proper adjustments.

[5]Results of the OECD study were summarized in the *International Letter* of August 27, 1982 published by the Federal Reserve Bank of Chicago.

exchange rate by domestic and foreign inflation rates, the monetary approach uses money demand and supply at home and abroad. It emphasizes the monetary determinants of exchange rates and deemphasizes real variables. As such it is more of a complement to PPP than a substitute.

The monetary approach begins with the money market equilibrium condition. The real supply of money is equal to the real demand for money:

$$\frac{M}{P} = L(i, y)$$

M is nominal supply of domestic money and L is the real demand function, which depends on the nominal interest rate (i) and the level of real income (y). Since i is the interest rate on bonds, a competing asset, the demand for money is inversely related to the interest rate. Money is assumed to be a normal good, so that an increase in income increases money demand.

A fundamental feature of the monetary approach is the direct link between the money and foreign exchange markets. An excess supply of money induces an excess demand for foreign exchange, which results in currency depreciation. Conversely, an excess demand for money leads to currency appreciation. An analogous expression describes equilibrium in the money market abroad:

$$\frac{M^\star}{P^\star} = L^\star(i^\star, y^\star)$$

After rearrangement, the money market equilibrium conditions can be interpreted as price-level equations:

$$P = \frac{M}{L(i, y)}$$

$$P^\star = \frac{M^\star}{L^\star(i^\star, y^\star)}$$

The price level is determined by the nominal money supply relative to the real money demand in each country. The sources of a price-level increase are an increase in the nominal money supply or a decrease in the real money demand. The latter may be caused by either an increase in the nominal interest rate or a decrease in real income. Assume that domestic and foreign bonds are perfect substitutes and that interest arbitrage is sufficient to equalize real interest rates at home and abroad.

$$r = r^\star$$

Real interest rates are equal to nominal interest rates minus the expected rate of inflation in that country:

$$i - \frac{dP^E}{P} = i^\star - \frac{d^\star P^{\star E}}{P^\star}$$

The difference between nominal interest rates at home and abroad can be interpreted as the difference between expected inflation rates in the two countries. If the home country is small, an increase in the home interst rate represents an increase in the expected inflation rate at home. Thus, an interest rate increase will induce an excess supply of money and currency depreciation.

Let there be two classes of goods, traded and nontraded. The money price level is a weighted average of the prices of traded and nontraded goods, where α is the budget share for traded goods:

$$P = \alpha P_T + (1 - \alpha) P_N$$

Let β represent the relative prices of traded and nontraded goods:

$$\beta = \frac{P_N}{P_T} \quad \text{or} \quad P_N = \beta P_T$$

The price-level equation can be rewritten by substituting for P_N:

$$P = \alpha P_T + (1 - \alpha)\beta P_T = [\alpha + (1 - \alpha)\beta]P_T = \gamma P_T$$

Where γ is defined as the term in brackets:

$$\gamma = [\alpha + (1 - \alpha)\beta]$$

Notice that γ increases when β increases. β can rise either because of an increase in the price of nontraded goods or a decrease in the price of traded goods. The latter might occur either because of an increase in supply due to technical change or factor accumulation or a decrease in domestic demand for traded goods. The price of traded goods may also fall because of a change in market structure from monopoly to competition. There will be an analogous expression for the price level in ROW:

$$P^\star = \gamma^\star P_T^\star$$

Let commodity arbitrage equalize prices of traded goods:

$$P_T = \Pi P_T^\star \quad \text{or} \quad \Pi = \frac{P_T}{P_T^\star}$$

The exchange rate can be expressed in terms of the domestic and foreign price levels and the home and foreign relative price terms:

$$\Pi = \frac{P}{P^\star} \frac{\gamma^\star}{\gamma}$$

Finally, the price level terms can be replaced by the ratios of money supply to money demand:

$$\Pi = \frac{ML^\star(i^\star, y^\star)}{M^\star L(i, y)} \frac{\gamma^\star}{\gamma}$$

This equation is the basic statement of the monetary approach to the exchange rate. It explains the exchange rate in terms of money supply, money demand, and a relative price term at home and abroad.

The equation can be interpreted as saying that the home currency will depreciate if there is (1) an increase in the home money supply, (2) a decrease in home money demand, or (3) a decrease in the home relative price of nontraded goods or opposite changes in the three ROW variables.

According to the hypothesis an increase in the money supply will bring about depreciation before it increases the price level. It is hoped that this feature will overcome the sluggishness of prices that may be responsible for short-run deviations from PPP. A decrease in home money demand can bring about depreciation either as a result of an increase in the interest rate or a decrease in real income. Under the current assumptions, an increase in the interest rate is a signal that inflationary expectations have increased. As a result, the demand for domestic money decreases and the home currency depreciates. A controversial implication is that higher interest rates (tight credit) weaken the home currency. This point will be discussed in Section 19.6. A reduction in real income induces currency depreciation by reducing money demand. It follows that real economic growth should be associated with currency *appreciation*.

This implication conflicts with the popular notion that real economic growth weakens a currency by increasing imports relative to exports. According to the monetary approach, real income growth simultaneously increases imports and induces a capital inflow. The increased supply of foreign exchange from the capital inflow exceeds the increased demand for foreign exchange coming from imports, and the currency appreciates. Finally, any economic change that decreases the relative price of nontraded goods will bring about currency depreciation. The monetary approach is like PPP in that it stresses the monetary determinants of exchange rates, but it does not exclude real factors entirely. Real income influences the exchange rate through its effect on money demand. Relative price effects enter through the ratio of nontraded to traded goods prices.

19.6 INTEREST RATES
AND EXCHANGE RATES

The relationship between the exchange rate and the interest rate is a complex one. A common view is that tighter credit strengthens a currency. For example, in the first half of 1982, Western European political leaders blamed high U.S. interest rates for the strength of the dollar and the corresponding weakness of their countries' currencies. The mechanism underlying this position is that high interest rates will attract capital flows, which add to the demand for the currency. Conversely, the monetary approach implies that higher interest rates depreciate a currency by signaling that greater inflation is expected in the future. If these contradictory views of the interest rate-exchange rate relationship are not sufficiently confusing, an investment advisor has a third alternative. "If rates go higher, it helps the dollar on a real rate of return basis; if rates go lower it reflects confidence that the U.S. will shortly experience a decline in the rate of inflation. So, either way, the dollar benefits." [6]

What is puzzling about the interest rate-exchange rate relationship? It is important to distinguish between nominal and real interest rates. The difference between the two is the expected inflation rate. An increase in the nominal interest rate could indicate an increase in the real interest rate, or it could indicate an increase in inflationary expectations. In the former case, capital should be attracted to the country, and the currency should appreciate. In the latter case, the demand for money should decrease, and the currency should depreciate.

Part of the puzzle is that changes in nominal interest rates are difficult to interpret. If they signal an increase in real rates, the currency will appreciate. If they signal an increase in inflation expectations, the currency should depreciate. What remains is an empirical question as to whether observed changes in nominal rates have been dominated by changes in the real rate or changes in inflationary expectation.

One interpretation of recent U.S. experience is that before October 1979 changes in inflation expectations dominated. [7] Increases in nominal interest rates were associated with dollar depreciation. This evidence supports the monetary approach. Since 1979, changes in nominal interest rates have been dominated by changes in real interest. Thus, higher nominal rates have been associated with dollar appreciation. This episode conflicts with the monetary approach.

What might explain a change in the relationship in 1979? The Federal Reserve announced a change in its operating procedures in October 1979. The new procedures increased the importance of controlling the money supply and deemphasized control of interest rates. As a consequence, real interest rate

---

[6] Prudential-Bache, *The Money Manager*, February 2, 1981, p. 12.

[7] Dallas Batten, "Foreign Exchange Markets: the Dollar in 1980," *Review*, Federal Reserve Bank of St. Louis, April 1981.

changes have dominated fluctuations in nominal rates. Increases in nominal rates have signaled an increase in real rates, and the dollar has appreciated. It remains to be seen whether this pattern will continue.

19.7 EXPECTATIONS, ASSET MARKETS, AND EXCHANGE RATE VOLATILITY

The perspective of the monetary approach helps to explain exchange rate volatility. In the 1970s, exchange markets have been more volatile than would have been predicted by PPP. Money and foreign exchange are durable assets whose behavior is more like that of other assets than commodities. Exchange rates follow the random walk behavior of stock prices rather than the sluggish adjustment pattern of national inflation rates. Although exchange rates have fluctuated more than inflation differentials have, the former have not fluctuated more than relative stock market indices have. Changes in expectations are an important source of price fluctuation in asset markets. Because of their durability, asset prices depend on expected future values as well as current values of explanatory variables. Strictly speaking, the current exchange rate depends on the current money supply and the expected future money supply in all subsequent periods. A similar statement can be made about money demand and relative prices.

None of these future variables can be known for certain, and expectations change as new information reaches the market. Elections, wars, or changes in personnel at the central bank may be a signal of a change in future monetary policy. Any of these or similar events or simply rumors about them can alter the current exchange rate in the same way as they influence daily stock prices. Since the future exchange rate depends on the future money supply, ability to forecast money should be helpful in forecasting the exchange rate. If a central bank has inside information about its future monetary policy, the bank might have an advantage in forecasting exchange rates.

This argument has been made as to why a float managed by a central bank might be more stable than a free float with private speculators. In the United States, the central bank's information advantage may be quite small. The Federal Reserve is required by Congress to announce its money supply target to the public six months in advance. The target is stated as a range, and partly because of random factors, the realized money supply may be a surprise to the Fed.

A strong currency is popularly interpreted as a symbol of success of a government's economic policy. Politicians attempt to influence the rate by their public statements. It is not uncommon for politicians to denounce the foreign exchange market for undervaluing the national currency. It has become traditional for government officials to deny that a devaluation is forthcoming, even days or hours before it occurs. Market participants have learned to expect such denials. In June 1982 there were strong rumors that the French franc would be devalued. When President Mitterand scheduled a press conference, it was anticipated that he would announce a devaluation. The government then scheduled an earlier press conference to deny that the purpose of the original conference was to announce a devaluation. Within days the franc was devalued. It has been said that if a government denial of an impending devaluation is excessively vehement, the market interpretation is that the devaluation is coming soon. Because expectations respond to new information, prices in asset markets are more volatile than are aggregate commodity price indices.

19.8 MONETARY APPROACH TO THE BALANCE OF PAYMENTS

The variability of a floating exchange rate is explained by the monetary approach to the exchange rate. The same principles are applicable to the balance of payments under a fixed rate system. Many countries have chosen compromise monetary systems for which the exchange rate is sometimes fixed and sometimes floating. These mixed systems can be analyzed using the concept of exchange market pressure. It combines the features of the monetary approach to the exchange rate and the monetary approach to the balance of payments. Exchange market pressure combines price changes and quantity changes.

The monetary approach to the balance of payments is applicable to the broadest concept of the balance of payments, the monetary reserve balance. Recall from Chapter 16 that the monetary reserve balance is

$$B_R = \frac{dR}{dt} = B_{ca} - K$$

It includes all foreign exchange transactions except government transactions in foreign exchange. Notice that it attempts to explain the combined behavior of the current account without attempting to separate the individual components. This level of aggregation distinguished it from the elasticities approach of Chapter 18, which attempts to explain the balance on goods and services. Begin by expressing the money supply as the sum of monetary reserves and domestic credit

$$M = R + D \quad \text{or} \quad R = M - D$$

When these stocks are expressed as changes per unit time, it can be seen that the monetary reserve balance is the difference between the change in the money supply and the change in domestic credit:

$$B_R = \frac{dR}{dt} = \frac{dM}{dt} - \frac{dD}{dt}$$

The relationship can be written in terms of percentage changes:

$$\frac{dR}{R} = \frac{1}{\rho}\frac{dM}{M} - 1 - \frac{dD}{D}$$

where $\rho = R/M$.

The money market equilibrium condition is again

$$\frac{M}{P} = L(i, y) \quad \text{or} \quad P = \frac{M}{L(i, y)}$$

These conditions can be combined to yield the following expression for the percentage change in monetary reserves:

$$\frac{dR}{R} = \frac{1}{\rho}\left(\frac{dP}{P} + \eta_{Li}\frac{di}{i} + \eta_{Ly}\frac{dy}{y}\right) - \left(\frac{1-\rho}{\rho}\right)\frac{dD}{D}$$

The elasticities η_{Li} and η_{Ly} represent the change in money demand with respect to the nominal interest rate and real income, respectively. η_{Li} is negative and η_{Ly} is positive. An increase in reserves, dR/R, indicates a balance-of-payments surplus. The surplus will be greater (1) the faster the growth of real income, (2) the slower the growth of domestic credit, (3) the slower the growth of nominal interest rates, and (4) the faster the rate of inflation. The paradoxical effect of inflation on the surplus is explained by the separate domestic credit variable. Otherwise, the explanatory variables play the same role as in the monetary approach to the exchange rate.

Monetary expansion depreciates the exchange rate, and expansion of domestic credit causes a balance-of-payments deficit. Domestic credit appears as an explanatory variable instead of the money supply, because the latter is not under the control of the central bank with fixed rates. Real economic growth induces a surplus under fixed rates and appreciation under floating rates. Increases in nominal interest rates induce a balance-of-payments deficit under fixed rates and depreciation under floating. The rationale is that higher interest rates represent an increase in expected inflation.

The monetary approach can be applied to situations in which only the exchange rate changes or only the balance of payments changes. The concept of exchange market pressure is an attempt to extend the basic principles to situations in which both the exchange rate and the quantity of reserves are changing. During the Bretton Woods period, most of the changes were in reserves, but there were infrequent large exchange rate adjustments. During the recent managed float, exchange rate changes are more common, but reserve changes are not negligible. The basic idea is that the foreign exchange market is disturbed by changes in real income, domestic credit, and interest rates and that exchange market pressure is a measure of the magnitude of these shocks.

In Figure 19-2 the initial equilibrium is at A along F_1^d and F_1^s. Let there be a shift in F^d to F_2^d caused by an outside disturbance. If the exchange rate remained fixed at Π_1, the magnitude of the disturbance would be measured exactly by the loss of reserves $AB = R_1 R_2$. Under floating rates the reserve change would not measure the disturbance, since the entire excess demand would be eliminated by the price change from Π_1 to Π_2.

Instead of a pure price policy $(\Pi_1 \Pi_2)$ or a pure quantity policy $(R_1 R_2)$, suppose that the government accepted a small devaluation $(\Pi_1 \Pi_3)$ and a small reserve loss $(R_3 R_4)$. The disturbance is not measured by either the reserve change or the exchange rate change, but it can be measured by a kind of average of the two. The devaluation can be expressed as a percentage of the initial rate, and the reserve change can be expressed as a percentage of the money supply (dR/M). An equation explaining the determinants of exchange market pressure is the following:

$$\frac{d\Pi}{\Pi} - \frac{dR}{M} = \frac{dD}{M} - \frac{dP^\star}{P^\star} - \frac{dy}{y}$$

Exchange market pressure represents a kind of composite of balance-of-payments surplus and currency appreciation. If the exchange rate is constant, the reserve change captures all the pressure. If there is no intervention, the

FIGURE 19-2   Exchange Market Pressure

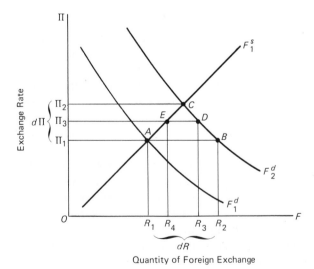

Quantity of Foreign Exchange

appreciation captures all the pressure. The left-hand side measures the pressure or tendency for the home currency to depreciate. If the government refrains from selling reserves $(dR = 0)$, the currency will depreciate whenever the right-hand side is positive. Alternatively, if the exchange rate is to be held constant, the government must lose reserves.

For example, let domestic assets of the central bank (dD/M) rise by 10 percent, given foreign prices and real income. There must be a 10 percent increase in the price of foreign exchange, a 10 percent decrease in foreign exchange reserves, or a combination of the two. Similarly, pressure for depreciation of the home currency would be caused by a decrease in foreign prices or a decrease in domestic income. Since it is derived from the monetary approach, one should not be surprised to see domestic credit, inflation, and real income growth as explanatory variables. The basic ideas have been applied successfully in empirical studies of Canadian and Brazilian currency experience.[8]

19.9 REAL VARIABLES AND THE CURRENT ACCOUNT

The strength of PPP and the monetary approach is that they incorporate the important monetary determinants of exchange rates, but their weakness is their failure to incorporate satisfactorily real variables. The balance of payments on current account is a traditional summary of the real variables that affect the exchange rate. A current account surplus is expected to induce currency appreciation, and a deficit is associated with depreciation. Since the current account includes exports, imports, and transfers, it could incorporate a wide variety of real factors. Technical change, factor accumulation, income growth, market structure, and commercial policy could all affect the exchange rate through the current account. None of these variables plays a prominent role in the monetary approach or PPP. However, it was pointed out in Chapter 16 that some information about real variables may reach the foreign exchange market before it appears in the published balance of payments accounts.

When the foreign exchange market processes the information, the exchange rate will change. When the same information appears later in the balance-of-payments accounts, it is no longer news, and it will not alter the exchange rate. An implication is that expected changes in the current account have no effect on the exchange rate. However, if the balance of payments contains information not processed by the foreign exchange market, the an-

---

[8] See Lance Girton and Don Roper, "A Monetary Model of Exchange Market Pressure Applied to the Postwar Canadian Experience," *American Economic Review*, September 1977; and Michael Connolly and José Dantas da Silveira, "Exchange Market Pressure in Postwar Brazil: An Application of the Girton-Roper Monetary Model," *American Economic Review*, June 1979.

nouncement of this news will affect the market. It is important to distinguish between the expected and unexpected components of the current account. Only the unexpected portion should influence current exchange rates.

This hypothesis can be expressed as

$$\frac{d\Pi^U}{\Pi} = \frac{d\Pi}{\Pi} - \frac{d\Pi^E}{\Pi} = F(B_{ca}^U)$$

where the unexpected component of the current account is the difference between the actual and expected changes in exchange rates. The hypothesis cannot be empirically tested in this form because two of the variables are not directly observable. However, the expected rate of depreciation can be represented by the observed interest differential:

$$\frac{d\Pi^E}{\Pi} = i - i^\star$$

The exchange rate equation can be rewritten as

$$\frac{d\Pi}{\Pi} = \frac{d\Pi^E}{\Pi} + \frac{d\Pi^U}{\Pi}$$
$$\frac{d\Pi}{\Pi} = i - i^\star + B_{ca}^U$$

The unexpected current account can be represented by the deviation from some standard forecast, and the hypothesis is empirically testable. If the market expected 10 percent appreciation and the actual appreciation was 10 percent, the balance-of-payments term should have no explanatory power. However, if the market expected 6 percent appreciation and the actual rate appreciated by 10 percent, the current account should help to explain the residual. Some empirical work has supported the hypothesis that balance-of-payments news influences the exchange rate.[9]

19.10 RELATIVE REAL INTEREST RATES

The preceding discussion assumed that real interest rates were equalized by international borrowing and lending. Equalization will occur if foreign and domestic bonds are perceived by investors as being perfect substitutes, and if there are no restrictions on capital flows. However, if home and foreign bonds are

---

[9] See Rudiger Dornbusch, "Exchange Rate Economics: Where Do We Stand," *Brookings Papers on Economic Activity*, 1980.

imperfect substitutes, real interest rates will differ. The international real interest rate differential will depend on relative supplies of bonds denominated in home and foreign currency. If bonds are imperfect substitutes, investors may want to hold portfolios that are diversified between domestic and foreign currency. Once an optimum portfolio is established, the equilibrium will be disturbed by changes in the balance on current account and changes in relative supplies of domestic- and foreign-currency–denominated assets.

Suppose that ROW experiences a current account surplus. The surplus represents an increase in net foreign assets, which is a form of wealth. The increase in wealth will increase the demand for foreign currency–denominated assets, and the foreign currency will appreciate. The appreciation will restore portfolio balance by increasing the share of foreign currency assets in total world wealth. Thus the balance of payments on current account may alter the exchange rate through its effect on national wealth.

Fiscal policy may also influence the exchange rate by altering the composition of asset portfolios. Suppose that the government in ROW has a budget deficit, which is financed by issuing new bonds. This fiscal policy increases the relative world supply of foreign currency–denominated bonds. World asset portfolios are out of equilibrium; there is an excess supply of foreign bonds. Equilibrium will be restored by depreciation of the foreign currency, which reduces the relative value of foreign bonds. Thus, a foreign budget deficit will cause the foreign currency to depreciate. It should be emphasized that relative asset supplies are relevant to world portfolio equilibrium. A foreign fiscal deficit accompanied by an equal domestic deficit will leave relative asset supplies unchanged, and it will not alter the exchange rate. Similarly, a foreign deficit, accompanied by a larger domestic deficit, would increase the relative supply of domestic bonds and cause the foreign currency to appreciate. This point is relevant to fiscal policy in the 1980s. Much public concern was expressed about large budget deficits in the United States, while at the same time the dollar appreciated substantially in 1981 and 1982. Since relative asset supplies are relevant for portfolio balance, the simultaneous existence of large foreign deficits should not be ignored. (See Chapter 22 for data on fiscal policy.)

SUMMARY

This chapter has examined the sources of shifts in foreign exchange supply and demand curves. Purchasing power parity explains exchange rate changes in terms of relative inflation rates. PPP calculations can be used to adjust exchange rate biases that occur in national income comparisons. Short-run deviations are partly due to sluggishness of commodity prices in the short-run. The monetary approach attempts to overcome this problem by substituting money supply and money demand for the price-level variables. It is difficult to interpret changes in nominal interest because they may represent a change in inflationary expectations or they may represent a change in the real interest rate. The two changes have opposite effects on the exchange rate.

Exchange rate volatility more closely resembles the behavior of stock prices than commodity prices. Expectations are an important determinant of asset prices, such as foreign exchange rates. The monetary approach can also be employed to analyze the balance of payments under fixed exchange rates. The concept of exchange market pressure can be used to study mixed systems, which employ changes in both exchange rates and reserves. Real economic variables may influence the exchange rate via the current account balance. However, the influence should be limited to the portion of the current account that is not expected by the foreign exchange market. If domestic and foreign bonds are imperfect substitutes, changes in relative real interest rates may alter the exchange rate.

REFERENCES

ARGY, VICTOR. *The Postwar International Money Crisis: An Analysis*. London: George Allen and Unwin, 1981. Chapter 20 analyzes portfolio balance and the exchange rate. Advanced discussion of exchange rate determination.

BALASSA, BELA. "The Purchasing Power Parity Doctrine: A Reappraisal." *Journal of Political Economy*, December, 1964. A study showing how the use of market exchange rates distorts international income comparisons.

BIGMAN, DAVID, and TEIZO TAYA, eds. *The Functioning of Floating Exchange Rates: Theory, Evidence, and Policy Implications*. Cambridge, Mass.: Ballinger, 1980. A collection of papers on aspects of floating exchange rates.

BRITTAIN, BRUCE. "Tests of Theories of Exchange Rate Determination." *Journal of Finance*, May 1977, pp. 519–529.

CASSEL, GUSTAV. *Money and Foreign Exchange After 1914*. New York: Macmillan, 1923. Cassel's exposition of purchasing power parity.

CONNOLLY, MICHAEL, and JOSÉ DANTAS DA SILVEIRA. "Exchange Market Pressure in Postwar Brazil: An Application of the Girton-Roper Monetary Model." *American Economic Review*, June 1979. Application of the exchange market pressure concept to Brazil.

CLARK, PETER B., DENNIS E. LOGUE, and RICHARD JAMES SWEENEY, eds. *The Effects of Exchange Rate Adjustments*. Washington, D.C.: U.S. Department of Treasury, 1977.

DORNBUSCH, RUDIGER. "Monetary Policy Under Exchange Rate Flexibility." In *Managed Exchange Rate Flexibility: The Recent Experience*. Federal Reserve Bank of Boston, Conference Series, No. 20, 1978. Discussion of the asset market approach to the exchange rate.

———. *Open Economy Macroeconomics*. New York: Basic Books, 1980. Advanced textbook that discusses purchasing power parity in Chapter 8.

———. "Exchange Rate Economics: Where Do We Stand," *Brookings Papers on Economic Activity*, 1980. Survey of literature on exchange rate determination.

FRENKEL, JACOB A. "Purchasing Power Parity: Doctrinal Perspective and Evidence from the 1920s." *Journal of International Economics*, May 1978. Empirical study of the 1920s experiment with floating exchange rate.

———. "The Collapse of Purchasing Power Parities During the 1970s." *European*

Economic Review, February 1981. Emphasizes larger deviations from PPP in the 1970s than in the 1920s.

————. "Flexible Exchange Rates, Prices, and the Role of 'News': Lessons from the 1970s." *Journal of Political Economy*, August 1981. Emphasizes the effects of new information on exchange rates.

————, and HARRY G. JOHNSON, ed. *The Monetary Approach to the Balance of Payments*. London: George Allen and Unwin, 1975.

————, and HARRY G. JOHNSON, eds. *The Economics of Exchange Rates: Selected Studies*. Reading, Mass.: Addison-Wesley, 1978. A collection of empirical studies on exchange rate determination.

GAILLIOT, HENRY J. "Purchasing Power Parity as an Explanation of Long-Term Changes in Exchange Rates." *Journal of Money, Credit, and Banking*, August 1970. Empirical study of purchasing power parity.

GIRTON, LANCE, and DON ROPER. "A Monetary Model of Exchange Market Pressure Applied to the Postwar Canadian Experience." *American Economic Review*, September 1977. Application of the concept of exchange market pressure.

HUME, DAVID. "Of Balance of Trade." In *International Finance: Selected Readings*, Richard Cooper, ed. Harmondsworth: Penguin, 1969. Original statement of the price-specie flow mechanism.

HUMPHREY, THOMAS. "Explaining Exchange Rate Behavior: An Augmented Version of the Monetary Approach." *Economic Review*, Federal Reserve Bank of Richmond, June 1981. An exposition of the monetary approach to the exchange rate.

INTERNATIONAL MONETARY FUND. *The Monetary Approach to the Balance of Payments*, Washington, D.C.: IMF, 1977. A collection of papers by members of the Fund staff.

ISARD, PETER. "How Far Can We Push the Law of One Price?" *American Economic Review*, December 1977.

————. *Exchange Rate Determination: A Survey of Popular Views and Recent Models*, Princeton Studies in International Finance, No. 42. Princeton, N.J.: Princeton University Press, May 1978. A survey of exchange rate theories.

JOHNSON, HARRY G. "The Monetary Approach to Balance of Payments Theory." In *Further Essays in Monetary Economics*, Harry G. Johnson, ed. Cambridge, Mass.: Harvard University Press, 1973. Exposition of the monetary approach to the balance of payments.

KRAVIS, IRVING, ZOLTAN KENESSEY, ALAN HESTON, and ROBERT SUMMERS. *A System of International Comparisons of Gross Product and Purchasing Power*. Baltimore: Johns Hopkins University Press, 1975. The first of a three-volume study of national income comparison sponsored by the World Bank and the United Nations.

————, ALAN HESTON, and ROBERT SUMMERS. *International Comparisons of Real Product and Purchasing Power*. Baltimore: Johns Hopkins University Press, 1978. Second volume of the international income comparison.

————, and ROBERT E. LIPSEY. "Price Behavior in the Light of Balance of Payments Theories." *Journal of International Economics*, May 1978. An analysis of purchasing power parity.

————, ALAN HESTON, and ROBERT SUMMERS. *World Product and Income: International Comparisons of Real Gross Domestic Products*. Baltimore: Johns Hopkins University Press, 1982. Final volume of the international comparison study.

KREININ, MORDECHAI, and LAWRENCE OFFICER. *The Monetary Approach to the Balance of Payments*, Princeton Studies in International Finance, No. 43. Princeton, N.J.: Princeton University Press, November 1978. A survey of the literature on the monetary approach.

MARRIS, ROBIN. "Is EC Really Richer Than Us?" *Europe*, March–April 1981. Popular discussion of national income comparisons.

MCKINNON, RONALD I. *Money in International Exchange: The Convertible Currency System.* New York: Oxford University Press, 1979. Chapter 6 deals with purchasing power parity.

OFFICER, LAWRENCE H. "The Purchasing Power Parity Theory of Exchange Rates: A Review Article." International Monetary Fund *Staff Papers*, March 1976. Survey of the literature on purchasing power parity.

PIGOTT, CHARLES. "The Influence of Real Factors on Exchange Rates." *Economic Review*, Federal Reserve Bank of San Francisco, Fall 1981. An empirical study emphasizing the real determinants of exchange rates.

SACHS, JEFFREY D. "The Current Account and Macroeconomic Adjustments in the 1970s." *Brookings Papers on Economic Activity*, 1:1981. Discussion of the effects of the current account on the exchange rate.

SCHADLER, SUSAN. "Sources of Exchange Rate Variability: Theory and Empirical Evidence." International Monetary Fund *Staff Papers*, July 1977.

YANG, JAI-HOON. "Comparing Per Capita Output Internationally: Has the United States Been Overtaken?" *Review*, Federal Reserve Bank of St. Louis, May 1978. Discussion of market exchange rates and national income comparison.

YEAGER, LELAND. *International Monetary Relations Theory, History, and Policy.* New York: Harper & Row, 1976. Discusses the accuracy of PPP during earlier experiments with floating rates.

CHAPTER TWENTY
PERMANENTLY FIXED
EXCHANGE RATES

20.1 INTRODUCTION
TO ALTERNATIVE
MONETARY SYSTEMS

Chapters 17 and 18 analyzed the economics of floating exchange rates. The extreme opposite monetary regime is one characterized by permanently fixed rates. Although no monetary institutions are strictly permanent, some exchange rate changes are so unlikely that economic agents treat the exchange rates of the associated currencies as if they were permanently fixed. This chapter will consider the economic effects of fixed exchange rates. Two examples of fixed rate systems are commodity money, such as a gold standard, and a monetary union, such as the arrangement among the 50 United States. Some aspects of the historical international gold standard will be reviewed.

The evolution of the U.S. monetary system from bimetallism to paper money will be considered. Price-level adjustment under a gold standard will be analyzed for a closed economy. The real resource cost of operating a gold standard will be considered. The effect of a gold standard on exchange rates will be shown for an open economy. The effect of the balance of payments on the money supply will be examined. The current and prospective monetary role of gold will be considered. Finally, the economic effects of monetary union will be analyzed for paper money systems.

Under fixed exchange rates, the money supply and aggregate demand are altered by the balance of payments. This chapter will emphasize the effect of aggregate demand on the money price level for given levels of national income and employment. Chapter 21 will discuss the effects of aggregate demand changes on real income and employment.

A strict gold standard is one way of achieving fixed exchange rates. A paper (fiat) money system in which exchange rates are fixed has similar characteristics. If the exchange rates are permanently fixed, the system becomes a monetary union. For example, the 50 United States can be thought of as a monetary union. This chapter will analyze the economics of fixed exchange rates with special reference to the gold standard and monetary union.

Because all markets are related, equilibrium in any single market depends on prices in all markets. Foreign exchange market equilibrium depends not only on the price of foreign exchange, but also on the average price of goods, wages and labor, and the quantity of money. In general equilibrium, all markets clear. There is a kind of economywide budget constraint called Walras' law, which says that if all markets except one are in equilibrium, the remaining market must be in equilibrium also. Because the residual market is always in equilibrium, one of the money prices in the economic system is redundant. One nominal price may be set arbitrarily, and equilibrium in all markets may still be achieved.

Another way of stating the condition is that market equilibrium depends on relative prices rather than on money prices. Any one price can be fixed, but all the remaining prices must adjust to it to achieve relative equilibrium prices. The selection of which price or nominal variable to fix determines the nature of the monetary system.

A fixed exchange rate system is one in which the nominal exchange rate is fixed and all other nominal variables must adapt to it to clear all markets. In particular, in a fixed exchange rate system, the money price level, money wages, and the money supply must be free to adjust to the fixed exchange rate. The implication for economic policy is that a government's decision to fix the exchange rate implies loss of control over inflation, money wages, and the quantity of money. Given the fixed exchange rate, the remaining nominal variables are determined in the rest of the world. It is important to recognize that a fixed exchange rate may be achieved only by accepting flexibility of other economic variables. Since floating rates have already been analyzed in Chapters 17 and 18, it is appropriate to compare the economic characteristics of the two systems.

Consider the major alternative monetary system. Aggregate all goods, assets, and factors of production such that all economic activity takes place in either the foreign exchange market, the goods market, the money market, or the labor market. Denote the excess demands for foreign exchange, goods, money, and labor as F, X, L, and N, respectively. Let Π represent the money exchange rate, P the money price level, M the nominal money supply, and W

the money wage. In market equilibrium, quantity demanded equals quantity supplied; that is, excess demand equals zero. The equilibrium condition for the economy may be represented as

$$
\begin{aligned}
\text{foreign exchange:}\quad & F(\Pi, P, M, W) = 0 \\
\text{goods:}\quad & X(\Pi, P, M, W) = 0 \\
\text{money:}\quad & L(\Pi, P, M, W) = 0 \\
\text{labor:}\quad & N(\Pi, P, M, W) = 0
\end{aligned}
$$

If all the markets except one are in equilibrium, the remaining market must also be in equilibrium, making one market and one nominal variable redundant. The choice of the variable to fix (numeraire) determines the nature of the monetary system. A fixed exchange rate system is one in which Π is fixed, and P, M, and W must adjust to bring about the equilibrium relative prices Π/P, Π/M, and Π/W. If more than one nominal variable is fixed, there is no assurance that general equilibrium will be reached. Disequilibrium could exist because there are not enough adjustable relative prices to eliminate all excess demands and supplies.

The gold standard was an important historical example of a fixed exchange rate system. Under a gold standard, flexibility of money prices, money wages, and the money supply are necessary to clear all markets. A monetary union is another example of a fixed exchange rate system, and the 50 states of the U.S. are a particular monetary union.

Three alternative monetary systems may be obtained by letting the exchange rate vary and fixing either P, M, or W. All three are flexible exchange rate systems, but they have different characteristics. First, consider fixing the money price level of goods and services. It means the price level variable is set by forces outside the economic system (exogenous), and it is not permitted to respond to economic forces, such as excess demand. Thus, the money price level could be fixed forever, or it could be permitted to rise or fall at some rate unrelated to economic conditions.

Most governments have a stated policy of trying to stabilize the price level. This goal was formalized in the United States by the Employment Act of 1946. The implication of fixing the price level is that the exchange rate, money supply, and money wages must adapt to it. One cannot fix both the exchange rate and also the price level in the long run. For example, under a fixed exchange rate, if the price level is set too low relative to the trading partner's prices, a balance-of-payments surplus will increase the money supply and the price level. If prices are set too high, a payments deficit will induce a monetary contraction, and prices will fall. The pressure to import inflation or deflation may be eliminated only by floating the exchange rate.

A second alternative to fixed rates is a monetary system that fixes the money supply and permits a flexible exchange rate, a variable price level, and flexible money wages to adapt to it. The money supply could be constant, or it could increase or decrease at a rate unrelated to economic conditions. An example of this system is the proposal by Milton Friedman that the Federal Reserve increase the money supply at a constant rate.[1] Such a system is sustainable only under floating exchange rates. If a fixed money growth rate were implemented under fixed rates, the country would experience a balance-of-payments deficit or surplus depending on whether money growth was faster or slower than in other countries. The surplus or deficit would alter the money supply, interfering with the fixed money growth target.

Friedman's rule would remove discretionary authority over the money supply from the Federal Reserve. Some critics of U.S. monetary policy since 1973 have blamed the Federal Reserve for capitulating to political pressure and causing inflation. They have proposed a kind of "monetary constitution" that would limit the options of the central bank in the same way that the Constitution limits the behavior of the Congress and the president. Friedman's proposed rule would be one form of monetary constitution. A fixed exchange rate system, such as that found with gold standard, would be an example of an alternative system.

The third kind of monetary system with floating rates would be achieved by fixing money wages outside the economic system. Real wages would remain flexible, provided that the exchange rate, prive level, and money supply adapted to money wages. Much of the work associated with John Maynard Keynes (1883–1946) treated money wages as if they were determined by political or sociological conditions unrelated to the demand and supply of labor. In some countries, money wages are set directly by the government or by negotiations with a national labor union. Full employment and equilibrium in all markets can be achieved in such a system, provided that the other nominal variables adjust passively. For example, if money wages rise more rapidly than in other countries, a real wage consistent with full employment can be achieved if the money supply and price level rise at a similarly rapid rate. To avoid a balance-of-payments deficit, the currency must also depreciate.

Some people have this system in mind when they refer to a cost-push or wage-push inflation. The term is somewhat misleading, because monetary accommodation is a necessary condition for the inflation. Thus, policymakers are free to select a target value for one and only one of the four variables. If more than one variable is fixed, there is no mechanism to clear all the markets. For example, if a government chooses fixed exchange rates, the country must accept the same rate of inflation as partner countries. An attempt to achieve fixed rates and stable prices would fail.

[1] Milton Friedman, *A Program for Monetary Stability.* New York: Fordham University Press, 1959, Chapter 4.

20.2 THE HISTORICAL INTERNATIONAL GOLD STANDARD

A gold standard is one way in which to achieve fixed exchange rates between currencies. Each government fixes the price of gold in terms of its own national money, and indirectly the currency exchange rates are fixed. Any commodity or group of commodities could be substituted for gold, but gold has been the historically important monetary commodity. If exchange rates are permanently fixed, nominally separate currencies become a single currency in fact. Lower transactions cost is an advantage of a single currency, since it permits all values to be expressed in a single unit. The economic advantages of a single currency have been compared with the advantages of a single language.

The historical gold standard coincided with a period of relative prosperity. The world price level showed no significant upward or downward trend, and international trade was relatively free of government barriers. There has been much debate about whether the gold standard was the cause of prosperity or whether the relationship was an historical coincidence. Even people who attribute some of the prosperity to gold question whether conditions in the 1980s are sufficiently similar to earlier conditions to justify a return to the gold standard.

There is not complete agreement about the relevant dates of the international gold standard.[2] One reason for disagreement is that different countries participated at different times. Also certain countries were partial participants in the sense of obeying some of the rules of a gold standard but not others. At least some countries followed some of the rules from 1821 to 1971. In 1821 Great Britain restored convertibility of the pound into gold following the Napoleonic wars. In 1971, when the United States declared the dollar inconvertible into gold for foreign central banks, the Bretton Woods system broke down. In the eighteenth century Britain and many other countries, including the fledgling United States, were on a bimetallic standard of silver and gold. Following 1821 several countries ceased using silver as money, and by 1880 most countries of the world had adopted some form of gold standard.

Although some skeptics deny that a true gold standard has ever existed, virtually all writers agree that the purest historical gold standard existed dur-

---

[2] For a discussion of the historical gold standard, see Michael David Bordo, "The Classical Gold Standard: Some Lessons for Today," *Review*, Federal Reserve Bank of St. Louis, May 1981; or Richard N. Cooper, "The Gold Standard: Historical Facts and Future Prospects," *"Brookings Papers on Economic Activity,* 1982. The term "historical gold standard" usually refers to a portion of the nineteenth and twentieth centuries, but gold was used as money much earlier. For example, a gold inflow was said to have caused inflation in Cairo in 1324. On his famous pilgrimage to Mecca, Mansa Musa, the king of Mali, spent and gave away so much gold "that he upset the value of goods on the Cairo market." See Basil Davidson, *A History of West Africa* (Garden City, N.Y.: Doubleday, 1966), p. 58.

ing the years 1880 to 1914. This period prior to World War I was characterized by relatively free trade and free factor movements. Some writers have
stressed the importance of international capital flows and the role of London
as the world financial center. The period was also characterized by rapid economic growth and stable prices.

The gold standard broke down during World War I as the European
countries suspended gold convertibility. The United States continued convertibility for residents, but gold exports were banned between 1917 and 1919. Even
though the dollar was fixed in terms of gold, it was floating against Western
European currencies, most of which followed a managed float until 1925. The
United Kingdom returned to gold convertibility in 1925 at the prewar price.
An attempt was made to revive the gold standard from 1925 to 1931, but the
attempt was ended by the Great Depression. The period from 1925 to 1931 is
sometimes called the Gold Exchange Standard, because central banks held some
of their reserves in the form of foreign exchange (pounds and dollars) to economize on gold.

World War II and the Great Depression were marked by major currency
devaluations (e.g., the United Kingdom in 1931, the United States in 1933)
and extensive controls on trade and payments. The Bretton Woods system from
1946 to 1971 contained a monetary role for gold, but the dollar came to play a
more prominent role. The dollar was linked to gold directly, but other currencies were linked indirectly through the U.S. dollar. The United States held
gold reserves, and other countries held primarily dollar reserves. The system
was closer to the gold exchange standard than to the gold standard operating
between 1880 and 1914. An example of the U.S. government's limited commitment to gold was the Treasury's policy of converting dollars into gold for
foreigners but not for U.S. residents. Private ownership of gold by Americans
was banned in 1933.

In 1971 gold lost its small remaining significance in international finance
when dollar convertibility ended for foreign central banks. Congress formally
devalued the dollar, first to $38 in 1971 and then to $42.22 in 1973. However,
these specific prices had no economic significance, since gold was not traded at
these prices. Later Congress abolished the concept of an official gold price.
The International Monetary Fund also abolished the official role of gold. Although gold has had no formal significance in the international monetary system since 1971, disappointment with the performance of floating rates has led
some people to suggest a return to a gold standard.

20.3 THE UNITED STATES
AND GOLD

The U.S. Constitution of 1789 delegates to the federal government the right
"to coin money and regulate the value thereof." Following the examples of
England and Western Europe and the recommendation of Secretary of the

Treasury Alexander Hamilton, the United States adopted a bimetallic money. The dollar was defined to be fixed amounts of either gold or silver. After considerable study of earlier prices of gold and silver, Hamilton decided that the correct ratio was 15 ounces of silver per ounce of gold. The American Coinage Act of 1791 defined a dollar as equal to either 371.25 grains of fine silver or 24.75 grains of fine gold, a ratio of 15 to 1. This ratio is equivalent to a price of silver of $1.293 per ounce and a gold price of $19.395 per ounce.

Earlier experience with bimetallism indicated the importance of proper prices at the mint. If the official mint prices undervalued one metal relative to its market value as bullion, the undervalued metal tended to disappear from circulation as money. People receiving the officially undervalued money ("good money") had an incentive to melt it down and sell it as bullion. Debts were more cheaply paid in the form of the officially undervalued money ("bad money"). The tendency for a single metal to circulate as a medium of exchange under bimetallism was known as Gresham's law, after Thomas Gresham (1519–1579), a financial advisor to Queen Elizabeth I of England. It is commonly stated as "Bad money drives out good money."[3]

Gresham's law is a special case of the principle that arbitrage tends to prevent two prices from coexisting in a single market. In spite of Hamilton's careful calculations, Gresham's law soon caused gold to be driven out of monetary circulation in the United States. Even though the initial 15-to-1 mint price ratio was consistent with relative prices in bullion markets, conditions changed to make the ratio a disequilibrium price. As the market price ratio moved to $15\frac{1}{2}$ to 1, it became profitable to melt gold coins and export gold bullion. Even though the United States was on a nominal bimetallic standard in the early years of the republic, it was on a de facto silver standard from 1792 to 1834.

To encourage the circulation of gold, the mint price was adjusted in 1834. The new mint price of 16 to 1 attacted gold to the mint, but it drove silver out of circulation as money. The new mint ratio of 16 to 1 was accomplished by raising the gold price to $20.67 per ounce while keeping silver at $1.293. Thus, the dollar was devalued with respect to gold. Since the market price ratio was still $15\frac{1}{2}$ to 1, the new mint ratio made it profitable to melt silver coins and export silver bullion. The main message of Gresham's law is that any fixed mint ratio will become inconsistent with market prices, since the latter respond to changes in supply and demand. This fundamental weakness of bimetallism caused it to be replaced by monometallic money.

The country was on a de facto gold standard from 1834 to 1933 with minor exceptions. Gold convertibility was suspended from 1838 to 1843 following the Panic of 1837, and gold exports were banned during World War I, but the main deviation from the gold standard was the Greenback period, from 1861 to 1878. Because of inflation during the Civil War, convertibility of the dollar

---

[3] The principle had been recognized by some people for centuries. The medieval writer Nicole Oresme wrote about it, as did the Greek playwright Sophocles in *The Frogs*.

into gold was suspended, and the dollar depreciated in terms of both gold and foreign exchange. Prices rose and the currency declined until 1866. Because of the wartime inflation, restoring convertibility of the dollar required either a higher gold price (dollar devaluation) or price deflation. A policy of price deflation was chosen, and prices fell from 1866 until convertibility was restored at the prewar gold price in 1878. The Greenback period was an unintentional experiment with floating exchange rates. The price level continued to decline after convertibility was restored, and the question of deflation versus inflation became an important political issue.

Silver was formally demonetized by the Coinage Act of 1873. Those favoring inflation advocated transforming the monetary standard from gold to silver. William Jennings Bryan and his Populist Party became the champions of a free silver movement. They described the demonetization of silver as the "Crime of '73." In one of his famous speeches, Bryan accused his opponents of "crucifying the country on a cross of gold."

The dollar remained convertible into gold until 1933, but it floated against Western European countries from World War I until 1925, because of European inconvertibility. A major change in U.S. monetary standard occurred in 1933, when President Franklin Delano Roosevelt devalued the dollar. Devaluation involved raising the official price from $20.67 per ounce to $35.00. The nominal price of $35 had been roughly constant since 1834. The immediate effect was to depreciate the dollar relative to other gold standard currencies. However, the United Kingdom had already left the gold standard in 1931, and other countries devalued their currencies also. Eventually, it became clear that all currencies can be devalued relative to gold, but not all currencies can depreciate relative to each other.

Before the Roosevelt administration raised the official gold price, all U.S. residents were forced to sell their gold to the government for $20.67 per ounce. Thus, the Treasury realized a capital gain on the gold stock. Private ownership of gold by U.S. residents was banned from 1933 until 1975, except for those commercial activities (e.g., jewelry and dentistry) licensed by the government. Trading of gold on organized markets was prohibited, and gold clauses in contracts (promises to pay an amount of money with fixed gold value) were declared unenforceable. The domestic money supply was no longer closely linked to the quantity of monetary gold. Even though the U.S. monetary system retained some features of a gold standard until 1971, the commitment to gold was much weaker after 1933.

The United States was one of the sponsors of the Bretton Woods (New Hampshire) conference of 1944, whose objective was to end the monetary disorder experienced during the Great Depression and World War II. A common view was that part of the earlier monetary disorder was attributable to floating exchange rates.[4] The result of the conference was the creation of the Interna-

---

[4] An example of this unfavorable view toward floating was an influential League of Nations study by Ragnar Nurkse, *International Currency Experience* (Geneva: League of Nations, 1944.)

tional Monetary Fund and an adjustable peg monetary standard known as the Bretton Woods system. Details of the system will be considered in Chapter 21, but the important features for the present discussion are (1) a system of mainly fixed exchange rates and (2) a continuing commitment to gold. Each member country was obliged to fix the price of its currency in terms of either gold or the U.S. dollar, and it was required to maintain that price within a narrow margin. Since most countries chose to fix the dollar price, which was fixed in terms of gold, most currencies had an indirect link with gold under the Bretton Woods agreement.

The dollar price of gold remained at $35 per ounce because of the U.S. Treasury's willingness to trade at that price with nonresidents. The Treasury accumulated gold immediately after World War II, and in 1949 the United States held 75 percent of the world's official gold stock. From that point U.S. gold reserves declined continuously, and in 1970, they were only 30 percent of world gold reserves. As the U.S. gold stock dwindled, a decision was made to stop supporting the private gold market abroad at the price of $35.

In 1968 the so-called "two-tier system" was implemented as an attempt to separate the private gold market, centered in London, from the foreign official gold market. Thus, the Treasury continued to promise to convert dollars into gold at the $35 price for foreign governments, but not for foreign private traders. The London price immediately rose, and the average private market price in 1968 was $39.26 (see Table 20-1). This attempt at price discrimination depended on foreign governments' refraining from buying gold at the U.S. Treasury for $35 and reselling it in London for a higher price. As the U.S. gold stock dwindled and foreign official dollar holdings increased, the U.S. Treasury continued to promise convertibility. Indeed, the promise continued even after U.S. gold reserves fell below dollar holdings of foreign governments. In August 1971 gold convertibility of the dollar ceased, and it has never been restored.

Following inconvertibility of the dollar, the gold price rose on private markets (see Section 20.8), and exchange rates and money supplies have not been related to gold since then. Notice in Table 20-1 that the private market price of gold rose to $40.81 in 1971 and $58.16 in 1972. However, in terms of dollars of constant purchasing power, the gold price remained low after the 1971 declaration of inconvertibility. The column labeled Consumer Price Index uses 1967 as the base year (1967 = 100). Thus, the same bundle of goods that cost $100.00 in 1967 cost $38.80 in 1933 and $265.10 in 1981.

Since the nominal price of gold was approximately fixed at $35.00, the real price (see last column) declined continuously from $90.21 in 1933 to $30.90 in 1970. The nominal increase in 1971 raised the real price to $33.64, but it was the second lowest real price since 1933. The secular decline in the real price made monetary gold more scarce by discouraging new production and encouraging nonmonetary demand. Congress raised the official gold price first to $38.00 an ounce in 1971 and again to $42.22 in 1973.

TABLE 20-1   Price of Gold, 1933–1983

YEAR	CURRENT DOLLARS PER OUNCE LONDON	CONSUMER PRICE INDEX (1967 = 100)	CONSTANT 1967 DOLLARS
1933	$ 35.00	38.8	$ 90.21
1934–62	35.00		
1963	35.09	91.7	38.27
1964	35.09	92.9	37.77
1965	35.13	94.5	37.17
1966	35.17	97.2	36.18
1967	35.19	100.0	35.19
1968	39.26	104.2	37.68
1969	41.09	109.8	37.42
1970	35.94	116.3	30.90
1971	40.81	121.3	33.64
1972	58.16	125.3	46.42
1973	97.33	133.1	73.13
1974	159.25	147.7	107.82
1975	160.96	161.2	99.85
1976	124.82	170.5	73.21
1977	147.72	181.5	81.39
1978	193.24	195.4	98.89
1979	306.67	217.4	141.06
1980	607.87	247.8	246.30
1981	459.75	265.1	173.43
1982	375.80	289.1	129.99
1983 (June)	400.25	245.5	135.45

Source: International Money Fund, International Financial Statistics Yearbook, 1980, and International Financial Statistics, June 1983.

The first increase followed the Smithsonian agreement of December 1971, which established a new set of fixed exchanges with a depreciated dollar. Then-President Richard Nixon described these new rates as immutable, but by 1973 it became clear that they were not sustainable. The dollar was devalued a second time, but in March 1973 the European Economic Community countries adopted a joint float against the dollar. Other major countries followed, and the dollar depreciated on currency markets.

Later, as generalized floating became a fact of life, Congress abolished the concept of an official gold price. Congress also changed some earlier legislation that gave gold some monetary significance. Private ownership and trade were permitted in 1975. The requirement that the quantity of Federal Reserve notes be linked to gold reserves was abolished in 1968, and gold clauses in contracts became permissible again.

Part of the official gold reserve was auctioned to the private market during the Carter administration, but the future of the remaining inventory remains uncertain. At the end of 1981, the U.S. government held 264 million ounces of gold, which had a 1981 market value of more than $120 billion.[5]

A U.S. Gold Commission was appointed in 1982 by President Ronald Reagan to study the future monetary role of gold. A strong majority of the commission recommended that the United States not return to any form of gold standard. The commission was a response to the 1980 Republican Party platform that made an oblique reference to a return to the gold standard. Certain members of Congress have also expressed their support for a gold standard.[6]

20.4 THE GOLD STANDARD AND THE PRICE LEVEL

Two important economic features of the gold standard are (1) determination of the price level and (2) determination of the exchange rate. To separate the two issues, first consider the determination of the money price level under a gold standard for a closed economy. Under a gold standard, there is a tendency for price-level changes to be self-correcting. Inflation induces a decrease in the monetary gold stock, while deflation increases the money supply. The first requirement of a gold standard is that the government define its money as a fixed quantity of gold (e.g., 2 ounces per dollar). The inverse of the gold content ($0.50 per ounce) is the mint price of gold, at which the government must be willing to buy and sell unlimited amounts of gold.

The government's commitment to be the residual buyer and seller means that the demand and supply of gold become infinitely elastic at the mint price. The price of gold cannot fall below the mint price because the government will buy any private surplus. The price cannot rise above the mint level because the government will satisfy any private shortage. The government's obligation can be satisfied by providing all residents with free access to the mint and permitting them to melt coins and export bullion.

If there were no coinage fee, no residents would ever sell gold bullion for less than the mint price, since they could always receive that price from the government. If a fee equal to the marginal cost of coinage (called brassage) were charged, the market price of gold could fall until it equaled that mint

---

[5] U.S. holdings were 28 percent of official world reserves. Other countries with large official reserves were West Germany with 95 million ounces (10 percent), Switzerland with 83 million ounces (9 percent), France with 82 million ounces (9 percent), and Italy with 67 million ounces (7 percent).

[6] Included in that group are Senator Jesse Helms of North Carolina and Congressmen Jack Kemp of New York and Ron Paul of Texas. The official report of the Gold Commission is available as *Report to Congress of the Commission on the Role of Gold in the Domestic and International Monetary Systems*, 1982.

price minus the coinage fee. If the government charged a fee in excess of cost to earn revenue (called seigniorage), the price of bullion could fall farther. Similar forces would limit price increases for gold bullion. Without a coinage fee, the market price could not rise above the mint price. A tendency for the market price to rise would be offset by people melting gold coins and selling them for their greater value as bullion. If a coinage fee equal to the cost were charged, the price of gold could rise by an amount equal to the fee before it became profitable to melt coins.

The effects of an increase in the gold supply are shown in Figure 20-1. Initial supply and demand curves are G_1^s and G^d. The equilibrium is at point A, where the mint price (P_M) equals the market price. Let there be a small decrease in the price of gold, perhaps from a new discovery, that shifts supply from G_1^s to G_2^s. If there is no coinage fee, the market price of gold will remain at P_m, and the money supply increases by $AB = G_1 G_2$. The private excess supply of AB at P_m will be sold to the mint. However, if there is a coinage fee (f), the market price can fluctuate between $P_3 = P_m + f$ and $P_2 = P_m - f$ without inducing coinage. With a coinage fee the market price will fall to P_4 without inducing coinage, since the net price paid by the mint is $P_2 = P_m - f$. It is not profitable to buy gold bullion for P_4 in the market and resell it to the mint for the lower price of P_2. Thus, the effect of a gold discovery on the money supply and the market price of bullion depends partly on the coinage fee.

Now consider a larger gold discovery that would shift supply from G_1^s to G_3^s. In the absence of a coinage fee, the price would remain at P_m and the money supply would increase by AF. With a coinage fee the price would fall to P_2 before it became profitable to take gold to the mint. At P_2 there is an excess supply of DE, which would be profitable to coin. The money supply would increase by $DE = G_4 G_5$. For similar reasons, the market price of gold could rise to P_3 before it became profitable to melt coins.

FIGURE 20-1   Gold Supply and Coinage in a Closed Economy

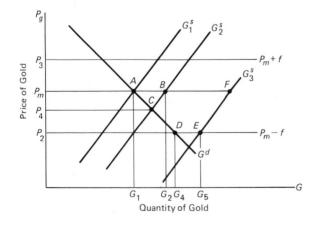

The same economic effects could be achieved by letting convertible paper money circulate as the medium of exchange. The government would be obliged to convert paper into gold and gold into paper at a fixed price. The government could charge a conversion fee that would have the same effects as a coinage fee. The government's obligation to convert money into gold has the effects of (1) limiting the money supply and (2) limiting the price of gold bullion.

A characteristic of the gold standard is that it tends to dampen price level changes. It contains built-in forces that tend to restrain both inflation and deflation. Because the money price of gold is constant, the relative price of gold varies inversely with the price level. Thus, inflation lowers the relative price of gold and deflation increases it. Since gold mining is a commercial activity, the supply of gold depends on the relative price, which moves inversely with the price level. Gold is used both as money and for nonmonetary purposes, and the nonmonetary demand depends on the relative gold price. When the price level increases, the quantity of newly mined gold decreases and the quantity of gold demanded for nonmonetary purposes increases. These two forces tend to reduce the amount of gold that is used as money.

The depressing effect of a price-level increase on the money supply is part of the automatic adjustment mechanism under gold. Conversely, a decrease in the price level would increase the relative price of gold, which would increase the quantity of gold mined and decrease nonmonetary demand. It would become profitable to melt nonmonetary demand and convert it to money. In this way price deflation would be self-correcting by increasing the money supply. A gold standard contains self-correcting forces, but the strength of the forces is an empirical question.[7] Specifically, their strength depends on the elasticity of supply of newly mined gold and the elasticity of demand for nonmonetary gold. The greater are these elasticities the greater will be the price-level stability in response to economic disturbances.[8]

With respect to the price level, one should distinguish between the trend in prices and fluctuations around the trend. During the historical gold standard there was no significant trend in prices, but there was fluctuation around the trend, whose magnitude depended on these elasticities. The trend in prices depends on the forces that shift gold supply, nonmonetary demand, and the demand for money. In the case of gold supply, the trend price depends on new gold discoveries (e.g., California gold rush, Alaska, South Africa), technological change (e.g., cyanide process), and factor accumulation.

A larger money supply may be created from a given gold stock by adopting a fractional gold reserve. The demand for gold depends on the prices of substitutes in nonmonetary uses and real income growth. Thus, any forces that

---

[7] A good analytical paper on the gold standard is Robert Barro, "Money and the Price Level Under the Gold Standard," *Economic Journal*, March 1979.

[8] For an analysis of commodity money standards see Milton Friedman, "Commodity Reserve Currency," in his *Essays in Positive Economics* (Chicago: University of Chicago Press, 1953).

increase the supply of gold or decrease the demand for gold tend to increase the price level. The European discovery of America added to the European supply of precious metals and resulted in the so-called "price revolution" in Europe. Michael Bordo compared price stability during the gold standard period with the paper money standard after World War II for both the United States and the United Kingdom. He concluded that the gold standard provided greater price stability in the long run but greater price instability in the short run.[9]

20.5 THE SOCIAL COST OF THE GOLD STANDARD

What is the cost to society of gold or any commodity money compared with that of paper money? The social cost of using gold as money is the forgone opportunity cost of the gold. For a closed economy, gold could be used for industrial or artistic purposes; in an open economy, it could also be exported. The social or opportunity cost has two components: (1) the cost of the existing stock and (2) the cost of adding to the gold stock. In the case of the inherited stock of gold bullion that has already been mined, the historical mining costs are irrelevant. Since they have already been borne, they are not relevant to current decisions. However, gold is durable, and the cost of using it for money in each period is the forgone interest on the inherited stock.

The second component of social cost is the cost of adding to the gold stock to satisfy the demand for additional real cash balances as the economy grows. As real income grows, the demand for all normal goods including real money balances will increase. Additional money demand may be satisfied by (1) increasing the nominal money supply at a constant price level, (2) accepting price level deflation for a constant nominal money supply, or (3) employing some combination of monetary expansion and price-level deflation.

The options may be expressed in terms of the equation of exchange,

$$MV = Py$$

where V is the income velocity of money. It may be written in percentage changes:

$$\frac{dM}{M} + \frac{dV}{V} = \frac{dP}{P} + \frac{dy}{y}$$

[9] Michael David Bordo, "The Classical Gold Standard: Some Lessons for Today." *Federal Reserve Bank of St. Louis Review*, May 1981.

To simplify calculations, suppose that money demand grows at the same rate as income that is, $dV/V = 0$. The additional demand for real cash balances caused by real income growth may be satisfied by

1. Constant money supply and price deflation:

$$\frac{dM}{M} = 0 \quad \text{and} \quad \frac{dP}{P} = \frac{dy}{y}$$

2. Stable price level and monetary growth:

$$\frac{dP}{P} = 0 \quad \text{and} \quad \frac{dM}{M} = \frac{dy}{y}$$

Either the price level falls at the rate of income growth or the nominal money supply increases at the same rate. In the latter case, the social cost of supplying the additional money is

$$C_2 = dM = \frac{M\,dy}{y} = (\frac{M}{y})(\frac{dy}{y})y$$

The cost of supplying the additional money depends on (1) the ratio of money to income (the inverse of income velocity), (2) the rate of real economic growth, and (3) the initial income level. Consider an example:

$$\frac{M}{y} = 0.25, \quad \frac{dy}{y} = 0.04, \quad y = \$1{,}200 \text{ billion}$$

The annual cost of adding to the gold cost would be

$$dM = (0.25)(0.04)(1{,}200) = (0.01)(1{,}200)$$
$$= \$12 \text{ billion per year}$$

Expressed as a percentage of GNP the total cost is

$$\frac{C}{y} = \frac{dM}{y} = \frac{M}{y}\frac{dy}{y} = (0.25)(0.04) = 0.01$$

The annual cost would be 1 percent of initial GNP. The cost of gold must be compared with the cost of providing paper money, which is borne partly by the central bank, the Treasury, and private banks.

A problem with estimating the cost of paper is that each of these institutions performs other functions, which makes it difficult to allocate costs between those functions and money production. Whether 1 percent of GNP is large depends on what it is compared with. Traditional estimates of the annual cost of all monopolies in the U.S. economy show the cost at far less than 1 percent of GNP. If growth in money demand were satisfied by falling prices instead of monetary growth, the social cost would not be smaller. The cost of adding to the stock would be lower, but the forgone cost of the existing stock would be greater. Because of falling prices, the same number of ounces of gold would be worth more of other goods and services.

One could reduce the social cost of a gold standard by holding fractional gold reserves against money. If the fraction is variable, the government acquires some discretionary power over monetary policy that it lacks under a 100 percent reserve gold standard. The evolution of the world's monetary system from a gold standard to paper money with floating rates may be described as a gradual reduction in the fractional gold reserves. The standard commodity could be gold, silver, bricks, or some bundle of commodities, but the social cost would be the same. The only difference would be the distribution of rents accruing to owners of the standard commodity.

20.6 GOLD AND FIXED EXCHANGE RATES

Fixed exchange rates between national currencies is the most important feature of a gold standard for international trade. The operation of an international gold standard requires at least two countries with monetary systems based on gold. This point seems obvious, but it is not always recognized by some proponents of a unilateral U.S. commitment to gold. A single country may fix the gold price and link its money supply to gold, but that country will have floating exchange rates unless other countries also link their national currencies to gold.

Suppose that two countries do adopt a gold standard. Each government must determine the gold content of its money, which indirectly establishes the mint price of gold. Let the home country be the United States and the foreign country be the United Kingdom. Let the United Kingdom define the pound to be equal to 2 ounces of gold and let the United States define the dollar to be equal to 1 ounce of gold:

$$\Pi_{\pounds G} = G2$$
$$\Pi_{\$G} = G1$$

The implied mint prices of gold in the two countries are

$$\Pi_{G\pounds} = \pounds.5$$
$$\Pi_{G\$} = \$1$$

Each government must be willing to buy and sell unlimited amounts of gold at the mint price. Both must also permit gold exports and imports. It does not matter whether gold coins circulate as money or whether paper money circulates, provided that 100 percent of the gold reserves are held and paper is convertible at a fixed price. The actions of the U.K. and the U.S. central banks and private arbitragers will establish fixed exchange rates between currencies. Unlike the Bretton Woods system, neither central bank is obliged to deal in foreign currency. The obligation of each government is to trade gold against its own currency. The two mint prices of gold will indirectly establish the following exchange rate between the currencies:

$$\Pi_{£\$}^M = \frac{\Pi_{G\$}}{\Pi_{G£}} = \frac{\$2}{£1} = \$2 \text{ per pound}$$

This is an indirect exchange rate, since neither the U.K. nor U.S. central banks will exchange dollars for pounds at this price. It is the rate that arbitragers obtain by converting one currency into gold and then trading gold for the remaining currency. It is a special case of triangular arbitrage, where one of the assets is gold.

To see why the mint exchange rate $\Pi_{£\$}^M$ is the equilibrium rate, consider the trading opportunities available to arbitragers. First, assume there are no transportation costs. The maximum possible price of pounds in the exchange market is $\Pi_{£\$} = \$2$. No traders will pay more, because they may always obtain £1 for $2 through the following transactions:

1. Buy $G1$ for $2 at the U.S. mint.
2. Ship $G1$ from the United States to the United Kingdom.
3. Sell $G1$ for £1 at the U.K. mint.

Dollars have been exchanged indirectly for pounds. The opportunity to pay dollars in the United States and receive pounds in the United Kingdom establishes a perfectly elastic supply of pounds at a price of $2.

It may also be shown that $\Pi_{£\$} = \$2$ is the minimum price that traders will pay for pounds. Arbitragers may always sell $2 for £1 indirectly using the following sequence of transactions:

1. Sell £1 for $G1$ at the U.K. mint.
2. Ship $G1$ from the United Kingdom to the United States.
3. Sell $G1$ for $2 at the U.S. mint.

Since all suppliers of pounds may obtain this price, they will not sell for less. The two mint prices establish a perfectly elastic demand for pounds at the price of $2.

The equilibrium in the foreign exchange market is shown as point A in Figure 20-2. The demand curve F_1^d is drawn for the initial gold stock in the

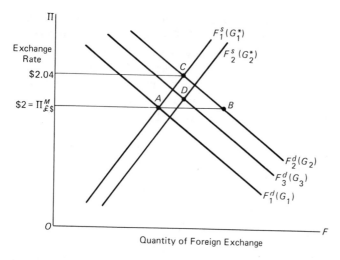

FIGURE 20-2   Gold Standard Adjustment

United States, while F_1^s is drawn for the initial gold stock in the United Kingdom.

Consider the gold standard adjustment to an increase in the demand for foreign exchange that shifts F^d from F_1^d to F_2^d. The excess demand of AB will induce a dollar depreciation to $2.04, where there is a temporary equilibrium at point C. This exchange rate is the direct price between pounds and dollars. The mint exchange rate of $2.00 is an indirect rate that is also available. Since two prices now exist in the same market, arbitragers have an incentive to buy pounds for $2.00 indirectly and sell pounds for $2.04 directly. Pounds may be bought for $2.00 using the following transactions:

1. Buy $G1$ for the $2 in United States.
2. Ship $G1$ for the United States to the United Kingdom.
3. Sell $G1$ for £1 in the United Kingdom.

The net effect of arbitrage is to transfer gold from the United States to the United Kingdom. Since gold is money, the money supply decreases in the United States and increases in the United Kingdom. The monetary changes will shift demand to $F_3^d(G_2)$ and supply to $F_2^s(G_2^*)$, and the dollar will appreciate. Gold flow from the United States will continue until the equilibrium exchange rate returns to $2.00. Depreciation of the dollar is arrested by the gold outflow from the United States. Any pound price above $2.00 will induce gold exports from the United States. Similar logic will demonstrate that any pound price below $2.00 will induce gold imports into the United States.

The same kind of adjustment would occur with a paper money standard and fixed exchange rates. The excess demand of AB would be met by sales of foreign exchange by the central bank, which would buy an equivalent amount of domestic money. In the absence of sterilization, the foreign exchange demand curve would shift to the left. Gold standard adjustment substitutes the profit-motivated behavior of private arbitragers for the foreign exchange intervention of central banks.

So far the costs of transporting gold have been ignored. The effect of transport costs is to reduce the volume of gold flows and permit some limited flexibility of the exchange rate. The maximum and minimum exchange rates are determined by the gold export and import points.

Figure 20-3 shows the gold standard adjustment to an increase in foreign exchange demand when there are costs of transporting gold between the United States and the United Kingdom. Let the transport cost be $TR = \$0.02$ per ounce of gold. This additional cost now raises the indirect buying price that arbitragers must pay for pounds from \$2.00 to \$2.02. This maximum price of pounds becomes the gold export point for the United States. Similarly, the additional transport costs lower the indirect selling price of pounds from \$2.00 to \$1.98. This minimum price becomes the gold import point for the United Kingdom. The maximum and minimum prices may be determined by working through the same sequence of transactions considered above with the addition of transport costs.

1. Maximum $\Pi_{\pounds\$} = \Pi_{\pounds\$}^{M} + TR = \$2.02$
    a. Buy $G1$ for \$2 in the United States.
    b. Ship $G1$ from the United States to the United Kingdom for $TR = \$0.02$.
    c. Sell $G1$ for £1 in the United Kingdom. Thus, $\Pi_{\pounds\$} = \$2.02$.
2. Minimum $\Pi_{\pounds\$} = \Pi_{\pounds\$}^{M} - TR = \$1.98$
    a. Sell £1 for $G1$ in the United Kingdom.
    b. Ship $G1$ from the United Kingdom to the United States for $TR = \$0.02$.
    c. Sell $G1$ for \$2 in the United States. Thus, $\Pi_{\pounds\$} = \$1.98$.

FIGURE 20-3   Transport Costs and Gold Points

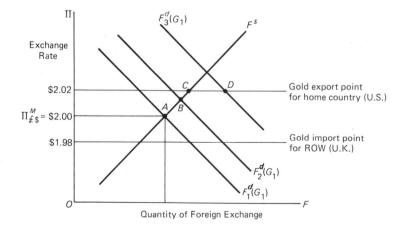

The equilibrium exchange rate must lie between \$2.02 and \$1.98:

$$\Pi_{£\$}^M - TR \leq \Pi_{£\$} \leq \Pi_{£\$}^M + TR$$
$$\$1.98 \leq \Pi_{£\$} \leq \$2.02$$

The indirect net buying price is the gold export point:

$$\Pi_{£\$}^M + TR = \$2.02$$

The indirect net selling price is the gold import point:

$$\Pi_{£\$}^M - TR = \$1.98$$

The two prices taken together are the gold points, which determine the range of permissible exchange rate fluctuation under the gold standard.

The effect of the gold points is shown in Figure 20-3. A small increase in the demand for foreign exchange from F_1^d to F_2^d will increase the exchange rate above \$2.00 but below \$2.02. However, this depreciation of the dollar will not induce a gold outflow from the United States because the arbitrage gain is less than the cost of transporting gold. However, a larger increase in demand to F_3^d would induce a gold outflow. The price of pounds would rise to \$2.02, and at that price, there is an excess demand for pounds of CD. The price of \$2.02 is the gold export point, and CD units will flow from the United States to the United Kingdom. The gold outflow will decrease the U.S. money supply, shifting F^d to the left. The gold inflow will increase the U.K. money supply, shifting F^s to the right. Gold will continue to flow, shifting F^d and F^s, until the excess demand for pounds is eliminated.

The gold flow is part of David Hume's price-specie flow mechanism. The adjustment process is symmetrical for decreases in foreign exchange demand. Small decreases will lower the price of pounds, but at \$1.98, it becomes profitable to import gold into the United States. Notice that the gold export and import points are analogous to the gold minting and melting points for a closed economy. Within the gold points the exchange rate fluctuates, and at the gold points the money supply fluctuates.

Gold points based on transport costs do not permit a central bank to carry out a discretionary monetary policy. However, if the government can manipulate the gold points, there is some scope for monetary policy. There is some evidence that the Bank of England managed the gold standard by manipulating the gold points. Manipulation refers to changing the effective buying and selling prices of gold. For example, the United States may sell gold for \$2, but it may require payment before delivery of gold. The length of the waiting period and the interest rate determine the cost in forgone interest. The central bank may charge an explicit fee, which raises the gold export point. It may sell gold but ban gold exports (e.g., during World War I in the United States).

The extreme policy is to refuse to sell gold, that is, declare inconvertibility. This policy was carried out during the Greenback period. In addition to manipulating the gold points, the Bank of England used interest rate policy to influence capital flows. As an alternative to a gold outflow, the central bank could attract capital by raising interest rates. Raising the Bank of England's discount rate was said to be an effective way to attract funds to London.

The gold standard achieved fixed exchange rates by pegging national currencies directly to gold. It could also be achieved by pegging currencies to silver or any other commodity. The rate of world inflation would depend on the demand and supply of the standard commodity. Fixed rates could also be achieved with paper money by pegging all national currencies but one to the remaining national currency. The dollar became the de facto key currency in the Bretton Woods system, which will be considered in Chapter 21. In the case of a dollar standard, the world inflation rate would be determined by monetary policy in the United States. A final alternative for achieving fixed exchange rates is to peg all national currencies to an international money, such as special drawing rights (SDRs) created by the IMF. In this case the Fund's rate of SDR expansion would determine the world inflation rate.

20.7 THE GOLD STANDARD, THE MONEY SUPPLY, AND THE RULES OF THE GAME

Under a strict gold standard, the government has no control over the money supply. In a closed economy the quantity of money is determined by the demand and supply of gold. In an open economy, the national money supply depends on the balance of payments. Any forces that would cause an excess demand for foreign exchange would lead to a gold outflow and a decrease in the money supply. Conversely, anything leading to an excess supply of foreign exchange would induce a gold inflow and increase the money supply.

Since the gold standard was not a system enacted by law, there were no formal rules. Nevertheless, there were some informal "rules of the game" that were followed by participants in varying degrees. All governments were obliged to declare a mint price of gold and to be prepared to buy and sell unlimited amounts of gold at that price. Residents were free to bring gold to the mint, melt coins, and export gold. If money consisted of 100 percent gold coins, the money supply would change automatically when gold was minted or melted, imported or exported. If fractional reserve money circulated, the money supply would vary with gold reserves.

Systematic sterilization of gold flows violated the spirit of the rules of the game. It broke the link between the money supply and the balance of payments. Manipulating the gold points would be another violation. A strict gold standard provides no scope for discretionary monetary policy. As central banks developed, they acquired more authority, and the rules of the game were violated more frequently.

Even before 1914 there was evidence of limited but systematic manipulation of gold flows by central banks.[10] Later the experience of the Great Depression and a change in economic thinking inspired by John Maynard Keynes convinced most policymakers that the gold standard rules were anachronistic. According to the new view, central banks should stabilize national economies through an active monetary policy that would add to private demand during recessions and subtract from demand during business expansions.

This notion of countercyclical demand management cannot be reconciled with the passive monetary policy inherent in the gold standard. Although the post–World War II Bretton Woods system retained a formal role for gold, the rules of the game were not taken very seriously. However, the poor performance of demand management in the 1970s combined with macroeconomic research that criticized Keynesian thought has revived interest in the automatic characteristic of the gold standard.

20.8 THE CURRENT STATUS OF GOLD

Under floating exchange rates that have prevailed since 1973, gold has no official monetary significance. Gold does not directly determine currency exchange rates or national money supplies. No currencies are convertible into gold. Special drawing rights are not linked to gold. Most governments and the IMF hold gold inventories that they have inherited from the past. At the end of 1981, the United States held official gold reserves of 264 million ounces with a market value of $121 billion. Total world gold reserves were 952 million ounces or $438 billion at market prices. Both the United States and the IMF auctioned part of their gold in the private market, but they retain sizable reserves. From 1976 to 80 the IMF auctioned 25 million ounces (one-sixth of its stock) for 4.6 billion, which it distributed as aid to low-income members. The IMF also returned another 25 million ounces to members in proportion to their quotas. This formula returned a disproportionate amount of gold to high income countries, but initial gold contributions of countries were based on the same formula.

Because of high inflation rates since 1973, there is renewed political interest in returning to a gold standard or some form of commodity money. Some countries may be reluctant to sell their reserves for this reason. The private gold market has been quite volatile. As shown in Table 20-1, the gold price rose rapidly in 1973 and 1974. It declined in 1976 and sharply increased from

---

[10] See Arthur I. Bloomfield, *Monetary Policy Under the International Gold Standard, 1880–1914* (New York: Federal Reserve Bank of New York, 1959).

$148 in 1977 to $193 in 1978 and to $307 in 1979. The price rose farther in 1980 to an average of $608, and at one point during the year, the price was near $900 per ounce. The price dropped sharply in 1981, and by June 1982 the price had fallen to nearly $300 per ounce. By June 1983 it had returned to $400 per ounce. In one sense gold has become just another mineral, like silver and copper. However, because of its previous monetary role and possible future role, the gold market may reflect economic conditions that other commodity markets do not.

It is widely believed that the gold market is more sensitive to political events than are other markets. The announcement of a war, revolution, or political assassination usually causes the gold price to rise. There is at least one financial advisor whose gold price equation contains a political instability index. The index is an attempt to quantify events such as wars and revolutions that might have indirect economic effects. War does not cause inflation directly, but the traditional wartime finance is inflationary.

The gold market could be a sensitive barometer of inflationary expectations. However, it is difficult to explain the sharp gold price decreases in 1981 and 1982 in terms of inflation expectations. The largest gold producing countries are South Africa and the Soviet Union. However, since current production is small relative to the existing gold stock, fluctuations in price are dominated by demand changes rather than the current production.

The gold price has shown a trend upward since 1971, but it has been volatile. It has been quite responsive to interest rates, which are the opportunity cost of holding gold. At a gold price of $500 and an interset rate of 20 percent (experienced in 1981), the annual cost of holding an ounce of gold is $100 per year. Speculators would not hold gold unless they expected the price to rise to $600 within a year. However, at an interest rate of 10 percent, speculators would hold gold even if they expected the price to rise only above $550 per ounce.

There have been periods when gold speculation would have been profitable and others when it would have been ruinous. If speculators acquired gold for $35 per ounce in 1933 and sold it at the end of 1980 for $500, they would have received a 5.95 percent compound annual rate of return, which is not substantially different from the yield on financial assets. Gold is widely traded on organized spot and futures markets in London, New York, Chicago, and Winnipeg. There is evidence that the forward gold price is an unbiased, although inaccurate, forecast of the subsequent spot price.

Would a gold standard be a useful monetary system in the 1980s? The answer depends partly on how well the alternative systems perform. The traditional case against gold is that it has an unnecessarily high real resource cost. It accomplishes fixed exchange rates, but that could be done as easily with paper money. It provides an automatic balance-of-payments adjustment process, but that is a feature of all fixed rate systems. It assigns control of the money supply to the gold market rather than to central bankers. Although gold contains a built-in adjustment mechanism, it would not permit modern counter-cyclical monetary policy. Whether that feature is a virtue or a vice depends on the success of discretionary monetary policy.

In recent years critics have blamed central bankers for destabilizing the world monetary system. As an alternative to paper money, the private gold market is not necessarily a source of stability. New discoveries and technical change in the gold industry are difficult to forecast. The major gold producing countries, South Africa and the USSR, are vulnerable to economic and political instability.

Gold does provide a kind of monetary constitution that restricts the authority of the central bank. The same goal could be achieved by imposing a rule on the central bank. The Federal Reserve is a creation of Congress, and the legislature could impose a monetary rule at any time. Friedman's constant rate of growth of the money supply is one example of such a rule.

Some gold advocates have proposed that the United States unilaterally adopt a gold standard. However, if no other countries followed, the United States would continue to have floating exchange rates. At what level should the gold price be set? In a brief period between 1980 and 1982, the price fluctuated between $300 and $900. If the price is set too high, there will be a large private excess supply. The U.S. government will buy large amounts of gold, create an equivalent amount of money, and cause more inflation. If the price is set too low, there will be a large private excess demand. The United States will sell large amounts of gold from reserves (if they are large enough), reduce the money supply by an equivalent amount, and impose deflationary pressure on the economy. After a long enough period of adjustment, the economy could adapt to any nominal price of gold. Specifically, the money price level, money wages, and the money supply would have to adapt to the mint price. However, if the official gold price chosen were far from equilibrium, the transitory adjustment cost could be substantial.

There has been a revival of political interest in the gold standard in the United States, but proponents remain a small minority. As discussed in Section 20.3, a large majority of the 1982 U.S. Gold Commission opposed a monetary system based on gold.

20.9 MONETARY UNION AND FIXED EXCHANGE RATES

One institutional device for achieving fixed exchange rates is either gold or another commodity standard. Any commodity money standard severely restricts a nation's monetary independence. The world money supply is determined by the market for the standard commodity, and each nation's money supply is determined by its balance of payments.

Fixed exchange rates may be achieved with paper money if each currency is pegged to some national or international paper money such as dollars or SDRs. If one currency is permanently pegged to another, an effective monetary union results. Most monetary unions are also political unions, but they need not be. The merger of the 13 American colonies made them a monetary union. The 50 United States and Puerto Rico are a monetary union, even though Puerto Rico does not have the same political status as do the states. Belgium and Luxembourg are a monetary union.

The British Commonwealth was once a monetary union, but many members have adopted their own currencies with floating exchange rates. Panama has achieved an effective monetary union with the United States by permanently fixing the exchange rate between the balboa and the U.S. dollar (1 balboa per dollar). The members of the European Economic Community have proposed a full monetary union, and they have moved toward union by narrowing the range of exchange rate variation between member currencies. All national central banks will surrender autonomy, and eventually they will be replaced by a single EEC central bank.

What are the benefits and costs of monetary union? Transactions costs are reduced by expressing all values in a single unit, and exchange rate uncertainty is eliminated. The absence of exchange risk promotes free capital mobility. Mobile capital has been cited as an important source of economic development in Puerto Rico. The development of Panama as a regional banking center has been attributed to the fixed rate with the dollar. Balance-of-payments problems are rarely noticed within a monetary union, because there is an automatic adjustment process. Because of the automatic adjustment, there is little reason to use commercial policy to solve balance-of-payments problems. Hence, monetary union is compatible with free trade.

In addition to the advantages, monetary union has some costs. The country or region loses autonomy over its money supply and exchange rate as policy variables. The exchange rate is permanently fixed with the union, and it varies against the rest of the world. When the dollar appreciates, it appreciates for all 50 states plus Puerto Rico, Panama, and any currencies linked to the dollar.

Suppose that the source of appreciation is a high world price of wheat that increased the value of Kansas wheat exports. The dollar appreciation will make the exports of all other regions of the union less competitive on world markets. It will also make imports more competitive in all parts of the dollar area. Automobile producers in Michigan will become less competitive because they belong to a currency union in Kansas. If Michigan had a separate currency, the Michigan dollar could remain fixed against the rest of the world whereas the Kansas dollar could appreciate.

One problem is that exchange rates between regions of a union move up and down together even though economic conditions may differ between unions. For this reason factor mobility between regions is important. When factors of production are immobile, there may be economically depressed regions. If the monetary union is a single country, fiscal transfers may be made to depressed regions.

If the union consists of separate countries, fiscal transfers are more difficult to accomplish. Members of a monetary union lose autonomy not only over exchange rate policy, but also over the money supply. They must accept the same rate of inflation or deflation as the rest of the union. If part of the union is experiencing a recession with high unemployment, they may prefer a more expansionary monetary policy than the rest of the union. However, the monetary union may have only one monetary policy for all regions. If the regions are part of a single nation, each region may attempt to influence the common monetary policy through its political representatives. If separate countries are involved, the problem of satisfactory representation emerges. Panama is affected by U.S. monetary policy, but it has no direct influence over the policy. A separate country could use commercial policy as a kind of indirect monetary policy. For example, Panama could use tariff policy to alter the domestic money supply, but this would distort relative prices, production, and consumption.

A final cost to a national member of a currency union is the forgone interest from holding noninterest-bearing foreign money. Traditionally, national governments have used their right to issue noninterest-bearing currency as a source of revenue. However, if foreign money pays competitive interest, as many modern deposit accounts do, there is no loss of income from using foreign money.

The plan for a European monetary union is an ambitious undertaking that has made some progress, but it has also encountered serious problems. The first step toward an eventual full monetary union was to narrow the range of exchange rate variability between member currencies. During the Bretton Woods period, proponents of monetary union complained that the dollar was the de facto international currency in Europe. They attributed the dollar's importance partly to the fact that the dollar fluctuated less against any European currency than any two EEC currencies fluctuated against each other. They proposed to continue the Bretton Woods exchange margin against the dollar but to adopt a narrower band of exchange rate fluctuation between EEC currencies. This policy was commonly described as the "snake in the tunnel." The wider range against the dollar was interpreted as a kind of tunnel within which individual currencies could fluctuate in the manner of a snake. After the breakdown of Bretton Woods, the proponents of a European monetary union advocated a joint EEC float. Indeed, the beginning of the EEC's joint float in March 1973 is usually taken as the end of the Bretton Woods system.

The idea of a joint float was formalized in March 1979, when the European monetary system (EMS) came into being. Progress toward union has been difficult. The United Kingdom has never participated in the EMS, and Greece, which became an EEC member in January 1981, had not joined the EMS as of the end of 1982. There have been several major exchange rate changes within the EMS. The French franc and Italian lira were devalued in June 1982, which was the second major currency change in eight months.

The next step in the plan is to create a European monetary fund and, eventually, a single central bank with a single currency. Currently each country retains its own central bank and its own national monetary policies. Partly because of differences in national monetary policies, national inflation rates of EEC members have shown considerable divergence. (See Chapter 22 for data.) Germany, The Netherlands, and Belgium have tended to have less inflation, whereas France, Italy, and the United Kingdom have tended to have more.

As a result of these monetary differences, as well as real economic differences, there has been pressure for exchange rates to change. Success for a European monetary union seems unlikely as long as national central banks are free to conduct their own policies. There has been much discussion of coordinating monetary policies, and European central bankers meet regularly at the Bank for International Settlements, but significant differences remain. If agreement can be reached about a target inflation rate, will it be the German inflation rate or the Italian rate?

It has been said that greater monetary union cannot be achieved until there is greater political union. If the German monetary policy is adopted throughout the EEC, Italians may complain about currency appreciation and excessively high unemployment rates. If the Italian monetary policy is adopted, Germans may complain about currency depreciation and excessive unemployment. With current political institutions, aggrieved citizens in one country may find it difficult to influence the EEC's monetary policy.

SUMMARY

Fixed exchanged rates may be achieved either with commodity money or paper money. The gold standard was historically the most important system of commodity money. General economic equilibrium may be achieved if one nominal variable is fixed by policy. Fixing the gold price requires variability of the money supply, price level, and money wages. The U.S. monetary system incorporated most features of a gold standard from 1791 to 1933, with some features continuing until 1971.

A gold standard limits exchange rate flexibility to a range within the gold points, which are determined by the cost of transporting gold between countries. An important characteristic of the gold standard is that the money supply is beyond the control of the government. A nation's money supply depends on its balance of payments, and the world money supply depends on the gold market.

A significant cost of the gold standard is that real resources must be used to serve as money. Gold has been completely demonetized in the United States and the rest of the world since 1971.

Dissatisfaction with recent inflation rates has revived interest in the gold standard, but no important moves have been made to restore gold to a monetary role. A monetary union provides many of the same features as a gold standard, and the proposed European monetary union is an important attempt to achieve union.

REFERENCES

ABKEN, PETER. "The Economics of Gold Price Movements." *Economic Review*, Federal Reserve Bank of Richmond, March–April 1980.

ALLEN, POLLY REYNOLDS. *Organization and Administration of a Monetary Union*, Princeton Studies in International Finance, No. 38. Princeton, N.J.: Princeton University Press, 1976.

BARRO, ROBERT. "Money and the Price Level Under the Gold Standard." *Economic Journal*, March 1979. Theoretical analysis of the properties of a gold standard.

BLOOMFIELD, ARTHUR I. *Monetary Policy Under the International Gold Standard, 1880–1914*. New York: Federal Reserve Bank of New York, 1959. Study emphasizing the amount of discretionary monetary policy that occurred under the gold standard.

BORDO, MICHAEL DAVID. "The Classical Gold Standard: Some Lessons for Today." *Review*, Federal Reserve Bank of St. Louis, May 1981. Empirical study comparing the gold standard and recent monetary experience.

———, and A. J. SCHWARTZ, eds. *A Retrospective on the Classical Gold Standard, 1821–1931*. Chicago: University of Chicago Press, 1983. Proceedings from a conference on the gold standard sponsored by the National Bureau of Economic Research.

BROWN, WILLIAM A. *The International Gold Standard Reinterpreted, 1914–1934*. New York: National Bureau of Economic Research, 1940.

COOPER, RICHARD N. "The Gold Standard: Historical Facts and Future Prospects." *Brookings Papers on Economic Activity*, 1:1982. Discusses the gold standard and other commodity reserve proposals.

DEVRIES, T. *On the Meaning and Future of the European Monetary System*, Princeton Essays in International Finance, No. 138. Princeton, N.J.: Princeton University Press, September 1980.

FISCHER, STANLEY. "Seigniorage and the Case for a National Money." *Journal of Political Economy*, April 1982. Advanced analysis of the amount of revenue a country might receive from its key currency status.

FRIEDMAN, MILTON. "Commodity Reserve Currency." In his *Essays in Positive Economics*. Chicago: University of Chicago Press, 1953. Thorough analysis of commodity reserve money.

———, and ANNA JACOBSON SCHWARTZ. *A Monetary History of the United States, 1867–1960*. Princeton, N.J.: Princeton University Press, 1963. Massive monetary history that includes the gold standard period.

HARBERGER, ARNOLD. *"Reflections on the Monetary System in Panama."* In *Chicago Essays in Economic Development*, David Wall, ed. Chicago: University of Chicago Press, 1972.

HART, A. G. "The Case as of 1976 for International Commodity Reserve Currency." *Weltwirtschaftliches Archiv.*, Band 112, Heft 1 (1976).

HAWTREY, R. G. *The Gold Standard in Theory and Practice*. London: Longmans, Green, 1947.

HIRSCH, FRED. "Influences on Gold Production." International Monetary Fund *Staff Papers*, November 1968.

INGRAM, JAMES C. *Regional Payments Mechanisms: The Case of Puerto Rico.* Chapel Hill: University of North Carolina Press, 1962.

———. "Some Implications of Puerto Rican Experience." In *International Finance*, Richard Cooper, ed. Baltimore: Penguin, 1969. Discusses the effects of fixed exchange rates between the United States and Puerto Rico.

INTERNATIONAL MONETARY FUND. *International Financial Statistics Yearbook.* Washington, D.C.: IMF, annually. Each issue contains a 30-year time series on private market gold prices and official gold holdings by country.

JASTRAM, ROY W. *The Golden Constant.* New York: John Wiley, 1977.

JOHNSON, HARRY G. "Equilibrium Under Fixed Exchange Rates." *American Economic Review*, May 1963. Analyzes a fixed exchange rate system as an attempt to achieve the advantages of a single money.

———. *Economic Policies Toward Less Developed Countries.* Washington, D.C.: The Brookings Institution, 1967. Chapter 7 and Appendix F analyze commodity reserve money.

———. "The Panamanian System." In his *Further Essays in Monetary Economics.* Cambridge, Mass.: Harvard University Press, 1973.

———, and ALEXANDER SWOBODA, eds. *The Economics of Common Currencies.* Cambridge, Mass.: Harvard University Press, 1973.

KEYNES, JOHN MAYNARD. "The Economic Consequence of Mr. Churchill." In his *Essays in Persuasion.* New York: W. W. Norton, 1963. Keynes argued that Britain's return to the gold standard in 1925 at the prewar gold price required a 10 percent price deflation.

LINDERT, PETER. *Key Currencies and Gold, 1900–1913*, Princeton Studies in International Finance, No. 24. Princeton, N.J.: Princeton University Press, 1969.

LIPSCHITZ, LESLIE, and ICHIRO OTANI. "A Simple Model of the Private Gold Market, 1968–74: An Exploratory Econometric Exercise." International Monetary Fund *Staff Papers*, March 1977. A formal analysis of the private gold market.

LOONEY, ROBERT. *The Economic Development of Panama: The Impact of World Inflation on an Open Economy.* New York: Praeger, 1976.

LUKE, JOHN C. "Inflation-Free Pricing Rules for a Generalized Commodity-Reserve Currency." *Journal of Political Economy*, August 1975. Advanced analysis of the theoretical properties of a commodity reserve money.

MCCLOSKEY, D. N., and J. R. ZECHER. "How the Gold Standard Worked, 1880–1913." In *The Monetary Approach to the Balance of Payments*, Jacob Frenkel and Harry G. Johnson, eds. Toronto: University of Toronto Press, 1976.

MCKINNON, RONALD I. *Money in International Exchange: The Convertible Currency System.* New York: Oxford University Press, 1979. Appendix is on commodity reserve currency proposals.

MORGENSTERN, OSKAR. *International Financial Transactions and Business Cycles.* Princeton, N.J.: Princeton University Press, 1959.

MUNDELL, ROBERT. "A Theory of Optimum Currency Areas." *American Economic Review*, November 1961. A revised version appears in Mundell, *International Economics.* New York: Macmillan, 1968. Discusses aspects of a monetary union.

NURKSE, RAGNAR. *International Currency Experience.* Geneva: League of Nations, 1944. Interprets floating exchange rates as contributing to monetary disorder during the interwar period.

PALYI, MELCHIOR. *The Twilight of Gold, 1914–36.* Chicago: Regnery, 1972. A favorable interpretation of the historical gold standard.

BANCO NAZIONALE DEL LAVORO. *Quarterly Review*, Rome, September 1980. Most of the issue devoted to European monetary union.

Report to Congress of the Commission on the Role of Gold in the Domestic and International Monetary Systems. Washington, D.C.: U.S. Government Printing Office, 1982.

SALANT, S., and DALE HENDERSON. "Market Anticipations of Government Gold Policies and the Price of Gold." *Journal of Political Economy*, August 1978. Analysis of the effect of government gold sales on the private gold market.

TREZISE, PHILIP, ed. *The European Monetary System: Its Promise and Prospects*. Washington, D.C.: The Brookings Institution, 1979. Collection of papers on European monetary unification.

TRIFFIN, ROBERT. *Gold and the Dollar Crisis*. New Haven, Conn.: Yale University Press, 1960. Discussion of the weaknesses of the gold exchange standard.

WARREN, GEORGE, and FRANK PEARSON. *Gold and Prices*. New York: John Wiley, 1935. Statistical study of gold and the price level, whose authors apparently influenced the U.S. government to devalue the dollar in 1933.

WHITAKER, J. K. "An Essay on the Pure Theory of Commodity Money." *Oxford Economic Papers*, November 1979.

CHAPTER TWENTY-ONE
THE ADJUSTABLE
PEG SYSTEM

21.1 THE ADJUSTABLE
PEG AS A COMPROMISE
SYSTEM

Freely floating exchange rates and permanently fixed exchange rates are two extreme types of monetary systems for an open economy. In one case, the price of foreign exchange does all the adjusting; in the other case, the quantity of foreign exchange or gold does all the adjusting. Under floating rates, the central bank has complete control over the money supply, but with fixed rates, it has no control over the money supply. With floating rates, traders face continuous foreign exchange risk, but with permanently fixed rates, there is no foreign exchange risk. The adjustable peg system is a compromise between the extremes of permanently fixed and freely floating rates. It is an attempt to retain some of the stability of fixed rates, while adding some of the flexibility of floating.

Proponents of the adjustable peg would say that the system avoids the excessive rigidity of fixed rates and the disorderly instability of floating rates. Critics contend that the adjustable peg retains the worst features of both extreme systems. The adjustable peg notion is associated with the Bretton Woods monetary system that prevailed from 1946 to 1973. The system is a compromise in the sense that exchange rates are fixed some of the time but not all of the time. It was also an historical compromise in that it was a transition between the earlier commodity money and the later paper or fiat money. In the

Bretton Woods system, national money remained linked to gold, but only indirectly through the U.S. dollar.

We will treat the adjustable peg as if it were distinctly different from fixed and floating rates. However, since the difference lies in the frequency of exchange rate adjustment, it is a difference in degree rather than in a kind. As the frequency of exchange rate adjustment increases, the system approaches a managed float and eventually a free float. In the opposite direction, as rate changes become more rare, the system approaches fixed rates.

An important characteristic of the adjustable peg is that policymakers have discretionary control over the exchange rate. They must devise a rule to determine when to change the exchange rate and when to hold it constant. A conscious exchange rate policy is an unavoidable obligation. With respect to exchange rate policy, both freely floating rates and permanently fixed rates are automatic rather than discretionary. If the exchange rate is always fixed or floating freely according to market forces, central bankers have no scope for choice. Permanently fixed rates and freely floating rates are both automatic systems; the adjustable peg and managed floating are discretionary systems. It follows that people who are skeptical of the efficacy of discretionary policy tend to favor the former policies. People who have confidence in the effectiveness of discretionary policy tend to favor the latter systems.

Business cycles are relevant to the choice between automatic and discretionary monetary systems. In the long run, national income and its rate of growth are determined by aggregate supply variables such as technology and supplies of capital and labor. These supply factors determine a nation's production possibilities curve. However, in the short run, real income and employment fluctuate in response to aggregate demand variables such as consumption demand, investment demand, monetary and fiscal policy. During a recession an economy operates inside its production possibilities curve. Unemployment exceeded 10 percent in the United States during the recession of 1982, and joblessness was unusually high throughout the world. The Great Depression was an extreme example of the effect of aggregate demand on real income. Unemployment reached 25 percent of the labor force in the United States. A message of John Maynard Keynes (1883–1946) was that discretionary monetary and fiscal policy might be employed to offset business cycle fluctuations in aggregate demand. To the extent that deficient aggregate demand could be offset by expansionary monetary policy, a discretionary policy would be preferable to an automatic system. However, if discretionary monetary policy amplified business cycle fluctuations, an automatic system would be preferable. This chapter will consider some issues related to monetary and fiscal policy and real income fluctuation in an open economy.

Chapter 20 analyzed fixed exchange rate systems, which contain an automatic balance-of-payments adjustment mechanism. A balance-of-payments deficit automatically induces a contraction of the money supply, whereas a surplus brings about monetary expansion. Changes in the money supply alter the aggregate demand for goods and services. If full employment continuously prevailed in the labor market, aggregate supply would be perfectly inelastic with respect to the price level. In that case fluctuations in aggregate demand would bring about fluctuations in the price level without altering real income and employment.

Foreign disturbances that alter the balance of payments would affect the price level but not real income. However, real business cycles are a fact of life, and changes in aggregate demand do alter real income and employment as well as the price level. Thus, balance-of-payments deficits that reduce aggregate demand may reduce real income and employment. Concern about the potential loss of real income caused by a reduction in demand led many governments to abandon the automaticity associated with permanently fixed exchange rates. The fear among policymakers was that gold standard adjustment to a deficit would consist of unemployment rather than price-level deflation. This chapter will analyze the adjustment of real income to changes in aggregate demand induced by the balance of payments.

Currency devaluation is an alternative policy response to a payments deficit. The adjustable peg system was designed to provide policy makers with a choice in responding to deficits. They could reduce aggregate demand or they could devalue, depending on the economic circumstances. This chapter will provide an economic analysis of the adjustable peg system. It will describe important institutions in the system. The key currency role of the dollar and the economic functions of the IMF will be examined. The policy problem of simultaneously achieving internal and external balance will be presented. Aggregate demand policy may be divided into monetary and fiscal policy. The effect of monetary and fiscal policy will be compared under both fixed and floating exchange rates. Direct controls on trade and payments will be considered as an alternative to aggregate demand policy and exchange rate adjustment. The adjustable peg system was replaced by floating exchange rates in 1973, but the International Monetary Fund remains an important institution. The current and future role of the IMF will be considered.

21.2 THE BRETTON WOODS SYSTEM

The Bretton Woods conference, held in July 1944, was designed to devise a plan for the postwar international monetary system. It was a compromise in that it retained some fixity of exchange rates and a monetary role for gold yet permitted some adjustment of exchange rates and a major role for the U.S. dollar. The actual Bretton Woods system evolved so that the system operating in the 1960s was quite different from the system planned by the monetary architects in 1944. The conference was presented with a British plan and an American plan, authored by John Maynard Keynes and Harry Dexter White, respectively. Both plans called for a new International Monetary Fund, but they differed with respect to the power vested in the IMF.[1]

The Keynes plan for a clearing union would have given the fund greater authority to lend money to deficit countries. Since the United States was expected to be a net lender following the war and the United Kingdom was expecting to be a borrower, it is not surprising that the U.S.-sponsored plan offered credit on less generous terms than the U.K. plan. The White plan was adopted as the basis of the new adjustable system.

The new monetary system would be administered by a new institution, the International Monetary Fund, to be located in Washington, D.C. There were 30 initial members, and the number had grown to 144 by February 1982. The main obligation of member countries was to declare and maintain fixed exchange rates, called par values, except under extraordinary circumstances. The term "peg" refers to the fixed par value, and the term "adjustable" refers to the opportunity to devalue or revalue one's currency upward.

Each member was obliged to inform the Fund of the par value of its currency either in terms of gold or U.S. dollars. Each country was required to intervene in the gold or dollar market to keep the actual value of its currency within 1 percent of par value. In fact, all countries except the United States declared their par values in dollars, held reserves primarily in dollars, and intervened by trading dollars against their own currency. Because of the prominent role of the U.S. dollar, the Bretton Woods system is sometimes called the gold-dollar standard. The idea of substituting foreign exchange for gold was formally advocated at the Genoa conference in 1922. The resulting system is called a gold-exchange standard, and the gold-dollar standard is a special case. Notice that the 1 percent band around par value permitted limited exchange rate flexibility analogous to the gold points of a gold standard. Countries would defend their par values by holding reserves of dollars or gold and by borrowing from the IMF.

Availability of credit depended on country quotas, which were related to a nation's importance in trade.[2] The United States received the largest quota. Loans were conditional, and conditions became more stringent as a country's debtor position increased. Initial loans, within the so-called "gold" or "reserve tranche," were virtually automatic. A country's gold tranche was determined by its initial gold contribution to the Fund. Larger loans, which fell within the credit tranches, were subject to increasingly stringent conditions. Conditions were related to monetary and fiscal policies that were compatible with elimi-

---

[1] For details of the two plans, see J. Keith Horsefield, ed., *The International Monetary Fund, 1945–1965*, Vol. I Chronicle. Washington, D.C.: IMF, 1969. (Washington, D.C.: International Monetary Fund, 1977).

[2] Initial country quotas were determined by a formula suggested by the U.S. Treasury that included GNP, monetary reserves, imports, and variance in reserves.

The initial U.S. Quota was 37 percent of the total, and quotas were adjusted every five years. Quotas determine voting power, and 15 percent of the total votes constitutes a veto on certain key issues. At the end of 1982, the United States retained 19.5 percent of the total voting power, which was sufficient for a veto.

nating balance-of-payments deficits that initiated the loan. Since loan conditions often consist of telling national governments to cut budgets, raise taxes, and decrease the money supply, they are not popular with debtors.[3] If the Fund discovers that loan conditions are being violated, payment of funds may be withdrawn from the borrower. In 1982 the Fund cut off payment on 25 percent of the loans approved because conditions were not being met.

Initially the IMF was empowered to extend credit, whose amount was limited by member subscriptions, but it could not create money. The power to create special drawing rights was not acquired until 1970.[4] Voting power in the IMF was based on member quotas, which gave the United States veto power over major changes. By tradition, the managing director of the IMF has been a European. In 1982 the sixth director was Jacques de Larosière, from France. The World Bank, a sister institution, was created at the same time, and its head has always been an American. A. W. Clausen replaced Robert McNamara in 1982.

The original intention was that the IMF would make short-term loans for balance-of-payments purposes. The World Bank would make long-term loans related to economic development. Although it was clear that the purpose of the IMF was to promote fixed exchange rates, the Articles of Agreement did permit changes in par value. Exchange rate adjustment was permitted only under conditions of "fundamental disequilibrium." The difficulty of giving the phrase a clear, operational meaning was one of the major shortcomings of the Bretton Woods system. The problem is inherent in all discretionary systems, including a managed float. If there is an excess demand for foreign exchange, when should the price change and when should the central bank intervene?

Many attempts were made to define the concept of fundamental disequilibrium. For example, it might refer to a permanent deficit rather than to a temporary one. Presumably, a crop that was reduced by bad weather would be a temporary disturbance. It might refer to real economic disturbances rather than monetary ones. A successful OPEC cartel would be a real disturbance that would create a fundamental disequilibrium for both importing and exporting countries. Presumably differential inflation attributable to expansionary monetary, policy would not be a fundamental disequilibrium.

A third possible interpretation of fundamental disequilibrium is the policy dilemma problem of achieving internal and external balance. A policy dilemma exists if aggregate demand policy cannot be used to achieve both inter-

---

[3]When Mexico borrowed $3.9 billion from the IMF in November 1982, the following condition was imposed: the budget deficit of 16.5 percent of GNP was to be reduced to 8.5 percent in 1983 and to 3.5 percent by 1985. The government must also reduce subsidies to private business, freeze government hiring and wage increases, follow tight credit policies, and increase prices of goods produced by government-owned enterprises. See *The Wall Street Journal*, January 11, 1983, p. 56.

[4]The IMF's Board of Governors approved the SDR plan in September 1967. The First Amendment to the Articles of Agreement establishing an SDR facility took effect in July 1969 after being approved by three-fifths of the membership representing four-fifths of the total voting power (quotas) in the IMF. The first distribution of SDRs occurred in January 1971.

nal and external balance. The most common policy dilemma encountered is the combination of a balance-of-payments deficit and domestic unemployment. The Bretton Woods system was a discretionary system, and the failure to provide guidance or exchange rate policy by defining fundamental disequilibrium more precisely was a major shortcoming of the system.

The Articles of Agreement give the impression that the IMF would play an active role in approving or disapproving of par value changes, but in fact it played a passive role. Governments altered par values when they found it expedient to do so, and they informed the IMF after the fact. The IMF had little power to sanction members. They could refuse loans or declare a country to have a "scarce currency," which authorized other members to discriminate against them. But this procedure was never used. A common interpretation of Bretton Woods experience is that (1) exchange rates became more rigid than they were intended to be and (2) there was a built-in devaluation bias. Exchange rate adjustment is one form of adjustment, and reluctance to use it implies more frequent use of other adjustment policies such as trade controls, reserves, and aggregate demand.

A common criticism is that the Bretton Woods system lacked a satisfactory adjustment process. In those instances when par values were changed, devaluation by deficit countries was more common than was appreciation by surplus countries. The same adjustment bias took the form of deficit countries' increasing trade controls and pursuing deflationary demand policies more than surplus countries reduced trade barriers and expanded aggregate demand.

One of the early critics of the Bretton Woods adjustment process was Robert Triffin. He argued that the system put more pressure on deficit countries to deflate than surplus countries to inflate. His solution to the alleged deflationary bias was to provide a means to increase the supply of world reserves. He advocated that the IMF become a world central bank with the power to create monetary reserves. The Articles of Agreement permitted a uniform increase in the gold price in terms of all currencies with the approval of 85 percent of member votes. This source of liquidity was never used. It is ironic that the Bretton Woods system collapsed soon after the IMF created the first SDRs (1970), and the system broke down because of world inflation rather than because at deflationary pressure.

21.3 THE DOLLAR
AS A KEY CURRENCY

In the Bretton Woods system, the dollar did not play the same role as did other national currencies. It was the numeraire in terms of which most par values were expressed. IMF loans could be repaid either in gold or dollars. It was the currency of intervention in the sense that most central banks exchanged dollars for their own currencies to maintain the par value. The choice of the dollar as the numeraire and intervention currency implied that the exchange rate margin between the dollar and any other currency was narrower than the margin between any two nondollar currencies. If each country maintained a range of 1 percent on either side of its par value with the dollar, the total range of 2 percent would result in a 4 percent range between any two no-dollar currencies. This practice may have encouraged residents of ROW to denominate contracts in dollars even when not trading with the United States. Foreign exchange reserves were held in the form of dollars. Acquiring dollar reserves constituted a loan to Americans that was resented by some world leaders, especially French President Charles de Gaulle. Whether the loan constituted an income transfer to the United States depends on the interest paid on dollar reserves to foreign central banks relative to the interest rate earned by American banks.

Dollar reserves of foreign central banks were and are invested primarily in interest-bearing assets, such as Treasury bills and certificates of deposit rather than in noninterest-bearing currency and demand deposits. Indeed, a major motive for holding dollar reserves instead of gold is that dollar assets pay interest and gold does not. Thus, the system contained an asymmetry between countries. The $n-1$ member countries pegged to the dollar and held dollar reserves, and this obligation imposed a certain discipline on the policies in those countries. The remaining country, the United States, pegged to gold and held gold reserves.

The obligation to convert dollars into gold may have imposed a similar discipline at one time, but in the final years of Bretton Woods, it did not. After it became evident that all official dollar reserves could not be converted into gold, the system was transformed into a de facto dollar standard. Convertibility of the dollar was not necessary to retain fixed exchange rates. With n currencies there are only $n-1$ exchange rates that need to be fixed. Without dollar convertibility, the role of the United States in a fixed exchange rate system would have been to determine the rate of growth of world monetary reserves. Because of the link between reserves and national money supplies, the United States would have determined the world rate of inflation.

The system collapsed in 1971 not so much because of dollar inconvertibility but because the rate of growth of dollar reserves was considered excessive. Without dollar convertibility, the gold dollar standard would have become a dollar standard. The United States would have faced no balance-of-payments constraint. Any deficit would have been automatically financed by foreign accumulation of dollars. De Gaulle referred to this practice as an "exorbitant privilege."

The key currency role of the dollar offered some disadvantages to the United States. U.S. balance-of-payments deficits were necessary to provide for growth in world reserves. However, growth in dollar reserves relative to limited U.S. gold holding undermined confidence in the convertibility of the dollar. To the extent that U.S. policies were directed toward the confidence problem, there was pressure to pursue deflationary demand policies and impose trade controls. The same point can be expressed in a slightly different way. The gold

TABLE 21-1   World Monetary Reserves, 1973–1981 (in billions of dollars)

	1973	1975	1976	1977	1978	1979	1980	1981
TOTAL RESERVES	211.2	280.7	304.2	364.3	421.5	632.0	755.4	667.5
Foreign exchange	101.5	137.4	160.3	200.3	221.2	246.2	293.3	304.6
Share of foreign exchange	48%	49%	53%	55%	52%	39%	39%	46%
Value of gold*	94.7	121.9	117.5	137.8	177.8	361.5	433.5	325.2
Gold (million ounces)	1,018	1,018	1,013	1,015	1,022	930	938	952.3
Special drawing rights	8.8	8.8	8.7	8.1	8.1	12.5	11.8	16.4
Reserve positions in the fund	6.2	12.6	17.7	18.1	14.8	11.8	16.8	21.3
Share of SDR	4%	3%	3%	2%	2%	2%	2%	2%

*Value at the London market price.

Source: International Monetary Fund, 1981 Annual Report, p. 65; and International Financial Statistics, December 1982.

exchange standard was an attempt to economize on gold by substituting paper money. The system could not simultaneously retain confidence that all dollars would be converted into gold. Perhaps the confidence problem was less serious than people thought at the time. It was often said that foreign central banks would not hold dollar reserves if they expected the dollar to depreciate. The behavior of central banks since the float seems to contradict that proposition.

Table 21-1 shows that during the period of floating, central banks continue to add foreign exchange to their reserve portfolios and that most of the foreign exchange is dollars. From the beginning of the float in 1973 to May 1981 foreign exchange holdings more than tripled from SDR 101.5 billion to SDR 304.6 billion. In addition to possible dollar depreciation, foreign central banks also have a chance for dollar appreciation. If the chance of dollar depreciation is greater, credit markets should reward holders with higher interest income. The fact that the dollar has remained a prominent key currency in spite of incovertibility and floating indicates that confidence in the dollar remains strong.

A final disadvantage of key currency status is that the United States had no direct control over exchange rates. The United States could alter the official gold price, but it had no direct impact on currency exchange rates. If the United States raised the gold price by 10 percent and if all countries continued to peg to the dollar, all currencies would depreciate by 10 percent against gold without any change in exchange rates.

Exactly this situation was faced in August 1981 when the Nixon administration attempted to depreciate the dollar. The dollar was declared inconvertible into gold, but this action had no direct effect on the dollar price of pounds, marks, and other currencies. These prices were under the control of the other $n-1$ governments. It was the duty of Secretary of Treasury John Connolly to persuade other countries to appreciate against the dollar. He offered an incentive by imposing an across-the-board tariff on all imports, which he promised to rescind for those countries that appreciated. Other central banks responded with alacrity. The Group of Ten countries agreed to a new set of exchange rates at the Smithsonian conference in December 1971. The key currency country could influence exchange rates indirectly through tariffs and fiscal policy, and it did not have the same direct control as did other countries. Producers of exportable products, including agriculture, claimed that the key currency status of the dollar led to overvaluation, which inhibited exports.

21.4 LIQUIDITY, THE IMF, AND THE DOLLAR

In the Bretton Woods system members with balance-of-payments deficits or surpluses that were not considered fundamental disequilibria were obliged to maintain fixed exchange rates. Defending the exchange rate required some combination of aggregate demand policy, trade controls, and the use of monetary reserves. After the war, governments were less willing to use monetary policy to defend the exchange rate than they were during the gold standard period. A common criticism of the Bretton Woods system is that it lacked a satisfactory adjustment mechanism. Memories of the Great Depression were clear, and governments were optimistic that aggregate demand could be manipulated to yield a higher average level of output and employment than was possible with an automatic policy. The use of trade controls to defend the currency imposes well-known costs that were discussed in Chapters 7 and 8. Consequently, monetary reserves were an important part of the Bretton Woods system.

A broader term, liquidity, was used to indicate both reserves owned by central banks and also ready access to credit, which could be used to defend exchange rates. The liquidity problem was how to ensure that total world liquidity would grow at the optimum rate. If it grew too slowly, there would be deflationary pressure and greater trade controls. If it grew too rapidly, there would be inflationary pressure in the world. Price-level deflation would have generated additional real reserves, but the experience of the Great Depression convinced many people that deflation would also bring a reduction of real output.

A major reason that gold reserves were not increasing is that the real price of gold had declined. Gold was less profitable to produce and cheaper to use for nonmonetary purposes because of the rising price level combined with the constant price of gold at $35 per ounce. In terms of 1967 dollars, the relative price of gold declined from $90.21 in 1933 to $30.90 in 1970 (see Table 20-1). The decline in the relative gold price was one reason for the alleged "shortage" of monetary reserves. Under the gold standard rules, a decline in the relative gold price would cause a reduction in the money supply and price level. In the postwar period, those monetary rules were no longer being followed. Therefore, growth of world liquidity required an increase in nominal reserves, and it would not come from gold. The only alternative sources were dollars, credit, or IMF money. An elaborate system of credit arrangements was worked out with the IMF and among central banks, which included the General Arrangements to Borrow[5] and currency swaps. The United States attempted to borrow on better terms by issuing Treasury bonds denominated in marks. The first issue occurred when Robert Roosa (Roosa bonds) was undersecretary of Treasury and a later issue (Carter bonds) occurred during the Carter administration.

The IMF extended credit to deficit countries, but the credit was extinguished when loans were repaid. Finally, at the Rio de Janeiro Conference of

---

[5] In 1962 the Group of Ten agreed to lend a fixed amount of money to the IMF that would be lent again to countries needing liquidity. The Group of Ten consists of Belgium, the United Kingdom, Canada, France, West Germany, Italy, Japan, Sweden, the Netherlands, and the United States. Switzerland had observer status. In January 1983 the size of the emergency fund of the General Arrangements to Borrow was increased to $19 billion.

1967, the Fund was authorized to create a limited amount of reserves called Special Drawing Rights. SDRs worth $10 billion were to be created in three installments beginning in 1970. SDRs were paper money issued by the IMF to member governments. Central banks could use SDRs to defend exchange rates by selling them to member governments, which were obliged to exchange them for currency. For example, suppose that the pound sterling was tending to depreciate. The Bank of England could sell SDRs for dollars to a central bank designated by the IMF and then sell dollars for pounds in the foreign exchange market. Newly created SDRs were distributed to members in proportion to quotas. The U.S. share of total quotas in 1971 was 23 percent, a decline from 37 percent in 1946. Thus, the United States received the largest amount of SDRs.

This scheme of distributing the largest amounts of new money to the wealthiest countries has been controversial. An alternative scheme of distributing most or all of newly created SDRs as aid to low-income members was proposed and rejected by high-income countries as inflationary. It was argued that linking aid and reserve creation would give those countries most likely to spend reserves a vested interest in voting for larger allocations.[6] Some $10 billion worth of SDRs was created between 1970 and 1972. Partly because of the resulting inflation, no new SDRs were created until 1979. In December 1978 the Fund was authorized to create SDR $12 billion between 1979 and 1981. The SDR was initially valued in terms of gold and dollars, when the two were linked.

In June 1974 the SDR was linked to the market value of a "basket" of national currencies. Specifically, the SDR was redefined to equal a weighted average of the 16 major currencies of the world. The weights were based on the shares of the countries in international trade. Thus, the SDR became a kind of composite currency whose value fluctuated with daily exchange rates. In 1976 the IMF abolished the official status of gold. It returned one-sixth of its gold to members in proportion to quotas and sold another one-sixth to the private market, using the proceeds as aid to poorer members. The use of 16 currencies was found to be cumbersome, and the basket was reduced to 5 currencies in January 1981. The currencies and their relative weights are U.S. dollar, 42 percent; German mark, 19 percent; British pound, 13 percent; French franc, 13 percent; and Japanese yen, 13 percent.

Daily values of the SDR appear in *The Wall Street Journal*, and a time series of values appears in *International Financial Statistics*. The value of an SDR in terms of dollars is shown in Table 14-3 for recent years. Initially, the SDR was used exclusively in transactions between governments. Now it has a market-determined value, and it has begun to be used in private transactions as

---

[6] Even though SDRs were not distributed as aid, some of the proceeds of IMF gold sales were. Some 25 million ounces of gold was auctioned for $4.64 billion over a four-year period ending May 1980. The proceeds were distributed as aid to the 104 developing countries that were members at the time.

well. Since an SDR consists of fixed amounts of five major currencies, it provides investors with an easy means of diversifying their portfolios. A group of seven major London banks began offering certificates of deposit denominated in special drawing rights in 1981.[7] They are sold to institutional investors in minimum amounts of 1 million SDRs. An organized secondary market has developed, and the SDR interest rate is based on the weighted average of interbank interest rates for the five countries.

The major source of growth in monetary reserves during the Bretton Woods period was the U.S. dollar. Rapid growth of dollar reserves contributed to the downfall of fixed exchange rates and the world inflation of the 1970s. Somewhat surprisingly, the growth of dollar reserves has continued at a rapid pace during the current period of floating exchange rates. Triffin's concern was that the Bretton Woods system would collapse because insufficient reserves would bring about deflationary pressure and trade controls. He feared that macroeconomic policy would be devoted to trying to eliminate balance-of-payments deficits without regard to domestic unemployment.

There was a period of slow economic growth, employment problems, and U.S. capital controls, but the collapse of the Bretton Woods system was ultimately brought about by inflationary pressure rather than by deflation. Balance of payments deficits and inflation in the United States, combined with rapid growth in monetary reserves and inflation in the rest of the world, brought an end to fixed exchange rates. Since world liquidity took several forms, no single institution was responsible for total world liquidity. For years IMF officials who feared a shortage of world reserves sought the authority to create reserves. By the time they received authority and exercised it, inflationary conditions already existed in the world. In retrospect the period from 1970 to 1972 was the worst time to add to world liquidity by creating SDRs. Thus, reserve creation of the IMF added to world inflation, although SDR creation was small relative to U.S. balance-of-payments deficits.

Although the world monetary system had become a de facto dollar standard by the late 1960s, Federal Reserve did not determine monetary policy with the world price level in mind. Other countries first attempted to avoid importing inflation by sterilizing the increase in dollar reserves, but the quantity was excessive. Increased integration of world capital markets made sterilization difficult. No one consciously planned to end the Bretton Woods system, and the currency realignments of 1971 and 1973 were desperate attempts to save the system from collapse. However, economic conditions made it expedient to let currencies float in March 1973.

[7] The group includes Barclay's Bank, Chemical Bank, Citibank, Hong Kong and Shanghai Bank, Midland Bank, Westminister Bank, and Standard Chartered Bank. For a discussion of the private use of SDRs, see Dorothy Meadow Sobol, "The SDR in Private International Finance," *Quarterly Review*, Federal Reserve Bank of New York, Winter 1981–1982; and Warren L. Coats, Jr., "The SDR as a Means of Payment," International Monetary Fund *Staff Papers*, September 1982.

21.5 THE POLICY GOALS OF INTERNAL AND EXTERNAL BALANCE

Two goals of modern economic policy are the achievement of internal and external balance. External balance refers to a stable price level and full employment. Under the gold standard or permanently fixed exchange rates, external balance is achieved only by sacrificing control over internal variables.

In his 1923 *Tract on Monetary Reform*, Keynes described the problem as a choice between "stability of the gold price and stability of the price level." If the rest of the world has inflation, a gold standard country will import gold and inflation. The money supply will automatically adapt to bring about external balance. Floating exchange rates permit a government to choose an inflation rate, including price stability, but it loses control over the exchange rate. A fixed rate system permits a government to choose its exchange rate, but it loses control over the inflation rate.

Since both extreme systems are automatic, policymakers are not confronted with a regular choice between stable prices and a stable exchange rate. However, the adjustable peg requires the policymaker to regularly choose between using aggregate demand policy to achieve a stable price level or a stable exchange rate.

The policy problem of how to achieve internal and external balance was formalized by James Meade in 1951.[8] A country seeking to maintain fixed exchange rates may not achieve both internal and external balance unless it is lucky. In the absence of exchange rate adjustment, aggregate demand policy may eliminate certain combinations of disequilibria but not others. The intractable combinations are called policy dilemma cases. In the dilemma cases, the use of aggregate demand policy to achieve internal balance magnifies the external imbalance. Conversely, the application of demand policy to achieve external balance increases the internal imbalance. The general problem is that two policy goals may not necessarily be satisifed with only one policy instrument, in this case demand policy. In the dilemma cases either one goal will not be satisfied or another policy instrument, such as exchange rate adjustment, must be employed.

The policy problem is illustrated in Table 21-2. Internal and external balance are defined as zero excess demand for goods and foreign exchange, respectively. Positive excess demand for goods can be interpretated as inflationary pressure and negative excess demand as deflationary pressure. When price-level deflation is combined with downward rigid wages, the result is unemployment. Positive excess demand for foreign exchange can be interpreted as a balance-of-payments surplus and negative excess demand as a payments def-

---

[8] James Meade, *The Balance of Payments*. London: Oxford University Press, 1951

TABLE 21-2 Achieving Internal and External Balance

CASE	EXCESS GOODS	DEMAND FOREIGN EXCHANGE	PROPER POLICY
1	+	+	Reduce aggregate demand
2	−	−	Increase aggregate demand
3	−	+	Devalue
4	+	−	Appreciate

icit. In this case the appropriate measure of the balance of payments is the monetary reserve balance.

Table 21-2 lists the four possible combinations of excess demand and supply that can exist in the two markets. The first two cases are the easy or nondilemma cases for policymakers. They involve excess demand in both markets or excess supply in both markets. Both combinations of disequilibria can be eliminated merely by changing aggregate demand policy with a fixed exchange rate. In case 1 there is excess demand for both goods and foreign exchange. The situation may be described as inflationary pressure plus a balance-of-payments deficit. The appropriate policy is to reduce aggregate demand, since it will reduce excess demand in both markets. Notice that a permanently fixed exchange rate would automatically induce this solution. Gold or monetary reserves would decline, and the money supply would automatically contract. A possible cause of the initial disequilibrium would be expansionary monetary policy. Reversing the initial mistake would be the appropriate policy. Another possible cause of excess demand in both markets would be a financial innovation that reduced the demand for money. Reducing the money supply would be the appropriate response.

Case 2 is simply the opposite of case 1. There is excess supply in both goods and foreign exchange markets. The situation can be described as deflationary pressure or unemployment combined with a balance-of-payments deficit. This is another nondilemma case, since aggregate demand policy is sufficient to solve both problems. Increasing aggregate demand would eliminate deflationary pressure and reduce the payments surplus. Again, a permanently fixed exchange rate would automatically induce the appropriate expansionary monetary policy. Gold or reserves would accumulate, and the money supply would expand. A possible cause would be deflationary domestic monetary policy, and reversing the policy would be an appropriate response to the problem. Another possible cause of the problem would be an increase in the demand for money, and an automatic increase in the money supply would be an appropriate response. Recall from the discussion of managed floating that, if all disturbances originate in the money market, a fixed exchange rate is optimal.

The remaining two situations cannot be solved as easily. Because there is excess demand in one market and excess supply in the other market, simply changing aggregate demand policy is not sufficient to solve both problems. Cases 3 and 4 are called the policy dilemma cases. In case 3, there is an excess supply of goods and an excess demand for foreign exchange. The situation may be described as unemployment combined with a balance-of-payments deficit. It is a situation that many countries experienced during the Bretton Woods period, including the United States during the early and mid-1960s.

It has been suggested that this combination (and case 4) of problems would have been a useful way to define the Fund's concept of fundamental disequilibrium. The dilemma is that if aggregate demand policy is used to solve one problem, it necessarily aggravates the remaining problem. With unemployment the appropriate policy for internal balance is an increase in aggregate demand. However, demand expansion will increase the balance-of-payments deficit. Internal balance can be achieved only at the expense of external imbalance. Given the balance-of-payments deficit, the appropriate policy is to reduce aggregate demand. However, demand contraction would exacerbate domestic unemployment. External balance may be achieved only at the expense of internal imbalance.

According to Meade, case 3 cannot be solved without an additional policy instrument. Under the adjustable peg system, case 3 is a justification for currency devaluation. Devaluation would increase exports relative to imports and switch domestic and foreign demand onto domestic goods and labor. A possible cause of case 3 would be a reduction in foreign demand for the home country's exports, which would induce both a payments deficit and deflationary pressure at home. Export demand may decline for macroeconomic reasons, such as a foreign recession or contractionary aggregate demand policy abroad. Alternatively, it may decline for reasons associated with trade, such as a change in comparative advantage (e.g., permanent loss of an export market) or an increase in trade barriers facing exports.

Case 4 is the opposite of case 3. It is the second policy dilemma situation, because there is an excess demand in one market and an excess supply in the other. Specifically, an excess demand for goods is combined with an excess supply of foreign exchange. There is inflationary pressure in the goods market and a balance-of-payments surplus. Internal balance would require a reduction in aggregate demand, but contraction would increase the balance-of-payments surplus. External balance would require an increase in demand, which would increase the inflationary pressure. Aggregate demand policy cannot simultaneously bring about both internal and external balance. Since case 4 represents the opposite kind of disequilibrium from case 3, the appropriate policy is currency appreciation. By making foreign exchange cheaper, the appreciation will reduce the payments surplus and switch foreign and domestic demand into foreign goods.

The conditions of case 4 could have been used to complete the definition of "fundamental disequilibrium" under Bretton Woods. A possible cause of case 4 would be an increase in foreign demand for exports, for example, "export boom." Examples are Switzerland, Germany, and Japan during the 1960s and 1970s, oil exporters after 1973, and South Korea during the war in Vietnam. Export demand may increase because of an autonomous business expansion (or a war that damages export rivals) or because of foreign aggregate demand policy. It may also increase for reasons related to international trade, such as a change in commerical policy or comparative advantage. As the policy problem is stated here, cases 3 and 4 cannot be solved by using aggregate demand policy with a fixed exchange rate.

Mundell has proposed splitting aggregate demand into monetary and fiscal policy, which would provide the authorities with an additional policy instrument.[9] Instead of simply increasing or decreasing aggregate demand, the authorities could employ an optimal monetary-fiscal policy mix. The analytical difference between monetary and fiscal policy is that they have opposite effects on interest rates. To analyze the effects of monetary and fiscal policy in an open economy, we must employ an explicit macroeconomic model.

21.6 MONETARY AND FISCAL POLICY IN AN OPEN ECONOMY

In the long run real national income is determined by the aggregate supply of goods and services. The determinants of aggregate supply were considered in Part I of this book. They are technology and supplies of labor and capital. Given those determinants of aggregate supply, long-run fluctuations in aggregate demand will alter the price level but not real output and employment. This long-run characterization of the economy can be called full employment, and it is shown in Figure 21-1.

The initial equilibrium is at point A along AD_1 and AS_1. The money price level is P_1, and real national income is y_1. The aggregate supply curve AS_1 is vertical at y_1, which represents full employment income. The money supply, government spending, and taxes are constant along AD_1. Monetary expansion will increase the price level without altering real income.

Let an increase in the money supply shift aggregate demand from AD_1 to AD_2. The excess demand of AB will induce a price increase to P_2 and a new equilibrium at point C; at C all product prices and money wages will have increased in the proportion P_2P_1/OP_1, but real output will be constant at y_1, and real wages and total employment will be constant. Notice that if aggregate supply slopes upward, as does AS_2, the same monetary expansion would increase

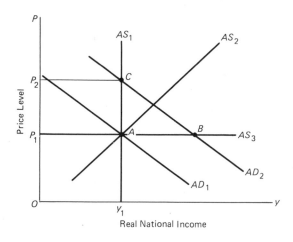

FIGURE 21-1   Price Level and Real Income with Full Employment

both real output and the price level. The extreme opposite of continuous full employment can be represented by the horizontal aggregate supply curve AS_3. In that case, all shifts in aggregate demand bring about changes in real income without any change in the price level.

Since much of the interest in the problem of achieving simultaneous internal and external balance arises from concern about short-run fluctuation in output and employment, it will be assumed in the remainder of this chapter that the aggregate supply curve is horizontal. It is a convenient simplification for analyzing certain problems, but it cannot be justified in the long run. Given a perfectly elastic aggregate supply, real income is completely determined by the aggregate demand for goods and services. Aggregate demand can be expressed as a function of monetary and fiscal policy variables. The effect of monetary and fiscal policy on internal and external balance will be analyzed in terms of IS and LM curves, which represent equilibrium in the goods and money market.

Analysis of monetary and fiscal policy in an open economy requires that the markets for domestic money, goods, and foreign exchange be represented separately. In Figure 21-2 the LM curve represents the combinations of interest rates (r) and real income (y), at which the demand for domestic money (L) equals the supply of money (M):

$$M = L(r, Y)$$

Since the interest rate on bonds is the opportunity cost of holding money, the demand for money is inversely related to the interest rate. Since money is a normal good, the demand for money is positively related to real income. A negatively sloped LM curve can be drawn for a given money supply. Consider

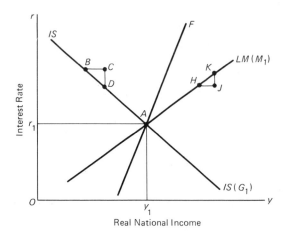

FIGURE 21-2   General Equilibrium in Money, Goods, and Foreign Exchange Markets

point H along LM. An increase in real income to point $\mathcal{J}$ would cause an excess demand for money, which would be eliminated by an increase in the interest rate to point K. Thus, the LM curve has a positive slope. An increase in the money supply will shift LM to the right. The IS curve shows the combinations of interest rates and real income at which the demand for goods equals the supply of goods (y). Demand may be represented by the sum of private demand for consumption and investment goods and government spending (G):

$$y = f(r, y) + G$$

Under the assumption that private demand is inversely related to the interest rate and positively related to real income (private goods are normal), the IS curve will have a negative slope.[10] Consider point B on the IS curve. An increase in the supply of goods from B to C will create an excess supply, which will be eliminated by a decrease in the interest rate from C to D. Thus, IS will have a negative slope, and its position will be determined by G. An increase in G will shift IS to the right.

In Figure 21-2 the intersection of LM and IS represents simultaneous equilibrium in the money and goods market. However, given the assumption about aggregate supply, the income level y_1 does not necessarily represent full employment and internal balance. The determination of external balance requires consideration of the foreign exchange market.

The foreign exchange market is in equilibrium when the demand for foreign exchange equals the supply, which occurs when official monetary reserves of foreign exchange are constant:

[10]To ensure that IS has a negative slope, the marginal propensity to spend on consumption and investment goods must be less than 1.

$$F^d = F^s$$
$$B_{ca} = K \quad \text{and} \quad \frac{dR}{dt} = 0$$

To simplify the problem let transfers be zero, which implies that the current account equals the balance on goods and services:

$$B_{gs} = K$$
$$E - I(y) = K(r)$$

Let exports depend on foreign income, which is given to the home country. Since imports are a normal good, the volume of imports depends on domestic income. The change in imports associated with a change in income is called the marginal propensity to import. It will be denoted I_y. Both exports and imports depend on the exchange rate, which is taken as given. Let domestic and foreign bonds be imperfect substitutes, so that relative interest rates can vary. The foreign interest rate will be given to the country, and the capital outflow will depend on the domestic interest rate. An increase in the interest rate r will decrease the capital outflow. The coefficient measuring the response of capital flows to the interest rate will be denoted K_r, and it will be negative.

In foreign exchange market equilibrium, the current account surplus (B_{cA})

FIGURE 21-3 Foreign Exchange Market Equilibrium

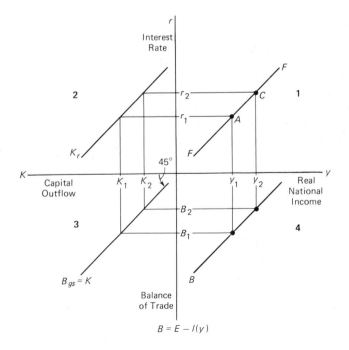

equals the capital account deficit (K). The separate relationships for the current and capital accounts and foreign exchange market equilibrium are shown in Figure 21-3. The object is to show how the FF curve, which represents foreign exchange market equilibrium, depends on capital and current accounts. Quadrant 1 of the diagram shows FF as a function of the interest rate and national income. Quadrant 2 shows capital outflows as a function of the interest rate. Its slope represents the assumption that capital outflows are a decreasing function of the interest rate. The slope of the K curve depends on the capital mobility coefficient K_r. Quadrant 3 shows equilibrium as a 45-degree line, indicating equality of the current account surplus and the capital outflow. Quadrant 4 shows the current account balance as a decreasing function of income. Since imports are the only variable component of the current account, it shows how imports vary with income. The slope of the B curve depends on the marginal propensity to import (I_y).

The relationship between the components may be seen by deriving the FF curve. Consider the interest rate r_1. At r_1 the capital outflow will be K_1. At that rate of capital outflow exchange market equilibrium requires a current account surplus of B_1. Given the marginal propensity to import, a surplus of B_1 is consistent with a level of income y_1. Thus, the point A at interest rate r_1 and income level y_1 represents foreign exchange market equilibrium. The capital outflow at r_1 equals the current account surplus at y_1. Point A is one point on the FF curve. A second point can be found by considering a second interest rate r_2. At r_2 the capital outflow is K_2. The required current account surplus is B_2, which occurs at income level y_2. Thus, point C representing interest rate r_2 and income level y_2, is a second point on the FF curve. Repeating the process at other interest rates will generate a positively sloped FF curve, whose exact slope depends on the capital mobility coefficient (Kr) and the marginal propensity to import (I_y).[11] In the extreme case of zero capital mobility, the FF curve is vertical. In the opposite case of perfect capital mobility, the domestic interest rate must equal the foreign interest, and FF is horizontal at that rate. In between these extremes, the FF curve can take any positive slope. In particular, it can be either steeper or flatter than the LM curve. Now the FF curve can be combined with the IS and LM curves to determine general economic equilibrium.

21.7 MONETARY
AND FISCAL POLICY
WITH FIXED EXCHANGE RATES

Let us consider the effect of aggregate demand policy on internal and external balance, when the exchange rate is fixed. Since much of the interest in the policy problem arises from concern about short-run employment changes, let

---

[11] The algebraic derivation is in the chapter appendix.

there be an excess supply of labor whose employment depends on aggregate demand. Aggregate supply will be represented by a horizontal curve such as AS_3 in Figure 21-1. Changes in income in the IS-LM-FF diagrams may be interpreted as real income changes up to full employment. The IS and LM curves taken together determine aggregate demand. The reason for splitting aggregate demand into two components is to show the separate effects of monetary and fiscal policy on external balance. An increase in aggregate demand will increase real output and employment, but it will also affect external balance.

Consider the internal and external effects of monetary policy, as shown in Figure 21-4. From an initial equilibrium at A, where the goods, money, and foreign exchange markets are all in equilibrium, let the money supply increase from LM_1 to LM_2. There is a quasi-equilibrium at B, where income has increased to Y_B and the interest rate has fallen to r_B. At Y_B the interest rate is too low for equilibrium in the foreign exchange market, and there is a balance-of-payments deficit.

The central bank must sell reserves for domestic money to avoid currency depreciation. As the money supply contracts, LM will shift to the left, and it will return to A in long-run equilibrium. The central bank may resist the leftward movement of LM through sterilized intervention as long as it is willing and able to lose reserves.

In the short run under fixed exchange rates, monetary policy will lower the interest rate and increase income. In the long run the government cannot control money, interest rates, or income. The shifting of the LM curve in response to balance-of-payments deficits or surpluses represents the automatic adjustment mechanism associated with a permanently fixed exchange rate. In the extreme case of perfect capital mobility, the FF curve will be horizontal,

FIGURE 21-4   Monetary Policy with Fixed Exchange Rates

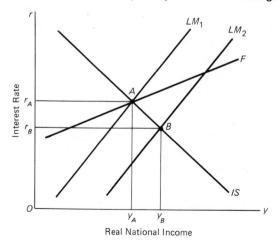

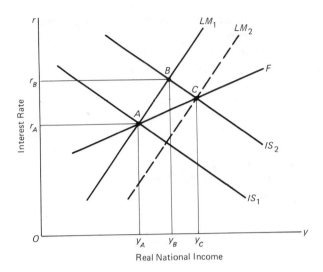

FIGURE 21-5   Fiscal Policy with Fixed Exchange Rates

and the central bank will be unable to control the money supply even in the short run.

The effect of fiscal policy is shown in Figure 21-5. The initial equilibrium at A is disturbed by an increase in government spending. The IS curve shifts from IS_1 to IS_2, yielding a quasi-equilibrium at B. Both the interest rate and income have increased, but there is an excess supply of foreign exchange at y_B. To prevent appreciation, the central bank must acquire reserves with newly created money. This fiscal-policy-induced monetary expansion will increase the money supply to LM_2. In the long-run equilibrium at C, all three markets are in equilibrium. In contrast to monetary policy, fiscal policy can affect income. A reason for the difference is that the two policies have different effects on the balance of payments. Monetary expansion causes a deficit, which brings about a secondary contraction of the money supply. Fiscal expansion induces a surplus, which brings about a secondary expansion of the money supply. The exact effects of fiscal policy depend on the slope of FF, which depends on the capital mobility coefficient and the marginal propensity to import. If FF is steeper than LM (as shown in Figure 21-6), fiscal expansion will induce a deficit and monetary contraction. It is left to the reader to show this case. The capital mobility coefficient (K_r), one of the determinants of the slope of FF, will vary by country. Its magnitude depends on characteristics of private capital markets as well as on the severity of government capital controls. Thus, one would expect K_r to be larger between Canada and the United States than between Uganda and the United States.

Mundell's solution to the problem of achieving internal and external balance under fixed rates is shown in Figure 21-6. The initial situation at point A is case 3, where there is unemployment and a balance-of-payments deficit. Ac-

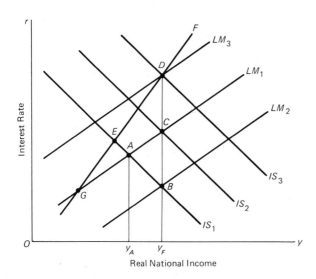

FIGURE 21-6   Policy Mix

tual income y_A is less than full employment income y_F. The interest rate r_A is too low for equilibrium in the foreign exchange market. It is a dilemma case because an increase in aggregate demand will move the economy toward internal balance, while moving it away from external balance. An increase in the money supply by itself will increase income, but it will also increase the balance-of-payments deficit. Let monetary expansion shift LM to LM_2. Full employment prevails at B, but the payments deficit is larger at B than at A.

Similarly, monetary contraction to point E would achieve external bal-

FIGURE 21-7   Devaluation and the Policy Dilemma

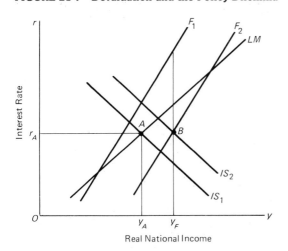

ance at the expense of internal balance. The exclusive use of fiscal policy would not solve the problem either. An increase in government spending would shift IS to IS_2. The quasi-equilibrium at C represents full employment and a balance-of-payments deficit. Conversely, a reduction in government spending sufficient to reach point G would achieve external balance at the expense of internal balance. Although neither monetary policy nor fiscal policy will resolve the dilemma by itself, a proper policy mix will achieve both goals, while preserving a fixed exchange rate.

According to Mundell a judicious combination of fiscal expansion and monetary contraction will solve the problem. An increase in government spending to IS_3 combined with a reduction in the money supply to LM_3 will yield point D, which represents simultaneous equilibrium in all three markets. The monetary policy associated with LM_3 and the fiscal policy associated with IS_3 is called the optimum monetary-fiscal mix. Contractionary monetary policy is directed at external balance, whereas expansionary fiscal policy is directed at internal balance.

The concept of an optimal monetary-fiscal policy mix has some logical shortcomings. In the model, monetary and fiscal policy are distinguished by their effects on interest rates. Monetary expansion lowers rates while fiscal expansion raises them. However, empirical evidence from the last decade indicates that monetary expansion does not lower nominal interest rates, and it may not lower real rates either. A second point is related to interest-sensitive international capital flows. It has been argued that capital attracted by higher interest rates will be a one-period stock adjustment rather than a regular annual capital flow. A third issue related to the policy mix is whether achieving exter-

FIGURE 21-8   Monetary Policy Under Floating

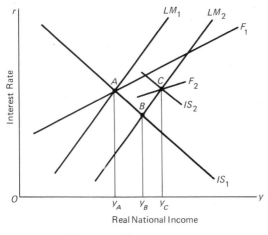

Initial monetary effect = $y_A y_B$

Induced devaluation effect = $y_B y_C$

nal balance through a high interest rate policy distorts domestic savings and investment choices.

The same policy dilemma may be solved by currency devaluation. Devaluation will increase the demand for domestic goods and labor yet increase the supply of foreign exchange. The geometrical effect of devaluation is to shift both IS and FF curves to the right. The effect of devaluation is shown in Figure 21-7. At the initial point A there is a balance-of-payments deficit (r_A too low) with unemployment ($y_A < y_F$). Devaluation will shift both *IS* and *FF* to the right until they intersect at B with full employment income y_F. Both the balance-of-payments deficit and unemployment have been eliminated. Since the money market is not in equilibrium at A, a complementary monetary policy is necessary to achieve full equilibrium. This case could represent fundamental disequilibrium that was used to justify devaluation under the Bretton Woods system.

21.8 MONETARY AND FISCAL POLICY UNDER FLOATING EXCHANGE RATES

In cases where no dilemma exists, aggregate demand policy is sufficient to achieve both internal and external balance. In the cases of dilemma either an exchange rate adjustment or a monetary fiscal policy mix is required to satisfy both goals. Since the world has abandoned the adjustable peg for floating rates, it is instructive to compare the effects of monetary and fiscal policy under the two different policy regimes. It will be shown that prudent policies under fixed exchange rates are not necessarily prudent under floating exchange rates. To see the significance of exchange rate policy, let us reconsider the impact of monetary and fiscal policy under floating exchange rates. The geometrical effect of floating is to shift the *IS* and *FF* curves until the exchange market clears. Depreciation shifts both curves to the right; appreciation shifts them to the left. The primary effect of monetary and fiscal policy will be followed by a secondary effect of the exchange rate change.

First, consider monetary policy under floating rates. In Figure 21-8, the initial equilibrium is at A. A money supply increase shifts LM_1 to LM_2. There is a quasi-equilibrium at B with a balance-of-payments deficit. The increase in income caused by the initial monetary change is $y_A y_B$. Under floating rates, the deficit will induce a currency devaluation that shifts IS_1 to IS_2 and F_1 to F_2. The final equilibrium is at point C, where the income level y_C is greater than y_B. Thus, the devaluation has added to the initial income increase by $y_B y_C$. The conclusion is that floating exchange rates magnify the effect of monetary policy on aggregate demand and income. The effect is symmetrical for monetary contraction.

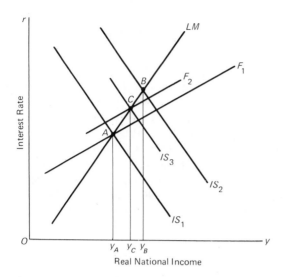

FIGURE 21-9 Fiscal Policy Under Floating

The effect of floating on fiscal policy is shown in Figure 21-9. Note that the FF curve is drawn flatter than LM, indicating a relatively high degree of capital mobility. Fiscal expansion shifts IS_1 to IS_2, yielding a quasi-equilibrium at B. Income increases from y_A to y_B. At B there is an excess supply of foreign exchange that induces a currency appreciation. Cheapening of foreign exchange shifts both IS and FF to the left. The final equilibrium is at point C where IS_3, F_2, and LM intersect. Because currency appreciation reduced income by y_B y_C, the total effect of fiscal policy on income is smaller under floating than under fixed exchange rates. These results depend on the relative slopes of LM and FF. It is left to the reader to show that, when FF is steeper than LM, fiscal expansion will induce currency depreciation. The exchange rate change will shift IS and FF to the right, magnifying the initial increase in income.

There is a special case that may be relevant to highly integrated economies such as the United States, Canada, and Western Europe. Suppose that capital is perfectly mobile between the home and foreign economies. The domestic interest rate must equal the foreign interest rate, and the FF curve is horizontal as shown in Figure 21-10. At any interest rate below r_A, everyone wants to borrow at home and lend abroad. The opposite is true at rates above r_1. Fiscal expansion will shift IS_1 to IS_2. At point B income has increased to y_B, but there is an excess supply of foreign exchange. The excess supply is caused by the capital inflow induced by high domestic interest rates. The appreciation will shift IS_2 to the left until it coincides with IS_1 at A. It cannot stop before then because the capital inflow and appreciation will continue as long as the domestic interest rate is above the foreign rate. In this extreme case

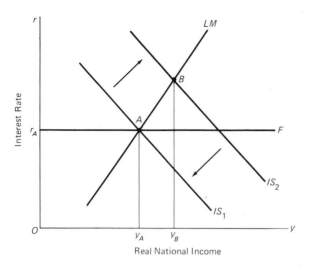

FIGURE 21-10   Fiscal Expansion and Perfect Capital Mobility

of perfectly mobile capital and floating exchange rates, fiscal policy has no effect on national income. The reader can amend Figure 21-8 to show that perfect capital mobility magnifies the effect of monetary policy on income. Thus, the effects of monetary and fiscal policy under floating rates may be quite different from the effects under fixed rates.

The analysis has referred to the effects of monetary and fiscal policy on national income and the foreign exchange market. The same economic model shows the effects of other economic disturbances on the same markets. There have been major financial innovations in recent years that have produced new substitutes for money. These innovations can be analyzed as a reduction in the demand for money, which shifts the *LM* curve to the right. The effects are then identical to those of an increase in the money supply. Not all money supply disturbances are attributable to monetary policy. If private banks change their reserve holdings or the nonbank public changes its currency holdings, the money supply will change without any change in the monetary base. All disturbances affecting money demand or money supply will have a greater effect on income under floating exchange rates than under fixed rates. If all economic disturbances originate in the money market, national income will be more stable if the exchange rate is fixed than if it floats.

In the case of the market for goods, there are many disturbances besides fiscal policy. Changes in consumption spending, investment spending, and export demand will all shift the *IS* curve. Unlike money market changes, disturbances in the goods market have a smaller effect on income under floating rates than under fixed rates (when *FF* is flatter than *LM*). Thus, the optimal exchange rate policy depends partly on the source of economic disturbances.

It was pointed out in connection with the optimal managed float that

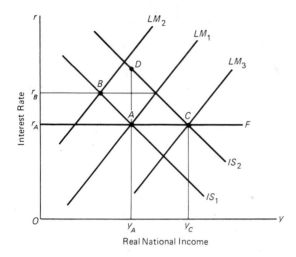

FIGURE 21-11   Effect of a Policy Mistake

knowledge of the source of economic disturbances is valuable, but it is not easy to acquire. For example, it is very difficult for policymakers to discern on a given day whether weakness of the dollar is due to a shift of *IS*, *LM*, or something else. If a mistake is made in identifying the source of a disturbance, the resulting policy will be a mistake, and government policy will destabilize the economy.

Figure 21-11 shows a case in which a goods market disturbance is mistaken as a monetary disturbance. Let the central bank perceive a tendency for interest rates to rise. It is interpreted as a increase in money demand which would shift LM_1 to LM_2. If the diagnosis were correct, a policy of increasing the money supply just enough to hold the interest rate constant would stabilize income at y_A. However, the diagnosis is wrong, and the true source of interest rate pressure is an increase in investment demand, which shifts IS_1 to IS_2. The monetary increase necessary to hold *r* constant shifts LM_1 to LM_3. Instead of stabilizing income at y_A, the effect of policy has been to destabilize income to y_C. Income stabilization would require contractionary fiscal policy that would return the goods market curve to IS_1.

21.9 SPECULATION AND THE ADJUSTABLE PEG

Par value changes under the Bretton Woods system were less frequent in practice than they were expected to be. Depreciation was more common than appreciation. Between 1947 and 1970, there were more than 200 devaluations and 5 appreciations. Most adjustments were delayed to the point where market participants knew the direction of change. If a central bank regularly loses reserves, exhausts its line of credit at the IMF, imposes trade controls, and permits its currency to float to the bottom of the permissible Bretton Woods band, it is a good candidate for devaluation. Such situations did occur, and they provided speculators with low-risk profit opportunities. On a given day there was a very high probability that a weak currency would either depreciate or remain constant in value, while appreciation could be ruled out. The situation has been described as a "one-way option."

The comparable probabilities of depreciation and appreciation are quite different under floating. The effect of this kind of speculation is to increase the probability of depreciation by shifting the foreign exchange demand curve to the right. The speculation was destabilizing in the sense of making it more difficult for central banks to defend par values. On the other hand, the same speculation may have been stabilizing in the sense of moving the exchange rate toward its equilibrium level.

One reason that governments defend overvalued currencies is that devaluation carries a political stigma. It is commonly interpreted as a signal of economic mismanagement. In a study of the effects of devaluation, Richard Cooper found that governments instituting devaluation often fell and finance ministers usually lost their jobs.[12] The redistribution effect of devaluation is one reason for the controversy. Devaluation increases the domestic currency prices of exportables and importables. Consumers of these products are adversely affected, and producers appear to receive windfall profits. Often governments attempted to mitigate the redistributive effect of devaluation by liberalizing imports and taxing exports following devaluation. Such policies also mitigate the allocative effect of devaluation.

Another reason for controversy is the effect on certain creditors. Resident borrowers with liabilities in foreign exchange take a capital loss in domestic currency. Partly because of this effect, bankruptcies tend to rise following devaluation. To the extent that the devaluation was expected by credit markets, there may have been an offset in the form of a lower foreign currency interest rate. In an attempt to nullify the destabilizing speculation that was encouraged by the operation of the Bretton Woods system, controls on capital flows were extensive.

21.10 EXCHANGE CONTROLS

Exchange control refers to regulation of the conversion of domestic money into foreign money. A currency that is free of exchange controls is called convertible. The U.S. dollar is almost entirely free of exchange controls. A currency

---

[12]Cooper analyzed 24 devaluations between 1953 and 1966. In 30 percent of the cases, the government fell within a year of the devaluation. In a control group, only 14 percent of governments fell. Sixty percent of finance ministers lost their jobs within a year after devaluation, while only 18 percent of a control group experienced turnover. See Richard N. Cooper, *Currency Devaluation in Developing Countries*, Princeton Studies in International Finance, No. 86 (Princeton, N.J.: Princeton University Press, June 1981).

subject to extensive controls is called inconvertible. The Soviet ruble is an example of an inconvertible money. In between these extremes there are many degrees of exchange control or convertibility.

Immediately after World War II virtually all Western European currencies were inconvertible. One of the first goals of the IMF was to persuade its members to establish convertibility. The IMF stressed the importance of current account convertibility, which was achieved by Western Europe in 1958. Convertibility on current account refers to unrestricted use of money to pay for imported goods and services. By distinguishing between current and capital account convertibility, the IMF implicitly sanctioned the use of capital controls for countries with balance-of-payments problems.

Exchange controls, also called controls on payments, are restrictions on the use of money. Trade controls, such as tariffs and import quotas, are controls on the purchase of goods. Exchange and trade controls can be used to accomplish the same goals. Sometimes the choice between the two policies depends on the cost of administration. Trade controls are typically administered by customs officials. Exchange controls are usually administered by the central bank or an agency that regulates private banks. Exchange controls can take an infinite variety of forms. Only the major types will be reviewed here. The interested reader should consult the IMF's annual report on exchange controls for more detail.[13]

Controls are an alternative to price rationing. If the exchange rate is free to vary, exchange controls have no function. Figure 21-12 shows the home currency with an overvalued exchange rate at Π_1. The private excess demand of AB could be eliminated by devaluation to Π_2. If price rationing were used,

FIGURE 21-12   Exchange Controls

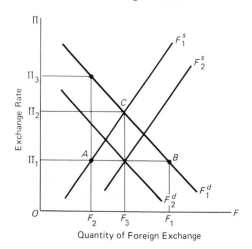

Quantity of Foreign Exchange

[13] The IMF's volume is entitled *Annual Report on Exchange Restrictions*.

there would be no need for controls on trade or payments. An alternative to devaluation is trade controls in the form of tariffs or quotas on trade. Instead of a devaluation in the proportion $\Pi_2\Pi_1/O\Pi_1$, the government could impose a tariff and an export subsidy at the same rate on all goods. The tariff would reduce demand for foreign exchange from F_1^d to F_2^d, and the export subsidy would increase foreign exchange supply from F_1^s to F_2^s. The combined tariff-export subsidy would have the same effect as the devaluation.

It was shown in Chapter 8 that quotas can be substituted for tariffs. It was shown in Chapter 9 that a set of domestic taxes and subsidies can be substituted for taxes on trade with the same economic effects. Thus, domestic fiscal measures would be another way to eliminate the excess demand $F_1F_2 = AB$.

Finally exchange controls are a way of directly rationing the OF_2 units of foreign exchange supplied among the demanders who seek OF_1 units. The buyer is required to have a license to buy a specified quantity of foreign exchange for a specified use at the official price. By specifying the permissible uses, the government obtains some authority over the content of imports. Instead of a single rate, the authority may specify multiple exchange rates. By charging different prices for different uses of foreign exchange, the authority effectively imposes a differential tariff and export tax.

On the import side, it is common to distinguish categories of necessities and luxuries, with a less favorable rate for the latter. On the export side, it is standard practice to pay a less favorable rate to firms selling products for which the country may have some monopoly power. For example, it has been traditional for Brazil and Colombia to pay an unfavorable exchange rate to coffee exporters. This practice is an effective export tax. Exchange control may distinguish between resident accounts and nonresident accounts with a fixed rate for one group and a market clearing rate for the other. The United Kingdom, which operated such a system for many years, ended it in 1981. Current account transactions may take place at one rate, and capital transactions may take place at a different (usually less favorable) rate.

In 1982 Argentina attempted to administer a complex system of 17 multiple exchange rates ranging from 7,000 pesos per dollar to 40,000 pesos per dollar. At the same time a black market rate of 60,000 pesos tempted wheat exporters to smuggle their product out of the country. Another popular form of exchange control is an advanced deposit requirement. Importers seeking foreign exchange must pay for a fixed percentage of the desired foreign exchange during a specified period in advance of delivery, and they are paid a noncompetitive interest rate on their deposit. The practice amounts to a de facto devaluation. The amount of the implicit price increase is greater (1) the larger the percentage of payment required, (2) the earlier payment is required, and (3) the lower (often zero) the interest rate paid on the deposit.

A problem with exchange controls and all price fixing schemes is that some potential buyers are willing to pay more than the legal maximum price rather than go without the product. In Figure 21-2 buyers would be willing to purchase $\Pi_1 B$ units of foreign exchange, but only $\Pi_1 A$ units are offered for sale. Buyers who are unable to obtain the additional AB units they seek would be willing to pay as much as Π_3 for another unit. Sellers (e.g., exporters) would be willing to sell for any amount greater than the official price of $O\Pi_1$. The problem for the exchange control authority is how to prevent these two groups from arranging mutually profitable trades at some price between Π_1 and Π_3.

In all cases a black market does develop, and the practical problem is how to keep it within manageable proportions. Every unit of foreign exchange supplied to the black market reduces the supply (F_1^s) to the legal market, which makes the rationing problem more severe.[14] Exchange control has an enforcement cost. A set of bureaucrats must scrutinize banks, tourists, postal transactions, invoices and barter trade.

Transfer pricing is a device by which multinational firms may circumvent exchange controls. Capital may be exported from a country subject to exchange control by charging an affiliate in that country an artificially high price for intrafirm imports or paying them an artificially low price for intrafirm exports. To detect violations, exchange controllers must establish an "arm's-length" price for each intrafirm transaction.

21.11 THE IMF AFTER THE BRETTON WOODS SYSTEM

The adjustable peg system associated with Betton Woods ended in 1971, but the IMF has survived as an international institution. It is still trying to adapt to new economic circumstances. Although the Articles of Agreement explicitly forbade floating exchange rates, floating was the policy of most members after 1973. The IMF finally legitimized floating by amending the charter at the Jamaica conference in 1976. In place of par values, the IMF claimed the authority to exercise firm surveillance over exchange rates. The only effective power the IMF has over exchange rates is through the conditions it attaches to loans. The IMF continues to make loans for balance-of-payments purposes even with floating.

The IMF also administers special facilities such as the compensatory Finance Facility (established 1963), the Buffer Stock Financing Facility, and the Oil Facility. IMF officials have discussed changing the nature of its loans, and in 1982 it made a large loan to India that was not directly related to the balance of payments. If the IMF makes longer-term loans for development purposes, the division of labor between the IMF and the World Bank will become less clear.

The number of member countries continues to grow. As of February 1982,

---

[14] A comprehensive set of black market exchange rates is published in *Pick's Currency Yearbook*. New York: Pick Publishing Corporation.

there were 144 members, including the People's Republic of China, Rumania, and Hungary. An application from Poland was pending. Poland's case is interesting in light of its serious problem of repaying external debt.

The IMF continues to promote SDRs as an international money. A new allocation of SFRs occurred from 1979 to 1981, which doubled the quantity outstanding. However, they remain a negligible fraction of total world reserves (see Table 21-1). In 1973 SDRs comprised 4 percent of world reserves, and in 1981 they were only 2 percent of reserves. When reserve positions in the IMF are added to SDRs, IMF comprised 5 percent of world reserves in 1981.

For many years the IMF has sought control over the growth of world reserves, but gold and dollars have dominated. The IMF proposed a Substitution Account through which governments could exchange dollar reserves for SDRs. Implicit in the scheme is the idea that many dollar reserves are unwanted ("dollar overhang") and that central banks could be easily persuaded to sell them for IMF money. A conflict arose over whether the dollar value of SDRs should be guaranteed against depreciation, and who should pay for such a guarantee. The IMF proposed that the United States pay for the guarantee, but the United States refused. In view of the substantial depreciation of SDRs in terms of dollars in 1981 and the first half of 1982, the cost of a guarantee would have been substantial.

Although the official role of SDRs remains limited, their private use as a unit of account has expanded. However, the appeal of the SDR as a private unit of account comes from the fact that it is merely a name for fixed amounts of the five major currencies of the world. As such, its value depends more on the economic policies of the United States, Japan, West Germany, the United Kingdom, and France than it does on the policies of the International Monetary Fund.

SUMMARY

The adjustable peg monetary system is a compromise between the extremes of freely floating rates and permanently fixed rates. It was set up at the Bretton Woods conference, and it lasted from 1946 to 1971. The system was based on par values that would be fixed except under extraordinary conditions known as funadmental disequilibrium. Fixed parities were to be defended by monetary reserves, credit from the Fund, and monetary-fiscal policy. The system encountered the problems of developing a satisfactory adjustment mechanism, providing for growth in liquidity, and providing confidence in the key currency, the U.S. dollar. The dollar played a special role as a key or reserve currency. The system of fixed rates eventually collapsed because of an excess supply of dollars in the world.

The twin policy goals of internal and external balance cannot necessarily be satisfied under fixed exchange rates. An appropriate monetary-fiscal policy mix is an attempt to achieve both goals without altering the exchange rate. Monetary and fiscal policy may have quite different effects under fixed and floating exchange rates.

Exchange rate adjustment was undertaken reluctantly under the Bretton Woods system, which encouraged destabilizing speculation. In the absence of an effective adjustment mechanism, exchange controls were widely used. The international monetary system continues to evolve after the demise of the Bretton Woods system, and the new role of the International Monetary Fund is yet to be determined.

REFERENCES

ABRAMS, RICHARD. "Federal Reserve Intervention Policy." *Economic Review*, Federal Reserve Bank of Kansas City, March 1979.

ALIBER, ROBERT Z., ed. *The Political Economy of Monetary Reform*. Chicago: University of Chicago Press, 1977.

———. *The International Money Game*, 4th ed. New York: Basic Books, 1983.

BERNSTEIN, E. M. *Reflections on Jamaica*, Princeton Studies in International Finance, No. 115. Princeton, N.J.: Princeton University Press, April 1976.

BIRNBAUM, E. A., and M. S. QUERESHI. "Advance Deposit Requirements for Imports." International Monetary Fund *Staff Papers*, November 1960.

BRYANT, RALPH C. *Money and Monetary Policy in Interdependent Nations*. Washington, D.C.: The Brookings Institution, 1980. Comprehensive study of technical aspects of international monetary policy.

COATS, WARREN L., Jr. "The SDR as a Means of Payment." International Monetary Fund *Staff Papers*, September 1982. Discusses actual and potential use of SDRs in private markets.

COHEN, B. J. *Organizing the World's Money*. New York: Basic Books, 1977.

COOMBS, CHARLES. *Arena of International Finance*. New York: John Wiley, 1976. Monetary history by a central banker.

COOPER, RICHARD, ed. *International Finance*. Baltimore: Penguin, 1969.

———. *Currency Devaluation in Developing Countries*, Princeton Studies in International Finance, No. 86. Princeton, N.J.: Princeton University Press, June 1971. Analysis of the effects of devaluation in a set of low-income countries.

DAM, KENNETH W. *The Rules of the Game: Reform and Evolution in the International Monetary System*. Chicago: University of Chicago Press, 1982.

DeVRIES, MARGARET GARRITSEN. *The International Monetary Fund 1966–71: The System Under Stress*, Vol. I, *Narrative;* Vol. II, *Documents*. Washington, D.C.: International Monetary Fund, 1977. History of the Fund toward the end of the Bretton Woods period.

DORNBUSCH, RUDIGER. *Open Economy Macroeconomics*. New York: Basic Books, 1980. Advanced textbook.

FISCHER, STANLEY. "Seigniorage and the Case for a National Money." *Journal of Political Economy*, April 1982.

FLEMING, MARCUS. "Domestic Financial Policies Under Fixed and Under Floating Exchange Rates," International Monetary Fund *Staff Papers*, November 1982.

GARDNER, R. N. *Sterling-Dollar Diplomacy*, 2nd ed. New York: McGraw-Hill, 1969. A study of the founding of the Bretton Woods system.

GILBERT, MILTON. *Quest for World Monetary Order*, New York: John Wiley, 1980.

GRUBEL, HERBERT G.   "The Demand for International Reserves: A Critical Review of the Literature." *Journal of Economic Literature*, December 1971. Survey of the demand for reserves.

HALM, G. N.   *Jamaica and the Par Value System*, Princeton Studies in International Finance, No. 120. Princeton, N.J.: Princeton University Press, March 1977.

HORSEFIELD, J. KEITH, ed.   *The International Monetary Fund, 1945–65*, Vol. I, *Chronicle;* Vol. II, *Analysis*. Washington, D.C.: International Monetary Fund, 1969. History of the Fund during the early period.

INTERNATIONAL MONETARY FUND.   *Annual Reports*, Washington, D.C., annually. Source of recent data on international finance and policy.

———.   *Annual Report on Exchange Restrictions*, Washington, D.C., annually. Report listing detailed exchange controls by country.

———.   *Staff Papers*. June 1979. The issue contains a bibliography on the IMF.

KEYNES, JOHN MAYNARD.   *A Tract on Monetary Reform*. London: Macmillan, 1923. Chapter 4 discusses the alternative goals of stable prices and stable exchange rate.

KRUEGER, ANNE.   *Foreign Trade Regimes and Economic Development: Liberalization Attempts and Consequences*. Cambridge, Mass.: Ballinger, 1978.

MARSHALL, JORGE.   "Advance Deposits on Imports." International Monetary Fund *Staff Papers*, April 1958. Discusses advance deposit requirements as a form of exchange controls.

MASON, E. S., and R. E. ASHER.   *The World Bank Since Bretton Woods*. Washington, D.C.: The Brookings Institution, 1973.

MEADE, JAMES E.   *The Balance of Payments*. London: Oxford University Press, 1951. Modern classic on the macroeconomic problems of an open economy. Part II deals with the problems of internal and external balance. Part V deals with direct controls on trade and payments.

MEIER, GERALD M.   *Problems of a World Monetary Order*, 2nd ed. New York: Oxford University Press, 1982. Contains detailed information about the international monetary system since World War II, including hotel rates at the Mt. Washington Hotel that hosted the Bretton Woods conference.

MICHAELY, MICHAEL.   *The Responsiveness of Demand Policies to the Balance of Payments*. New York: Columbia University Press, 1971. Empirical study of the use of monetary and fiscal policy to achieve internal and external balance.

MUNDELL, ROBERT A.   *International Economics*. New York: Macmillan, 1968. Collection of papers on international monetary issues.

NURKSE, RAGNAR.   *International Currency Experience: Lessons of the Interwar Period*. Geneva: League of Nations, 1944. An influential, unfavorable interpretation of floating exchange rates.

PICK, FRANZ.   *Pick's Currency Yearbook*, New York: Pick Publishing Corporation. Annual source of black market exchange rates.

ROLFE, SIDNEY E., and JAMES BURTLE.   *The Great Wheel: The World Monetary System*. New York: Macmillan, 1973.

SCAMMELL, W. M.   *The International Economy Since 1945*. New York: St. Martins, 1980. An international monetary history.

SCHULTZ, GEORGE P., and KENNETH W. DAM.   *Economic Policy Behind the Headlines*. New York: W. W. Norton, 1977. Chapter 6 is on international monetary policy.

SOBOL, DOROTHY MEADOW.   "The SDR in Private International Finance," *Quarterly Review*, Federal Reserve Bank of New York, Winter 1981–1982. Recent developments in the use of SDRs in private markets.

SOLOMON, ROBERT.   *The International Monetary System: 1945–1976*. New York: Harper & Row, 1977.

SOUTHARD, FRANK A., Jr. *The Evolution of the International Monetary Fund*, Princeton Studies in International Finance, No. 135. Princeton, N.J.: Princeton University Press, December 1979.

STERN, ROBERT M. *The Balance of Payments: Theory and Economic Policy*. Chicago: Aldine, 1973. Advanced textbook on macroeconomic problems of an open economy.

SWOBODA, ALEXANDER. "Equilibrium, Quasi-equilibrium, and Macroeconomic Stabilization Policy Under Fixed Exchange Rates." *Quarterly Journal of Economics*, February 1972.

SWOBODA, ALEXANDER, and HANS GENBERG. "Gold and the Dollar: Asymmetries in World Money Stock Determination, 1959–1971." In *The International Monetary System Under Flexible Exchange Rates*, R. Cooper et al., eds. Cambridge, Mass.: Ballinger, 1982.

TEW, BRIAN. *The Evolution of the International Monetary System, 1945–77*. New York: John Wiley, 1977.

TRIFFIN, ROBERT. *Gold and the Dollar Crisis*. New Haven, Conn.: Yale University Press, 1960. Analysis of the inherent weakness of the Bretton Woods system.

———. *The World Money Maze: National Currencies in International Payments*. New Haven, Conn.: Yale University Press, 1966. Detailed international monetary history from the end of World War II to 1966.

WHITMAN, MARINA. *Policies for Internal and External Balance*, Princeton Studies in International Economics, No. 9. Princeton, N.J.: Princeton University Press, 1970. Survey of the literature on monetary and fiscal policy under fixed and floating rates.

WILLIAMSON, J. *The Failure of World Monetary Reform, 1971–74*. New York: New York University Press, 1977. Discussion of the attempt to rescue the Bretton Woods system.

APPENDIX: THE DERIVATION OF IS, LM, AND FF CURVES

1. *Goods Market Equilibrium.* Equilibrium exists in the goods market when the private demand for goods plus government spending equals the supply of goods:

$$f(r, y) + G = y$$

Differentiation and rearrangement of terms will yield the slope of the *IS* curve in r, y space for a given value of G:

$$f_r dr + f_y dy + dG = dy$$
$$\frac{dr}{dy} = \frac{1 - f_y}{f_r} \quad \text{for } dG = 0$$

This *IS* curve has a negative slope when $f_r < 0$ and $f_y < 1$.

2. *Money Market Equilibrium.* The money market is in equilibrium when the demand for money equals the supply of money:

$$M = L(r, y)$$

Differentiation and rearrangement of terms will yield the slope of the money market equilibrium curve for a given value of M:

$$dM = L_r dr + L_y dy$$
$$\frac{dr}{dy} = -\frac{L_y}{L_r}$$

The *LM* curve has a positive slope since $L_r < 0$ and $L_y > 0$.

3. *Foreign Exchange Market Equilibrium.* Equilibrium exists when the goods and services surplus equals the capital outflow:

$$E - I(y, \Pi) = K(r)$$
$$dE - I_y dy + I_\Pi d\Pi = K_r dr$$

The slope of *FF* for a given exchange rate is

$$\frac{dr}{dy} = -\frac{I_y}{K_r} \quad \text{for } d\Pi = dE = 0$$

The *FF* curve slopes upward for $I_y > 0$ and $K_r < 0$. The relative slopes of *FF* and *LM* depend on the four variables: I_y, K_r, L_r, and L_y.

CHAPTER TWENTY-TWO
WORLD INFLATION

22.1 INTRODUCTION

The topic of this chapter is world inflation and its transmission between countries. The historical experience with world inflation will be reviewed. Inflation rates vary across countries as well as over time, and cross-sectional variation will be considered. Prominent explanations of variation in inflation will be reviewed. Popular explanations include monetary policy, growth of money substitutes, fiscal policy, currency depreciation, commodity prices, and fluctuations in private demand. The mechanism that transmits inflation between countries depends on the prevailing exchange rate regime. The transmission mechanisms under the gold standard, the adjustable peg, and floating exchange rates will be compared.

One of the determinants of world inflation is the world money supply, which depends partly on the stock of world monetary reserves. The components of world monetary reserves and their rate of growth will be analyzed. Since the interaction of demand and supply determines prices, the demand for monetary reserves will also be studied. It is a demand by central banks to hold reserves, which is analogous to the demand to hold money by householders and business firms.

Chapter 21 introduced the potential policy conflict between internal and external balance. This chapter will consider whether the abandonment of the adjustable peg system has led domestic price-level goals to dominate exchange rate goals in the determination of monetary policy. A simple hypothesis is that a nation's money supply will be primarily determined by foreign reserves under a fixed exchange rate regime, but money will be primarily determined by the domestic assets of the central bank under floating exchange rates. Finally, the development of substitutes for national money will be considered as an explanation for inflation. In particular, the determinants of the world stock of Eurodollars will be analyzed.

22.2 EXPERIENCE
WITH WORLD INFLATION

A single country or a small group of countries may experience inflation at the same time that most of the world has stable prices. In that case, one would expect the cause of inflation to be domestic or regional rather than worldwide. For example, the period 1950 to 1969 was a period of relatively stable prices in the world. For the world as a whole, the average annual rate of inflation was 3.7 percent for the two-decade period. Nevertheless, particular countries experienced substantial inflation during this period. The average inflation rates for Uruguay and Bolivia were 43.0 percent and 41.3 percent, respectively. During the same period, Brazil, Chile, and Argentina experienced inflation rates of 35.1 percent, 28.2 percent, and 26.4 percent, respectively.

In view of the stable prices in the rest of the world, these inflations would have to be considered national or regional. However, before one concludes that inflation is a "Latin American disease," inflation rates for the rest of Latin America should be considered.

Rates for 16 Latin American countries are presented in Table 22-1. Inflation in Guatemala and Venezuela averaged 1 percent per year for the same period. Eight of the 16 countries listed had inflation rates of less than 5 percent per year. The 8 countries with lower inflation rates averaged 2.3 percent per year, whereas the higher-inflation group averaged 25.5 percent. Whatever economic forces brought about inflation in one group either were not present or did not have the same impact on the second group.

The distinction between high- and low-inflation countries in Latin America has survived the demise of the Bretton Woods system. In 1980 the average world inflation rate was 11.5 percent, while the rates in Argentina,[1] Brazil, and Chile were 114.1 percent, 75.1 percent, and 62.6 percent. In 1980 the inflation rates in Guatemala, Venezuela, and Costa Rica were 13.4 percent, 14.6 percent, and 8.5 percent, respectively.

One question to be considered in this chapter is, What determines whether a given inflation will be strictly local or regional or whether it will be worldwide? The statistical question is what determines the cross-section variation in

---

[1] Because of sustained high inflation rates in Argentina, the denomination of the average currency note becomes intractable. Periodic currency reforms occur in which 1 unit of new money is defined to be equal to many units of old money. In January 1983 1 new peso was defined to be equal to 10,000 old pesos. A similar monetary reform was implemented in 1967.

TABLE 22-1   Latin American and World Inflation, 1950–1969

COUNTRY	MEAN INFLATION RATE (PERCENT PER YEAR)	COUNTRY	MEAN INFLATION RATE (PERCENT PER YEAR)
Uruguay	43.0%	Ecuador	3.0%
Bolivia	41.3	Honduras	2.1
Brazil	35.1	Costa Rica	1.9
Chile	28.2	Guatemala	1.1
Argentina	26.4	Venezuela	1.1
Paraguay	12.5	El Salvador	0.3
Colombia	9.2		
Peru	8.5	First eight	25.5
Mexico	5.3	Last eight	2.3
Nicaragua	3.4	Latin America	13.9
		World	3.7

Source: Robert Vogel, "Inflation in Latin America," American Economic Review, March 1974; and International Monetary Fund, International Financial Statistics.

inflation among countries in a given year? The related economic question is, What is the nature of the mechanism that transmits inflation from one country to another? Is the transmission mechanism significantly different under fixed and floating exchange rates? If it is different, then we might expect the dispersion of national inflation rates to be different in recent years than it was before 1973. A specific hypothesis is that national inflation rates will diverge more when exchange rates float. Thus, one set of questions considered in this chapter is the determination of national inflation rates at a point in time.

A second set of questions involves the variation of inflation over time. Large quantities of gold and silver were shipped to Europe following the discovery of America. The resulting European inflation in the sixteenth century contrasted so sharply to the previous and subsequent periods that it has been called the "price revolution." Most major inflations since then have been associated with wartime finance. Wartime destruction of people and property puts some upward pressure on prices by reducing real income and the demand for money. However, the main source of inflationary pressure is the manner in which war has traditionally been financed. Governments have chosen not to raise taxes as much as spending, and the resulting budgetary deficits have usually been financed by monetary expansion. Examples of wartime inflation are the American Revolution, Napoleonic wars, American Civil War, World War I, World War II, and the Korean conflict. The current worldwide inflation that began in the early 1970s may be the most significant peacetime inflation since the price revolution.

Table 22-2 shows annual world inflation rates reported by the International Monetary Fund for the period 1950 to 1983. The world inflation rate is the average of national inflation rates weighted by the shares of countries in

TABLE 22-2   World Inflation Rates, 1950–1983

YEAR	PERCENT PER YEAR	YEAR	PERCENT PER YEAR
1950	0.3%	1970	6.0%
1951	9.6	1971	5.9
1952	3.9	1972	5.8
1953	1.3	1973	9.6
1954	1.1	1974	15.3
1955	1.0	1975	13.4
1956	3.5	1976	11.1
1957	3.9	1977	11.4
1958	4.2	1978	9.7
1959	3.2	1979	12.0
1960	2.8	1980	15.5
1961	2.6	1981	14.1
1962	3.6	1982	12.8
1963	4.0	1983 (April)	13.3
1964	4.6		
1965	5.0		
1966	5.1		
1967	4.2		
1968	4.4		
1969	5.1		

Source: International Monetary Fund, *International Financial Statistics Yearbook, 1980,* pp. 58–59; and *International Financial Statistics,* September 1983, p. 51.

world income. The average world inflation rates for the decades of the 1950s and 1960s were 3.2 percent and 4.1 percent, respectively. The rate accelerated to 10.0 percent in the 1970s, and it averaged 14.1 percent for the first three years of the 1980s.

With respect to inflation, the years in the 1970s and 1980s appear to be significantly different from the previous 20 years. More specifically, an inflationary change appears to have occurred in 1973, which has not been reversed yet. To the nearest percentage point, world inflation jumped from 6 percent in 1972 to 10 percent in 1973, and it has not fallen below double digits since then.

An obvious question is, What caused the increase in inflation over time? This chapter will consider some alternative explanations. We have seen that there was a major change in the world monetary system at the time, as the Bretton Woods system was replaced by floating exchange rates. Some critics contend that floating rates cause inflation directly. An alternative explanation is that the fundamental monetary and fiscal policies that made the Bretton Woods system unworkable have caused both floating exchange rates and world inflation. Some real economic disturbance, usually described as supply shocks, also occurred around 1973. The success of OPEC in raising world petroleum prices is the most prominent example. Accordingly, some people have attributed the recent inflation to commodity market conditions that are unrelated to monetary developments.

Since World War II, the only two worldwide inflations have been the one associated with the Korean conflict and the inflation since 1973. The Korean experience involved a sharp acceleration of inflation followed by a sharp deceleration. The world inflation rate jumped from zero in 1950 to 9.6 percent in 1951 (see Table 22-2). It dropped to 3.9 percent in 1952 and was near 1 percent in each the next three years. Although brief, it was a widespread inflation. U.S. inflation was 8 percent in 1951, and most industrial countries of the world had rates exceeding 10 percent in that year. Following the Korean conflict, the world had an extended period of relatively stable prices. For the 20-year period 1953 to 1972, the average world inflation rate was 3.9 percent, and it was below 6 percent in every year.

The inflation since 1973 is significant in several respects. First, the inflation rate accelerated substantially relative to the experience of the previous 20 years. The prolonged period of price stability may have led people to expect price stability to continue. Thus, the actual inflation may have also been an unexpected inflation. Second, the inflation was extremely widespread. Although individual countries were affected differently, the inflation rate in every country of the world accelerated significantly. Because of the pervasiveness of inflation, a satisfactory explanation cannot rely on solely national causes. A third feature of the inflation is its durability. As noted, the world inflation rate has exceeded 10 percent every year since 1973. This persistence distinguishes it from the short-lived worldwide inflation of the Korean conflict. A fourth feature, also mentioned, is the absence of a major war to influence monetary and fiscal policy. U.S. military involvement in Vietnam may have had some economic impact in the early 1970s, but it cannot explain the worldwide inflation because of its limited duration and the small number of countries involved.

In spite of the comprehensive nature of the recent inflation, significant differences between countries are apparent. Over the period 1950 to 1979, the average world inflation rate was 5.9 percent. However, this average conceals considerable variability between individual countries and country groups. The set of industrial countries had a 4.6 percent inflation rate, and the non-oil developing countries had a 13.6 percent rate. However, the substantial variation in inflation rates among developing countries indicates that poverty, by itself, does not cause inflation. Over the same 20-year period, Asian developing countries had 6.4 percent inflation, whereas Western Hemisphere developing countries (mostly Latin America) had 24.1 percent. Some low-income countries, such as India and Pakistan, have had low inflation rates, whereas others, such as Uruguay, Bolivia, and Chile, have had high inflation rates. The higher average inflation rate in low-income countries is sometimes explained by the administrative ease of using inflation as a source of government revenue. There is an administrative cost of collecting all taxes, and it has been said that the administrative cost of an income tax, sales tax, or property tax is relatively greater in low-income countries.

Differences in the cost of collecting taxes may explain differences in average inflation rates, but they do not explain differences between low-income countries or changes in inflation over time. Why is it more costly to collect taxes in Latin American than in India and Pakistan? Why did Brazilian inflation increase from 12.7 percent in 1973 to more than 100 percent in 1981?

One explanation for differential national inflation is whether a currency is tied to another currency for which prices are stable. An example of the importance of exchange rate policy is the experience of Mexico and Panama. Both currencies were linked to the dollar for an extended period before 1973. Mexico has effectively floated since 1973, whereas 1 Panamanian balboa continues to exchange for 1 U.S. dollar. All three currencies were linked, and Panama and Mexico experienced roughly the same inflation rates as the United States. Since the peso began to float, the Mexican inflation rate has diverged sharply from the U.S. and Panamanian rates.

Table 22-3 shows the inflation rates for the United States, Mexico, and

TABLE 22-3   Inflation in the United States, Mexico, and Panama, 1951–1981

YEAR	UNITED STATES	MEXICO	PANAMA	YEAR	UNITED STATES	MEXICO	PANAMA
1951	8%	13%	4%	1970	6%	5%	3%
1952	2	15	1	1971	4	5	2
1953	1	−2	−1	1972	3	5	5
1954	0	5	0	1973	6	12	7
1955	0	16	0	1974	11	24	17
1956	1	5	0	1975	9	15	6
1957	4	5	0	1976	6	16	4
1958	3	12	0	1977	7	30	5
1959	1	3	0	1978	8	17	4
1960	1	5	0	1979	11	18	8
1961	1	2	1	1980	14	26	14
1962	1	1	1	1981	10	28	7
1963	1	1	1	1982	6	59	4
1964	1	2	2				
1965	2	4	1				
1966	3	4	0				
1967	3	3	1				
1968	4	1	2				
1969	5	4	2				

Source: International Monetary Fund, *International Financial Statistics Yearbook, 1983.* Washington, D.C., pp. 69–71.

Panama from 1951 to 1982. Panama has had a fixed exchange rate with the U.S. dollar since 1904. Mexico devalued the peso in 1954 and kept the rate fixed at 12.5 pesos per dollar through 1970. A devaluation occurred in 1971, and Mexico has operated a de facto managed float since 1973. During the period of fixed rates from 1954 to 1970, Mexico experienced approximately the same inflation rate as the other two countries. Very similar inflation rates occurred in spite of substantial economic and political differences between the three countries. Inflation rates converged because the fixed exchange rate imposed similar monetary policies on the countries. Excessive monetary expansion in Mexico led to a balance-of-payments deficit, a loss of reserves, and monetary contraction.

In 1973 inflation accelerated in all three countries, but it increased more in Mexico. Since 1973, Mexico has pursued an independent monetary policy, the peso has floated, and inflation has been substantially higher than in the other two countries. In most years since 1973, Mexican inflation has been more than twice the rate in the other two countries, and in 1982 the inflation rate in Mexico was nearly 10 times the rates in the U.S. and Panama. Panama has retained a fixed exchange rate with the dollar, and its inflationary experience has been very close to that of the United States. After extremely stable prices in the 1950s and 1960s, inflation increased in the 1970s. It reached a local maximum of 17 percent in 1974. Inflation declined until the acceleration of 1979 and 1980. In the United States, inflation increased until 1974 and declined until the acceleration of 1979 and 1980. Exchange rate policy helps to explain inflation differences between countries that are similar in other respects.

The average rate of inflation has been less in industrialized countries than in low-income countries. However, the inflation experience of this group has been far from homogeneous. The countries of Western Europe have many economic and political similarities. The European Economic Community is an accomplished customs union, and European monetary system is a formal attempt to achieve a common currency. On these grounds one might expect inflation rates in Western Europe to converge to a single rate. Instead, it appears that two informal but distinct currency blocs are emerging. Some EEC members are in one bloc and some are in the other. Table 22-4 shows the recent inflation rates for the two groups.

The low-inflation group seems to follow the German mark. The group includes the contiguous countries of Belgium, The Netherlands, Austria, Switzerland, and West Germany. In the last five years, the average inflation rates have ranged from 3.2 percent to 6.7 percent. Even though exchange rates are formally floating, there has been little variation within the group. The high-inflation countries include the four Scandinavian countries, the United Kingdom, France, and Italy. Their average inflation rates have ranged from 9.5 percent to 15.4 percent, and in each year inflation for the high group has been more than twice the rate of the low group. Since four members of the high group belong to the EEC, and three members of the low group also belong to

TABLE 22-4   Inflation in Western Europe, 1978–1982

	1978	1979	1980	1981	1982
Low-inflation group					
Belgium	4.5%	4.4%	6.7%	7.6%	8.7%
West Germany	2.8	4.1	5.5	5.9	5.3
The Netherlands	4.1	4.2	6.5	6.7	5.9
Austria	3.6	3.7	6.3	6.8	5.4
Switzerland	0.8	3.6	4.1	6.5	5.7
Mean	3.2	4.0	5.8	6.7	6.2
High-inflation group					
France	9.1	10.7	13.3	13.3	12.1
Italy	12.1	14.7	21.2	17.8	16.5
United Kingdom	8.3	13.4	18.0	11.9	8.6
Denmark	10.1	9.6	12.3	11.7	10.1
Finland	7.8	7.5	11.6	12.0	9.3
Norway	8.0	4.9	10.7	13.7	11.4
Sweden	9.9	7.3	13.7	12.1	8.6
Mean	9.3	9.7	14.4	13.2	10.9
United States	7.5	11.3	13.5	10.4	6.2
World	9.5	11.9	15.4	14.1	12.3

Source: International Monetary Fund, *International Financial Statistics Yearbook,* 1983, p. 69.

the EEC, it is easy to see why the EMS has had trouble establishing fixed exchange rates. Even though the two groups are not formal organizations, relatively uniform monetary policies have emerged within each group.

Just as poverty does not cause inflation, neither does high-income guarantee price-level stability. Differences between the inflation rates of these two relatively homogeneous groups of countries can be explained by differences in their monetary and fiscal policies. Notice that the notion of energy dependence does not explain the inflation differential. The two net exporters of oil, Norway and the United Kingdom, are both in the high-inflation group.

Inflation rates for selected individual countries since 1970 are shown in Table 22-5. Most countries followed the broad pattern in which inflation accelerated in 1973 and 1974, declined from 1975 to 1978, and increased again in 1979 and 1980. The world average followed that pattern, as did the averages for industrial countries and less developed countries. The individual country observations also followed the same pattern of acceleration in 1973 and 1974, followed by a four-year decline, and acceleration again in 1979 and 1980. It is the uniformity of the pattern over time that has led people to describe it as a worldwide inflation. The same uniformity has led people to search for a common explanation of inflation in all countries.

Although the timing of inflation changes followed the same pattern nearly everywhere, the magnitude of changes was quite different. Saudi Arabia and

TABLE 22-5 World Inflation Rates, 1970–1982

	1970	1971	1972	1973	1974	1975	1976	1977	1978	1979	1980	1981	1982
World	6.0%	5.9%	5.8%	9.6%	15.3%	13.5%	11.0%	11.2%	9.6%	12.1%	15.5%	14.1%	12.3%
Industrial countries	5.6	5.1	4.5	7.5	13.1	10.8	7.9	7.9	6.8	9.2	12.0	10.0	7.5
Less developed countries	9.2	10.2	13.8	22.5	28.5	26.4	28.3	29.1	24.7	30.1	37.5	34.7	34.3
United States	5.9	4.3	3.3	6.3	10.9	9.2	5.8	6.5	7.5	11.3	13.5	10.4	6.2
Canada	3.4	2.8	4.8	7.5	10.9	10.7	7.5	8.0	9.0	9.2	10.1	12.4	10.8
Japan	7.6	6.2	4.4	11.8	24.3	11.9	9.3	8.1	3.8	3.6	8.0	4.9	2.6
France	5.8	5.5	6.2	7.4	13.7	11.7	9.2	9.5	9.2	10.7	13.3	13.3	12.1
West Germany	3.3	5.4	5.5	6.9	7.0	5.9	4.5	3.9	2.6	4.1	5.5	5.9	5.3
Italy	4.8	5.0	5.7	10.8	19.1	17.0	16.8	17.0	12.2	14.7	21.2	17.8	16.5
Switzerland	3.6	6.5	6.7	8.8	9.7	6.7	1.7	1.3	1.1	3.7	4.0	6.5	5.7
United Kingdom	6.3	9.4	7.3	9.1	16.0	24.2	16.5	15.9	8.3	13.4	18.0	11.9	8.6
Saudi Arabia	0.2	4.4	4.4	16.6	21.4	34.6	21.6	11.3	−1.6	1.8	3.2	2.8	N.A.
Spain	5.8	8.1	8.3	11.4	15.7	16.8	15.1	24.5	19.7	15.6	15.6	14.5	14.4
Sweden	7.1	7.5	6.0	6.7	9.9	9.8	10.3	11.4	9.9	7.3	13.7	12.1	8.6
Norway	10.8	6.1	7.3	7.3	9.4	11.7	9.1	9.2	8.1	4.9	10.7	13.7	11.4
Belgium	3.9	4.3	5.4	6.9	12.7	12.7	9.2	7.1	4.5	4.4	6.7	7.6	8.7
Austria	4.3	4.7	6.3	7.7	9.5	8.5	7.3	5.5	3.6	3.7	6.3	6.8	5.4
Iran	1.6	4.2	6.5	9.8	14.3	12.7	11.3	27.3	11.6	10.5	20.7	24.2	18.7
Australia	3.9	6.0	6.0	9.4	15.1	15.1	13.5	12.2	7.9	9.1	10.2	9.6	11.2
Mexico	5.0	5.5	4.9	12.0	23.8	15.7	15.1	29.0	17.5	18.2	26.4	27.9	58.9
The Netherlands	3.8	7.4	7.9	8.0	9.6	10.5	8.8	6.4	4.2	4.2	6.5	6.7	5.9
Brazil	22.3	20.2	16.5	12.7	27.6	28.9	42.0	43.7	38.7	52.7	82.8	105.5	98.0
India	5.1	3.3	5.2	17.8	27.8	5.6	−7.8	8.5	2.5	6.3	11.5	13.0	7.9
Pakistan	4.3	10.0	5.4	23.0	26.6	20.9	7.2	10.1	6.7	9.5	11.7	13.8	7.4
Indonesia	12.6	4.4	6.3	31.0	40.6	19.1	19.8	11.0	8.4	19.4	21.0	12.3	9.5

Source: International Monetary Fund, *International Financial Statistics Yearbook*, 1983, pp. 69–71.

Mexico are two oil exporters whose inflation rate was around 4 percent in 1972. Inflation accelerated sharply in both countries, reaching a peak of 35 percent in 1975 in Saudi Arabia and 29 percent in 1977 in Mexico. However, in Saudi Arabia inflation had fallen to the neighborhood of 2 to 3 percent by 1979 through 1981, whereas in Mexico, it was in the neighborhood of 18 to 28 percent. In 1982, inflation exceeded 50 percent in Mexico, while it was close to zero in Saudi Arabia.

One other example of a differential impact is the comparison of Japan and Italy. The countries had similar inflation rates from 1970 to 1972. Inflation increased sharply and reached a peak of 24 percent in Japan and 19 percent in Italy. In Japan the rate was below 4 percent four years later, and the rate remained far below 10 percent from 1979 to 1982. Conversely, in Italy inflation never fell below 10 percent, and in the 1979–1981 period, it was near 20 percent. A completely satisfactory theory of inflation would explain both the pattern of similarity in the timing of inflation as well as the cross-sectional differences in magnitudes.

22.3 THEORIES OF INFLATION

The previous section presented some facts about world and national inflation. This section attempts to explain the basic determinants of world inflation. The next section deals with the mechanism that transmits inflation from one country to another. The equilibrium world price level can be expressed in terms of the money market equilibrium condition that world money demand equals world money supply:

$$\frac{M}{P} = L(i, y)$$

The world price level is determined by the ratio of the nominal world money supply and the real-world demand for money:

$$P = \frac{M}{L(i, y)}$$

Both the world price level and the world money supply are weighted averages of national aggregates. Eurodollars are not part of any country's national money supply, and the question of how to take account of them is considered in Section 22.5. Time series for both P and M are published in monthly *International Financial Statistics*. Inflation is an increase in the general price level, and it can be explained by those forces that either increase the money supply or reduce the demand for money. The money supply can be expressed as a product of the money supply multiplier (m) and the monetary base $(M_b$, called reserve money by the IMF). The base can be expressed as the sum of the central bank's domestic currency assets (D) and its foreign exchange reserves:

$$M = mM_b = m(D + R)$$

The money supply multiplier depends on the public's preferences for various monetary assets and the ratio in which banks hold reserves against their monetary liabilities. An increase in interest rates will reduce the demand for noninterest-bearing money, and it will reduce private banks' holdings of excess reserves. D represents the domestic currency assets of national central banks. The extent to which M is influenced by D is sometimes interpreted as a measure of a country's monetary independence. R consists of the stock of monetary gold under a gold standard. Nowadays, it also includes IMF money and foreign exchange, which is mostly U.S. dollars. The determinants of world reserves and liquidity will be discussed in Section 22.4. The world price level can be expressed as the ratio of the determinants of the world money supply to world money demand:

$$P = \frac{m(D + R)}{L(i, y)}$$

Collectively, the variables in the numerator will be referred to as the monetary determinants of inflation.

Real economic variables can influence inflation by altering the real demand for money. For example, financial innovation that creates new money substitutes will reduce money demand and increase the price level for a given money supply. A supply shock, such as monopolization of the world petroleum market, would put upward pressure on the world price level by reducing real income and the demand for money. Aggregate supply could also be reduced by an increase in money wages. Similarly, increases in consumption demand, investment demand, and fiscal policy could put upward pressure on the price level. These changes would reduce the demand for money by increasing interest rates.

In summary, monetary theories of inflation operate through an increase in aggregate demand induced by an increase in the money supply. Various real theories postulate a reduction in money demand as a result of either an increase in aggregate demand or a reduction in aggregate supply. Aggregate demand might increase because of an expansion of consumption demand, investment, or the demand for money. Aggregate supply might decrease because of monopolization of an important sector or an increase in money wages.

Many explanations of the recent inflation have been offered, and they can be analyzed in terms of the money demand and money supply framework. The monetary explanation of inflation cites the rapid increase in the world money supply in 1971 and 1972 as the cause of the 1973–1974 acceleration of inflation. The monetary explanation of the 1979–1980 increase in inflation is the increase in world monetary growth in 1977 and 1978.

Table 22-6 shows world inflation and world money supply growth. The inflation figures refer to wholesale prices, and both the inflation and money supply figures refer to the Group of Ten industrial countries. Inflation accelerated from 4.1 percent in 1972 to 12.9 percent in 1973 and 21.9 percent in 1974. The inflation rate subsided in the next four years, but it accelerated to 11.1 percent in 1979 and 13.5 percent in 1980. It is generally assumed that money affects prices with a lag, and this point is evident from comparing the inflation and money columns.

Money growth accelerated in 1971 (from 8.2 percent to 11.8 percent) and 1972 (12.7 percent), and the stimulus to aggregate demand increased inflation in 1973 and 1974. After subsiding for the next four years, money growth ac-

TABLE 22-6   World Inflation, Money, and Reserves, 1960–1980

YEAR	WORLD PRICE INFLATION* (PERCENT)	WORLD MONEY SUPPLY INCREASE† (PERCENT)	DOLLAR LIABILITIES OF THE UNITED STATES (BILLION DOLLARS)
1960	0.6%	7.0%	
1961	0.5	8.2	
1962	0.7	6.2	
1963	0.8	9.4	$ 11.9
1964	1.1	6.6	12.6
1965	1.5	7.9	12.1
1966	2.9	4.7	10.6
1967	0.3	8.4	13.1
1968	1.5	8.3	12.2
1969	4.0	5.0	11.3
1970	4.4	8.2	19.7
1971	3.1	11.8	47.9
1972	4.1	12.7	54.9
1973	12.9	7.6	59.8
1974	21.9	6.5	59.3
1975	7.5	9.2	59.5
1976	6.6	7.4	63.2
1977	6.6	10.3	93.2
1978	5.6	11.0	124.5
1979	11.1	7.6	103.9
1980	13.5	4.9	104.7

*Group of Ten countries.

†Wholesale prices for Group of Ten.

Source: Ronald I. McKinnon, "Currency Substitution and Instability in the World Dollar Market," *American Economic Review,* June 1982.

celerated in 1977 (from 7.4 percent to 10.3 percent) and 1978 (11.0 percent). According to the monetary explanation, this money supply expansion was responsible for the inflation of 1979 and 1980. The source of money supply expansion was an increase in dollar reserves of central banks, which will be discussed in Section 22.4.

All the nonmonetary theories require a mechanism for either reducing the demand for money or bringing about money supply accommodation of real disturbances. If the central bank passively increases the money supply in response to real shock, it is very difficult to make an empirical distinction between monetary and nonmonetary theories. For example, if the Federal Reserve increased the U.S. money supply every time there was an increase in the world price of oil, it would be difficult to distinguish between a monetary and a petroleum theory of inflation. Analytically, one would like to disentangle the separate effects of money and oil on the price level. In fact, the world has not provided analysts with well-controlled experiments that would permit discriminating between the two hypotheses. The behavior of world oil prices in the 1970s is shown here (repeated from Table 10-5):

Year	Money Price per Barrel	Year	Money Price per Barrel
1972	$ 2.57	1977	$13.29
1973	3.33	1978	13.29
1974	11.01	1979	18.67
1975	11.45	1980	30.46
1976	12.14	1981	34.02
		1982	31.26

The sharp increases in inflation of 1973 and 1974 occurred at the same time as did sharp increases in oil prices from $2.57 per barrel to $3.33 per barrel in 1973 and $11.01 in 1974. The second acceleration of inflation in 1979 and 1980 also coincided with sharp increases in oil prices from $13.29 per barrel in 1978 to $18.67 per barrel in 1979 and $30.46 per barrel in 1980. Oil prices and other supply shocks have been widely cited as a source of world inflation in the 1970s. Grain prices, which reached their peak in 1974, have also been cited as contributor to inflation.

A comprehensive index of primary commodity prices (including petroleum and grain), which is shown in Table 22-7, exhibits sharp increases in 1973 and 1974 and again in 1979 and 1980. Commodity price increases in 1973 and 1974 contrast sharply to prices in the previous 16 years, when they hardly moved. The high commodity prices of 1979 and 1980 contrast the lower prices in the earlier years (1975 to 1978) and subsequent years (1981 and 1982). Since primary products are factors of production, an increase in their prices has been interpreted as a source of cost-push inflation.[2] The observed correlation be-

[2] The book by Barry Bosworth and Robert Z. Lawrence, *Commodity Prices and the New Inflation* (Washington, D.C.: The Brookings Institution, 1982), emphasizes commodity prices as a source of inflation.

TABLE 22-7   **International Monetary Fund Commodity
Price Index, 1957–1982 (1975 = 100)**

YEAR	INDEX	YEAR	INDEX
1957	57.3	1970	57.8
1958	52.5	1971	55.0
1959	51.8	1972	62.3
1960	51.7	1973	95.5
1961	49.6	1974	122.2
1962	48.8	1975	100.0
1963	51.7	1976	113.2
1964	55.0	1977	136.6
1965	53.9	1978	130.3
1966	55.7	1979	151.7
1967	52.4	1980	166.4
1968	52.0	1981	142.0
1969	55.8	1982	125.8

Source: International Monetary Fund, *International Financial
Statistics Yearbook,* 1983. Washington, D.C., p. 93.

tween commodity prices and inflation does not imply causation. Inflation may
cause commodity prices, commodity prices may cause inflation, or they both
may be caused by other factors such as monetary expansion.

Another possible explanation for recent inflation is expansionary fiscal
policy. An increase in government spending relative to taxation will increase
aggregate demand. Interest rates will rise, reducing money demand and plac-
ing upward pressure on the price level.

Table 22-8 shows the budgetary deficits of the Group of Ten countries
expressed as a percentage of GNP. Budget deficits are not an entirely satisfactory measure of fiscal expansion, because tax revenue depends on the business
cycle. Thus, a recession could induce a budget deficit and give the mistaken
appearance of expansionary fiscal policy.

However, the 10-year time period is long enough to exceed a business
cycle, and the figures do represent a general pattern. In 1973, 4 of the first 17
countries had budget surpluses or a deficit of less than 1 percent of GNP. By
1975 all the surpluses were gone, and every country in the first 7 had a deficit
equal to at least 2 percent of GNP. The persistence of the deficits indicates
that they were not merely induced by the recessionary phase of a business cycle. By 1977, all 10 countries had budget deficits, and for the last five years
every country in the Group of Ten had a budget deficit equal to at least 2 percent of GNP. The general pattern is one of persistent fiscal expansion following 1973 and 1974. Variation in the deficits and their timing do not seem sufficient to explain the acceleration of inflation in 1973 and 1974 and 1979 and
1980. Perhaps the data indicate the effect of the absence of a fixed exchange
rate on fiscal policy. The deficits do represent a substantial increase in the stock

TABLE 22-8 Selected Industrial Countries: Central Government Financial Balances (percentage of gross national product)

	1972	1973	1974	1975	1976	1977	1978	1979	1980	1981
Canada	-0.5%	0.3%	0.7%	-2.3%	-1.8%	-3.5%	-4.6%	-3.5%	-3.7%	-2.1%
United States	-1.5	-0.4	-0.7	-4.9	-3.4	-2.6	-2.0	-1.2	-2.6	-2.7
Japan	-4.7	-5.3	-5.8	-8.9	-8.4	-7.3	-9.3	-9.0	-8.5	-7.8
France	0.4	0.6	0.3	-3.0	-1.1	-1.1	-1.5	-1.2	-1.3	-2.7
West Germany	-0.2	-0.5	-0.7	-3.6	-2.8	-2.2	-2.1	-1.9	-1.8	-2.6
Italy	-7.4	-8.3	-7.5	-10.7	-9.1	-9.0	-15.0	-11.2	-12.0	-12.8
United Kingdom	-2.5	-3.1	-4.2	-8.0	-5.5	-3.1	-5.1	-5.5	-5.0	-4.1
Weighted average of above 7 countries	-2.0	-1.5	-1.9	-5.6	-4.2	-3.6	-4.1	-3.4	-4.0	-4.1
Belgium	-3.7	-2.9	-2.8	-4.7	-5.0	-5.9	-6.0	-6.5	-8.6	-12.2
Ireland	-5.6	-6.9	-6.5	-16.3	-11.2	-10.2	-12.7	-14.1	-14.6	-16.9
Sweden	1.6	1.8	0.2	0.1	2.1	-0.8	-4.2	-6.2	-6.8	-8.0

Source: International Monetary Fund, *Survey,* March 22, 1982.

of government bonds, which should increase interest rates and reduce money demand. The persistent fiscal deficits may have encouraged central banks to buy more government bonds with newly created money. Thus, fiscal policy may have been partly responsible for the expansionary monetary policy that has been observed.

Some observers have attributed inflation to the floating exchange rate system. It has been said that the system places more pressure on deficit countries to depreciate than it places on surplus countries to appreciate. The depreciation bias is alleged to create inflationary pressure by increasing prices of importable and exportable goods. The increase in the prices of traded goods are said to create a kind of cost-push inflation. The idea that currency depreciation causes inflation was discussed in Section 18.7 in connection with the "vicious circle."

A shortcoming of the depreciation cost-push explanation is that it explains why a particular set of prices rises, but it fails to explain why other prices fail to fall. An increase in the prices of traded goods combined with a decrease in prices of nontraded goods is consistent with a stable price level. If the money supply is constant, relative prices should adjust without a change in the average price level. An extreme or strong version of the depreciation cost-push theory would imply the occurrence of inflation even if the money supply were constant. This explanation would require a mechanism that would reduce the demand for money. A weak version of the cost-push theory assumes that central banks accommodate any cost increase caused by depreciation. For a floating rate regime to produce an inflationary bias, central banks must be more willing to accommodate cost increases than they would be under fixed rates. In the presence of monetary accommodation, once cannot distinguish between currency depreciation and monetary expansion as the cause of inflation. Perhaps one reason for inflation's varying across countries is that central banks respond differently to the same external shocks.

22.4 INTERNATIONAL TRANSMISSION OF INFLATION

The previous section discussed the determinants of the average world inflation rate. In fact inflation varies from one country to another. This section will consider the factors that determine the dispersion of national inflation rates and the international transmission of inflation. The simplest transmission mechanism is the price-specie flow mechanism under the gold standard. Surplus countries acquire gold. Monetary expansion causes inflation, which tends to reverse the process. Deficit countries lose gold, and the price level declines. This mechanism was discussed in Chapter 20. One can think of an automatically adjusting *LM* curve shifting leftward along *IS* when there is a balance-of-payments deficit and shifting rightward when there is a surplus. A characteristic feature of a gold standard is that inflation or deflation is transmitted between countries by gold flows. An implication of this mechanism is that all national inflation rates tend to converge to the same rate.

Gold does not ensure price stability for the world, but it does bring about uniform price-level behavior for all countries. If a major gold discovery occurs in one country, inflation will occur in that country, and it will be imported by all other gold standard countries. The same transmission mechanism applies to all other fixed exchange rate sytems. Inflation is automatically transmitted from California to New York and other states by money flows. Inflation in all states tends to converge to a single rate. Inflation is transmitted in the same way to Puerto Rico and all countries that maintain fixed exchange rates with the dollar. As mentioned, Panama, which has retained a fixed exchange rate with the U.S. dollar since 1904, has had an inflationary experience almost identical to that of the United States. Mexico had a similar inflation rate for the nearly 20 years that the peso was pegged to the dollar.

The inflation transmission mechanism under the adjustable peg had some similarities to the gold standard, but it had differences as well. The set of countries that retained fixed exchange rates over long time periods had similar inflation rates. The set of countries that changed par values frequently had divergent inflation rates. Inspection of the divergent inflation rates of Latin American countries in Table 22-1 permits one to infer that currencies of the high-inflation countries depreciated frequently. Another difference is that sterilization was practiced more frequently under the adjustable peg system. Sterilized intervention permits a central bank to break the link between reserve changes and money supply changes. Because reserve stocks are limited, sterilization is only a temporary remedy.

Bretton Woods was a discretionary system that required a choice about whether to devalue when there was an excess demand for foreign exchange. If devaluation was ruled out, monetary contraction of the gold standard variety would eventually solve the balance-of-payments problem. For those countries choosing gold standard adjustment, national inflation rates should converge to a common rate. Other countries sought some monetary independence without altering the exchange rate. They attempted to employ sterilized foreign exchange market intervention. Sterilization was easier to implement in the immediate postwar years when capital controls were still pervasive. Eventually, capital controls weakened, and national credit markets became increasingly integrated.[3] As a result, sterilized intervention became less effective.

A simple empirical test of whether a country operates an independent monetary policy is to investigate the statistical relationship among the money

---

[3] Walter Salant has shown that the interest rate differential between the Group of Ten countries declined between the 1950s and 1970s. See Salant, "International Transmission of Inflation," in *Worldwide Inflation: Theory and Recent Experience*, Lawrence Krause and Walter Salant, eds. (Washington, D.C.: The Brookings Institution, 1977), p. 178.

supply (M), the domestic assets of the central bank (D), and foreign reserves (R). In the extreme case of complete monetary independence, M depends solely on D. Any potential effects of R on M are completely sterilized. At the opposite extreme is complete monetary dependence. M depends solely on R, as under the gold standard. A 1-unit change in monetary reserves induces a unit change in the money supply. Successful sterilization and monetary independence would permit a country's inflation rate to diverge from that of other countries. Conversely, monetary dependence would bring about convergence of national inflation rates. Evidence from the end of the Bretton Woods period indicated that only exchange rate adjustment permitted monetary independence.[4] For example, chronic deficit countries cannot implement rapid monetary expansion without devaluing their currencies.

With freely floating exchange rates, the money supply link between countries is broken. With fixed exchange rates, inflation-prone countries lose reserves and money, which tends to mitigate the inflation. With floating rates the currencies of more inflationary countries depreciate, without any effect on the money supply. Under a system of freely floating exchange rates, countries could have more monetary independence. National money supplies and inflation rates would be expected to show greater divergence than under fixed rates.

An hypothesis is that the period since 1973 would have exhibited more divergence of inflation rates than did the earlier Bretton Woods period. This hypothesis was discussed in Section 18.8, and the results are somewhat mixed. One reason is that Bretton Woods did not have strictly fixed exchange rates and the system since 1973 has not been a free float. In the earlier period, high-inflation countries such as Brazil and Argentina acquired monetary independence by devaluing frequently. The breakdown of Bretton Woods has not affected their behavior. Also the managed feature of the current system means that part of the link between money supplies and inflation rates remains intact. For example, there is a group of 40 currencies that remain formally linked to the dollar and have similar inflation rates.[5] Perhaps the true change in exchange rate arrangements has been smaller than it appeared. The link between national money supplies may be weaker than it was, but it has not been eliminated.

In addition to the money supply link, inflation can be transmitted through changes in the demand for money. Money demand depends on interest rates, which are linked by international mobility of capital. Currency substitution is another way in which inflation can be transmitted without changing the domestic money supply. Because of currency substitution, McKinnon has argued

---

[4]Project LINK has attempted to analyze the transmission mechanism by combining national econometric models of 31 countries. Some results are summarized in Walter S. Salant's paper "International Transmission of Inflation."

[5]Currency blocs are listed on the page entitled "Exchange Arrangements" in *International Financial Statistics*. In some cases there is a de facto link between currencies even when the arrangement is not formally acknowledged.

that U.S. inflation is better explained by the behavior of the Group of Ten money supply than by the U.S. money supply alone. An empirical study by Bordo and Choudhri has shown that floating exchange rates have not prevented the U.S. money supply from influencing Canadian inflation.[6]

Inflation may also be transmitted in other ways under floating exchange rates. Changes in the demand for goods (consumption, investment, or fiscal policy) in one country will alter the demand for the exports of partner countries. These real disturbances can alter interest rates, money demand, and inflation. However, it was shown in Chapter 21 (see Figure 21-10) that floating rates combined with capital mobility tend to mitigate these disturbances. In the case of perfect capital mobility (see Figure 21-11), shocks originating in the goods market are completely offset by floating. In general, if policymakers in one country base their monetary policy on conditions in another country, the inflation rates in the two countries will be linked. Fixing the exchange rate is one way of establishing the link.

Monetary policy coordination that produces similar growth rates in money will produce the same result. Several international institutions, such as OECD, the Group of Ten, the European monetary system, and the economic summits, are explicitly designed to coordinate policy. Basing the domestic money supply on the foreign interest rate will also transmit inflation between countries.

22.5 WORLD RESERVES AND WORLD MONEY

It was shown in Section 22.4 that the world money supply depends on the sum of domestic assets of central banks and monetary reserves. Since world reserves are a source of money growth, they are a potential source of world inflation. This section will consider the determinants of the supply and demand for reserves by central banks. The supply of world reserves can be expressed as the sum of three components: foreign exchange (R_F), gold (R_G), and IMF money (R_S):

$$R = R_F + R_G + R_S$$

The stock must be expressed in some common unit, and it is conventional to use the dollar as unit of account. Thus, R is the dollar value of world reserves. The value of each component depends on both price and quantity, and the prices are market determined:

$$R = \Pi_F F + \Pi_G G + \Pi_S S$$

[6] See Michael D. Bordo and Ehsan Choudhri, "The Link Between Money and Prices in an Open Economy: The Canadian Evidence from 1971 to 1980," *Review*, Federal Reserve Bank of St. Louis, August–September 1982.

F, G, and S are the quantities of foreign exchange, gold, and IMF money, whereas Π_F, Π_G, and Π_S are their respective dollar prices. Under the gold standard the money price of gold (Π_G) is fixed, and the relative price of gold varies inversely with the money price level. The supply of new gold and the demand for nonmonetary gold is determined by the relative price of gold. Governments are obliged to buy and monetize all gold brought to them. However, gold has no official status in the current monetary system. Its money price is market determined in the same way as prices of other minerals are. Therefore its relative price is not inversely related to the general price level.

In recent years an increase in inflationary expectations appears to induce an increase in the private market price of gold. Central banks inherited a stock of monetary gold, but they have not added to the stock in recent years.

Table 22-9 shows the behavior of the world's monetary gold stock from 1951 to 1983. The quantity grew slowly in the early period, reaching a peak of 1,194 million ounces in 1965. It declined continuously since then to a total of 938 in 1980. The market price was constant at $35 an ounce until 1968. The price has trended upward since then, but it has been quite volatile. In a two-

TABLE 22-9   Official World Gold Reserves, 1951–1983

YEAR	AMOUNT (MILLION OUNCES)	PRICE (PER OUNCE)	YEAR	AMOUNT (MILLION OUNCES)	PRICE (PER OUNCE)
1951	958	$35	1971	1,027	$ 41
1952	958	35	1972	1,018	58
1953	969	35	1973	1,020	97
1954	987	35	1974	1,019	159
1955	1,000	35	1975	1,018	161
1956	1,024	35	1976	1,013	125
1957	1,059	35	1977	1,015	148
1958	1,080	35	1978	1,022	193
1959	1,079	35	1979	930	307
1960	1,083	35	1980	938	608
1961	1,107	35	1981	952	398
1962	1,119	35	1982	947	457
1963	1,149	35	1983 (May)	947	416
1964	1,163	35			
1965	1,194	35			
1966	1,166	35			
1967	1,126	35			
1968	1,107	39			
1969	1,113	41			
1970	1,058	36			

Source: International Monetary Fund, *International Financial Statistics Yearbook*, June 1983, pp. 40–42.

year period between 1980 and 1982, the gold price fluctuated between $300 and $900 per ounce.

Agencies reporting the value of reserves are not in total agreement about how to value gold. Some agencies continue to use $35 or SDR 35, although the trend is toward using the current market price. Since the market price represents the amount of goods or currencies that holders can acquire with their gold, it ought to be the relevant value to holders. If a central bank's gold reserves double in value, it should make no difference to the bank whether the price doubles for a given number of ounces or the quantity doubles at a given price. Gold being valued at market price has led to a substantial increase in world monetary gold reserves since 1971.

The surges in the value of gold reserves roughly corresponds to the two incidents of acceleration in inflation. In 1973 gold reserves increased from $59.0 billion to $98.9 billion. The increase in one year was almost as large as the entire monetary gold stock in 1971. A larger increase to $162.0 billion followed in 1974. The value of monetary gold surged again in 1978 (from $150.2 billion to $197.2 billion), 1979 ($285.5 billion), and 1980 ($570.3 billion). These huge capital gains for central banks provided the opportunity for much more expansionary monetary policy. In 1981 the price of gold fell sharply, and by the middle of 1982, it had fallen to around $300, the level of 1979. The gold price recovered to $500 per ounce by January 1983. In summary, gold has been a major source of growth in world reserves since 1971. The rate of growth has been extremely volatile, and its growth is not directly under the control of any individual country or agency.

Since gold is held by central banks, it is a possible source of monetary expansion. Its price behavior has been similar to that of other commodities (see Table 22-7), but it retains some de facto monetary importance because it is the only commodity widely owned by central banks. If central banks determine money supplies on the basis of the money value of gold reserves, the current world monetary system contains a basic flaw that did not exist under the gold standard or Bretton Woods. An increase in the value of gold increases the money supply, which causes inflation. Inflation increases all prices, including gold, which induces another monetary expansion. A system in which the money supply is an increasing function of the money value of gold reserves is dynamically unstable. For the world monetary system to be stable, at least one nominal magnitude (e.g., M^s or Π) must be fixed. This same problem of dynamic instability is well known in connection with the "real bills" doctrine.

IMF money consists of special drawing rights plus reserve positions in the Fund. The administration of the fund does not have discretionary authority to vary the quantity of SDRs. The IMF is not a world central bank, although some reformers think it ought to be. Member countries must be consulted every time there is a new allocation of SDRs. Since the creation of additional SDRs requires approval by 85 percent of the member votes, the United

States retains veto power over new allocations. Only two new allocations have been made, and in each case the distribution was spread out over three years. SDR 10 billion was created from 1970 to 1972, and SDR 11.4 billion was created from 1979 to 1981. The SDR 21.4 increase was small relative to the increase in the value of gold and dollars.

However, the timing of the SDR creation was particularly unfortunate. The 1970–1972 allocation preceded the inflation of 1973 and 1974, and the allocation of 1979 to 1981 coincided with the acceleration of inflation in 1979 to 1981. It appears that the Fund contributed to both inflationary surges. The timing was ironic because Fund officials have complained that total world reserve growth is chaotic precisely because it is not under the control of any single agency. The IMF sought to gain exclusive control of reserve growth by (1) demonetizing gold and (2) proposing the dollar substitution account.

One cannot blame the Fund for recent growth in gold and dollars, but the institution has complete control over SDRs. In retrospect, it is difficult to find a worse time to add to world reserves than 1970 to 1972 and 1979 to 1981. It may be unduly harsh to evaluate the Fund's monetary judgment on the basis of two observations, but those skeptics who were reluctant to delegate more authority to the IMF have had their skepticism reinforced.

A fundamental problem related to the optimum quantity of SDRs is that there is disagreement about the purpose of SDRs. Some members advocate using SDRs as a means of aiding low-income countries rather than as a device for promoting price-level stability. If aid were accepted as the primary purpose of SDRs, a new allocation might be justified even if it resulted in more inflation. High-income countries with veto power have not yet accepted this position.

Section 22.3 considered the monetary explanation of the recent world inflation. The world money supply expanded rapidly and price inflation followed. Data on prices and money supply appears in Table 22-6. The surge in the world money supply can be attributed to the growth of world monetary reserves, particularly the foreign exchange component. Since the vast majority of foreign exchange reserves are dollars (some countries do not report the currency denomination of reserves), examination of the change in dollar liabilities of the United States to foreign governments gives some indication of the growth in foreign exchange reserves.

The major surge of dollar reserves in 1971 from $19.7 billion to $47.9 billion brought about inconvertibility of the dollar and the end of the Bretton Woods system. The next sharp increase in dollar reserves occurred in 1977 (from $63.2 billion to $93.2 billion) and 1978 ($124.5 billion). This reserve growth induced monetary expansion and inflation. Dollar liabilities of the United States shown in Table 22-6 are not identical with total dollar reserves in the world. Because of the Eurodollar market, some dollar reserves of central banks are not dollar liabilities of the United States. Those Eurodollar reserves are not

**TABLE 22-10   Foreign Exchange Reserves, 1951–1983
(in billions of SDRs)**

YEAR	FOREIGN EXCHANGE	YEAR	FOREIGN EXCHANGE
1951	13.5	1970	45.4
1952	14.0	1971	75.0
1953	15.4	1972	96.0
1954	16.5	1973	101.7
1955	16.7	1974	126.5
1956	17.8	1975	137.4
1957	17.1	1976	160.3
1958	17.1	1977	200.3
1959	16.1	1978	221.2
1960	18.5	1979	246.2
1961	19.1	1980	293.0
1962	19.9	1981	304.7
1963	22.7	1982	294.6
1964	24.2	1983 (May)	296.0
1965	24.0		
1966	25.7		
1967	29.4		
1968	32.6		
1969	33.0		

Source: International Monetary Fund, *International Financial Statistics Yearbook,
1981* and *International Financial Statistics,* June 1983.

reported directly, but the IMF publishes a series on total foreign exchange reserves, which includes dollar reserves at banks inside and outside the United States, as well as reserves denominated in other countries.

Those figures on total foreign exchange reserves appear in Table 22-10 denominated in SDRs. The figures confirm the impression gained from the data on dollar liabilities of the United States. Foreign exchange reserves surged by nearly $30 billion in 1971. The time series on foreign exchange reserves shows faster growth after 1971 than did the series on dollar liabilities of the United States. However, it also shows a sharp increase in 1977 (SDR 40 billion) and 1978 (SDR 21 billion). Both pieces of information are consistent with the monetary explanation of inflation.[7]

Total world reserves are the sum of three components: gold, IMF money, and foreign exchange. Their growth from 1970 to 1981 is shown in Table 22-11. It can be seen that the general pattern of growth was similar for all com-

---

[7]There is a curious divergence of the two series in 1980. The dollar liabilities series shows almost no increase, whereas the foreign exchange series shows an increase of more than SDR 40 billion.

TABLE 22-11 Total World Reserves, 1970–1981
(in billions of SDRs)

YEAR	IMF MONEY* (1)	FOREIGN EXCHANGE (2)	(3) = (1) + (2)	GOLD (MILLIONS OF OUNCES) (4)	VALUE AT MARKET PRICE (5)	TOTAL RESERVES (6) = (1) + (2) + (5)
1970	11	45	56	1,057	38	94
1971	12	75	87	1,026	42	129
1972	15	96	111	1,017	59	170
1973	15	102	117	1,018	95	212
1974	17	127	144	1,018	162	306
1975	21	137	158	1,018	122	280
1976	26	160	186	1,013	118	304
1977	26	200	226	1,015	138	364
1978	23	221	244	1,022	177	421
1979	24	246	270	930	362	632
1980	29	293	322	938	434	756
1981 (May)	34	310	344	939	385	729

*SDRs plus reserve positions in Fund.

Source: International Monetary Fund, *Annual Report, 1981*, p. 65.

ponents. Thus, growth in each reserve component reinforced the behavior of the others. The result was rapid growth of world reserves in 1971 and 1972 and again in 1977 and 1978. The resulting excess supply of reserves encouraged central banks to engage in expansionary monetary policy. Thus, inflationary episodes of 1973 and 1974 and 1979 and 1980 can be explained by the behavior of world reserves and world money.[8] The facts are consistent with this explanation, but they are also consistent with competing explanations. It is interesting to note that the initial surge of world reserves occurred while fixed exchange rates still prevailed. The second surge of reserves occurred under floating rates. Perhaps the world monetary system has changed less than formal appearances would indicate. In particular, the sustained growth of dollar reserves has surprised many observers.

22.6 DEMAND FOR MONETARY RESERVES

There is a predictable relationship between the money supply and the price level only if there is a stable demand function for money. In that case, an increase in the nominal supply of money will create an excess supply of real cash balances at the initial price level, which will be eliminated by an increase in the price level. The demand for monetary reserves by central banks is important for a similar reason. If central banks demand a certain level of real reserves, an increase in the nominal supply of reserves will bring about an excess reserve by expansionary monetary policy and a balance-of-payments deficit. However, the whole world cannot have a deficit, and the excess world supply of reserves is eliminated by price inflation.

The argument of the previous section that attributed an increase in the world money supply to growth in world reserves implicitly assumes a stable demand function for monetary reserves. What are the determinants of central bank reserve holdings?

A main function of a stock of monetary reserves is to permit the central bank to support some exchange rate. The desired exchange rate might be the par value of the Bretton Woods system, or it might be some temporary target under a managed float. Based on the function of intervening in the foreign exchange market, the demand for reserves is analogous to the transactions demand for money. Demand should depend on the opportunity cost of holding reserves, national income, the openness of the economy, and the variability of foreign trade. Opportunity cost is the difference between interest earned in the best alternative use and interest earned on reserve holdings.

[8] For more details, see the two papers by H. Robert Heller. "The International Monetary System and Worldwide Inflation," *Columbia Journal of World Business*, Fall 1976, and "International Reserves and Worldwide Inflation," International Monetary Fund *Staff Papers*, March 1976. McKinnon offers a similar explanation, emphasizing currency substitution. See "Currency Substitution and Instability in the World Dollar Market," *American Economic Preview*, June 1982.

The cost of reserve holding depends on the form in which reserves are held. Gold reserves pay no interest and certain transactions balances held as demand deposits are noninterest bearing. However, the vast majority of reserves have been held as interest-bearing dollars. Interest income has been one of the main reasons dollars replaced gold as a monetary reserve.

Because of the key currency or reserve role of the dollar, the question has been raised as to whether Americans received an interest-free loan from foreign central banks. Since most dollar reserves pay interest, the question of an interest-free loan can be easily dismissed. However, American banks and the Treasury would receive an income transfer or seigniorage if dollar reserves paid less than a competitive interest rate. Most dollar reserves are held in the form of Treasury bills or large certificates of deposit at commercial banks. Some of the deposits are at banks in the United States, and some are at Eurodollar banks outside the country. When the Treasury auctions bills, it must compete with domestic and foreign firms as well as foreign governments in the U.S. credit market. If the Treasury does not pay a competitive rate of interest, loanable funds will not be forthcoming. Is it possible for U.S. commercial banks to keep deposit interest rates artificially low?

The government has imposed a maximum deposit interest rate, called Regulation Q, on commercial banks since 1933. However, it was discovered in the early 1960s that when the Regulation Q ceiling was binding, foreign central banks moved their funds out of the country to the newly emerging Eurodollar market. Consequently, the deposit interest ceilings were removed for dollars held in the United States by foreign central banks. Foreign governments continue to have the option of holding deposits in the extremely competitive Eurodollar market, which has no interest ceiling and no legal reserve requirement. Some reserves are held in the form of SDRs, which paid less than competitive interest in the early years of their existence. Since 1981 when SDRs were defined as a basket containing five major currencies, they have paid interest rates closer to market rates. Thus, the demand for monetary reserves is inversely related to the opportunity cost of holding reserves, which depends partly on the form in which reserves are held.

Figure 22-1 shows the real demand for reserves as a function of forgone interest on reserves $i - i_R$. The demand curve is drawn for given values of other demand variables: income, openness, and trade variability. The initial supply of reserves (R^s) and price level (P_1) determine the position of the real supply curve. Equilibrium is established at point A, where the real demand for reserves equals the real supply. Let there be an increase in nominal reserves to R_2. At the initial price level and interest rates, there is an excess supply of reserves AB. Central banks will eliminate the excess supply by creating money, which will increase the world price level. Prices will rise until the initial level of real reserves is restored. In the diagram the increase in the price level will shift the curve R_2^s/P_1 to the left until it passes through point A. Alternatively, an excess demand for real reserves would create deflationary pressure. Robert

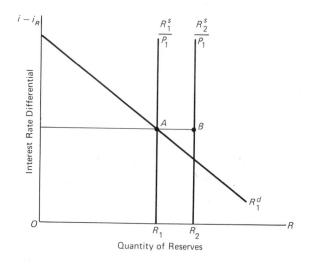

FIGURE 22-1   Demand for Monetary Reserves

Triffin and others feared that deflation would take the form of unemployment and lower real income rather than lower prices.

The other determinants of reserve demand are constant along each curve, and a change in each one of them is represented by a shift of R^d. National income (y) represents the scale of the economy, and the assumption is that reserve demand increases with income. Openness (O) is measured by imports relative to income. It is assumed that openness makes an economy more vulnerable to foreign disturbances, so that reserve demand is greater for a more open economy. Finally, greater variability (σ) of foreign trade is assumed to increase reserve demand.[9] Monetary reserves are a kind of buffer stock, and greater variability represents more frequent shocks to the foreign exchange market. Empirical studies have verified that central bank reserve demand has varied systematically as a function of these explanatory variables. Stable reserve demand equations have been estimated for both the fixed exchange rate period and the managed floating period. A shift in demand has been detected in 1972 and 1973, but not as large as might be expected as a result of a change from fixed exchange rates to floating rates. Frenkel concluded that "This finding led to the observation that economic behavior seems to be more stable than economic institutions."[10]

[9] Reserve demand can be summarized by the following equation:
$$R^d = i^\alpha y^\beta O^\gamma \sigma^\delta$$

Equations of this form have been estimated, and the superscripts represent the elasticities of demand with respect to each explanatory variable.

[10] Jacob Frenkel, "International Reserves: Pegged Exchange Rates and Managed Float," in *Carnegie-Rochester Conference Series on Public Policy*, supplement to *Journal of Monetary Economics*, Karl Brunner and Allen Meltzer, eds., Vol. 9 (1978).

Since the pattern of reserve demand under a managed float remains similar to the demand under pegged rates, the issue of optimal reserve supply remains as relevant under the new monetary regime as it did under the old system. Total reserve holdings of all forms continue to grow in spite of the increased flexibility of exchange rates. Perhaps foreign exchange market intervention is not the only motive for central bank reserve holding. For example, the increase in Saudi Arabia's dollar holdings may be explained by the desire to earn income from a diversified portfolio. Some reserve holdings may be explained by the same forces that explain private investments.

22.7 MONETARY POLICY AND DOMESTIC GOALS

The previous discussion emphasized the effect of monetary reserves on the world money supply and world prices. The world inflation of 1973 and 1974 can be explained by rapid growth of world monetary reserves in 1971 and 1972 that stimulated expansionary monetary policy. This explanation is consistent with traditional thinking about the transmission of inflation under fixed exchange rates. The European price revolution of the sixteenth century has been explained by growth in world monetary reserves.

Explaining the 1979–1980 inflation by the growth of monetary reserves is more perplexing because it occurred under a system of ostensibly floating exchange rates. Floating is supposed to permit greater monetary independence, which would make monetary reserves less important relative to the domestic component of money supplies. Indeed the traditional Viner-Robbins concern about the inflationary bias of floating rates is based on the dominance of the domestic component of the money supply over the foreign component.

It was assumed, that in absence of a fixed exchange rate, governments would use monetary policy for short-run political gains or as a convenient form of taxation. In terms of the money supply equation, $M = m(D + R)$, the hypothesis of Viner and Robbins is that, under floating exchange rates, changes in M will be dominated by changes in D. Monetary reserves should not be an important determinant of M. Monetary independence refers to the independence of M from R, and this relationship is supposed to be the source of the inflationary bias of floating exchange rates.

The paradox of the recent experience is that inflation and floating exchange rates have coincided apparently without monetary independence. Perhaps the current managed float and the Bretton Woods system are more similar than they appear. The adjustable peg of Bretton Woods permitted countries to have monetary independence in the long run provided that they were willing to adjust their exchange rates. In fact, such countries as Argentina, Brazil, and Chile had their monetary independence by employing frequent devaluation. The move to an international managed float may have had little impact on those countries that had already asserted their monetary independence under Bretton Woods.

The fact that the current system is not a free float means that it has retained some of the features of Bretton Woods. Central banks continue to hold reserves, and the rate of reserve growth affects monetary policy. Foreign exchange market intervention has been nearly as frequent for some countries as it was under Bretton Woods. However, the countries that have chosen active intervention are not those countries that chose monetary independence under Bretton Woods. They are largely the Group of Ten countries and others that have traditional monetary ties with them. The EEC countries have attempted to operate a joint float. Other European countries have informally followed the German mark. The Scandinavian currencies tend to stay in line with each other. There is a French franc bloc consisting mainly of former colonies. There is a dollar bloc of 40 countries whose currencies are officially tied to the dollar and a larger number that are formally pegged to the dollar. Another group of currencies is pegged to the SDR, which amounts to a partial peg to the dollar. These pegging arrangements imply sacrificing monetary independence. It may be more than coincidence that they have been chosen by the same set of countries that relinquished monetary independence under Bretton Woods.

22.8 EURODOLLARS AND WORLD MONEY

A monetary theory explains inflation in terms of changes in the money supply. Choosing the appropriate empirical measure of money is a persistent problem. In a closed economy, one must decide whether to include coins, paper currency, demand deposits, time deposits, and other liquid assets. The appropriate measure may also change in response to financial innovation. Central bankers have had to learn how to deal with negotiable certificates of deposit, repurchase agreements, and money market mutual funds. In an open economy, the problem is compounded by the existence of foreign currencies that substitute for domestic money. Because of currency substitution, it is possible that some aggregate including both domestic and foreign money is a better predictor of domestic inflation than is the domestic money supply by itself.

The problem of explaining the world inflation rate also requires a choice of the appropriate world money supply. The simplest approach is to add up all national money supplies, using market exchange rates to translate them into a common currency. The problem with this approach is that it omits Eurodollars and other external currencies. The problem is analogous to omitting traveler's checks or credit cards from the domestic money supply. The effect of the omission is to reduce the demand for the narrowly defined money.

Eurodollars are dollar-denominated deposits at banks outside the United States. Most of them do not appear in the money supply of the United States or the country in which the issuing bank is located. Thus, when the world money supply is obtained by adding the national money supplies of all countries, Eurodollars are excluded. Also excluded are the much smaller quantities of Europounds, Euromarks, and other external currencies. Although Eurodollars are time deposits, many have very short maturities, including overnight Eurodollars, which make them a good substitute for dollar deposits at U.S. banks. Since 1981 some Eurodollar deposits have been included in certain measures of the U.S. money supply.[11] Overnight Eurodollar deposits held by American nonbank residents at Caribbean branches of U.S. banks are included in the M-2 measure of the U.S. money supply. Term Eurodollars held by U.S. nonbank residents are included in a broader measure of the money supply, which the Federal Reserve has designated as L. However, Eurodollars held by foreigners are not included in any monetary aggregate.

If the Eurodollar market were small or stagnant, it might be harmless to ignore it. However, it is a large market, and the supply of Eurodollars is growing faster than is the U.S. money supply. Table 14-1 presents some figures on Eurodollars and the U.S. money supply. The U.S. figures are for M-1, the narrow definition of money, and broader definitions would result in a larger total. Let us consider the determinants of the Eurodollar supply.

The determinants of the Eurodollar supply can be expressed in the same way as the determinants of the domestic money supply in a simple fractional reserve banking system.[12] The domestic money supply can be written as a multiple of the monetary base, where the value of the multiplier (m) depends on the public's currency-deposit ratio (k) and the reserve-deposit ratio (r) of commercial banks:

$$M = mM_b = (\frac{1+k}{r+k})M_b$$

Similarly, the Eurodollar supply depends on the dollar base of the system $(R_\$)$, the public's Eurodollar deposit preferences (e), and the reserve-deposit ratio of Eurodollar banks (ρ). Define $M^\star$ as the world supply of dollars net of interbank deposits. M is the U.S. money supply, $E_\$$ is the Eurodollar supply, and $R_\$$ is the stock of reserves held by Eurodollar banks at U.S. banks. Since they are interbank deposits, they are excluded from the net supply of dollars. Since Eurodollar banks promise to convert Eurodollar deposits into deposits at U.S. banks on short notice, they must hold prudential reserves even though there

[11] For details see Edward J. Frydl, "The Eurodollar Conundrum," *Quarterly Review*, Federal Reserve Bank of New York, Spring, 1982.

[12] For more details on the fixed multiplier approach to Eurodollars, see Ronald I. McKinnon, *Money in International Exchange*, New York: Oxford University Press, 1979, Chapter 9. For a discussion of the variability of the coefficients that comprise the multiplier see Victor Argy, *The Postwar International Money Crisis: An Analysis* (London: George Allen and Unwin, 1981), Chap. 22.

are no legal reserve requirements. Let depositors hold some fraction (e) of each additional dollar in the form of Eurodollar deposit coefficient; among other things, it will depend on relative interest rates on Eurodollar and U.S. deposits:

$$E_\$ = eM^\star$$

The world supply of dollars is

$$M^\star = M + E_{\$} - R_\$$$

Let ρ be the reserve-deposit ratio of Eurodollar banks:

$$R = \rho E$$

These expressions can be combined in the following way:

$$E = eM^\star = e(M + E_\$ - R_\$) = eM + eE_\$ - e\rho E_\$$$
$$= \frac{eM}{1 - e - e\rho} = \frac{1}{1/e - 1 - \rho} M$$

The total stock of Eurodollars depends on the U.S. money supply and the two behavioral ratios representing the public's willingness to acquire another Eurodollar (e) and the reserve ratio of Eurodollar banks (ρ). In general the stock of Eurodollars will increase with the U.S. money supply, varying positively with e and inversely with ρ. The world dollar stock is the sum of the U.S. money supply and the stock of Eurodollars:

$$M^\star = M + R = M + eM^\star - R$$
$$= \frac{M - R}{1 - e}$$

The world dollar supply varies directly with the U.S. money supply and the Eurodollar deposit coefficient and inversely with Eurodollar reserves.

There has been much interest in the determinants of Eurodollar growth. The Eurodollar deposit coefficient is thought to be small and responsive to relative interest rates. The relevant rate is the risk-adjusted interest differential between U.S. and Eurodollar deposits. Eurodollars may be riskier because (1) they are not insured, (2) bank offices do not have direct access to discount borrowing at the Federal Reserve, and (3) they lie outside the legal jurisdiction of the United States.[13] The deposits may differ in other ways as well. Demand and small-denomination time deposits are not offered by the Eurodollar mar-

---

[13] For certain depositors, this feature may make the deposits less risky.

ket. Because of a more fully developed secondary market, U.S. certificates of deposit (CDs) may be more liquid than Eurodollar CDs. For these reasons, the two kinds of deposits are not perfect substitutes, and their interest rates may differ. Because of the absence of legal reserve requirements, Eurodollar banks have a cost advantage, which usually appears as a higher deposit interest rate.

It has been argued that Eurodollars are not perceived as being a safer asset, which would move the risk-adjusted interest rate in their favor. However, the 1982 failure of Banco Ambrosiano, a major Italian bank, has been interpreted as a symbol of the vulnerability of the entire Eurodollar system. This change might increase the Eurodollar deposit coefficient and contribute to expansion of the market. The reserve ratio is reputed to be quite low, which contributes to a larger multiplier.

Some observers have attributed Eurodollar growth to deficits in the U.S. balance of payments. Eurodollar growth is more closely related to the official settlements measure of the balance than the other measures, but the relationship is a loose one. Another explanation is based on the earnings and deposits of oil exporters. The argument is that world income was redistributed in favor of oil exporters, who have a higher Eurodollar deposit coefficient than do oil importers. If this argument were correct, an oil glut in the world should retard growth of the Eurodollar market. If Eurodollar growth is a source of world inflation, central banks can take it into account in determining their own monetary policy. Slower growth of national money could offset faster growth of Eurodollars.

A practical problem of adapting national monetary policy to Eurodollar growth is the lack of reliable and timely information about the size and growth of the market. Complete information about interbank deposits is not available. The best source of information about Eurodollars, the Bank for International Settlements, publishes data with a lag of three to six months.

While complete information about the quantity of Eurodollars is not easy to obtain, information about Eurodollar interest rates is more accessible. Since there is a large volume of interbank deposits, the interest rate at which banks are willing to lend dollars to other prominent banks is readily available. The well-known London interbank offer rate (LIBOR), which is the mean of the offer (lending) rates of six major London banks, has become the base interest rate for a wide variety of loans.[14] The creditworthiness of a borrower will determine the size of the premium that must be paid over the prevailing LIBOR.

It is not currently possible for central banks to adapt their week-to-week policy to Eurodollar developments, but that kind of fine timing may not be desirable anyway. However, central banks could adjust their long-run (e.g., year-to-year) monetary policy to Eurodollar developments in the same way as they adjust policy to expansion of credit cards and money market mutual funds.

---

[14] For details on LIBOR, see Gunter Dufey and Ian Giddy, *The International Money Market*, (Englewood Cliffs, N.J.: Prentice-Hall, 1978), pp. 52–54.

Eurodollars complicate monetary policy, but they do not present an insuperable problem for long-run monetary control.

SUMMARY

Inflation can be strictly national, or it can encompass the entire world. There are two separate sets of issues about inflation. First is the question of what determines variation in the rate of inflation over time. For example, What forces caused the stable prices of the 1950s and 1960s to become the inflationary period of the 1970s and 1980s? Second is the question of what determines variation in the rate of inflation across countries at the same time. Why is it that inflation exceeds 100 percent per year in Brazil, Argentina, and Israel at the same time it is 5 percent in West Germany and Switzerland?

Theories of inflation can be divided into those that stress increases in the supply of money and those that emphasize real forces that reduce the demand for money. Some nonmonetary theories that assume monetary accommodation by central banks are very difficult to distinguish from monetary theories. The transmission of inflation across countries may depend on the prevailing exchange rate regime. Fixed exchange rates provide a direct link between countries through adjustment of monetary reserves and money supplies. Floating exchange rates permit greater monetary independence, but interest rates and currency substitution provide a transmission mechanism.

World monetary reserves are a major determinant of the world money supply. Given the demand for reserves, an increase in supply will induce monetary expansion and world inflation. Rapid growth of world reserves occurred just prior to the acceleration of world inflation in 1973 and 1974 and 1979 and 1980. In addition to national money, Eurodollars are a money substitute that can add to inflationary pressure in the world. The policy problem caused by Eurodollars is analogous to the problem caused by the development of domestic money substitutes.

REFERENCES

ALIBER, ROBERT Z., ed. *National Monetary Policies and the International Financial System.* Chicago: University of Chicago Press, 1974. A collection of papers dealing with monetary independence and the exchange rate regime.

ARGY, VICTOR. *The Postwar International Money Crisis: An Analysis.* London: George Allen and Unwin, 1981. Part Three covers global inflation. Chapter 7 covers growth of the Eurocurrency system.

AUKRUST, ODD. "Inflation in the Open Economy: A Norwegian Model." In *Worldwide Inflation: Theory and Recent Experience,* Lawrence Krause and Walter S. Salant, eds. Washington, D.C.: The Brookings Institution, 1977. Discusses inflation in a small open economy.

BALBACH, ANATOL, and DAVID RESLER. "Eurodollars and the U.S. Money

Supply." *Review*, Federal Reserve Bank of St. Louis, June–July 1980. Considers technical effects of Eurodollars on the U.S. money supply.

BALL, R. J., ed.   *The International Linkage of National Economic Models*. Amsterdam: North-Holland, 1973. Several papers attempt to model the international transmission mechanism.

BASEVI, GIORGIO, and PAUL DEGRAUWE. "Vicious and Virtuous Circles: A Theoretical Analysis and a Policy Proposal for Managing Exchange Rates." *European Economic Review*, December 1977.

BATTEN, DOUGLAS. "Money Growth Stability and Inflation: An International Comparison." *Review*, Federal Reserve Bank of St. Louis, October 1981.

———. "Central Banks' Demand for Reserves Under Fixed and Floating Exchange Rates." *Review*, Federal Reserve Bank of St. Louis, March 1982.

BILSON, JOHN F. O. "The Vicious Circle Hypothesis." International Monetary Fund *Staff Papers*, March 1979. Analyzes the effect of exchange rate changes on inflation.

BHANDARI, J., and B. PUTNAM, eds.   The International Transmission of Economic Disturbances Under Flexible Exchange Rates. Cambridge, Mass.: M.I.T. Press, 1982.

BORDO, MICHAEL D., and EHSAN CHOUDHRI. "The Link Between Money and Prices in an Open Economy: The Canadian Evidence from 1971 to 1830." *Review*, Federal Reserve Bank of St. Louis, August–September 1982. An empirical study of currency substitution between U.S. and Canadian dollars.

BOSWORTH, BARRY P., and ROBERT Z. LAWRENCE. *Commodity Prices and the New Inflation*. Washington, D.C.: The Brookings Institution, 1982. Stresses real determinants of recent inflation.

BRYANT, RALPH. *Money and Monetary Policy in Independent Nations*. Washington, D.C.: The Brookings Institution, 1980. Comprehensive technical analysis of monetary policy in an open economy.

CAGAN, PHILLIP. "Imported Inflation 1973–74 and the Accommodation Issue." *Journal of Money, Credit, and Banking*, February 1980. Empirical study of foreign sources of U.S. inflation.

CIPPOLLA, C.   *Before the Industrial Revolution: European Society and Economy, 1000–1700*, 2nd ed. New York: W. W. Norton, 1980. Includes a section on the European price revolution.

CLINE, WILLIAM, et al.   *World Inflation and the Developing Countries*. Washington, D.C.: The Brookings Institution, 1982.

COHEN, BENJAMIN J. "International Reserves and Liquidity: A Survey." In *International Trade and Finance*, Peter B. Kenen, ed. Cambridge: Cambridge University Press, 1975.

DUESENBERRY, J. S., et al.   *The Brookings Quarterly Econometric Model of the United States*. Chicago: Rand McNally, 1965. Contains a section on the international transmission of inflation.

DUFEY, GUNTER, and IAN H. GIDDY. *The International Money Market*. Englewood Cliffs, N.J.: Prentice-Hall, 1978. Comprehensive analysis of Eurocurrency markets.

EMMINGER, OTTMAR. *The D-Mark in the Conflict Between Internal and External Equilibrium, 1948–1975*, Princeton Studies in International Finance, No. 122. Princeton, N.J.: Princeton University Press, 1977. Discusses German efforts to avoid imported inflation.

FIELEKE, NORMAN S. "The International Transmission of Inflation." In *Managed Exchange Rate Flexibility: The Recent Experience*, Federal Reserve Bank of Boston, Conference Series no. 20, 1978.

FRENKEL, JACOB. "International Reserves: Pegged Exchange Rates and Managed

Float." In Carnegie-Rochester Conference Series on Public Policy, supplement to *Journal of Monetary Economics*, Karl Brunner and Allen Meltzer, eds., Vol. 9 (1978). Comparison of reserve demand under the adjustable peg and managed float.

———. "The Demand for International Reserves Under Pegged and Flexible Exchange Rate Regimes and Aspects of the Economics of Managed Float." In *The Functioning of Floating Exchange Rates: Theory, Evidence, and Policy Implications*, David Bigman and Teizo Taya, eds. Cambridge, Mass.: Ballinger, 1980.

FRYDL, EDWARD J. "The Eurodollar Conundrum." *Quarterly Review*, Federal Reserve Bank of New York, Spring 1982. Discusses recent developments in the Eurodollar market.

GORDON, ROBERT J. "World Inflation and Monetary Accommodation in Eight Countries." *Brookings Papers on Economic Activity*, 2:1977.

GRUBEL, HERBERT. "The Demand for International Reserves: A Critical Review of the Literature." *Journal of Economic Literature*, December 1971. Survey of the theoretical and empirical literature on the demand for monetary reserves.

HELLER, H. ROBERT. "International Reserves and Worldwide Inflation." *International Monetary Fund Staff Papers*, March 1976. Explains inflation in terms of growth of reserves and money.

———. "The International Monetary System and Worldwide Inflation." *Columbia Journal of World Business*, Fall 1976. Reprinted in John Adams, ed., *The Contemporary International Economy: A Reader*. New York: St. Martins, 1979.

——— and MOHSIN KHAN. "The Demand for International Reserves Under Fixed and Floating Exchange Rates." International Monetary Fund *Staff Papers*, December 1978. Estimation of the demand for monetary reserves.

HUME DAVID. "Of the Balance of Trade" (1752). In *David Hume Writings on Economics*, Eugene Rotwein, ed. Madison: University of Wisconsin Press, 1970. Hume's statement of the price-specie flow mechanism.

INTERNATIONAL MONETARY FUND. *Annual Reports*, Washington, D.C., annually. Source of recent information on inflation, government policy, and IMF policy.

———. *Government Finance Statistics Yearbook*, Washington, D.C., annually. Source of data on government spending and taxation.

JOHNSON, HARRY G. "Secular Inflation and the International Monetary System." *Journal of Money, Credit, and Banking*, February 1973.

JOHNSTON, R.B. "Some Aspects of the Determination of Euro-Currency Interest Rates." Bank of England *Quarterly Bulletin*, March 1979. Discusses the relationship between Eurodollar and U.S. interest rates.

KRAUSE, LAWRENCE, and WALTER SALANT, eds. *World Inflation: Theory and Recent Experience*. Washington, D.C.: The Brookings Institution, 1977. Collection of papers analyzing world inflation.

MCKINNON, RONALD I. "Currency Substitution and Instability in the World Dollar Market." *American Economic Review*, June 1982. Monetary analysis of recent inflation.

MEISELMAN, DAVID, and ARTHUR LAFFER, eds. *The Phenomenon of Worldwide Inflation*. Washington, D.C.: American Enterprise Institute, 1975. Collection of papers on world inflation.

MILES, MARC. "Currency Substitution: Perspective, Implications, and Empirical Evidence." In *The Monetary Approach to International Adjustment*, Bluford H. Putman and D. Sykes Wilford, eds. New York: Praeger, 1979. Discusses the transmission mechanism under floating rates.

OBSTFELD, M. "Can We Sterilize? Theory and Evidence." *American Economic Review*, May 1982. Analysis of sterilization as a means of achieving national monetary independence.

PARKIN, MICHAEL, and GEORGE ZIS, eds. *Inflation in the World Economy.* Toronto: University of Toronto Press, 1976.

SALANT, WALTER S.   "International Transmission of Inflation," In *Worldwide Inflation: Theory and Recent Experience;* Lawrence Krause and Walter S. Salant, eds. Washington, D.C.: The Brookings Institution, 1977.

SCHWARTZ, ANNA JACOBSON.   "Secular Price Change in Historical Perspective." *Journal of Money, Credit, and Banking,* February 1973. History of inflation over the last 2,500 years.

SHAW, EDWARD S.   "International Money and International Inflation: 1958–1973." *Business Review,* Federal Reserve Bank of San Francisco, Spring 1975.

SWOBODA, ALEXANDER K.   *The Euro-Dollar Market: An Interpretation,* Princeton Studies in International Finance, No. 64. Princeton, N.J.: Princeton University Press, 1968.

————.   "Monetary Approaches to Worldwide Inflation." In *Worldwide Inflation: Theory and Recent Experience,* Lawrence Krause and Walter S. Salant, eds. Washington, D.C.: The Brookings Institution, 1977.

————.   "Gold, Dollars, Eurodollars, and the World Money Stock Under Fixed Exchange Rates." *American Economic Review,* September 1978. Analysis of the determinants of the world money supply.

VOGEL, ROBERT.   "The Dynamics of Inflation in Latin America, 1950–69." *American Economic Review,* March 1974. Empirical study of inflation.

WHITMAN, MARINA.   "Global Monetarism and the Monetary Approach to the Balance of Payments." *Brookings Papers on Economic Activity,* 3:1975. Survey of literature stressing the integration of world markets.

WILLIAMSON, JOHN.   "International Liquidity: A Survey." *Economic Journal,* September 1973. Survey of the literature on the adequacy of world reserves.

INDEX

BAD BLOOD

Arne Dahl is an award-winning Swedish crime novelist and literary critic. *The Blinded Man*, the first book in the internationally acclaimed Intercrime series, was published in 2012. *Bad Blood* is the second book in the series.

ALSO BY ARNE DAHL

The Blinded Man